I0819572

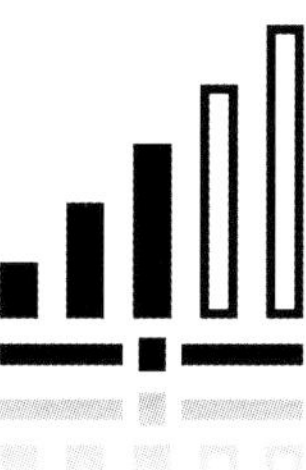

ON RECORD 1995 G. BROWN

CONTENTS

ON RECORD ENTRIES ARE NOT ORDERED ALPHABETICALLY, BUT ORGANIZED INTUITIVELY—A MIXTURE OF SEGUES BY MUSICAL GENRE OR STYLE.

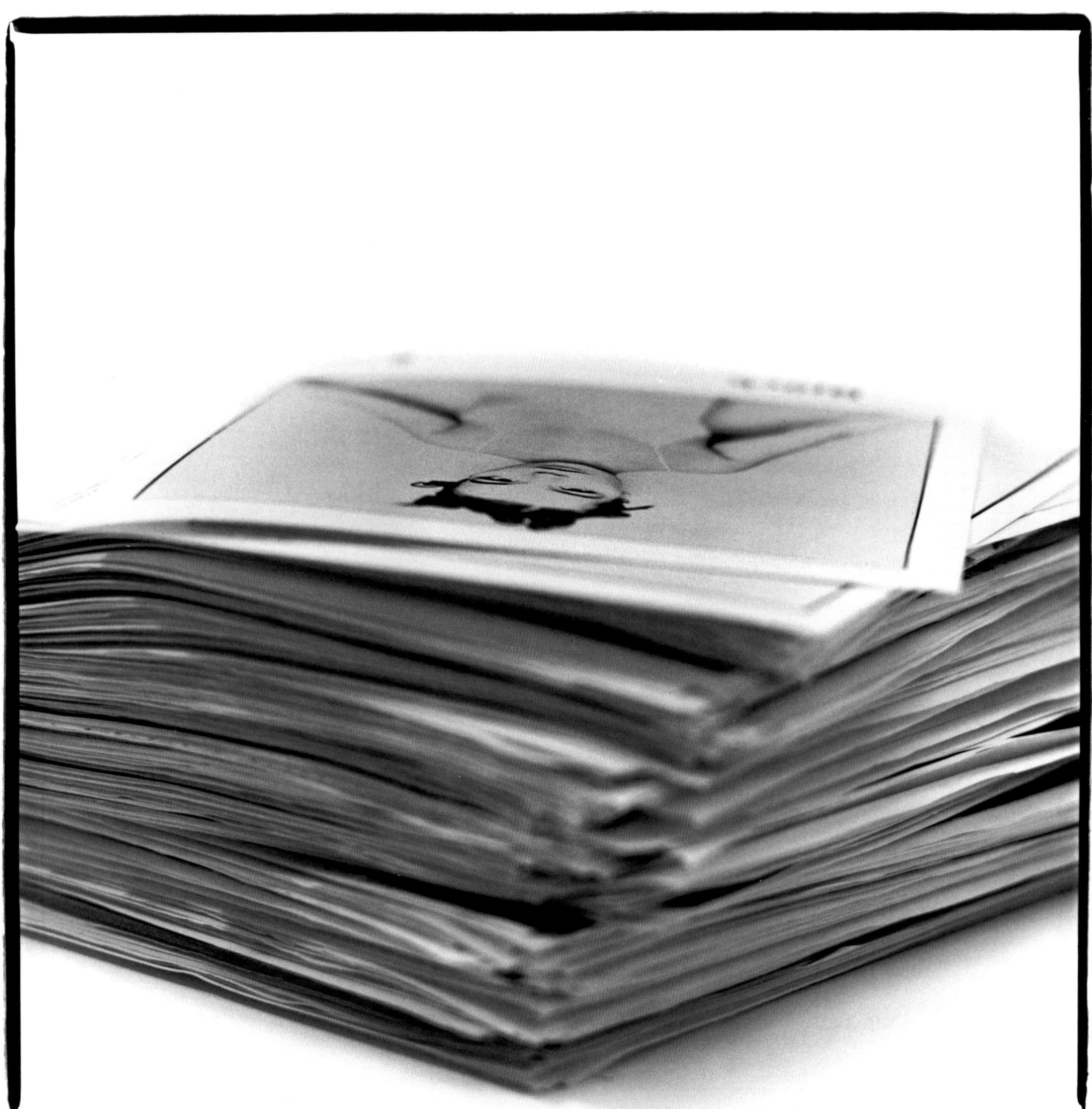

PHOTOGRAPH BY STEPHEN COLLECTOR

ON RECORD VOL.6 1995

MY ODYSSEY to influencing baseball history started in 1995, when the Colorado Rockies moved into their new home, Coors Field, after spending their first two seasons of existence at Mile High Stadium. Located in Denver's Lower Downtown neighborhood, the throwback ballyard quickly earned a reputation as a hitter's park—thanks in large part to the influence of the city's high elevation and semi-arid climate on the distance batted balls would travel. And we had players, collectively known as the Blake Street Bombers, who could rake. Whenever one of them would step into the batter's box, a snippet of a classic rock song blared over the P.A. system. And the walk-up songs seemed to work—how many times did Dante Bichette go yard after being pumped up to the strains of Peter Gabriel's "Sledgehammer," or Larry Walker send a moon shot into the upper deck to the tune of Ozzy Osbourne's "Crazy Train"?

Of course, pitcher development suffered commensurately. Time after time, I noticed pitching coach Frank Funk make his way to the mound for a conference with a member of his beleaguered staff. He wore No. 45, so the back of his uniform read "Funk 45." And it dawned on me—shouldn't it be "Funk 49," as in the James Gang's hit "Funk #49"? Wouldn't it be great, I wrote in *The Denver Post*, if fans could hear Joe Walsh's satisfyingly heavy rhythmed guitar riff whenever coach Funk left the dugout?

So I tracked down Funk and made a wild pitch, asking if he'd consider switching his number. "It wouldn't make any difference to me," he said. "I don't have an attachment to numbers of any kind."

But the impetus for change wasn't going to come from coach Funk—he'd never heard the James Gang's "Funk #49." "I like the mellow jazz—the Grover Washingtons, the George Bensons, the Earl Klughs," he explained. "I think I'll pass. I've already got everything marked No. 45. I don't want to have to do it again."

I figured that was the end of it. But as it turned out, Dan "Chico" McGinn, the Rockies' equipment manager, was a huge classic rock fan. He read my story—and he changed Funk's number to 49 without telling him. That's right, I impacted the culture of our national pastime. Sabermetrics can't measure my pride. I don't think the team ever played the song, though.

Arguably, more interesting things happened in the world of music in 1995. Alanis Morissette released her breakthrough *Jagged Little Pill*, and Foo Fighters and Radiohead issued consequential albums. It was a momentous year for indie rock and Britpop (Oasis, Blur, Pulp), while Coolio and Shaggy found the formula to a hit record with "Gangsta's Paradise" and "Boombastic," respectively. Jerry Garcia of the Grateful Dead passed away of a heart attack at age 53. The Rock and Roll Hall of Fame was dedicated in Cleveland, Ohio, and I was on the receiving end of a handshake from the Reverend Al Green in front of his hotel—it was as if someone took a catcher's mitt made out of lambskin and put it in a microwave for 30 seconds, an unimaginably warm, pillowy-soft greeting. I also got to access something most fans didn't—the opportunity to go to all the concerts and get all the new releases and press kits. I was and am a very lucky boy. Please allow me to share. — **G. Brown**

Alanis Morissette's *Jagged Little Pill*, the bible of girlish angst refined into alternative rock, topped the charts.

Billboard 200: *Jagged Little Pill* (No. 1)
Billboard Hot 100: "You Oughta Know" (#6); "Ironic" (#4); "You Learn" (#6)

WITH THE explosive "You Oughta Know," a lusty, combative declaration about love and betrayal, Alanis Morissette leapt onto the airwaves. The subject was a former boyfriend who'd gotten a new, older woman a little too quickly. Morissette worked herself into a lather, swooping from a vulnerable higher register into fiercely enunciated lyrics.

It was a defining musical moment, but the extreme emotions and sexual candor resulted in stereotypes of the Canadian singer-songwriter as an angry young woman. Radio listeners were then exposed to a wider range of confessional urgency with the hit singles from *Jagged Little Pill*, her debut album—"All I Really Want," "Ironic," "You Learn" and the self-affirmation of "Hand in My Pocket"—and Morissette came across more as a cheerful, confident and unpretentious pro than the ticked-off poetess of popular belief.

"The external world is always going to be filled with yin and yang," Morrisette mused. "The more people that are exposed to you, the more are going to love you and the more are going to hate you. It's mass."

Morissette created *Jagged Little Pill* with Glen Ballard, whom she met in early 1994. Having established himself in the pop world—co-writing Michael Jackson's hit "Man in the Mirror," producing Wilson Phillips—Ballard wanted to break out of that mold and create something keener and more incisive.

"I was finally in an environment where I was safe," Morissette said. "I was so connected with Glen on a cerebral level that I was able to write about things unapologetically and freely. People are focusing on my catharsis and my coming to terms with so many things—this whole stream-of-consciousness spiritual, inexplicable happening. But he was just as overwhelmed as I was."

Ballard wasn't, Morissette said, a hit-making producer scheming to create a grunge goddess. "People may think he went into it for impure reasons, but he would have been shooting himself in the foot. He came into this ready to do what he had always done—bring out the best an artist is capable of. Most of the time with Glen, he's playing electric guitar and I'm sitting on the floor, writing the melodies, lyrics and some of the chord changes at the same time. It was all pretty 'spew-ish.'"

Morissette's accomplishments—record-breaking multiplatinum sales for *Jagged Little Pill*, her near-sweep of the Grammy Awards—spoke for themselves, but detractors gave her heat for recording for Madonna's label (though she didn't begin looking for a company until the album was nearly complete), for being a former Nickelodeon child star (but who wasn't a different person at 15 than at 21?), even for the lyric of "Ironic," which indicated an improper definition of the adjective (would a song called "Vexing" or "Coincidental" have had quite the same ring?).

"When you're immersed in this, it has a way of either making you a defensive, wounded person or more filled with conviction about what you believe. I'm happy to say that it's helped me with the latter," Morissette said about the backlash. "It tests me constantly, daily. And after a while, when you keep coming out with what you feel are the right answers, what makes you feel peaceful, you just know that you always will." ■

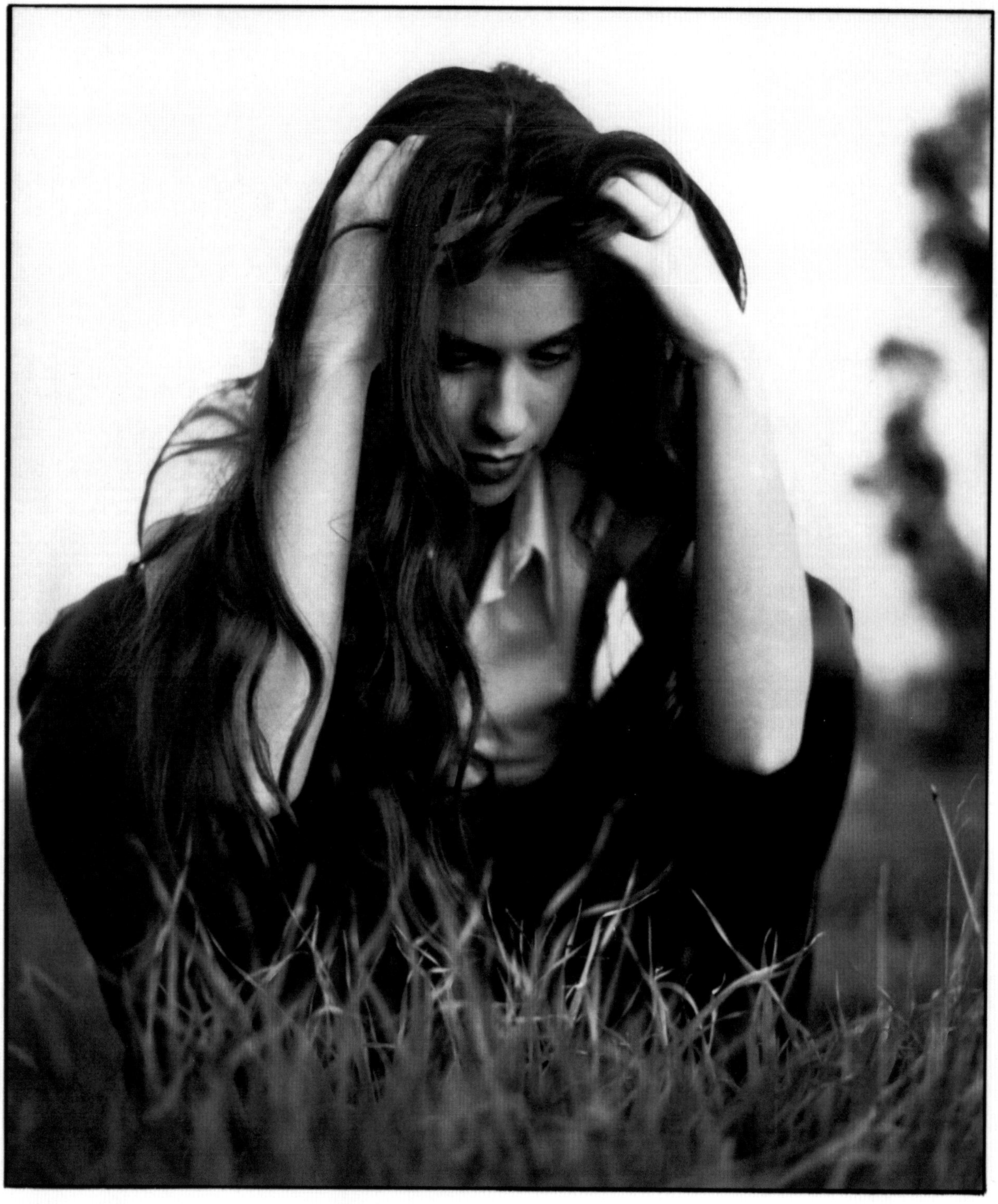

PHOTO CREDIT: John Patrick Salisbury

Alanis
Morissette

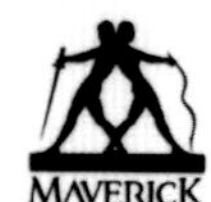

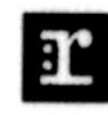

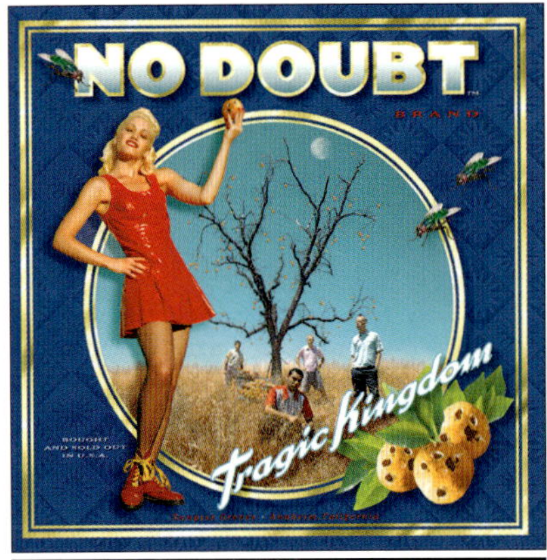

Billboard 200: *Tragic Kingdom* (No. 1)
Billboard Hot 100: "Just a Girl" (#23)

With "Just a Girl," "Spiderwebs" and "Don't Speak," No Doubt ruled the airwaves after scraping by for years.

AN EXPLOSIVE climb to high prestige—the album *Tragic Kingdom*, a peppy mix of punk, pop and ska, went on to hit No. 1—was a surprise to No Doubt's members, previously known by only a few hundred fans of the Southern California ska scene. The quartet was formed in 1987 by singer Gwen Stefani and her brother Eric, the band's keyboardist and creative heart in those days. Bass player Tony Kanal, who was born in India and raised in England, joined that spring, and for a while he was both the group's manager and Gwen's boyfriend.

"When the band started, Gwen was 17 and I was 16, a junior in high school," Kanal said. "We were always involved in booking clubs and recording demo tapes, doing it ourselves. Most of my business knowledge came from my parents, but experience is the best teacher. We were heavily influenced by the 2-Tone ska scene from England—the set was composed of covers of Madness, the Specials, the Selecter. We started writing our own material, experimenting with different styles of music."

"For the first five years of the band, we never even made records because we couldn't afford to go into the studio," Gwen Stefani added. "Being a live band is what kept us going, the fun part of our week."

Then forces nearly drove No Doubt apart. Original lead singer John Spence committed suicide; a self-titled debut album of whimsical, lively girl-sung pop was released in 1992, but it died as a surfeit of angst-filled alt-rockers grumped their way to fame; Eric Stefani left to become an animator for *The Simpsons*, and Kanal and Gwen Stefani ended their seven-year romance.

Now consisting of Kanal, Gwen Stefani, guitarist Tom Dumont and drummer Adrian Young, No Doubt considered disbanding, but the group resolved to complete *Tragic Kingdom* (the title referred to life in the suburbs surrounding Disneyland).

Finally, the time and place for No Doubt's pop smarts had arrived. *Tragic Kingdom* sold millions, and mainstream and alternative airplay for the lively radio nuggets "Spiderwebs," the cheerful "Just a Girl" and the power ballad "Don't Speak" was inescapable. "Don't Speak" was one of several candid songs that Stefani wrote to mend her broken heart after Kanal dumped her. Naturally, everyone looked for him to be ashamed when the public was singing along to real-life story lines.

"People expect a reaction onstage when we play songs about personal relationships," the garrulous ex chuckled. "But I've got to separate myself from the lyrics. I'm standing there thinking about how good I can play my bass on this song to make it sound better."

If there was a problem, it was that all four members had fought together for success, but the midriff-baring Stefani was the star. With her sulky voice and glamorous looks, she got honored and slavered over at the expense of her bandmates.

"I open up magazines and find myself cropped out of photos," Kanal admitted. "When you're in a band, it's not just about the music—I've been married to three other people for years. Then there are record companies, agents and attorneys to deal with. We've found a decent balance, and we're taking advantage of it. After experiencing tough times, you appreciate good fortune." ■

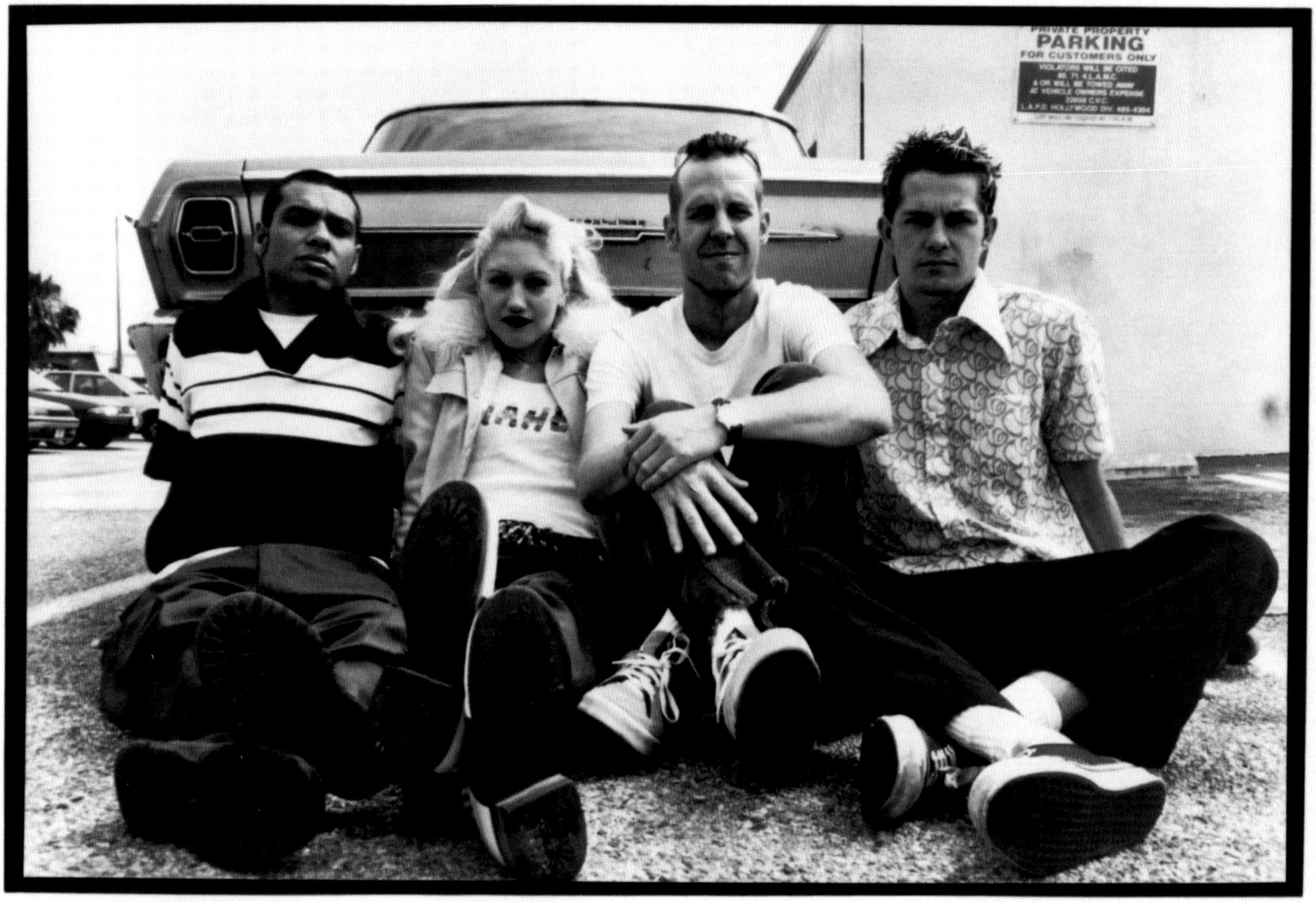

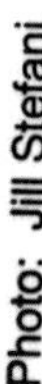

TONY KANAL **GWEN STEFANI** **TOM DUMONT** **ADRIAN YOUNG**

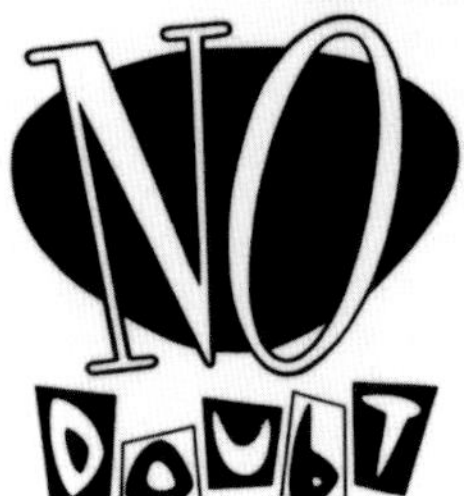

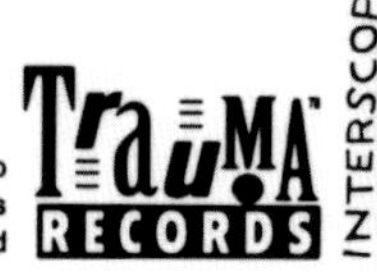

INTERSCOPE RECORDS®

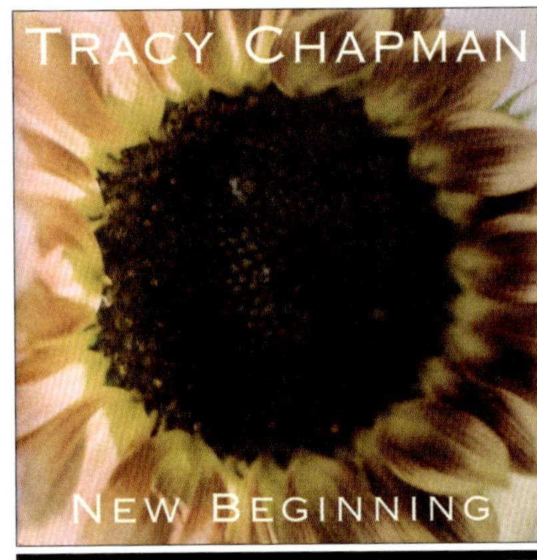

Billboard 200: *New Beginning* (#4)
Billboard Hot 100: "Give Me One Reason" (#3)

"Give Me One Reason" recaptured the impressive narrative command of Tracy Chapman's introspective songs.

IT WASN'T typical MTV fare—a young Black woman singing sharp, no-nonsense folk songs that displayed a strong political conscience and passionate looks at personal struggles. But with her 1988 debut album and the signature hit "Fast Car," a gripping treatise on impaired dreams, Tracy Chapman turned the pop world on its ear. Within a year, she had picked up three Grammys and was a conspicuous presence on Amnesty International's "Conspiracy of Hope" tour with Sting and Peter Gabriel.

Yet the demands of instant international celebrity didn't quite agree with Chapman. The previously little-known singer had been raised in Cleveland and spent time playing in Boston coffeehouses while attending Tufts University. It was a cliché—an artist had his or her whole life to write songs for a first album, and six months for the second. *Crossroads*, the follow-up to Chapman's debut, went platinum, but it didn't compare. *Matters of the Heart* in 1992 was disappointing artistically and commercially. Most fans relegated Chapman to cult status.

So Chapman deliberately deescalated her career, partly out of fear that she was being caught up in the machinery of the music biz. She moved to the Bay Area and put together a five-piece band. *New Beginning* provided a restrained, effective contrast to the bombast of formulaic rock bands and slick studio creations. Chapman's deep grainy voice was as quietly authoritative and powerful as ever, and her lyrics dealt with conflicts of love or good old social relevance. Her bluesy "Give Me One Reason" was an atypical hit from the album.

"I think I would, in some way, be involved in causes even if I wasn't a musician—it would make its way into my life to try and help people or raise consciousness," Chapman said. "I don't know exactly where it all comes from. It may be that I myself have benefited from the interest and charity of other people at different times in my life. I just know that I'm not alone in my struggles, whether it be trying to deal with people's racist or sexist attitudes, or the feelings that come from being disrespected."

Don Gehman's simple production accompanied Chapman's set of noble, calm meditations.

"You can have some of the most expensive equipment at your disposal and go make a really bad record," Chapman said. "And someone in their garage can make a pretty amazing record today. So it's a funny little balancing act I go through, trying not to make things too complicated, but at the same time making sure I'm availing myself of the best. Music will always be a part of my life, but I'm not sure I'll always want to make records, and I can't say that I like the road enough to want to be out there all the time." ■

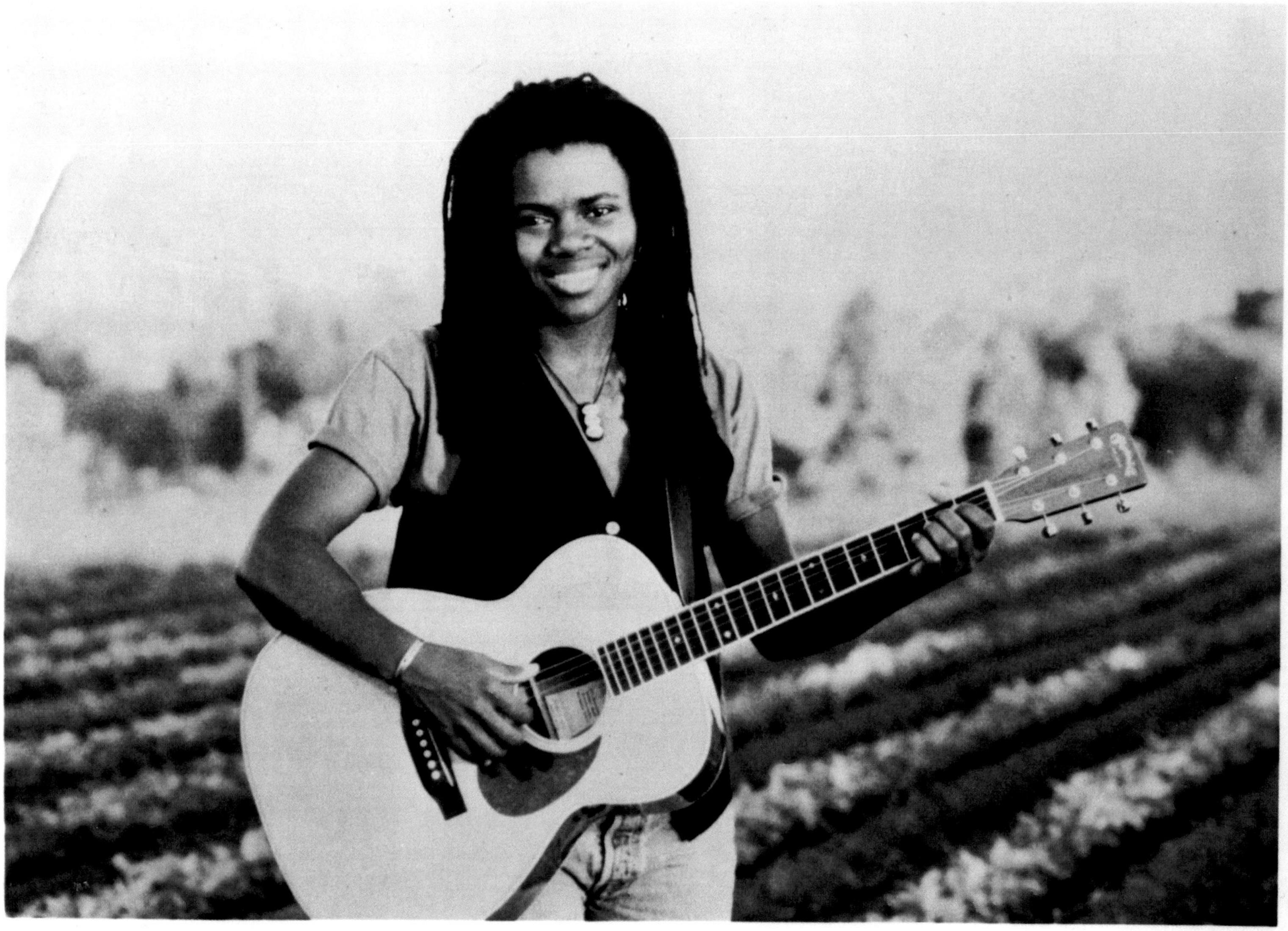

PHOTO CREDIT CHRISTINE ALICINO

TRACY CHAPMAN

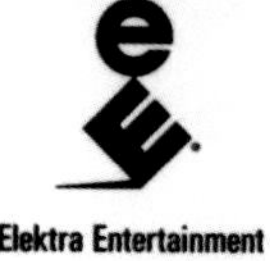

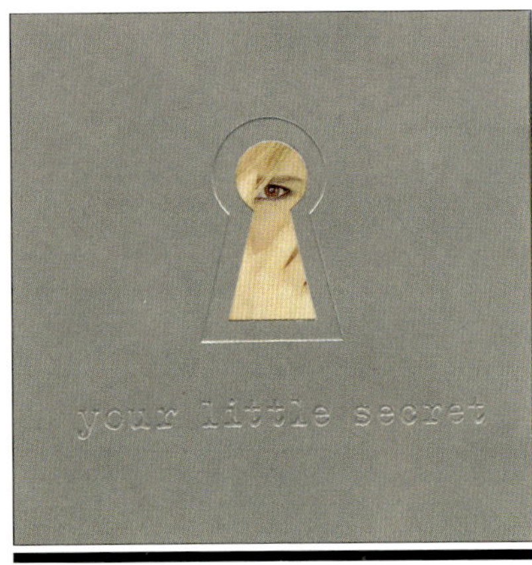

Billboard 200: *Your Little Secret* (#6)
Billboard Hot 100: "I Want to Come Over" (#22); "Nowhere to Go" (#40)

Issuing *Your Little Secret,* Melissa Etheridge was lauded for her lyrical intensity and assertive performing style.

FIVE MILLION fans had picked up Melissa Etheridge's fabulously successful *Yes I Am.* Her fifth release, *Your Little Secret*, came on the heels of that mainstream breakthrough album.

"I'm trying to understand my place in American pop culture," Etheridge mused. "You can only be new once. The funny thing is, I got to be new on my fourth album. Which is actually a good thing, because I have a body of work to back it up. I didn't think about the follow-up. I just went along with how I'd been doing it. I was constantly writing and I got songs and I recorded them and I put the album out.

"In retrospect, the only thing I would have done is wait a little longer. I'm selling just as many *Yes I Am* albums as *Your Little Secret* albums. If those were combined, I'd be much higher in the numbers game that's played, the perception in the business."

Your Little Secret debuted in the Top 10 on *Billboard*'s album chart. The songs were fueled by Etheridge's familiar themes—longing, sometimes tormented views of love and relationships. She set up an atmosphere of drama and unreachable desire on the ballad "I Want to Come Over." In the raw, rocking title track, she reached for tough-gal swagger.

"What inspired me was Joe Cocker," she explained. "When I played Woodstock '94, I was on stage when he opened it with 'With a Little Help from My Friends,' and I was one massive goose bump. That scream is a classic rock 'n' roll primal thing, and I said, 'I want to find that in me when I make this album.' Doing that song, I just screamed at the end and went, 'Oh, there it is!'"

The yearning "Nowhere to Go" came from Etheridge's hometown of Leavenworth, Kansas. "I took a look back inside myself. I felt that I'd come to a certain point in my writing—maybe I had been a little eager to get into my future and I neglected to open up certain parts of my past, my Midwestern upbringing."

Etheridge was impossible to ignore. If she wasn't on tour, she was singing at the Rock and Roll Hall of Fame opening or being feted on *MTV Unplugged* or gracing the cover of *Rolling Stone*. Or officially coming out—"I became the big lesbian spokeswoman," she said with a laugh.

"I have a lot of guidance, people I listen to. But in the end, all I really have is my gut. People aren't going to talk about my manager or my record company, they're going to talk about me and the decisions I make. When the album came out, it was dealt with as music, and I received reviews not mentioning my lifestyle at all. I really appreciated that. I've got a real strong sense that I'm on a definite career road. I've seen it in the audiences. I'm on solid ground." ■

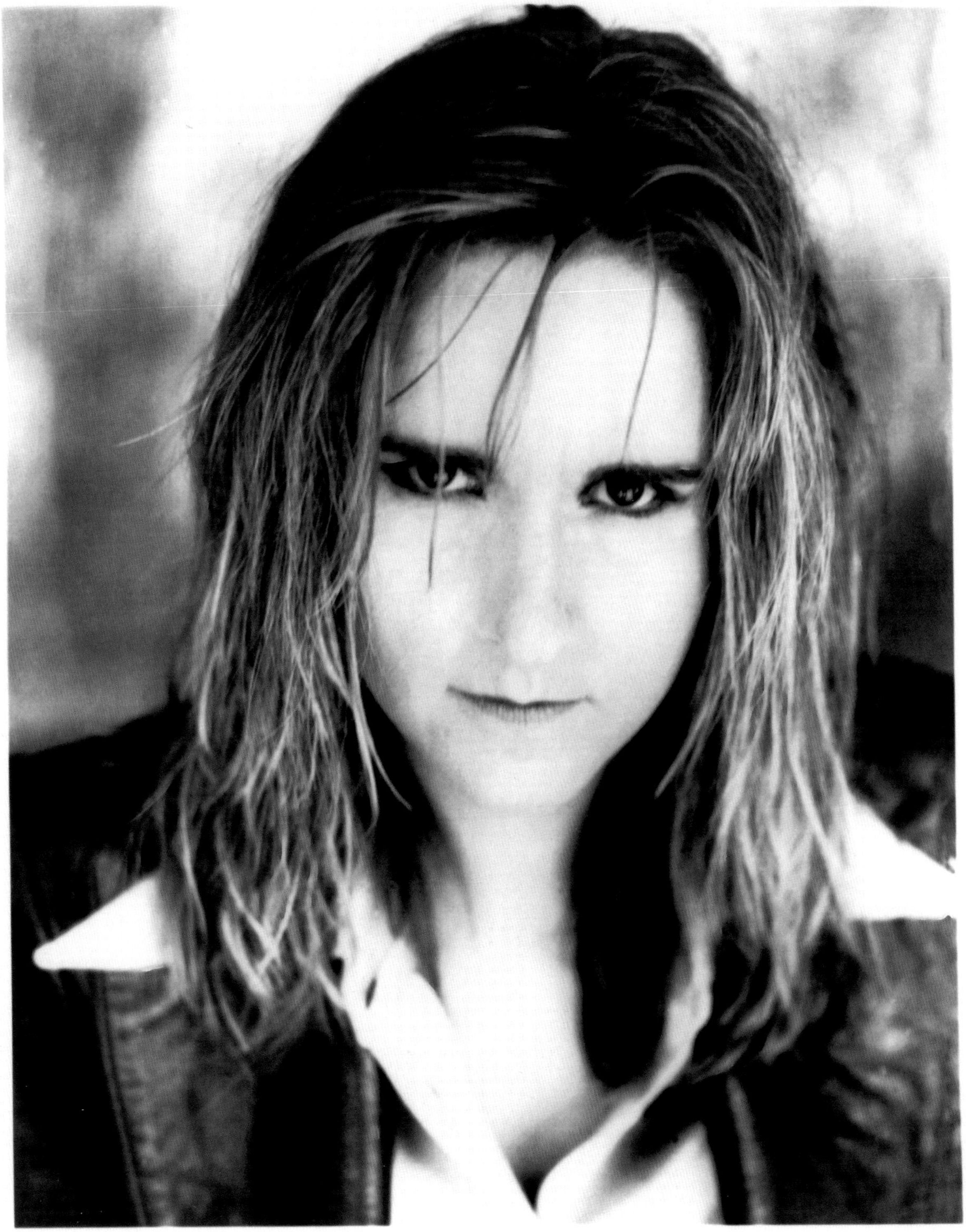

W.F. LEOPOLD
MANAGEMENT

melissa etheridge

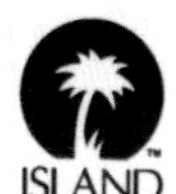

Photo Credit: Frank Ockenfels

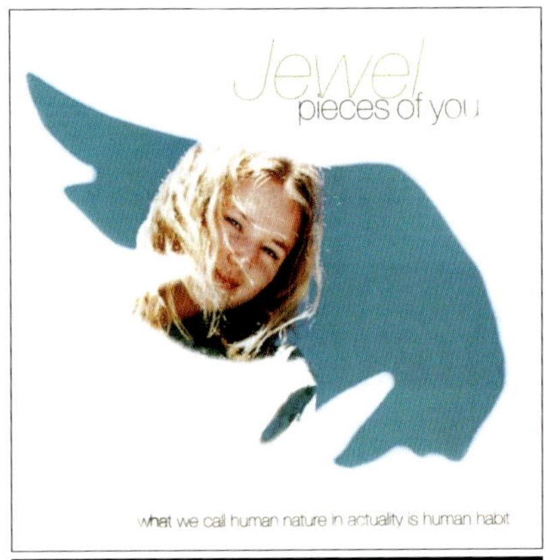

Billboard 200: *Pieces of You* (#4)
Billboard Hot 100: "Who Will Save Your Soul" (#11); "You Were Meant for Me" (#2); "Foolish Games" (#2)

A raw, sparsely produced album, Jewel's folksy *Pieces of You* became one of music's all-time top-selling debuts.

EVERYBODY KNEW Jewel as a fair-haired, rags-to-riches folk diva. Sometimes she sounded like an innocent. Other times she gave off the assurance of a show-biz veteran.

"I got into this knowing who I am and why I'm doing it," Jewel said. "It wasn't for approval or to discover myself. Everything's been relative to my spirit and my intent."

Jewel Kilcher (she went by her first name only) grew up on an Alaskan homestead with no television or running water, but she wasn't new to performing. As a little girl, she began gigging in dives with her parents. At 18, she was living out of a Volkswagen bus in San Diego, strumming her beat-up acoustic guitar on the streets for change and playing open-mike nights at clubs.

"By that age, singing and writing were what I was best at, versus marble carving and other interests," she explained. "I knew that I could make a living and have the biggest influence, and it's the most alive medium. A lot of the arts—poetry, dance, visual art—are dying on a mass scale."

In 1994, an Atlantic Records executive saw Jewel's act at a coffeehouse and signed the hippie to a contract. She was just 19 when she recorded *Pieces of You*, which spawned the smash hits "Who Will Save Your Soul," "You Were Meant for Me" and "Foolish Games," songs that were by turns sincere and loopy.

"All of the writers I've admired over the years have been confessional—the Bukowskis and the Nerudas, people whose lives you really understood," Jewel said. "We change each other and ourselves only by doing that. I don't want to stand still, but I also don't think my feelings are unique—it's not like I'm being *that* naked."

When *Pieces of You* was released, expectations were modest, and the album initially failed to chart. Jewel owed her success to an unusually patient campaign from her record company and nonstop touring. Fans flocked to her shows to hear her energy and fire come out. Embodying delicate acoustic melodies and alternately ethereal and gutsy vocals, she was also a personable raconteur, a shrewd mimic and a skillful yodeler.

"I mix it up every night—I've always done that just to keep things interesting for myself," she explained. "I have over 250 songs. I just have to write. I can't exist without it."

Having "real adults" in her life had paid off, Jewel noted. "I realize how much my background prepared me for what I'm doing. My dad taught me professionalism—without all those years of bar singing, I couldn't have pulled off playing in front of 2,500 people in between the Ramones and Everclear with just me and my guitar. My mom is my other half—she works so closely with me. I'm going out to the public, but she's the foundation. I'm really the tip of the iceberg." ■

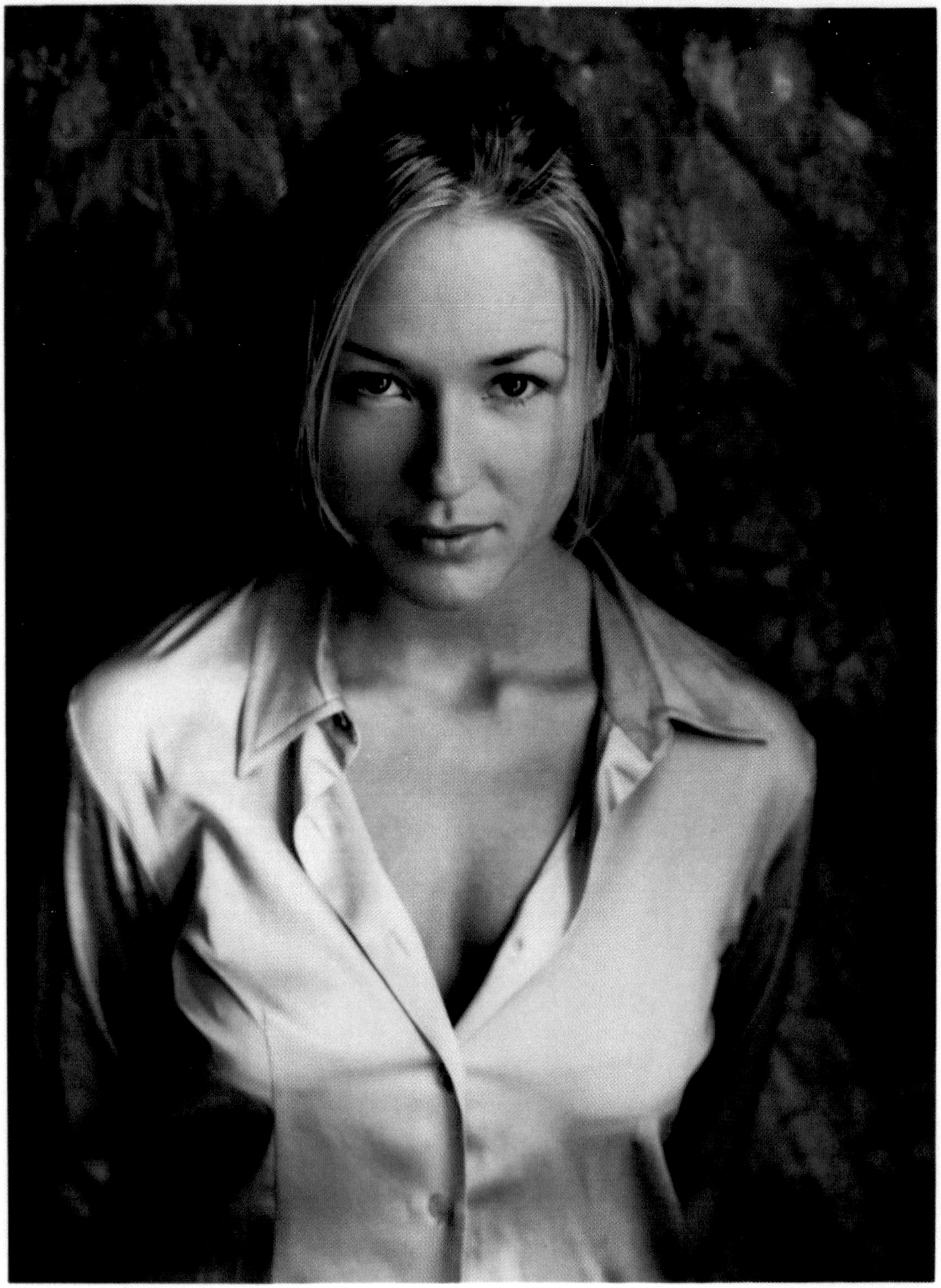

Jewel

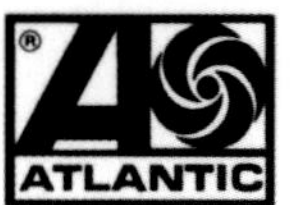

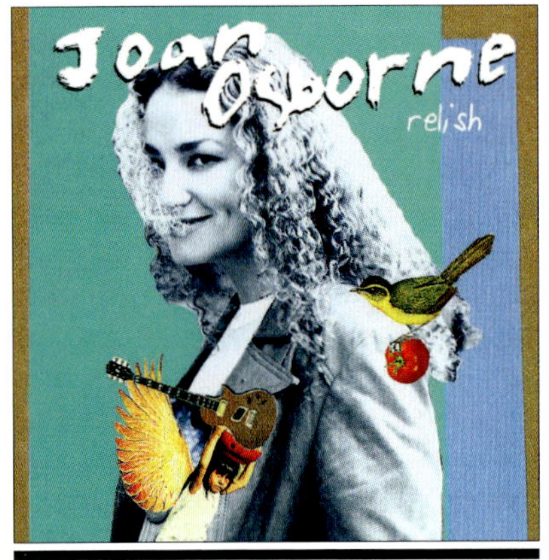

Billboard 200: *Relish* (#9)
Billboard Hot 100: "One of Us" (#4)

Warbling about God being "One of Us," Joan Osborne plugged into a monumental radio and video sensation.

WITH PROUD curves and fiery assurance, Joan Osborne's music and persona emphasized both earthiness and glamour. "I'm hoping to establish myself as an artist with a different perspective on everyday sexual politics and love, something with its own particular power," she said.

"I realized I could sing about six years ago. I'd been studying filmmaking at New York University. I happened to live on a street with a blues bar on the corner. I went in late one night and had a beer, and the piano player was still there. A friend dared me to get up and sing a song, so I sang Billie Holiday's 'God Bless the Child.' The piano player suggested that I come back for an open-mike night, and I discovered a whole new scene. I was always into the aspects of writing—journals and even long, complicated letters were my means of expression—so songs came naturally."

The Kentucky-raised Osborne earned a reputation as queen of New York's East Village clubs, touring diligently in the Northeast and releasing two indie recordings on her own Womanly Hips Music. With producer Rick Chertoff and collaborators Eric Bazilian and Rob Hyman (of the Hooters and Cyndi Lauper's *She's So Unusual* fame), she created the compelling major-label debut *Relish* and became a star. A key element, the hit single "One of Us," imagined God as an ordinary guy. The song and *Relish* earned Osborne seven Grammy nominations.

Guitarist Bazilian wrote "One of Us." "Eric brought in a recording that was almost like a Leonard Cohen thing—he was using a very deep, gravelly voice and it had almost a doomed air about it," Osborne explained. "The only way I could make it work for me was to do it from a place of real innocence. I pictured it as a daydream of this character sitting on a bus, watching all the people, and suddenly seeing the universality in very ordinary things. Those are really interesting eyes to see the world through."

The way Osborne delivered her own songs was bluesier and gutsier than the hesitant, timorous voice on her breakthrough hit. She bellowed confidently on the rollicking "Right Hand Man," and the vision of the mandolin-charged "St. Teresa" dominated the album—Osborne had allowed a hypnotist friend to put her under in an effort to relieve writer's block, and the resulting song was inspired by Saint Teresa of Ávila.

"She was a nun in the 16th century who started having visions of hell and heaven, going into convulsions. This was at the time of the Spanish Inquisition—she thought she was being possessed by the devil. So she went to her superiors at the church, and they instructed her to write down in detail everything she was going through in the trances—these really amazing manuscripts of mystic literature. The song is about that saint, but it's about other things as well." A paean to a streetwalker? "I don't want dictate a listener's experience."

MTV and VH1 got behind "St. Teresa," airing the video. "VH1 wants us to bleep out the word 'hash,' though, which is pretty hypocritical of them," Osborne noted. "They could show a half-naked woman being beat up, yet I can't have the word 'hash.' But the whole song doesn't turn on that one word." ■

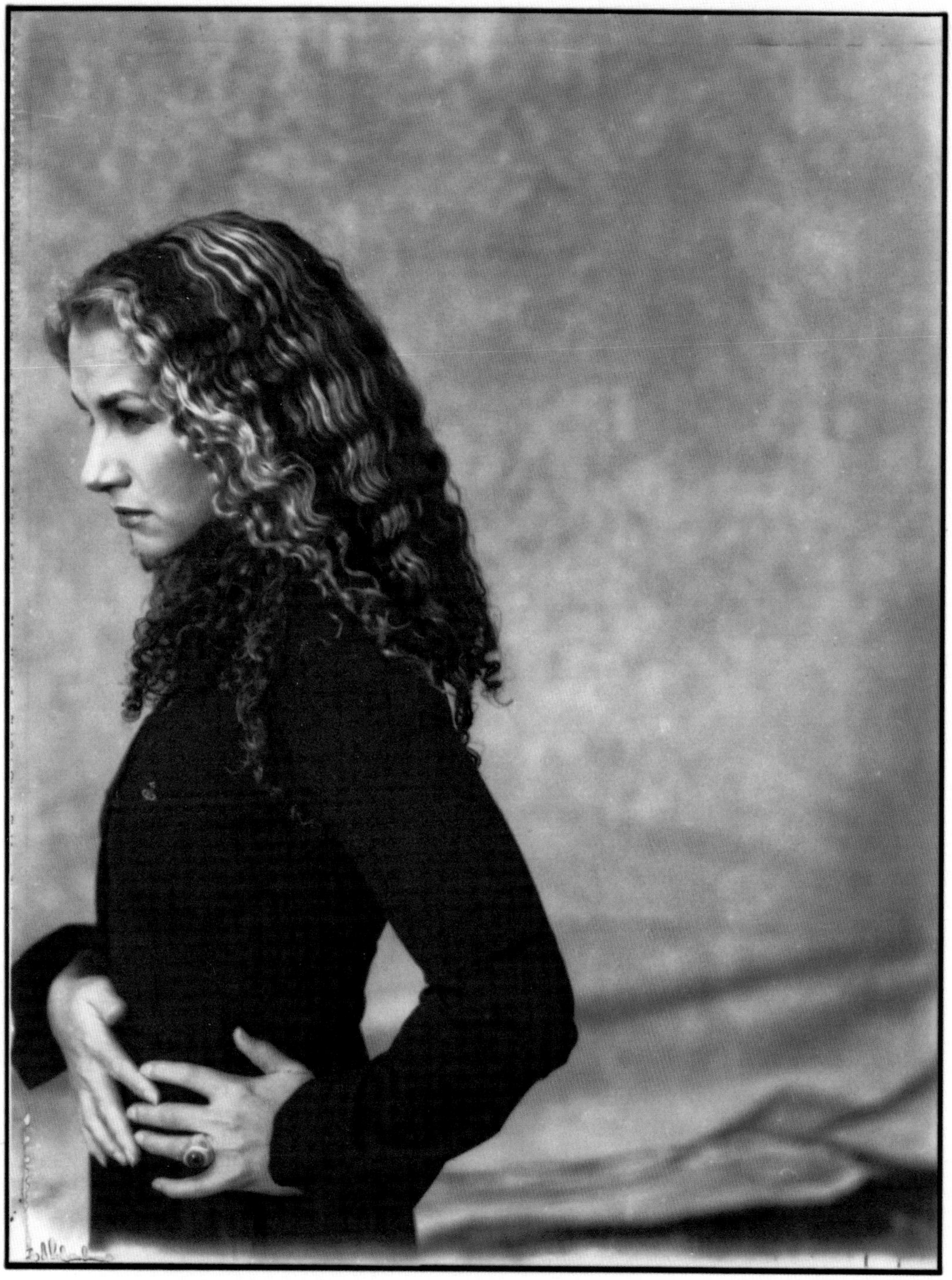

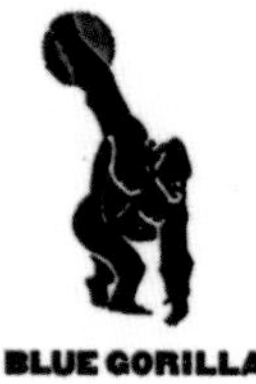

Joan Osborne

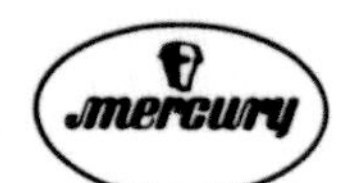

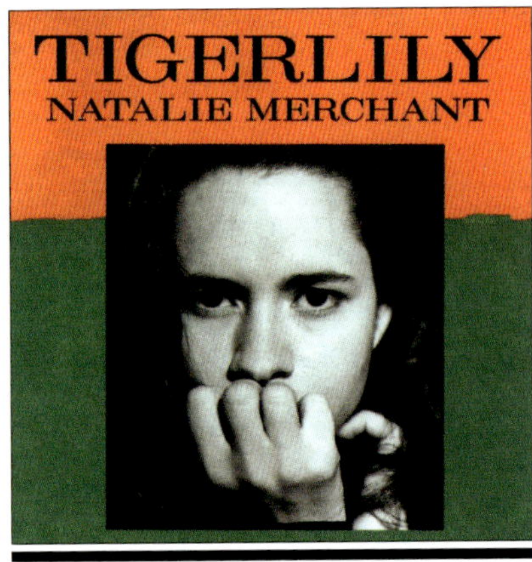

Billboard 200: *Tigerlily* (#13)
Billboard Hot 100: "Carnival" (#10); "Wonder" (#20); "Jealousy" (#23)

Formerly the force behind 10,000 Maniacs, Natalie Merchant began her solo career with the album *Tigerlily*.

HER DISTINCTIVE voice and waiflike activist image put 10,000 Maniacs on the map. And then, at the folk-pop group's peak, after six albums as lead vocalist and primary lyricist, Natalie Merchant quit.

"It was hard to do," Merchant said. "There are very few artists, especially women artists, who have been able to leave their bands and make successful records on their own. The odds were against me."

But Merchant made the most of it. Her self-produced solo debut *Tigerlily* sold more than 4 million copies, the hits "Carnival," "Wonder" and "Jealousy" defining her sentimental writing style.

Merchant's decision was a long time coming. "I joined the Maniacs when I was 17," the 31-year-old singer said. "It would have been lazy for me to stay in a situation where I was secure but creatively unchallenged. That's what the Maniacs had become. We had a following—we could put out a record, and we had a good feeling we could sell around a million—and that was very comforting in this business. With all the interesting and creative musicians I know who are waiting on tables for a living, it was a scary thing to leave."

In the fall of 1993, Merchant bought a house, began writing songs and assembled a band of young players to make *Tigerlily*, even though she'd been pressured to record with a seasoned producer and studio musicians to guarantee radio airplay. The album's appeal lay in its subtlety—there was a sensuousness that her Maniacs work lacked.

"I wanted to make a very natural-sounding record, as little production as possible," Merchant explained. "I borrowed money and paid for this record by myself. I worked with people who had never even walked into a recording studio before. I took a lot of risks, all to preserve the innocence of the process, to prevent it from becoming too synthetic and contrived. I wanted to rediscover what it was like to put a band together and play in clubs. I did all that, and there was something very charming about it."

Merchant earnestly cared about causes, but she was breaking away from her socially conscious reputation. "I always thought it was more subversive and subtle than that, except in a few cases—and they were probably my least successful songs," she said, laughing. "Most of the people who enjoyed 10,000 Maniacs find this to be a very natural evolution, and they're looking forward to what I do next. This isn't the defining record of my solo career. It's just what I did in the year after I left 10,000 Maniacs. There's a lot of room for experimentation, and I hope I'm versatile enough to make records different from this one. I think I am." ■

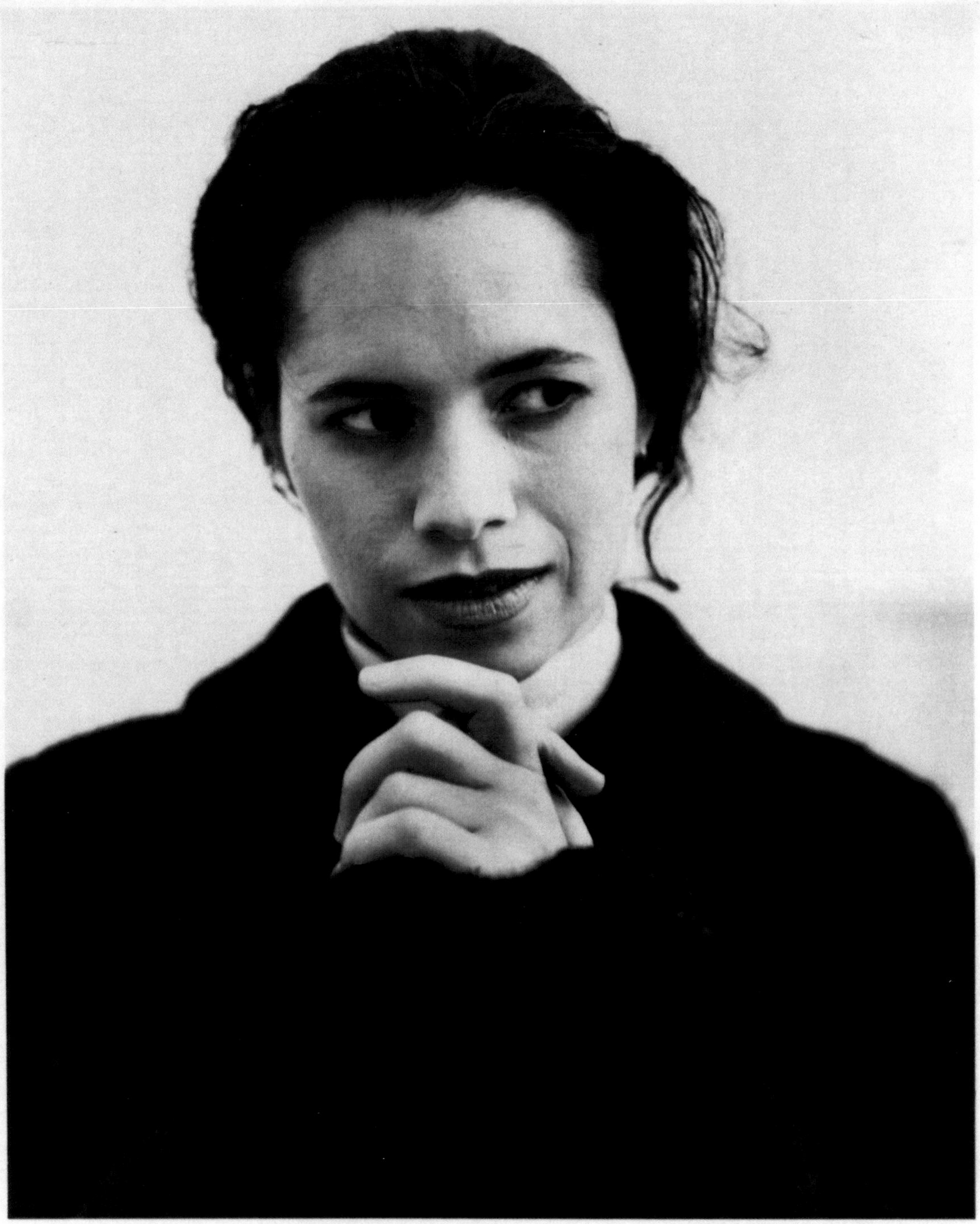

PHOTO CREDIT DANA LIXENBERG 1995

NATALIE MERCHANT

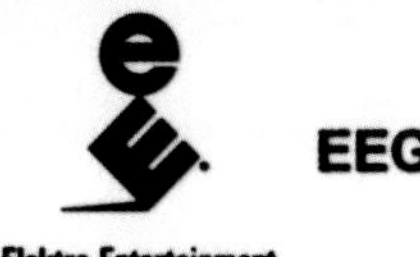

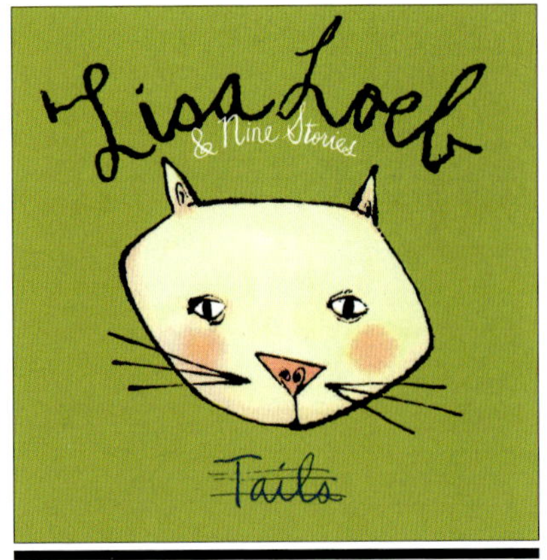

Billboard 200: *Tails* (#30)
Billboard Hot 100: "Stay (I Missed You)" (No. 1);
"Do You Sleep?" (#18); "Waiting for Wednesday" (#83)

Lisa Loeb & Nine Stories' debut album *Tails* delivered on the promise of a plaintive hit, "Stay (I Missed You)."

REMARKABLY, AT the time Lisa Loeb was propelled into the spotlight—"Stay (I Missed You)," her hit song off the *Reality Bites* soundtrack, climbed to the top of the charts and scored a Grammy nomination—she was an unsigned artist. Yet the singer-songwriter with the signature cat-eyed tortoiseshell glasses seemed smart and stable.

"There are different definitions of succeeding in the music business," Loeb mused. "Selling tons of records can be a success, but it's not as satisfying as being able to write songs or having a room full of people like the music."

Loeb established a reputation in New York for solo acoustic performances and electric gigs with her backing band, Nine Stories (named after the J.D. Salinger collection). She sold a demo tape at shows before her friend and neighbor, actor Ethan Hawke, suggested to *Reality Bites* director Ben Stiller that he use her gentle song "Stay (I Missed You)" in his movie. Loeb made a famed video (shot by Hawke, she drifted through an empty apartment), and the confessional ballad became No. 1 before she could put together a debut album.

Every major record company bid for her services, and the conventional industry wisdom held that a full-length release should be rushed into stores to capitalize on the hit's momentum. Instead, Loeb and producer Juan Patiño hunkered down in his apartment studio for eight months of meticulous work. *Tails* was sophisticated folk-pop, intimate and vulnerable. The single "Do You Sleep?" was written while Loeb was in her senior year at Brown University, where she studied comparative literature. "I'm not the type who can finish a song in 20 minutes after something has happened to me," she said. "Sometimes it takes years until it feels right."

"Stay" was included as well, closing the album. "It has a fake Motown thing happening," Loeb explained. "I was thinking about Daryl Hall & John Oates when I started writing it—I heard Daryl Hall was looking for new songs, and I love his voice. I thought I'd like to be a songwriter who writes for other people—'Whoa, it would be cool for him to have a song like "Sara Smile" or "Rich Girl."' I wrote the music and some of the lyrics for 'Stay,' then the Daryl Hall opportunity went away and I had a fight with my boyfriend. I finished the song in a few months. I exaggerated a little and then added things that had nothing to do with it!"

Loeb's lyrics and girlish voice captured the vicissitude of romance. Had she been dumped a lot? "Not really," she admitted. "I like writing about the saddest or most frustrated or confused way things could possibly be, to share those feelings without scaring people away. For me, it's important to use the art form not necessarily to be about me, but to have other characters. It makes me uncomfortable and nervous when it seems so direct that it's self-indulgent. I couldn't imagine writing everything from my personal experience. You don't have time to have that many personal experiences." ■

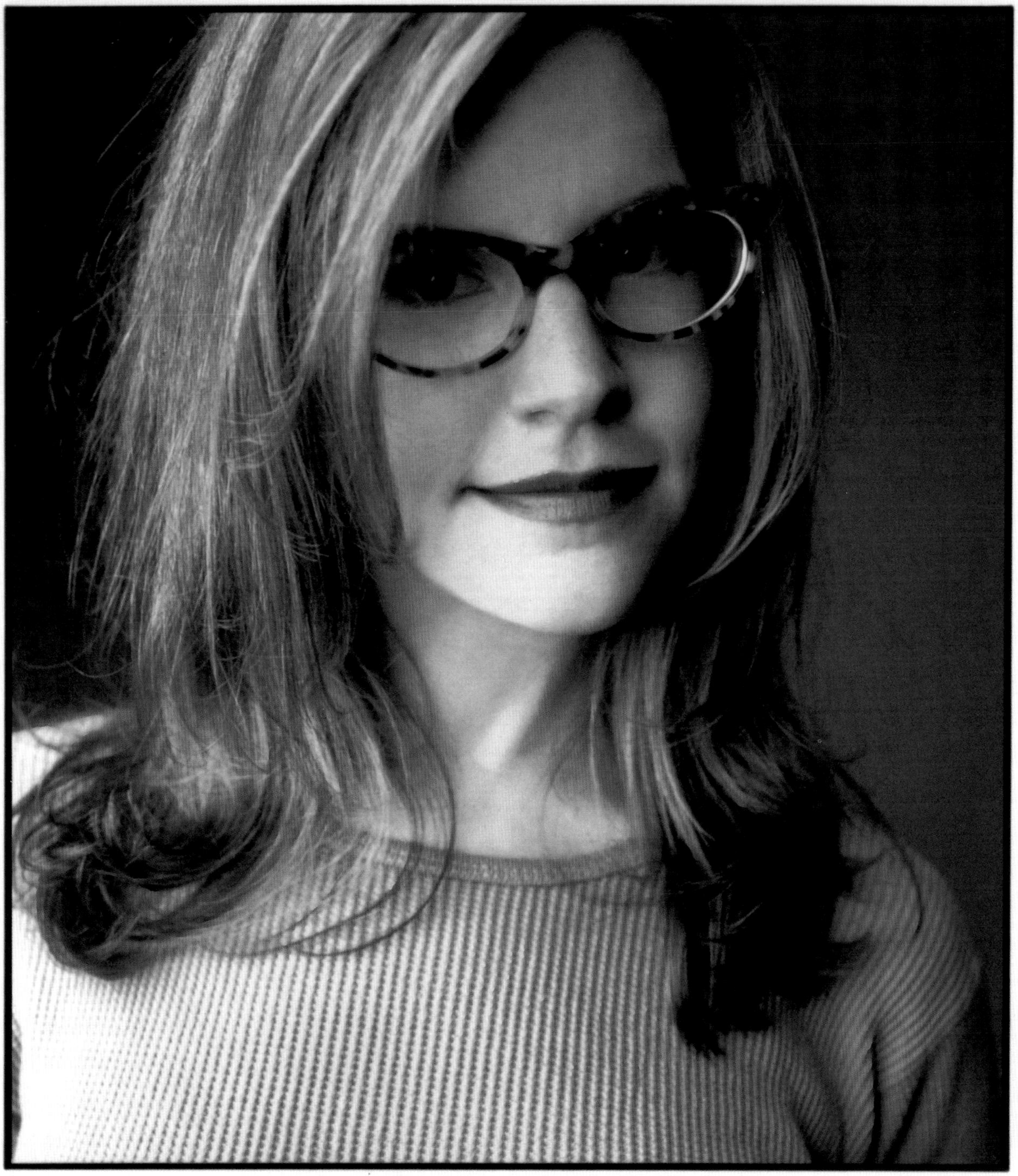

Photo Credit: Mark Seliger

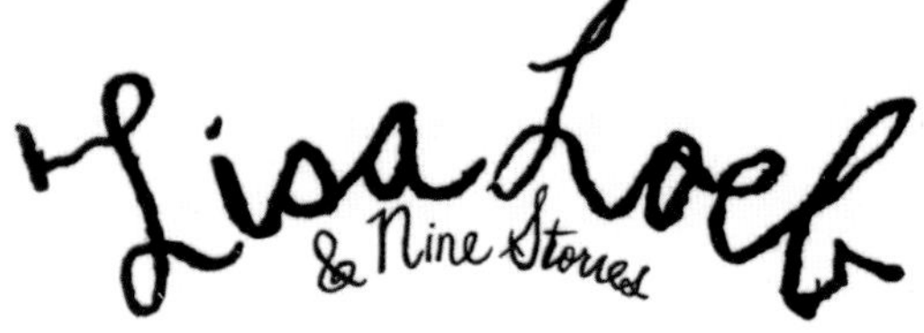

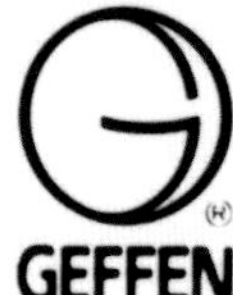

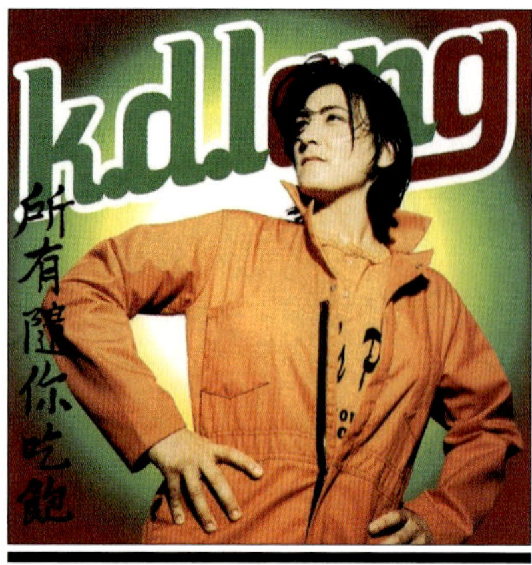

Billboard 200: *All You Can Eat* (#37)

On *All You Can Eat*, Canadian singer **k.d. lang** carried on with brazen pop sensibilities and adroit torch music.

BLESSED WITH one of the most distinctive, dazzling voices in pop music, k.d. lang's star rose during the period of her platinum album *Ingénue*. She won three Grammys, notably 1992's Best Female Pop Vocal Performance for the single "Constant Craving." She was also subjected to intense attention. A "Meat Stinks" ad campaign for the People for the Ethical Treatment of Animals earned the Canadian vegetarian repudiation from both the beef industry and her hometown in southern Alberta. She publicly declared she was gay in an article in *The Advocate*.

But it did no harm to the singer's career. "People are going to think what they want to think—they're going to interpret who I am in terms of their own experiences," lang said. "You can't fight that. You've got to live your life. There are so many untruths out there about me—it doesn't really matter. What really matters is when my music provokes an emotional response. Now I have no cards up my sleeve. I've got nothing left to talk about. I have to date a man to get some more publicity. Just kidding."

For two years, lang gave up her place in the spotlight to clear her head. She retreated to Canada and re-emerged with the album *All You Can Eat*. "I made a conscious decision to lay lower, not to go for the short-term," she explained. "To me, my career hasn't even started. Whatever it's going to be, it will probably be in my later years. Film, painting, production, whatever—I'm totally open. I don't want to be a pop artist necessarily."

Produced with longtime collaborator and guitarist Ben Mink, *All You Can Eat* told the tale of an evolving romance, and she crooned soft, sensuous gay love songs—"World of Love," "Sexuality" and "If I Were You," the only single. The album showed no traces of the country-outlaw stylings that launched her career.

"We didn't have a clear map of what we were doing, but we didn't want to make another *Ingénue*—that was the No. 1 priority," the chanteuse explained. "We had exhausted ourselves in terms of lushness and being over-the-top with the strings and the arrangements. It's a subtle record—no one's going to argue that with me. We wanted to do something simpler and funkier, make a seductive, sexy record with the lyrics a little more upfront.

"With *All You Can Eat*, I've avoided a lot of pressure—I've also sold about 10 percent of what I sold with *Ingénue*, but I've avoided it! For some reason, as I've developed as an artist, I have a bigger aversion to formulaic creativity. I don't like when an artist makes the same record over and over because it's selling. If that's really what they do, then that's cool, but for me, I'm way too musically promiscuous." ■

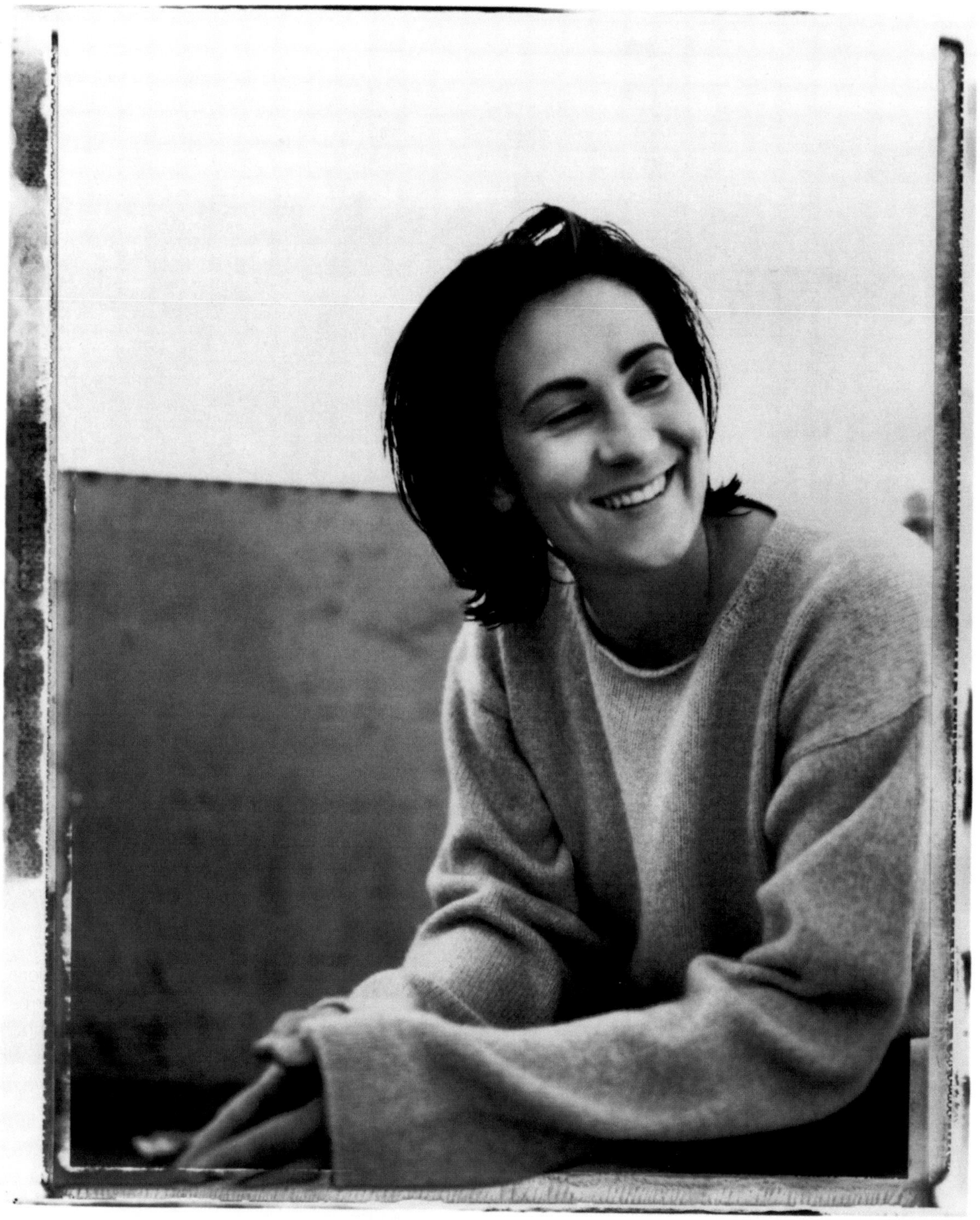

PHOTO CREDIT: Guzman

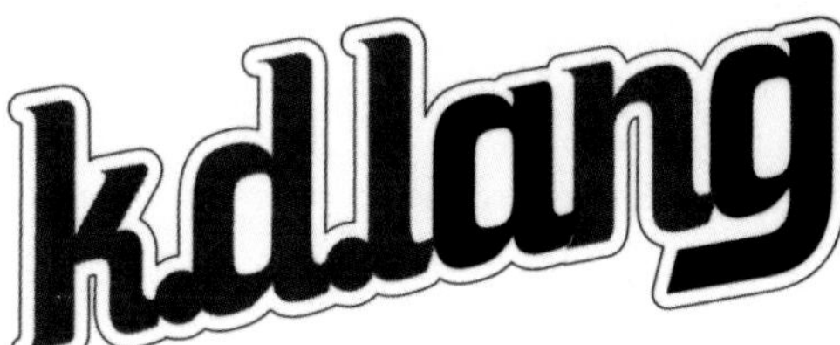

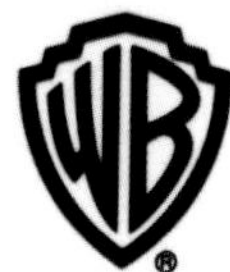

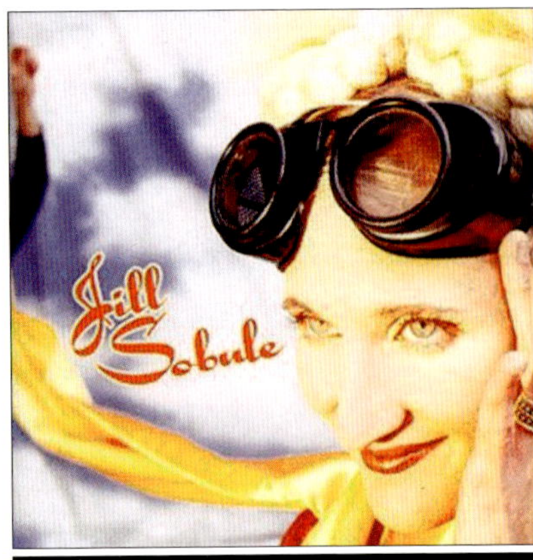

Billboard Hot 100: *"I Kissed a Girl"* (#67)

Singer-songwriter Jill Sobule found pop success when her endearing "I Kissed a Girl" passed by social taboos.

IN THE song "I Kissed a Girl," two women compare notes about their jerky boyfriends and end up dabbling in the act described as "just like kissing me, only better." Thus, Jill Sobule managed to tackle a controversial topic with disarming wit and style, and thanks to a wacky video (featuring famed male fashion model Fabio playing a sometime sweetheart described as "dumb as a box of hammers") that got heavy airplay on MTV and VH1, "I Kissed a Girl" garnered a lot of publicity—and took on a novelty-song stigma.

Sobule, a clever songwriter with anecdotal approach to lyrics, didn't understand why her ditty caused such an uproar—WYHY, a radio station in Nashville, broadcast parental advisories before playing it—but she refused to fuel the fire by confirming whether it was as autobiographical as it appeared.

"It's a pretty innocent comedy song," Sobule said. "I mean, it reminds me of a bad Nineties version of *Love, American Style*. It certainly isn't a Melissa Etheridge 'Yes I Am' thing, you know? I had one guy ask me in an interview, 'So, is it fact or fiction, heh-heh?' I said, 'It's over, and I'm ashamed of it, and I don't want people to know—but it was an affair I had with the wife of a very important Republican congressman with a new high position in government.'"

The alternative folk singer grew up in Denver in the Sixties. Despite her Jewish upbringing, she was enrolled in Catholic school for the strict discipline. She played and quit the electric guitar as a child; then, studying at the University of Colorado, she started singing and playing acoustic, but she never had the nerve to play her songs for other people. Spending her junior year abroad, she played her first public gigs in the streets of Seville, Spain.

She headed back to the US and started shyly playing in front of audiences, migrating between Denver, New York City and Nashville before a showcase gig led to her discovery and a recording contract. Her 1990 debut, *Things Here Are Different*, produced by Todd Rundgren, was all but unheard in the States. She opened Joe Jackson's tour and completed a follow-up album with him as producer, but her record company turned it down and released her from the contract.

"Then my management dropped the ball, and I couldn't get arrested. It was a complete disaster, really bleak," Sobule said. "And then it just happened out of nowhere, as a fluke."

By way of a lawyer acquaintance, she came to the attention of Atlantic Records. *Jill Sobule* was permeated with her melodic instincts and wry whimsy. With "I Kissed a Girl," she pondered the innocent yet seditious notion of same-sex attraction. The satirical "Supermodel," which referenced an eating disorder, was featured prominently in *Clueless*, Amy Heckerling's 1995 hit teen comedy film.

"I wish I'd never had to do two years of being completely disillusioned and in poverty, but it made me a better person," she said. "This is actually the first thing that I've been really proud of. Not many people get one chance to do this. I feel pretty amazed that I get another." ■

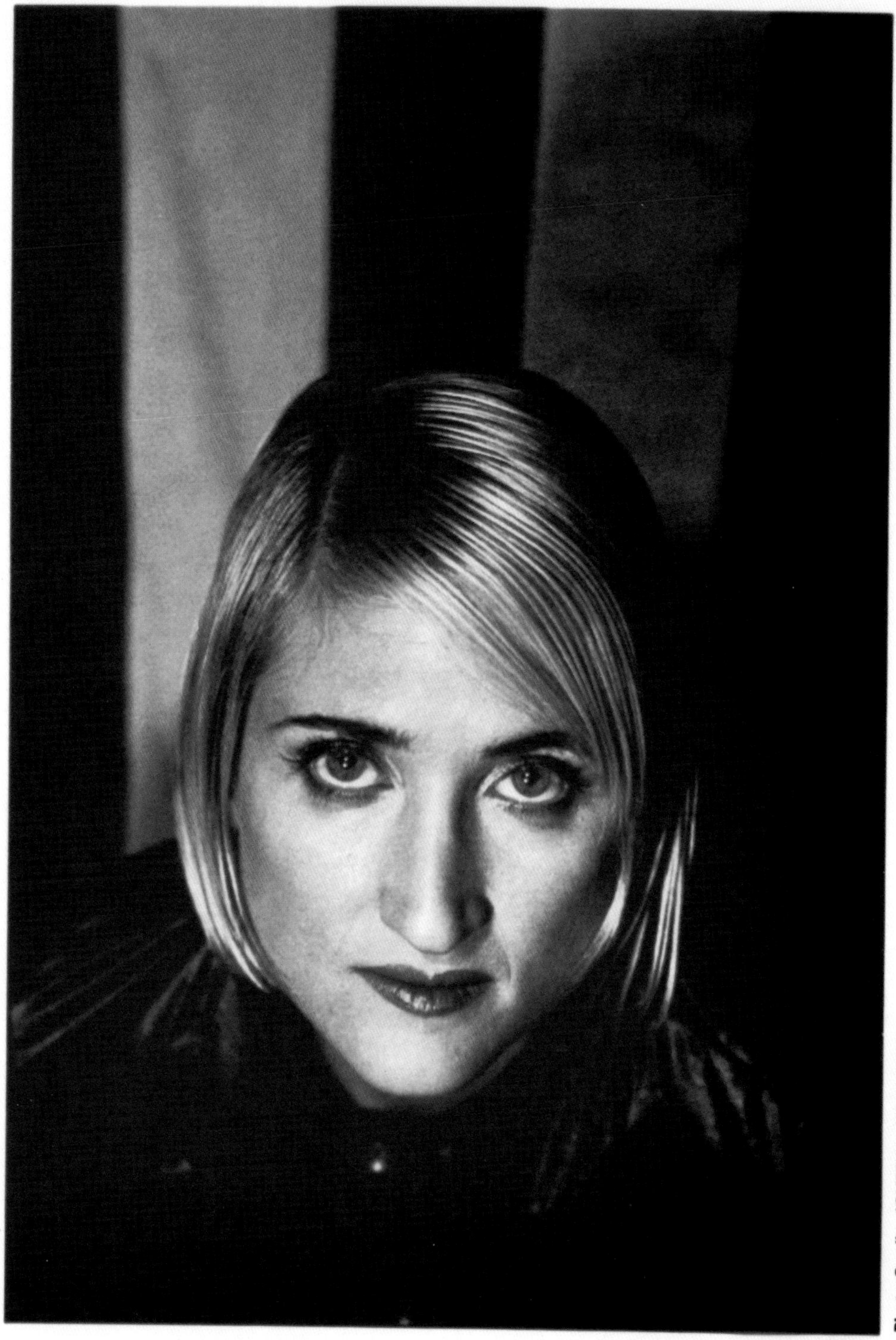

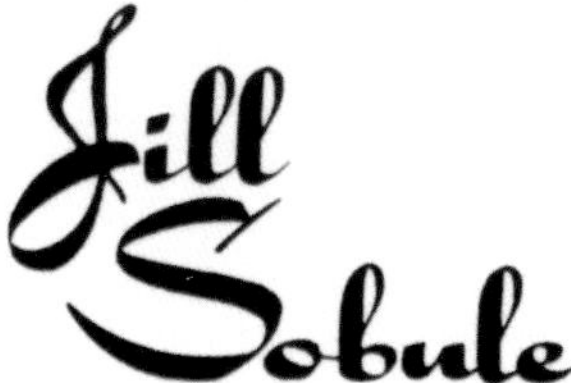

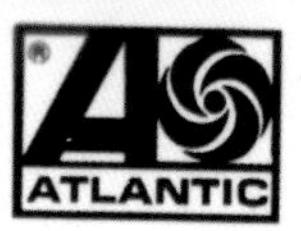

Photo Credit: JOHNNY HERNANDEZ

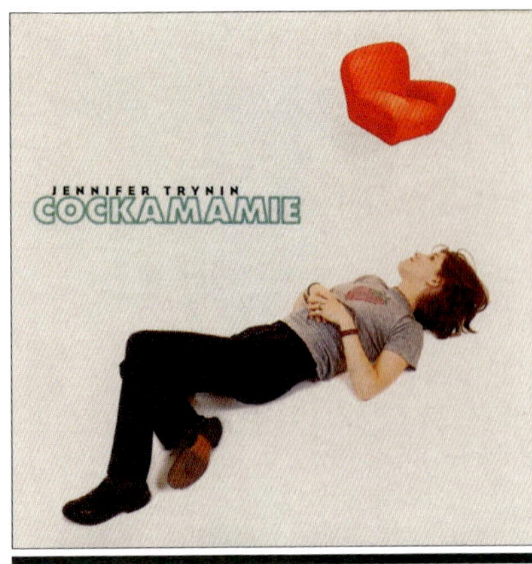

Jennifer Trynin's catchy "Better Than Nothing" portended long-term success, but album sales proved otherwise.

AFTER SEVEN years of slogging it out in the Boston music scene, Jennifer Trynin was running her own desktop publishing business when she recorded *Cockamamie*, an exercise in tough, smart guitar-pop.

"I recorded the album the only way I've ever done stuff, on my own with tons of different people—you do what you can to slap it together, and whoever shows up plays on the track," Trynin said.

Cockamamie earned enough attention to bring about a bidding war between major labels looking for the next high priestess of indie rock. Warner Bros. re-released the album as originally recorded, and "Better Than Nothing" did well on radio and MTV—the single reached at #15 on *Billboard*'s alternative chart. But Trynin had some attitude when it came to label executives and the album's promotion.

"I figured out how to make a name for myself on a local level. I'm beginning to realize it's going to take me a while to suss out how to do it on a much larger scale," she said. "All this has been a little wacky and distracting, an extremely hard adjustment. If I change, this is all gonna fall apart."

Cockamamie deserved a wider audience, but despite positive reviews, the album failed to do well. Trynin described the experience as "a little like tooling around on your bike only to awake in a semi going 90 and not knowing how to drive."

"In the end, if you're not proud of your songs and yourself, pack it in, because this ain't worth it—it's just not that much fun. People say, 'Don't sell out.' I'm thinking, 'Sell out to what?' This is extremely hard work, and you get embarrassed and angry all the time. People think they know you and they don't. It's not the party I signed up for, anyway." ■

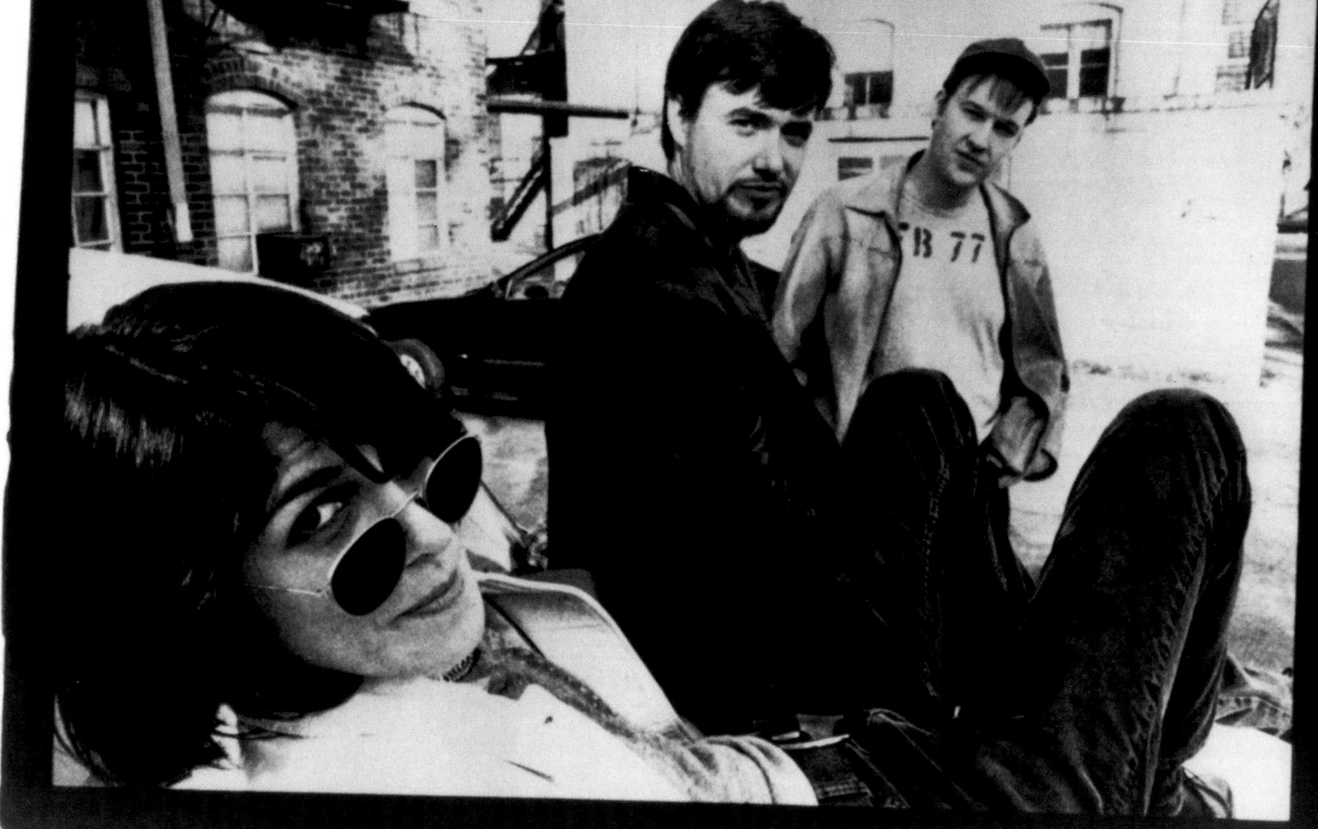

PHOTO CREDIT: Jonas Kahn

JENNIFER TRYNIN

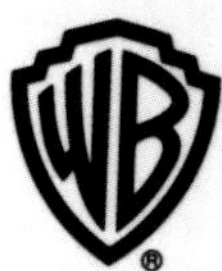

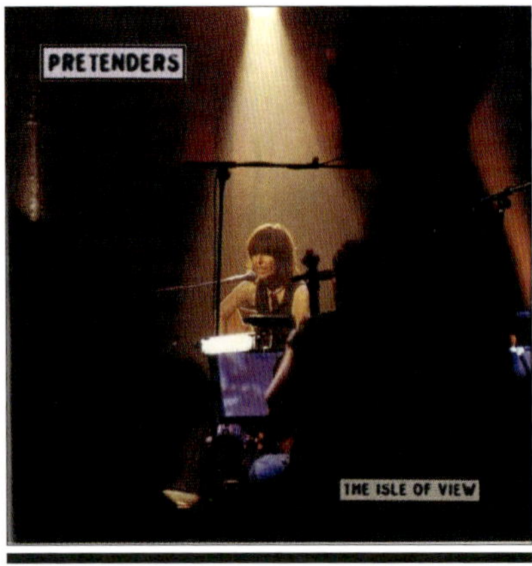

Billboard 200: *The Isle of View* (#100)

Classic **Pretenders** tracks were fashioned in all-acoustic arrangements on *The Isle of View*, a dynamic live album.

MUCH HAD transpired since the 1979 debut of the Pretenders. Two founding members had died, and original drummer Martin Chambers had returned after an absence of nine years.

But Chrissie Hynde was still fronting the band and influencing how women rocked. Her impeccable pop smarts and no-nonsense sexual bravado remained remarkably undiminished on the band's 1994 release *Last of the Independents*, a triumphant return to form.

"There's a sense of nostalgia every time I get on a stage," Hynde said. "I'm a rock 'n' roll person. After a few years off, I'm just fucking dying to get into a hotel—to be honest, domesticity doesn't really suit me that well. I'm not trying to carve out a career for myself or leave something behind to become immortal. I am just trying to goof off, hang out, get by, get onstage and rock. I've never felt like I had to prove anything. I only wanted to be in a band."

The motivation for *The Isle of View* emerged during the sessions for *Last of the Independents*. "We cut a version of 'Angel of the Morning' to use as a B-side," Hynde explained. "Stephen Street, who produced the track, suggested we use the Duke Quartet, whom he's worked with in the past. The sound of the strings meshed with the band so well that the idea of working with that kind of instrumentation stayed with me."

After touring in support of *Last of the Independents*, the group wanted to keep working. Hynde and Pretenders guitarist Adam Seymour began culling the Pretenders' catalog and found that material formed from the electric exchange of bass-drums guitar took on new dimensions in an unamplified approach.

"It was great to strip back these songs to their bare essentials, to take away all the studio touches and refinements and hear them in their most basic form," Hynde said. "I think that's a good test of any song, to see if it stands on its own."

The next step was incorporating the Duke Quartet into the acoustic setting. Recorded before a live audience at London's Jacob Street Studios, *The Isle of View* captured the Pretenders in a stylistic changeup. "Instead of sticks, Martin at one point was playing drums with two ball point pens," Hynde revealed. "Everybody had fun, doing whatever it took to make the music work. I like to think of the Pretenders as a group somewhere in midcareer. We've got time to try all sorts of things. I don't think of this album as some kind of drastic departure—we'll always be a rock 'n' roll band. This is just a way of keeping things fresh." ■

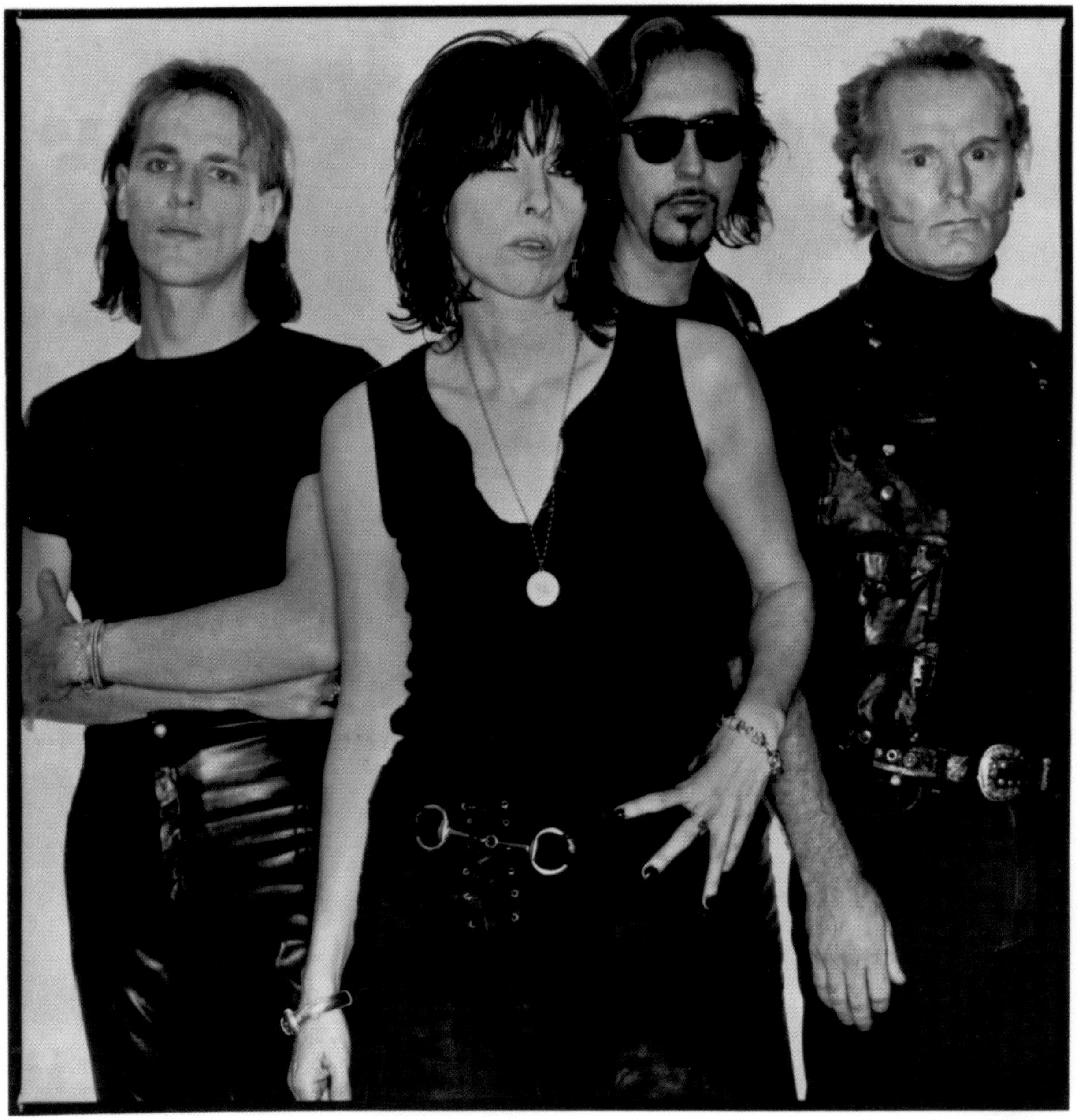

PHOTO CREDIT: Gavin Evans

PRETENDERS

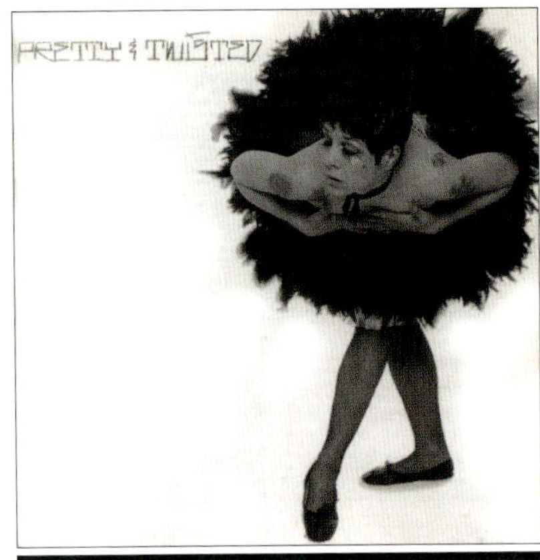

Having put Concrete Blonde on the shelf, the enigmatic cult heroine Johnette Napolitano forged Pretty & Twisted.

FOR SIX years and five albums, Johnette Napolitano was the vocalist, songwriter and bassist fronting Concrete Blonde. But after a 1994 tour, she broke up the acclaimed Los Angeles punk band and introduced a new endeavor, Pretty & Twisted.

"I nearly broke down at rehearsal when we started sounding good—'I don't believe this, this is exactly what I'm hearing in my head,'" she said. "And I feel bad about saying that, because I do love my old band. I felt equal measures of guilt, joy and peace. I didn't know what to do with my life at the point that I left Concrete Blonde. There were hard times when I thought I was going to go nuts—'I made a big mistake, I don't know what I'm doing, I put too much pressure on myself.' There are a lot more women playing music in bands since I started. What do people expect of me? It's very easy to get confused if you have too much input."

Initially, Napolitano began recording a solo project at her home studio in the Silver Lake area of Los Angeles. But the time came to assemble a new band lineup—Pretty & Twisted featured former Wall of Voodoo guitarist Marc Moreland and drummer Danny Montgomery. The group's self-titled debut album included five tracks Napolitano penned with Moreland, but she also turned to other collaborators. Chris Bailey from Australia's Saints helped with the lyrics to "¡Ride!" "Singing Is Fire" was a Charles Bukowski poem set to music.

Bukowski "was very much the voice of L.A. to me when I was in my twenties, the early, wild years, which he captured better than anyone," Napolitano explained. "I had to go through everything he'd ever done and find something where he repeated a word at least four or five times—then it was a point he was trying to make, and I could make it a chorus. I can't play the same stuff I played 10 years ago. I'm older and not as angry about the same things. The music is darker, moodier, more intense, but it's not juvenile. It's where I am now."

Napolitano hadn't laid Concrete Blonde to rest completely—she was still working with guitarist Jim Mankey on an album with longtime friends Los Illegals, an East L.A. Chicano punk band.

"Jim is playing a lot of flamenco guitar, and I get to write in Spanish, something the American record companies have always had a problem with me doing," she said. "So it's nice—Jim and I are in a band together, but it's not our band. We're just a group of friends again. I'm pretty happy—the kind of happiness that comes after you had something in mind germinating for years and then fear of chasing the wrong rainbow. But if you really do believe, it's all yours. People can call you crazy, but nobody can stop you." ■

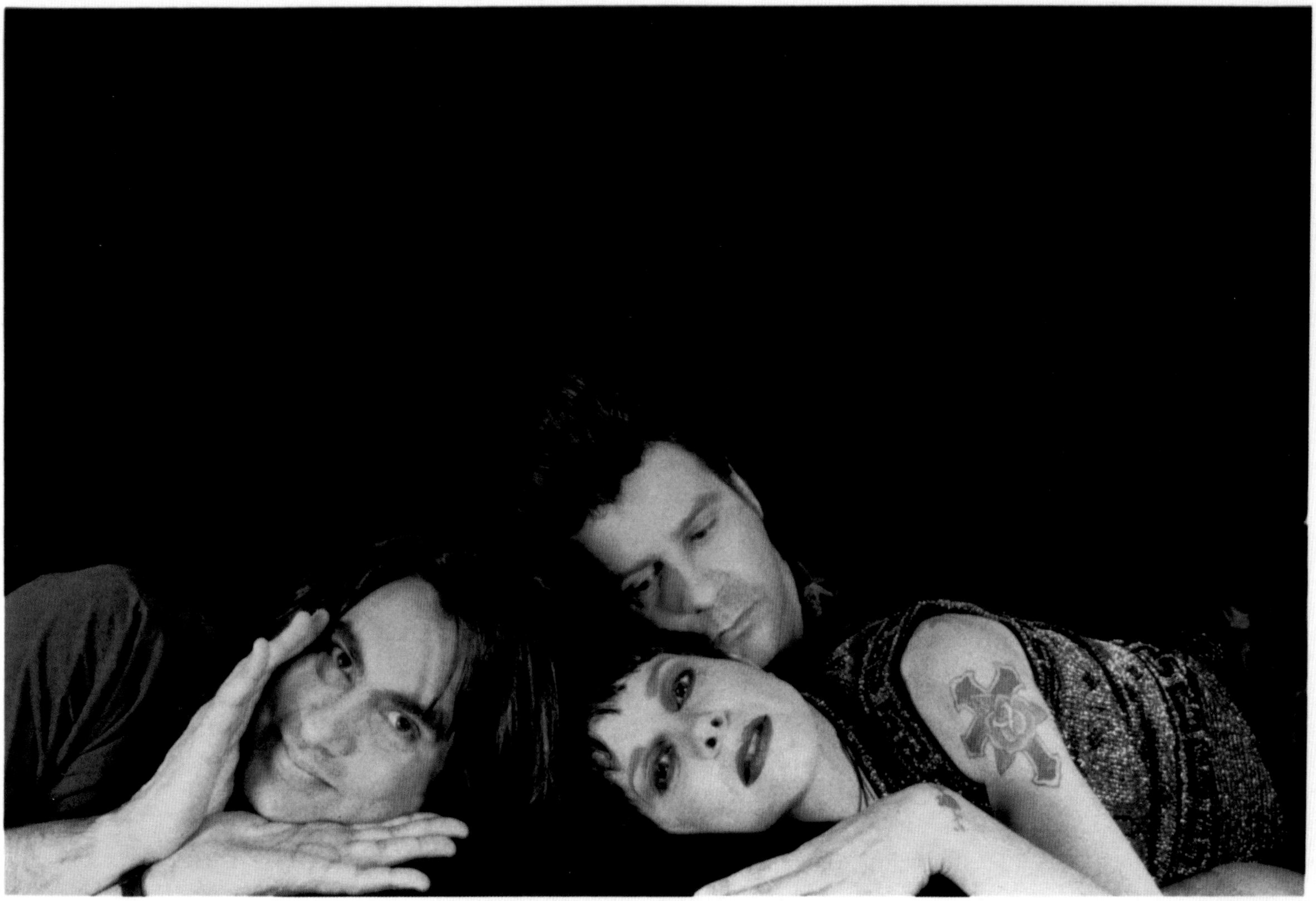

PHOTO CREDIT- Portia S.R. Liles

PRETTY & TWISTED

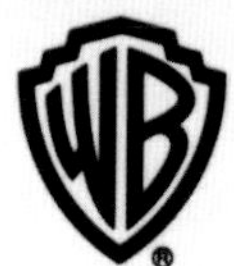

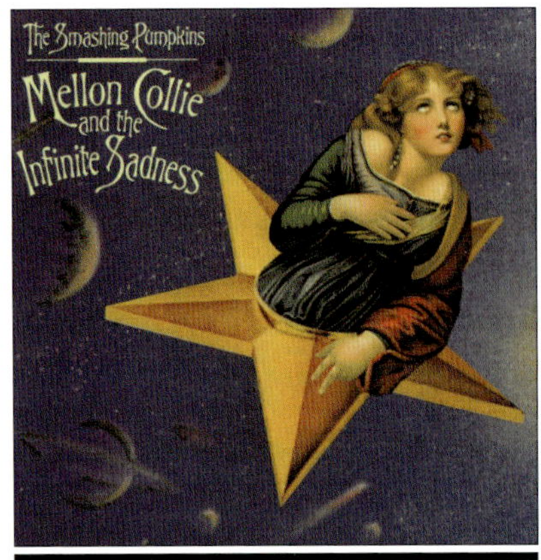

Billboard 200: *Mellon Collie and the Infinite Sadness* (No. 1)
Billboard Hot 100: "Bullet with Butterfly Wings" (#22); "1979" (#12); "Tonight, Tonight" (#36); "Thirty-Three" (#39)

The Smashing Pumpkins emerged as grunge-rock's heavy hitters with *Mellon Collie and the Infinite Sadness.*

IN THE wake of Nirvana's *Nevermind*, the Smashing Pumpkins were the first non-Seattle alternative band to hit the mainstream. The Chicago rockers gained a strong following with 1991's *Gish*, and 1993's *Siamese Dream*, featuring the radio staple "Today," put them over the top.

But the success was nearly obscured by the foursome's difficult past, a reputation as "the poster children for dysfunctional America." Obsessive singer-songwriter-guitarist Billy Corgan decided to play most of the guitar and bass parts himself on *Siamese Dream*, which created tension in the band.

"When Billy and I started the band eight years ago, we wanted to get away from three-chord Midwestern rock, like the Replacements," guitarist James Iha said. "We didn't want to be another average band, we wanted to make something more dramatic. It was a culmination of a lot of different things we liked back then—the Cure and the Smiths, and Black Sabbath. We wanted to get bigger and bigger, but we didn't think we were going to be the biggest rock band in the world."

After the Pumpkins' headlining stint on the 1994 Lollapalooza tour, Corgan—who never hid his love for Sixties and Seventies classic rock—boasted he would make a sprawling, ambitious double-CD that would be Pink Floyd's *The Wall* for Generation X. *Mellon Collie and the Infinite Sadness* was the masterpiece the Pumpkins crafted. The 28 songs on the album were entertaining and diverse, careening from dense, tortured metal ("Where Boys Fear to Tread") to delicate ballads (the majestic "Tonight, Tonight") to even long, trippy art-rock pieces ("Porcelina of the Vast Oceans"). Corgan and Iha stretched out on several dynamic guitar workouts.

"There was just no way to finish the record as a one-man band—it was important that everyone gave their two cents worth on every track," Iha said. "By the time the recording was getting close to finished, you could see the depth that the record might have. This is probably the epic of the band's career—trying to encapsulate all these different styles and yet still be a Nineties rock band."

Corgan seemed more conflicted and wretched than ever—in "Bullet with Butterfly Wings," he shrieked "Despite all my rage, I am still just a rat in a cage"—and his brutally confessional lyrics probed his emotional detachment.

"We're not easy to understand," Corgan said. "I'm not every teenage girl's vision of what they want to bring home to mom. Yes, we're a little strange, and what we feel and believe is a little different, so it's not always an easy conversation. We're not given the respect critically or culturally that we deserve, but we feel we're doing something unique."

With *Mellon Collie and the Infinite Sadness*, the Smashing Pumpkins had bragging rights to the best-selling double-CD release of all time. "It's good that the record sold a lot," Iha said. "That validates the band to a lot of would-be detractors." ■

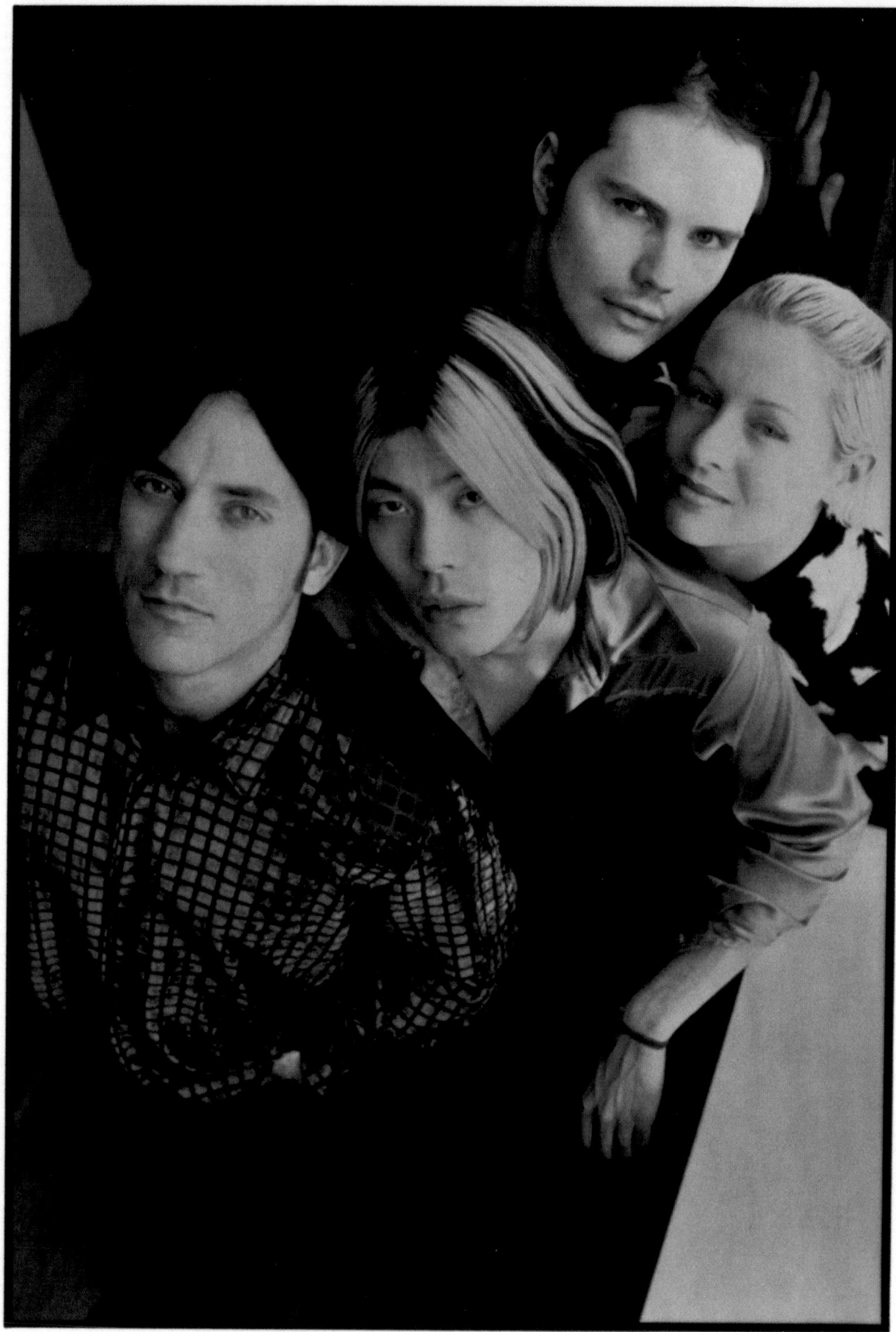

Photo Credit: Danny Clinch 9/95

The Smashing Pumpkins

Virgin

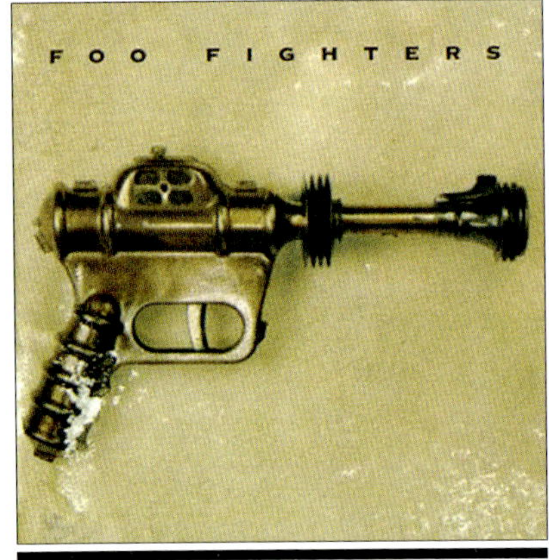

Billboard 200: *Foo Fighters* (#23)

Pulling himself out from the shadows of Nirvana, Dave Grohl surprised the public by establishing Foo Fighters.

IT SEEMED anachronistic to refer to Dave Grohl as the drummer for Nirvana—not because his contributions to that pioneering grunge band weren't significant, but because his post-Nirvana project, Foo Fighters, enjoyed so much success. Rather than fade away in the aftermath of Kurt Cobain's 1994 suicide, Grohl traded in his drum kit for a guitar and a microphone and formed an enterprise that provided him an opportunity to deliver aggressive, radio-friendly pop-punk.

Foo Fighters had a smart, energetic sound—there was a knack for urgent chord progressions and a love of distortion. Layered guitar sounds and some real precise bashing punched up the joyous "This Is a Call," which garnered heavy alternative- and album-rock airplay. "For All the Cows" took off after the slowed-down verses. "Big Me," a gentle pop-flavored melody, enjoyed crossover success.

Grohl sang and wrote every song and played virtually every note on the project. By his admission, *Foo Fighters* was simply a collection of his own demos that he cobbled together.

"In 1990, I was living in Seattle and I'd just joined Nirvana," he explained. "My friend Barrett Jones was sick of living in Virginia, where the two of us grew up. He had this eight-track studio—he recorded my first punk rock band. I said, 'You should move out here, it's really nice, we'll get a house.' So he moves out and he brings the eight-track. Any time, I could go down in the basement and say, 'Hey, Barrett, will you turn this thing on? I've got an idea.' It was just an experiment, all for fun. You buy the reel of tape for $45, bring it back to the studio and you can put whatever you want on. We were making speed-metal songs, country songs, funk songs, just fucking around. That went on for years. I wasn't recording for anyone else to hear because I couldn't stand my singing voice. I gave my mother a tape. That was about it.

"After Nirvana was over, I thought maybe I'd take my 12 favorite songs out of the 30 I'd recorded and release it on my own label, maybe 10,000 copies on vinyl, and have it be totally anonymous so that people would buy this record and think, 'Who's this band? I've never heard of them before. Where are they from?' But Foo Fighters turned into a totally different thing."

The debut was a runaway hit, selling 2.5 million copies worldwide and earning all kinds of accolades and awards (it was the readers' choice for Album of the Year in both *Rolling Stone* and *Spin*). When it came time to take the show on the road, Grohl put together a band, fleshing out Foo Fighters to include Pat Smear on guitar and former Sunny Day Real Estate members Nate Mendel (bass) and William Goldsmith (drums).

Grohl explained the band's name—the term "foo fighters" was coined during the end of World War II to describe strange "glowing red" phenomena spotted by U.S. Air Force flyers patrolling German skies. ■

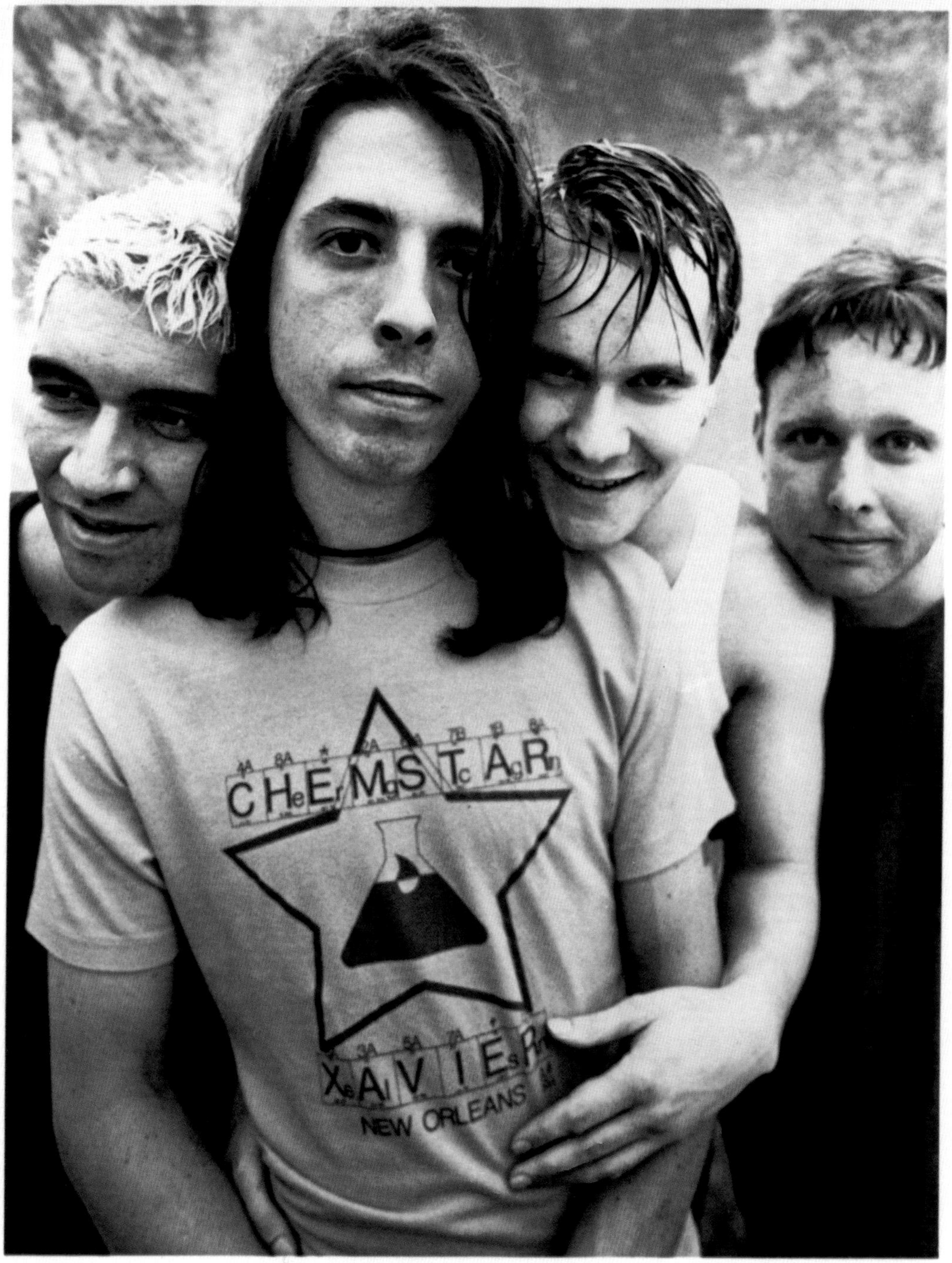

Photo credit : Tony Mott © 1996

L - R : Pat Smear, Dave Grohl, William Goldsmith, Nate Mendel

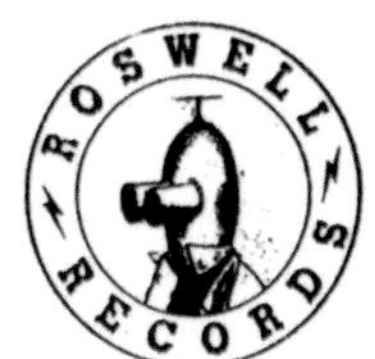

FOO FIGHTERS

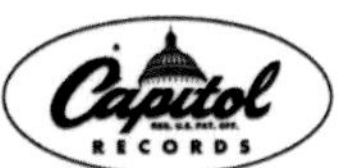

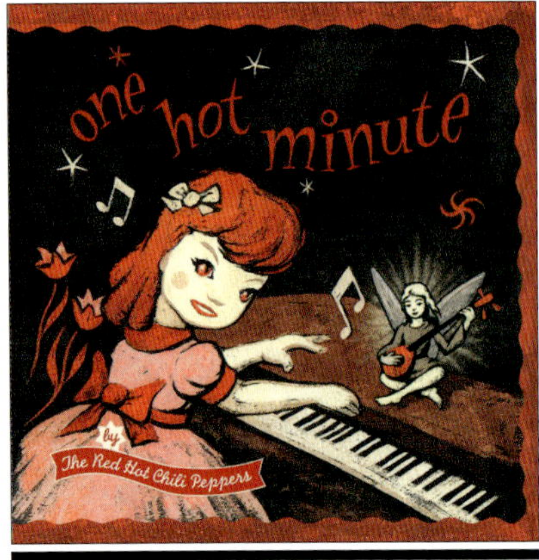

Billboard 200: *One Hot Minute* (#4)

Joining the lineage of Red Hot Chili Peppers guitarists, Dave Navarro took part in the album *One Hot Minute*.

ONCE THEY were irrevocably associated with muscular, sloppy slabs of hormonally pumped-up punk-funk and barrages of four-letter words. Oh, and performing naked except for strategically placed tube socks. Then the Red Hot Chili Peppers were catapulted from underground cultdom to the heights of alternative-rock fame when 1991's *Blood Sugar Sex Magik* generated two smash singles, "Give It Away" and "Under the Bridge."

It had taken four years to follow up the multiplatinum album. *One Hot Minute* was the first release to feature the newest guitarist—Dave Navarro, the former Jane's Addiction mainstay. Guitarist had been a revolving-door position with the Peppers following Hillel Slovak's 1988 death from an accidental overdose. Navarro was charming and animated, but he turned reserved when stating his difficulty integrating with the band. He had never listened to a Chili Peppers record before he joined. He hated funk music and basketball, both Chili Peppers commodities. He respected his new bandmates' legend, but he wasn't daunted by it.

The Chili Peppers first approached Navarro in 1992—the band was headlining Lollapalooza that summer, but guitarist John Frusciante abruptly announced that he was quitting for stress-related reasons. Navarro wasn't available at the time, but after a series of short-term replacements, he joined the band. His first gig was Woodstock '94, where the members stole the show by wearing giant light bulbs over their heads.

"I personally don't like doing stuff like that. Once we got out there, it was terribly uncomfortable," Navarro said. "I was more interested in playing a good show than being combative about something as ridiculous as that, so I just went with it."

Many fans thought the whelming presences of lead singer Anthony Kiedis and bassist Flea wouldn't allow Navarro to have an effect on the band's sound, but he brought more to the table than anyone since Slovak. Navarro's roots were in Zeppelin-influenced rock—it was his nature to take up more space, and he had moments of flashy brilliance. *One Hot Minute*, a mix of slamming workouts and skewed ballads, featured the singles "Warped," the poignant "My Friends" and "Aeroplane," a poppy paean of celebration.

Navarro had heard remarks about how his big-rock stylistic preferences had gotten the Chili Peppers away from their characteristic funk-metal floor-shaking grooves. "In fact, I have an easier time with the old material than the new material," he said. "Playing the old songs is fun—I have no emotional connection to them whatsoever. I'm in a cover band, simple."

For more than a decade, the Peppers had staked their careers on camaraderie. The charming and animated Navarro valued that, but he valued the music as well.

"The whole reason I picked up the guitar was to escape reality, human beings. So I don't try to emulate or fit in with anyone else. I just focus on whatever it takes to leave the planet for a while. I'm not really concerned with being a wacky Chili Pepper for those 75 minutes onstage."

After the tour in support of *One Hot Minute*, the band parted ways with Navarro. ■

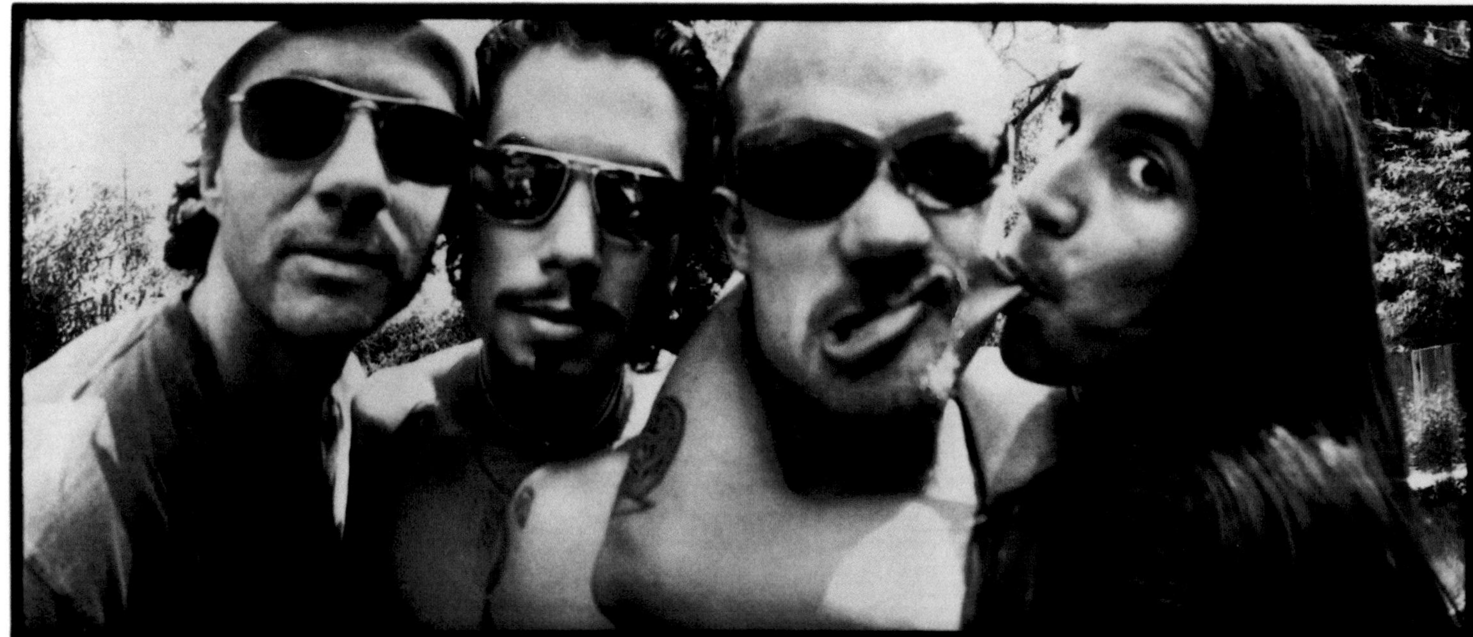

PHOTO CREDIT: Marina Chavez

Chad Smith Dave Navarro Flea Anthony Kiedis

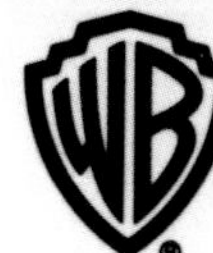

Red Hot Chili Peppers

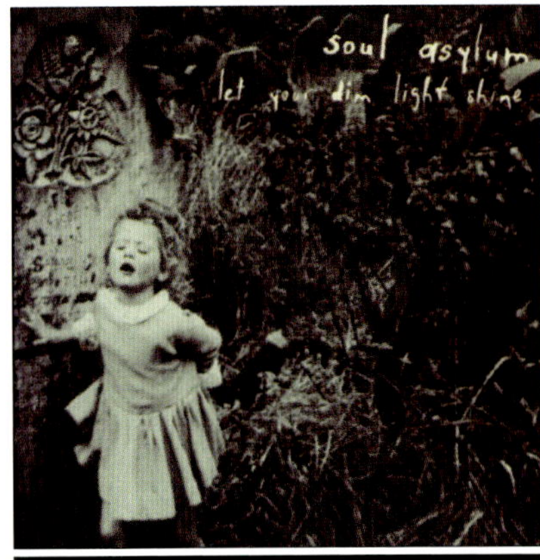

Billboard 200: *Let Your Dim Light Shine* (#6)
Billboard Hot 100: "Misery" (#20); "Promises Broken" (#63)

Managing to juggle ascendancy with credibility, Soul Asylum scored a platinum album, *Let Your Dim Light Shine.*

AFTER A decade of banging away in tiny clubs, longtime cult favorite Soul Asylum had its breakthrough. The 1992 album *Grave Dancers Union* went multiplatinum and yielded the Grammy-winning "Runaway Train," a sad hit about unwanted kids that got the world all warm and runny. Suddenly everyone was seeking Soul Asylum. But the long road to success made the Minneapolis quartet suspect of the star-making machinery.

"During those 10 years, Pearl Jam and the Black Crowes and Living Colour and the Pixies all opened for us. We were going, 'Geez, what about us? Don't we have any talent?'" guitarist Dan Murphy said. "We're not trying to keep Soul Asylum a secret anymore. We already went through that."

But *Let Your Dim Light Shine* was the first time Soul Asylum had put out a record to lofty expectations. And they were met. The band sounded dynamic thanks to the production of Butch Vig (Nirvana). The guys could still be loud and unrestrained, but they could also knock out Tom Petty-like acoustic pop. The hit "Misery" sounded like another song about self-loathing for disaffected twentysomethings: "They say misery loves company/We could start a company and make misery/Frustrated Incorporated…"

"But 'Misery' is us making fun of ourselves as much as anybody," Murphy said. "We're on Sony fucking Music—Frustrated, Inc. The humor isn't lost on us."

Another bright moment was the clever "Just Like Anyone." The guitars were gutsy, and the words charted a girl's emotional epiphany—in an outhouse.

"It's a weird, strange story-song—pondering existence when you're sitting on the bowl," Murphy said. "But that's a common experience for everybody. I do some of my best thinking when I'm in that pose. Musically, it's got a lot of Soul Asylum elements. There's a lot of tension—it's staccato for the verses and just explodes in the big chorus."

The album put Soul Asylum in an awkward position with irritable alternative rockers who had previously championed the band but now charged it had gone soft. Singer and guitarist Dave Pirner was a regular in the gossip sections for his relationship with movie star Wynona Ryder, but Murphy said Pirner was "still the same bunch of guys that he was before.

"This record has been so misunderstood. People aren't reacting to the music as much as they are to what they've heard about the band. We've slowly learned how to play better together. That's really the only change. We've become more of a band and less of a contest to see who can play the most shit at the same time."

Murphy laughed. "Unfortunately, the other style of music that I'm a fan of is in vogue right now—the loud, punk-rock guitars, the angst and spitting. Someday we're gonna get it right, and then the world's in trouble!" ■

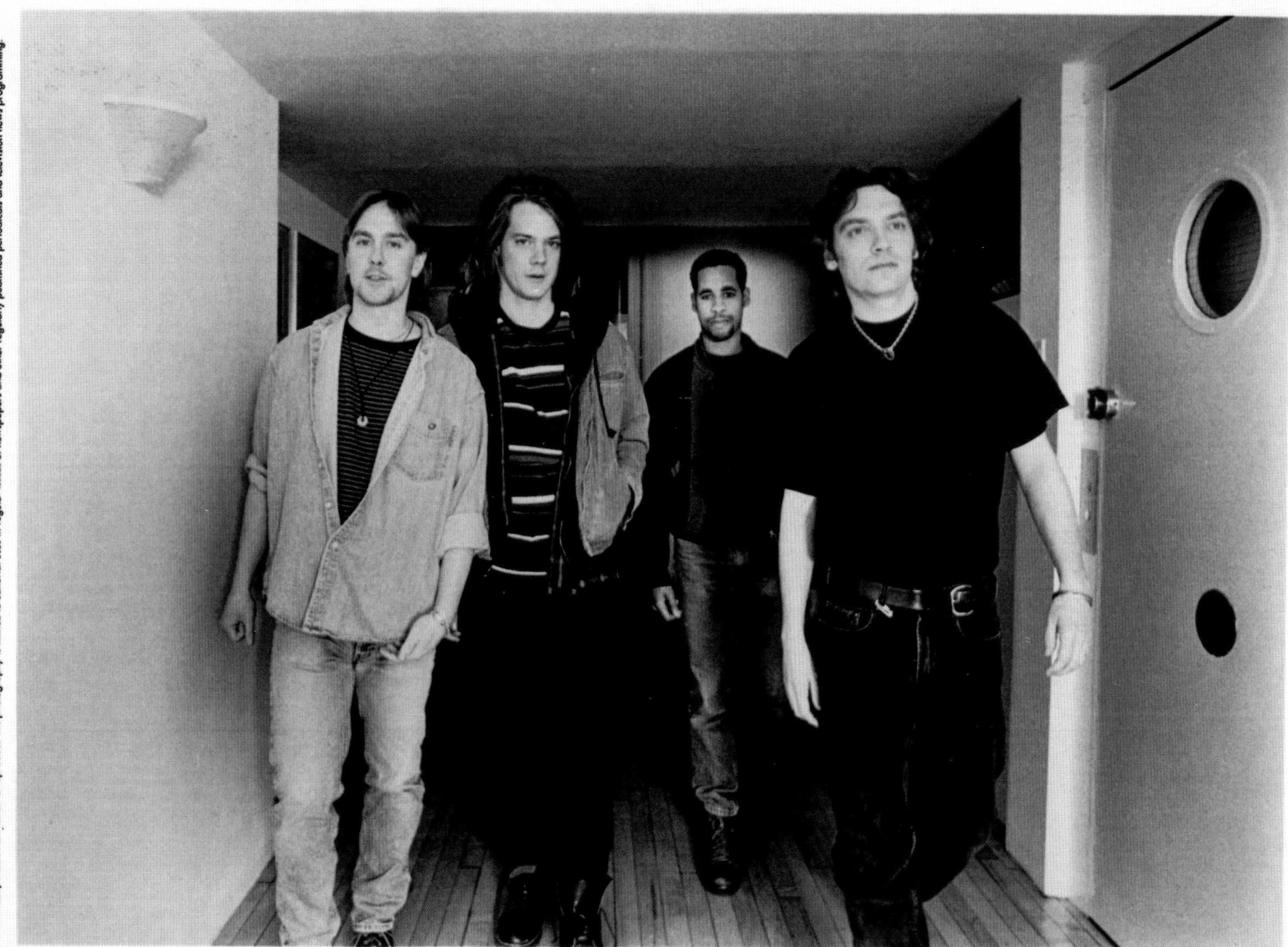

PHOTOGRAPH: KAREN MASON

Dan Murphy Dave Pirner Sterling Campbell Karl Mueller

Management: Danny Heaps
For Addis/Wechsler & Associates
Los Angeles, CA
Phone: 213-954-9000
Fax: 213-954-9023

SOUL ASYLUM

COLUMBIA
9504

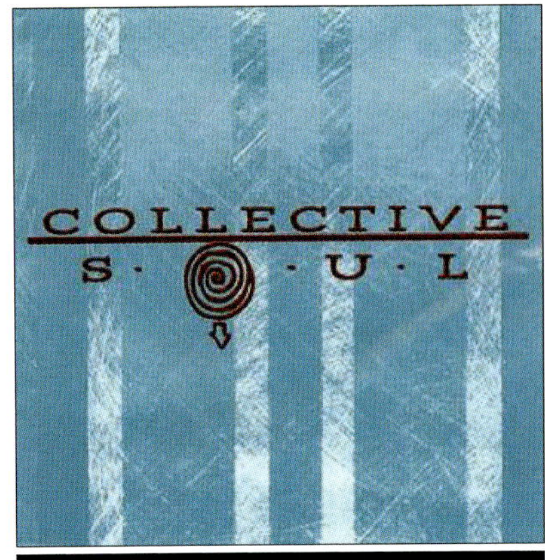

Billboard 200: *Collective Soul* (#23)
Billboard Hot 100: "December" (#20); "The World I Know" (#19)

Spawning five mainstream rock hits, a self-titled sophomore endeavor proved Collective Soul's crossover appeal.

COLLECTIVE SOUL was initially fettered with the "alternative" label, but the Georgia-based quintet was enjoying a heyday as a guitar-pop alternative to grunge, punk and hard rock.

"A critic called us 'the Bachman-Turner Overdrive of the Nineties,'" singer, guitarist and songwriter Ed Roland said. "Those comparisons don't bother me—we owe a great debt to classic rock. Looking back on the past year, I'm shocked but grateful."

That was because the debut album *Hints, Allegations and Things Left Unsaid* was basically Roland's demo—after a dozen years of assembling and playing with various lineups trying to get a record deal, he had given up on success. "I got discouraged and disenchanted," he admitted. "I was locked in a basement, sitting with a drum machine and writing songs for other bands to play."

He put together *Hints* and one of the tunes exploded. A college radio station began playing "Shine," which created a hometown buzz. Then a commercial station in Florida broke the song—16,000 copies of a self-distributed album were sold in two months. The news intrigued a major label, which picked up *Hints*, sweetened the mix and re-released it, and "Shine"—the most requested song in the country in 1994, a massive smash played on every radio format—propelled it to platinum status.

"But when I was asked to perform live, I had to round up a band," Roland said.

He regrouped his younger brother Dean and Ross Childress on guitars, Will Turpin on bass and Shane Evans on drums, and Collective Soul (Roland came across the name in Ayn Rand's book *The Fountainhead*) did the bonding thing on the road.

"*Hints* just wasn't a true representation of the band—*Collective Soul*, our new album, is actually our first official record," Roland said. "I'm still the songwriter, but it's evident that we collaborate well."

The Beatles-esque "December," the symphonic ballad "The World I Know" and "Where the River Flows" each reached No. 1 on *Billboard*'s album rock chart, detailed by Roland's penchant for engaging, hooky melodies, layered harmonies and subtle percussion work. The anthemic "Gel" and the funky "Smashing Young Man" were other radio-ready songs, featuring punchy and precise three-guitar interplay.

"We were asked to do 'Gel' for *The Jerky Boys* soundtrack, and we were like, 'Who are the Jerky Boys? We thought it was pretty funny that we'd contributed this song about the coming together of mankind for this movie about these guys making prank phone calls," Roland recounted.

"We're from Stockbridge, a very small town a half-hour outside of Atlanta—everybody knows everybody. I used to fight with my parents over rock 'n' roll when I was a teenager. Now they watch MTV all the time. Family and friends are more excited than we are. That's the best part about having my dream come true." ■

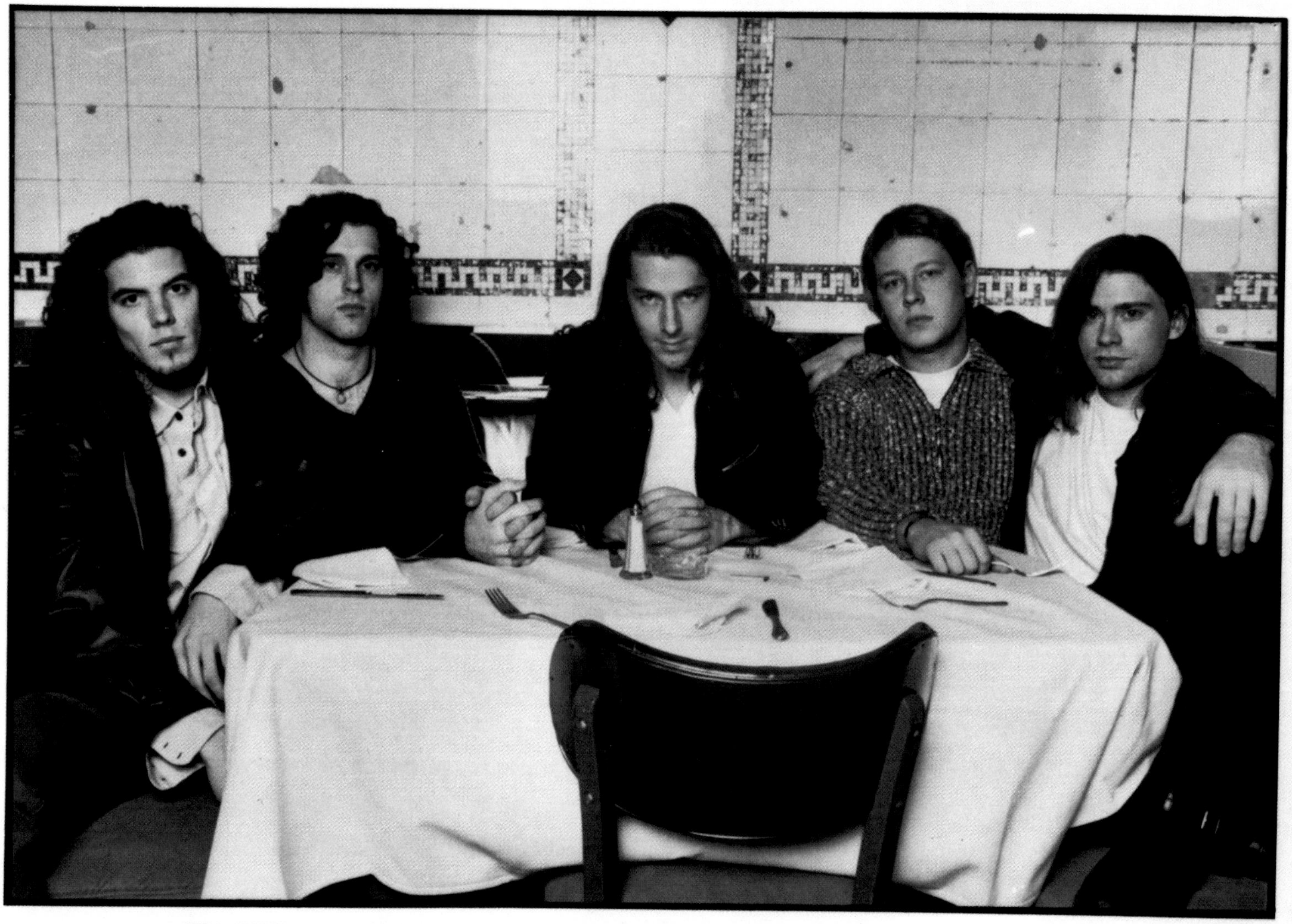

WILL TURPIN DEAN ROLAND ED ROLAND SHANE EVANS ROSS CHILDRESS

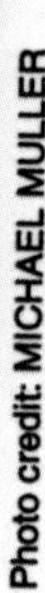

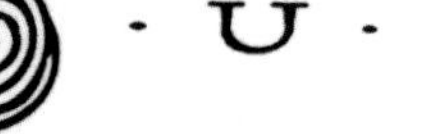

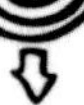

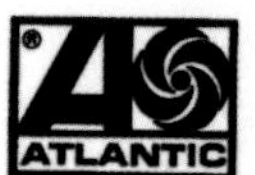

Billboard 200: *A Boy Named Goo* (#27)
Billboard Hot 100: "Name" (#5); "Naked" (#47)

With *A Boy Named Goo* and the wistful smash "Name," Goo Goo Dolls were in the grip of a new level of success.

FOR MANY new rock contenders, bursting into the limelight wasn't a capricious event, it was a testimony to persistence and drive. In the nine years since the Goo Goo Dolls got together in their hometown of Buffalo, New York, "America's best-known unknown band" struggled through relentless touring and record-industry woes. Things didn't look any brighter when a fifth album, *A Boy Named Goo*, barely made a dent on the radio.

But the Goo Goo Dolls' scrappy charm paid off. "Name," the third single from *A Boy Named Goo*, finally turned around the blue-collar trio's fortunes when, after a steady climb, the acoustic ballad reached No. 1 on *Billboard*'s modern rock and album rock charts. The song's aching, folk-tinged tone was a departure from the band's usual blend of pop-flavored punk and infectious, anthemic rock, crossing over to pop and adult contemporary radio. Guitarist and vocalist Johnny Rzeznik topped off all his songwriting with savvy street smarts and the realization that the best years may be behind.

"As far as being a technical musician goes, I was always real shitty. I think I took two or three lessons," Rzeznick, who was orphaned at 15 and studied to be a plumber, said. "It sounds weird, but from the first time I could actually play the damn guitar, I just wanted to write songs. So I did! And lots of 'em were bad!"

Some thought "Name" was a Replacements/Paul Westerberg ripoff. Rzeznik didn't understand it. "We're definitely from the same school, but different classrooms. The funny thing about the Replacements is that they were touted as one of the most influential bands of our time. And then the second that someone is influenced by them, they get slammed!"

Many fans felt the great "Flat Top," a hard-driving common-man protest about the TV news, would be the hit. "It's about insomnia, being oversaturated," Rzeznik explained. "As a society, I don't think we're in any worse predicament than we've ever been in. The world has been ending since it started. It's just that the television coverage has gotten so much better. CNN is 24-hour-a-day negativity. Everybody's obsessed with it because your average Joe's life is so freaking boring that he needs the drama of the ebola virus in his home every night. I have to shut myself down or I go crazy."

A Boy Named Goo went well past platinum, and the Goo Goo Dolls (they were stuck with the dumb name—Rzeznik came up with it when he was 19 and drunk) tried to adjust gracefully. But there were changes—drummer Mike Malinin replaced George Tutuska following the recording of the album, and there were legal troubles (the group filed a breach of contract suit with their label).

"I look at our career as having three stages—drunk, hungover and sober," Rzeznik said with a laugh. "I wouldn't exactly say we're in our sober phase now, but we are dead serious about making the best music we can." ■

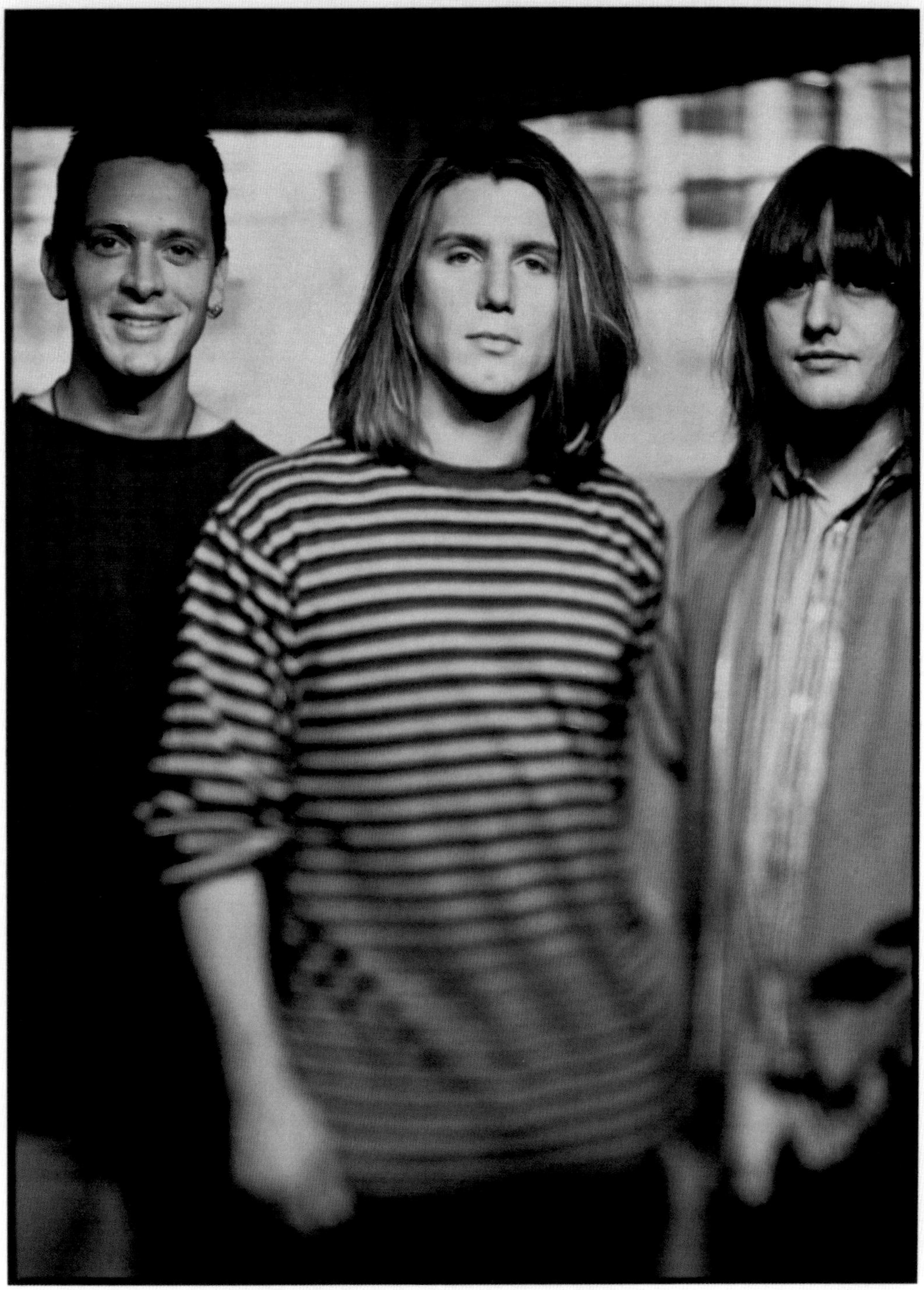

Photo Credit Frank Ockenfels

GOO-GOO-DOLLS

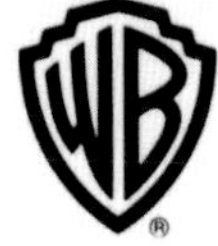

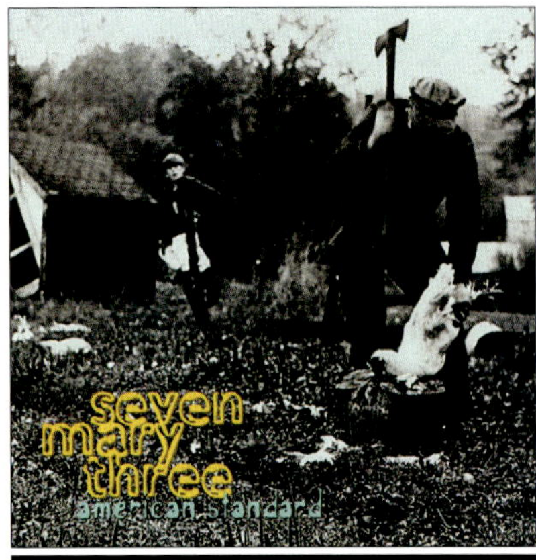

Billboard 200: *American Standard* (#24)
Billboard Hot 100: "Cumbersome" (#39)

The fashionably grungy "Cumbersome" propelled Seven Mary Three's *American Standard* to platinum prestige.

ON THE surface, Seven Mary Three, a college band out of Virginia, wasn't that different from thousands of other promising groups. But a commercial radio station in Orlando, Florida began playing the song "Cumbersome" from the quartet's independent CD. It got the band a record deal, and Seven Mary Three re-recorded the songs and created *American Standard*. The rest of the nation's stations started airing the newer version of "Cumbersome"—and the track peaked at No. 1 on *Billboard*'s Album Rock Tracks chart.

"It's a Cinderella story," vocalist Jason Ross said. "When we wrote the song, we felt that it had a good groove. It's catchy, no two ways about it. But we didn't expect it to take on a life of its own."

Jason Pollock's melodic guitar riff propelled the tune, and Ross trilled the lyrics in a coarse baritone: "I have become cumbersome to this world/I have become cumbersome to my girl..."

"I was young and in one of those relationships that didn't pan out, and I decided I wanted to write a song about it. It was the first one with heavy guitars where we were gonna rock, kick it," Ross said. "I'm glad we had the perspective of two guys who knew very little about playing the guitar and singing in a band. We were writing solely on emotion, not any kind of theory, and it was really fun. I've had 15-year-old guys come up to me and say they love the song, and I've had 40-year-old waitresses with three kids come up to me and say, 'My life has become cumbersome, too,' and they're serious about it. It gives me a lot of satisfaction knowing that they can take it wherever they want to take it."

"Cumbersome" wasn't a word that ordinarily turned up in rock songs, and the second single, "Water's Edge" (about a young woman's fatal abduction), was culled from one of Ross' creative writing assignments in college. Ross acknowledged that his degree in English from the college of William & Mary may have benefited his songwriting.

"I don't think you need an education to understand or enjoy music—that's an elitist view. But just from a personal standpoint, I found traditional literature appealing when I was younger. I enjoy the closure that it offers, where stories have a beginning, a middle and an end. There's a point to everything. When I tried to become a songsmith, that's the part that I brought over from my education—the importance of a narrative, of not just describing detail but humanizing inanimate things so that people can connect with them."

So did Seven Mary Three's somewhat mysterious moniker have a didactic interpretation?

"To tell the truth, we were sitting around watching *CHiPS* on TV, some crazy scene in the heat of action, and someone said, '7 Mary 3 to the rescue'—it was the blond officer's call sign," Ross confessed. "We thought it was a cool name." ■

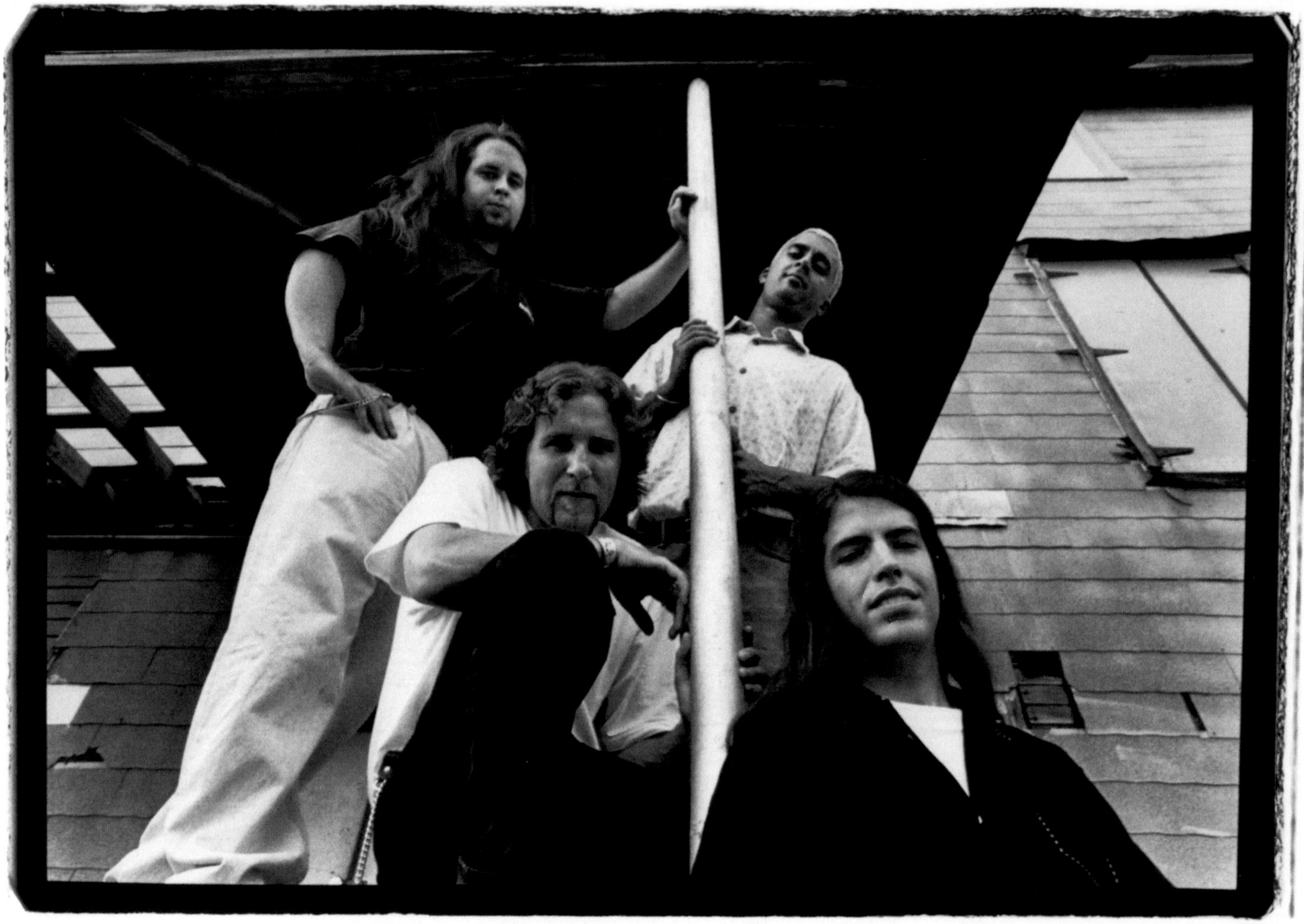

Photo Credit: Ben Gray

CASEY DANIEL JASON ROSS GITI KHALSA JASON POLLOCK

seven mary three

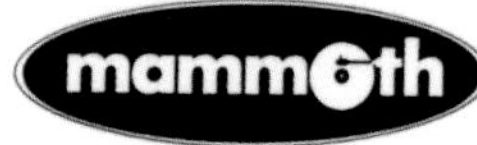

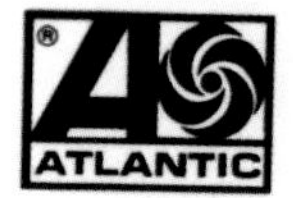

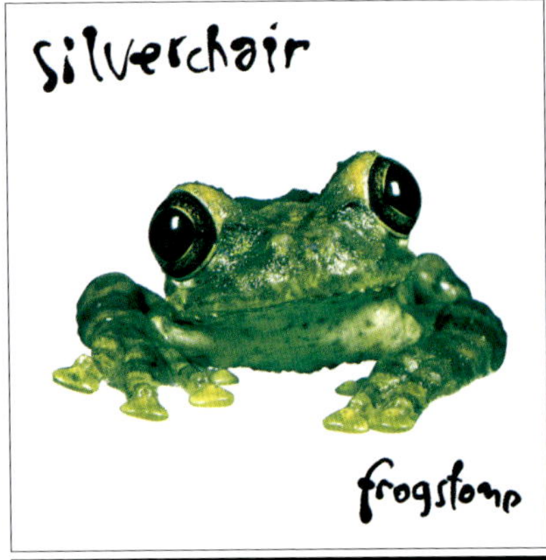

Billboard 200: *Frogstomp* (#9)

Buoyed up by the single "Tomorrow," the Australian trio Silverchair quickly soared to international stardom.

DANIEL JOHNS had heard all of the joke nicknames for his band: Silverhighchair…Soundkindergarden…Nirvana in Pajamas. Silverchair sold millions of albums worldwide, but no one was able to ignore the fact that the guys weren't old enough to buy cigarettes.

"The most unfair thing is people who think I have a limited range of life experiences, that it's not possible to have feelings at 16," vocalist and guitarist Johns said. "But go ask any teenager if they can be pessimistic or resentful or angry, and they'll fucking tell you!"

Johns thought he would grow up to be a surfer or a plumber. With bassist Chris Joannou and drummer Ben Gillies, he went from jamming in a garage in a small Australian town to winning a demo-tape contest run by a TV show. The prize was a day in a recording studio, where the teen threesome recut "Tomorrow," an anthemic track that could have been a Pearl Jam song.

The session launched a startlingly rapid climb. The debut album *Frogstomp* entered the Australian charts at No. 1, and Silverchair swept the Australian Record Industry Awards (the Aussie equivalent of the Grammys). In America, the grungy "Tomorrow" became the most played song of 1995 on modern rock radio, and "Pure Massacre" turned into a radio and MTV hit as well. *Frogstomp* reached double platinum status, establishing Silverchair as the most potent rock export from Down Under in a decade.

The band's music drew upon straightforward, familiar elements of the Seattle sound—the quiet verses and hyper choruses, the forceful percussion and mighty guitars, the angst, energy and attitude of the lyrics. "But from the start, the main influence on us was Black Sabbath and Led Zeppelin," Johns explained. "We only started getting into the other stuff later." ■

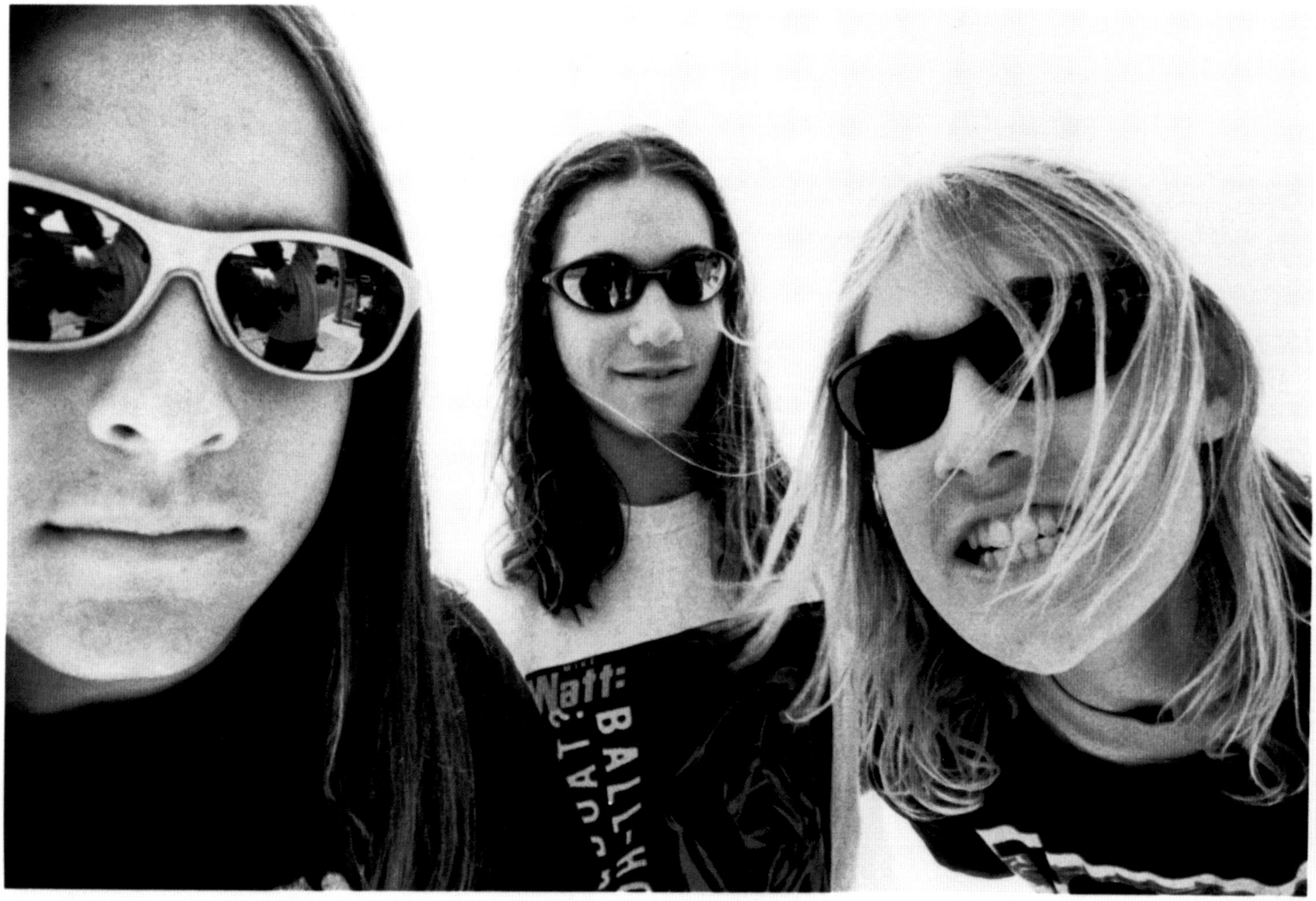

PHOTO CREDIT: JOHN DUNNE

BEN GILLIES
(DRUMS)

CHRIS JOANNOU
(BASS)

DANIEL JOHNS
(GUITAR, VOCALS)

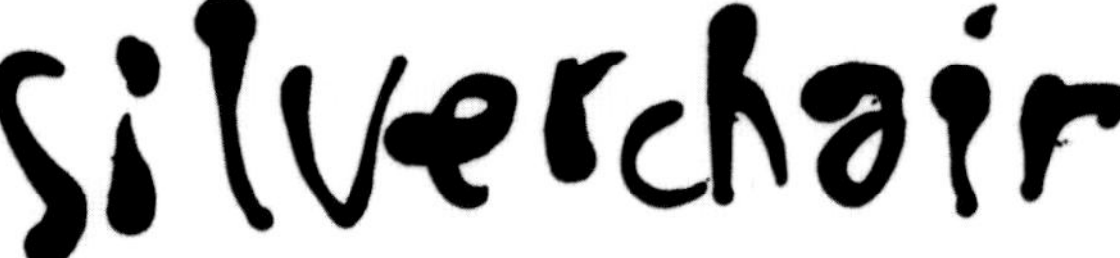

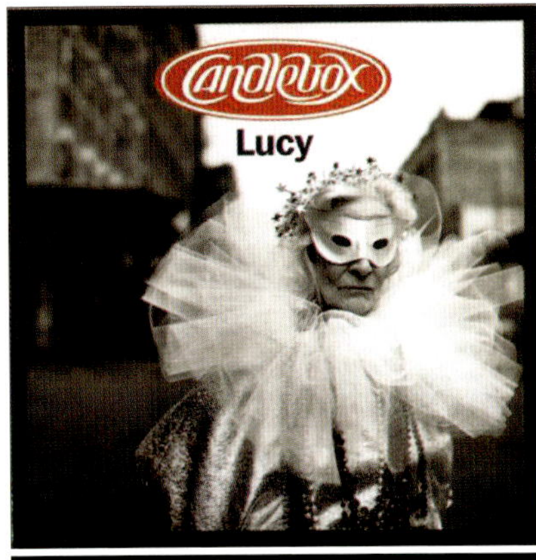

Billboard 200: *Lucy* (#11)

The backlash from the grunge faithful was well underway by the time Candlebox returned with its second album.

THE SOUND of Candlebox—classic rock songcraft with a fervent grunge edge—took off in 1994. The Seattle-based band's self-titled debut album sold almost 4 million copies, led by two breakout songs, "You" and the power ballad "Far Behind." Hitting the road for 18 months and playing Woodstock '94 helped sell the record.

But Candlebox repulsed some cynics who said the quartet knocked out dismayingly derivative drudgery, a generic take on a smarter brood of Seattle guitar bands (Pearl Jam, Soundgarden). And every reporter asked about Madonna, since Candlebox recorded for her label, Maverick Records, instead of Sub Pop, the independent label linked with the Seattle sound.

"It took place from day one," singer Kevin Martin said. "There are bands that avoid it and bands that don't. And we didn't avoid it. We're just one of those bands that take a bunch of shit."

It wasn't easy making it over that sophomore hump. The album *Lucy* built on the band's signature intensity, but with less studio polish. Martin sang "Simple Lessons," the angry opening track, like a man possessed. It was about his relationship with his brother.

"It was Easter Sunday," Martin explained. "I was at home with my family, everyone was in the living room. I was cleaning up in the kitchen and thinking about Dennis. He's dyslexic, he had a learning disability as a child. It was an uphill battle for him. When I was growing up, there was a competition between us. I was the baby who got away with everything, and he was the older brother who was dealing with his own demons. I went downstairs to my computer and wrote the lyrics in five minutes and went back to the studio that night. We did three takes and that was it—it was right there in my head."

The subdued middle section in "Understanding" revealed a more elastic, dynamic arrangement than anything the band had previously done. Candlebox shot the video almost entirely underwater in Key West with film director Gus Van Zant (*To Die For*, *My Own Private Idaho*, *Drugstore Cowboy*). At one point, Martin sang submerged for 56 straight seconds without coming up for air. "I've been scuba diving for a couple of years," he shrugged. "And quit smoking!" ■

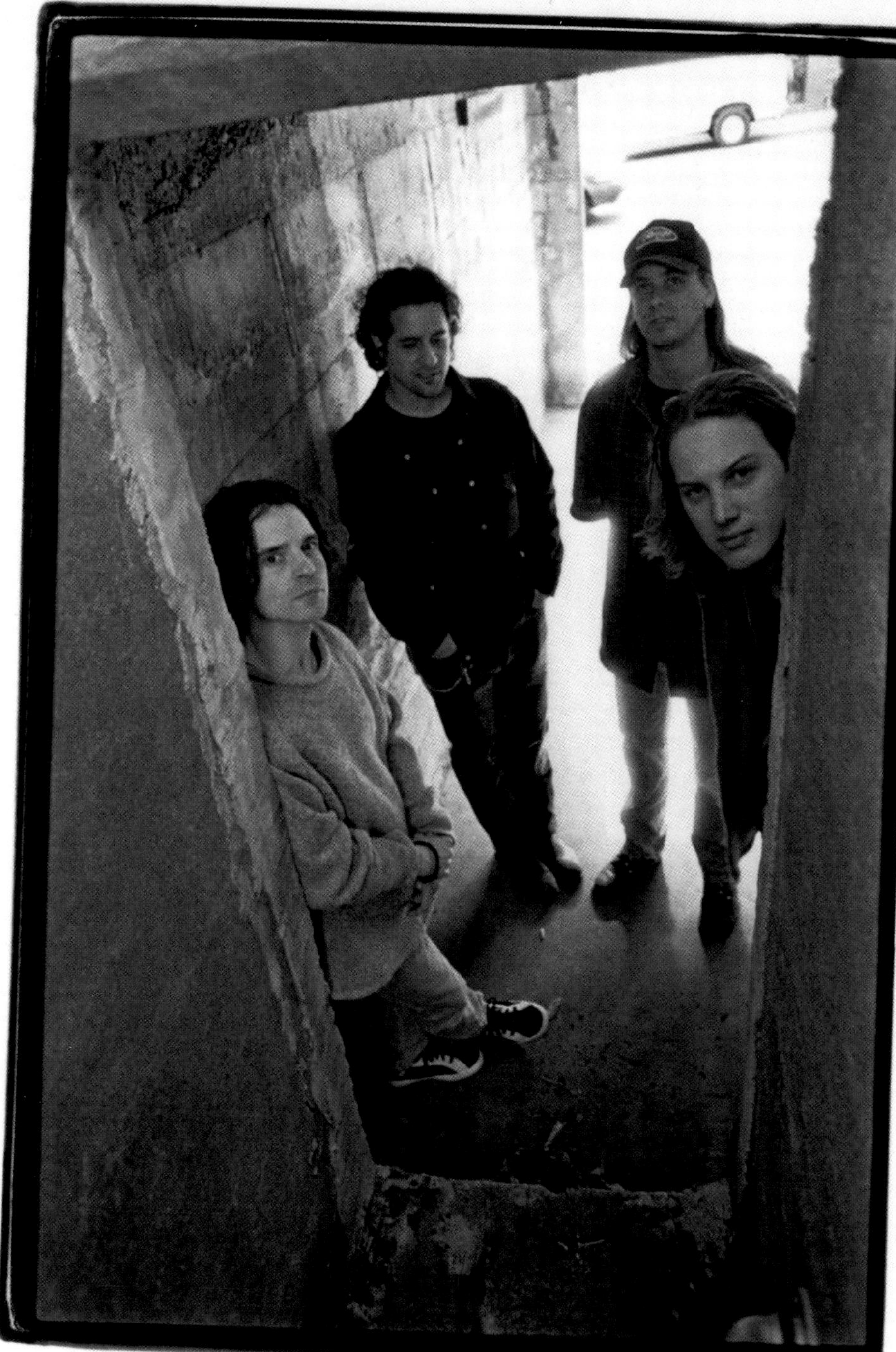

PHOTO CREDIT· Danny Clinch

Scott Mercado Bardi Martin Peter Klett Kevin Martin

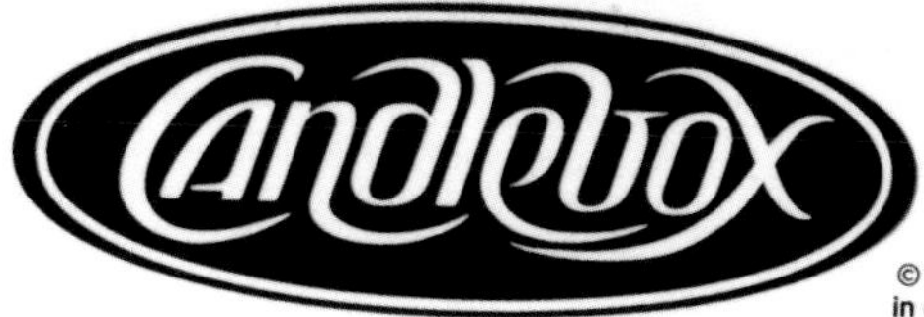

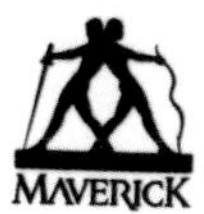

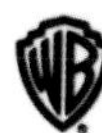

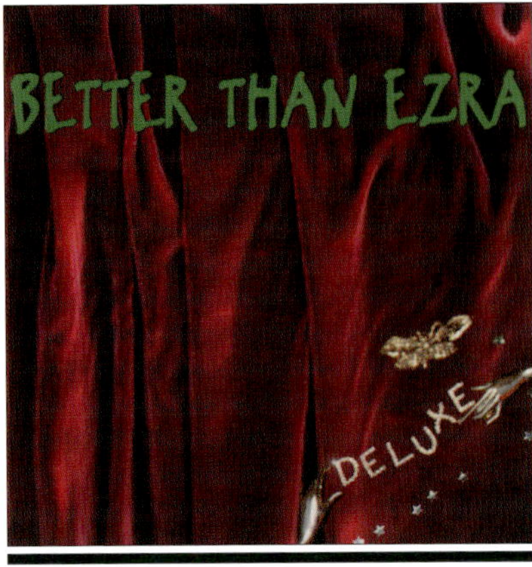

Billboard 200: *Deluxe* (#35)
Billboard Hot 100: "Good" (#30); "Rosealia" (#71)

The Louisiana trio Better Than Ezra exulted in commanding radio and MTV rotation with the ubiquitous "Good."

FORMED IN the late Eighties, Better Than Ezra drew substantial crowds on the local circuit in Baton Rouge. But after the death of guitarist Joel Rundell, BTE took time off, and singer-songwriter Kevin Griffin spent a year in Aspen, returning to the South to play shows every few months. He found that the band's audience had increased enough (the "Ezralites," as fans christened themselves) to support moving to Los Angeles with bassist Tom Drummond and drummer Cary Bonnecaze.

The three members originally released *Deluxe* on their own Swell Records in 1993, selling the CD when they moved back to Louisiana and started touring the state. A South by Southwest conference show paid off—Better Than Ezra signed with Elektra Records, which re-released *Deluxe* as the band's major-label debut. A critic described the album as "kinda like a car wreck in which Creedence Clearwater Revival runs over R.E.M."

"We knew we were good enough, and people in the South loved us, but we felt like there was a jinx with the band," Griffin said. "It was almost tongue-in-cheek. We used to laugh—'Guys, look, it's not in the cards, it's not gonna happen.' But we never realized how important it was to get our act together musically and businesswise. Finally, after doing that, everything came together the way we wanted it to."

"Good" helped push *Deluxe* to platinum status—the song climbed to No. 1 on *Billboard*'s Modern Rock Tracks chart and #3 on the Mainstream Rock Tracks chart. "'Good' is a nice introduction to the band," Griffin said. "It could be a 'Dear John' tale. It's certainly about a relationship ending. But I haven't decided if it's about the person who's finding the note saying, 'It was good living with you,' or if it's written in the letter."

"Good" was still fun to play, Griffin said. "It's always been a favorite of ours, an instantly likeable sing-along. But now it is people's first introduction to the band. We second-guess every move we make—'Gosh, is it too poppy, does it give the right impression of what Better Than Ezra is about?' I think the rest of our songs are a little lusher musically. 'Good' was an exercise in writing a song that had four chords, and using dynamics to give the illusion that you're doing different parts when in fact you're playing the same thing."

Griffin, Drummond and Bonnacaze were sharing a house in New Orleans that served as home, office and rehearsal space. "I grew up on rock 'n' roll in Monroe, the northern part of Louisiana—it's like Anywhere, USA, as far as rural areas go," Griffin said. "In New Orleans, there's so much heritage to draw from, and for me, it's an untapped resource. On subsequent albums, I think you'll hear more of that distinct regional flavor coming through. But hopefully it'll be completely skewed and twisted. I mean, we're not gonna turn into Buckwheat Zydeco." ■

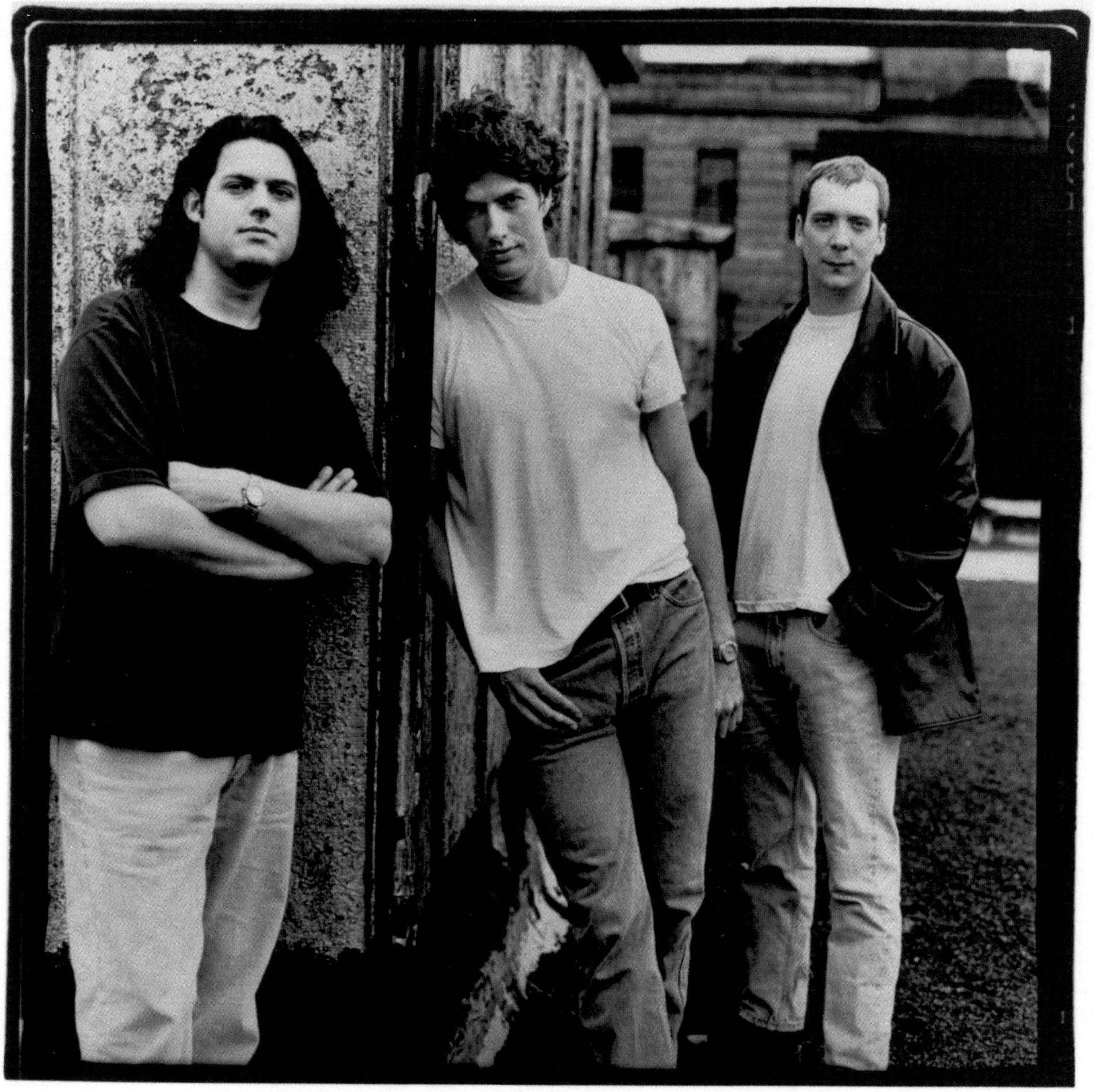

PHOTO CREDIT JOSEPH CULTICE

L R : TOM DRUMMOND, KEVIN GRIFFIN, CARY BONNECAZE

BETTER THAN EZRA

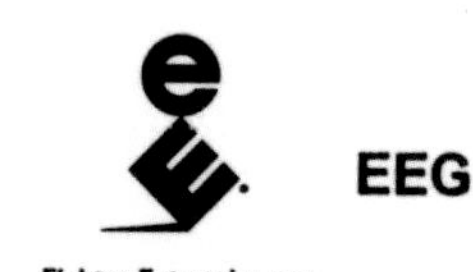

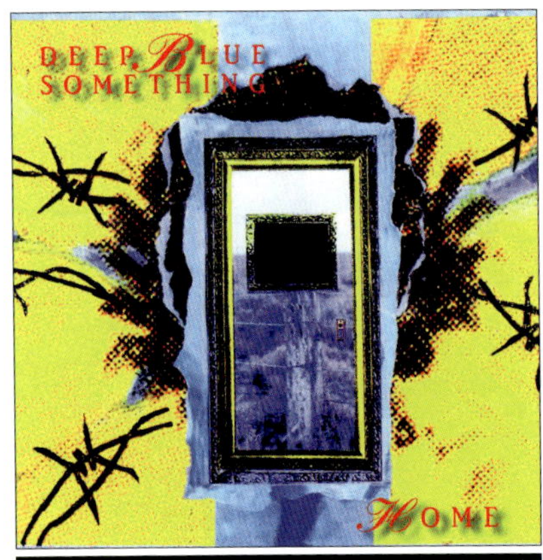

Billboard 200: *Home* (#46)
Billboard Hot 100: "Breakfast at Tiffany's" (#5)

The pop smash "Breakfast at Tiffany's" forced Deep Blue Something to be pigeonholed as a one-hit wonder.

SINGER AND bassist Todd Pipes of Deep Blue Something was exasperated with his adoring public.

"You'd be amazed at the number of people who say, '"Breakfast at Tiffany's" is my favorite song—so who's Tiffany?' I'm going, 'Man, come on! It's about a movie! Can't you read it in the lyrics—"I think I remember the film"—and see it in the video?' And they go, 'Gee, can you rent it?'"

In "Breakfast at Tiffany's," the protagonist tried to convince his girlfriend that they should stay together because they "both kinda liked" the same Audrey Hepburn film. He sounded so wimpy that it was irresistible.

"I was watching *Roman Holiday* on TV—I'm a big Hepburn fan, I thought she was so cool," Pipes explained. "But for a song title, I'd been kicking around another movie she starred in, *Breakfast at Tiffany's*, which Henry Mancini did the score for. It's got a more romantic ring to it. The song came out of my head in 15 minutes."

The huge success of "Breakfast at Tiffany's" at pop radio stations—it reached the Top 5 on the charts—made many modern rockers recoil from Deep Blue Something. But the members—Pipes, his younger brother Toby (guitar, vocals), Kirk Tatom (guitar) and John Kirkland (drums)—considered themselves an alternative act, like the "ethereal 'goth' thing of the Eighties."

"That's when I really got into things like the Smiths and Echo & the Bunnymen and the Cure," Toby Pipes said. "I thought, 'If they can do that with a guitar, then I'm gonna give it a go.' 'Breakfast at Tiffany's' wasn't a big part of the show when we were first playing around. I've been hating it—'Uh-oh, we're gonna be this new little pop sensation.' But at least we're not playing to 20 people like we used to."

"Breakfast at Tiffany's" was Deep Blue Something's only hit; the lack of follow-up singles from the album *Home* led to inactivity. The band had formed at the University of North Texas in Denton, circa 1992.

"People from the Dallas region dig the local music. The radio stations play it, even compete about it. That's pretty cool," Toby Pipes said. "And it goes from Jackopierce to the Toadies, Tripping Daisy, the Nixons. Everybody tries their hardest not to sound like the band next door." ■

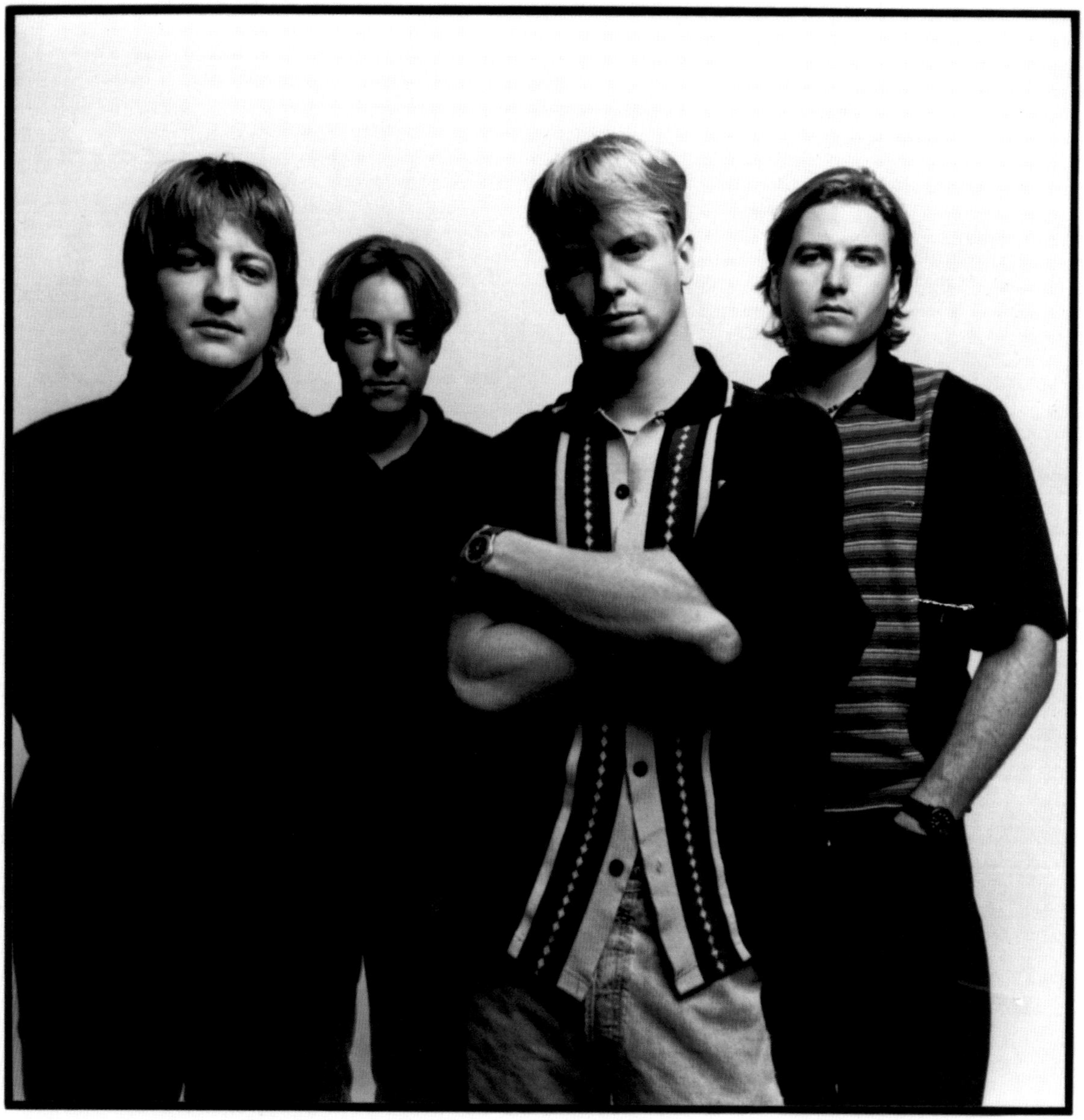

Photo credit: James Bland

Toby Pipes | Kirk Tatom | Todd Pipes | John Kirtland

DEEP BLUE SOMETHING

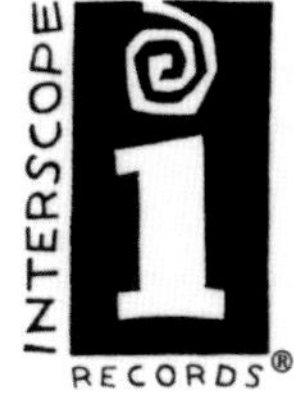

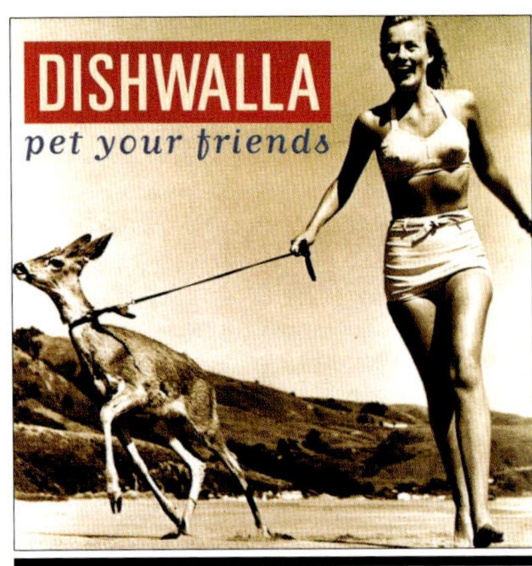

Billboard 200: *Pet Your Friends* (#89)
Billboard Hot 100: "Counting Blue Cars" (#15)

With the hit "Counting Blue Cars," Dishwalla emerged from obscurity to become one of the year's hottest acts.

A CHART-TOPPING smash on rock and alternative radio, Dishwalla's "Counting Blue Cars" was sung from the perspective of an inquisitive child, posing the question—what if God is a she? "Tell me all your thoughts on God/I'd really like to meet her…"

But according to vocalist and keyboardist J.R. Richards, the convention that any god would have to be a male Caucasian was entrenched.

"There have been a lot of different reactions," he said. "People will find whatever they want in it, and I respect that, I suppose. But we get some knuckleheads who will stand out in front of our shows condemning everybody to hell that walks inside—that's happened in Texas and Florida. I get some pretty irate letters, people quoting Scripture for me. The point is that when you grow up, you're taught by society that things should be referred to in a certain way and never really challenged. It's meant to be a positive 'question authority' song. And it's got a good melody!"

Dishwalla—the name refered to a "pack of entrepreneurial nomads" who invaded remote villages in India, set up satellite dishes and wire-pirated cable television into the homes of simple folk—formed in 1992. Diverse, seemingly incompatible elements—pop, classic rock, alternative and soul—fit into the sound on *Pet Your Friends*, Dishwalla's debut album. It languished for nearly a year before "Counting Blue Cars" finally took off on radio stations everywhere, becoming the most-played rock track of the year, according to the trade publication *Radio & Records*.

But the Santa Barbara-based band then had to prove it wasn't a one-hit wonder. "Charlie Brown's Parents," the next single, built in intensity after starting out like a Queen ballad. Another fine song, it was a metaphor for the way adults converse and manage to say nothing at all, a reference to the indecipherable banter of the celebrated cartoon character's folks: "It feels like I'm talking to Charlie Brown's parents…"

Richards wrote it after a long day. "I was watching *Star Trek* and people kept banging on my door, trying to sell me something or convert me to some religion or join some political party. I was like, 'Man, leave me alone.' It's weird talking to people that you can communicate with—you're both speaking English—but you really can't relate to them in any way."

In terms of sales, "Charlie Brown's Parents" failed to sustain the success achieved by "Counting Blue Cars."

"It totally blows," Richards said. "You figure, 'Okay, we had a huge hit, it should be easy to get another song played on the radio.' That's total bullshit. They don't hang with bands, there's no loyalty at all. It's frustrating that they don't follow up—'People really loved this one song and dug this band, so let's play some other stuff by them and see what happens.' They tend to go for the flavor of the day." ■

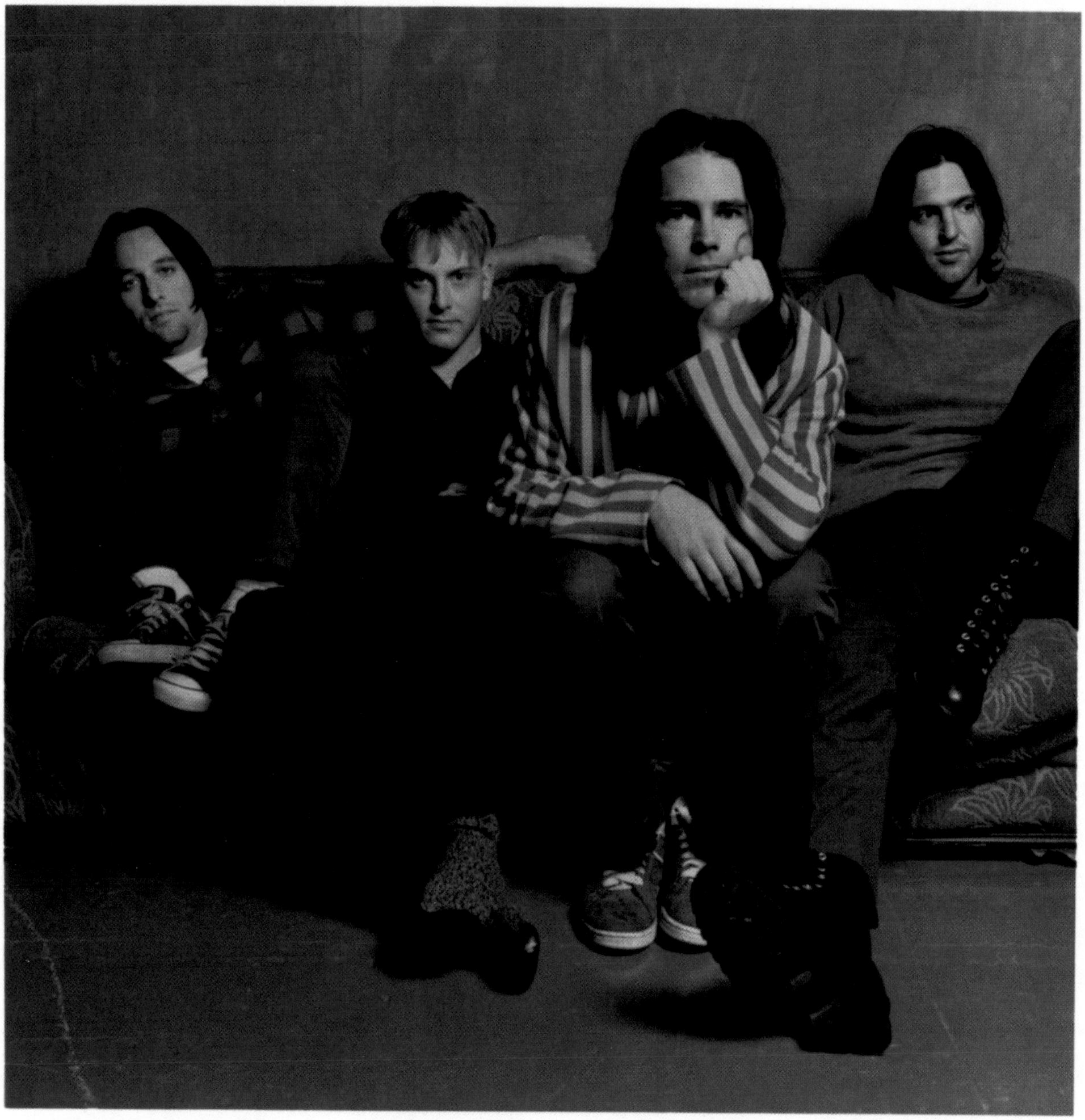

Photo: Michael Lavine 4/95

George Pendergast Scot Alexander J.R. Richards Rodney Browning

DISHWALLA

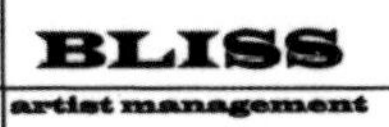

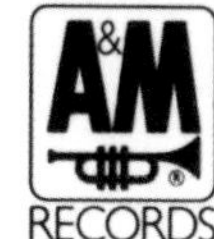

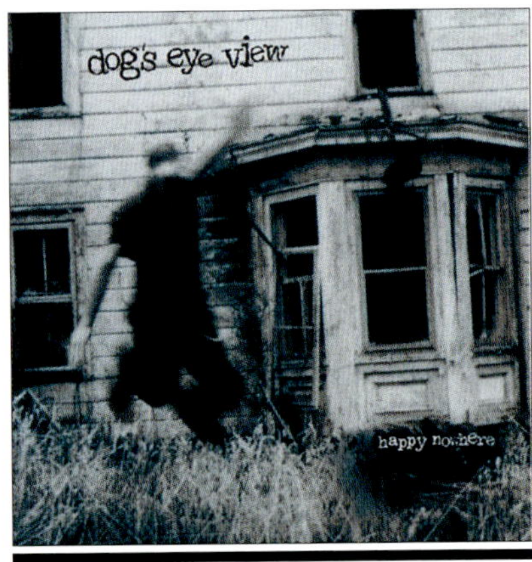

Billboard 200: *Happy Nowhere* (#77)
Billboard Hot 100: "Everything Falls Apart" (#66)

Concocted by Peter Stuart, Dog's Eye View's "Everything Falls Apart" found success at multiple radio formats.

ON RADIO and MTV, "Everything Falls Apart" by Dog's Eye View became a favorite. Peter Stuart, the frontman and guitarist, had masterminded a smart hit—the sound was uplifting, but the lyrics teemed with troubling emotions.

"That's the joy of pop music, my favorite thing about the Smiths and early Aztec Camera," Stuart said. "You rope in people with the melody and bouncy drum beat of it, and then before you know it, people are singing, 'The devil is in my pants…Wait, how did I get that lyric in my mind?' Ha!"

A New York native, Stuart developed his craft in Chicago (where he had a basement apartment with a "dog's eye view"), and for four years he worked his way up the club circuit. He found himself spending a large part of 1994 on tours with Counting Crows and Tori Amos, and his solo acoustic performance as an opening act wowed the audiences.

"I gravitated toward songwriting because it was an immediately gratifying form of communication," Stuart explained. "I'm always suspect of people who sit down and try to say something. It makes sense if you're an essayist. But if you're a songwriter with an agenda, I don't necessarily believe it when I listen. I sit down and play guitar and mumble along with it and start singing words, and I'll form a song around that.One of the things I used to do when I was out opening for Tori Amos and Counting Crows, if I was losing the audience, I'd take a suggestion of a word and I'd just put a song together on the spot.

"It can't be overstated how much that helped my development, going from playing once every two weeks in a New York City coffeehouse to playing in front of 300 to 1,000 people every night for months. After a while you go, 'Yeah, this is what I do, here I am,' instead of 'Um, I'm here to play tonight, please listen.'"

In addition, by the end of the tour Stuart had sold more than 6,000 homemade demo tapes. He wound up with a record deal and created *Happy Nowhere*, Dog's Eye View's big-label debut. It marked his first time working with a band, which he put together as a vehicle for songs he had written long before the group existed. The album yielded "Everything Falls Apart."

"There's a Chinua Achabe book called *Things Fall Apart*, so the phrase was in the back of my mind," Stuart said. "I was in New Orleans for a week and feeling pretty fragile at the end of it, realizing that, no matter how good things are, I always tend to see the seedy underbelly of it. All these people running around drinking and having fun—all I could picture was how miserable they'd be the next morning. All these nice buildings and houses, but because it's so close to sea level, they're all disintegrating, crumbling into the ground. I wrote the whole song on the plane heading home. The last verse was my imagining that God is just some guy who keeps letting things get messed up in the world because it keeps him busy. I've found that when you're completely in love and life couldn't be better, you go out and have an affair to throw a wrench in the works. Because when things are easy and comfortable, it's boring." ■

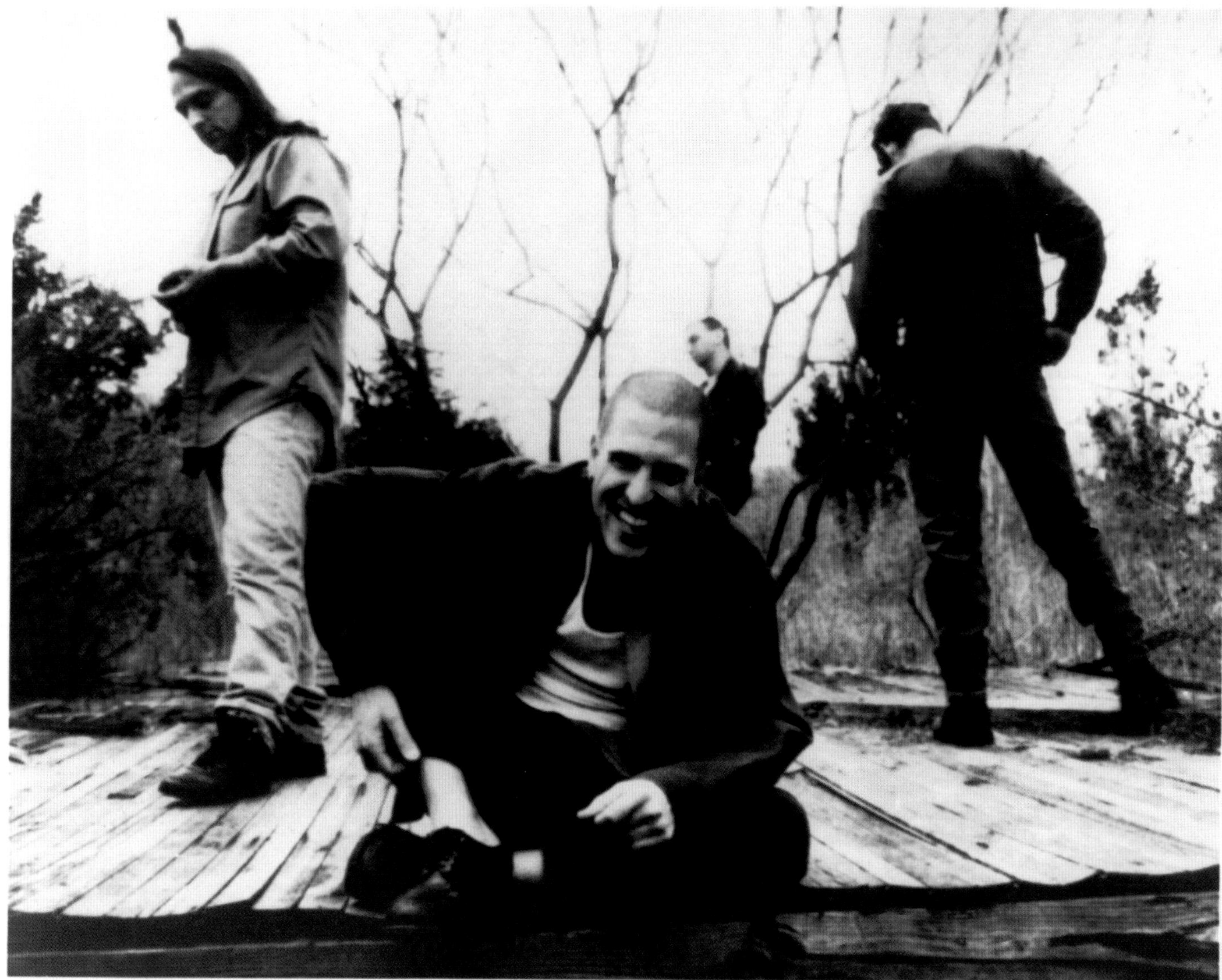

PHOTOGRAPH: CHRIS STROTHER

dog's eye view

COLUMBIA
9507

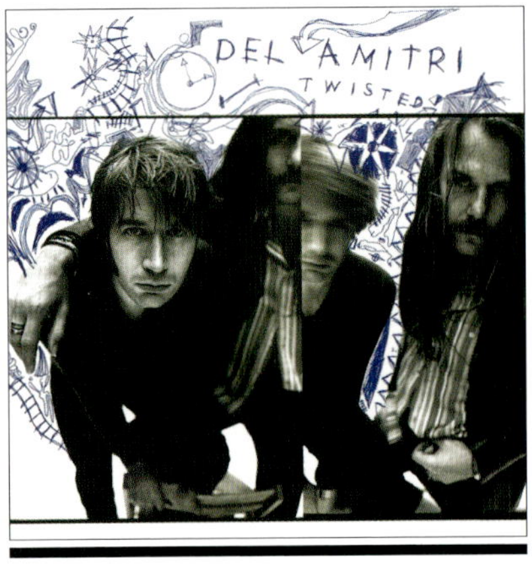

Billboard 200: *Twisted* (#170)
Billboard Hot 100: "Roll to Me" (#10)

Something set apart Del Amitri's charming "Roll with Me" for classic rock fans who weren't living in the past.

CLASSIC ROCK wasn't just an era of music. It was a style that had its own class of Nineties practitioners like Counting Crows, Hootie & the Blowfish—and Del Amitri.

"We even get played on some classic rock radio stations, right next to Led Zeppelin and Billy Joel," guitarist Iain Harvie admitted with self-deprecating humor. "We're pretty old-fashioned. It's unlikely that we'll ever be perceived as an alternative act—when I look at that scene, we're quite irrelevant."

But Del Amitri heated up Top 40 radio, MTV and VH-1. The guitar-driven melodies were memorable, and frontman Justin Currie's warm, romantic rasp of a voice brought the articulate, expressive words to life.

"The one advantage to having never been hip for even a short period is that you can never really go out of fashion," Currie said. "If you play in a pop band and you have a couple of hits, all you can hope to do is write songs and make records in a way that interests you. The rest is up the gods. If you worry about maintaining a level of success, you'll go very gray and become very depressed. You'll suffer from nonexecutive stress and you'll have to be checked into a hospital fairly soon!"

Del Amitri's first albums spawned the radio hits "Kiss This Thing Goodbye" and "Always the Last to Know." For its fourth release, *Twisted*, the Scottish quintet practiced and arranged the songs as they were being written. Currie and Harvie moved the band and their equipment into a rented house in the English countryside. They got more work done because everyone didn't leave at the end of the day. The no-frills "Roll to Me," which reached the Top 10 in the US charts, resulted from the relaxed way of recording, beginning while the members where working on another song.

"It's the most obviously poppy thing on the record," Currie said. "Writing pop songs is probably the easiest thing in the world. All you need is spare time, really. Their construction is fairly Neanderthal, which is what I like about them. I don't think it's a great art. You learn to express things in your own way, and you try to point it there, I suppose. It's not something I like to think about. It's just something I enjoy doing."

The inviting "Driving with the Brakes On," "Here and Now" and "Tell Her This" also became popular with fans. But image? None, except that Currie and Harvie sported sideburns just inches shy of muttonchops.

"We only know about six chords," Harvie laughed. "It would be a total sham to pretend that we're anything other than straight-in-the-middle rock or pop music. But within that, there's crap and there's good stuff. And I think we're the good stuff." ■

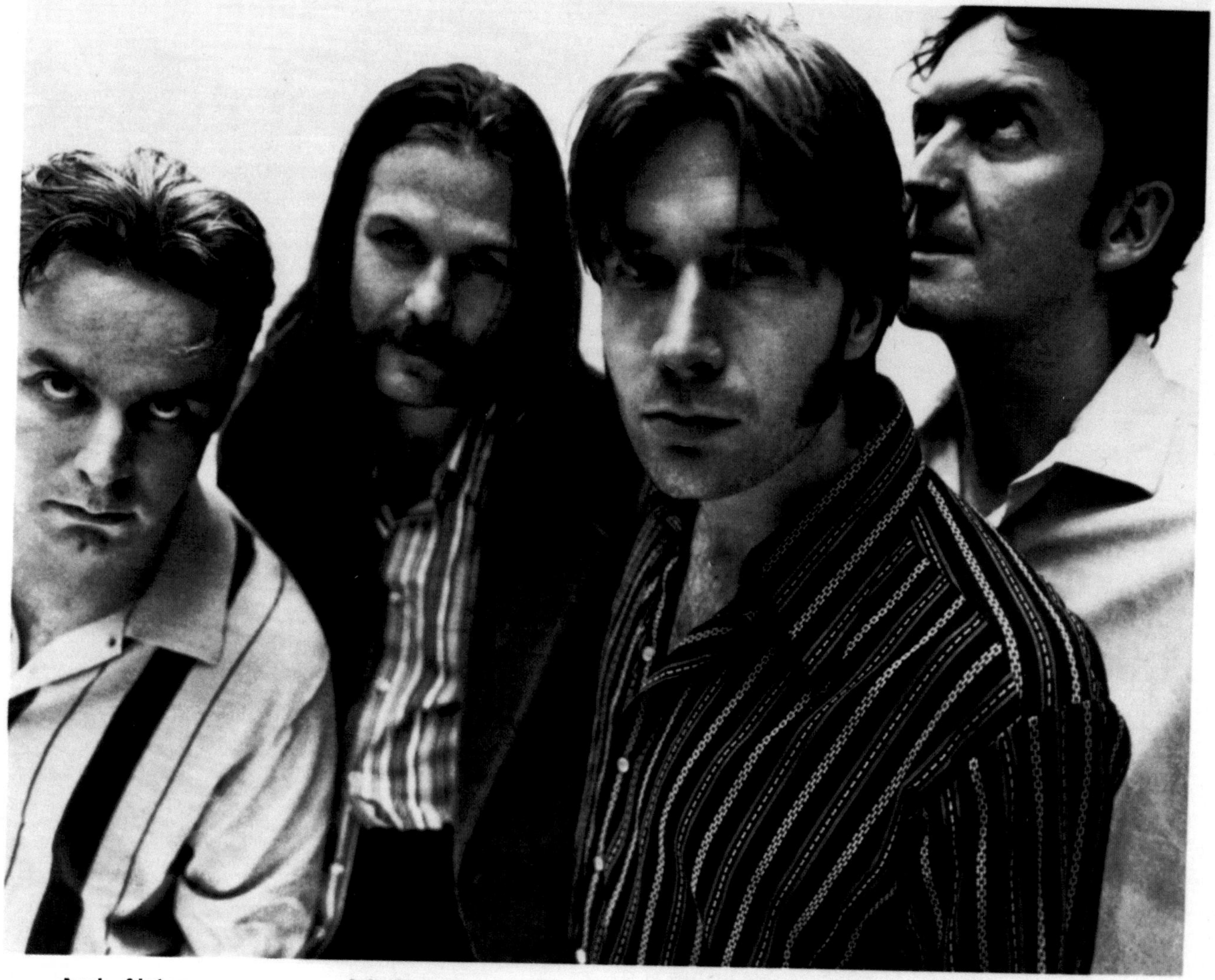

Andy Alston Iain Harvie Justin Currie David Cummings

Del Amitri

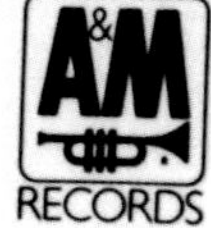

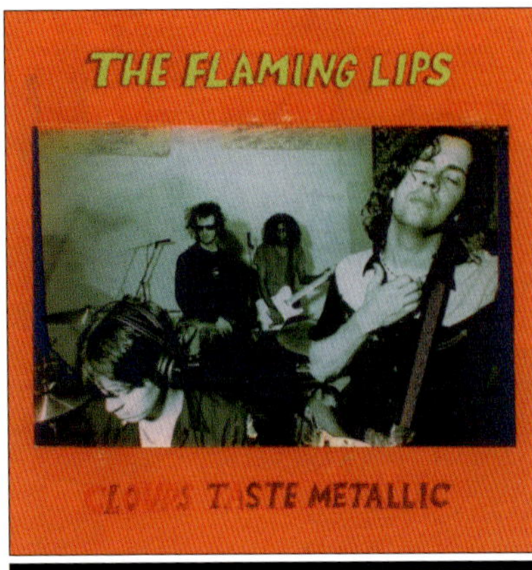

The Flaming Lips' *Clouds Taste Metallic* sustained the Oklahoma-based band's witty, ingenious blend of sounds.

THINGS HAD changed for the Flaming Lips. Lead singer/guitarist Wayne Coyne and bassist Michael Ivins had been transforming noise fragments into quirky, homemade power-pop for over a decade, but it had taken six albums of exploring the fringes of the consciousness of American culture for the band to wiggle into the mainstream.

"She Don't Use Jelly"—a catchy ditty from 1993's *Transmissions from the Satellite Heart*—broke out of MTV and became a fluke hit nearly two years later. The song owed its success partly to its strong novelty value—it was about toast, tangerines and Vaseline. Appearances at Lollapalooza and on the teen drama TV series *Beverly Hills 90210* followed.

"When *90210* called up and said, 'We want the Flaming Lips to play the Peach Pit,' we thought it was a joke—but a joke like you can't afford to pass up, so we said, 'Sure! Great! We'll do it in a second!'," Coyne recalled. "We really didn't know who Tori Spelling or any of the stars were. If it was 1973 and it was the Brady Bunch, we'd know."

The Flaming Lips' seventh album, the densely constructed *Clouds Taste Metallic*—full of stories about birds, brains, giraffes, sub-atomic molecules, travels to other worlds and other oddities—received critical acclaim. But "Bad Days" (a remix was featured in *Batman Forever*, introducing Jim Carrey's Riddler to the audience) and "This Here Giraffe" had limited chart success.

"It's kinda weird," Ivins said of the up-and-down surge in popularity. "We've always taken the attitude that we're gonna be in a band no matter what happens—this is what we do. Industry people were willing to look around and say, 'They're not giving up, so let's not give up.' It's easy to fall into watching the charts, and sometimes it's interesting to follow along, but that's lame in the whole scheme of things. People get wrapped up in this idea of 'Let's make a hit.' It's just music. Why is everybody making a big deal about it? Let's get on with it."

The band's hometown was the site of the Oklahoma City bombing, a domestic terrorist attack on the Alfred P Murrah Federal Building.

"We were in the middle of recording, and we heard the bombing—we live eight blocks north and four blocks west of where it happened," Ivins said. "It was weird to watch on TV as it was happening right down the street. You read about (the 1993 bombing of) the World Trade Center and it seemed a million miles away, even though I'd driven right by it. This doesn't seem real—it's Oklahoma City, what do you do with that?" ■

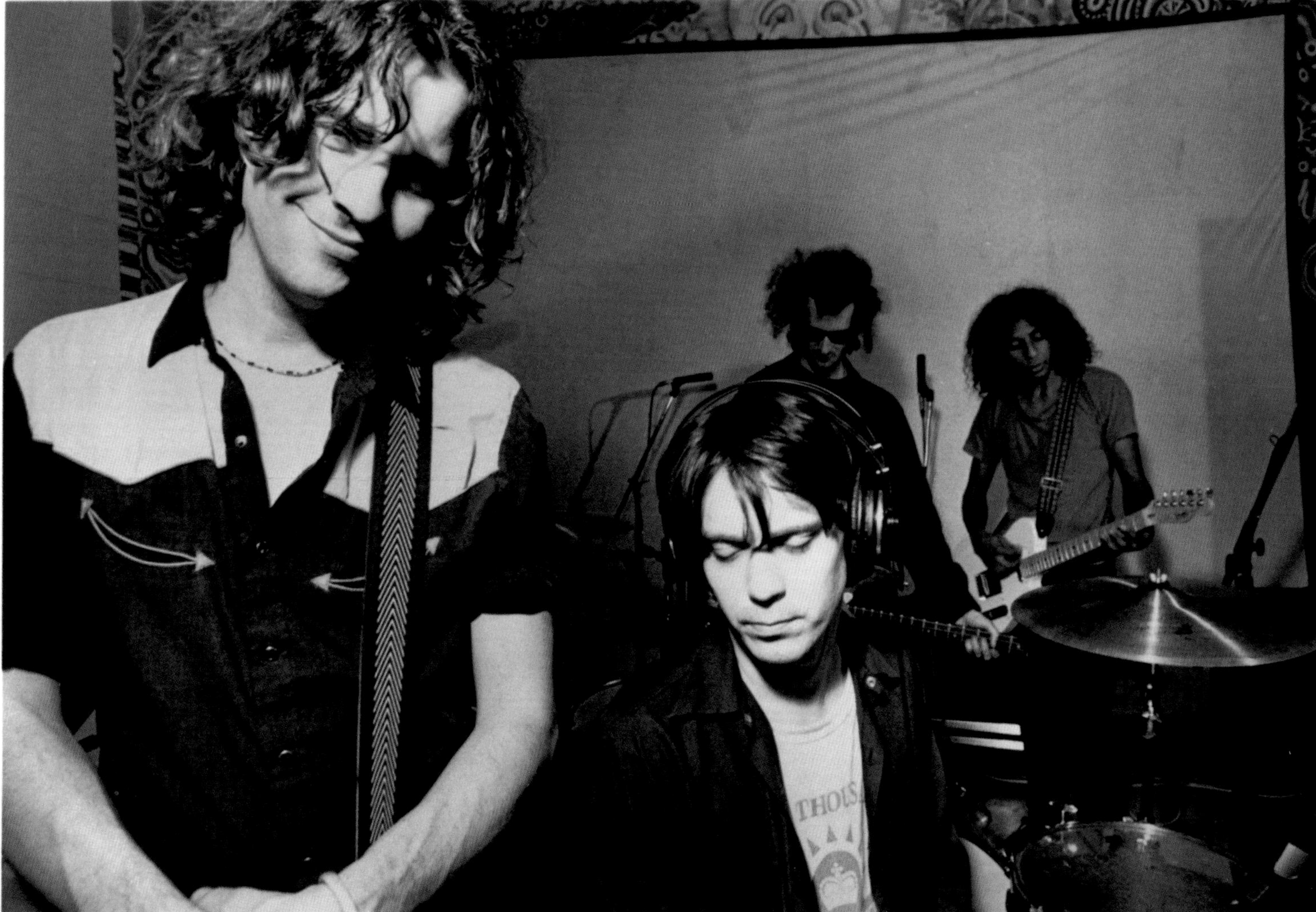

PHOTO CREDIT: J. Michelle Martin

Wayne Coyne Steven Drozd Michael Ivins Ronald Jones

The Flaming Lips

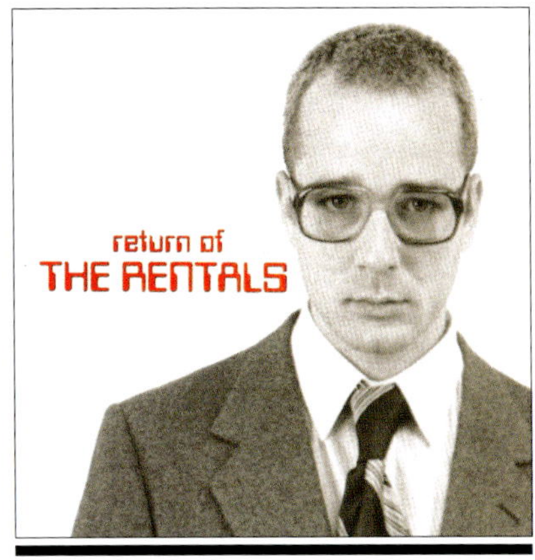

Billboard Hot 100: *"Friends of P."* (#82)

The Rentals notched a surprising radio hit, but "Friends of P." didn't sound like modernized guitar-driven rock.

RIDING THE crest of dweeb rock as the bass player for Weezer wasn't enough for Matt Sharp, so he created the Rentals and put out *Return of the Rentals*, a debut album led by the single "Friends of P."—which peaked at #7 on *Billboard*'s Modern Rock Tracks chart.

"I wasn't ready to have anything put on the Weezer record. When these songs were finished, they sort of made up a whole," Sharp explained. "Why not put them out? This record wasn't intended to be played on the radio or have any exposure. It's very lo-fi, low-budget. We made it for ourselves, and I'm glad people are being nice and supporting it. It's pretty shocking."

"Friends of P." was distinguished by the sound of a squealing, cheesy synthesizer straight out of the new-wave music made in the late Seventies. "They were slagged even when they were popular," Sharp said. "It wasn't preplanned. We were recording, and we went back to change some things, and Tom (Grimley, co-producer) brought his old keyboards. We tried a couple of different things and settled on this one I really liked. And we used it over and over again."

The dry-witted Sharp passed on revealing the identity of P.

"I've heard all kinds of things. People bring up Johnny Depp's band (P.), but it doesn't have anything to do with him. Prozac. The proletariat. Punk rock. I like it—I'd rather have people come up with their own thing."

Sharp co-directed a video for "Friends of P." that cost $400—shot in black and white, it used off-center closeups, offbeat edits and Russian subtitles. MTV added it. "Usually a video costs the same as the record," Sharp said. "All my friends chipped in and we tried to figure it out together—how to get the camera to work!"

The Rentals included vocalist Cherielynn Westrich and featured Weezer bandmate Pat Wilson and Petra Haden of That Dog. Sharp insisted that the band was more than just a side project—"I've lost far too much sleep for it to be called that"—but his involvement didn't mean he had left Weezer.

"Rivers (Cuomo, Weezer's singer and guitarist) and I are best friends, so we try to help each other. But it changes my plans. I probably won't end up recording the next Rentals record for only $10,000. We'll do a bigger production." ■

Matt Sharp   Cherielynn Westrich

THE RENTALS

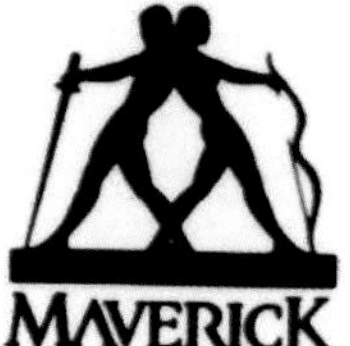

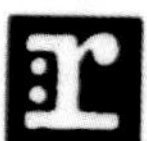

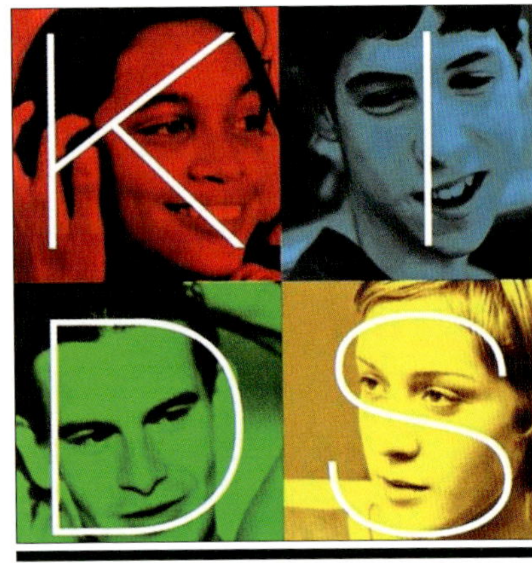

Billboard Hot 100: "Natural One" (#29)

"Natural One," a song credited to Folk Implosion, became an unlikely Top 40 triumph for Sebadoh's Lou Barlow.

IN THE indie-rock pantheon, "lo-fi" pioneer Lou Barlow sat near the top. And he didn't even have a reservation.

"When I started playing, there was a distinct underground, and it was never going overground—no one ever thought it would or could," Barlow said. "And things got a little screwed up over the last couple of years. Those boundaries really got blurred."

In 1989, Barlow was thrown out as Dinosaur Jr.'s bassist. He had been making home tapes with his friend Eric Gaffney, who suggested they pursue their project as Sebadoh. Barlow became alternative rock's most notoriously sensitive-cerebral deity, writing beautiful love-hate songs about losing the girl.

And he was considered a trailblazer of the lo-fi movement, an approach to crappy sound quality that indie fans equated with honesty. Like Barlow cared—whoever thought that not having enough money to make the music sound good would become the cool trend?

"There's been shit like that forever. I grew up listening to Young Marble Giants, and the English post-punk movement in the late Seventies, and where Sonic Youth came from. 'You're the godfather of lo-fi!'—I'm more like the nephew. For me, it was a mix of aesthetics and necessity. In order to put songs together and really feel like I was accomplishing something, I needed to spend a lot of time on it. And the only way I could do that was at home!"

Sebadoh's discography was one of the most convoluted and confusing in indie rock, including Barlow's ongoing studio collaboration with singer-songwriter John Davis as Folk Implosion (they met when Davis sent Barlow a fan letter). Folk Implosion's "Natural One," from the soundtrack to Larry Clark's controversial coming-of-age film *Kids*, became an unlikely radio hit. An eerie groove, it just cracked the Top 40 and earned a blip on the small screen as an MTV "Buzz Clip."

"That's what I like about pop music—you never know," Barlow said. "It was a wonderful little studio experiment that caught on—the funky drums, the slinky bass playing, the singing were a different approach than the folk-rock base of Sebadoh. But it softened people up to Sebadoh." ■

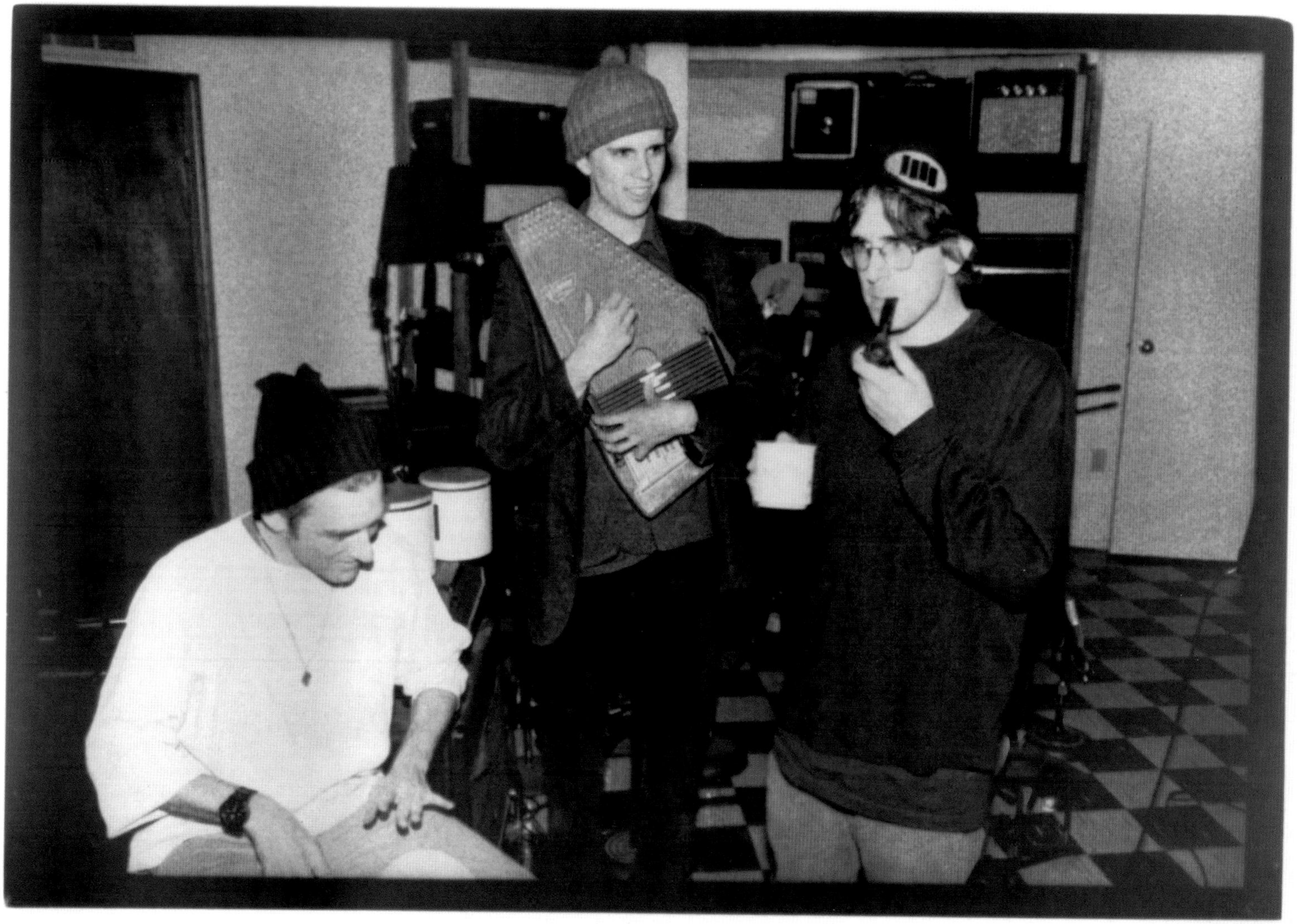

Photo Credit: Charles Miller

FOLK IMPLOSION

from the KIDS soundtrack

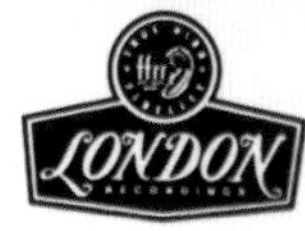

Billboard 200: *Example* (#171)

Despite suffering tragedy, For Squirrels released "Mighty K.C." as a single from its only major-label release.

A RISING young act out of Gainesville, Florida, For Squirrels—singer John Vigliatura, bassist Bill White, guitarist Travis Tooke and drummer Jack Griego—said that they were so committed to being in a band, they would play music "for squirrels." After touring the East Coast and establishing a following, the group was on the cusp of national recognition, signing to a major label and recording the album *Example* with noted producer and engineer Nick Launay.

A month before the album's scheduled release, while driving home from playing the CMJ Music Marathon at CBGB in New York City, the band's touring van blew a tire and crashed, claiming the lives of Vigliatura and White, along with their tour manager.

Example was released as planned and received wonderful support from college radio. The soaring guitar-pop of "Mighty K.C." became a radio hit, peaking at #15 on *Billboard*'s Modern Rock Tracks chart. The song, ostensibly about the death of Kurt Cobain—"It's the feeling of despair, but not to the point of giving it up," Vigliatura had said—took on a special significance given the band's fate.

"I lost my three best friends," Tooke said. "Jack and I lost our band, a piece of ourselves that will always be treasured but never regained." ■

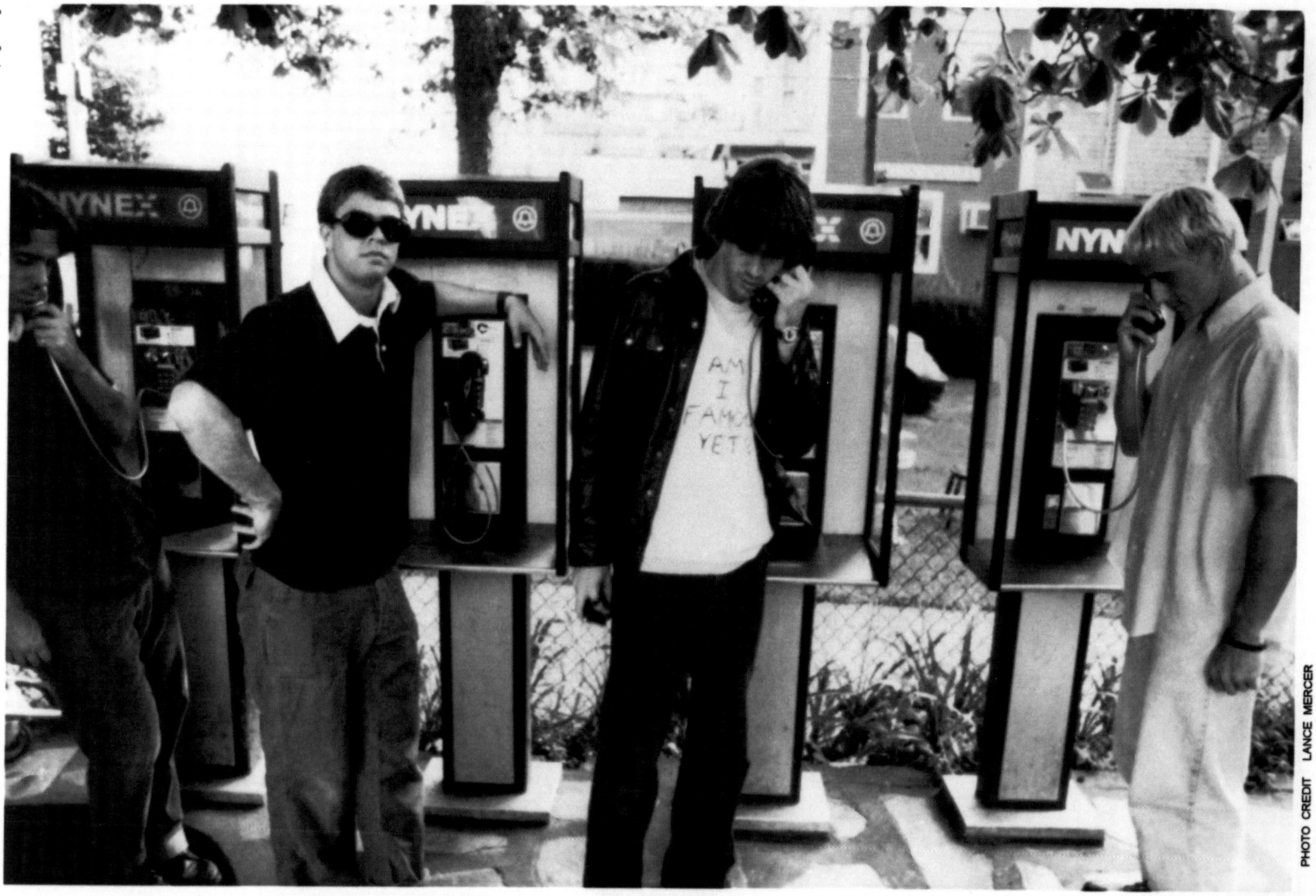

PHOTO CREDIT LANCE MERCER

BILL WHITE
BASS

JOHN FRANCIS VIGLIATURA IV
VOCALS

TRAVIS MICHAEL TOOKE
LEAD GUITAR

JACK GRIEGO
DRUMS

FOR SQUIRRELS

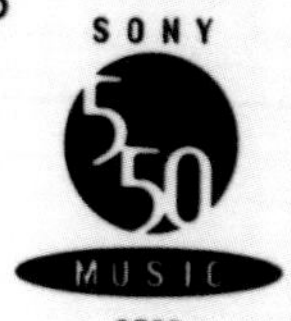

9509

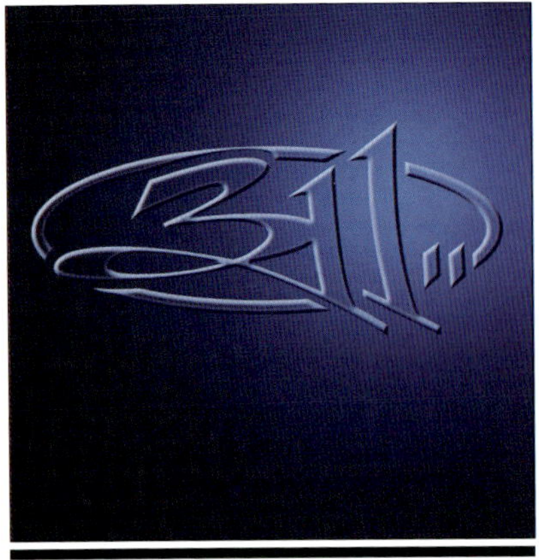

Billboard 200: *311* (#12)

311 combined hard work and opportunity, winning recognition in the rock-rap scene with a self-titled album.

NO RULES applied to rock music in the early Nineties. Bands took as many styles as they wanted and fused them—the intensity of rap, the bombast of metal, a touch of reggae. The five members of 311 labeled the genre "rock-style rap." But surprisingly, the group's rhythmic urban influences were offered by Omaha natives.

"We get a lot of amazed looks," drummer Chad Sexton admitted. "But the truth is, Omaha's a pretty big town—we get MTV. Once you have all that media influence, it comes back out in your writing."

Since forming in 1990, 311 had been on a steady climb toward success, perfecting its eclectic mix through three independently released records. The group eventually moved its base of operations to Los Angeles and caught the attention of Capricorn Records, known in the Seventies for its roster of Southern rock acts like the Allman Brothers Band and the Marshall Tucker Band.

"We're the only signing they have that's hard-edged alternative rock," Sexton noted. "It didn't look like we worked hard to get signed—we moved and got a record deal in four months. But we'd been working from Omaha, shipping a lot of our independent albums to all the college radio stations and record companies we could get through to. We were at our potential—we had a big following, we were kings of the scene, we couldn't go any further there. We had to move on. We found that in Los Angeles, the attitude is, 'Give me this'—they don't have a work ethic. We're proud to be from the Midwest."

Tied in with the surf/skate/snowboard culture associated with Southern California, 311 built on the early buzz that surrounded its frenetic, charged live performances, where the musicians weren't limited like rappers. "Our goal was to take rap and make it musical," lead vocalist Nick Hexum stated.

"Our music originates from our instruments—seeing the other players, adding the improvisational element—then we go to the studio and record it," Sexton added. "Rap is recorded in the studio, then they try to make it happen live—and a drum machine and some guys rapping with tapes isn't exciting to a lot of people."

The guys of 311 won the alternative-rock lottery with the singles "All Mixed Up," "Don't Stay Home" and their biggest hit, "Down." It took a manic year of touring for *311* (referred to by fans as "the Blue Album") to crack the Top 20, but it achieved double-platinum sales.

"We're ecstatic—we watch the charts every week to see how much MTV and radio play we're getting," Sexton said. "It's gratifying, but it doesn't change anything. We've been working on it for a while." ■

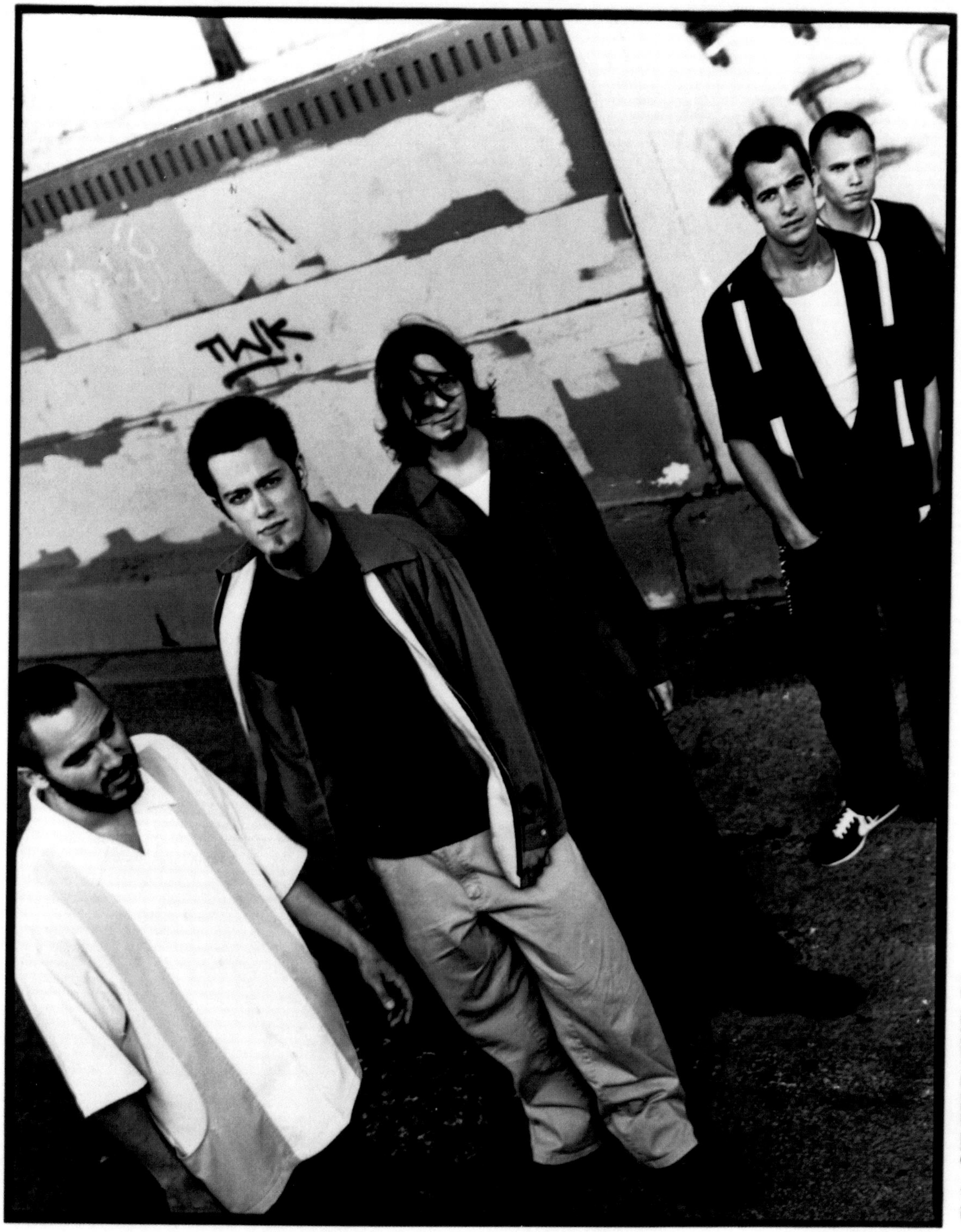

Photo: CATHERINE WESSEL (01)

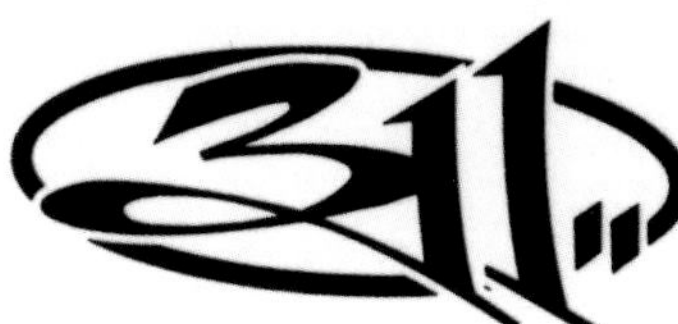

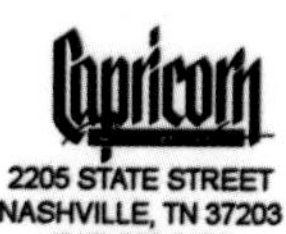

2205 STATE STREET
NASHVILLE, TN 37203
(615) 320-8470

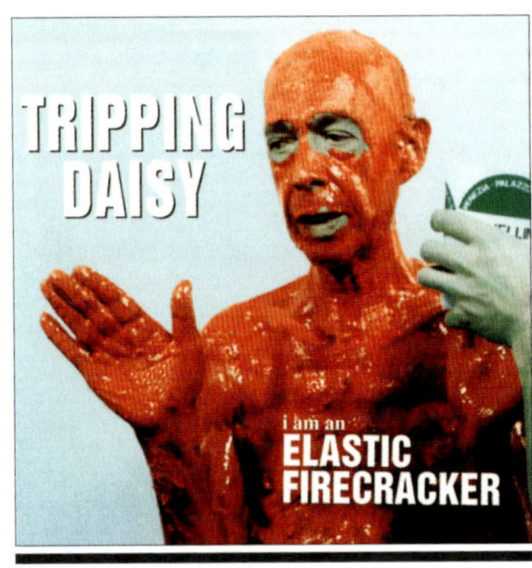

Billboard 200: *I Am an Elastic Firecracker* (#95)

With touches of pop and wiseass lyrics, Tripping Daisy's laconically amorous "I Got a Girl" got wide exposure.

FORMED IN Dallas, Tripping Daisy received a lot of attention for the album *I Am an Elastic Firecracker*. The fuse was lit with "I Got a Girl," a mind-blowing love song for legions of alterna-kids, reaching #6 on *Billboard*'s Modern Rock Tracks chart.

"I wrote the song, and it was no big deal—I didn't think anything about it," singer and guitarist Tim DeLaughter said. "We put it on the record and it opened the door for us. Radio wanted a song that was going to get a reaction. But I was kind of scared there for a while. That was people's first impression of us, and there's not another song on the record like that."

Radio stations then played the psyche-delirious "Piranha." "It's about those unnecessarily evil people out there who are constant obstacles, that's all," DeLaughter said. "I mean, I dealt with a piranha today at the hotel."

The ball got rolling when one of Tripping Daisy's first recordings, "Lost and Found," appeared on a compilation album put out by Dallas station KDGE-FM, garnering the band not only radio airplay, but an enthusiastic local following (they swept the *Dallas Observer*'s 1993 Music Awards).

"That area has a pretty healthy scene," DeLaughter said. "What's interesting is that there are a lot of really strong bands that sound completely different. Usually there's a band that has 10 other bands emulating them. That's not the case. You have metal and R&B. You have Reverend Horton Heat's rockabilly and the Toadies. It's extremely versatile."

The cover of *I Am an Elastic Firecracker* featured a harrowing image of a greased, bloody, melting Guglielmo Achille Cavellini (he was actually covered with red paint). Cavellini, an Italian cult hero, was one of the leading figures in mail art, an underground movement in which artists put their work on stamps and sent it to each other.

"I just thought Cavellini deserved the recognition," DeLaughter explained. "The picture is so striking—you don't know what it's about when you first look at it. I can identify with anyone who's trying to express themselves and make a living from what they love and what they do without being accepted in a way that would bring them success." ■

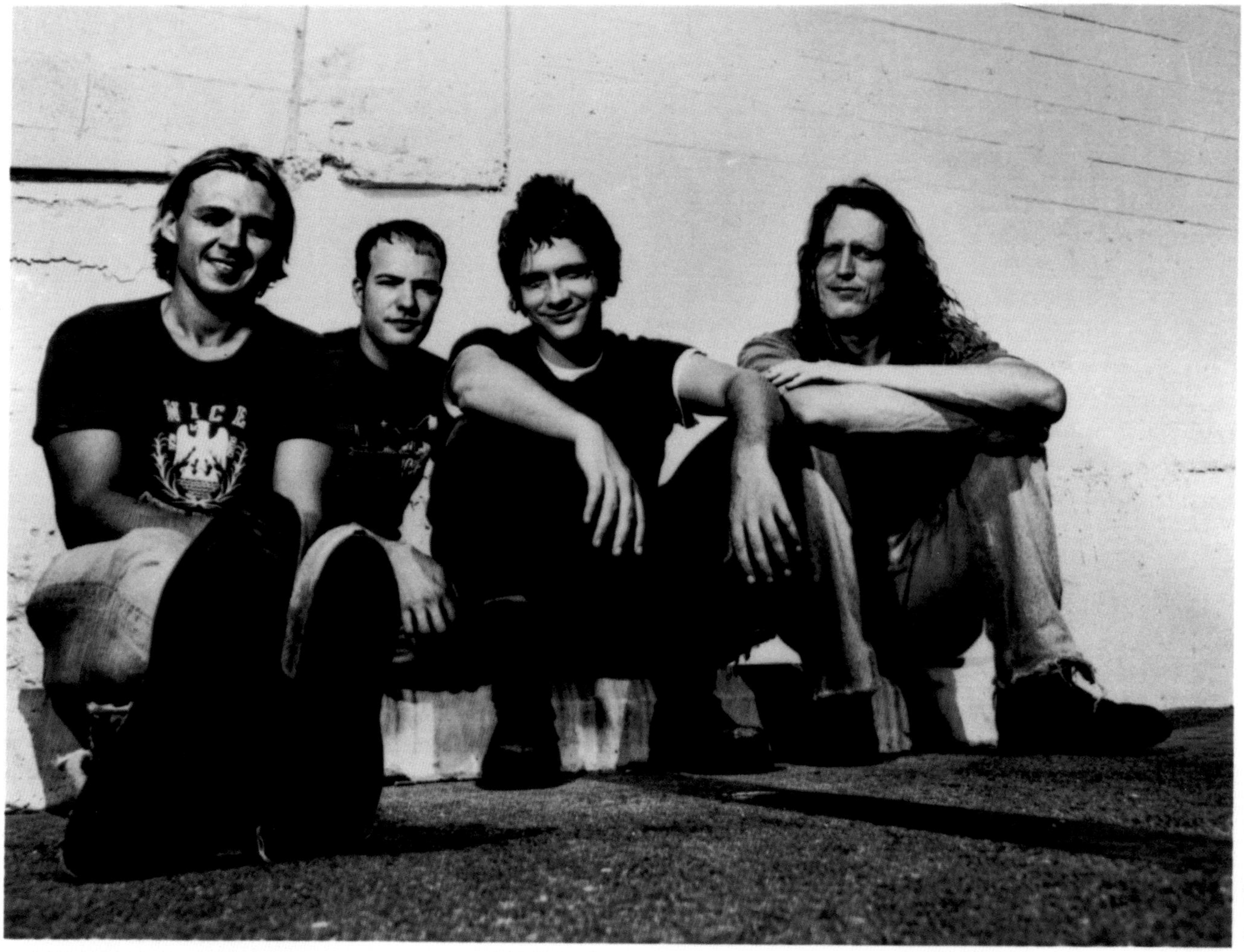

Photo Credit: John Falls

Wes Berggren Mark Pirro Tim DeLaughter Bryan Wakeland

TRIPPING DAISY

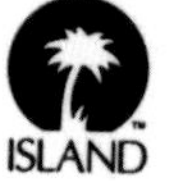

Billboard 200: *Resident Alien* (#49)
Billboard Hot 100: "In the Meantime" (#32)

With one bona fide hit, "In the Meantime," Spacehog made the most of its journey to the land of opportunity.

PEOPLE KNEW Spacehog from the cool, catchy single that recalled Mott the Hoople and Ziggy Stardust-era David Bowie. "In the Meantime" skyrocketed on modern-rock radio stations.

"We're adjusting. We've fallen into a ruin of drink and drugs and bad attitudes—separate helicopters to sound check, that sort of thing," drummer Jonny Cragg noted wryly.

Spacehog had found success in America before breaking in its mother country of England. The expatriated members—Cragg, lead guitarist Richard Steel, guitarist Antony Langdon and his younger brother Royston on lead vocals and bass—were animated and charming. But their entry into rock was with a multitude of obscure British bands that "all went horribly wrong," Cragg said.

"In the last decade, there's been a weighty history of nonachievement by British bands in America. We could all see that. A couple of years ago, I came over to New York just to hang out with a friend. I didn't have any kind of musical agenda at all. I packed my drumsticks just in case, but I hung out in the East Village and partied a little bit. It's a great place to lose yourself."

Cragg was stuck toiling at an espresso bar when he served Antony Langdon and discovered they both had the same Leeds accent and musical tastes. A short time later Royston joined and became the primary songwriter. After a failed attempt at working with another lead guitarist, Cragg coaxed his old friend Steel to fly to New York. Spacehog caused a buzz in the modish scene with spaced-themed songs and a logo designed by Mary Frey, who ran the downtown boutique Liquid Sky.

Resident Alien, the debut album, highlighted the band's "rocktastic" sound, and Cragg readily acknowledged the early Seventies glam-rock elements.

"Bowie, Mott, T. Rex—it's just a part of what we do, an ingredient. I think we cover a lot of other bases on the record, a reflection of the fact that we listen to a lot of different music—the Beatles, the Stones, funk, classic rock."

Resident Alien went gold. The standout track was "In the Meantime," which reached No. 1 on *Billboard*'s Mainstream Rock Tracks chart.

"It was literally the first song that we played as a band, that we jammed," Cragg said. "We recorded a demo of it in a jingle studio on 57th Street. It was an appalling, scratchy version with an incredibly happy, hopeful vibe. A guy who was doing music for the vampire movie *Nadja* heard it, loved it and put it on the film. And it was always something that spearheaded our live set. So we had the sensation that it was going to be the housewives' choice for a single." ■

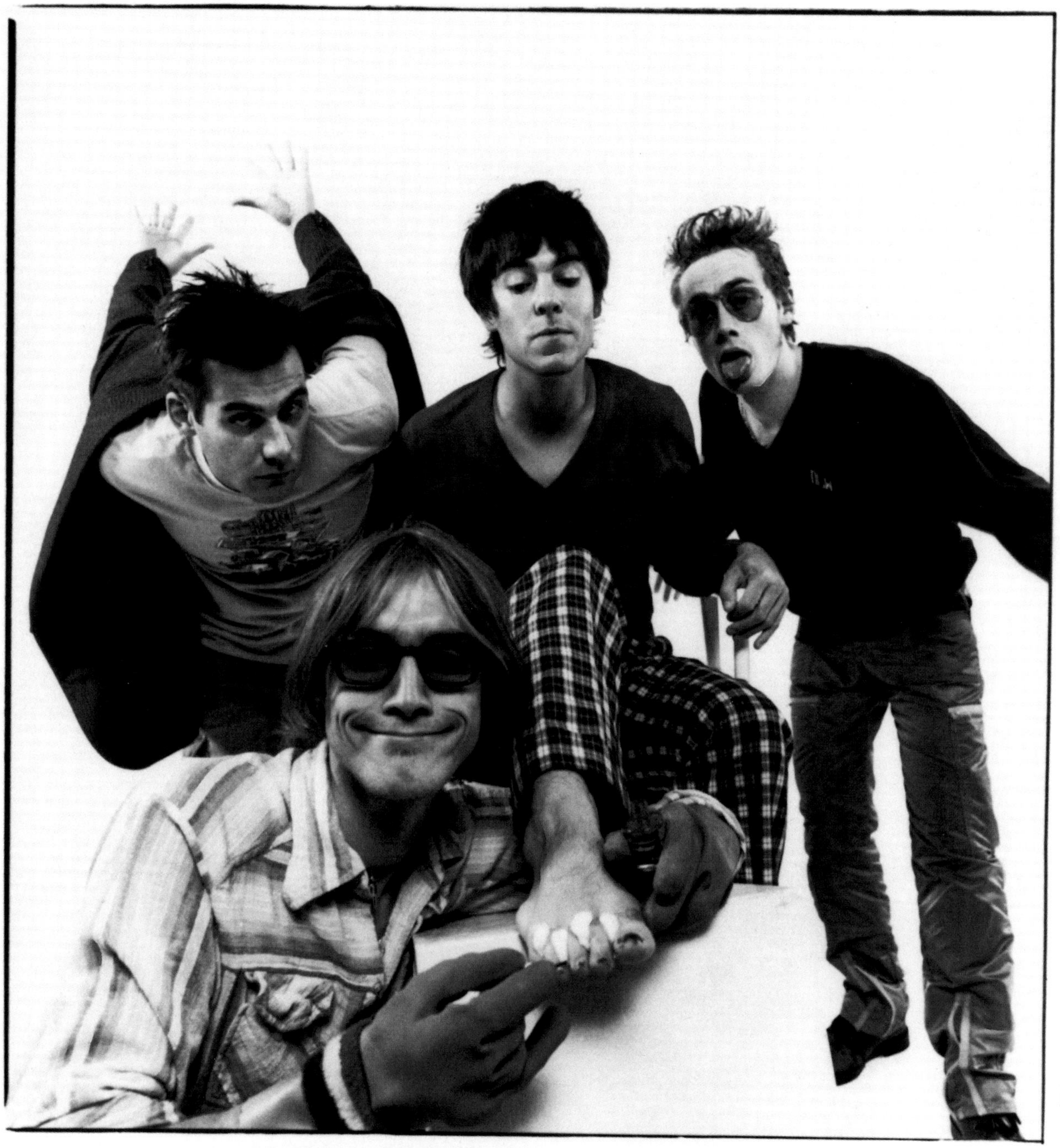

PHOTO CREDIT ELI HERSHKO / 1995

L - R : ANTONY LANGDON, RICHARD STEEL, JONNY CRAGG, ROYSTON LANGDON

SPACEHOG

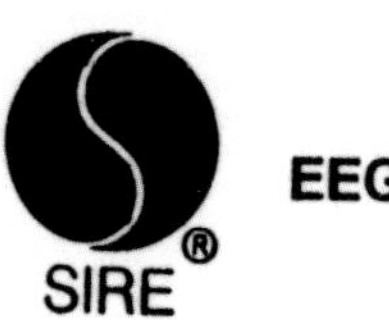

EEG

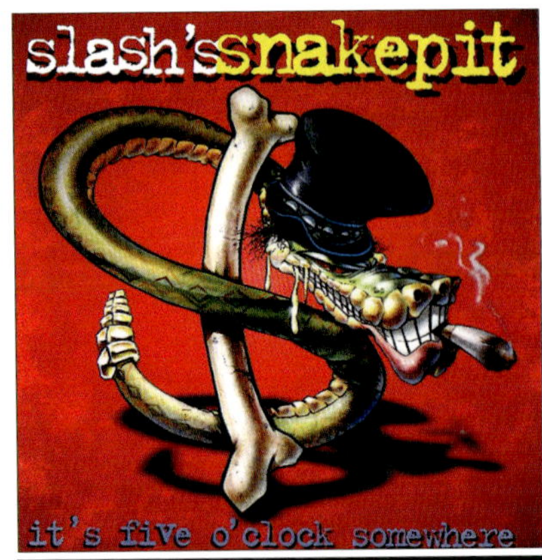

Billboard 200: *It's Five O'Clock Somewhere* (#70)

At odds over Guns N' Roses' path, when the bloom was off the Rose, Slash's Snakepit was born spontaneously.

ONE OF the biggest bands in the world, Guns N' Roses was usually embroiled in controversy engendered by Axl Rose's belligerence. Lead guitarist Slash had said he'd never do a solo album, but Slash's Snakepit was a "side project" band he formed.

"I'm having a really hard time with Guns right now," the laid-back Slash (real name Saul Hudson) admitted. "All of a sudden, Axl said, 'I want to work with different people' and kicked Gilby (Clarke, rhythm guitarist) out of the band. We were doing some cool stuff—and of course Axl wasn't there, because he never comes to rehearsal. I can't stand the guy he wanted to use, and that started a whole big rift. At the moment, that doesn't help my enthusiasm for Guns any better—or 'Eddie Vedder,' that's the joke we use."

Guns N' Roses' tour in support of the *Use Your Illusion* records had lasted 28 months, with 192 concerts in 28 countries. "Suddenly I came home," Slash said. "It's dangerous if I'm not working, because I get bored and I'm gonna fuck up—that's where my whole history of getting strung out on drugs comes from. So I built a studio in my house, and I started writing and demoing material. I played it for Axl and he said, 'I don't want to do that kind of music anymore.' Whoa, another big fuckin' kick in the nuts for me.

"And then Matt (Sorum, Guns N' Roses drummer) started coming over, and he'd give me drums to work with and get arrangements. Then Gilby brought a couple of songs—I'd really gotten used to hanging out with him, he's one of my best friends. I had a barbecue one night and Mike Inez (bass) from Alice in Chains walks in. I said, 'What are you doing here?' 'The limo driver said you were having a party.' 'Well, here's a beer.'

"All of a sudden, I have a band. You know how attorneys and managers play golf? We were just a bunch of friends hanging out and playing music."

Slash auditioned 40-odd singers, and former Jellyfish guitarist Eric Dover was included as vocalist. "With a mixture of vodka, Jack Daniel's and *Absolutely Fabulous* on the tube, we whipped out 14 songs in a week and had a great time doing it. Then Axl wanted the material back. I said, 'Dude, we've already finished the record.' He was like, 'There's no way you could do it that fast.' I said, 'You'd be amazed.'"

It's Five O'Clock Somewhere was a party starter album of Southern fried blues-rock. "Beggars & Hangers" featured a tasty, sharp-cut rhythm; Slash leaned into the dirty riffs with spontaneous, inebriated grace. With rock radio backing away from the traditional sound of Slash's Snakepit, the band toured in clubs and theaters.

"Guns N' Roses is a street band—we come from a 'non-existent existence,' just guys out there with nothing," Slash laughed. "Suddenly we're a stadium band. I haven't changed at all. On the other hand, Axl is really into this whole star status thing. So I'm having fun—there's no pressure, no one looking over my shoulder. We don't have that flamboyant lead singer trip going on. We all fell together—it's like a Cinderella story. But come the end of the tour, I'll be a pumpkin. Axl wants to do another album." ■

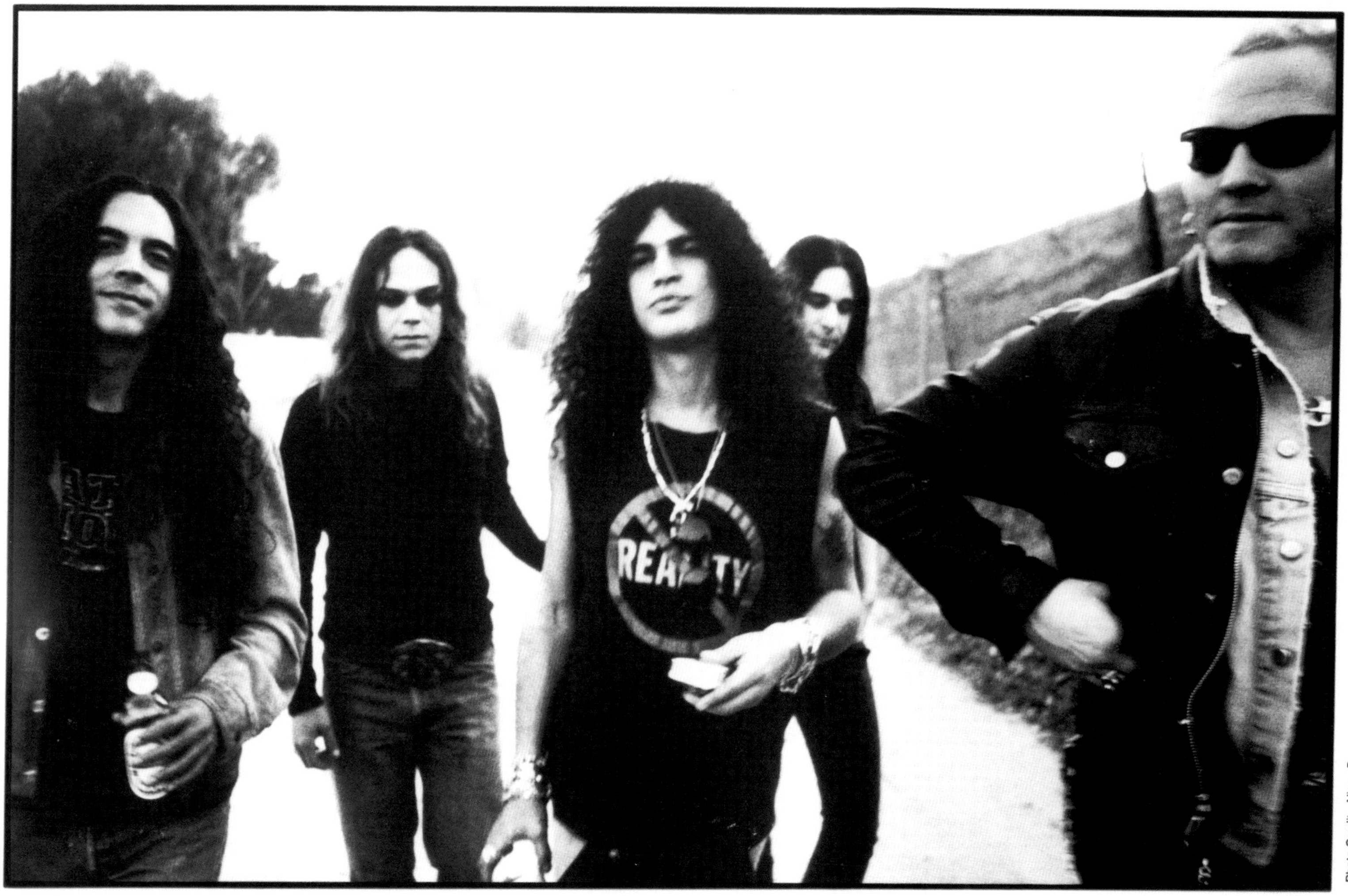

Photo Credit: Alison Dyer

Mike Inez Eric Dover Slash Gilby Clarke Matt Sorum

slash'ssnakepit

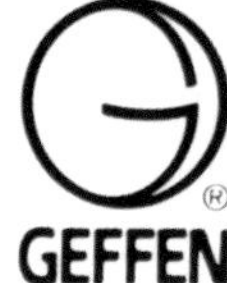

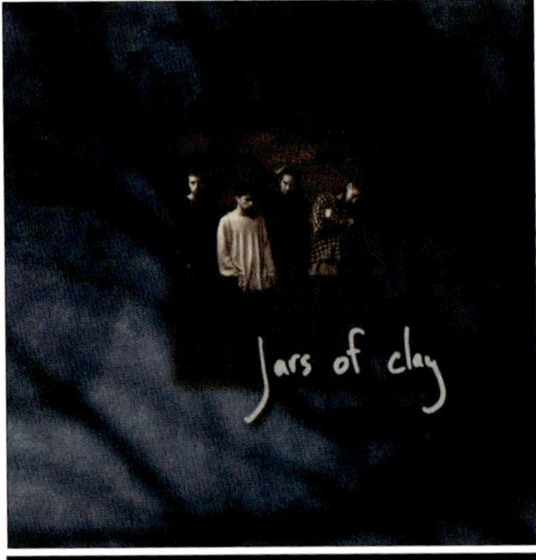

Billboard 200: *Jars of Clay* (#46)
Billboard Hot 100: "Flood" (#37)

Christian rock group Jars of Clay dispensed an unpredicted hit when "Flood" crossed over to the pop charts.

AFTER THE song "Flood" began to catch on with mainstream pop and alternative rock radio stations, Jars of Clay enjoyed a massively popular hit and platinum sales. But "Flood" was already a smash—on contemporary Christian music charts, making Jars of Clay the fastest-selling debut act in the history of that industry.

"A good Christian audience has stood behind us, and that's important to us," lead singer Dan Haseltine said. "But at the same time, we want to branch out. Hopefully people will tap into what we're doing for the musical content. MTV and secular radio stations aren't playing 'Flood' for the spiritual message."

Jars of Clay (the Nashville-based band took its name from the Bible verse 2 Corinthians 4:7) formed in 1993, when three of the guys were still students at Illinois' Greenville College. A demo earned them a spot in a Gospel Music Association contest where more than 200 artists vied for the Spotlight Award as "the best unsigned band." They won. Haseltine called the music "acoustically driven alternative pop," laced with lyrics about life and faith.

"The Christian music industry hasn't been around as long as mainstream music. It's still a very insecure medium in a lot of ways. For a long time, there was no originality to the songwriting. Everyone was trying to create a copy of a secular sound that was already out there."

The record company that signed Jars of Clay hired Adrian Belew, known for his work with David Bowie and King Crimson, to co-produce "Flood" from the group's self-titled debut release. The driving single dealt with a religious theme in a way unique to the modern rock glut but typical of Jars of Clay's music.

"Metaphorically speaking, it's a song about the way we let guilt weigh us down, let things pile up without any sort of relief. It's the cry of a person to save him from that," Haseltine said.

The band members were dealing pragmatically with ministry versus work. "We don't completely fit in with that contemporary Christian music description," guitarist Matt Odmark said. "We don't look like the average band, and our albums don't sound like the average record. A lot of music in our style of rock dodges the chance to communicate something meaningful. We react strongly in the opposite direction—we want songs that will come at your very sincerely, music that will be inspirational to people. It's a lot easier to throw down cool-sounding phrases and clever concepts than it is to dig around in your heart and say, 'These are the things that are moving me right now—how do I get them in song?'"

"A lot of people think if you're a Christian musician, you also have the ability to preach the gospel, like that's your main purpose onstage. But we fumble over our words regularly," Haseltine added. "We try to let the music speak, and hopefully our attitude. For a long time, Christians have been portrayed as very judgmental individuals with rigid dos and don'ts. Breaking down that stereotype is better than the gospel." ■

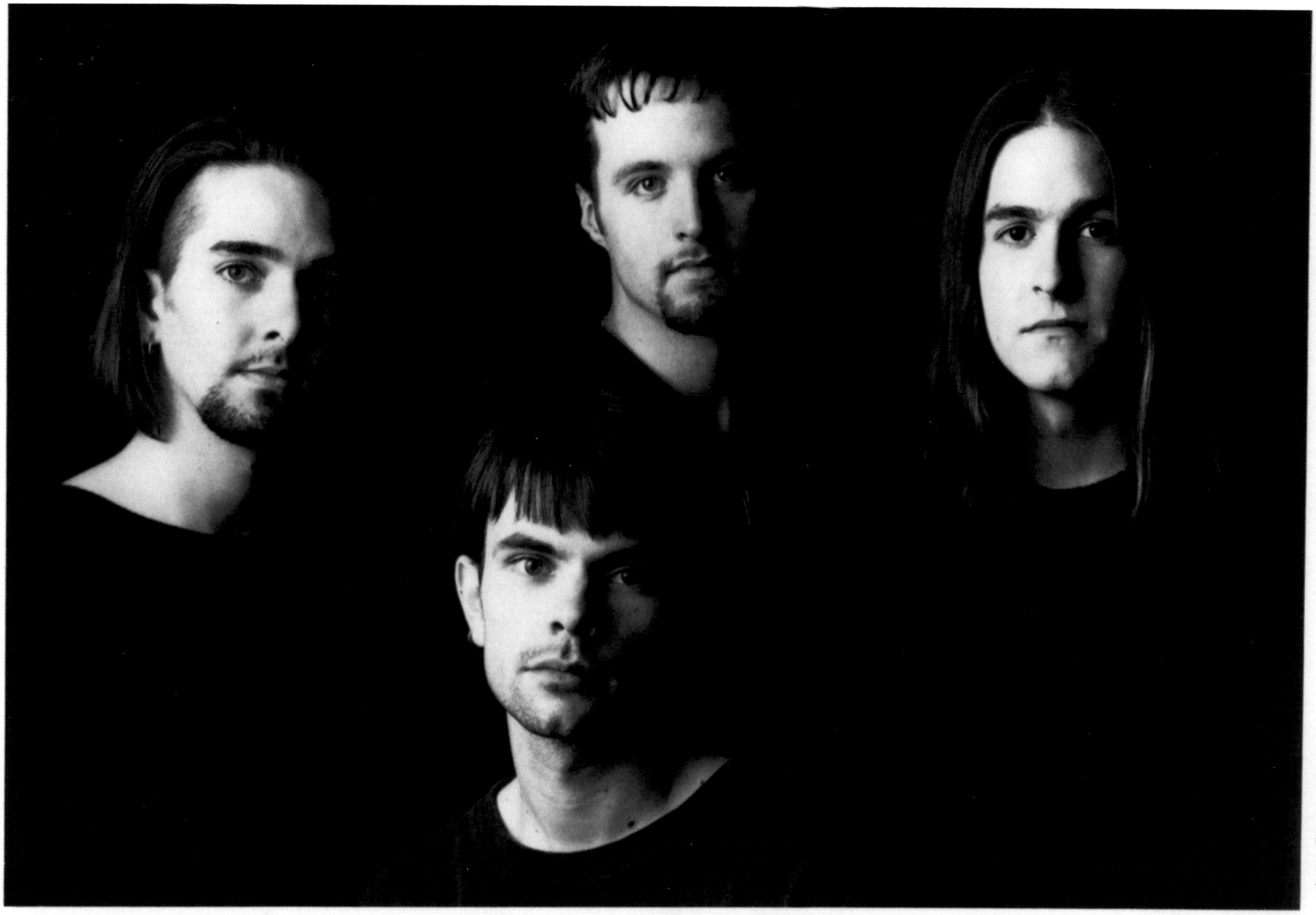

photo: Tamara Reynolds

Jars of clay

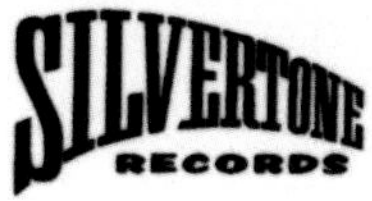

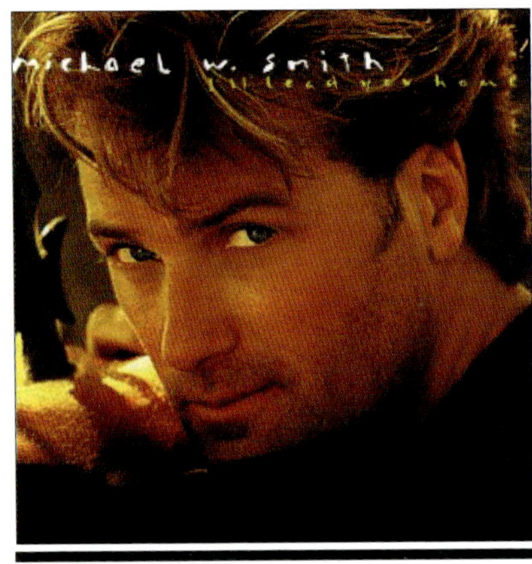

Billboard 200: *I'll Lead You Home* (#16)

The top-selling male artist in the contemporary Christian music genre, Michael W. Smith bore *I'll Lead You Home.*

A DEVOTION to the Christian music market had taken Michael W. Smith to remarkable places. His signature song "Friends" became a sentimental favorite for high school graduations and farewell celebrations all over the world. With 1991's "Place in This World," Smith enjoyed significant crossover success as a bona fide star, getting widespread exposure on pop radio, VH1 and MTV. It effectively validated his aspirations to get his message out to a wider audience, but his more religious fans feared that he was selling out to the more lucrative secular market.

"A lot of things have changed," Smith acknowledged. "With a wife and five kids, I certainly have more responsibilities. Some of the changes have not been easy, but I still feel like a kid myself, and I think I always will."

I'll Lead You Home, Smith's eighth studio album, combined the style of his mainstream releases with a touch of the faith values that continued to be a cornerstone of his life. He worked with Patrick Leonard, the production wizard whose credits included Madonna, Peter Cetera and Kenny Loggins. Leonard's layered synths and guitars gave Smith's honest lyrics a glistening, immaculate atmosphere.

"I've failed so many times that I've come to a point of not being afraid to write about it," Smith said. "You tend to write better songs when you just embrace life and experience some tough times."

I'll Lead You Home became the highest-debuting Christian release in the history of the *Billboard* 200, the chart ranking the most popular albums in the US. It also gave Smith his second Grammy win, in the Best Pop/Contemporary Gospel Album category. ■

MICHAEL W. SMITH

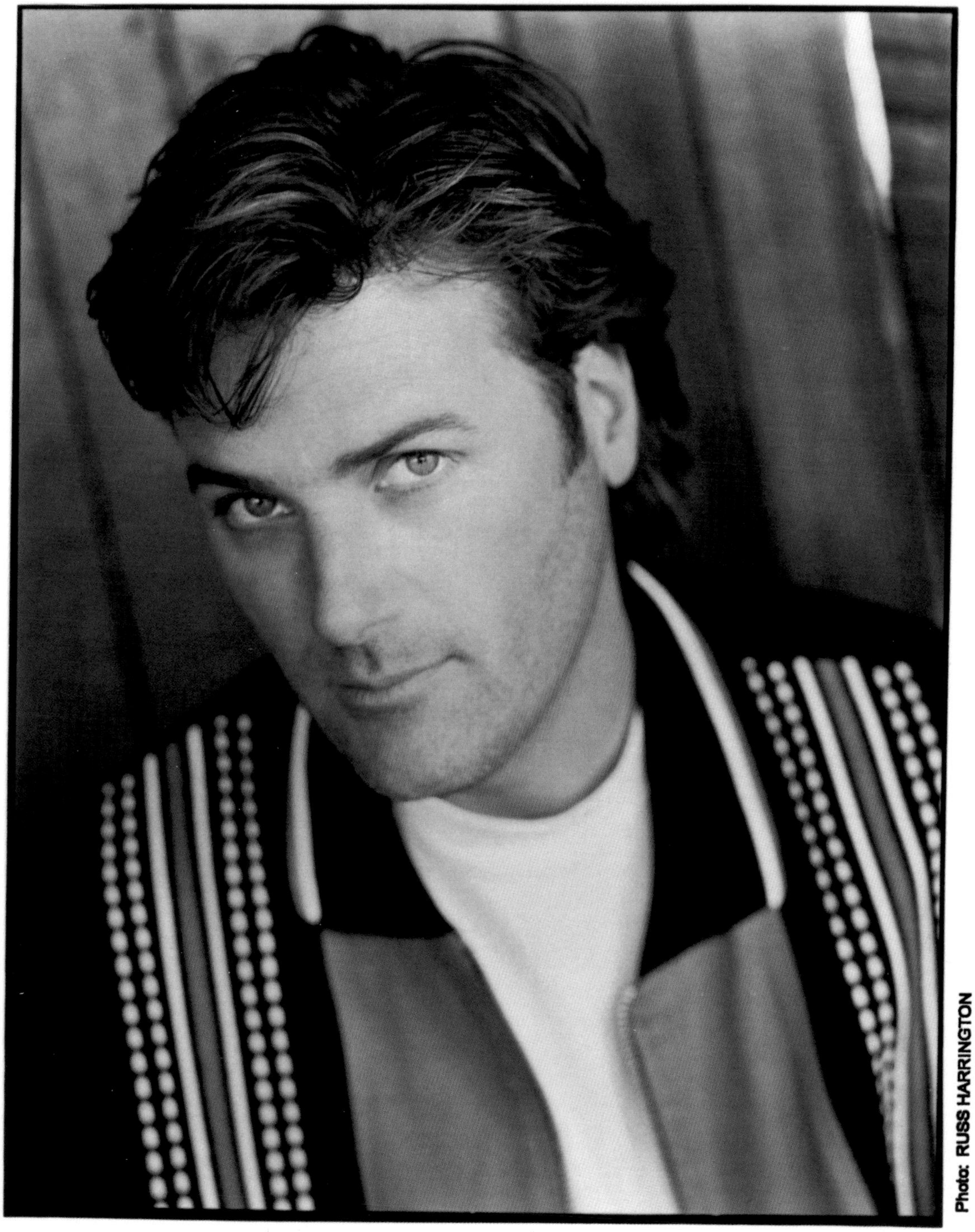

Photo: RUSS HARRINGTON

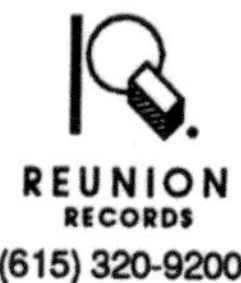

REUNION
RECORDS
(615) 320-9200

exclusive management:
BLANTON / HARRELL, INC.
2910 Poston Avenue
Nashville, TN 37203
(615) 327-9300

Billboard 200: *The Presidents of the United States of America* (#6)
Billboard Hot 100: "Peaches" (#29)

The Presidents of the United States of America received high approval ratings for their self-titled debut album.

THE PRESIDENTS of the United States of America made party music—not Republican or Democrat, but catchy, goofy punk-pop. Though the band was new, the three members—Dave Dederer, Chris Ballew and Jason Finn—were veterans of the famously pained Seattle music scene, and they emerged as the most popular band based in a city with a reputation for tortured tunes of misery and self-absorption.

"The whole grunge scene is less of a big deal in Seattle than it is everywhere else in the world," Dederer said. "We're part of a Northwest tradition of good-time, party-down rock bands that predates grunge, that's been going on for 30 years. We're entertainers, not artists."

The trio blasted through quick, quirky offerings on *The Presidents of the United States of America*. The wacky "Lump," a Top 10 track at alternative radio, was either about a brain tumor, a strange woman squatting in a swamp or utter nonsense. "Kitty" was a declaration of war on a cat that didn't want to be petted. The hit "Peaches" was a rustic ode to fruit.

"There's always been that fun element in whatever I've done," Ballew said. "I used to write more confessional trying-to-encompass-the-human-experience-in-a-hilarious-metaphor songs. Two years ago, I gave up the human experience part and just went for the hilarious metaphors. I never believed that any of the bands I was in would make records or go anywhere, so I never felt the pressure to be serious."

The hyperactive trio used peculiar instrumentation. Fast, noisy chords and tones were covered using only five strings between Bellew, who played a two-string basitar, and Dederer, who played a three-string guitbass (and Finn, who played no-string drums). Ballew got the idea of removing strings when he worked with Mark Sandman of Morphine in a band called Supergroup.

"It's been said that we want to sound like Aerosmith or AC/DC on toy instruments," Dederer said. "When Chris and I got together, his songs were all in this open tuning. I liked the sound of it. Our tunings are the same except I have another string that's higher. It's easier because you do most of the songs in one key and you can jump around. It's harder because you have to think about what you're trying to do. I have to hear something first and then figure out a way to play it."

On Presidents Day, MTV aired the group's concert at Mount Rushmore. "It was actually a gas, but conceptually it was a pain—a sophomoric promotional idea that put us in an uncomfortable position, and we were forced to accept it," Ballew said. "It's our fault. We chose to be called the Presidents of the United States of America; it was a reaction to the trend in one-syllable band names. But we don't like presidential references—we just think it's too obvious. We tried to diffuse it by painting ourselves red, white and blue on the inside of the record cover, thinking that would be it. But it didn't work out that way." ■

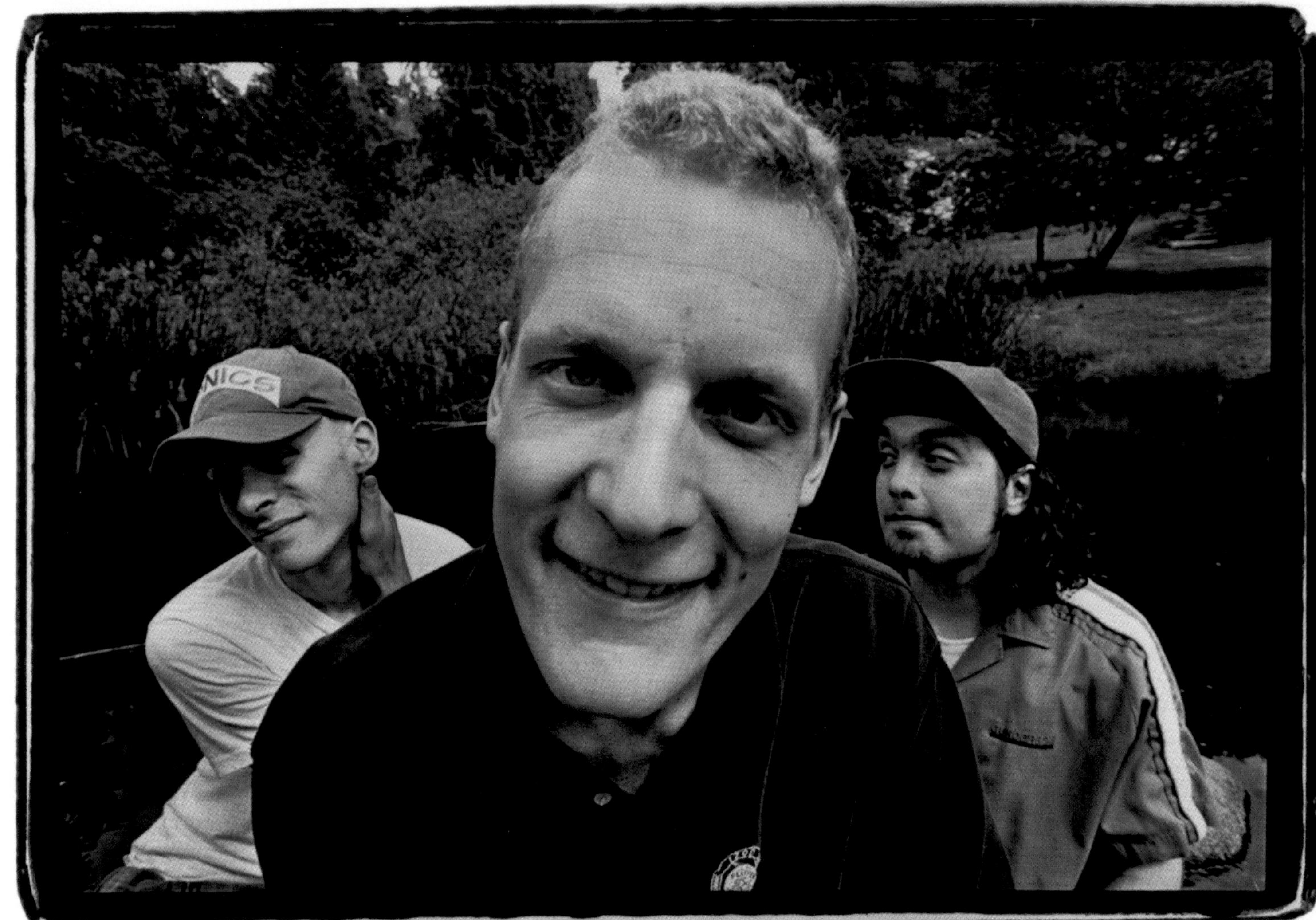

CHRIS BALLEW DAVE DEDERER JASON FINN

THE PRESIDENTS OF THE UNITED STATES OF AMERICA

COLUMBIA
9507

PHOTO CREDIT: Karen Mason

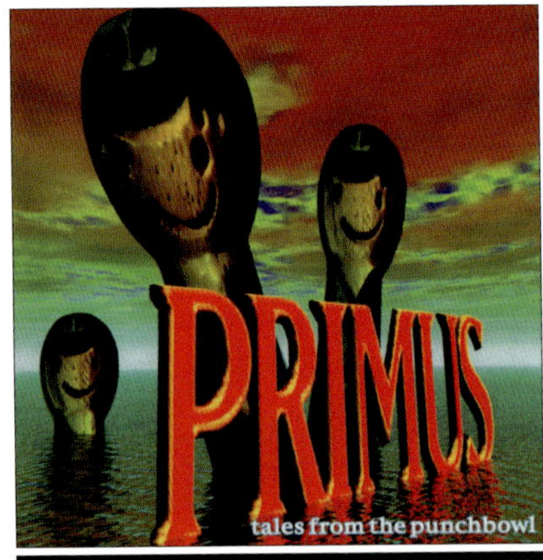

Billboard 200: *Tales from the Punchbowl* (#8)

Primus' penchant for warped subject matter and mutant musical chops turned up in "Wynona's Big Brown Beaver."

MOORED BY Les Claypool's spirited bass work and loony lead vocals, Primus had converted alt-metal quirkiness into rock stardom while maintaining a just plain weird essence. The band had scored marvelous concert spots, including a headlining stint on the 1993 Lollapalooza tour and highlighting Woodstock '94. Onstage, Primus' jamming was as whacked out as it was accomplished, with fractured rhythms and guitarist Larry Lalonde's skewed playing. "There's some real carpal tunnel parts on some of those things," Claypool laughed.

Primus released its fourth album, *Tales from the Punchbowl*, and made waves on alternative radio and MTV with the unforgettably titled "Wynona's Big Brown Beaver," an absurdist tale about, er, a mammal that sounded sneakily like the Charlie Daniels Band's "The Devil Went Down to Georgia" on bad acid.

"It's a pun, of course. And it's caused a certain Hollywood star some grief," Claypool said. "Actually, the whole beaver concept got into my head when I saw one as I was doing some fly-fishing. Wynona's just a name I had. It's just a happy, benign little song that's becoming extremely popular. People who haven't delved into the world of Primus experience that and think we're a silly band. But if you look at the album, 'Big Brown Beaver' is sandwiched between two songs that have very tragic characters. There's some dark, satirical subject matter in Primus music."

"Wynona's Big Brown Beaver" was nominated for the Grammy Award for Best Hard Rock Performance. The members of Primus also utilized some twisted technology in the song's video to create the image of themselves as plastic cowboy toys—they were fitted with prosthetics by a special-effects team famous for similar suits in Duracell battery commercials. ■

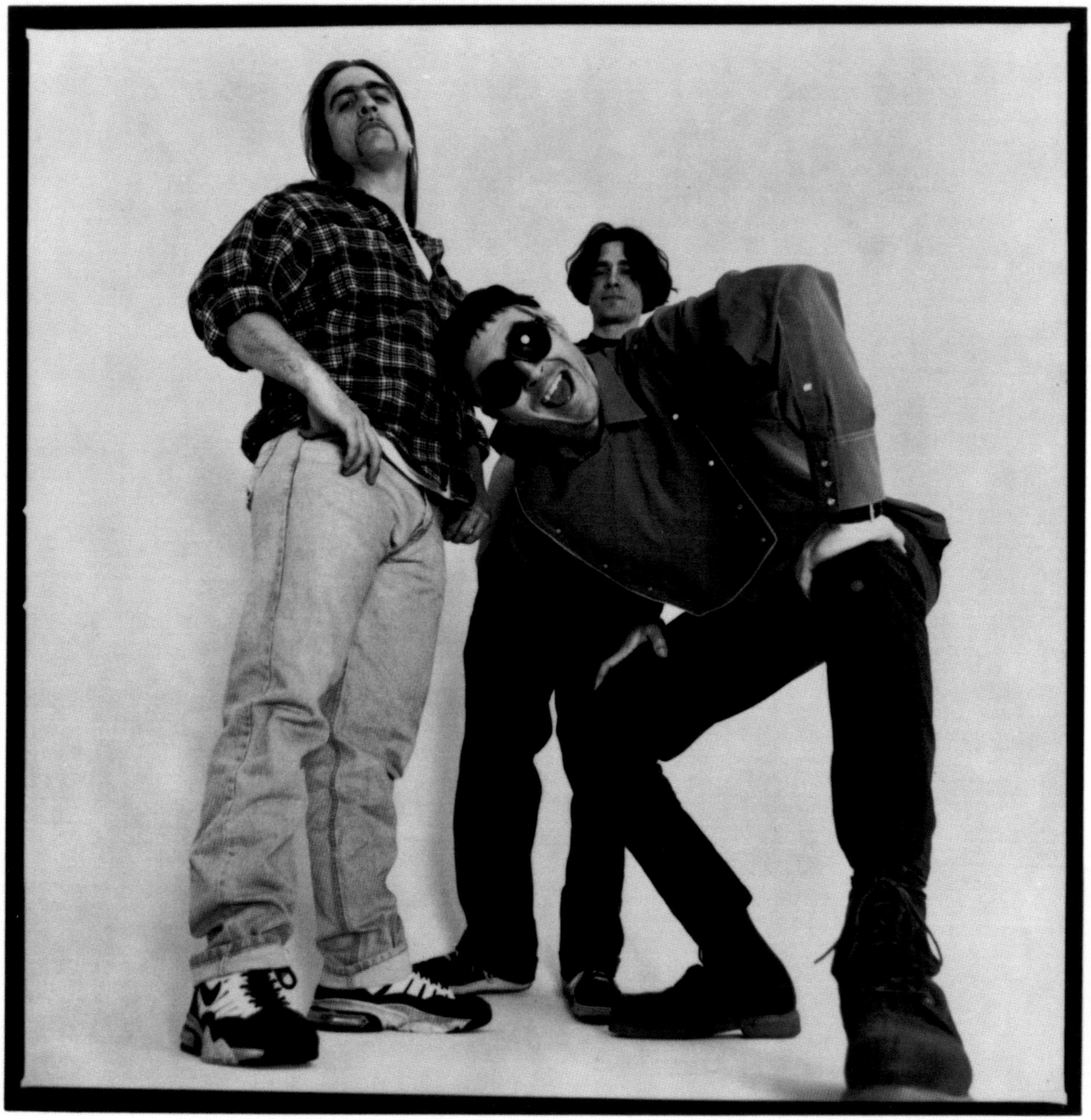

Photo credit: Michael Halsband

Tim Alexander Larry Lalonde Les Claypool

PRIMUS

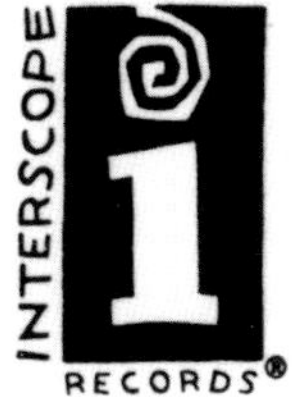

Billboard 200: *The Great Escape* (#150)

For Britain's accomplished Blur, being a nonentity in the States was a discouraging, distressing development.

THE BEATLES spearheaded the first British pop music invasion of America, but since those days, the most lauded UK bands—from T. Rex and Slade in the Seventies to Suede in the early Nineties—had found it hard to make more than a fleeting impact on the US market.

Blur was a phenomenon in the UK. The band's 1994 album, *Parklife*, racked up record-breaking sales and won the guys four BPI awards (British Grammys). The romping single "Girls and Boys" contributed their ascent to superstardom across Europe. But it failed to gain Blur a foothold in the States. Why was America suspicious of "Brit-pop" exports?

"Nobody in Britain says anything about American bands being too American," bassist Alex James said. "We made an album that completely changed the face of pop music in Britain. *Parklife* opened the door for a lot of other bands of our ilk to be successful—the mainstream is now in the hands of irresponsible, reckless young men like myself. So do you allow yourself to become Americanized? We wouldn't think of becoming North German to appeal to Germans. But for some reason there's just this fundamental sense which exists, that American culture is the standard. And that's not good for anybody. We wouldn't be happy, it would be soulless pretending to be something that we're not. If American people get it, well and good. I think good pop music always transcends everything. That's the great thing about it."

So Blur set about breaking through to kids in America, and the band anticipated success following the release of its next album. *The Great Escape* went straight to No. 1 on the British charts and sold more than 500,000 copies there in its first two weeks. "Country House" was deceptively bouncy, and "The Universal" was a first-class ballad. *The Great Escape* was Blur's first record to crack the US charts, debuting on the *Billboard* 200 at #150. But the album fell off entirely the next week.

"I think British pop has got something to offer," James said. "Last time we were here, it was all Hootie & the Blowfish and punk rock. Punk rockers are not very cool in England—we had all that ages ago. Now it just seems a bit silly. But I suppose it's something that you need to get out of your system."

"We've honed down our (US) audience to mostly loony Anglophiles who get it more completely than I get it—we've got to build on that," singer Damon Albarn added. "We can rock, but we can also pop. I've always felt that pop is a higher art form than rock. I'd hate to be in a rock band. It's like saying, 'I only drink beer,' when I like to drink sherry with ice sometimes. Pop is more cosmopolitan. There aren't many pop bigots. Rock is either Courtney Love or Pamela Anderson, isn't it?" ■

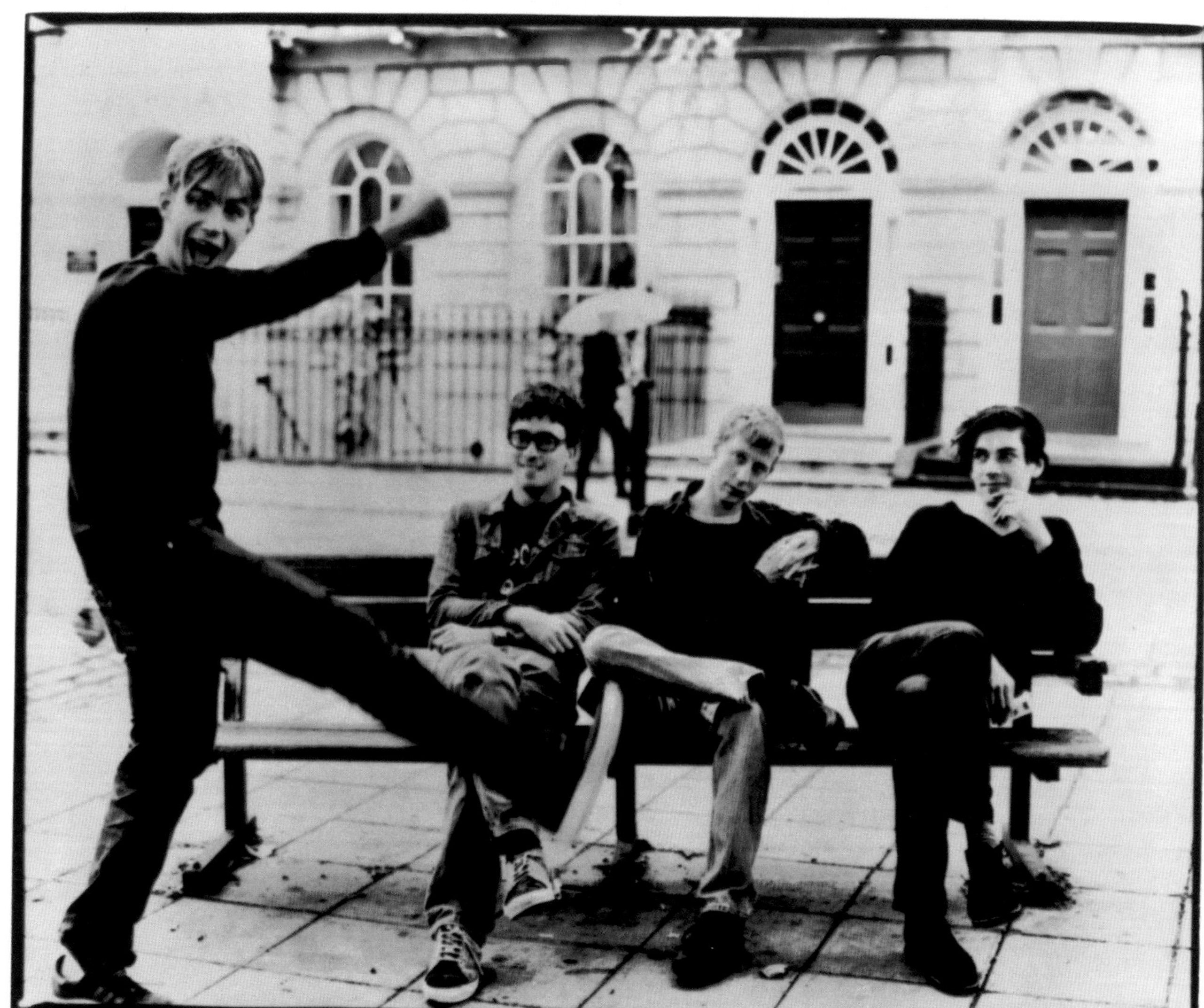

Photo Credit: Kevin Westenberg 10/95

BLUR

Virgin

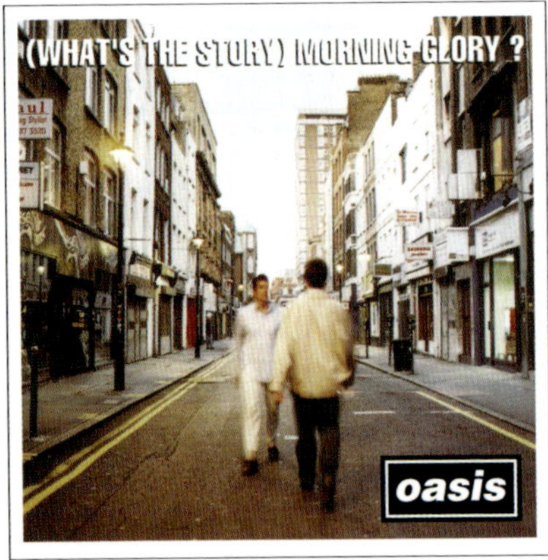

Billboard 200: *(What's the Story) Morning Glory?* (#4)
Billboard Hot 100: "Wonderwall" (#8);
"Don't Look Back in Anger" (#55)

At the pinnacle of its UK success, the tempestuous Oasis made waves in the US with the iconic "Wonderwall."

IN MID-NINETIES England, Oasis defined its generation, the most popular band since the Beatles—and the most volatile. Liam and Noel Gallagher, who fronted Oasis, never kept their infighting and wild lifestyles much of a secret. The contentious relationship between the feuding brothers and their brushes with the law turned Oasis into a virtual soap opera in the ruthless British tabloids.

In America? The rock music world needed some personality, some bratty stars, and Oasis' bad-boy behavior was a temporary remedy. What was so charming musically was the Gallaghers' profound Beatles influence—they made no bones about the impression that British Sixties guitar pop had made on them. *(What's the Story) Morning Glory?* sold more than 3 million copies and spawned a Top 10 single, "Wonderwall," and a seven-minute modern-rock anthem, "Champagne Supernova."

"I'd like a No. 1 record in America, right? But to be big there, you've really got to put a lot of time into it—or you've really got to be shit," Liam Gallagher said. "I mean that in the best way! You've got to be really tacky, or you've got to spend a lot of time there. And I don't know if I could live there."

Noel supplied Oasis' creative vision, writing the songs and the guitar parts. Singer Liam provided the defiant rock-star posturing. "We know what we're doing before we go in (the studio), and we just fucking go for it," Liam said. "But believe you me, I just sit in the back and have a couple of cigs—and when I'm ready to sing, I'm singing."

Onstage, Liam attempted to play the frontman with indifference—standing still, staring into space. "I'm only there to sing my songs," he said of his nonchalant vibe. "There's plenty of music going down. The day they should start worrying is the day I'm not fucking singing. There's no need for movement in our band. We're there for people to listen to the songs. If they want to move, they can do what they fucking want. If they don't want to move, then fine by me. I'm listening. To do leaping about, you've got to be prepared to do it every fucking night—for every gig, every tour for the rest of your fucking life. If you do it every now and again, then people are going to go, 'Oh, he's had a bad gig because he hasn't got his little dance routine together.' I'm not prepared to do that." ■

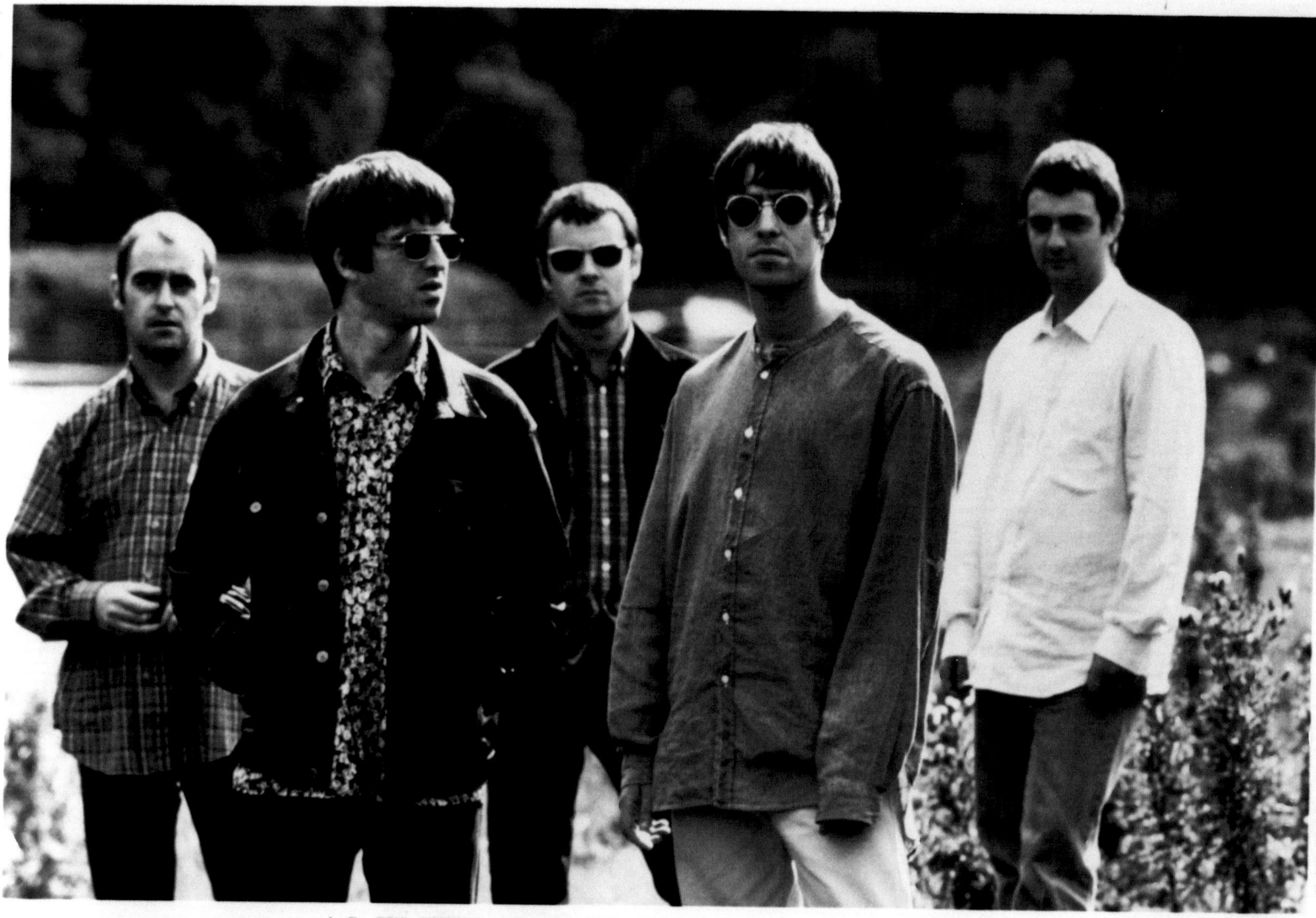

PHOTO CREDIT JILL FURMANOVSKY

L - R : PAUL ARTHURS, NOEL GALLAGHER, ALAN WHITE, LIAM GALLAGHER, PAUL MCGUIGAN

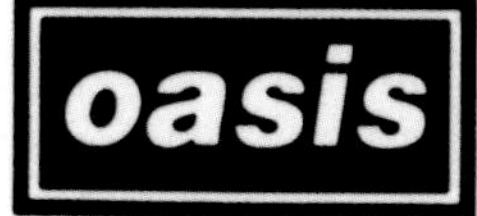

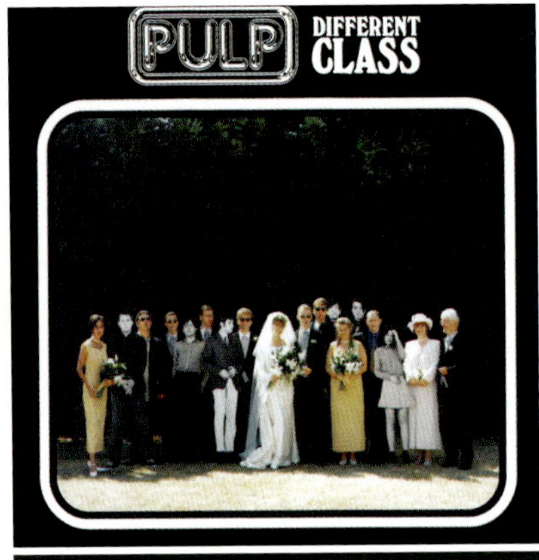

In the UK, a new superstar band stood in the wake of Oasis' success–Pulp, fronted by the fey Jarvis Cocker.

IN ENGLAND, Pulp had achieved multiplatinum status, but in the US, the introduction to Jarvis Cocker's band had been media coverage of his disruption of Michael Jackson's epic performance at the Brit Awards. Cocker, bored and frustrated, jumped on stage and pranced around Jackson's chorus line of children until security people removed him. In a press release, Cocker declared his spontaneous act was a form of protest against the industry's pandering to Jackson's pompous fantasies, "the way he sees himself as some Christlike figure with the power of healing."

"I don't regret doing it," Cocker said in his bored-to-tears Sheffield accent. "Just as long as people don't come to concerts to see the backside that was shoved in front of Michael Jackson's dancers."

The tall, thin Cocker was the kind of foppish pop icon that Brits couldn't help but react to. He'd wanted to reach celebrity status for as long as he could remember, leading different lineups of Pulp since his school days in northern England. It was only in 1995 that his persistence finally paid off. On *Different Class*, Pulp's breakthrough album—it entered the British charts at No. 1 upon its release—Cocker's witty, observant songwriting was a big asset. He explored the awkward realities of sex and life without financial security, and all of his pent-up emotions, aspirations and talents collided.

Pulp's signature song was "Common People," a story about being picked up by a patronizing rich girl who fancied slumming with the working-class world. Against a quirky synth-pop backdrop, she told Cocker's protagonist, "I want to sleep with common people like you." His reply: "I'll see what I can do."

"It's based on when I was at college in 1990," Cocker explained. "I always employ the time-lag mechanism in my songwriting, you see. That way, if you write about relationships, you're usually writing about a dead one. Writing about one that's still going on, you might get more grief."

Cocker considered the idea that his detailed narratives and theatrical delivery might be a drawback when it came to crossing the cultural divide between Britain and America.

"A lot of people say, 'Well, you're not about to make it in America because you're a very English-sounding band.' At least you can understand the words, which is a start. Even though the settings of the songs are English, it's about human beings in various stages of unhappiness, which happens both sides of the Atlantic. Most things in life are more pleasurable if you take it a bit slower. That's the philosophy we're bringing. We're attempting to seduce rather than pillage. We won't kick America's ass—we'll stroke it." ■

PULP

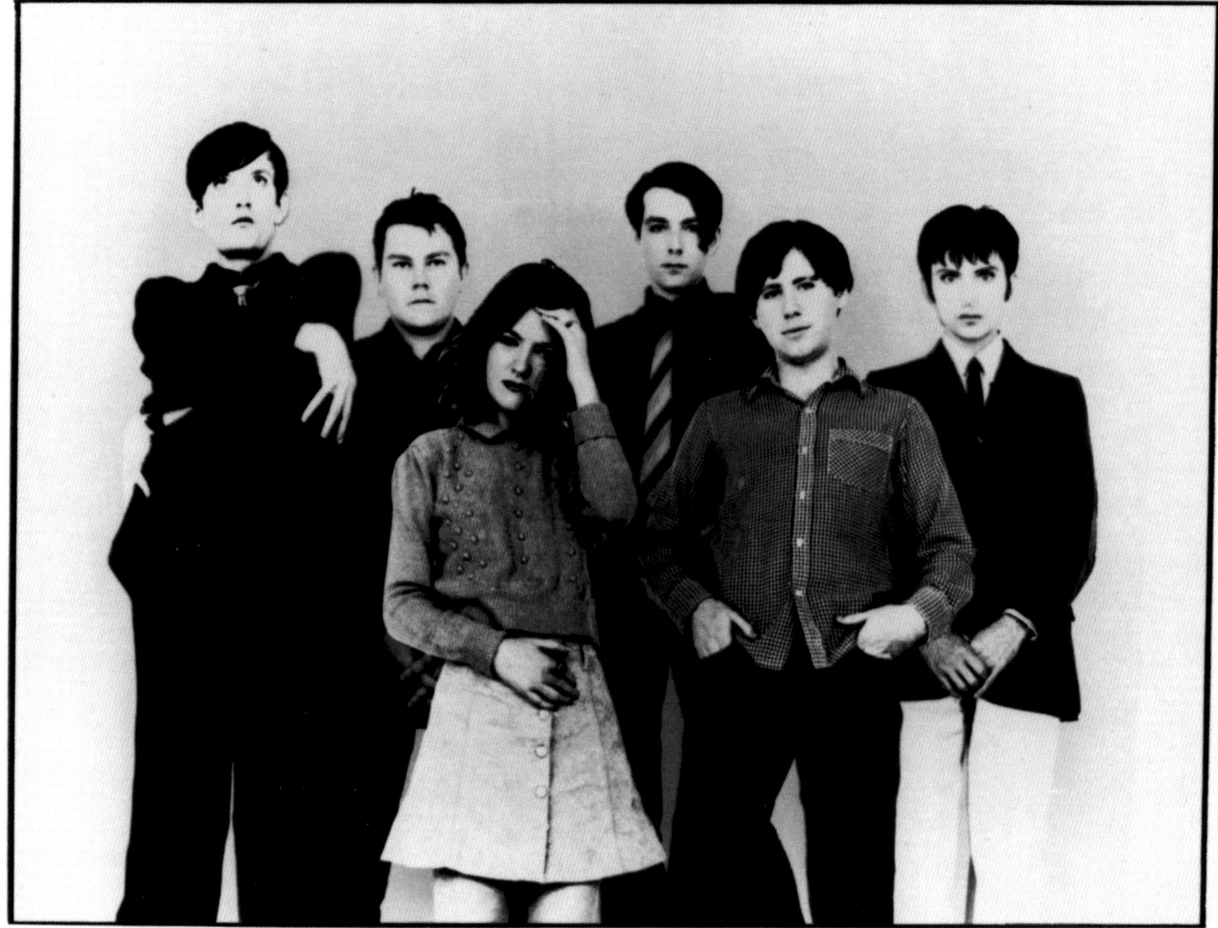

Jarvis Cocker Nick Banks Candida Doyle Steve Mackey Mark Webber Russell Senior

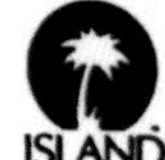

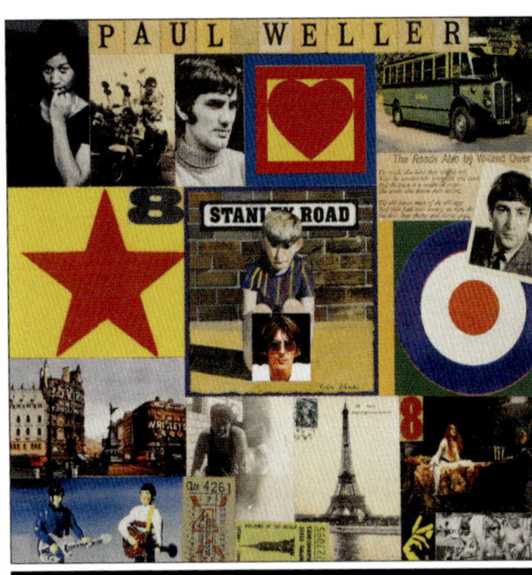

In a winding career path, *Stanley Road* was the latest undertaking for Paul Weller, one of Britain's musical icons.

A BELOVED and influential musical personality in his native Britain, Paul Weller had attained remarkable chart success and reverence among the public. In the US, the former Jam and Style Council member's stature was that of a cult figure.

"Yeah, I've never had a hit in the States, and it's unlikely I ever will," British rock's querulous uncle said. "But it's not like I've been there on a regular basis."

Next to the Clash, the Jam was the most enduring group to emerge from England's punk-rock class of 1977. The Who-inspired trio deftly mixed punk energy with catchy pop and soul-influenced melodies, and guitarist and singer Weller quickly established himself as a gifted lyricist able to look inward and outward. The Jam set the record for the most singles in the UK pop charts at one time, with 13, and became the first band to enter the charts at No. 1 with three different singles ("Going Underground," "Town Called Malice" and "Beat Surrender"). But in the US, no Jam single ever made the *Billboard* Hot 100.

"Because the Jam never got any kind of record action, we thought we never meant anything in the States," Weller said. "We were too young or stupid to realize it at the time, but there were a few gigs on the last tour where there was a buzz, which was a bit too late, because we were breaking up. And because we were such a big band in England, there was that measure of arrogance as well—'What are we doing wasting our time in America when we've got all this happening for us?'"

The Jam disbanded after six years, and Weller formed the Style Council shortly thereafter. All told, the cool and soulful duo had seven UK Top 10 hits, but only "My Ever Changing Moods" and "You're the Best Thing" (1984) charted in the US. The band folded in 1990.

Weller had released three albums under his own name since 1991. Many long-term devotees considered the third, *Stanley Road*—named after the street on which he had grown up in Woking—his best in years. The album took him back to the top of the British charts with songs like "The Changing Man" and the heartfelt balladry of "You Do Something To Me." Oasis guitarist Noel Gallagher joined Weller on a tour-de-force reading of Dr. John's voodoo-blues classic "I Walk on Gilded Splinters."

Even with the success of pop-punk and Brit-pop, Weller decided to stop attempting to break into the US market. But supporters who had gone that far with him found *Stanley Road* very gratifying.

"When I've been back to the States in recent years, I've met people who were kids when they went to see the Jam in '79. In hindsight, I realize those gigs did mean something. I'm just bowled over by the fact that there's still an audience, pockets of people who are really into it." ■

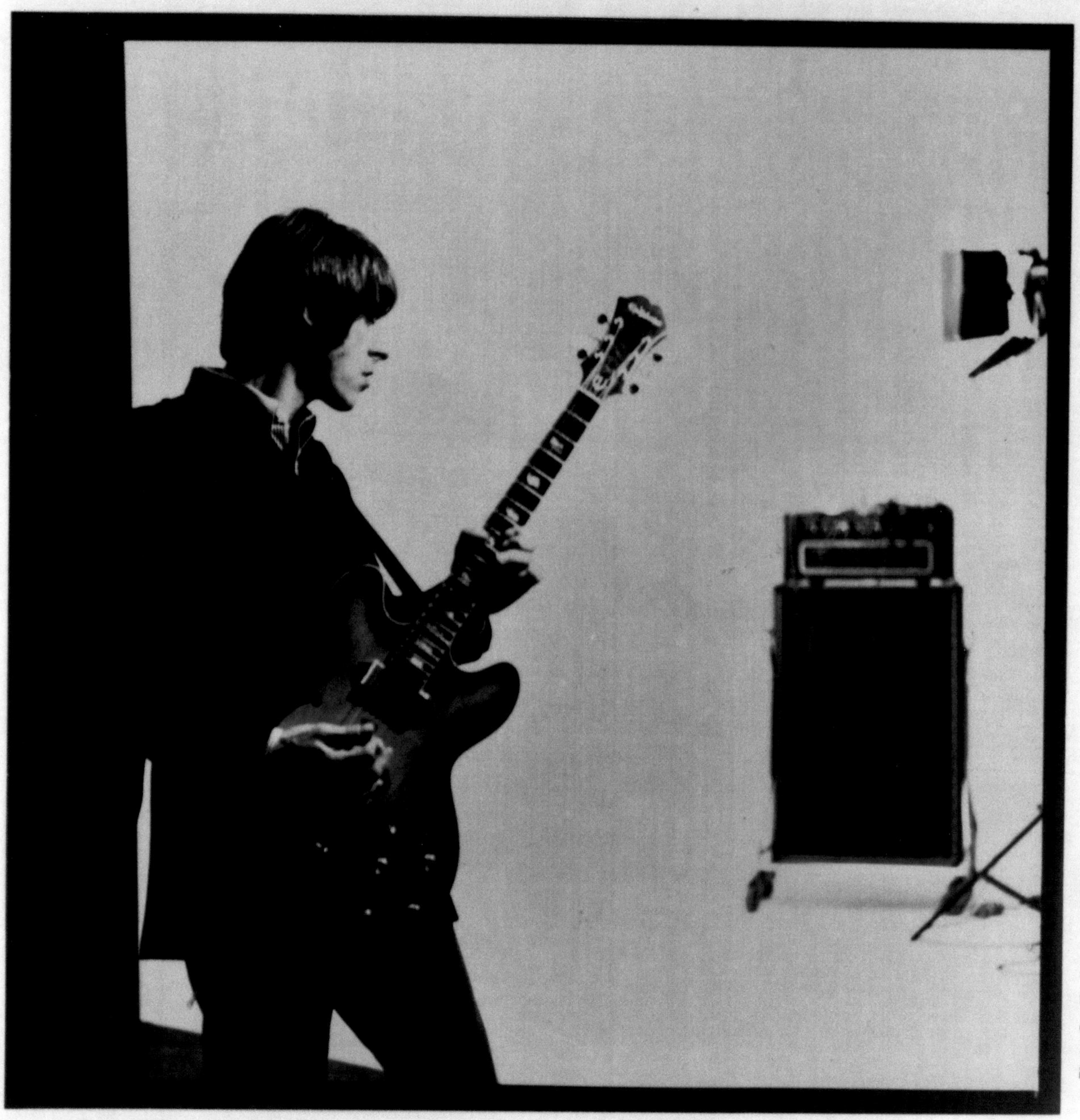

Photo Credit: Lawrence Watson

PAUL WELLER

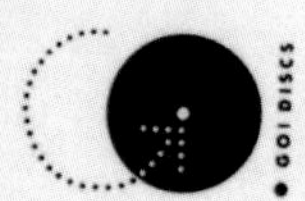

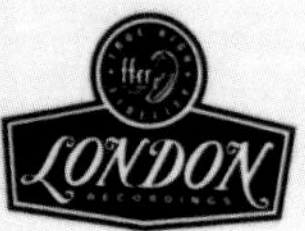

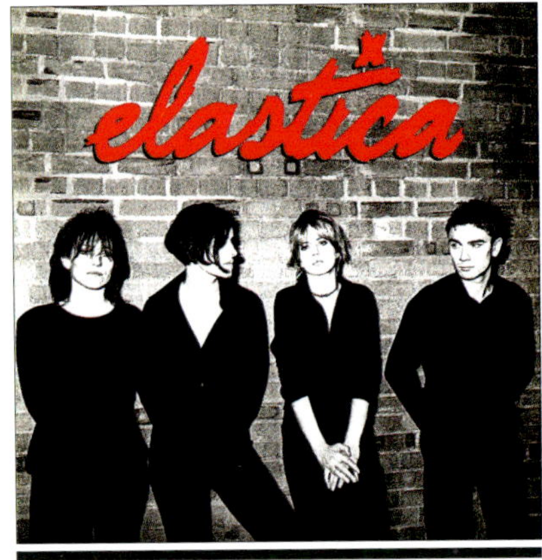

Billboard 200: *Elastica* (#66)
Billboard Hot 100: "Connection" (#53); "Stutter" (#67)

Elastica held sway over the rock scene with a No. 1 album in the UK and "Connection" erupting on US radio.

THE SAVING grace of the English music scene's "New Wave of the New Wave" was Elastica, three women and one guy reviving the craft of writing punky power-pop. The tasty single "Connection," which peaked at #2 on *Billboard*'s Modern Rock Tracks chart, featured singer Justine Frischmann holding her own against short, sharp washes of guitar jitters. The lyrics of "Stutter," another catchy joyride, were about a boyfriend's drunken impotence—"No need to whine, boy/Like a wind-up toy you stutter at my feet…It's always something you ate…Is it just that I'm much too much for you?"

The debut album *Elastica* balanced the style of the late Seventies with Nineties pop, all rolled into instantly familiar two-minute blasts. "We hear that a lot from people—'I start to like a song, and then it's over,'" Frischmann said.

The popular quartet was too young to remember the first New Wave. Frischmann stumbled on her brother's record collection when she was a preteen, and she was obsessed with the music of Wire, the Stranglers and Blondie. "He's 10 years older," she said. "When he left home and started a CD collection, he left his vinyl behind, and it all became important to me. Television, the Buzzcocks, XTC…"

Frischmann started playing guitar with Suede, but she bailed just before the band made it boffo in Britain. She launched Elastica with guitarist Donna Matthews, bassist Annie Holland and drummer Justin Welch, and their faces were plastered in British music weeklies less than six months after their first gig. "We didn't even have enough songs for an album," Frischmann said. "But I try to be practical about it. The whole music industry is a necessary evil you have to deal with if you want people to be aware of your music."

The band reeked of angular art-punk attitude on the cover of *Elastica*, but Frischmann, whose relationship with Blur frontman Damon Albarn made tabloid headlines, lacked nihilism. "It just depends on how you relate to stuff," she reasoned. "I worked in an office for a while and it drove me mad—that's the reason I formed a band. I don't know what else I'd be doing now, probably having babies. That would be a copout for me."

Frischmann, whose come-hither groans and snarls punctuated her detached vocal delivery, was trying to take Elastica's American breakthrough in stride. "Coming over here, the Nirvana phenomenon is amazing," she said. "Kurt Cobain is like Jesus." ■

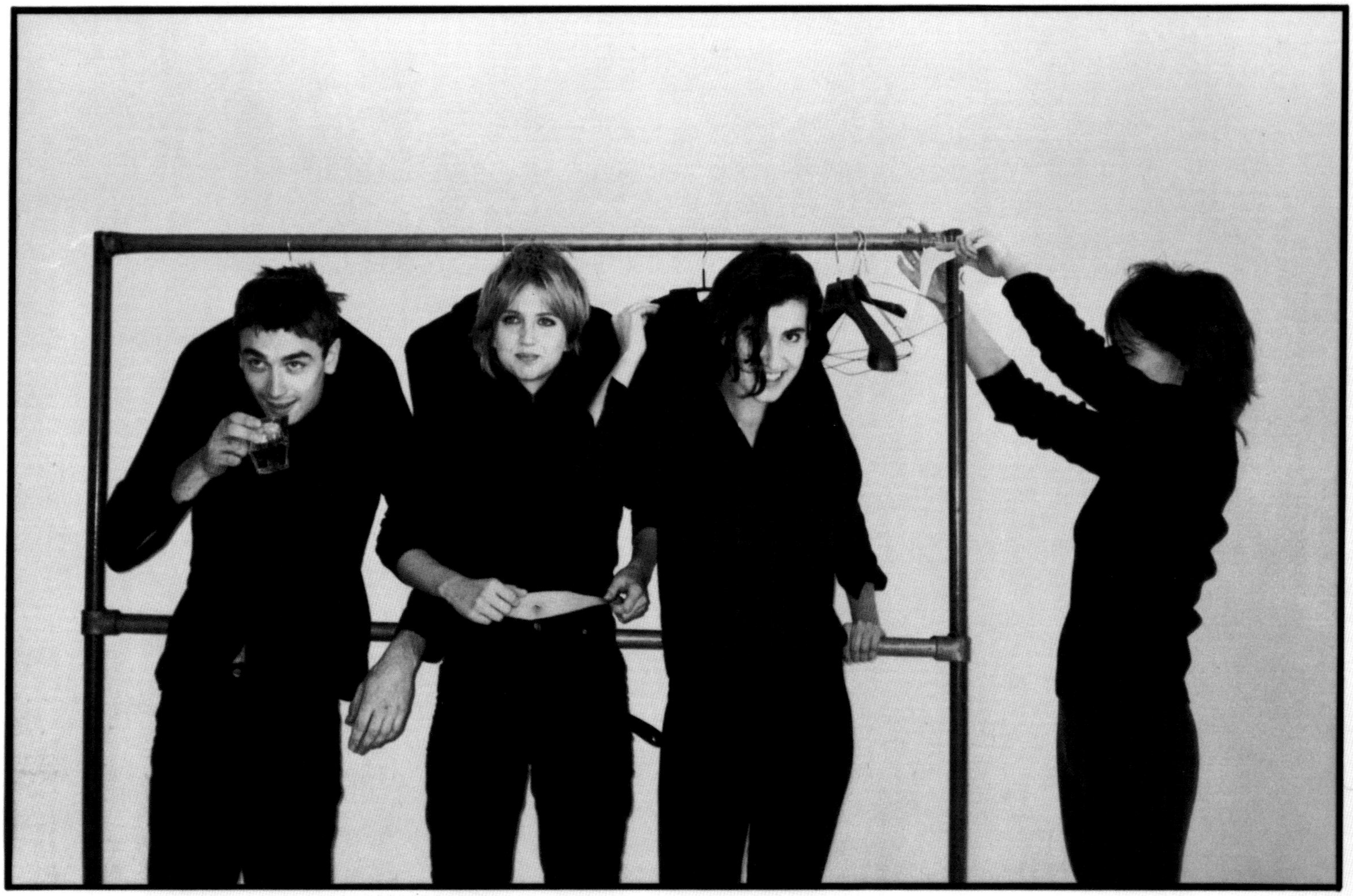

Photo Credit: Juergen Teller

Justin Welch | Donna Matthews | Justine Frischmann | Annie Holland

elastica

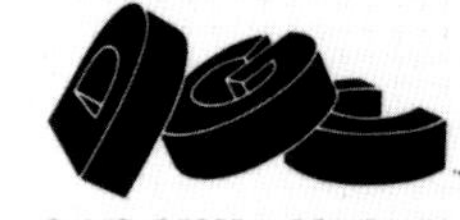

DAVID GEFFEN COMPANY

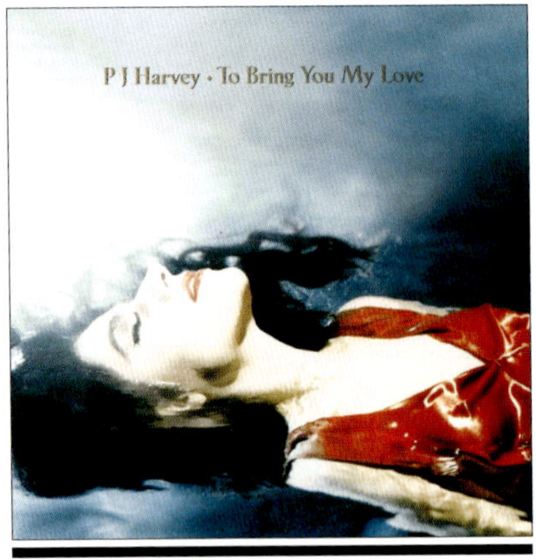

Billboard 200: *To Bring You My Love* (#40)

A moderate US hit, PJ Harvey's *To Bring You My Love* earned critical acclaim as a dark, dramatic masterwork.

SLINGING A guitar and leading a trio bearing her name, Polly Jean Harvey blew out of rural England in 1992. She presented a stark, simple image—wide eyes, thick brows, hair drawn back in a prim bun. The music on the debut album *Dry* was a raw folk-blues and rock hybrid characterized by layers of corrosive guitars. And the lyrics pulsated with the dark side of the female psyche, a cunning mix of romantic pain and carnal desire. It led to comparisons with Patti Smith, the Seventies priestess of confrontational art-rock.

"I grew up feeling shy, ugly, like a loner," Harvey confessed. "I was a late starter—I didn't go on a real date until I was 20. I was at art college learning sculpture when I started writing songs."

In America, the British trio was hailed by critics—*Dry* was chosen as one of the year's best albums by *Rolling Stone* magazine, and Harvey was named Best Songwriter and Best New Female Singer. But after her maiden tour in support of 1993's *Rid of Me*, Harvey parted ways with her original band members, put down her guitar to compose songs on keyboards and joined forces with new musicians and co-producers Flood (real name Mark Ellis) and John Parish.

"I wanted a completely different way of making records, so I played most of the instruments myself," she said. "I felt in complete control." The result was *To Bring You My Love*, a collection of confessional songs that candidly dealt with sexuality and relationships. Harvey reshaped her menacing sound, creating a "modern woman's blues." She danced with her demons on the ominous "Down by the Water"—her breakthrough in the US, it reached #2 on *Billboard*'s Modern Rock Tracks chart and received extensive rotation on MTV. And she concocted a sultry glam-rock persona—flashy dresses, feather boas, pop-star shades. Harvey earned multitudinous rave reviews and magazine covers, but she was notoriously taciturn in talking about the trauma her savage, obsessive lyrics revealed.

"From the year dot (since time began), music and art have dealt with an understanding of love," she explained. "Certainly, that is what the world is about. That is why, again and again, I turn to that topic—whether you're singing about love of another person or love of a tree or dog or making a painting, everything has to do with love. For me, it's endless as a source of inspiration. The most important thing to me is sticking to strong songwriting but approaching that in a slightly different, off-center way."

Harvey toured extensively in support of *To Bring You My Love*, and the steamy, explosive performances warranted all the attention. She slammed into songs with unnerving confidence and control, emanating imposing theatricality. It was hard for people to imagine such impassioned music coming from a petite woman.

"At the time of my first album, I was very anti-performance in a way—I only wore black clothes, I wore no makeup, I stood very still, completely opposite to what I'm doing now," she said. "Finding new ground to cover is the way I give myself some degree of satisfaction. I'm pushing my limits and finding out what I can do in my lifetime." ■

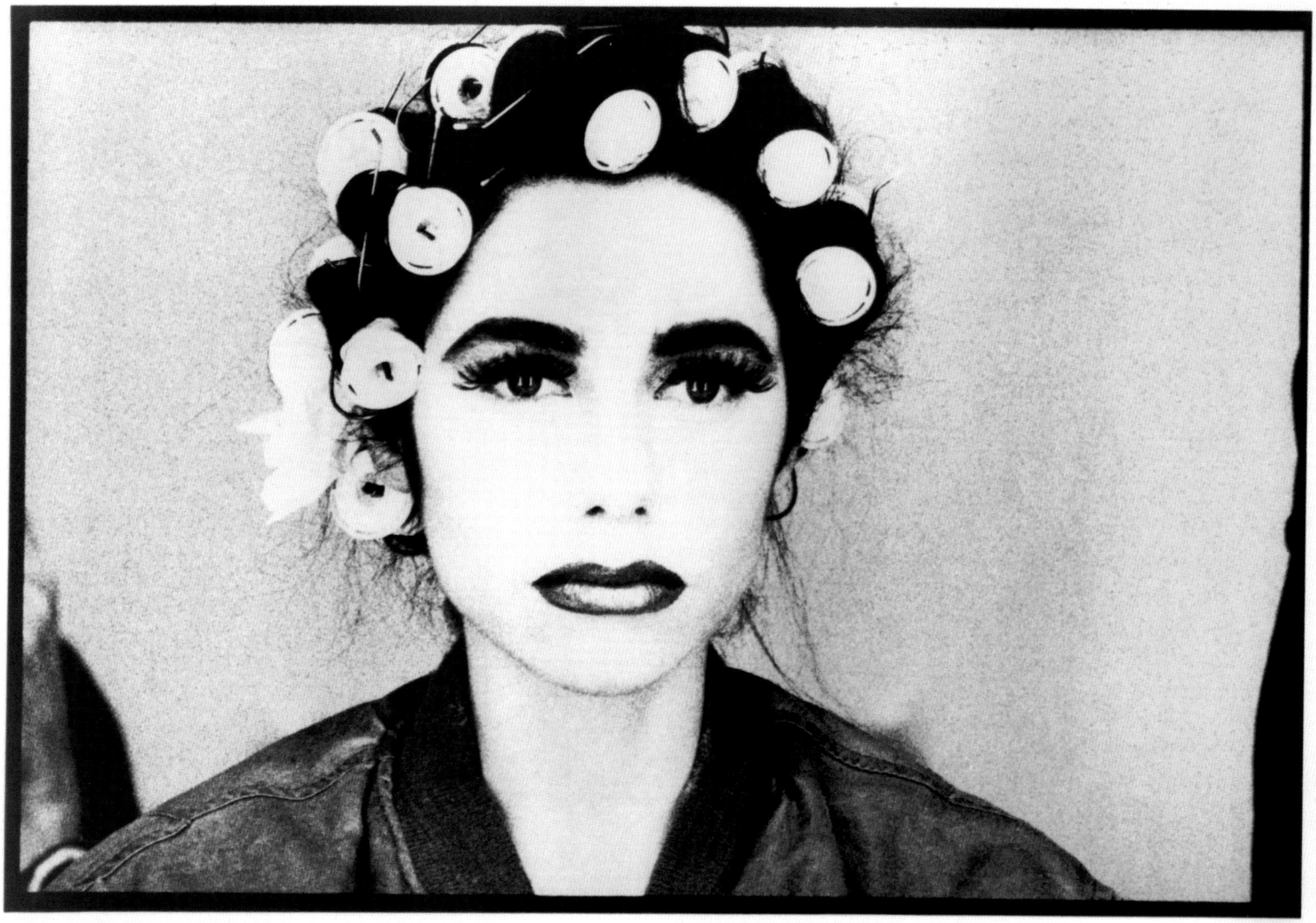

Photo Credit: Valerie Phillips

P J Harvey

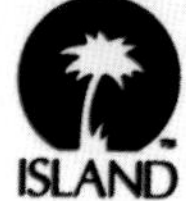

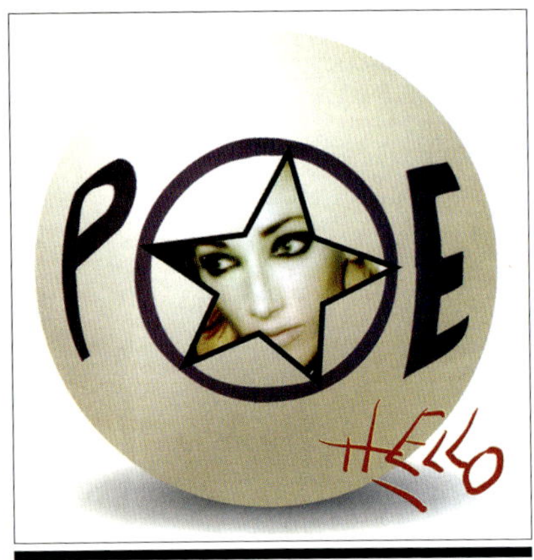

Billboard 200: *Hello* (#71)

Assimilating hip-hop samples and elements of electronica, the album *Hello* introduced music devotees to Poe.

AT 10 years old, Annie Danielewsky was tagged Poe after dressing up for a Halloween party as a character from her favorite bedtime story, Edgar Allan Poe's "The Masque of the Red Death."

"It's about a costume party where someone dresses as the plague, and the emperor ends up dying," Poe said. "So I came dressed as death—I was right at the age where you're starting to get morbid and thinking your parents are stupid—and I named myself Poe to give everyone a hint. And it stuck ever since. They all thought it was hysterical, but I was like, this is serious performance art!"

Then the native New Yorker went to high school in Provo, Utah. "It was a gorgeous place, but those school-bus Mormons took one look at my Sex Pistols t-shirt and hated my guts." Poe said. "And when I was 16, my parents split up and my mother left. So my time there was almost apocalyptic. I haven't figured out entirely what effect that phase of my life had on me."

The songs on Poe's debut album *Hello* didn't all sound alike, moving from loping dance beats to metallic guitars to swing-jazz to acoustic ballads. She recorded it with eight different co-writers and three producers working in seven studios, using a combination of computers and live musicians.

"There's this 'angry female' thing that's popular now, but my record is all over the place—and I like it that way," the Princeton graduate said. "Most of the writers and producers had never made a record in their life. Whoever happened to be around, if they had an idea, I gave them credit."

Poe coyly told listeners she wanted "to blow you…away" on "Angry Johnny," which reached #7 on *Billboard*'s Modern Rock Tracks chart. "It just popped into my head one day," she said. "I found myself singing it in my car for two weeks. It entertained me, so I recorded it. Sometimes a song comes out that's almost like a dream—I'll sit there and analyze it for a year and be like, 'What does that mean?'"

Poe sang about the inability to communicate with psycho men on the hip, funky "Trigger Happy Jack (Drive By a Go-Go)." "The songs all come from personal experience, but some are more specific than others. That song was initially sparked by this instance where a guy wanted me off the road and carjacked me with a gun in Los Angeles. I got away because my car was faster. Then this security officer escorted me home, and he proceeded to sit in the driveway all night, every night for a month. He might just be a nice guy, but he might be totally psychotic!" ■

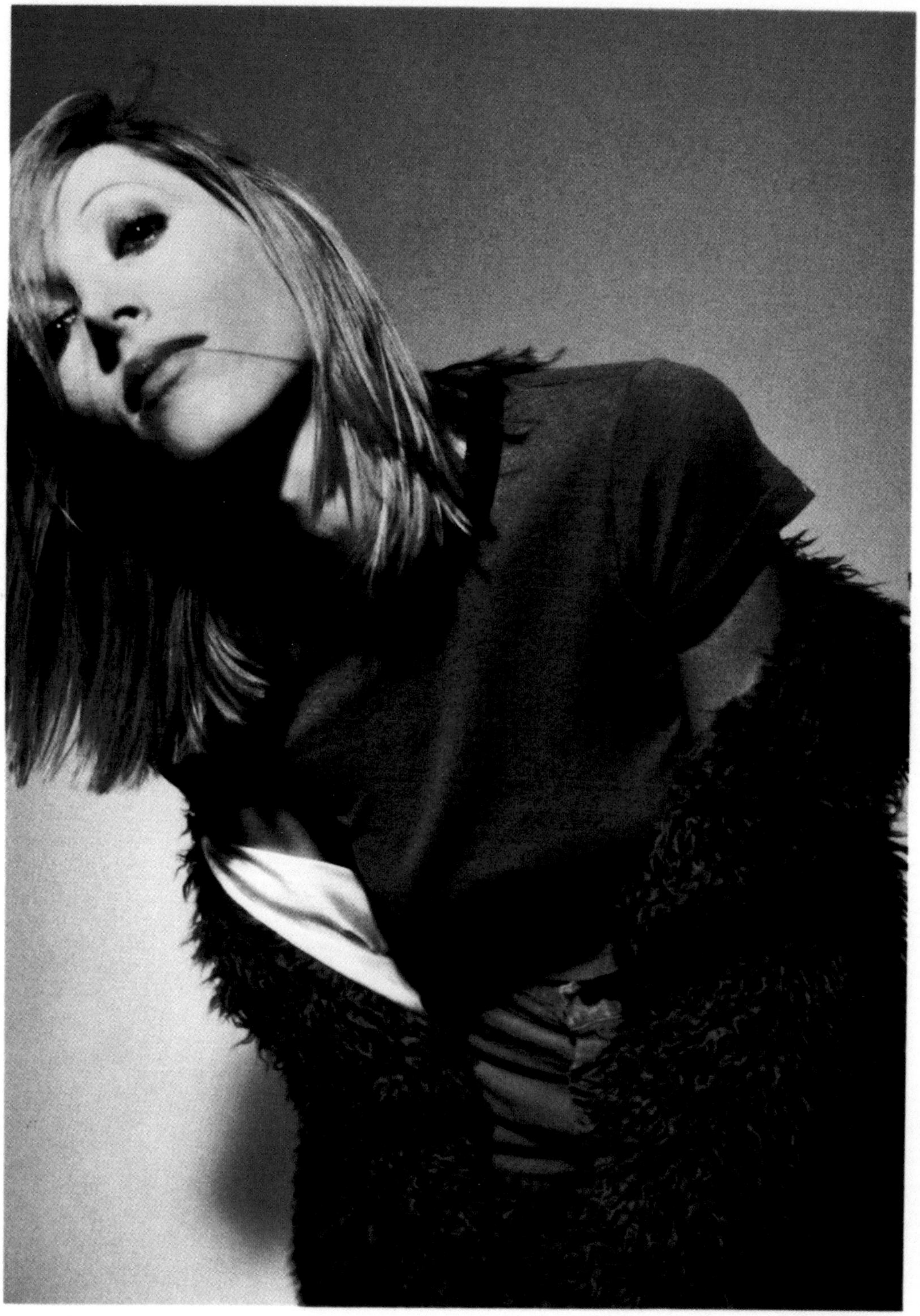

Photo Credit: Melanie Nissen

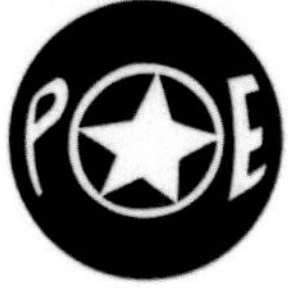

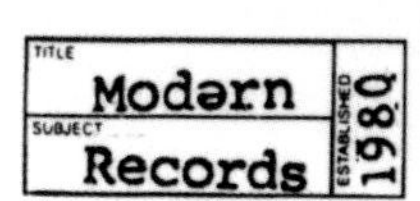

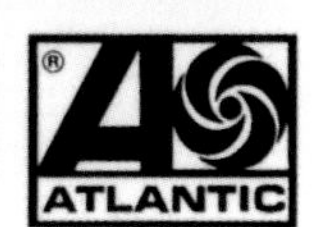

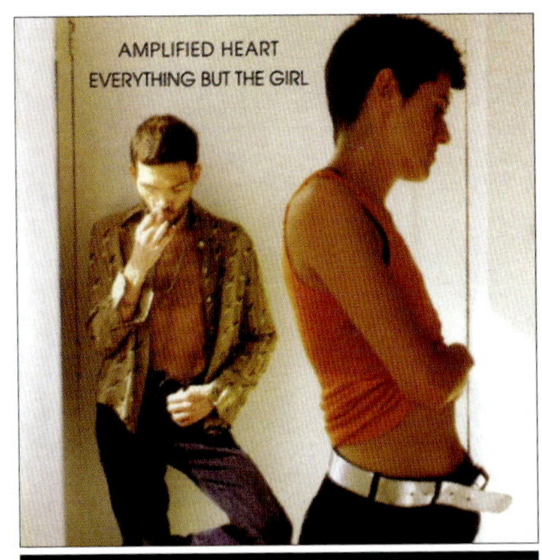

Billboard 200: *Amplified Heart* (#46)
Billboard Hot 100: "Missing" (#2)

Everything but the Girl's "Missing," remixed by Todd Terry, blossomed as a large-scale international sensation.

MUSIC FANS who'd grown tired of hearing about alternative rock's victim mentality discovered a happy story about Ben Watt and Tracey Thorn, known as Everything but the Girl.

Joining forces in 1982, lead singer Thorn and songwriter and multi-instrumentalist Watt played top-drawer melancholy tunes with bossa nova beats and souful neojazz undertones. But after six studio albums, the English duo remained an undiscovered treasure to US audiences. In 1992, Watt was stricken with a rare, often fatal autoimmune disease (Churg-Struss syndrome) that attacks the body's connective tissue and inflames vessel walls.

Deserved respect came when *Amplified Heart*, a primarily acoustic-driven set of tender, folk-jazz breakbeats, spawned a belated million-selling global hit. A year after the album's 1994 release, producer Todd Terry's thumping, melancholy house remix of the single "Missing" reached #2 in America and charted in a variety of radio formats. Watt's condition had improved, and Everything but the Girl became the UK's hottest pop act.

"There's a sense of rebirth in the air," Watt said. "People know the trials we've been through in our personal lives, and generally they're pleased for us that we've managed to draw some kind of strength and energy out of ourselves to create some music for them."

Watt's brush with death made him reassess his lyrics. "Coming out of my illness made me very aware of the vulnerability that we all have. Even within relationships that may be stable, we do inhabit the insides of our own heads so much of the time—even between the closest couples, there is a space."

Watt weighed in at barely 120 pounds. "They know how to restrain the illness—it's in the background now," he shared. "With careful monitoring, they hope it won't recur. But if it does come back and my immune system starts to over-respond again, hopefully they'll be able to see it coming. Nobody knows what the future is. It's a cutting-edge illness that's receiving cutting-edge treatment. Until the early Eighties, people were dying with this. People know that I'm incredibly skinny now. They see me and it's quite a shock. In *People* magazine, they misrepresented the fact that I tire quickly. It's not true. In fact, I almost have an increased appetite for work. We've probably worked harder in the last year than in the last five put together. There are some benefits. I feel very focused." ■

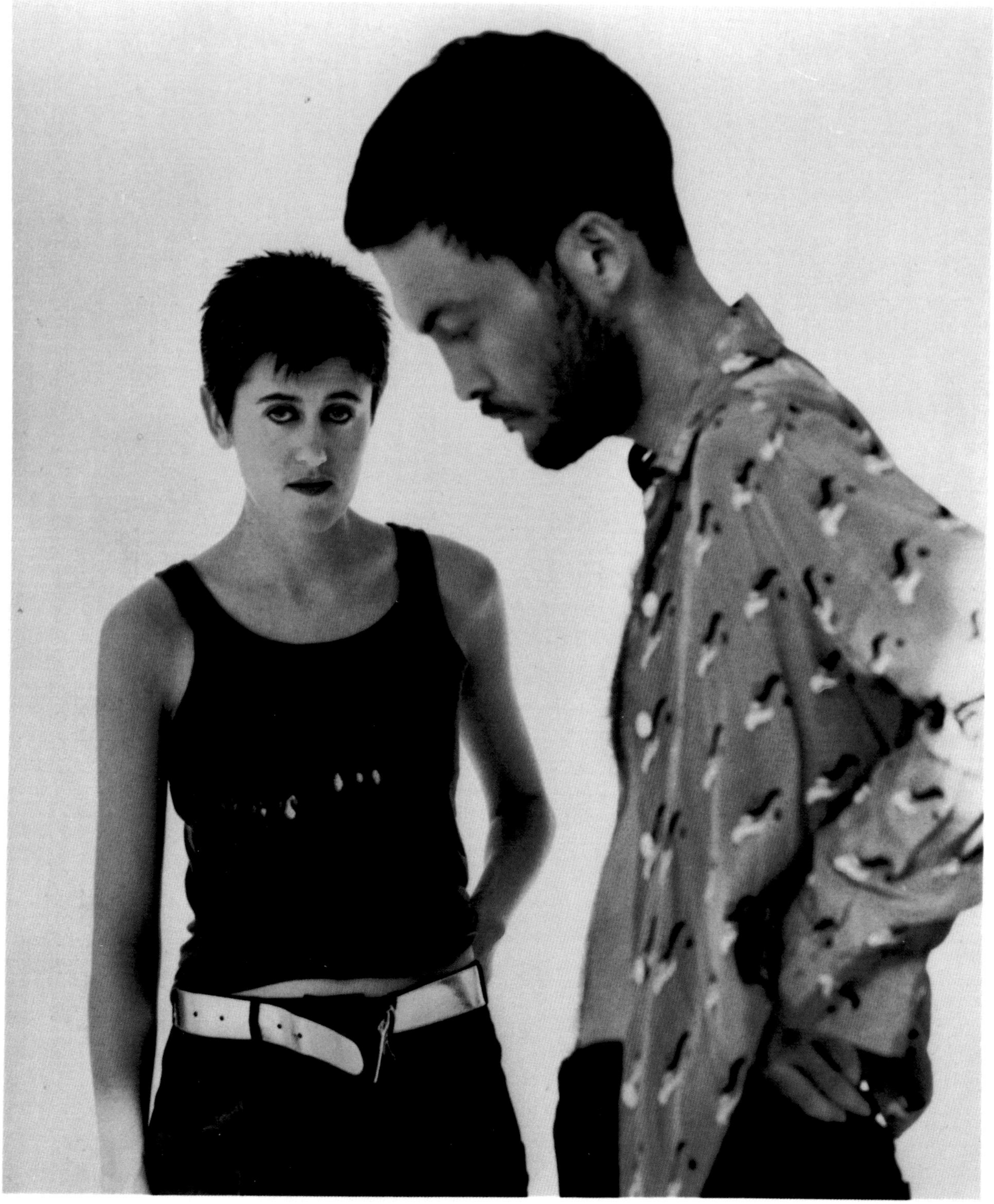

TRACEY THORN BEN WATT

EVERYTHING BUT THE GIRL

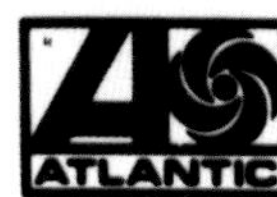

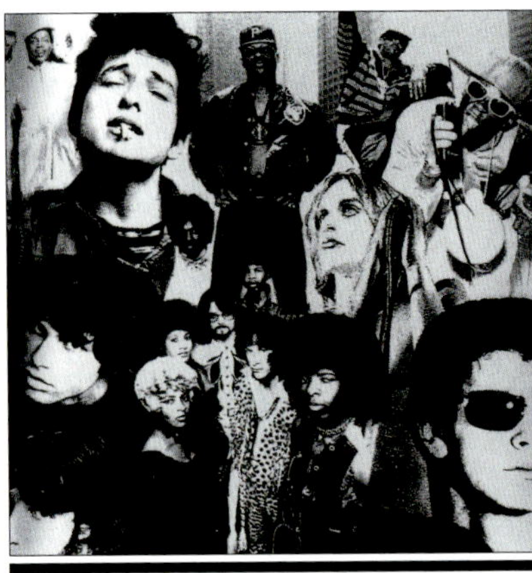

Billboard 200: *Thank You* (#19)

One of Britain's eminent new wave acts of the Eighties, Duran Duran returned with the cover album *Thank You*.

INSPIRED BY David Bowie and Roxy Music, school companions Nick Rhodes (keyboards) and John Taylor (guitar) formed Duran Duran in 1978 with friends. The five handsome lads from England became international pop stars through clever music videos, but by the late Eighties, the group had fallen out of favor. Nevertheless, with the 1993 hits "Ordinary World" and "Come Undone," Duran Duran enjoyed a resurgence in popularity.

For their next move, the band members went back in time with *Thank You*, an album of covers paying homage to their heroes, recorded in studios during their last tour.

"Nick and I have actually been talking about making an album like this since we were teenagers, inspired by Bryan Ferry's *These Foolish Things*, along with David Bowie's *Pin Ups* of the same year (1973)," Taylor recalled. "Both those albums were exclusively covering other people's songs—most of which we had never heard before. The idea that you could actually release an album with songs you liked by other people was very cool to me."

Rhodes suggested remaking Lou Reed's "Perfect Day" ("A perfect song—perfect lyrics, perfect melody. I wish I'd written it.") into a sleek soft-rock ballad. "Although we all grew up in the same musical era, we all have extremely varied tastes," Rhodes said. "It was important to the band that we all like (a song). We would actually start to record it, then convince the other band members."

The eclectic choices ranged from Sly & the Family Stone's "I Wanna Take You Higher" to Bob Dylan's "Lay Lady Lay." Melle Mel's "White Lines (Don't Do It)" featured backing vocals by the original artist. "Someone might suggest one song and the others would howl with derision! Occasionally a song would come up and everyone would say, 'Yeah, that would be great!,'" Taylor recalled. "'White Lines' first came up at a rehearsal for *The Tonight Show*. It was interesting to record on the tour. To have Grandmaster Flash and Melle Mel down with us for a day in the Big Apple was a major groove."

Thank You was brutally mocked among some sectors of the music press, but the poor reviews didn't faze frontman Simon Le Bon. "Singing other people's songs is great fun," he noted, "especially when you don't have to explain the lyrics to the rest of the band." ■

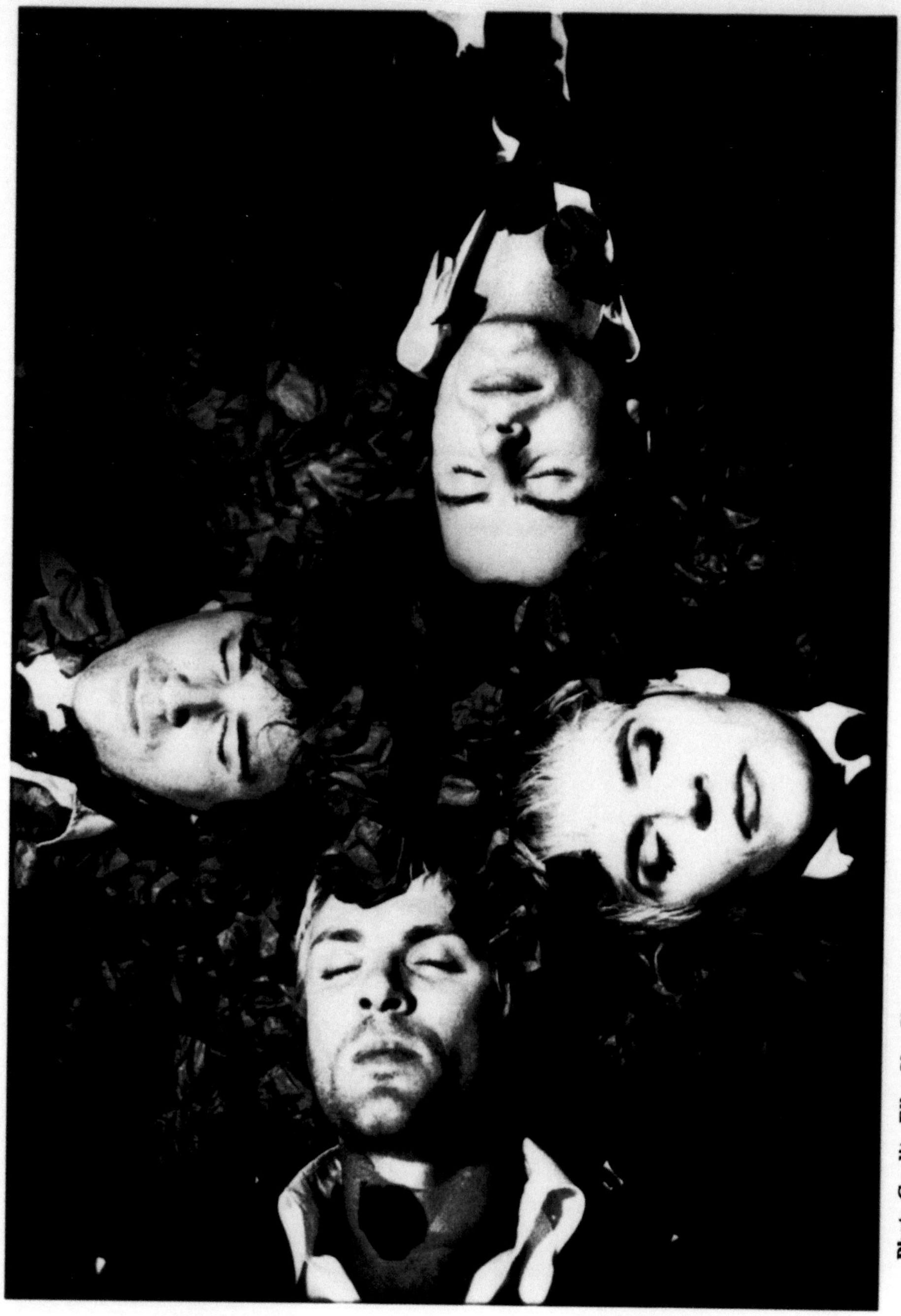

Photo Credit: Ellen Von Unwerth ©1994

Duran Duran

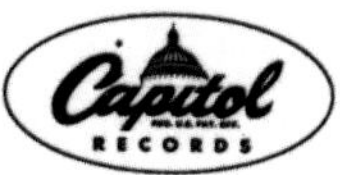

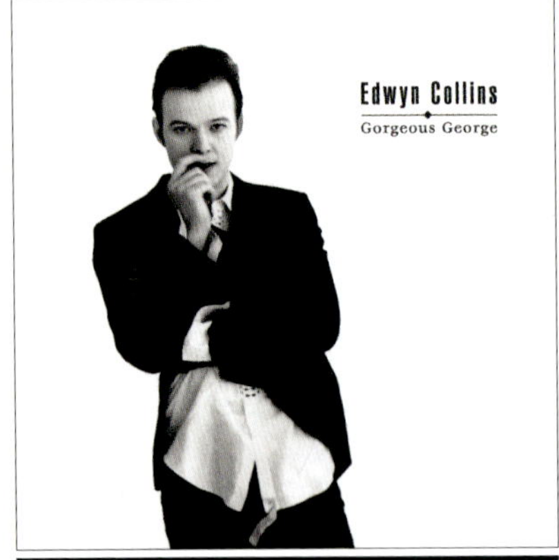

Billboard 200: *Gorgeous George* (#183)
Billboard Hot 100: "A Girl Like You" (#32)

The darkly clever "A Girl Like You" turned into a remarkable global hit for Scottish pop musician Edwyn Collins.

SECURING HEAVY broadcast exposure in the summer of 1995, Edwyn Collins' "A Girl Like You" was a spirited, blue-eyed soul groove with a glorious hook, but the production was irresistibly offbeat—lively vibraphone, wheezing synth effects and taut fuzz guitar. And Collins' deep, mannered croon was reminiscent of *Scary Monsters*-era David Bowie.

"The song was written very quickly. It started out as an experiment with a snare drum sample—I won't say from which record—and we looped it," Collins said. "We have a genre in the UK called 'northern soul'—quite a few people were into this club scene that revolved around a casino in the north of England. Enthusiasts got into basically bad Motown approximations and Seventies soul for break beats, what they call 'real groove.'

"I wanted that kind of feel, basically a Sixties rhythm section with Seventies Isley Brothers guitar. And then I wanted Eighties call-and-response between the vocal and what's actually a treated guitar that sounds like a vocoder—that's a techno sound, really. I wanted these different elements to make an intriguing whole. At the same time, I wanted it to have considerable atmosphere and sound moody, hence I used minor chords. So it strikes me odd that people see it as a summer single—it sounded quite melancholy when I finished it!"

Surprisingly, Collins' *Gorgeous George* album was the first of his career to be released in the US. Collins was the former leader of Orange Juice, a Glasgow-based band that played a coy, ingenious brand of "neo-pop" in the Eighties.

"Quite often we were described as 'charming,' which I suppose is a euphemism for 'You can't play for toffee,'" he said. "We had this youthful arrogance—we started the group when we were teenagers. We didn't like touring, so we didn't do any work abroad."

Orange Juice stayed together for five years and made a series of records. Embittered by the band's commercial failure, Collins called it quits. On his own, he released a couple of singles and albums. At the end of 1994, Collins finished construction of his own studio and completed *Gorgeous George* in nine weeks.

"I appreciate that, for the bulk of the American public, I'm a relative newcomer," Collins said. "At the same time, having self-produced this album, I think it's a good place for people to come in. I'm quite pleased with the way I sing and play now." ■

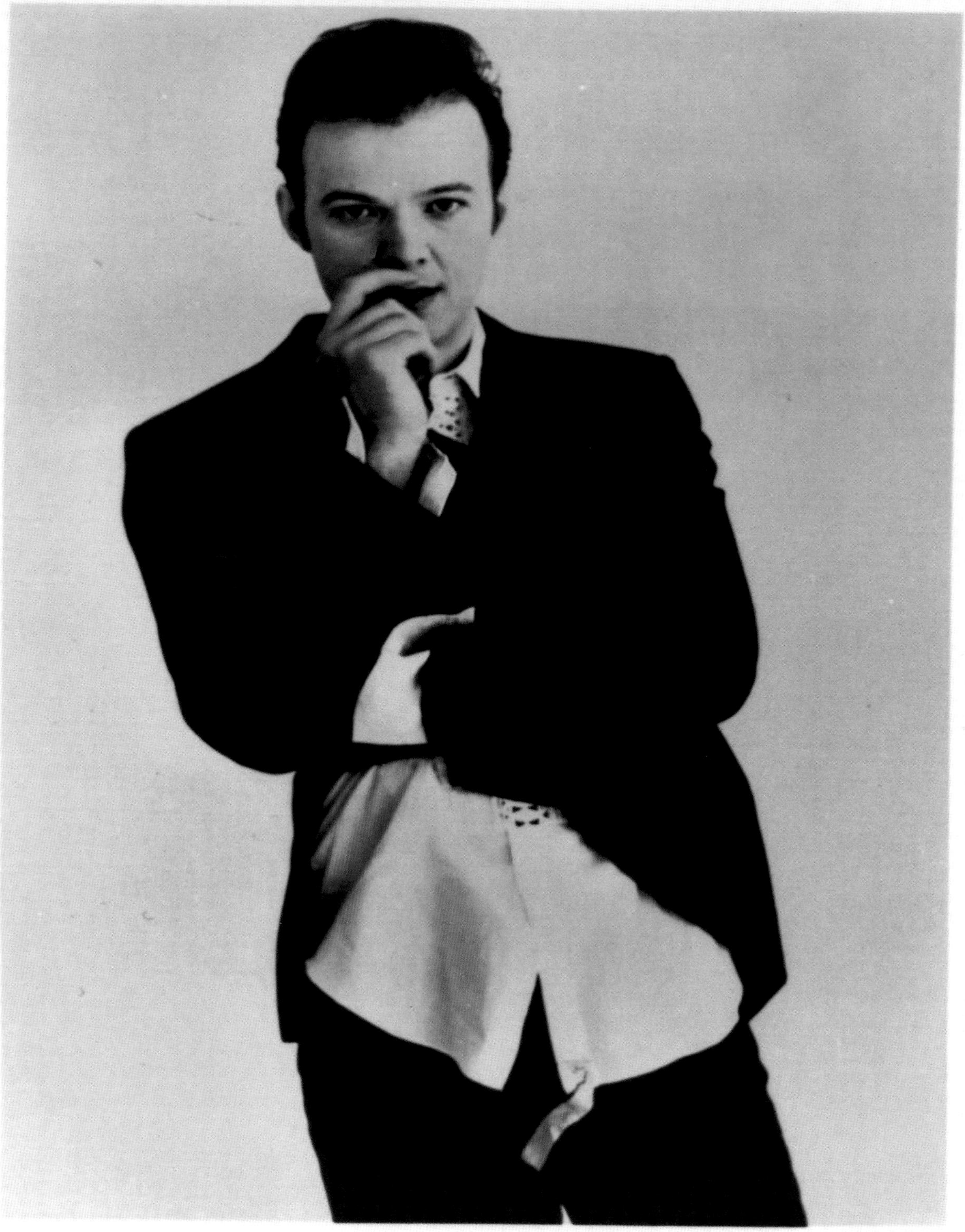

Photo by:
Gavin Evans

Edwyn Collins

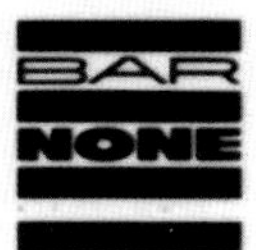

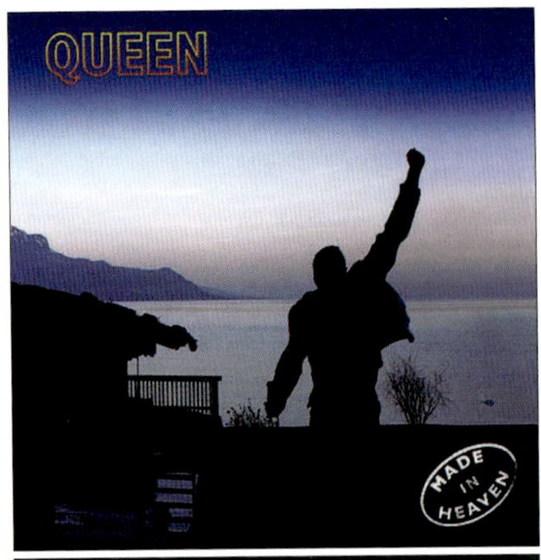

Billboard 200: *Made in Heaven* (#58)

Made in Heaven, Queen's final studio album, was issued four years after the death of singer Freddie Mercury.

WHEN QUEEN frontman Freddie Mercury passed away due to complications from AIDS in November 1991, the world mourned the loss of a vibrant and talented rock performer. Mercury had, however, been aware of his own mortality. In the last period of his life, he determined that he would record as many vocal and piano parts as he was physically capable of. Living close to the band's Montreux, Switzerland studio at the time, he would call on the rest of the band—guitarist Brian May, bass player John Deacon and drummer Roger Taylor—whenever he felt well enough to visit the studio.

"He would say, "Just write me anything, and I'll sing it, anything I can do—I'll give you as much material as I can,'" May said.

Mercury completed enough new components for the basis of another Queen album, *Made in Heaven*, released just shy of four years after his demise. The finishing work was constructed from Mercury's final sessions ("A Winter's Tale," "You Don't Fool Me"), material left over from the British band's previous studio albums ("Let Me Live," "Too Much Love Will Kill You") and re-worked material from the members' solo albums ("Heaven for Everyone").

The cover photo depicted a view from Mercury's home, across Lake Geneva at Montreux. *Made in Heaven* didn't take off in the US, but the album debuted at No 1 in the UK and topped the charts in the rest of Europe. ■

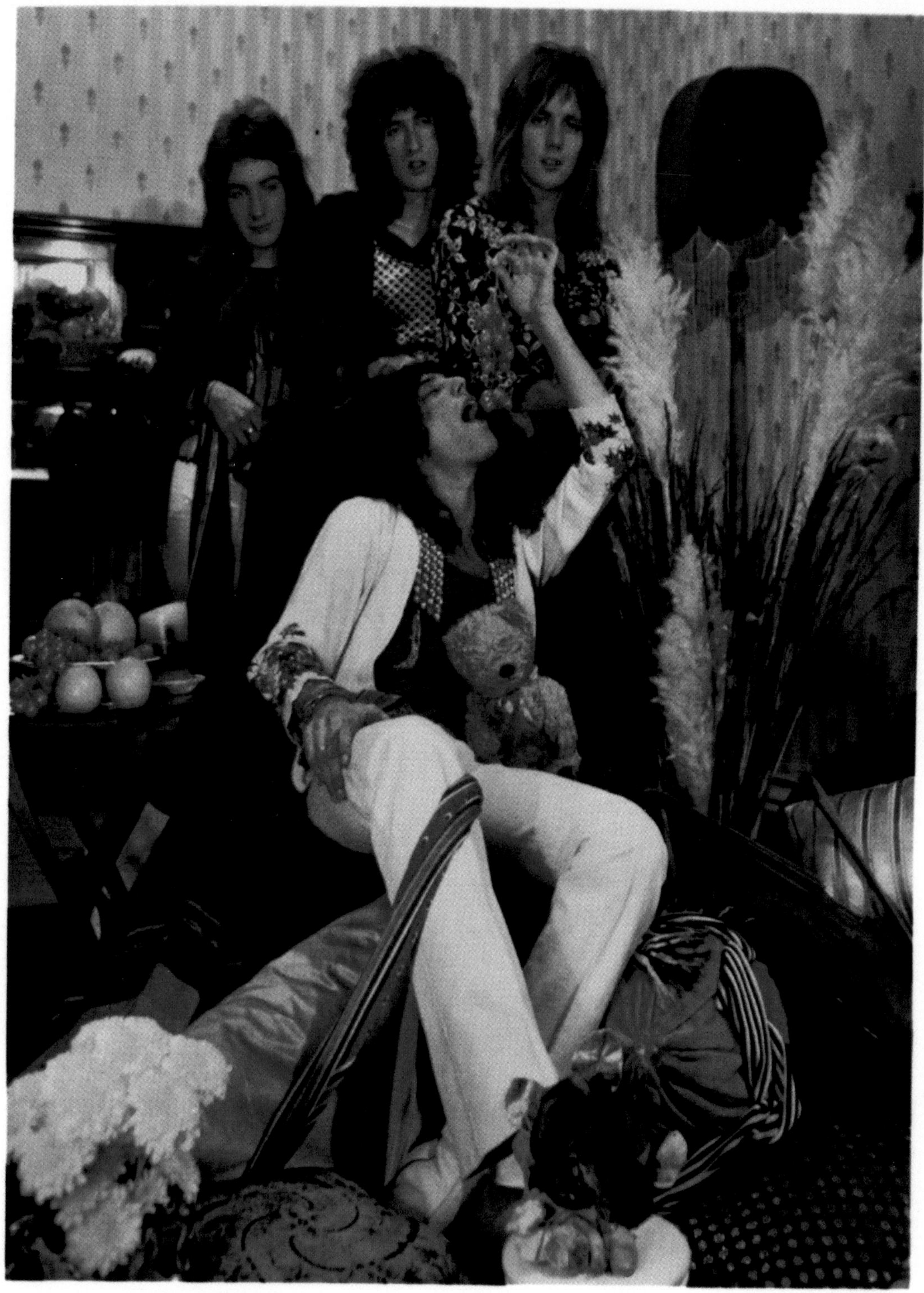

Photo Credit: Douglas Puddifoot

HOLLYWOOD records

QUEEN

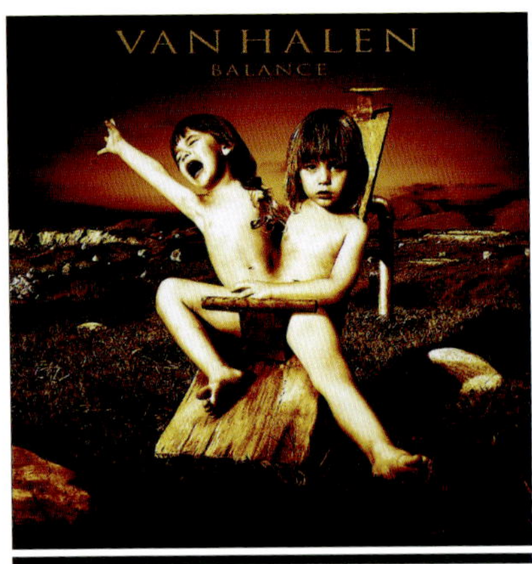

Billboard 200: *Balance* (No. 1)
Billboard Hot 100: "Can't Stop Lovin' You" (#30); "Not Enough" (#97)

Van Halen unleashed *Balance*, the celebrated group's fourth release to showcase lead vocalist Sammy Hagar.

THE MUSICAL focus of *Balance*, Van Halen's first collection of all new material since 1991's *For Unlawful Carnal Knowledge*, was on the most influential rock guitarist of a generation. Sporting facial hair and a trendy new crewcut, Eddie Van Halen whipped up another distinctive, incendiary blend of virtuoso moves and sheer Richter-ready propulsion. But his efforts were complicated by internal struggles. Asked about the meaning behind the title, he said, "It's about life being in balance—and how things have gotten out of balance."

"He went through a real bad period—limping and walking with a cane for a while," singer Sammy Hagar said. "He had stopped drinking and settled into a mellower groove, and it was tough after years of alcohol abuse—all of a sudden he started feeling aches and pains in his body."

Van Halen was diagnosed with avascular necrosis, the same condition that ended the career of two-sport star Bo Jackson. "But he's almost completely healed himself by taking it easy, and it's been nothing but positive for his playing—anyone's a better guitarist with both feet on the ground than three feet in the air," Hagar said. "I don't know if it's the sobriety or the hip, but I think it put him in a good position where he really had to concentrate."

Hagar, 47, hadn't slowed down any. "I still knock out 150 sit-ups and 50 push-ups a day, and I feel good about it. I've been a runner for a long time, and I'm heavy into mountain biking."

Eddie Van Halen's rumbling guitar engulfed Hagar's party-hearty ode, "Amsterdam," and on "Not Enough," he intertwined his high-flying six-string riffs and plaintive piano playing. "Don't Tell Me (What Love Can Do)" reached No. 1 on the *Billboard* Album Rock Tracks chart. But it was doubtful that the band would have had the confidence to do a song like "Can't Stop Lovin' You" before Hagar replaced David Lee Roth as Van Halen's frontman—the Red Rocker's rough-edged voice was silky, evocative and emotional.

"Some of the old headbangers are pissed off that we do songs like that," Hagar said. "But you have to be able to expand, do every form of art you know how to do. This band is now capable of doing a song with Eddie sitting at a piano and me singing. That's pretty special, I think. To not do that would be selling ourselves short."

Balance became Van Halen's fourth consecutive No. 1 album, but tensions between the singer and the band had grown considerably. It was the final release of the "Van Hagar" era. ■

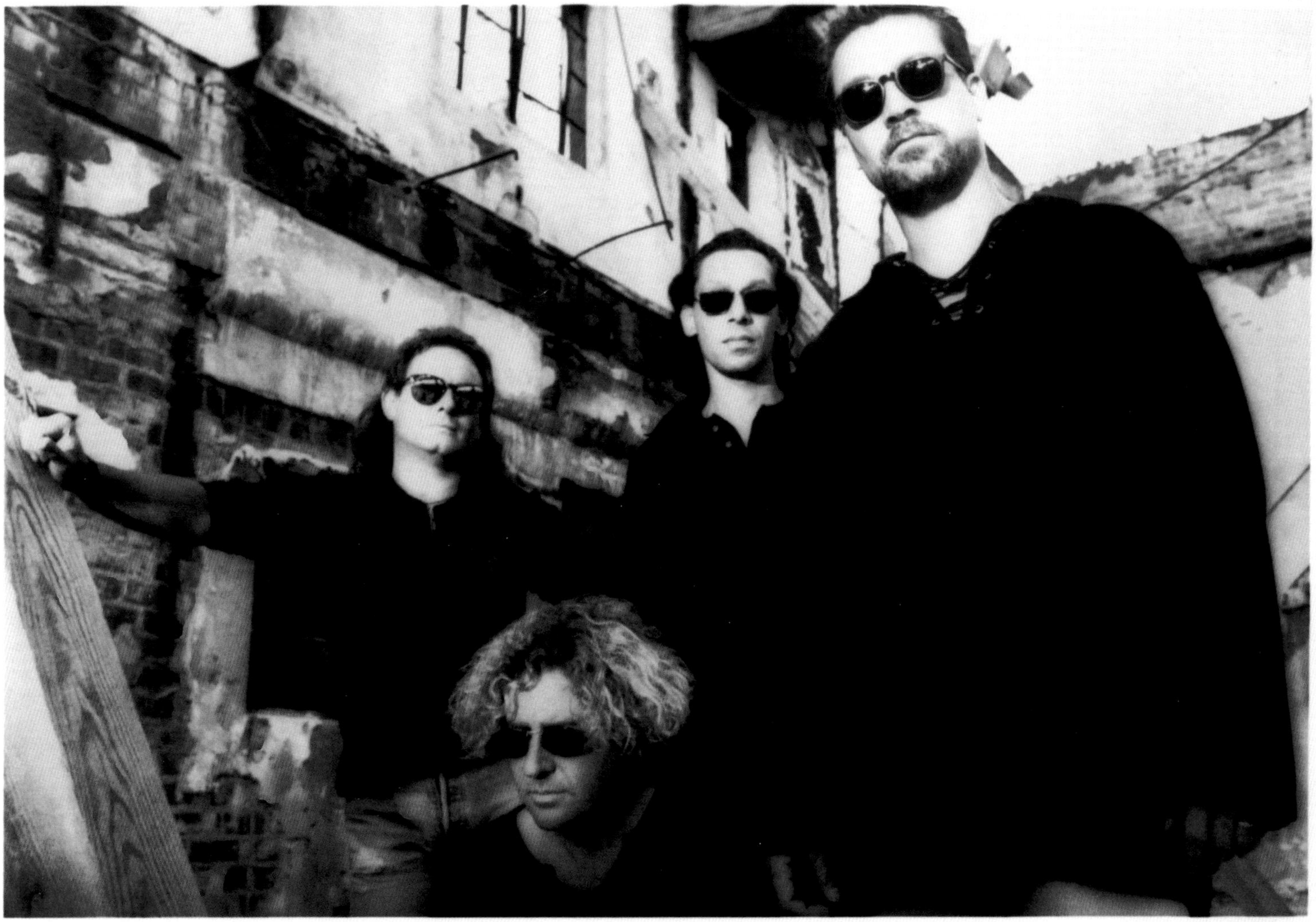

Photo Credit: Randee St. Nicholas

VAN HALEN

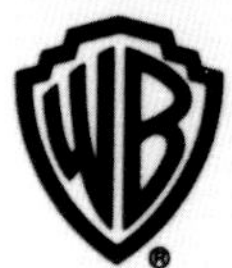

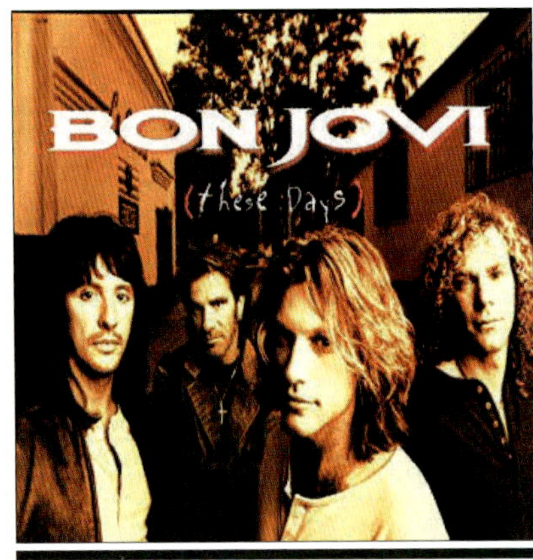

Billboard 200: *These Days* (#9)
Billboard Hot 100: "This Ain't a Love Song" (#14); "Something for the Pain" (#76); "Lie to Me" (#88)

With *These Days*, Bon Jovi proved to have greater staying power than other lite-metal sensations of the Eighties.

FUSING POPCRAFT and populism, Bon Jovi conquered the world in the late Eighties.

Slippery When Wet was the breakthrough in 1986, propelled by the hits "You Give Love a Bad Name" and "Livin' on a Prayer." *New Jersey* was another No. 1 album. But the band's commercial fortunes reached a standstill when fans flocked to grunge and indie-rock. According to the critics, Bon Jovi was dead—crashed and burned along with other pop-metal cohorts.

But music moves in cycles, and Bon Jovi's time had come again. The band bounced back in 1994 with *Cross Road* (a greatest-hits collection that sold 12 million copies worldwide) and "Always" (a Top 5 single). It re-established Bon Jovi among rock's top international acts.

"We don't worry about what's fashionable; we just go along our own merry path," singer Jon Bon Jovi said. "Because, ultimately, if I can't be true to myself, people are going to catch on and say I was full of shit. So it's just not worth it. In 1983, if I had worried about those kind of things, I would have made it a point to look like Boy George and Cyndi Lauper. And then in '93, when I would have had a goatee and work boots on, and somebody somewhere would have said, 'Well, who the hell is the real Jon Bon Jovi?"

The raw, gutsy approach Bon Jovi devotees had come to expect had matured. *These Days*, the band's sixth studio album, reflected what Bon Jovi did better than anybody—irresistible arena rock. The anti-ballad "This Ain't a Love Song," featuring a passionate vocal, screamed up the Top 40 charts, and the hook in "Hey God" proved the band wasn't finished with crisp, polished anthems. There was also the buoyant "Something for the Pain" and the moving power ballad "Lie to Me." *These Days* also proved to be a commercial success in European and Asian markets, producing four Top 10 singles in the UK.

"It's no superstar stuff, it's blue collar," the New Jersey rocker said. "I don't have the inside story about what Madonna does, and I'm not shooting heroin and killing myself like the guys in Seattle. But I was at the Super Bowl enough times..."

Bon Jovi was living in unpretentious domesticity—happily married to his high school sweetheart, the father of two. "I know that having a kid changed my life dramatically, but I don't think that it's related to what I do professionally, especially in the songwriting process," he said. "That works for some guys—Billy Joel has written some real nice ones—but I haven't felt that kind of necessity to sit down and write baby songs about my daughter." ■

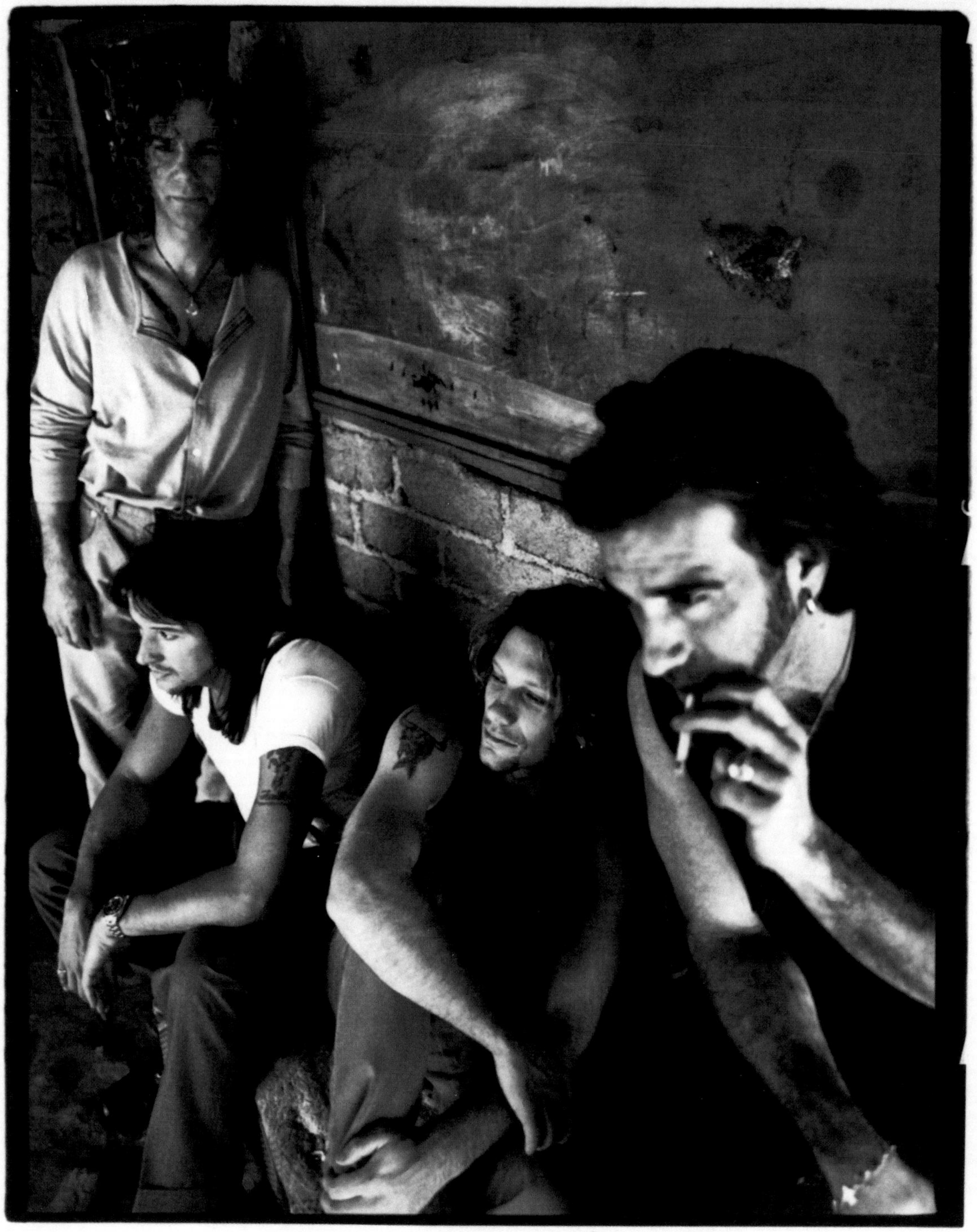

PHOTO CREDIT: MARK SELIGER

L R: DAVID BRYAN, RICHIE SAMBORA, JON BON JOVI, TICO TORRES

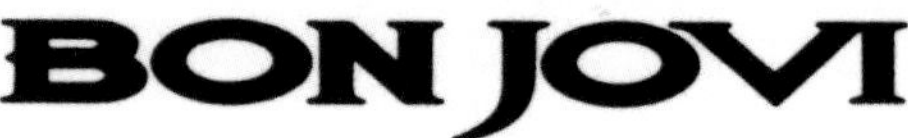

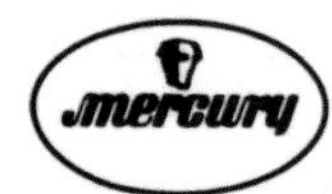

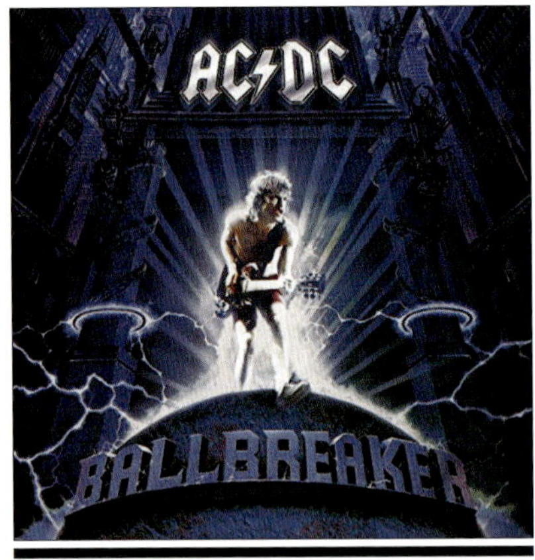

Billboard 200: *Ballbreaker* (#4)

When it came to sheer riffing power on the heavy, bluesy *Ballbreaker*, few disputed that AC/DC was without peer.

EVER SINCE the American release of the debut album *High Voltage* in 1976, AC/DC had paved a road into rock history with brain-smashing three-chord grooves, sandpaper vocals and a blue-collar appeal. The hit songs "Highway to Hell" and "You Shook Me All Night Long" were as good as raw, lewd, guilty-pleasure rock got.

Ballbreaker was promoted as the band's big comeback. Produced by Rick Rubin, it signified the first studio album in five years, and it was… the same old thing, anthemic songs hanging on potent fist-pumping riffs and lyrical insights celebrating the concerns of horny 15-year-olds—"Hard as a Rock," "Cover You in Oil." Lead guitarist Angus Young still viewed life through the eyes of a perpetual teenager, stomping around in his schoolboy outfit.

"Over the years, when we've released a record, people say, 'So, what do we get?' Well you get more of the same," the 40-year-old Young said with a laugh. "We know what we do best, which is playing rock 'n' roll music."

Ballbreaker marked the return of drummer Phil Rudd, and singer Brian Johnson's screeching vocals were even more throat-searing. But it was the dual-guitar assault of Angus and Malcolm Young that came off as heroic.

"A lot of people think it's my guitar, but it's all based around Malcolm—I'm color on top of his driving, hard-edged rhythm," Angus said. "We try to sound like one big guitar together. If you actually listen to it, it's two unique sounds even on the stage. Instead of saying, 'Okay, I've got all my speakers facing me,' we've got it cross-connected—I've got Malcolm coming out of my side, and he's also got speakers of me coming out his side. We constantly plug in and listen to each other.

"I'm mostly a fan of Chuck Berry. He took a bit of the blues and country and threw it all together and came up with rock 'n' roll. To me, he's as good as Shakespeare, because he's got some guitar signatures that are instantly recognizable and he's written some great lyrics. I think good poetry translates well into a song. That's what we do, sit with a few lines and juggle them around. A lot of it's tongue-in-cheek—we crack ourselves up."

Ballbreaker went platinum in the States, but fans had a hard time hearing it on the radio. AC/DC was in no man's land—alternative formats didn't find an arena-metal anachronism enticing, and classic formats wouldn't play anything new by the veteran Aussie band.

"Every time I've ever been on tour or made a record, they've always said, 'Well, people are into this or that now.' I always think, 'Geez, somebody makes a good car and it lasts years,'" Young said. "When one band is successful at a trend, record companies go out and sign another 500 of the same thing and then the radio format changes and it comes back to, 'Okay, what do we do now? Get the rock 'n' roll back!' I suppose it's that old saying, adapt or die! So maybe AC/DC is just decaying, a slow death—growing old disgracefully!" ■

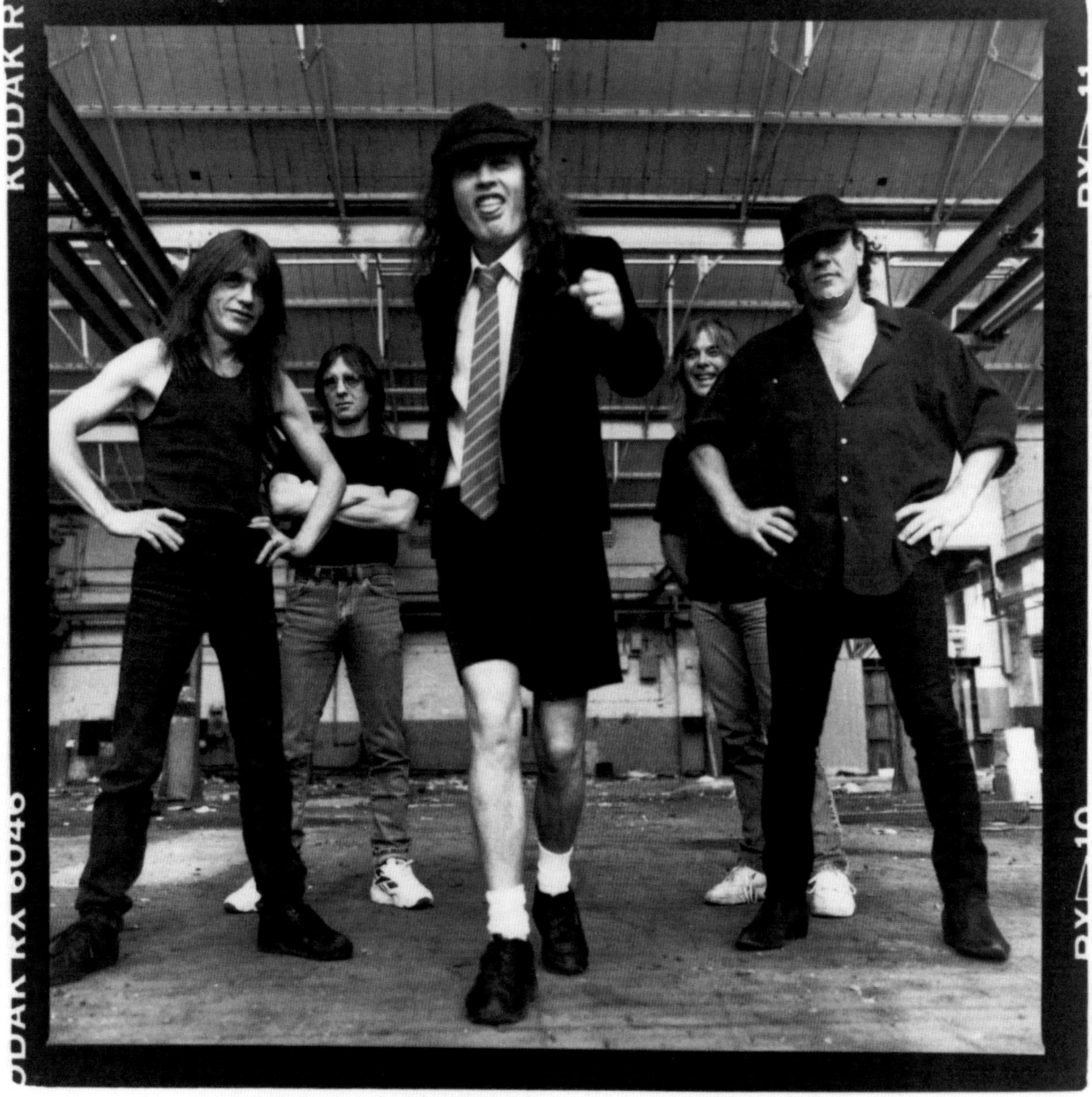

PHOTO CREDIT MICHAEL HALSBAND

L R : MALCOM YOUNG, PHIL RUDD, ANGUS YOUNG, CLIFF WILLIAMS, BRIAN JOHNSON

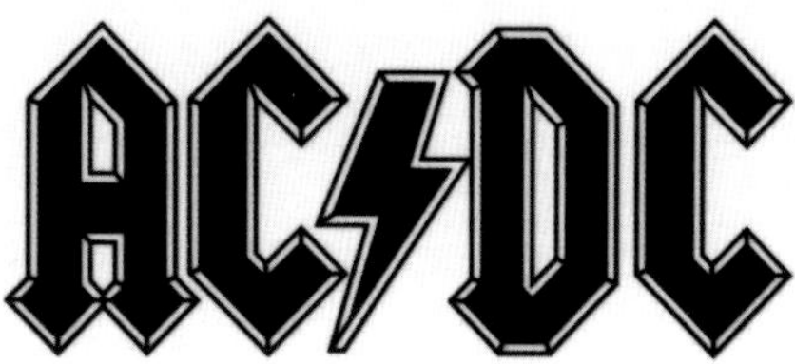

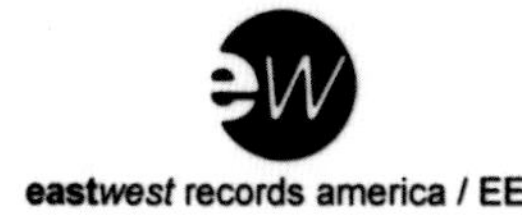

east*west* records america / EEG

Billboard 200: *Ozzmosis* (#4)

With *Ozzmosis*, Ozzy Osbourne was champing at the bit to restore his standing as metal's relentless ringmaster.

AFTER THE release of *No More Tears* in 1991, heavy-metal madman Ozzy Osbourne announced that he would retire from music. However, it was not to be—he returned with *Ozzmosis*, his first release in four years.

"I just wanted to step aside for a while and look at what I got," Osbourne explained. "In my heart of hearts, I knew I wouldn't retire forever. But by announcing it, it was a final decision—everybody thought, 'There's no use asking Ozzy to come out to Bulgaria.' I went home and had an open-ended schedule. I was a father and husband—I learned a great deal about commitment. I can honestly say that for one year in my life, I had no pressure. Had I not done it, I would have forever been going, 'I had the idea, and it's too late now.'

"But in hindsight, I don't know whether it was a good move. As the old saying goes, you never know what you've had until it's gone. I had too much time on my hands. I thought, 'What a stupid thing to do!' So I'm back. And I ain't gonna retire again."

Produced by Michael Beinhorn (Soundgarden, Red Hot Chili Peppers) and created with old friends like Zakk Wilde (guitar) and Geezer Butler (bass), *Ozzmosis* offered the witty "Perry Mason" (a swaggering take on the theme music that identified the venerable TV show) and the songs "See You on the Other Side" and "I Just Want You" in vintage Ozzified style. Many pundits were claiming that alternative music had eclipsed hard rock, but *Ozzmosis* debuted in the Top 5 of the *Billboard* album chart, the highest position of Osbourne's 25-year career.

"The album cover is spooky," he allowed. "I've been desperately trying to get far away from that unhinged image, not because I'm embarrassed about it, but because I want to move on. I'm not going to come out with short back 'n' sides and a pink suit and do disco music. But why should I, because I've done some crazy things in the past, have to sing about suicide or Satan for the rest of my life?"

Osbourne returned to performing, kicking off his "Retirement Sucks!" tour. The career retrospective included a few Black Sabbath songs.

"I'm very proud of my time in Sabbath, the early days," he said. "It was a long, long time ago. But kids come up to me and say, 'Ozzy, why'd you do this and that?' I don't know where it came from—it was absolutely a gift. We never consciously sat down in 1970 and thought, 'Well, we'll write the music now, and in 1995 people will look back on it as iconic.' I'm as surprised as anybody. The original Sabbath started out playing jazz-blues—our influences were Ten Years After, Jethro Tull, Fleetwood Mac, John Mayall's Bluesbreakers. But if you listen to how it developed, there's no kind of blues—we never recorded a twelve-bar blues song, ever. The guys would come up with the heavy riffs, and I'd try to put a melodic vocal line over the top if I couldn't I'd sing along with the riff, like 'Iron Man.' It was just innocence."

Osbourne had remained one of heavy metal's most influential and popular vocalists. "To me, this new music is old music played by younger kids," he said. "The vocal quality of a lot of the Seattle bands sounds like the Byrds, bands that were around in the Sixties. Nirvana was very Lennon-ish." ■

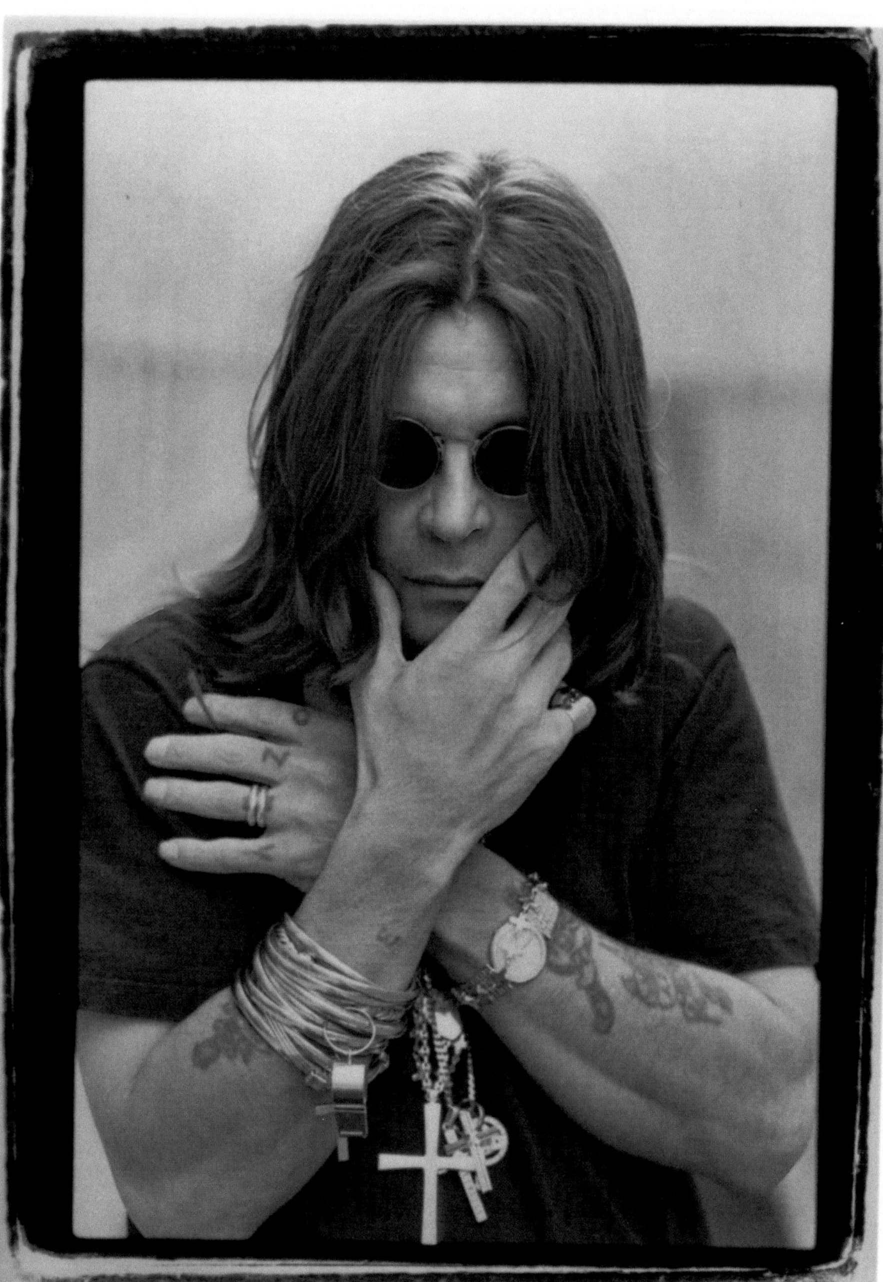

PHOTO CREDIT: GENE KIRKLAND

OZZY OSBOURNE

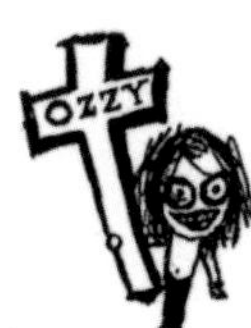

epic
9507

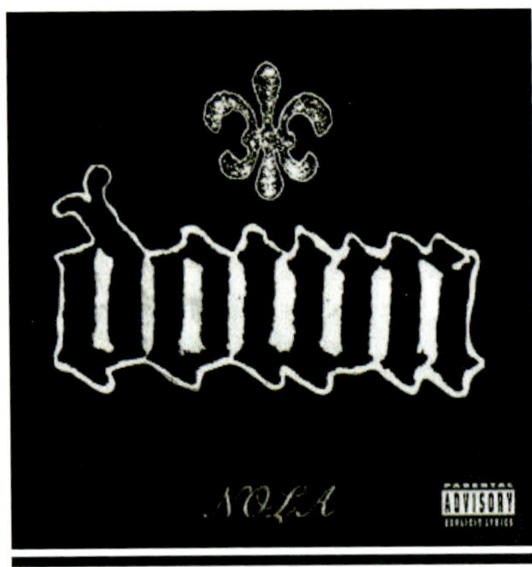

Billboard 200: *NOLA* (#57)

Down was perhaps the nearest thing to a supergroup that the metal underground had ever brought together.

A SIDE project formed by Pantera vocalist Philip Anselmo and Corrosion of Conformity guitarist Pepper Keenan, Down released *NOLA*, an impressive debut album. But loyal fans expecting that the group would specialize in extreme metal were sadly disappointed. The band took a no-frills approach to elements of classic rock, with prime ingredients of early Black Sabbath and Southern rock prevailing in the riffs. "Stone the Crow" (which reached #40 on the *Billboard* Mainstream Rock Tracks chart), "Lifer," "Bury Me in Smoke" and "Temptation Wings" were rough-edged, crude metal in the old-school sense—the stoner-rock feel, the swampy roots, the dirtbag patina.

Down traced its roots to 1991, when Anselmo and Keenan had taken time off from their respective bands and hooked up with second guitarist Kirk Windstein and bassist Todd Strange of Crowbar, and drummer Jimmy Bower of Eyehategod.

"We were all into the same shit, musicwise," Keenan said. "Down was going to be a band that was influenced by bands that were influenced by Sabbath, before it was cool to be influenced by Sabbath—Trouble, St. Vitus, the Obsessed, Witch Finder General, Pentagram. But it had to kick with that New Orleans groove, which I still find hard to explain, but you know it when you hear it—mainly, Jim, stoned, dropping that kick and snare behind the beat pushing along lazy and slippery guitar riffs."

The longtime friends made a three-track demo for underground trading. "Philip went back out with Pantera and I went back out with C.O.C. and we would play it for people and let them copy it and let their friends dub it, and their friends, just to see how far it would get through the underground. Soon after that I'd be in Montreal, talking to kids who had the damn tape. I even met some freak in Stockholm who had a Down shirt—a bootleg, but shit, I'd only made a dozen! Once Crowbar and Eyehategod got on the road, we had better distribution than a Columbian drug cartel. We recorded two more jam sessions and did the same thing."

Down eventually played a small concert in its hometown of New Orleans, and a record executive in attendance signed the band to a contract. *NOLA* went on to sell close to a half-mllion copies worldwide. Down supported the album with a 13-date concert tour before all members continued their full-time projects. ■

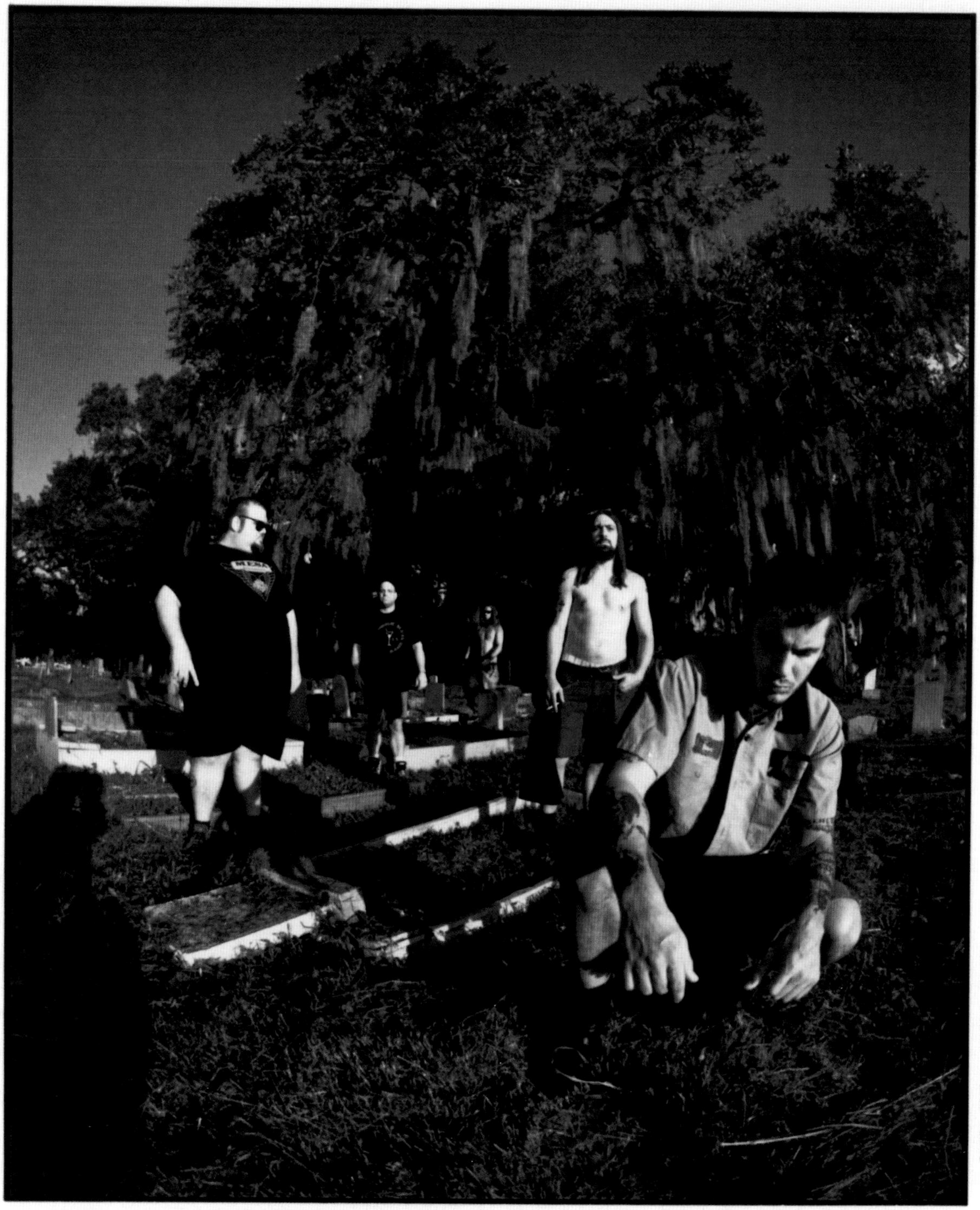

PHOTO CREDIT MICHAEL MILLER

L R : TODD STRANGE, KIRK WINDSTEIN, PEPPER KEENAN, JIMMY BOWER, PHILIP ANSELMO

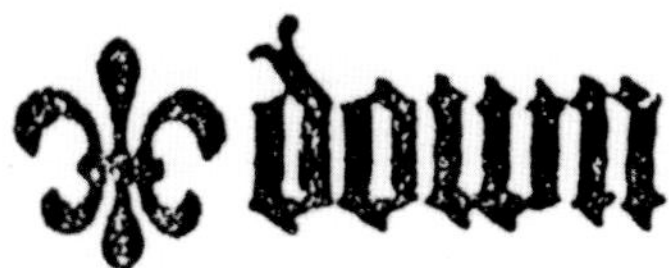

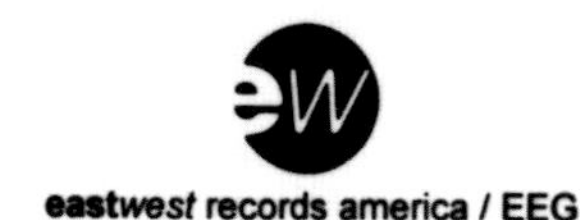

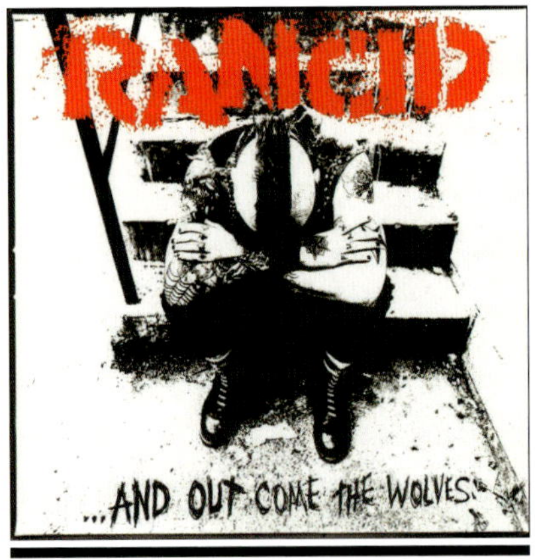

Billboard 200: *...And Out Come the Wolves* (#45)

Reviving mainstream interest in punk, Rancid took a platinum-selling turn with *...And Out Come the Wolves*.

SPORTING FLUORESCENT mohawks, menacing tattoos and clothes that screamed 1977 London, the members of Rancid were passionate punk diehards, and like other Northern California bands such as the Offspring, they found themselves at the forefront of the genre's user-friendly reawakening.

"People have a hunger now—for whatever reason, this music has gotten its day in court," greaser bassist Matt Freeman mused. "There are a lot of good records, and they're just happening to get played on the radio. We're close friends and we work really hard—we take this shit really seriously. We've got a hell of an opportunity here."

It didn't hurt that the band was led by sturdy, confident and charismatic guitarists Tim Armstrong and Lars Frederiksen, who traded lead vocals. Songs from *...And Out Come the Wolves*, the band's third album, were ecstatic sing-alongs—the chaotic sound was about having fun, but the lyrics were dead-serious tales of the explosive urban settings of Rancid's youth.

"It's not like growing up in middle America—you've got an incredible melting pot of people and cultures, and you can be just as alienated in a big city in the East Bay as in a farmhouse in Nebraska," Freeman said. "But we're not very nihilistic. It's this simple—if you're not privileged or didn't go to college, you're working some shitty job 40 hours a week just to survive and then going to shows at night. Band practice was something we built that was ours, an escape from the everyday world. It was a release—it helped us deal with everything else."

The centerpiece of *...And Out Come the Wolves* was "Time Bomb," which featured the bouncy ska-punk twist of *London Calling*-era Clash (and Freeman and Armstrong's roots in the band Operation Ivy). Critics claimed Rancid's playing imitated the British punk style developed in the late Seventies.

"In Europe, they say, 'You sound more British than American.' Okay, fine—that's what we're influenced by," Freeman said. "But if you listen closely, we're conversant with California hardcore bands. I don't think the Clash ever wrote songs like we did on the (preceding) *Let's Go* album with that fast-tempo beat, Bad Religion-style."

The audience was no longer a righteous minority—all sorts of folks, most of whom were cutting their teeth when the Clash's Joe Strummer had already begun barking, enjoyed Rancid's tuneful adrenaline surge.

"The crowd has changed a little bit. Before, it would be all punks. Now you get regular people. That's fine—we have an open-door policy," Freeman said. "You can have your own opinion. And I can have a worse job than explaining it." ■

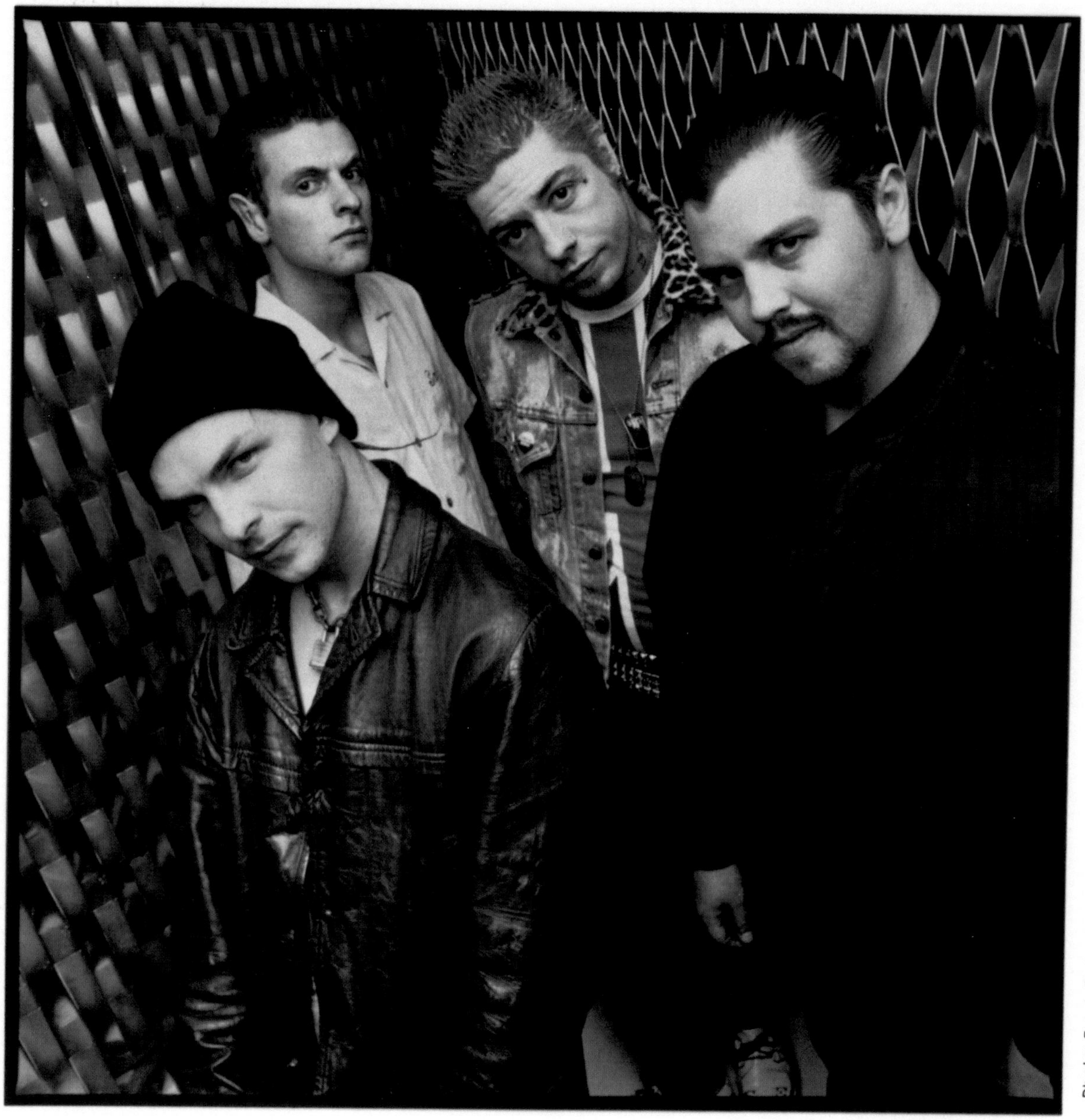

Photo: Frank Ockenfels

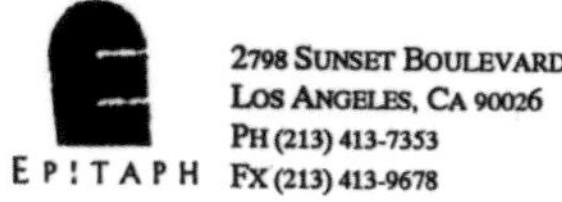

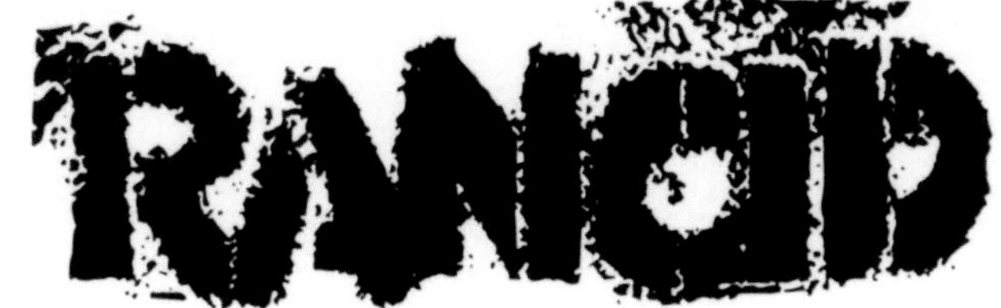

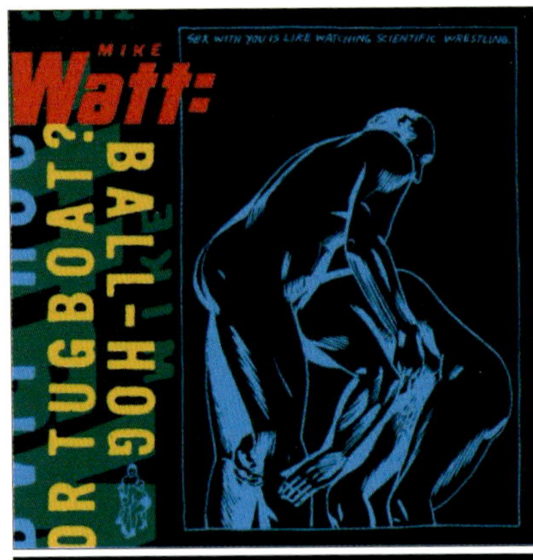

The solo album *Ball-Hog or Tugboat?* gained punk bassist Mike Watt his first exposure to mainstream fame.

MIKE WATT had accumulated many friends in his travels over the years, helping lay the foundation for punk's surge in popularity. He co-founded the Minutemen, a hard-core power trio with a jazz-funk edge. Along with Black Flag and the Circle Jerks, they formed part of the underground scene that united around Los Angeles-based SST Records through the Eighties. Watt's aggressive, athletic approach to his bass playing influenced bands from the Red Hot Chili Peppers to Fugazi.

But the Minutemen ended in 1985 when guitarist D. Boon died in a van crash. Watt was dragged back into music by Ed Crawford, a young fan and novice guitarist from Ohio. They formed fIREHOSE, got a major-label deal and kept touring in vans and recording on short money. The band called it quits in late 1994.

"I thought, 'What can I do that would really be different for me?' I tried to make it scary, playing with a bunch of different guys that don't live in my town," the garrulous Watt said. "It was therapy. I thought being intimidated might help me find an answer. I wanted a little chaos to bring myself out."

Seeing himself as "more of a rudder man or maybe a casting director than a front guy," Watt corralled a who's who of alternative rock for *Ball-Hog or Tugboat?*, his self-proclaimed wrestling record (the album credits were designed to look like a match card). Fifty-odd artists got into the ring with Watt, including Pearl Jam's Eddie Vedder, J Mascis of Dinosaur Jr, Nirvana's Dave Grohl and Krist Novoselic, the Red Hot Chili Peppers' Flea, the Lemonheads' Evan Dando, former Pixies leader Frank Black, Soul Asylum's Dave Pirner and the Beastie Boys' Mike D.

"Against the 70s" commanded attention, as Vedder sang Gen X lyrics—"The kids of today should defend themselves against the 70s/It ain't reality, just someone else's sentimentality." Watt blamed his own generation for "forcing youth away from the truth of what's real today. I was thinking to myself, 'I am the Seventies, look out for me—maybe you guys should live in your own time to be you.' I just remember when I was a kid and they were selling me *Happy Days* and *American Graffiti* and *Grease*, all that Fifties stuff. Didn't you feel weird, like, 'This is my dad's music'?"

Watt, who still looked like a punk rocker in his flannel shirt and close-cropped hair, was concerned that people didn't take the famous names attached to his all-star affair too seriously.

"Because it's on a big label, people think all these people were flown down to San Pedro and we had a *We Are the World* super-jam. It wasn't like that at all! I come from a tradition where the guys who are playing are in control." ■

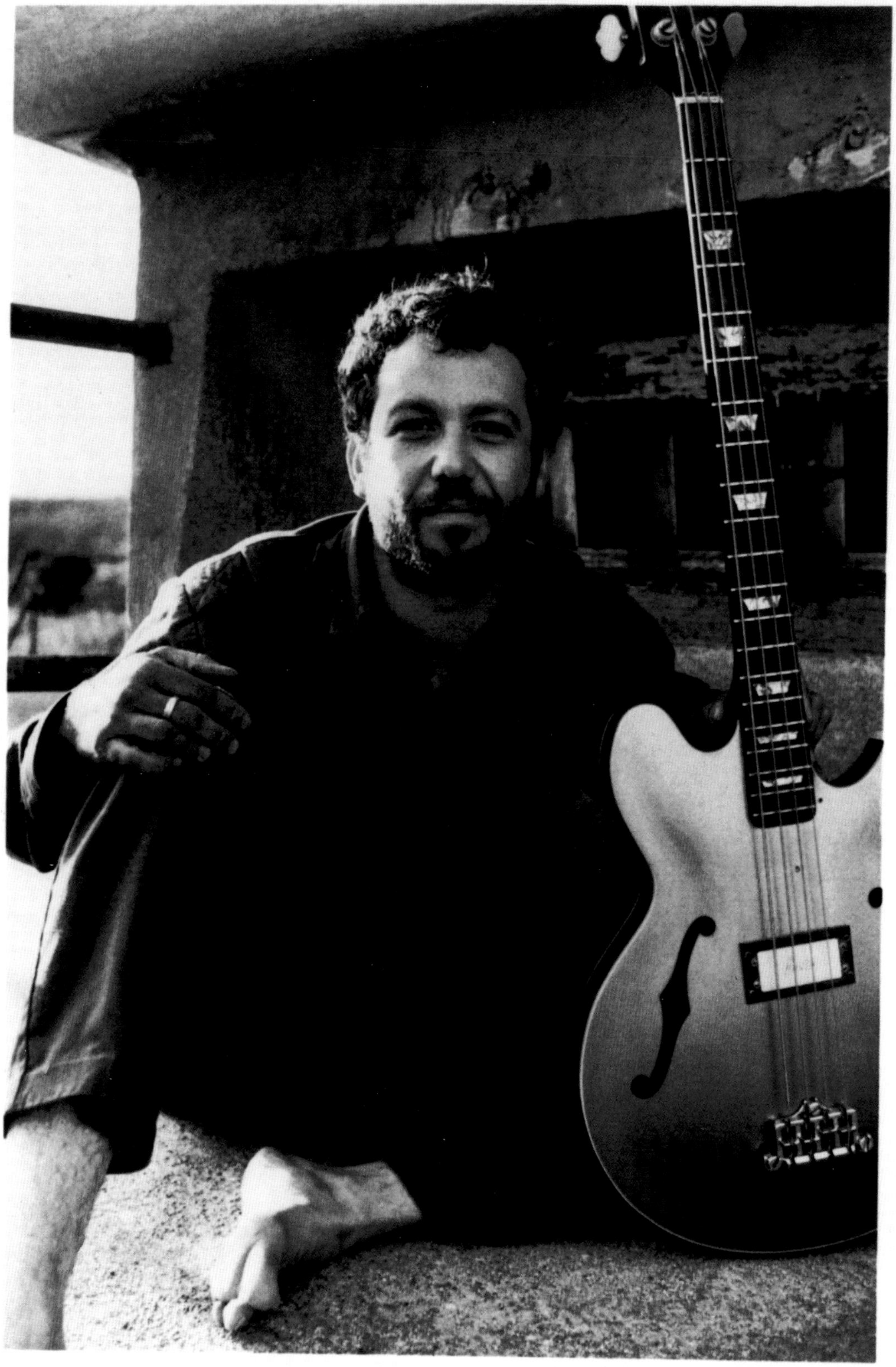

PHOTOGRAPH: JOHN EDER

mike watt: ball-hog or tugboat?

COLUMBIA
9410

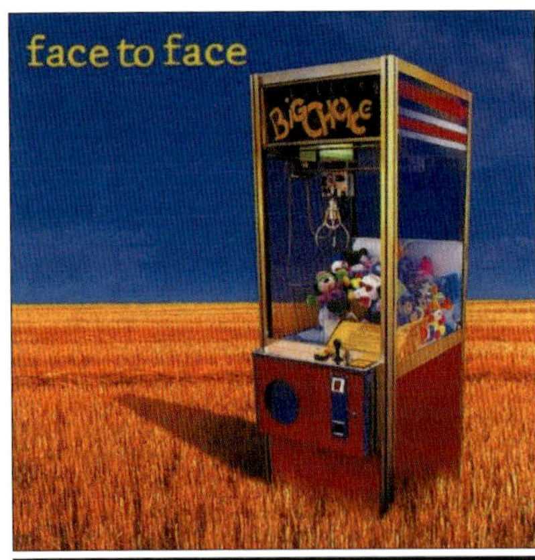

Filling the need for canorous punk-pop, the slamming "Disconnected" propelled Face to Face to the next level.

IN THE consumer-friendly return of punk, Face to Face was a viable commodity. The anthemic choruses and testosterone-pumping guitar chords of "Disconnected" and "A-OK" revived the spirited craft of the Clash in its prime.

"The ferocity and intensity of the old wave is definitely an influence," singer Trever Keith said. "But the social aspects of what they were singing about didn't really affect us much because we were pretty young then. That's what is so different about this new school of punk rock in the Nineties. Reagan's no longer president—we're dealing with a whole new set of problems."

Keith formed Face to Face in 1991 in his hometown of Victorville, California, and the band established a fan base with vigorous live shows, sharing the stage with Green Day and the Offspring. Like those heavyweights, Face to Face had aligned with a major label and recorded its first full-length album, *Big Choice*. "Disconnected" peaked at #39 on *Billboard*'s alternative songs chart—it had been previously released on an independent record label, but the band re-recorded it.

"It took us a day," Keith chuckled. "That included mixing and everything. You know, there's really not much to it. Either you know how to play it or you don't."

The radio hit was also made into a music video. It had made Face to Face "sell-outs" in the eyes of too-cool-for-you punks, but Keith saw nothing wrong with it.

"Punk sells records, but selling records isn't punk—that's the dichotomy," he shrugged. "The bands really can't help it if the corporate world comes around to liking that style of music again. We might as well abuse the corporate world to our advantage. Our goal was to get a record deal that would give us the ability to do this as a full-time job. All of us were working in construction. We all know what it's like to work hard. So, to me, if the music's good, you should be allowed to like it." ■

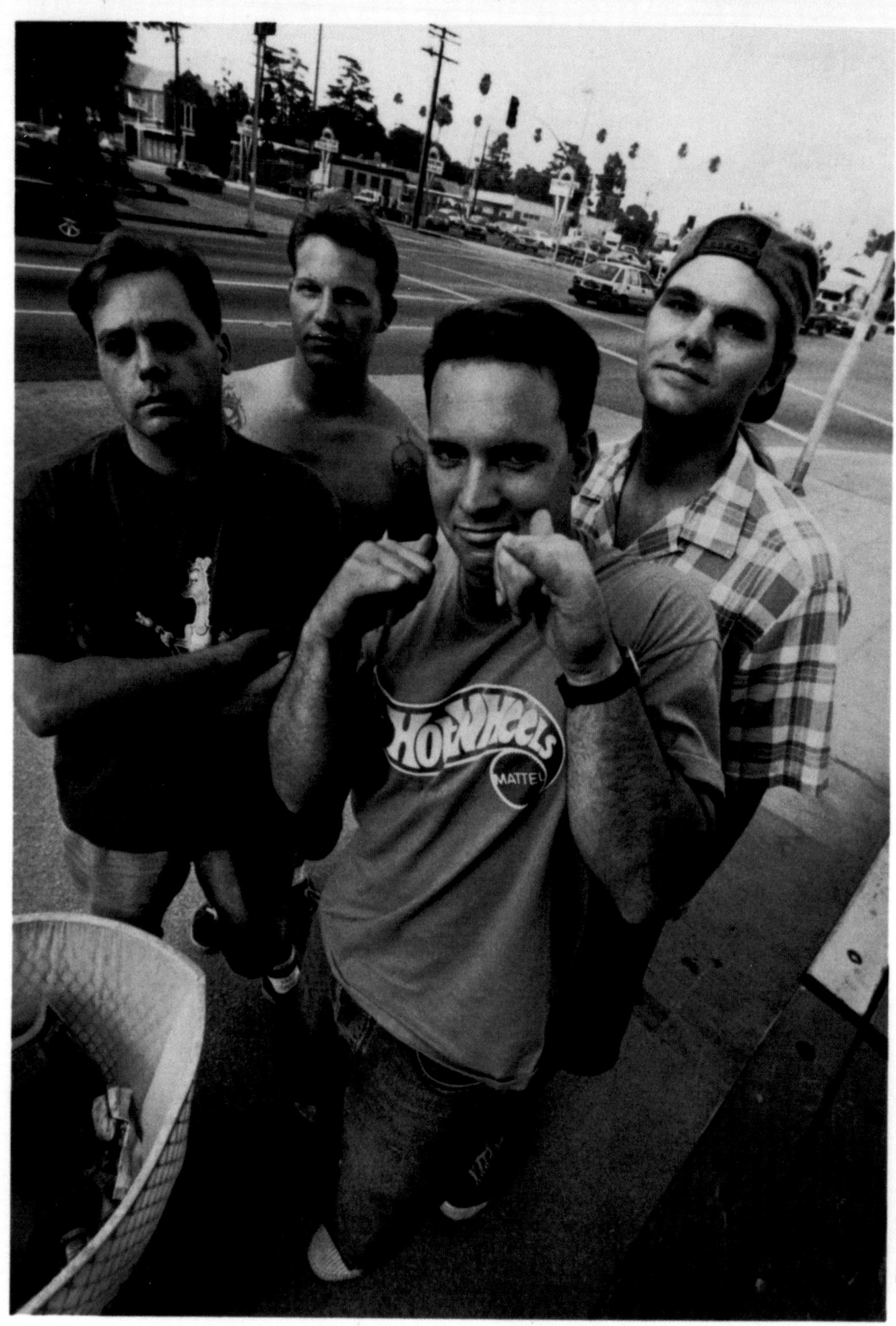

Photo Credit: Lisa Johnson

MATT RIDDLE CHAD YARO TREVER KEITH ROB KURTH

face to face

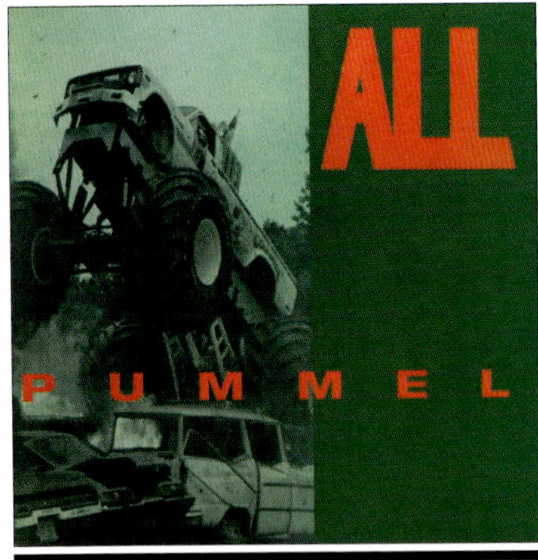

Punk rock band All financed a recording studio with money wangled from its major-label recording contract.

BILL STEVENSON got his start drumming for Black Flag, the original purveyors of the D.I.Y. rock ethic. While still in high school, Stevenson co-founded the Descendents, a near-legendary punk rock group which released eight albums before singer Milo Aukerman left in 1987 to pursue a doctoral degree in biochemistry. Stevenson then formed All with remaining Descendents Karl Alvarez and Stephen Egerton and recruited Chad Price for vocals, and they stayed the punk-pop course.

"But we left Los Angeles in '89 for all the obvious reasons—cost of living, pollution, crime, racial tensions, traffic," Stevenson said. "We landed in rural Missouri for four years, but we were in the middle of nowhere. So, Fort Collins, Colorado, was randomly chosen as a middle ground. We could just as well have landed in Austin, but the guys wanted to be in the mountains. Bands make decisions in weird ways."

All was signed to Interscope Records, a major label, and released *Pummel*. "The Nirvana/Pearl Jam revolution had happened on the radio, a distant cousin to punk rock, and the 'mall punk' thing with Green Day and Offspring was now popular, too," Stevenson noted. "So the world was finally cool with punk, and labels started coming after us. Interscope gave us ridiculous, life-changing money."

Pummel didn't sell enough copies to reach the *Billboard* charts, and disputes over marketing and promotion of the album ended the relationship quickly, but Stevenson had been astute enough to negotiate for two albums. The money from the short-lived agreement was used to purchase a 48-track board, and the band members designed and built their own recording studio, appropriately dubbed the Blasting Room, offering it to groups that were having a hard time finding a label to treat them right.

"We built it one step at a time—'Oh, let's buy a truck, a mixing board, a bigger one...' It seemed like the progression of the earthworm—we inched our way in, and somehow threw together a half-assed career," Stevenson said. "If you had told me when I was 15, 'So, Bill, you're going to co-own a studio and have a record label and your punk band is still going to be playing,' I would have just laughed and said, 'Well, first of all, I won't even be alive because I'm going to kill myself when I hit 30. And there's no way I'm still going to be a punker.' So all this took me by surprise." ■

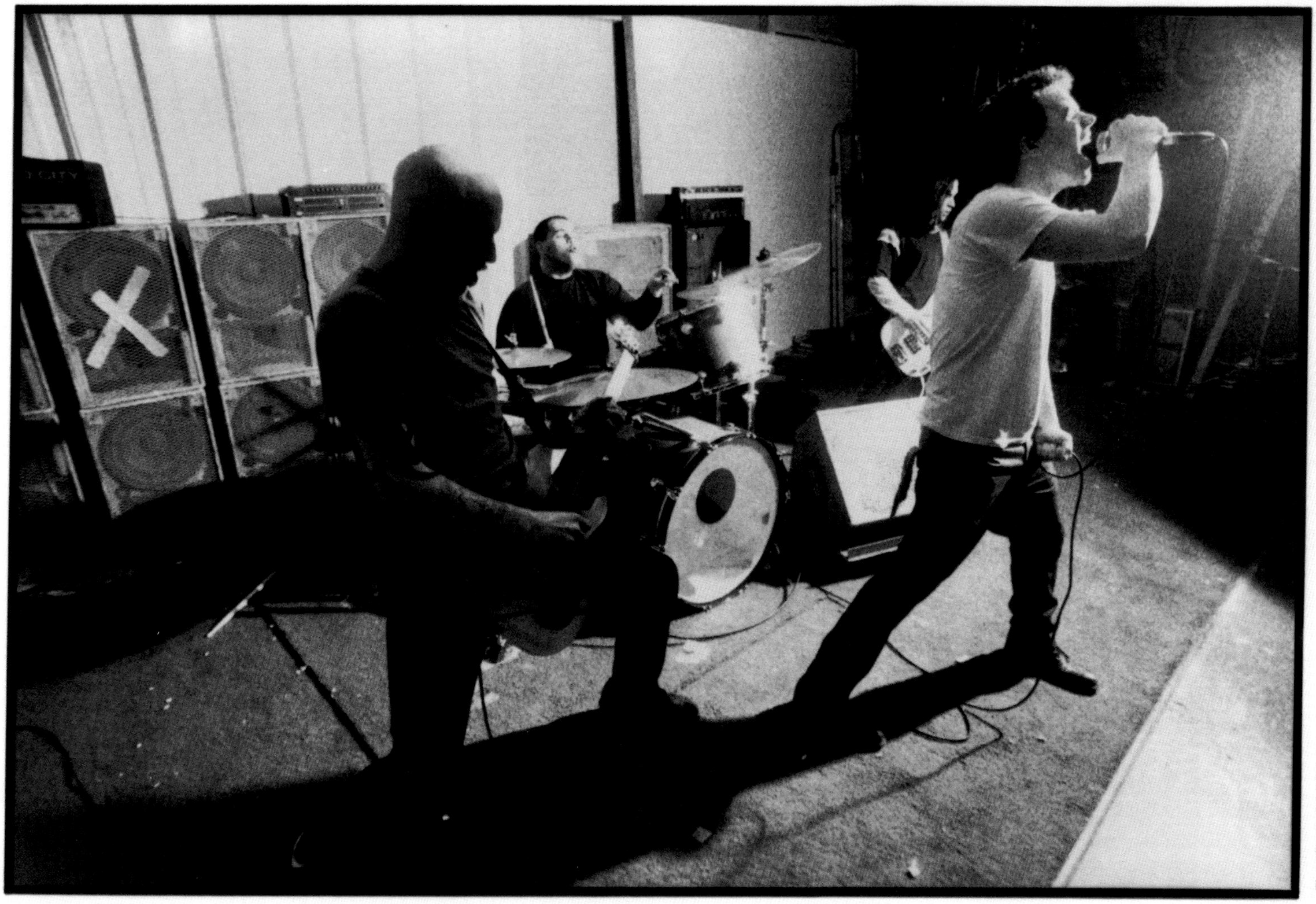

Photo Credit: Daniel Corrigan

Stephen Egerton Bill Stevenson Karl Alvarez Chad Price

ALL

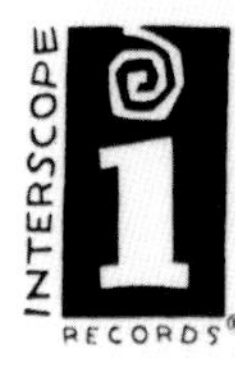

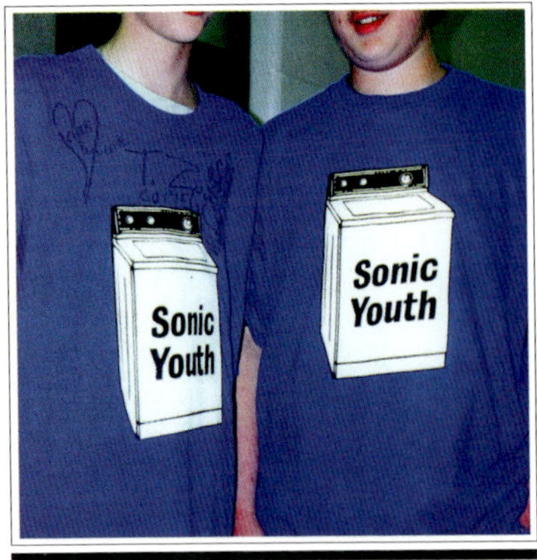

Billboard 200: *Washing Machine* (#58)

Hitting No. 1 on the college charts, Sonic Youth's *Washing Machine* managed to balance sounds and songs.

OVER THE course of nine albums, the members of Sonic Youth had gone from being obscure New York noise-rock makers to kingpins of the alternative scene. The band's early work was marked by a dissonant lassitude, which had to do with the hell they put guitars through—from distortion and feedback to unconventional tunings and physical abuse of the instrument.

"People would ask, 'How'd you get that sound?' Well, you get the wire used to string pianos with…," guitarist Lee Renaldo recalled.

But Sonic Youth moved toward a pop sensibility, incorporating a variety of moods with simple rhythms while reworking and refining their trademark textures.

"The more we stayed together and worked on the idea, the more sophisticated we became at constructing songs," guitarist and vocalist Thurston Moore said. "So, you had the people who were generally into us for being noise-mongers thinking we were selling out by getting more involved with songcraft. And a lot of people who started getting into us doing songs like 'Teen Age Riot' were not really that interested when we went off into more improvisatory worlds. It's a really weird balance—one we like working with."

Sonic Youth's *Washing Machine* didn't pander to the unenlightened. Renaldo's songs sounded like early Pink Floyd, slipping off into free-floating noise-play, dramatically cohering again at just the right moment. There was a lot of adventurous jamming—vocalist Kim Gordon's oblique title track popped out at around nine minutes.

"We were more interested in having high-energy action sound, just turning whatever that was into songs," Moore said. "By adding a verse and recording it and calling it a song, it was a song."

"The Diamond Sea" was Sonic Youth's hookiest tune yet. It also happened to be 20 minutes long—the pretty little ditty turned into an unhinged sonic rumination when it was least expected (an edit was serviced to radio stations). Sonic Youth spent the summer headlining Lollapalooza, and "The Diamond Sea" closed the sets, invigorating the band's three-guitar terrorism in the face of mainstream visibility.

"As far as I can tell, the general population is not that musically adventurous," Moore said. "Which is neither bad nor good, but that's just the way it is—they're into classic rock and that's where it stops. People aren't going to go out and buy Captain Beefheart albums, they're going to buy what they saw on TV. They take the most comfortable route, something accessible and easily assimilated. Sonic Youth surely isn't that." ■

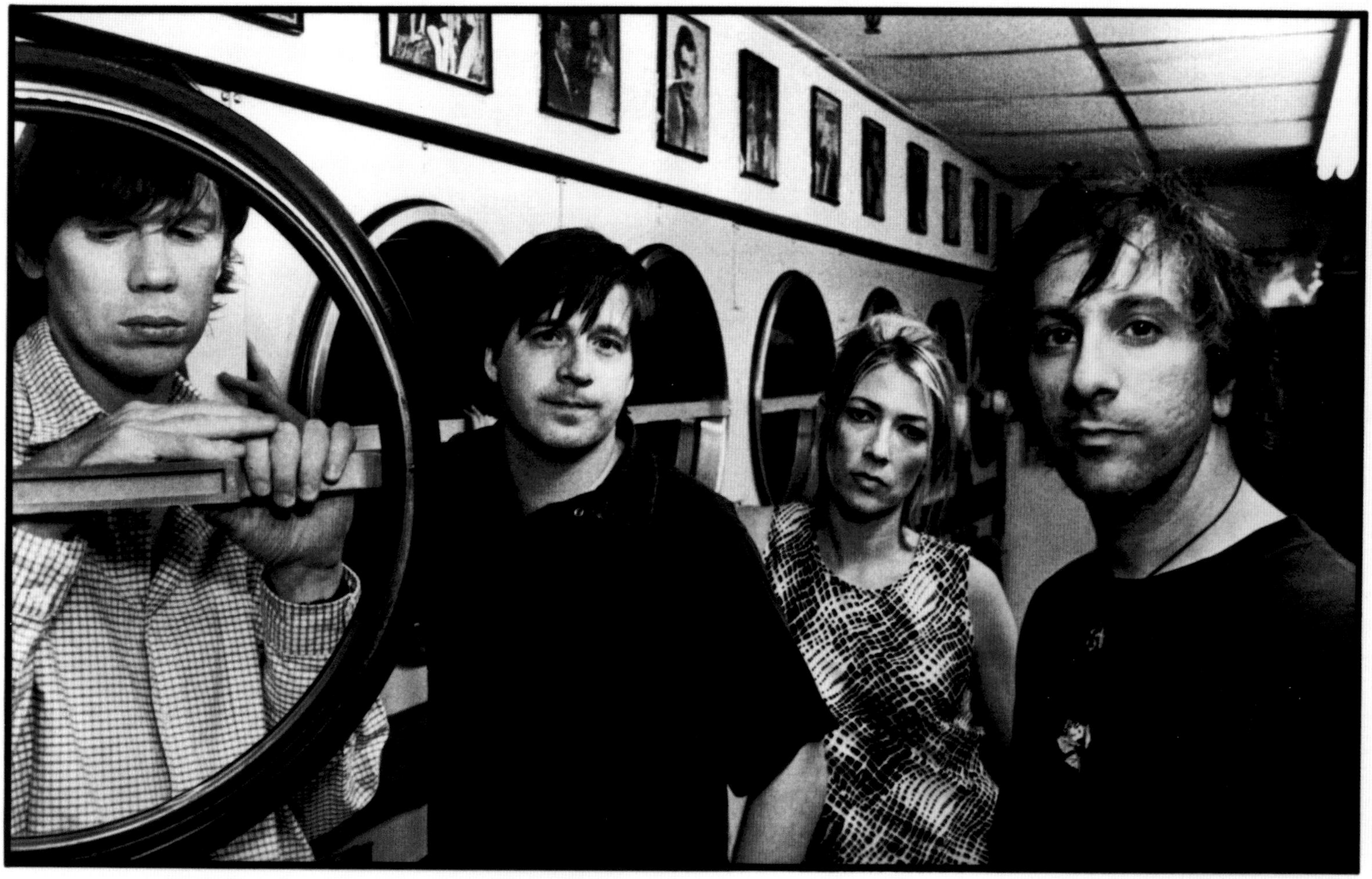

Photo Credit: Michael Lavine

Thurston Moore   Steve Shelley   Kim Gordon   Lee Ranaldo

Sonic Youth

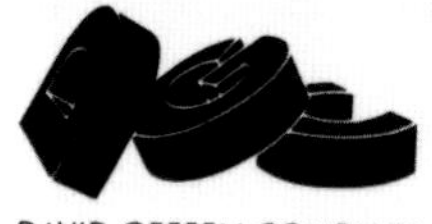

DAVID GEFFEN COMPANY

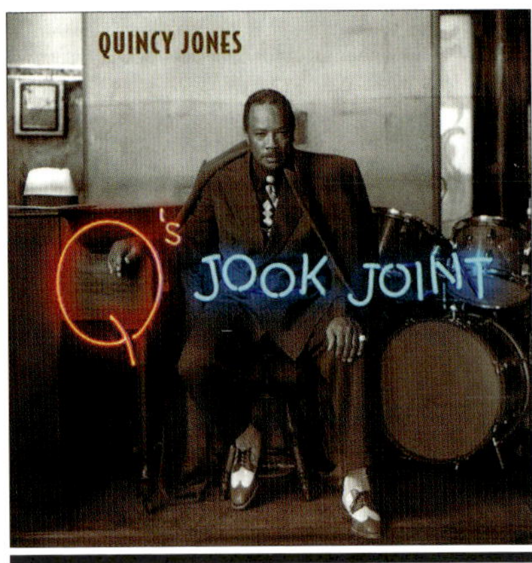

Billboard 200: *Q's Jook Joint* (#32)
Billboard Hot 100: "You Put a Move on My Heart" (#98); "Slow Jams" (#68)

An impresario in the most creative sense, the inimitable Quincy Jones put his heart and soul into *Q's Jook Joint*.

FOR MORE than 40 years, Quincy Jones had encompassed the roles of musician, composer, producer, arranger and conductor, illuminating much about the development of the African American musical tradition.

"I believe that in the coming years, the names Louis Armstrong, Duke Ellington, Count Basie, Miles Davis, Dizzy Gillespie, Sarah Vaughan, Ella Fitzgerald and Billie Holiday, to name a few, will be spoken with the same emotion, passion and respect as classical artists—Beethoven, Bach and Mozart," Jones said. "In deciding on the songs to put on this album, I started to think about the recordings that I really loved, that were due for a brand new 'do.'"

A mythological journey, *Q's Jook Joint* made reference to the back-woods club houses that flourished in rural America's Black communities after the abolition of slavery. The superbly crafted album jumpstarted a party, blending jazz, hip-hop, pop, funk and R&B productions.

"Musically, the American 'jook' is the most important place in the country—its sound joined together the secular and sacred," Jones enthused. "Suddenly, this album began to take on a whole new meaning. It became symbolic of that valued establishment."

Q's Jook Joint offered a cavalcade of collaborators, from all-stars like Ray Charles, Bono and Stevie Wonder to Jones' most recent discovery, a 19-year-old singer named Tamia. The album reached No. 1 on the *Billboard* jazz albums chart and won the Grammy Award for Best Engineered Album, Non-Classical.

"Please don't write any letters to me about the authenticity and correctness of this album," Jones said. "I studied the evolution and history of Black music and dance for 25 years, so I know how it all went down. If you want to take this trip, let all of your 'isms' and categorizations collapse." ■

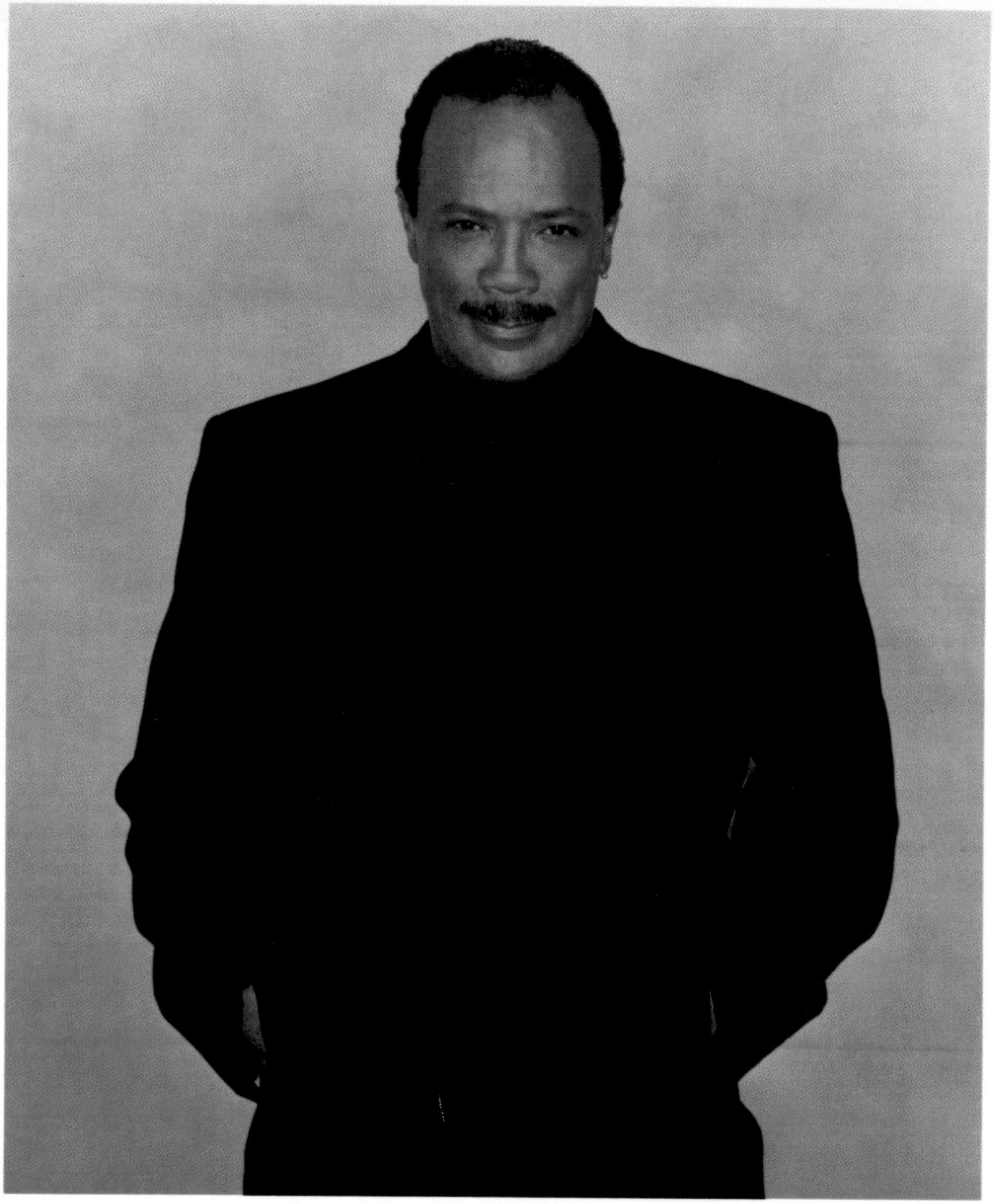

Photo Credit: Greg Gorman

QUINCY JONES

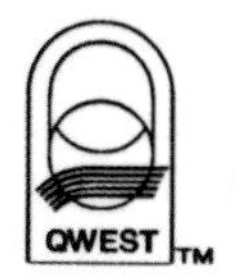

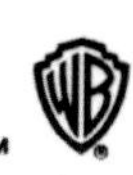

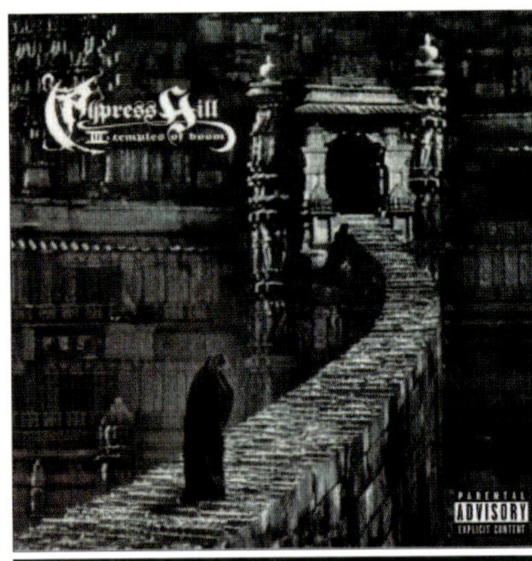

Billboard 200: *Cypress Hill III - Temples of Boom* (#3)
Billboard Hot 100: "Throw Your Set in the Air" (#45);
"Boom Biddy Bye Bye" (#87)

On *Cypress Hill III - Temples of Boom*, Cypress Hill's third platinum set, love of hip-hop and chronic came through.

HIP-HOP WAS a fiercely competitive world given to overnight successes and equally quick fades, but Cypress Hill had carved out a distinct niche. The California collective's trademarks were B-Real's recognizable nasal delivery, Sen Dog's booming braggadocio and producer DJ Muggs' mastery of taut beats. And "the bud"—the members of Cypress Hill were the first rappers to openly support cannabis legislation.

"I want to be known as more than just a pot group," B-Real (Louis Freese), a South Gate native of Mexican-Cuban extraction, said in his remarkably relaxed and understated manner. "We left so many songs about that off the new album so people would understand that we're musicians first and activists later. But when we come to town, there's still gonna be the get-high feeling—everybody wants to have a lot of fun."

With *Cypress Hill III - Temples of Boom*, the group turned towards darker, heavier moods with beats. Cypress Hill's gangsta instinct was represented on the anthemic "Throw Your Set in the Air." The song was about television, right? No, to "throw up a set" meant to flash hand signals that indicated gang affiliation, but B-Real insisted that the song was anti-gang. "If the kids were all getting into fights representing wherever they're from while the song goes on, then I wouldn't want to play it onstage. But we haven't seen one fight. A security guard in Canada got his ass whupped, but that was on his own."

"Illusions" was a bitter reflection that examined subtler musical ground. "It's a song that tries to help anybody who's trying to cope with the problems in their head," B-Real said. "They're not by themselves, there are other people out there with these same feelings. Maybe they can relate to a positive message."

Having rocked the Lollapalooza tours, the multiracial act was one of the few hardcore rap groups to achieve popularity in both ghetto neighborhoods and suburban developments. Some leaders within the hip-hop community had labeled Cypress Hill "sellouts."

"We want everybody to be down with our sound," B-Real observed. "It ain't about keeping it to one certain group. If we limit ourselves, we're just holding ourselves back. To move ahead, you've got to make music that everybody can feel a part of. Take advantage of the doors that were kicked the fuck open." ■

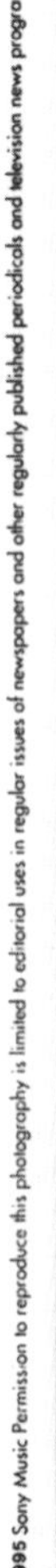

PHOTOGRAPH: KEN SCHLES

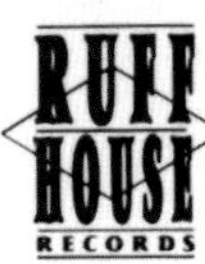

Management BUZZ TONE
646 North Robertson
Los Angeles, CA 90069
Phone: 310.657 9400
FAX. 310.657.0277

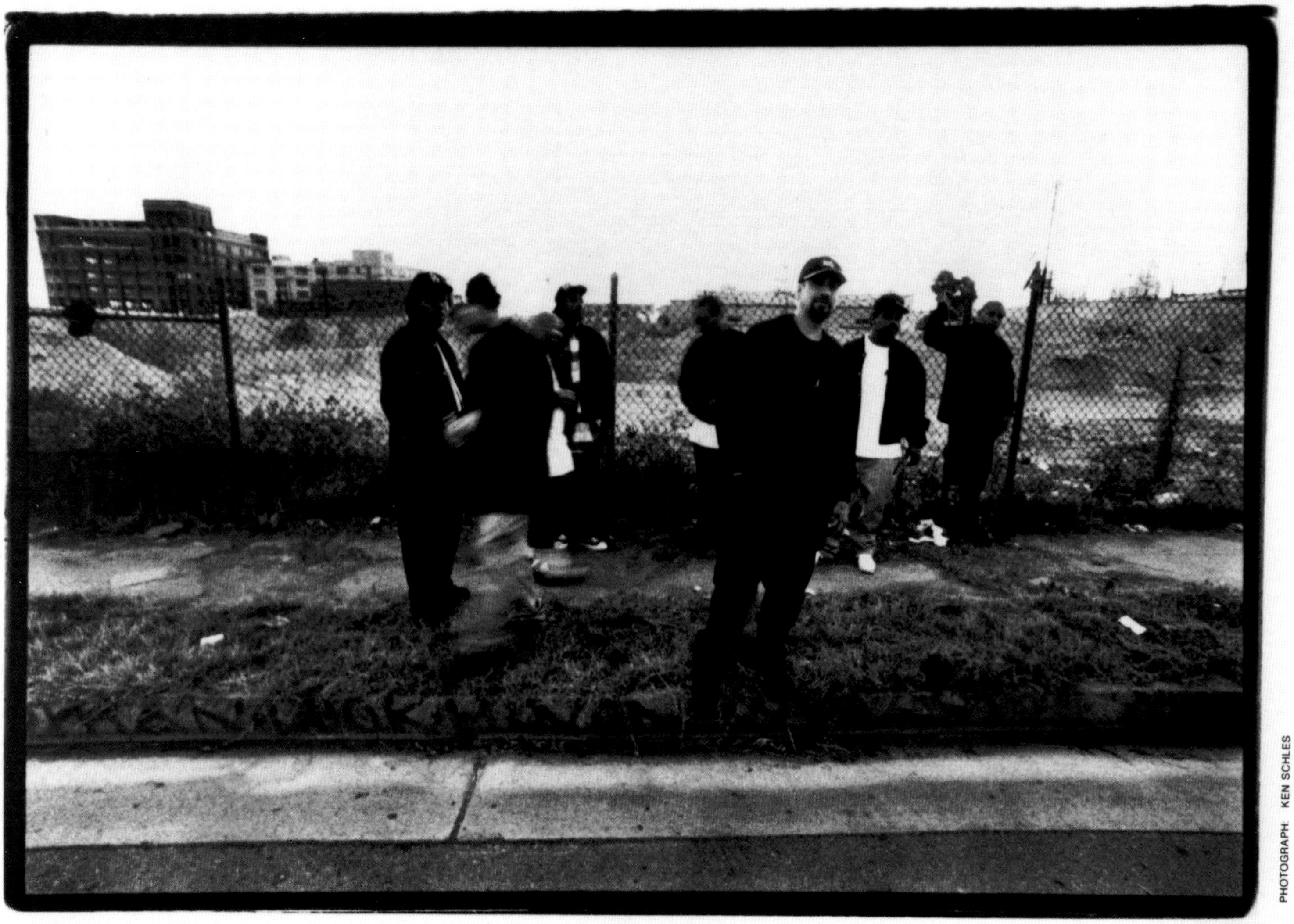

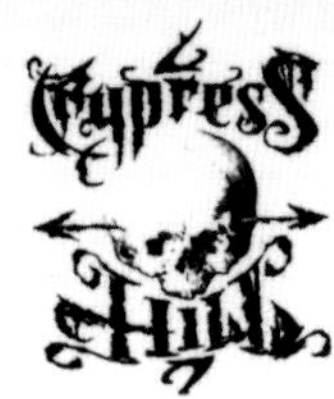

COLUMBIA
9506

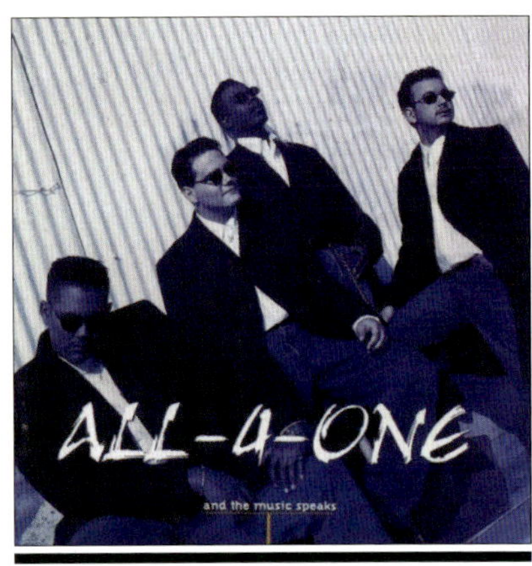

Billboard 200: *And the Music Speaks* (#27)
Billboard Hot 100: "I Can Love You Like That" (#5)

The mega-ballad "I Can Love You Like That" demonstrated All-4-One's reverence for spine-tingling harmonies.

CRANKING OUT romantic R&B hits, All-4-One had risen to the top of the vocal group pack, garnering a Grammy award and an American Music Award. People laughed, but karaoke might have been responsible.

Tony Borowiak, Jamie Jones and Alfred Nevarez had no significant experience beyond singing in church choirs, amateur nights and talent shows. At a karaoke contest in their native Antelope Valley (an hour north of Los Angeles), they met fellow contestant Delious Kennedy singing "Ebony and Ivory."

"I had just quit another group and come to town looking for a break in show business," Kennedy explained. "We competed against each other. We tied and then we both lost in the grand finals. But they decided to make their group a quartet and brought me in."

And as All-4-One, they were enjoying sweeter victories. *All-4-One*, 1994's debut album, took off. "So Much in Love," an update of the Tymes' 1963 doo-wop classic, scaled the Top 5, and a soulful cover of "I Swear"—a No. 1 country hit only a few months earlier by John Michael Montgomery—became the year's biggest-selling single.

And the Music Speaks, the multi-ethnic group's second album, featured "I Can Love You Like That," another remake of a country ballad popularized by Montgomery. It was one of the nation's top pop hits. Studio trickery—multitrack recording, pitch-shifting, overdubbing—couldn't replicate the sound of four voices blending.

"We did a lot more a cappella singing around one mike with the record," Kennedy, the oldest member at 24, said. "In this day and age of technology, you've always got to go back to what works. When I was young, my dad's basement was always the place to listen to music—he'd play Motown and the O'Jays and the Spinners and the Manhattans. I used to love to sing those songs. I grew up in the Eighties when the more synthesized sounds, flashy makeup and the big hair came in, but I still had the real scene going on in the basement. There was always a balance at home." ■

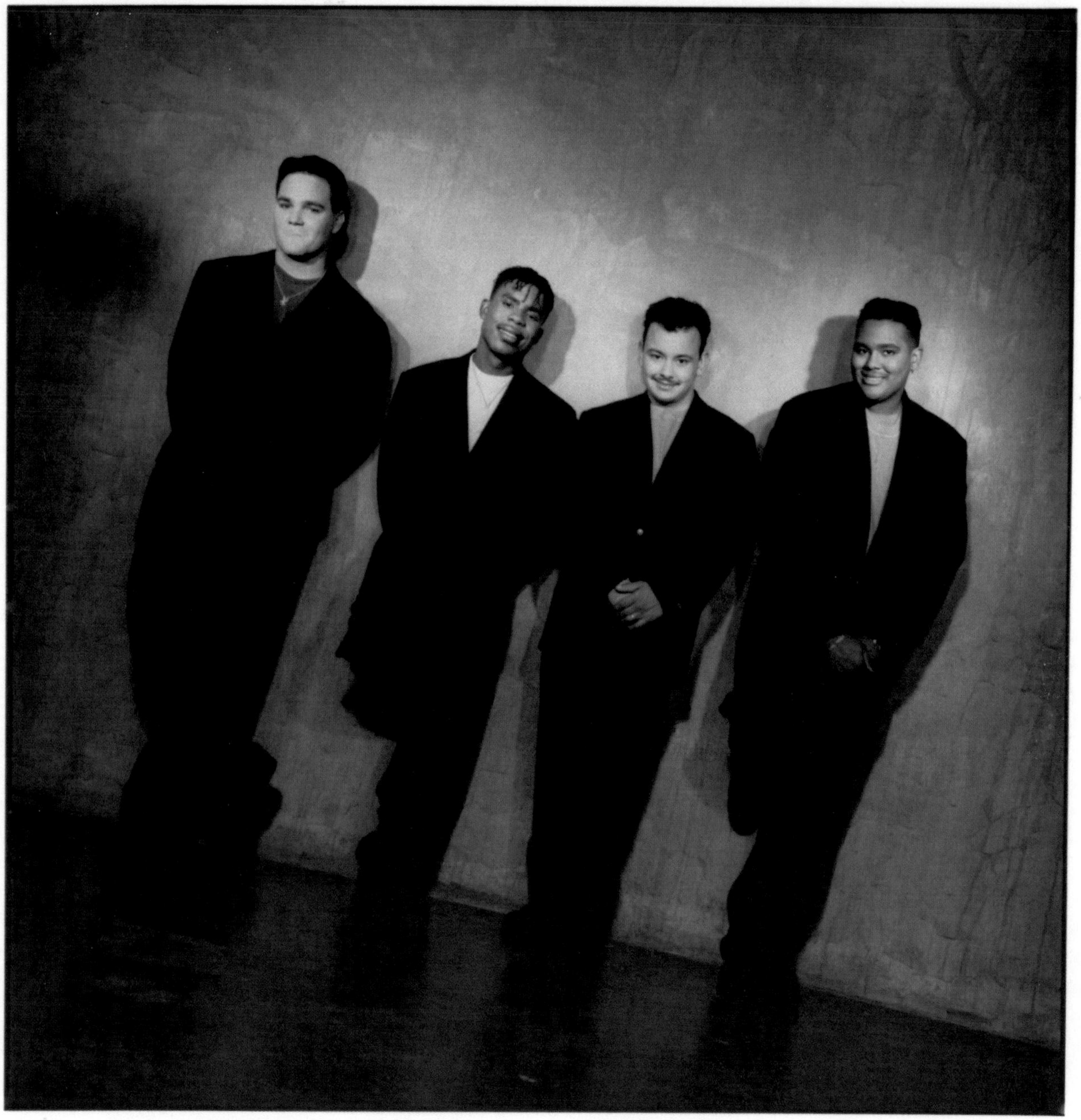

Photo Credit: Jeff Katz

TONY BOROWIAK DELIOUS ALFRED NEVAREZ JAMIE JONES

ALL-4-ONE

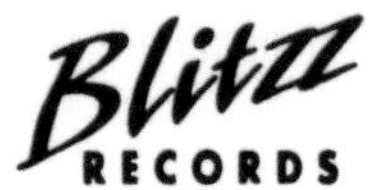

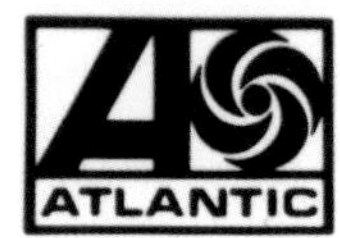

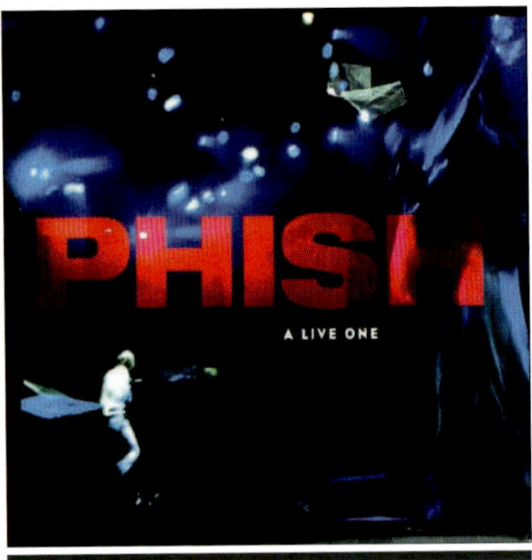

Billboard 200: *A Live One* (#18)

An official release to capture the true concert experience, *A Live One* became Phish's first million-selling album.

WITHOUT BENEFIT of a hit record, major radio airplay or videos in MTV rotation, the Phish phenomenon had risen—the band was one of the top 40 grossing acts, according to *Pollstar*. The popularity stemmed from its live shows. Loyal Phish Heads, a legion of neo-hippie kids who saw the band as a way of life, gravitated to the long, loose and humorous improvisations. Each Phish concert was different, with the band even transforming individual songs onstage.

A Live One, a double-live album, took the in-concert excitement onto the charts. Vermont's favorite sons selected a dozen songs from among 550 recorded during the 1994 fall tour.

"We toyed with the idea that it would be better to release an entire night," guitarist Trey Anastasio said. "But we encourage the taping of shows, so everybody's got that bootleg. We thought people would be interested in hearing our favorite moments of the tour, what our special night would have been. Technologically, things have changed. You used to pay big money trying to record a night on analog equipment—renting a mobile studio, using two-inch reels of tape that were only 15 minutes long. With modular digital multitrack recorders, it's much easier. You can capture an entire tour, you can record directly off the sound board, carry the recorders in a rack, the tapes are small and they record two hours."

A Live One included more than 130 minutes of music, and half of the tracks weren't found on Phish's five studio albums. There wasn't an emphasis on lean, tight songwriting craft. "There's a lot of jamming on the album. That's what fans like, that's what you don't hear on the others," Anastasio said.

A 30-minute version of "Tweezer" was expanded, diverted and deflected every which way. "That was the one song that was never in doubt," Anastasio insisted. "From the minute it hit the tape, we knew we were gonna put that on the album." Anastasio and bassist Mike Gordon's onstage trampolines and drummer Jon Fishman's frock were meant to be seen and not heard. ■

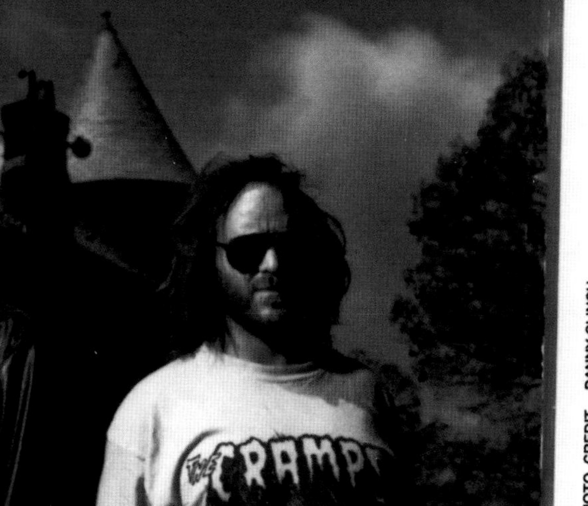

PHOTO CREDIT DANNY CLINCH

L R PAGE MCCONNELL, MIKE GORDON, TREY ANASTASIO, JON FISHMAN

PHISH

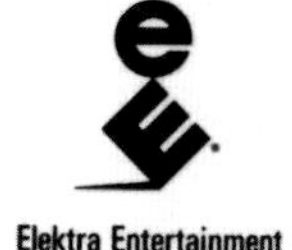

Elektra Entertainment

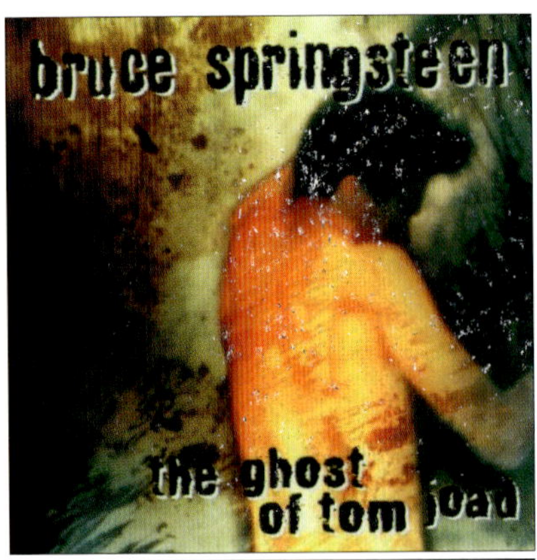

Billboard 200: *The Ghost of Tom Joad* (#11)

Bruce Springsteen's *The Ghost of Tom Joad* was inspired by forgotten segments of Americans in rural society.

OF ANY album Bruce Springsteen ever made, *The Ghost of Tom Joad* probably had the least mass appeal. But Springsteen had never been about numbers—it was his heart, soul and integrity that had made him one of rock music's most beloved artists. And he'd rarely packed more of a wallop than on the collection of low-key, downcast, near-acoustic songs.

"I just feel like I'm doing something out there that isn't being done by anyone else at the moment," the stocky artist acknowledged. "It's a good thing."

The Ghost of Tom Joad was named for the protagonist of John Steinbeck's classic American novel *The Grapes of Wrath*, Springsteen said, yet John Ford's great 1940 film was the basis for his work. The Joads were displaced Okies of the 1930s who moved west to get work as migrant fruit-pickers but only found oppression, disenchantment and death.

"I saw the movie when I was 26," Springsteen recalled. "The effect has resonated through the rest of my life. Joad was radicalized by the social injustice he confronted. I was sitting there thinking, 'Yeah, that's what I want to do. I want to do some work that gets into people's lives and means something, if I can.'" Springsteen described a scene in *The Grapes of Wrath*, interpreting it as a metaphor for the possibility of beauty and art in people's lives. "It asked a really important question—are there individual souls? Is individual salvation possible? Or do we all rise and fall together in some fashion?"

Some people thought the working-class New Jersey troubadour had become an upper-crust L.A. guy, making it harder for him to grapple with proletariat passions. But having mined his personal life for as many albums as he could, he'd rethought his role. To get back to the relevance that had been missing from his music in recent years, Springsteen connected the Depression-era setting with the present-day's increasingly disadvantaged masses, trying to put himself and his audience in touch with "a whole group of Americans whose lives and dreams have been basically declared expendable as part of doing business."

His affecting new songs—"Sinaloa Cowboys," "Balboa Park," "The Line" and the title track—offered a voice for those who seldom got heard. Some numbers, set along the California/Mexico border, forcefully depicted the misery of immigrants trying to escape poverty. It wasn't easy to be the Woody Guthrie for the baby boomers, but Springsteen hoped some of his compassion would rub off.

"This is something I really want to do, something I feel connected and committed to," he explained. "I'm always looking around for a song of some sort, a story. But more so than in the past, I'm looking to the outside."

The Ghost of Tom Joad won the Grammy for Best Contemporary Folk Album. ■

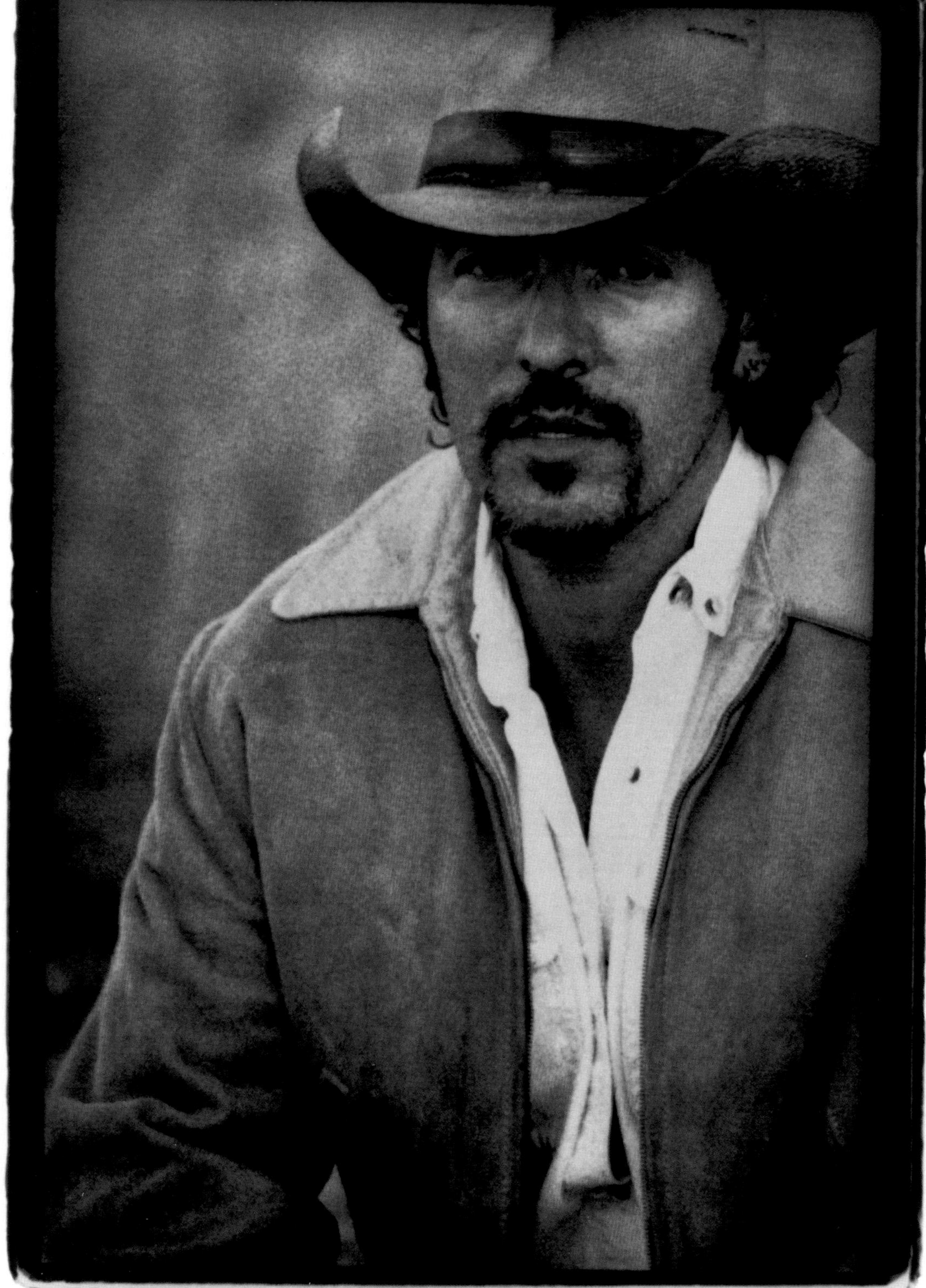

PHOTO CREDIT: PAM SPRINGSTEEN

BRUCE SPRINGSTEEN

COLUMBIA
9512

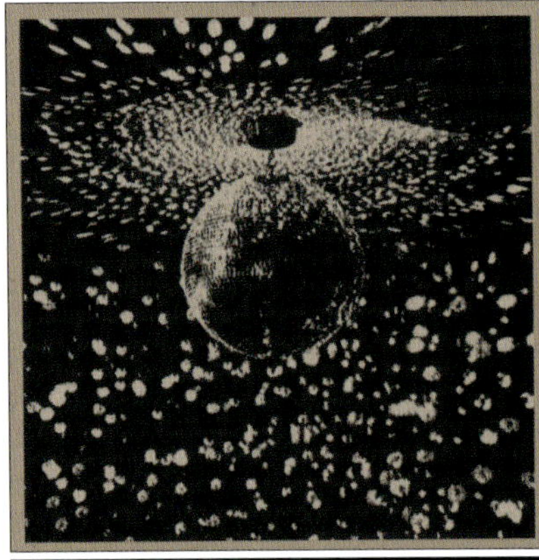

Billboard 200: *Mirror Ball* (#5)

Backed up by musicians from Pearl Jam, Neil Young issued the album *Mirror Ball*, recorded "live" in the studio.

ONE OF the leading creative figures in rock music, Neil Young was always looking for a new challenge. His oft-distorted electric guitar playing and customary deshabille had earned him the nickname "the Godfather of Grunge" and, still enamored with the grunge scene, led to his jamming with Pearl Jam. The members served as the backing band for Young's album *Mirror Ball*, and Pearl Jam's energy and spontaneity supported some of his best work.

"Records are all made the same way—a lot of people are trying to be perfect so they all sound finely crafted," Young said. "This takes a lot of time and, in the long run, is kinda useless. What I think is important is to get the songs out there and play music live. It's rock 'n' roll, play it all at once. If it sounds good, ship it. That's the way it all started, the way all great rock 'n' roll was fabricated."

There were plenty of deliciously mangled guitar sounds, but the songs—"Peace and Love," the powerful and appealing pop riff of "Downtown"—didn't come off like Pearl Jam's, and the band cautioned fans who would buy *Mirror Ball* expecting otherwise. Singer Eddie Vedder had the green light to do whatever he wanted, yet he only lent his voice to a couple of tracks.

Guitarist Stone Gossard was proud of the collaboration, but due to legal reasons, Pearl Jam's name was not allowed to be featured on the cover. "Some people wanted to call it *N.Y.P.J.*," he said. "But the suits in the legal department didn't think that was such a good idea."

1995 also marked Young's induction into the Rock and Roll Hall of Fame. Vedder did the honors at the ceremony, and the two performed "Act of Love."

"I gotta get my music out and make room for the next music," Young shared. "I gotta stay regular, you know what I mean? You just can't hold back, because we've got a lot to give, so here it comes. Why wait to be cool? Forget it." ■

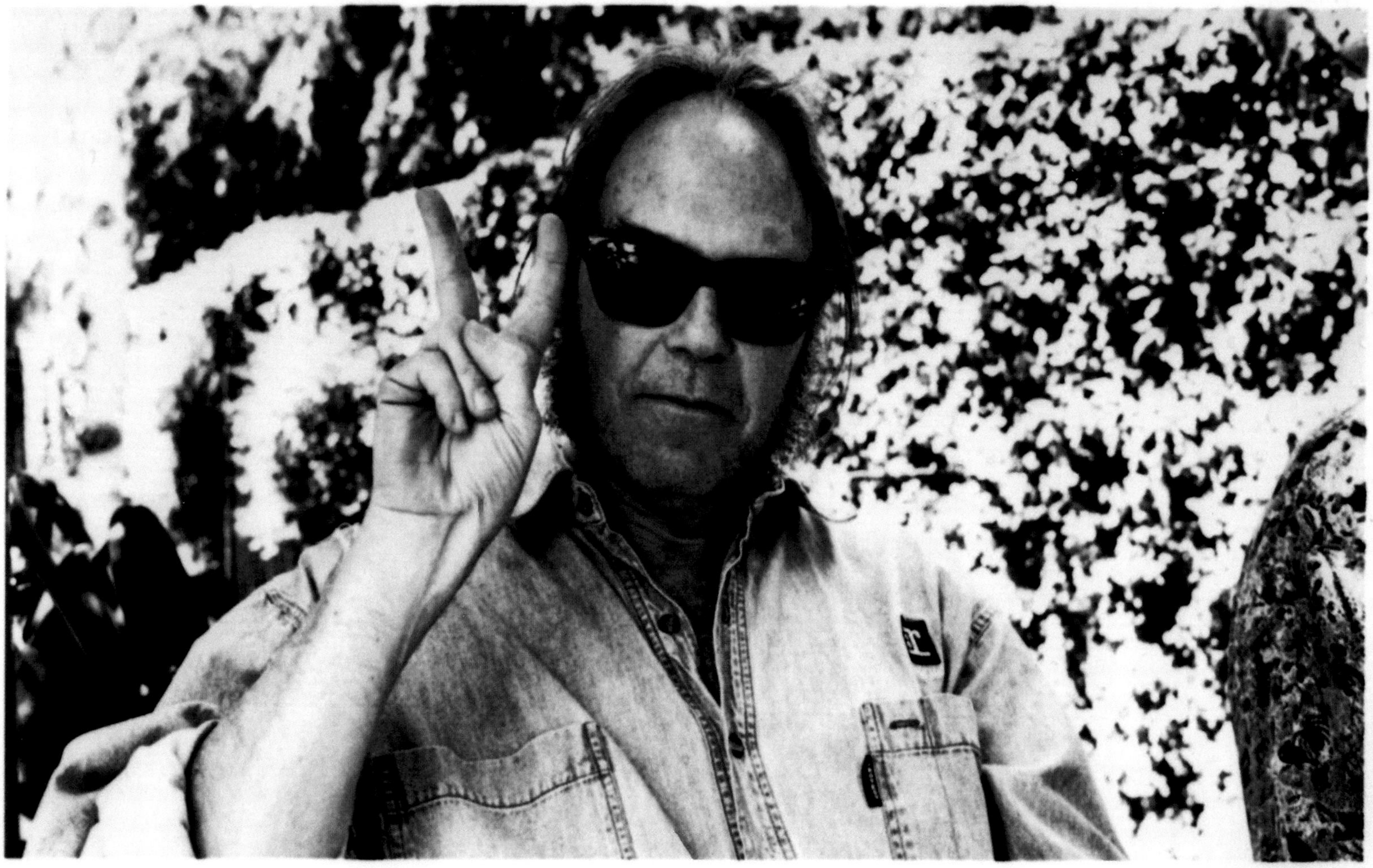

PHOTO CREDIT: Henry Diltz

Neil Young

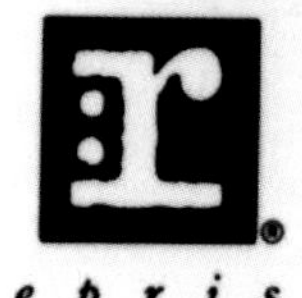

r e p r i s e

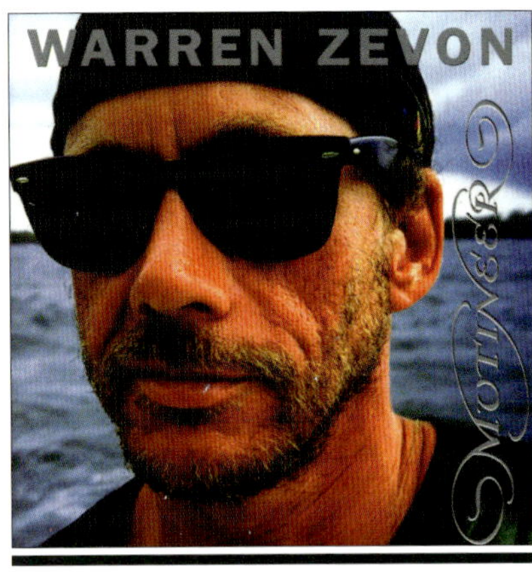

Warren Zevon, one of rock's most talented and significant performers, crafted a self-produced album, *Mutineer*.

EXCEPT FOR his only hit single, 1978's "Werewolves of London," Warren Zevon had a recording career that sometimes seemed to go on in spite of him. With no commercial prosperity to match his critical acclaim, the restless, sardonic singer-songwriter delivered *Mutineer*, another solid album.

"I started out with musical heroes who were in their 80s, so I didn't think of this as a youth deal," the droll Zevon said. "When the vast degrees of financial success aren't part of the equation, you hope the work is its own reward—hmm, that sounded like a method actor. But there's no reason why you'll suddenly stop doing good work."

The tough-guy sagas on *Mutineer* offered Zevon's trademark wit and cantankerous social commentary. "Poisonous Lookalike" was a dark, disturbed ode to love gone bad. A haunting metaphor built on pirate imagery drove the title track. And he co-wrote the sardonic "Rottweiler Blues" with journalist and best-selling crime novelist Carl Hiassen. It concerned a psycho survivalist arming himself for suburban life—Zevon sang sincerely about a dog that's "dreaming about…the promise of burglar blood."

Zevon produced the album himself, writing and recording in the loft of his Los Angeles apartment. With recent advances in digital recording equipment, he was able to work in relative isolation, laying down instrumental parts and vocals as the songs took shape.

"I will admit that a curious part of having this dream come true was feeling ashamed because I wasn't working as hard as I imagined the artist formerly known as Prince did in a home studio. I shuffled around nervously and ate and watched TV. It seemed to me I wasted a lot of time, but I was told, 'No, no, don't worry, it's part of the process, too.' Oliver Stone was supposed to have said, 'When anybody can make a movie, then it'll be an art form'—I presume he meant instead of the ability to take a very good lunch with the backers. I think we're close to the point where anybody can make a record."

To harmonize with the modern age, Zevon also appeared on interactive computer networks. "Reading these discussions has been one of the most brutalizing, degrading experiences of my life. We were never supposed to know how people react to the 'reproductive arts' like record-making, to know the first thing out of a kid's mouth when he comes through the door from Tower Records after buying your album instead of the new Soul Asylum. My daughter looked at the postings and said, 'I don't think you're supposed to read this, Dad.' It's like being McKinley standing outside the door of an assassins' convention." ■

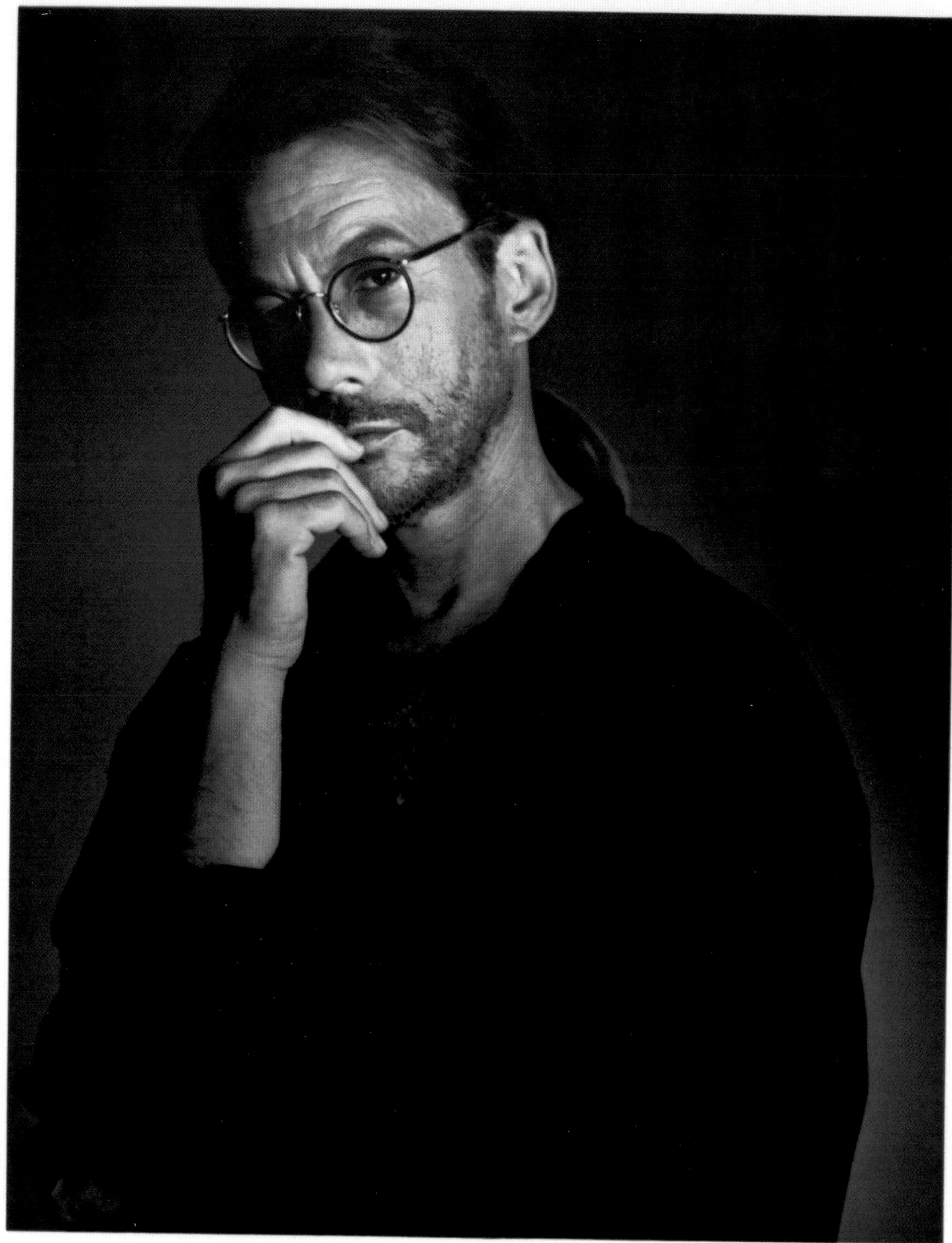

Photo Credit: Jonathan Exley

WARREN ZEVON

giant ™

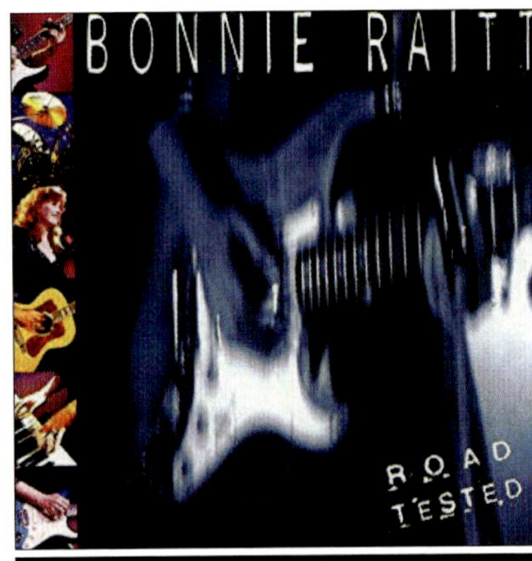

Billboard 200: *Road Tested* (#44)
Billboard Hot 100: "Rock Steady" (#73)

Fans had always known that Bonnie Raitt would pull out all the stops for her first-ever concert set, *Road Tested.*

IT DIDN'T bother Bonnie Raitt that it had taken 24 years into her recording career to release a live album.

"To me, it's a personal statement, like Little Feat did with *Waiting for Columbus*—a lot of times your fans want to hear something that's a mixture of great material with the band stretching out. I'm known for my live shows, but in the Eighties I didn't have a good enough relationship with my record company to give them a live record. I wanted to wait until I was on one that would treat me with enough respect."

Road Tested, a 22-track, double-disc package, included highlights of her early work—"Angel from Montgomery," "Love Me Like a Man"—and songs from the three multiplatinum studio albums that made her a star—*Nick of Time* (1989), *Luck of the Draw* (1992) and 1994's *Longing in their Hearts.* And some new songs, too.

"There's a Michael McDonald song that I really love called 'Matters of the Heart,'" Raitt said. "And there are some special guests. Bryan Adams wrote a song for me, 'Rock Steady,' that we recorded together. Bruce Hornsby came out and played on 'I Can't Make You Love Me.' And Kim Wilson from the Fabulous Thunderbirds played harp and sang on a song of his I've done for years since we used to double-bill, 'I Believe I'm in Love with You.' And there's a song with Ruth and Charles."

Ruth Brown and singer-songwriter Charles Brown had been Raitt's opening acts on her entire tour, using the shows to shed some light on R&B legends less acquainted with popular acclaim. Raitt's commitment went back to the late Sixties when she played on the Northeast folk scene, frequently appearing in concert with country blues figures like Mississippi Fred McDowell, Mississippi John Hurt, Sippie Wallace and Son House because her manager also represented them. It fueled her idea to become an authentic white blues performer.

Raitt dedicated her boundness spirit to garnering financing and visibility for unsung blues and R&B musicians. A founding member and vice chairwoman of the Rhythm & Blues Foundation, she fought what she had called a "racist" situation.

"I'm pushing to get some justice here," the eight-time Grammy winner said. "These artists don't need charity, they need their royalties—they either didn't have an agreement or didn't get proper statements, so they didn't get any health insurance. Now it's hard because they have a lot of pre-existing conditions.

"So what we're dealing with on a day-to-day basis is financial assistance—anything from new teeth to new instruments to rent to medical emergencies. We can't suddenly buy somebody a house or pay their IRS bill, but there are long-term care budgets. It's necessary for record companies and magazines making their livings from this music to make donations. I think it's long overdue. So many of the pioneers have passed away." ■

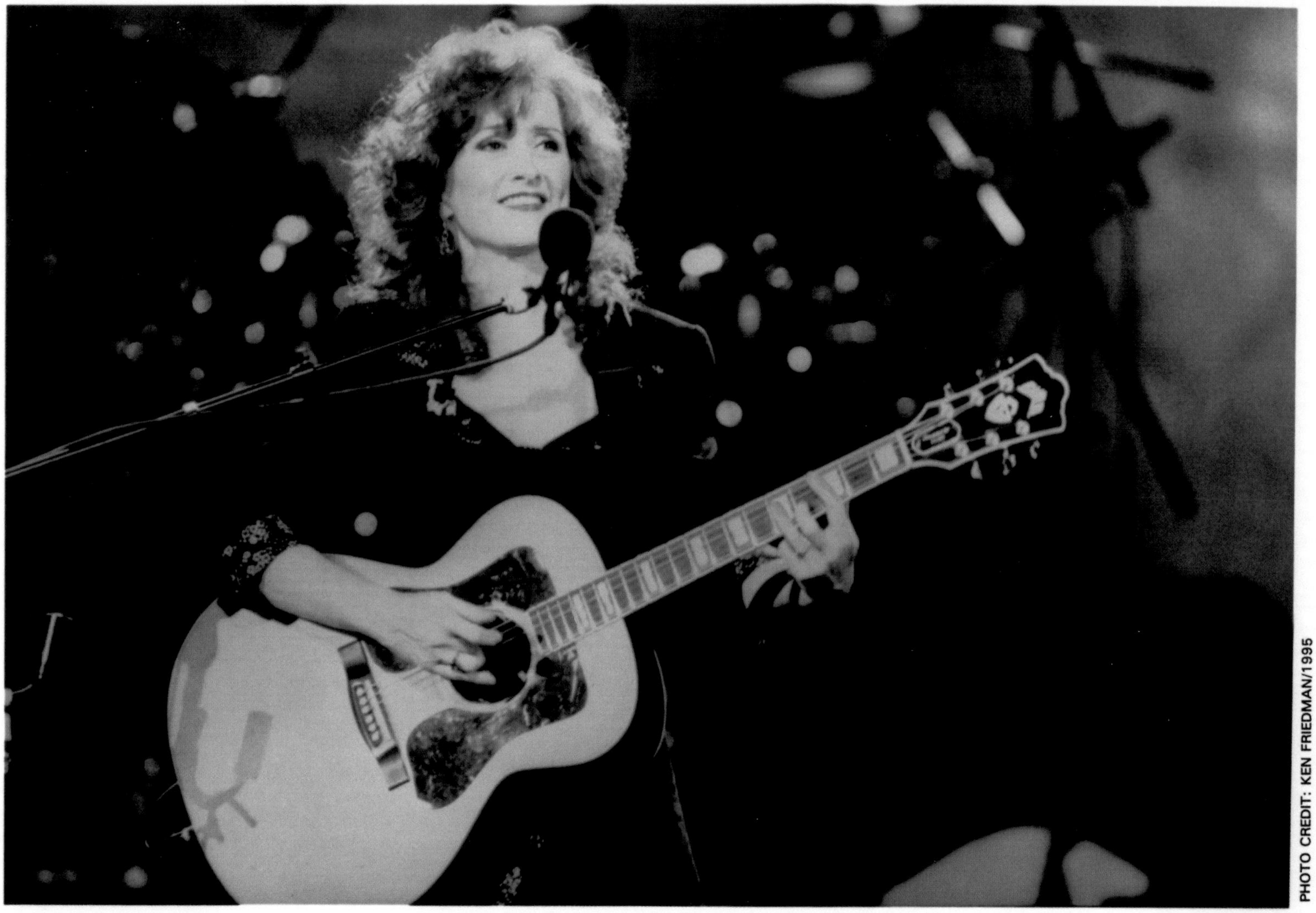

PHOTO CREDIT: KEN FRIEDMAN/1995

BONNIE RAITT

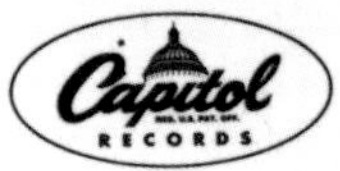

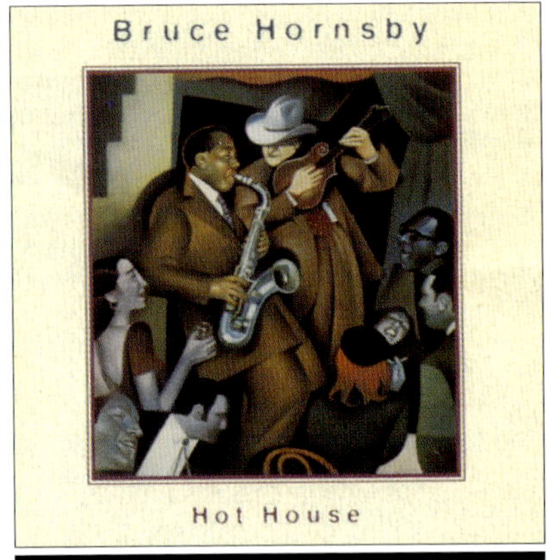

Billboard 200: *Hot House* (#68)
Billboard Hot 100: "Walk in the Sun" (#54)

Bruce Hornsby, a diverse, dauntless and collaborative voice in adult rock, promulgated his *Hot House* album.

SINCE THE release of *The Way It Is*, his 1986 smash debut album, Bruce Hornsby had created a nice musical life for himself. He recorded in his home studio in Williamsburg, Virginia, with the help of friends like Béla Fleck, Jerry Garcia and Pat Metheny. A sports fanatic, he performed the national anthem at sporting events along his tours. He made appearances on other artists' projects and sat in with the Grateful Dead.

"It's really the best part of what's happened to me," Hornsby said. "I've worn a lot of hats over the years, played a lot of different kinds of music."

Hot House, Hornsby's fifth album, struck a balance with the jazz elements of 1993's *Harbor Lights*. "That was the most inaccessible, least commercial record I'd made," Hornsby explained. "We played the Bakersfield County Fair and found out that Leon Russell was playing there the same night. We were sitting around shooting the breeze—'Hey, Horny-man, I really like that last record, all that "j" (jazz) you got going there.' And as I was leaving, he said, 'H! I just wanna say one thing before you go—don't forget the vulgate.' I said, 'The vulgate? What's that?' He said, 'The language of the people.' It was a typical, enigmatic Leon line. But as I walked away and started thinking about it, I knew exactly what he was saying—'Don't get too out there, don't get so highbrow in your music that you lose sight of your audience.'"

So Hornsby wanted to have his cake and eat it too. And he found his muse, reflected in the *Hot House* cover art—a drawing of jazz legend Charlie Parker playing with bluegrass legend Bill Monroe. "There was a time when swing music was the language of the people, the popular music of the day," Hornsby said. "Now that consciousness is very archaic in the white world of music. I wanted to see if I could make a swing-influenced record in 1995 and have it mean something, have it still be a party record."

The songs on *Hot House* melded different styles—"White Wheeled Limousine," featuring Fleck, fused folk with jazz, and the glossy "The Longest Night" paid tribute to the classic R&B sound of Sam Cooke. But more than half of them had swing grooves—"Hot House Ball" utilized the triplet feel of hip-hop, the modernized version of swing. The album opened with "Spider Fingers," a term Deadheads had given to the way Hornsby rapidly played the same note on piano. Garcia's guitar graced "Cruise Control."

Lyrically, Hornsby wove some good yarns on *Hot House*. "Walk in the Sun" was "about a guy who works in a strip joint and his girlfriend is one of the strippers." The video, shot in southern California, included appearances by members of the California Angels baseball team. "Big Rumble" nodded to his obsession with sports.

"We captured the festive quality of our live gig on this record much more than we have before," Hornsby said, noting an early performance tape he had found on the internet. "They're bootlegging my University of Miami senior recital from 1977—is that ridiculous, man? At least it doesn't suck too bad for happening 18 years ago." ■

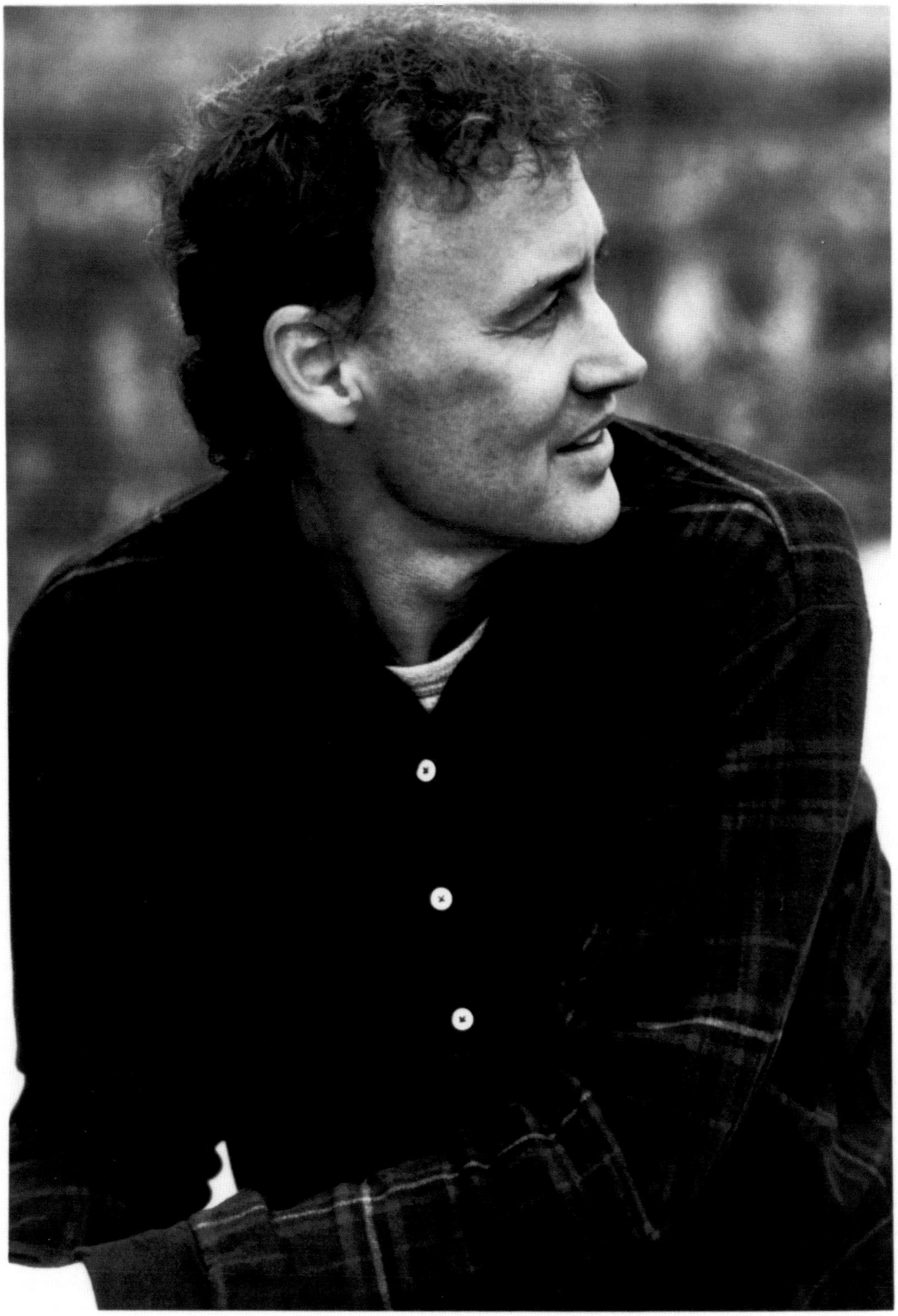

July 1995

Photo Credit: William Claxton

BRUCE HORNSBY

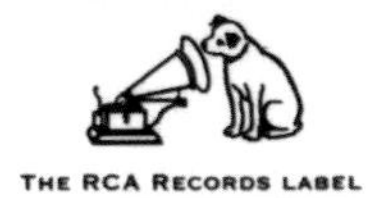

THE RCA RECORDS LABEL

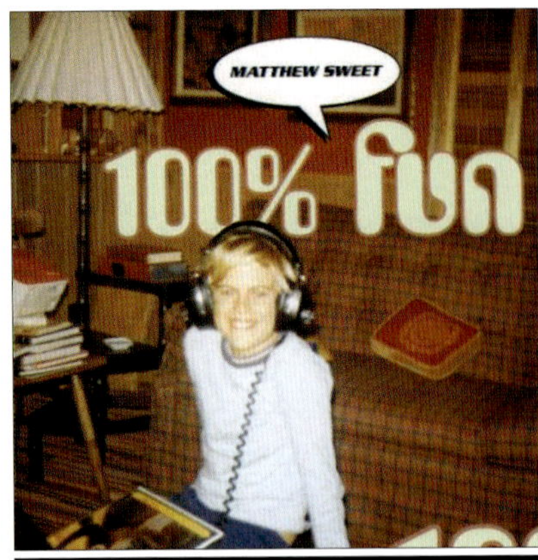

Billboard 200: *100% Fun* (#65)
Billboard Hot 100: "Sick of Myself" (#58)

The masterful Matthew Sweet kept the power-pop flame burning with the musical smarts of "Sick of Myself."

A CHAMPION of power-pop, Matthew Sweet delivered a breezy mix of guitar-heavy hooks with just enough emotional angst on his 1991 breakthrough album *Girlfriend*.

"The kind of music I do is a limited realm," Sweet said. "There are only so many people that are getting into thoughtful embraces with records, trying to feel their own lives through them."

He'd written a new favorite—"Sick of Myself," from his third album, *100% Fun*. An exuberant hit that one critic called "a compelling paean to self-loathing," Sweet and drummer Ric Menck composed the tune during a jam in the studio. "It's not a song I intellectualized a lot when I wrote it—it kinda popped out," Sweet said.

The lyric articulated the wonderment and insecurity that flourishes in the wake of infatuation. What counted was Sweet's raucous guitar and Menck's bashing—and *two* false endings.

"The actual take might have been the second time we played it," Sweet explained. "Ric ended on the wrong beat, so I kept motioning to him to do it again, to make a piece that was the right length that we could cut in. That's why we did multiple endings. It wasn't even a serious recording. When we went in and listened back to the take, we just liked the free feeling in it. So I overdubbed the bass and guitars to go along with the track the best I could. It really sounds like the band messing up!"

With its spirited mix of rock spontaneity and pure pop charm, "Sick of Myself" reached #2 on *Billboard*'s Modern Rock Tracks chart.

"It felt good to put it first on the record," Sweet said. "We thought it'd make a good alternative single, and it seemed to have this life of its own right out of the box. The record company did an edited version, too, and that made me mad. Nobody will use it." ■

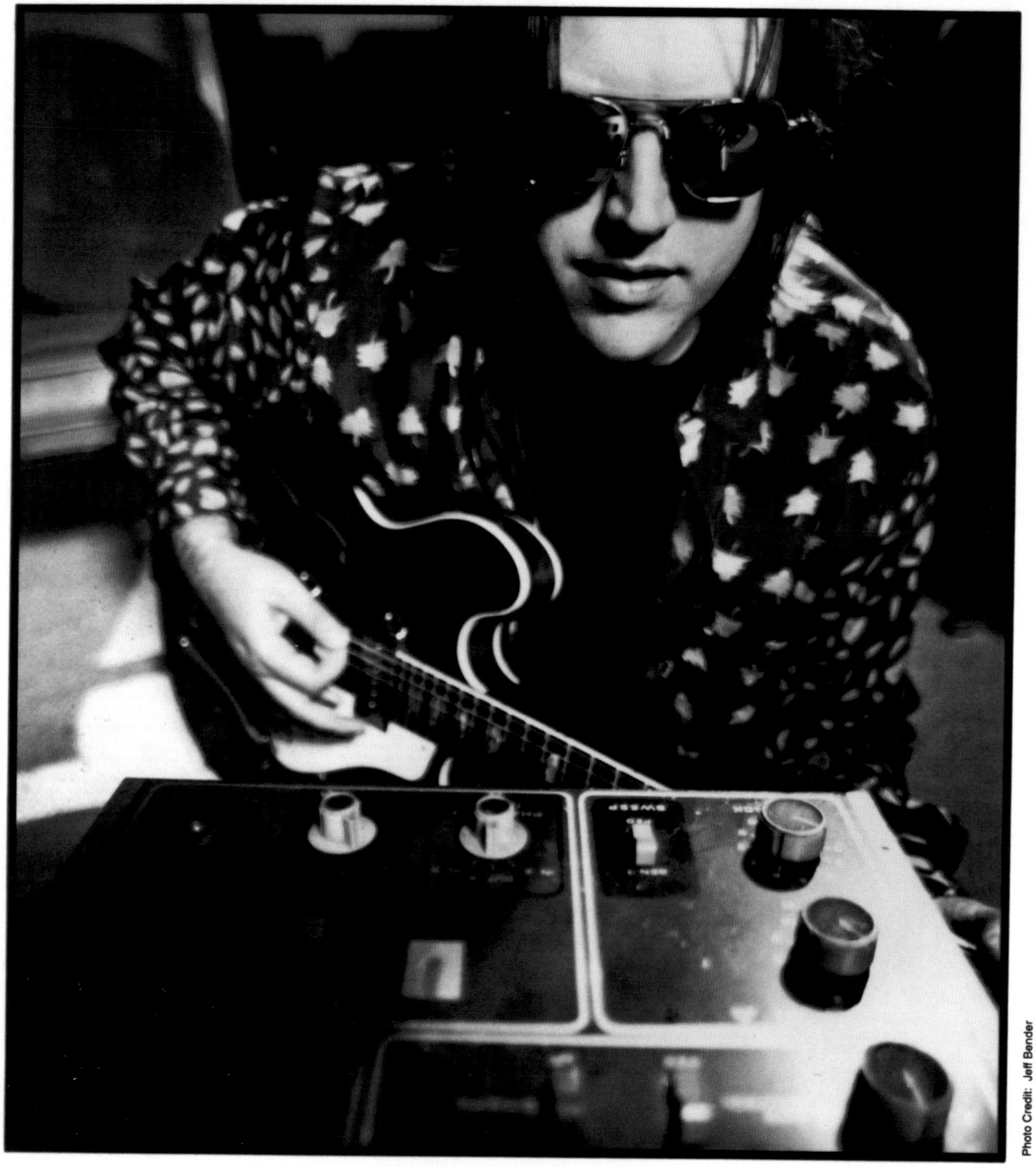

Photo Credit: Jeff Bender

MATTHEW SWEET

Management:
RUSSELL CARTER ARTIST MANAGEMENT

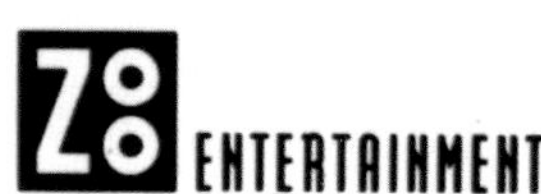

6363 Sunset Boulevard, Hollywood, California 90028 TEL 213 468 4200 FAX 213 468 4207

9501

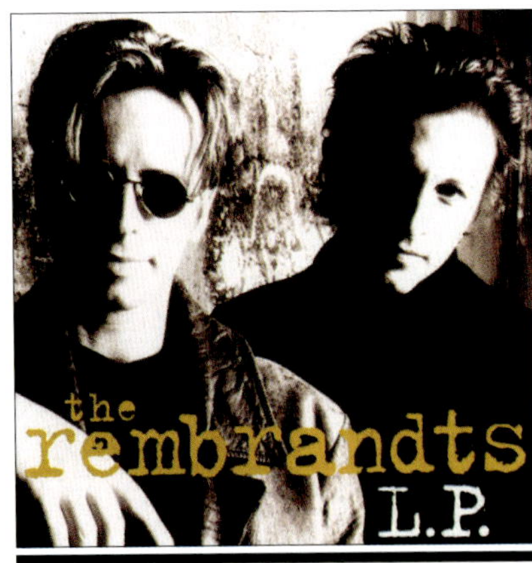

Billboard 200: *L.P.* (#23)
Billboard Hot 100: "I'll Be There for You"/"This House Is Not a Home" (#17)

The Rembrandts' melodic brand was retained on "I'll Be There for You," the theme for the Gen-X sitcom *Friends*.

THE REMBRANDTS—the Los Angeles-based duo of Danny Wilde and Phil Solem—used their guitars and voices like two brothers, writing, arranging and producing songs strong on the classic pop elements of layered harmonies and catchy melodies. The forte of the "brainy-pop" standard bearers could be traced directly to the Beatles and the Everly Brothers.

"We do it because we love it, not because it sounds like the Beatles," Wilde said. "If it's meant as a compliment, great. If not, so what? We're beyond that now. I would prefer for us to be called alternative, but we're pigeonholed as a pop band. But that's cool—when I grew up, it was pop music on the radio."

The Nineties began with Wilde and Solem, who were both in originally in the band Great Buildings, working up some new songs in a garage studio. The first new tune Wilde demoed, "Just the Way It Is, Baby," turned out to be his "proudest moment"—it led to a record deal and landed as the hit from the Rembrandts' self-titled debut album. A second album, *Untitled*, contained a modest single, "Johnny Have You Seen Her."

The Rembrandts' third album, *L.P.*, featured the theme song from the television smash comedy series *Friends*. The producers for the show had approached the duo about singing the opening theme, and they obliged. The show became a runaway hit, radio demanded a full-length version of the brief effervescent theme, and one was added to *L.P.* at the last minute as a "hidden track." The song was credited to the show's co-producers, David Crane and Marta Kaufman, as well as Kaufman's husband, composer Michael Skloff and lyricist Allee Willis, and Solem and Wilde.

The Rembrandts suddenly were transformed into a pop-culture behemoth, a shock to the principals. Wilde described it as "a double-edged sword. We've certainly benefited in terms of people knowing who we are. On the other hand, there's a part of me that's always wanted to be respected, not only as a singer but as a songwriter. When something like that comes around and it's the biggest thing that's ever happened in your life and you really didn't have much to do with the success of it, that's a weird sensation. I remember Jim Kerr of Simple Minds complaining about '(Don't You) Forget About Me' (the defining song in the 1985 hit film, *The Breakfast Club*). At the time I wondered why he wasn't happy about it. Now I understand his ambivalence." ■

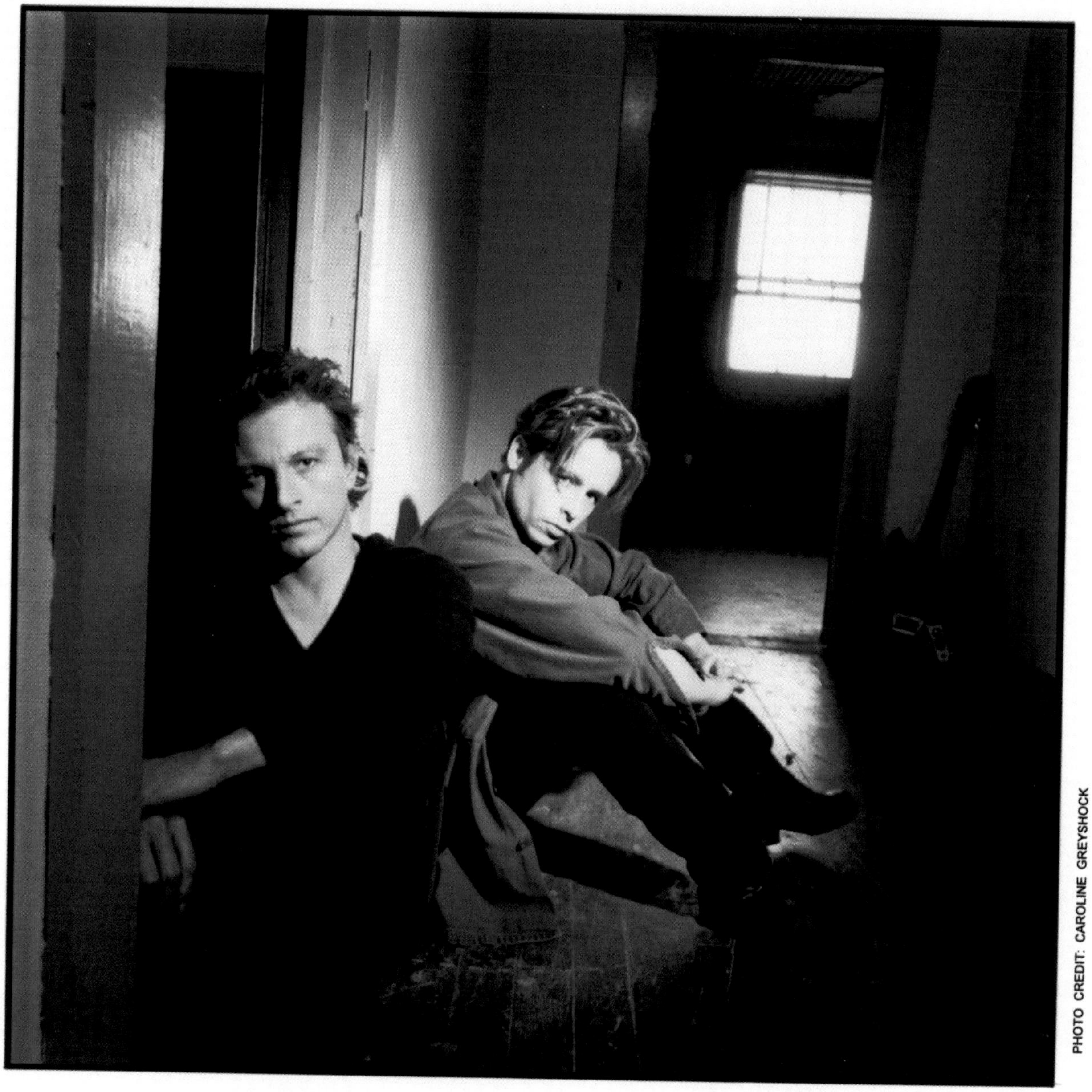

PHOTO CREDIT: CAROLINE GREYSHOCK

DANNY WILDE PHIL SOLEM

the rembrandts

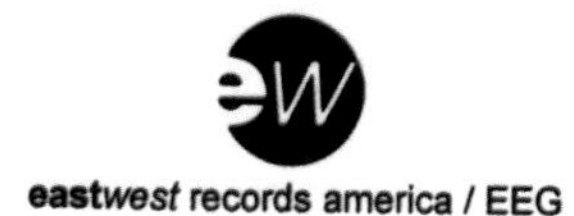

east*west* records america / EEG

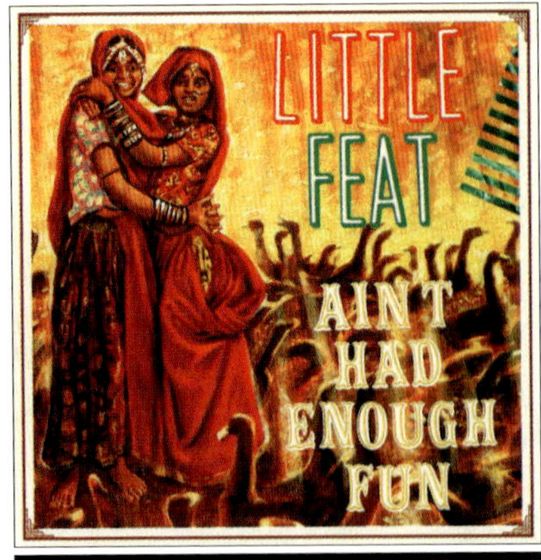

Billboard 200: *Ain't Had Enough Fun* (#154)

The addition of female vocalist Shaun Murphy provided Little Feat with a new attribute on *Ain't Had Enough Fun*.

EVER SINCE Little Feat's arrival in the Seventies, the quirky California group had set the standard for the multi-hyphenated musical form ("New Orleans R&B-funk-boogie," for example). Founder Lowell George's most memorable flights—"Easy to Slip," "Dixie Chicken," "Willin'"—were fueled by crazy inspiration, and with that rich concept, Little Feat built a fanatical cult following. After George's death in 1979, the band took a hiatus, resurfacing in 1988 to rekindle the magic for fans. The absence of George left a void, but the musical direction was guided by the faultless keyboard playing of keyboardist Bill Payne and the considerable talents of Richie Hayward (drums) and Paul Barrere (lead vocals and guitar).

Ain't Had Enough Fun, Little Feat's 12th release, found the band sailing above the norm again with a new singer, Shaun Murphy. She was a former session singer for Bob Seger, Eric Clapton and Bruce Hornsby, and her raspy voice added an invigorating twist to the band's time-tested rock 'n' roll gumbo. Murphy first met Payne and guitarist Fred Tackett during Seger's last tour in 1986. She'd already sung backup on three Little Feat albums by the time she first appeared as co-lead vocalist. Murphy brought a blues influence, pulling the band in a funky direction. The guys invited her to take a more prominent role in recording, and she helped write four songs on *Ain't Had Enough Fun*.

"I purposely put Shaun in the forefront on this record. I love what she does for this band," Payne said. "In general, she's really refocused our efforts on what this thing is about, which is musicianship. She comes in totally prepared. She's a real pretty lady, too, so there's that thing going where you want to perform well in front of her."

The results of the collaborative effort could be heard on "Shakeytown," a driving boogie with a touch of gospel backing vocals. "I had a couple of years to think about it," Payne said. "Little Feat is a great live group. How do you get it on tape? One of the prime factors was making sure that we erred on the side of performance rather than perfection. And there was a concentrated effort to make music that jumped and had some fire to it. The grooves had to be fun."

Little Feat dedicated the album to Neon Park, the band's longtime cover artist who had died after a long battle with Lou Gehrig's disease. Little Feat had survived trials that would have overpowered weaker hearts, engendering a sense of maturity and confidence few bands ever obtained.

"I always call this band 'the experiment in terror'—we've lived up to it in the last 25 years," Payne said. "The opportunity to work is more important to me than any dreams of popularity. I was sitting around the house trying to figure out why this band isn't more popular than it is, which is stupid, because people either don't know us or love the hell out of us.

"As it turns out, we've got plenty of popularity. Our music is all over the place when you think of sporting events and film trailers and commercials and people we've backed up who've sold gazillions of records. The sound of this band is pretty well known, but nobody out of the loop will go, 'Oh, that's Little Feat.' If we could get everybody to do that...I wouldn't live in Beverly Hills, but I could afford to." ■

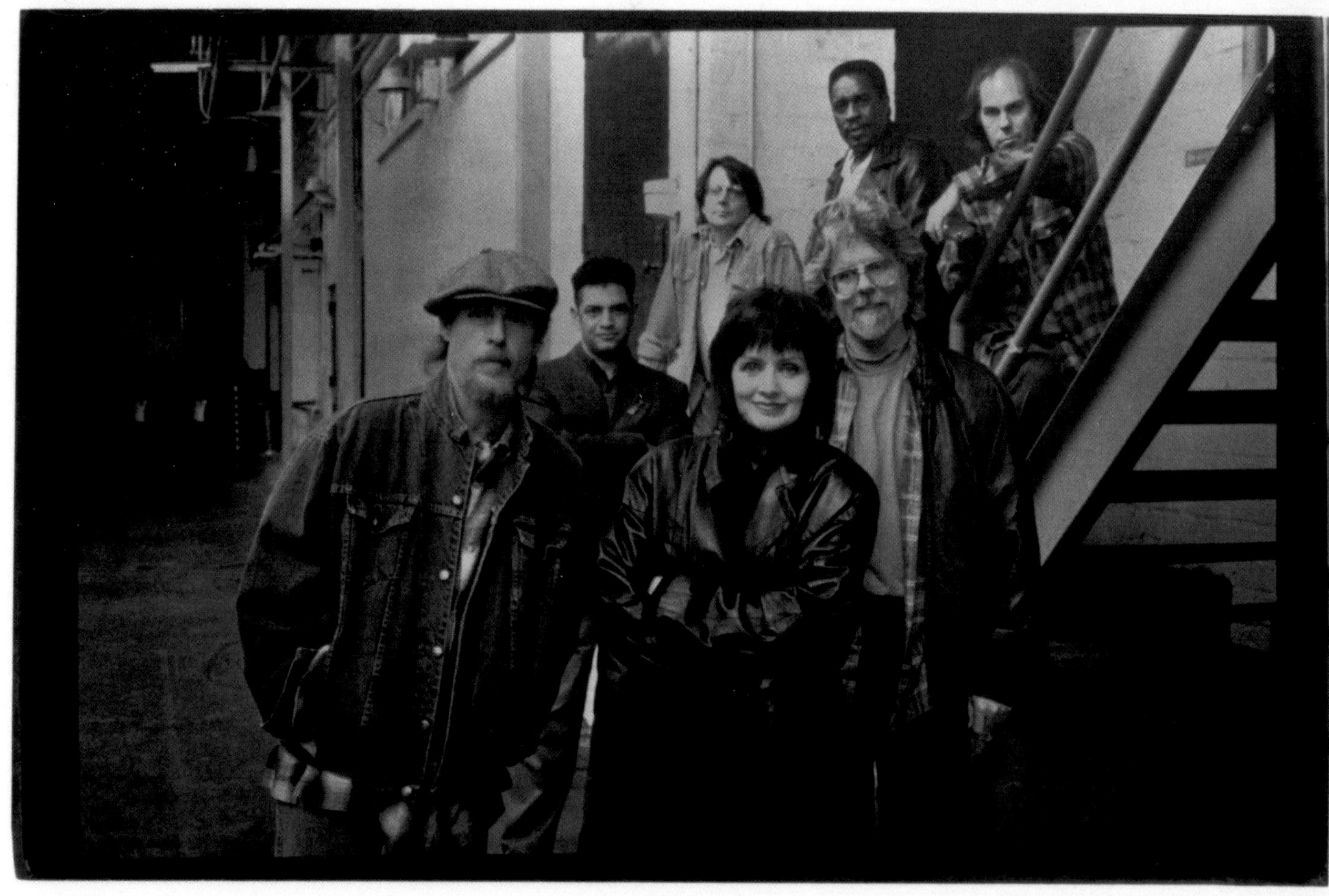

Photo Credit: Dennis Keeley

L to R: (front) Paul Barrere, Shaun Murphy; (middle) Ken Gradney, Fred Tackett; (back) Richie Hayward, Sam Clayton, Bill Payne.

LITTLE FEAT

PETER ASHER MANAGEMENT INC.

644 NORTH DOHENY DRIVE, LOS ANGELES, CALIFORNIA 90069 · 213 273-9433

ZOO ENTERTAINMENT 6363 Sunset Boulevard, Hollywood, California 90028 TEL 213 468 4200 FAX 213 468 4207

9503

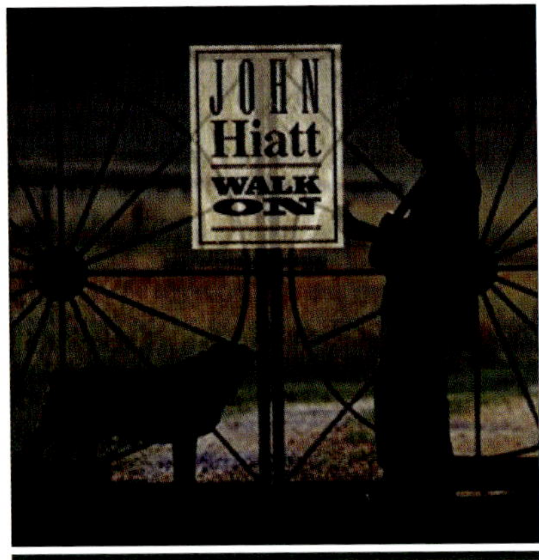

Billboard 200: *Walk On* (#48)

The album *Walk On* was the latest example of John Hiatt's exceptional and remarkably underappreciated talent.

THOUGH HE'D never attained superstar status, John Hiatt had enjoyed a career that spanned more than 20 years, uncommon in its persistency and longevity. After several near misses and a battle with alcoholism, he finally established his widening reputation in the late Eighties with *Bring the Family* and *Slow Turning*, albums that skewered his preconceptions of adulthood, filled with delightful and impassioned paeans to shaping up and settling down.

"I've had this funny little career," he said. "We keep growing in terms of people that hear the music, we're always moving forward. If I was backpedaling, I'd knock it on the head. But I feel like my best work is still in front of me. I've never been more committed to the music than I have been in the last four years. Maybe that's a feature of being 43 years old and sensing that there's a beginning and an end to things, getting while the getting's good."

Walk On was Hiatt's 13th album. The prolific singer-songwriter, who usually wrote at home, composed the songs during the tour in support of 1993's rocking *Perfectly Good Guitar.*

"It was out of necessity," he said. "We were on the road for about 14 months. The 22 hours a day that you're not onstage get kinda gray after a while, like a blur. It's a weird existence. I was looking for some inspiration. To save my sanity, I just started writing in hotel rooms and dressing rooms as a diversion. I think that's why the music contrasts from the last record. There's a lot of sexual longing and coming-and-going stuff in there."

Hiatt's hallmark sense of style, intelligence and humor revealed itself on the searing "Cry Love" and the countrified "Ethylene," a jaunty love song. The raucous "Shredding the Document" railed against talk-show culture, and several meditations concerned wrestling with his old demons, not as some enigmatic abridgment but in the context of pondering the contour of memories and experiences. His friend Bonnie Raitt joined him on the soulful "I Can't Wait."

"I couldn't figure out how to sing that song, it had me baffled," Hiatt said. "I tried this falsetto thing, and it worked great, we got a bag on it—I started feeling like Pops Staples or something. Bonnie came to mind as playing that Mavis Staples role—not really a duet but throwing in a line here and there."

Hiatt's fine band featured new guitarist and mandolin player David Immergluck from Camper Van Beethoven, who helped generate a bigger-than-life acoustic sound. "The first time I ever played with him was while we were rolling tape on an early song we cut. He played that wacky pedal steel through some kind of stomp box—it sounds like woodpeckers on acid. I thought, 'Well, I think he'll work out okay.'" ■

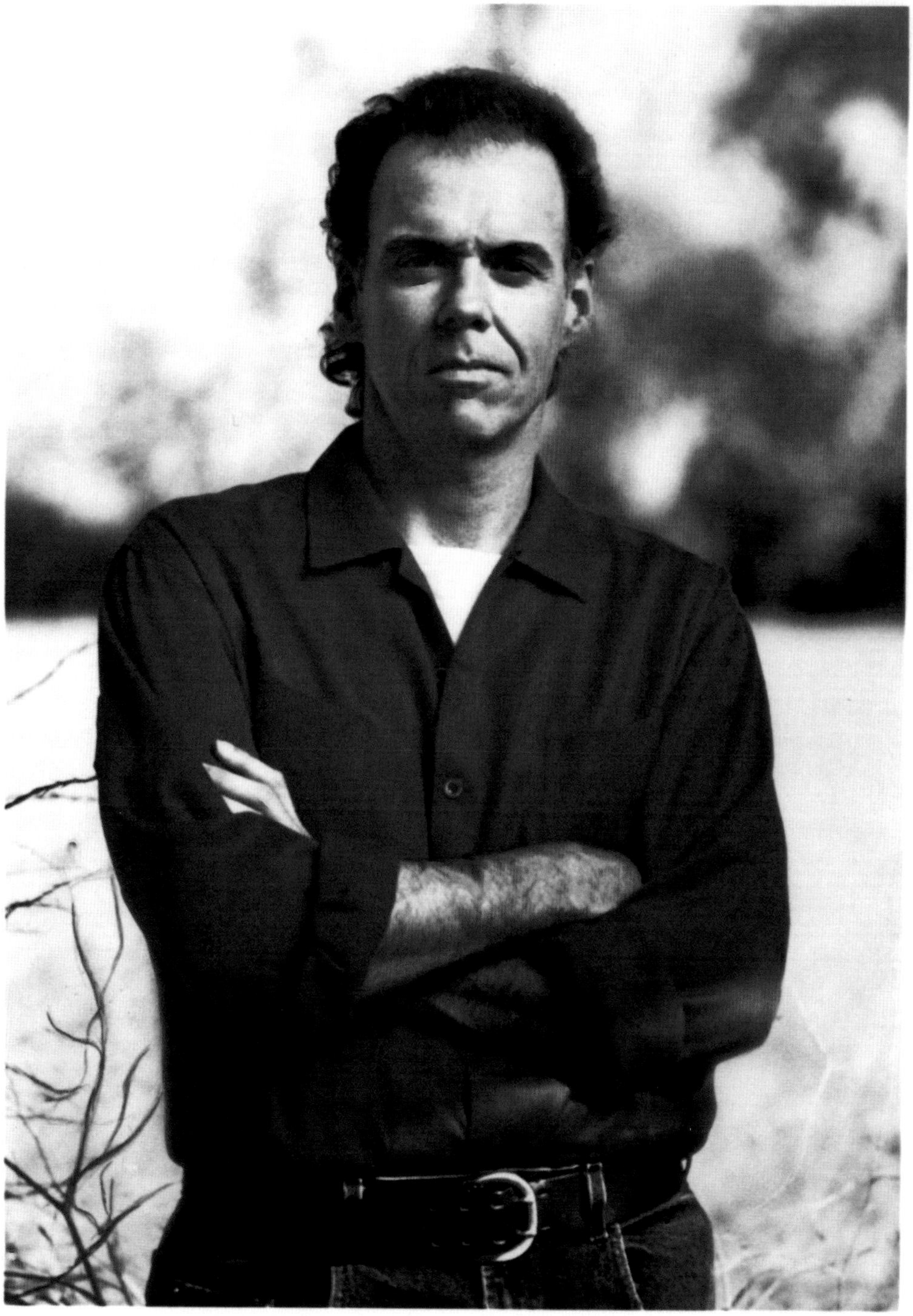

Photo credit: Lester Cohen © 1995

JOHN · HIATT

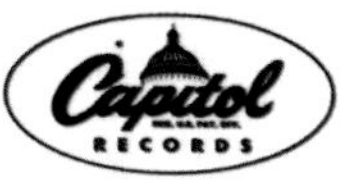

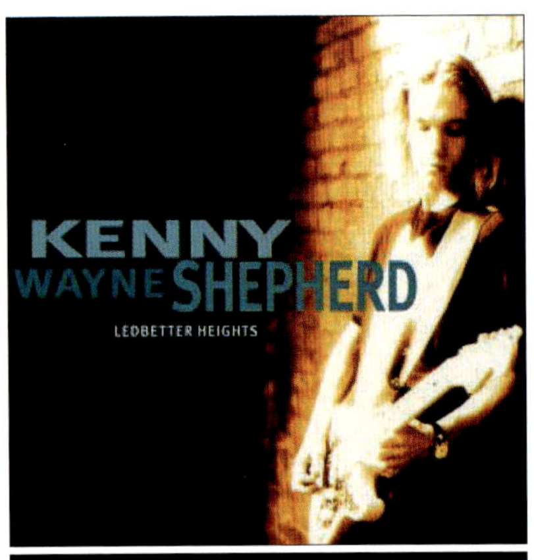

Billboard 200: *Ledbetter Heights* (#108)

Guitarist Kenny Wayne Shepherd dazzled audiences, critics and fellow players on his debut, *Ledbetter Heights*.

"**THE NEXT** Stevie Ray Vaughan" was a phrase thrown around about countless young blues guitar hopefuls. Eighteen-year-old Kenny Wayne Shepherd emerged as a legitimate successor.

There was no doubt about Shepherd's talent or commercial potential. The Louisiana native had traded licks with icons like B.B. King and Robert Cray, opened a few dates for the Eagles and Bob Dylan and landed an official endorsement deal with Fender Guitars. Onstage, his long, straight blond hair hid his baby face every time he looked down at his vintage reissue 1961 Stratocaster. The fiery blues-rock sound recalled the poised, forceful, smart style of his hero.

"Anybody that's doing this kind of music is gonna get compared to Stevie Ray Vaughan, especially somebody like me, who was heavily influenced by him," Shepherd said. "But Stevie's owed a lot of credit. He's the one who's really responsible for a lot of the attention the blues is getting."

Shepherd started playing guitar at age 7, and at 13 the blind bluesman Bryan Lee brought him onstage in New Orleans. "I don't know who I got this gift from—nobody in my family plays anything," Shepherd said. "I believe it's something you're blessed with. But I was surrounded by a lot of the music business. I'm managed by my dad, who was a radio station programmer for 25 years. This project's been going on a lot longer than most people know. The whole idea was conceived when I was 14 years old, and it's been building and building since then. When I went into the studio, I knew what I wanted it to sound like."

Ledbetter Heights, Shepherd's debut album, topped *Billboard*'s blues chart, and the single "Déjà Voodoo" became the most requested song on mainstream rock radio stations. "Born with a Broken Heart," a tribute to legendary guitarists, adopted a Vaughan-like seething groove. On Bukka White's "Aberdeen," Shepherd picked up an acoustic guitar for some tasty Delta slide riffs, then plugged in and kicked into the tune's second half. But wasn't life experience an important element in traditional blues?

"I don't think that's necessarily a big deal," Shepherd said. "I know I've got many years ahead of me, more maturing to do. But I have things to dwell on now. Everybody gets their feelings hurt, everybody gets upset, and that's what the music is about, dealing with problems. I don't think it's a matter of age; it's a matter of point of view."

The hype had created high expectations for Shepherd, but he remained undaunted. "I sang one song on this record just to let everybody know that I'm working on it, but right now, I feel like I can do more with my hands than I can with my voice," he said. "You can't compare the stress levels to a normal job, because it's a whole new environment and set of rules to get used to. But I would rather be doing this than having to wake up every day and be somebody at a big nine-to-five company." ■

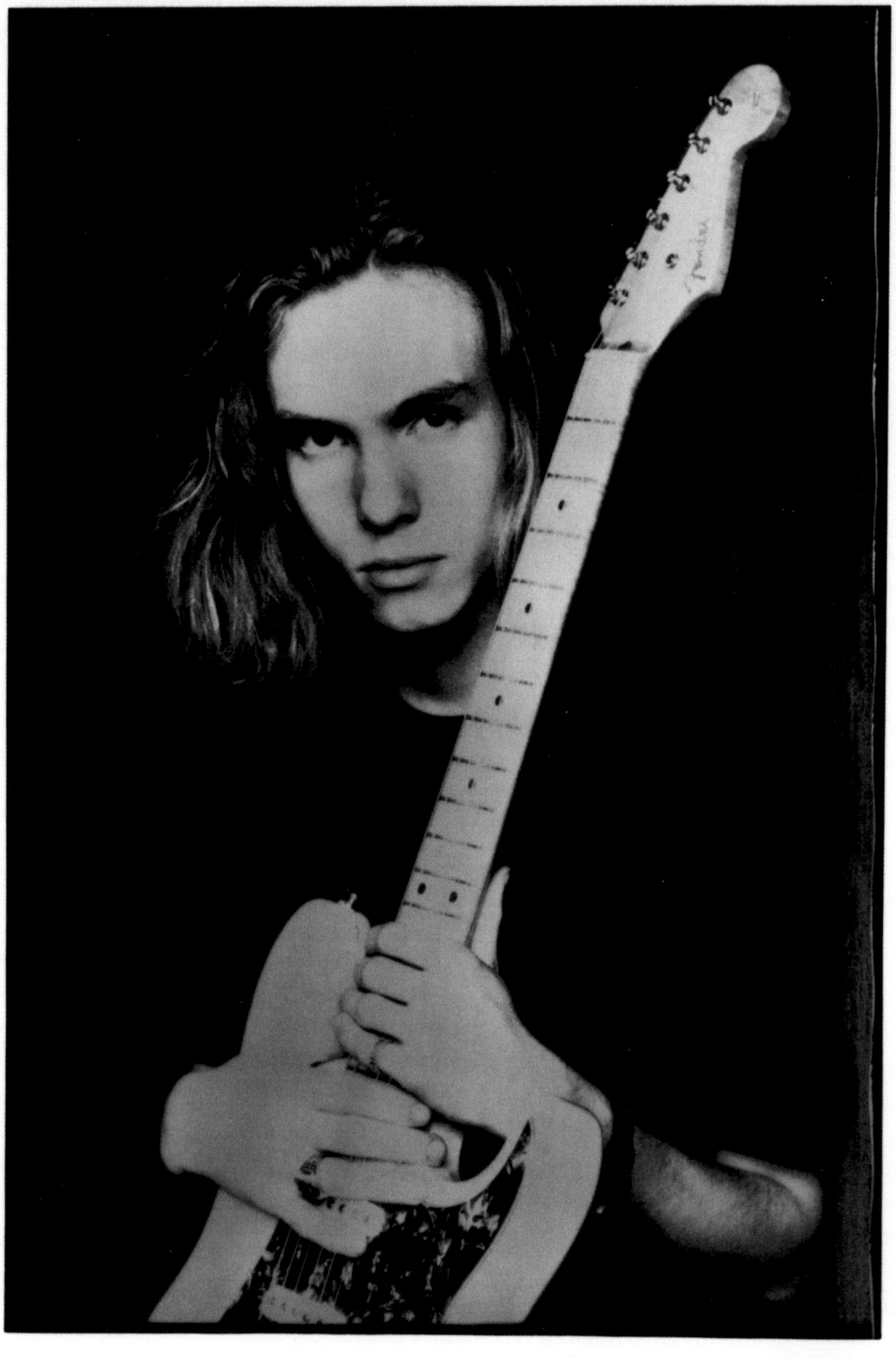

Photo Credit: Caroline Greyshock

Kenny Wayne Shepherd

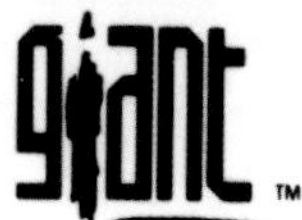

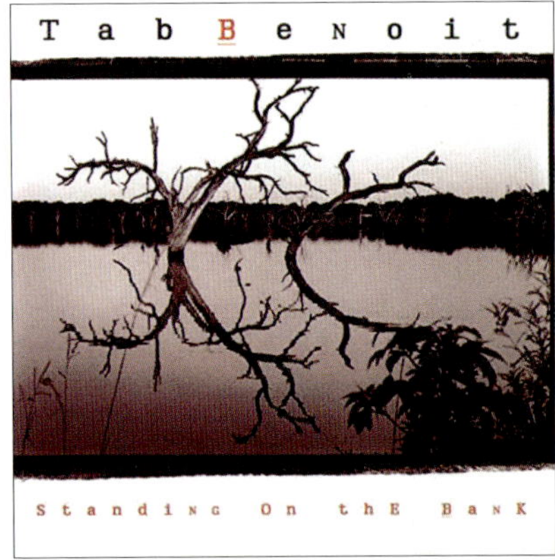

Tab Benoit's emotional discreteness in playing the blues gave his set *Standing on the Bank* a striking vivacity.

A SELF-TAUGHT Louisiana bluesman, Tad Benoit was raised in Houma, a small Gulf Coast oil town. "I had a book that showed you how to play chords," he said. "After I learned the first three, I got rid of the book." He gained acceptance at Tabby's Blues Box and Heritage Hall, a run-down, shotgun-style brick building where the proprietor of the club told him, "If you play the blues, you'll always have a job."

Benoit ventured off to New Orleans and soon landed a recording contract with Texas-based Justice Records. Hitting the road hard, he watched the attendance at his concerts increase—his live performances were defined by his raunchy, crisp Telecaster licks. Every young white blues guitarist had to endure comparisons with the late Stevie Ray Vaughan, and Benoit was no different.

"I didn't aspire to be the 'next' anybody. I played in my room by myself for a long time before I played in front of people," he said. "Stevie Ray got to more people with the blues that anybody in recent years. His licks were pretty simple and straightforward, but nobody plays with that fire. What you're hearing is my interpretation of all the blues I've heard, from B.B. King to Guitar Slim, Buddy Guy, Albert King, Albert Collins, Freddie King. And that's the same place Stevie Ray got his stuff from."

Benoit seemed intent on blazing his own trail. Instead of going off into blues-rock territory, he took a step backward technologically—*Standing on the Bank*, his third album, captured his Cajun-influenced blues by recording live directly to two-track, an unforgiving "first take" method.

"It's almost impossible to be as spontaneous in the studio as at a gig, but I've always tried," Benoit said. "When you record like this, everybody's working at the same time. The whole band is playing, and the producer and engineer in the booth are mixing. Everybody knows you have one shot—'Let's slam it,' that's the feeling."

Six of Benoit's original songs were interspersed with covers of songs by Leon Russell, Willie Dixon and Blind Lemon Jefferson. "Rainy Day Blues" was a duet with Willie Nelson, his occasional golf partner.

"It's his blues song—we just got in the studio and plugged in," Benoit said. "It's hard to play when Willie Nelson is sitting there. That's one of the reasons I play music, to meet guys like him." ■

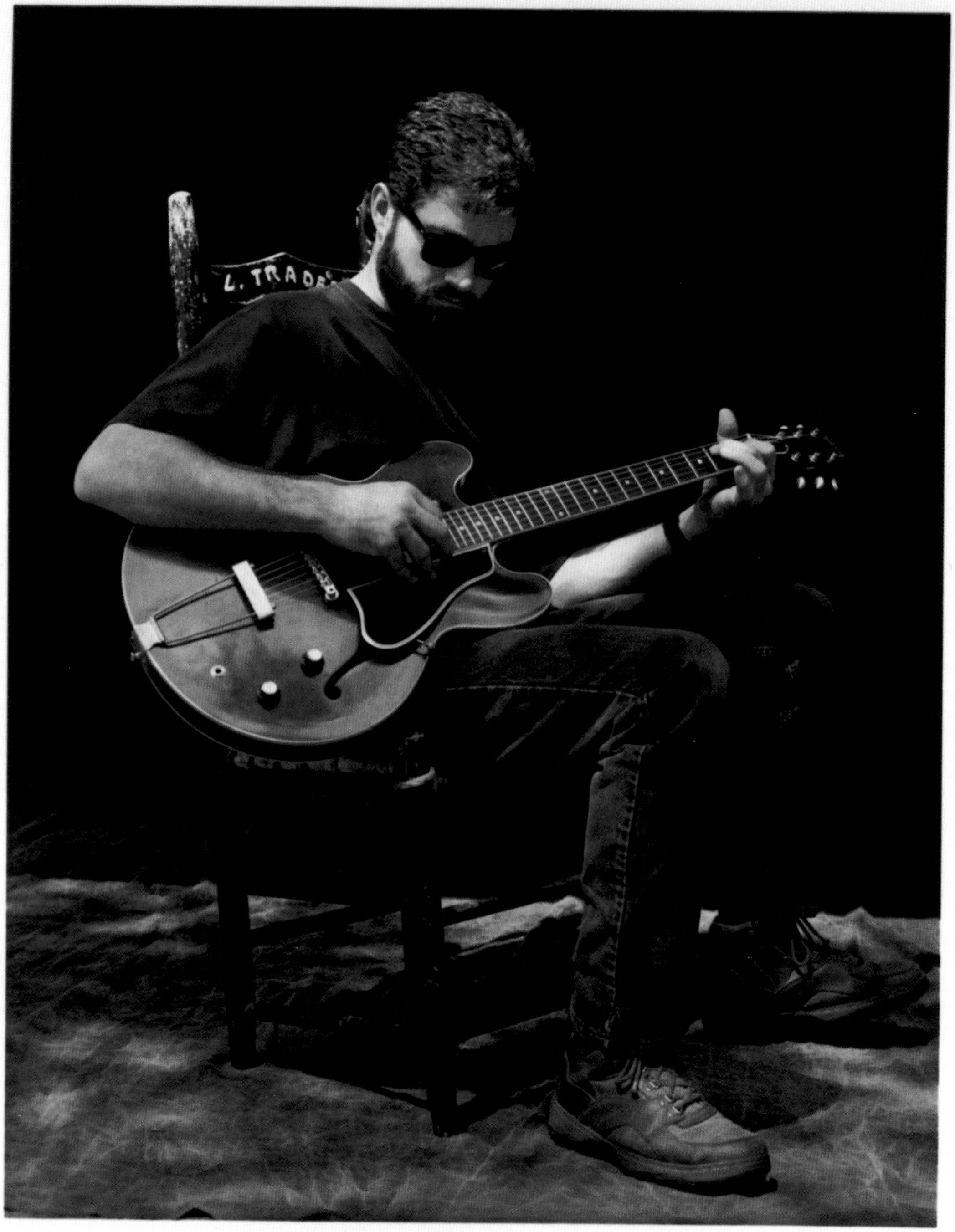

TAB BENOIT

Ruby Artist Management 504 876 5181

Photography by Wyatt McSpadden

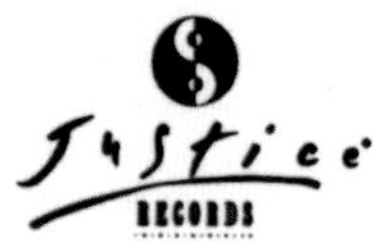

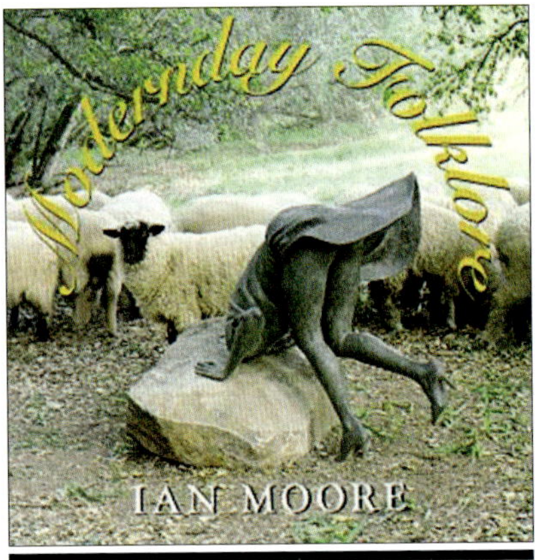

Austin-based blues-rocker Ian Moore revamped his initial image with his blazing work on *Modernday Folklore*.

IN THE years after Stevie Ray Vaughan died, new claimants to the title of Texas guitar hotshot were a dime a dozen. But Ian Moore was worth watching closely.

"It's real hard being a guitarist playing blues out of Austin—you're gonna get that tag," the former Joe Ely sideman said of the inevitable comparisons with Vaughan. "The stereotypes come with the way you're marketed. Stevie Ray used to tell me, 'People did that to me—they'd say I was just another Hendrix.' Worse things have been endured."

Moore had earned opening spots for the Rolling Stones and ZZ Top when Capricorn Records signed him in the early Nineties. Barely out of his teens, he was already considered a veteran of the Austin scene. The label sought to build up the budding guitar prodigy, capitalizing on his flashy blues-rock licks.

But for the most part, the slender, long-haired Moore hated that guitar-hero tag, which didn't really reflect his musical sensibilities. So he was "building a story," in music biz parlance.

"You never know who's going to have the vision," Moore said. "Before I signed with Capricorn, I talked with Interscope and had a big fight with the president—'You're going to make what we want, a Texas guitar-rock album, nothing else.' And EMI had left me in limbo—they were trying to make me feel good about being there because they had George Thorogood and Huey Lewis, but what do I have in common with those two bands? It seems if you have any roots at all, you're in for a tough ride."

Cutting his third album, *Modernday Folklore*, Moore looked toward a more expansive sound. He jolted fans with tunes that referenced classic Southern rock, soul and even New Orleans funk. The album landed his tom-tom-powered "Muddy Jesus" on the album-rock radio charts, a song that followed Moore's belief that modern religion and society were invariably skewed, depicting Jesus "as a fast-talking, snake-oil salesman in Juarez who's determined to get across the Mexican border."

"I'm not some Los Angeles metal boy," he said. "Honestly, aside from Hendrix and a little Cream and Led Zeppelin, I never really listened to rock 'n' roll. I've spent my life always trying to get back to where the music started, trying to define myself as an individual, no parameters. I felt it in school with my peers, and I feel it even stronger now. My vision of who I am isn't as narrow as other people's. It isn't a problem with people who have seen me several times—they know the moods I have, the sides of my character." ■

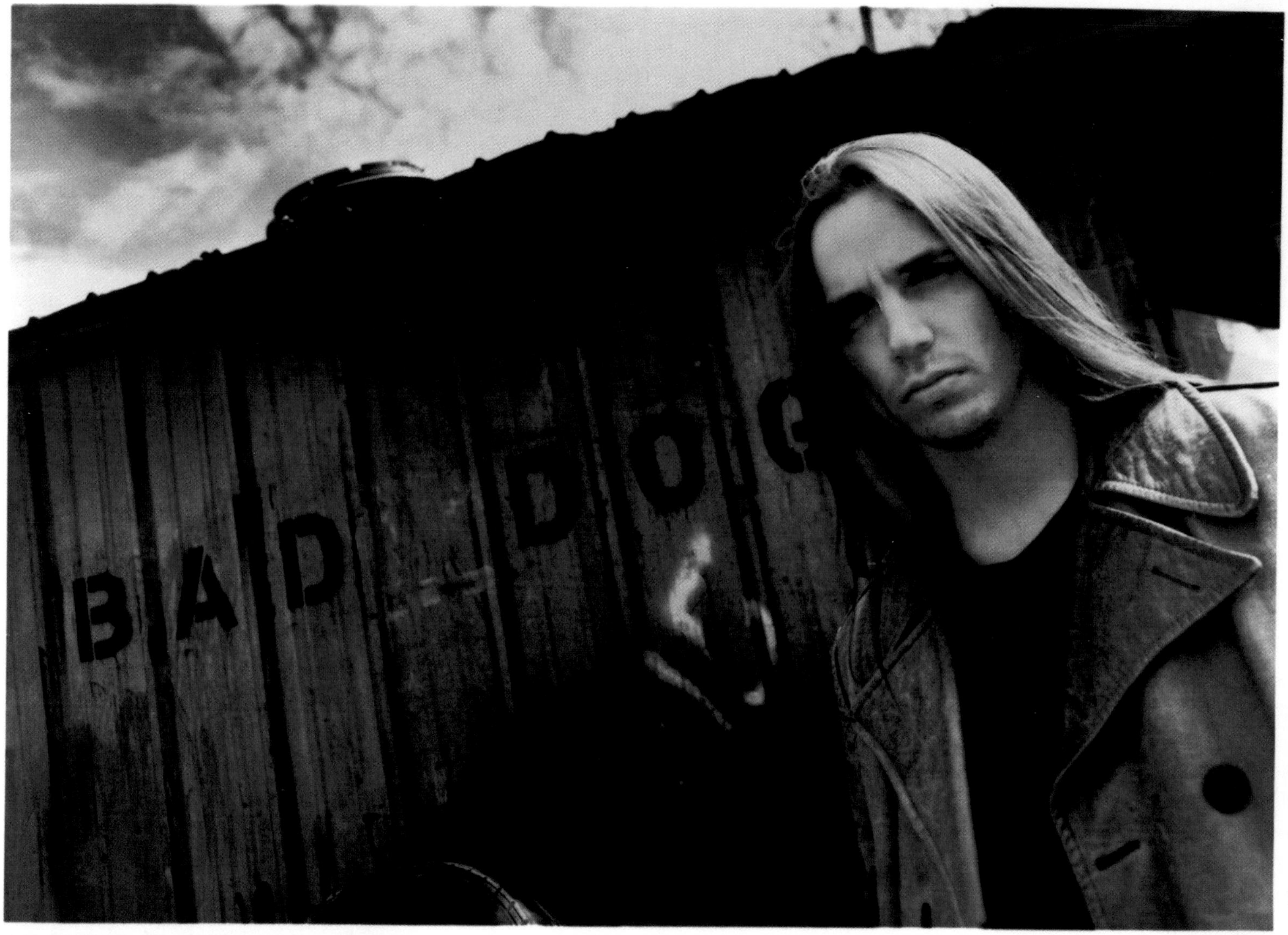

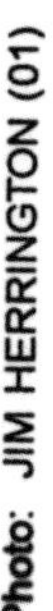

IAN MOORE

Capricorn

2205 STATE STREET
NASHVILLE, TN 37203
(615) 320-8470

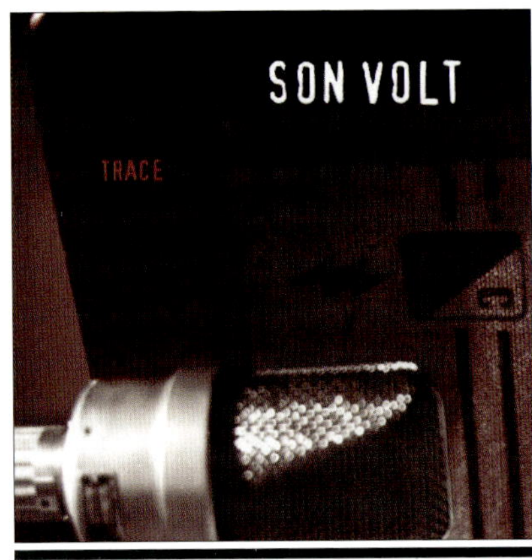

Billboard 200: *Trace* (#166)

Formed by Jay Farrar following the breakup of Uncle Tupelo, Son Volt distilled alt-country greatness on *Trace*.

MANAGING TO convey the vision and spirit of country-rock in the early Nineties, Uncle Tupelo disseminated a blend of urban grit and rural keening. Led by the songwriting team of Jay Farrar and Jeff Tweedy, the Midwestern band released three critically acclaimed albums and built a national following through touring. But in 1994, Uncle Tupelo unexpectedly packed it in when Farrar decided to exit. Tweedy regrouped as Wilco.

"It just seemed like the band had run its course," Farrar said. "There wasn't a lot of creativity or communication anymore."

With Son Volt, his new band, Farrar turned Uncle Tupelo's distinctly American roots-rock sound on its edge. The album *Trace* highlighted the dynamics between folk-country purity, loud riffs and homespun values. As a songwriter, Farrar was the shining light of a trend that had given way to a new set of buzz words—"rural contemporary," "no depression," "hip county," "y'allternative"...

"...'Insurgent country,' whatever—I should keep a list," Farrar said in a slow, laconic manner. "It's interesting to hear the names they keep coming up with. But being put at the forefront of a so-called movement isn't something I'm real comfortable with. Bands have been playing this type of music all along. It just seems to go in cycles as to when people pay attention to it."

Trace included Farrar's choicest songs to date. The edgy anthem "Drown," a minor rock radio and college hit, rocked like raved-up Neil Young. While writing the album, Farrar spent a lot of time driving up and down I-55, hoping to capture what he called "the rhythm of the mighty Mississippi River." The members of Son Volt were scattered all over the map—brothers Jim and Dave Boquist (the bassist and guitarist) were long-time Minneapolis scene veterans, original Tupelo drummer Mike Heidorn lived in St. Louis, and Farrar was based in New Orleans. During his trips to rehearse, Farrar filtered images of aimlessness, wandering and late-night radio into his work.

"Doing all that solitary driving seems to be a good thing to do, as far as songwriting goes," Farrar explained. "I guess I never had enough tapes to listen to, so the radio was interesting—it was more of a gamble to try and find something. Late at night there's not a whole lot on, but I picked up this AM station, WWL that comes out of Louisiana. From midnight to 6, they had this show called 'The Road Gang'—they'd play older country music and truck-driving songs. Some of those elements wound up in my songs."

Trace was recorded before Son Volt had ever performed live. On tour, Farrar had the stage presence of drying paint, but "the shah of shy" moved to the front of the stage. "I wanted to concentrate more on rhythm guitar playing, and I enjoy it a lot, but singing every song was something I had to get acclimated to. I'm not completely comfortable with it, but it does offer a lot of freedom. It's not something I think about!" ■

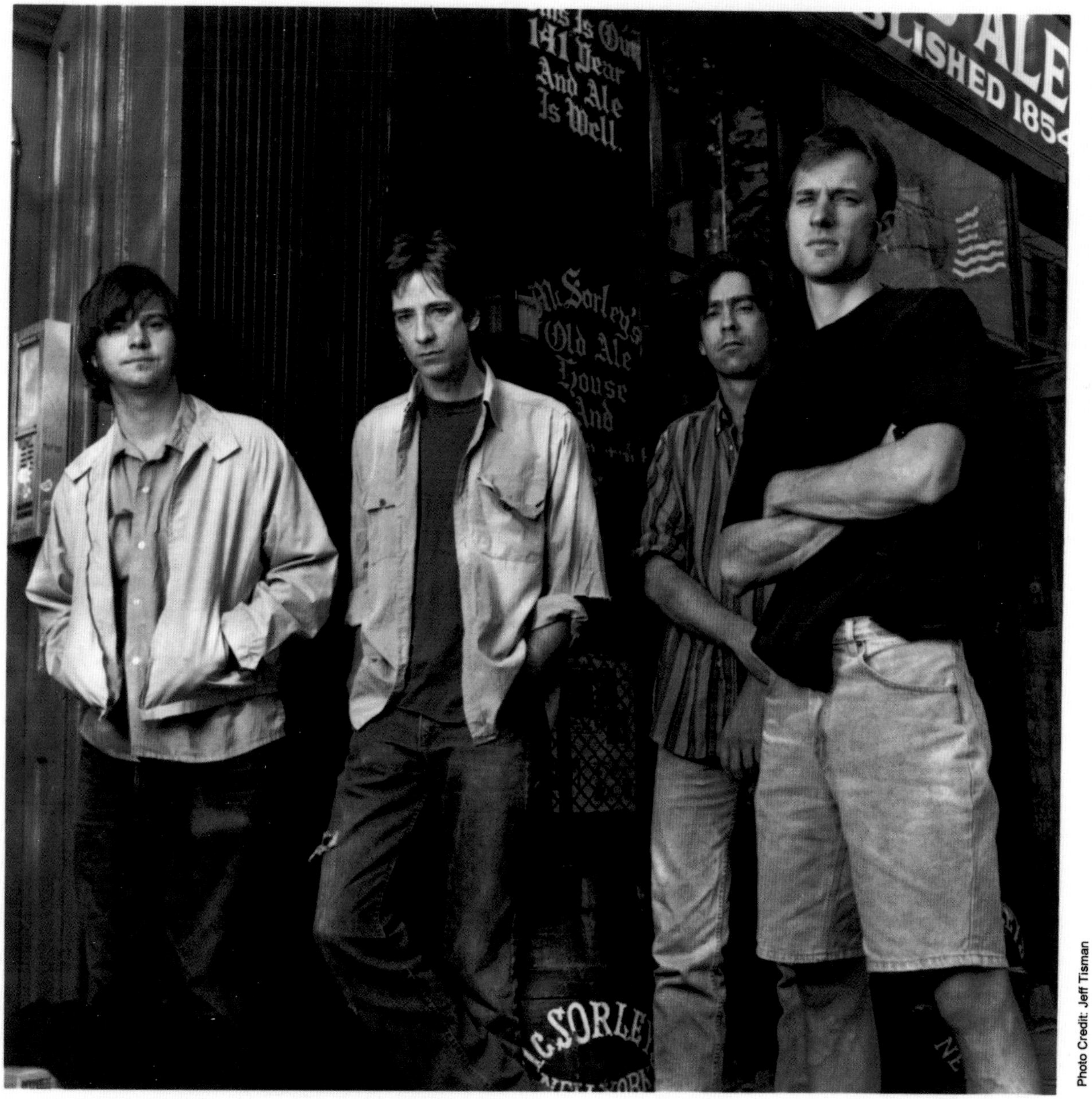

Photo Credit: Jeff Tisman

Jay Farrar Jim Boquist Dave Boquist Mike Heidorn

SON VOLT

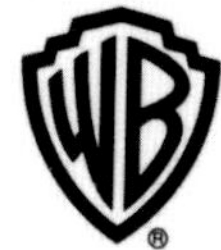

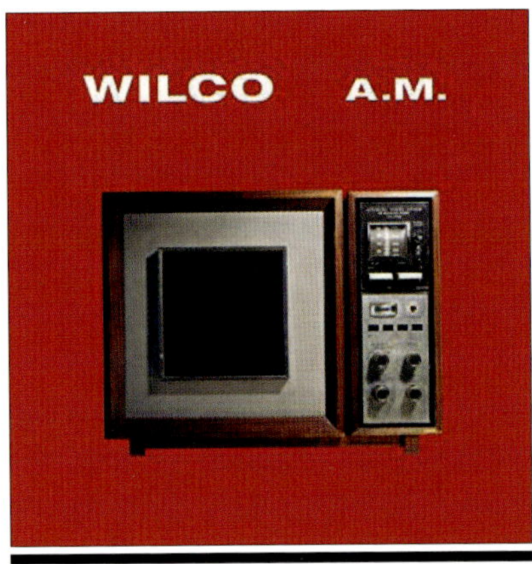

After the cessation of the seminal roots band Uncle Tupelo, Jeff Tweedy and the remaining members set up Wilco.

AS A member of Uncle Tupelo, Jeff Tweedy would contribute a half-dozen songs to one of the group's albums; the rest were penned by bandmate Jay Farrar. Together they worked up a blend of twangy country music with punky guitar noise. After Uncle Tupelo abruptly disbanded in 1994, Farrar started Son Volt while Tweedy regrouped with the rest of the Uncle Tupelo lineup and founded Wilco.

"There's no acrimony, but I'm sure a rivalry exists between us," Tweedy said. "Even though Jay had his reasons for leaving, both personal and creative, we were really thrown for a loop. It took us a little while to find our footing again."

Bassist Jay Stirratt, who was also a member of Uncle Tupelo, said his old group was just a vaunted cult band. "People ask me if it was a post-punk roots revival thing. I always though Uncle Tupelo could turn people on. I knew the albums would be liked—it was fun to be in for a while. Sometimes making a few records and breaking up is the best thing for a pseudo-legend."

A.M., Wilco's seductive debut album, picked up where Uncle Tupelo left off. The band was equally adept at bashing out catchy country ramblings and punchy alternative-rock values with exuberance and humor, displaying an unaffected, modest quality. "Box Full of Letters," a typically loose tale of tribulation and remorse, featured Tweedy's deadpan vocal and dueling guitar riffs. It was obvious—Tweedy was a guy who loved to spin one up and monitor his record collection.

"I used to work in a record store, and I still spend all my spare time listening to music," he said. "There are so many classic albums out there, works of genius that nobody's ever heard of for whatever reasons. I can't figure out why people wouldn't buy those instead of ours!"

A.M. was the kind of album that gave roots rock a good name—Tweedy had an acute understanding of Americana idioms—but he couldn't fathom why every review of Wilco mentioned Gram Parsons' influence.

"People use Gram Parsons as the country-rock name to drop like they use the Velvet Underground as the alternative-rock name to drop. I don't think they've even heard Gram Parsons' music. I mean, why not Neil Young? In my mind, he did more to advance what Wilco is doing now." ■

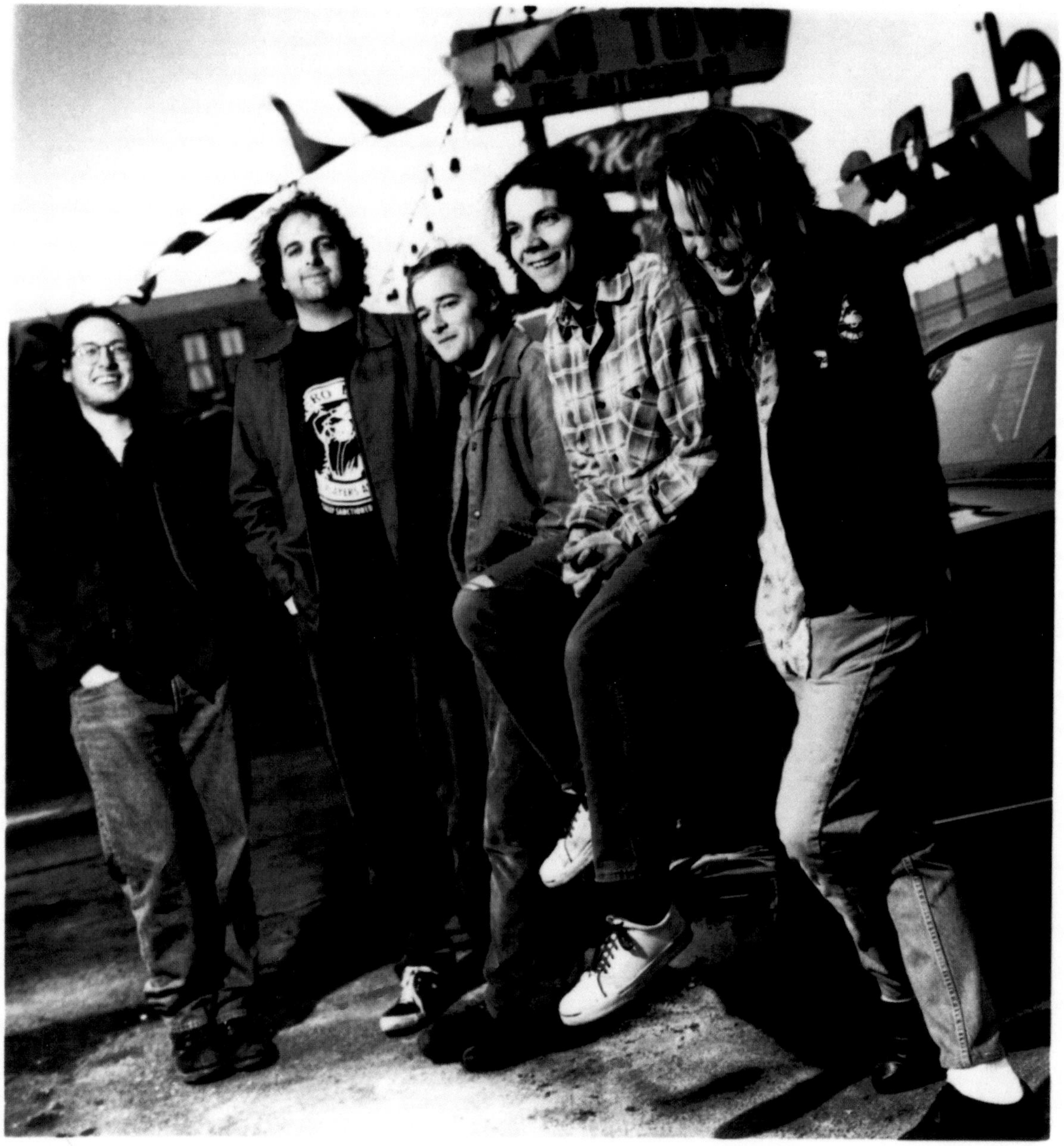

Photo Credit Brad Miller

Max Johnston Ken Coomer John Stirratt Jeff Tweedy Jay Bennett

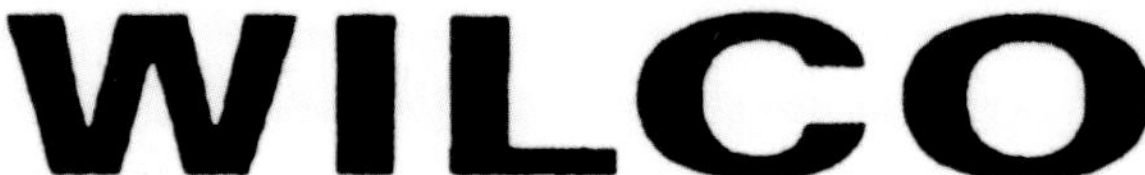

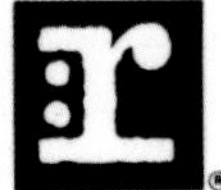

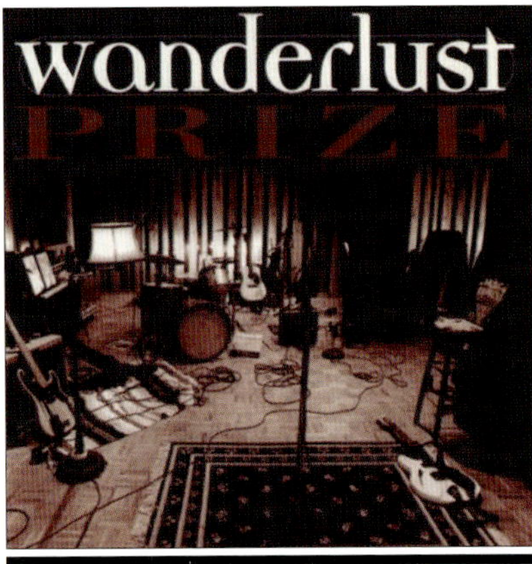

Amid a surfeit of alternative-rock groups, Wanderlust acknowledged classic influences on the hit "I Walked."

WANDERLUST'S MUSICAL language was jangly Rickenbacker guitars, well-harmonized choruses and melodic hooks with an edge. It spoke to a heritage that stretched back as far as the Byrds and the Beatles, from Big Star to Teenage Fanclub. Vocalist and guitarist Scot Sax made no apologies.

"It's like you dress a certain way because of the way you were brought up and the town you live in," he said. "You can either wear acid-washed jeans, which were in for about a year, or wear classic jeans that were in when you were a kid, an adult—forever. Our songs aren't like anybody else's, but the style in which we're playing them is reminiscent of the Seventies and Sixties—that's when the only albums I listen to were made. I can't help it. I feel embarrassed when we run into radio people and I'm not familiar with any of the new bands. I grew up listening to David Bowie and Bob Dylan and Queen and Fleetwood Mac. I love that kind of music so much that it's tough to go on to other stuff."

Wanderlust formed in 1993, signed to a label rather quickly and recorded *Prize* for less than some groups spent on catering. A buzz developed around the Pennsylvania quartet when the debut album was released—the rousing single "I Walked" hit pay dirt, reaching #28 on *Billboard*'s album rock chart.

"The band pokes fun at me because I'm the laziest of the four guys—'You don't walk anywhere!'" Sax laughed.

When Sax's older brother by ten years was growing up and there would be turmoil in the house, he would go out and walk all night. "I remember him not being home too often," Sax said. "I talked to my mom and asked, 'Am I accurate on this?' They're not happy memories for her. My brother isn't a confrontational person. If things were rough, it was like running away from home for a night—he came back the next morning. He felt it was therapeutic. He'd feel himself starting over just as the day does. I've since had my own times like that."

Displaying the genre's intelligence and sophistication, "I Walked" described how to let it go—"it" being an emotional decision or a lover. Sax's brother was now a family man running a hair salon.

"I look up to him for a lot of things," Sax said. "When I was little, he hipped me to a lot of the best music in the world, the stuff that I still listen to today. I was just totally mesmerized, and I still am—that's the most exciting thing in the world to me. Stages are about five feet higher than the floor, and you should realize that when you get on one. It's been tough playing clubs in Philadelphia over the years—I would have that star attitude and it didn't always go over well with the other bands, but I always felt like getting onstage was a big thing, and I played it up. It's so great now to do across the country what I've been doing in my hometown. It's a big part of the dream." ■

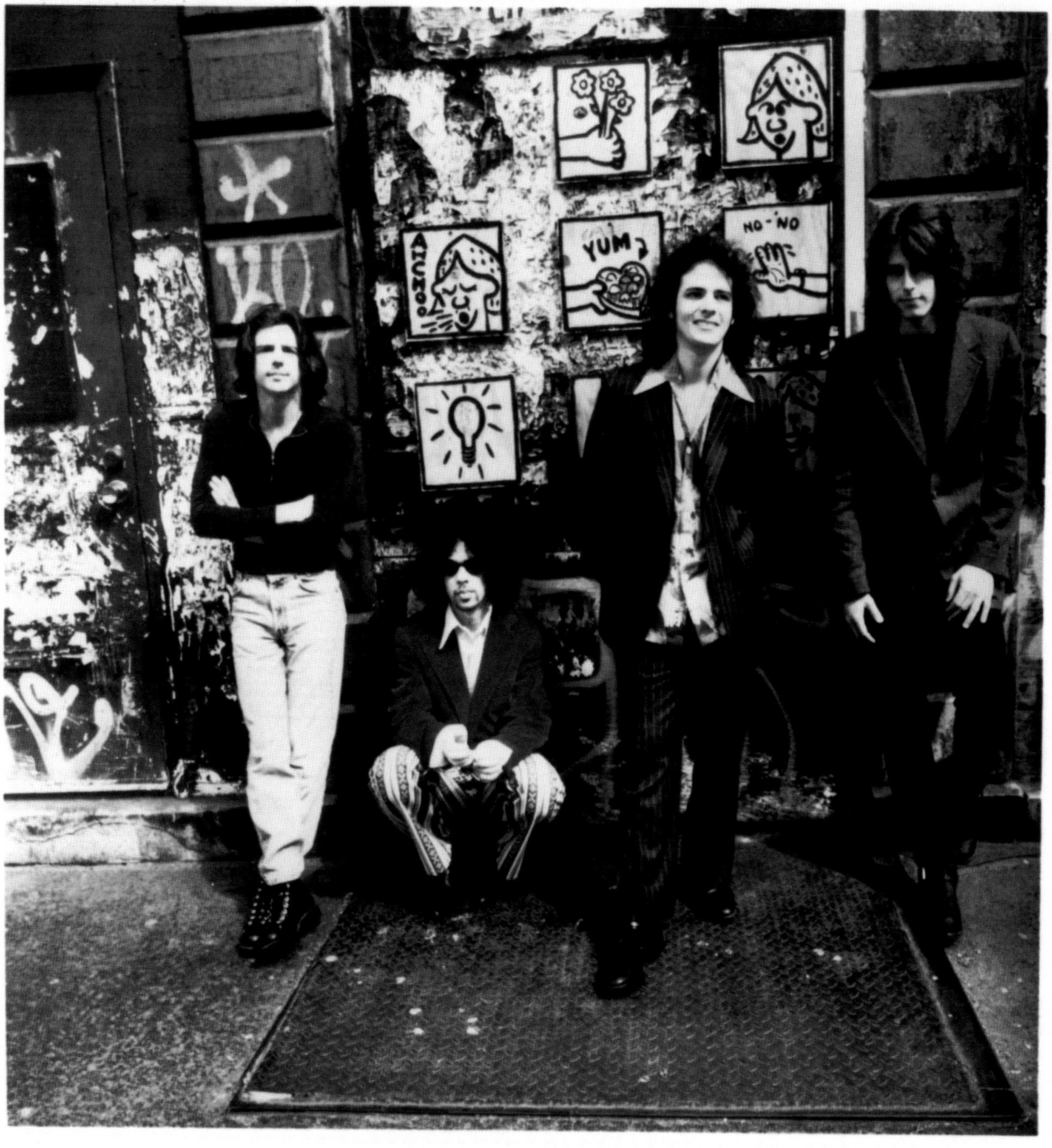

Wanderlust

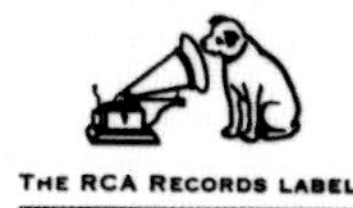

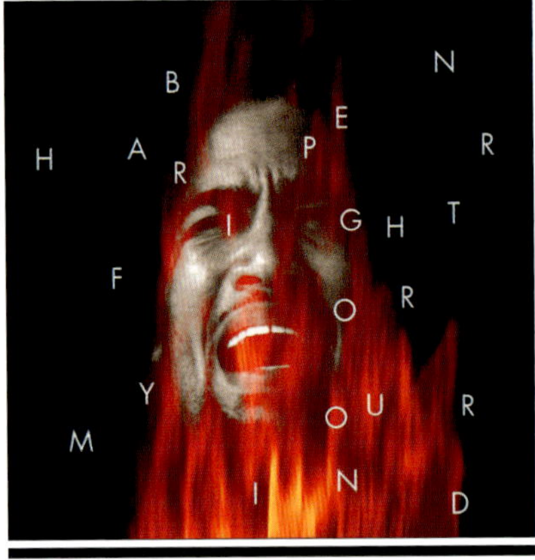

Advancing his principles, *Fight for Your Mind*, Ben Harper's sophomore album, became a college radio favorite.

ON THE jam-band scene, Ben Harper's organic, passionate approach drew rapt attention from a growing following of "Benheads." His music was hard to categorize, but its impact was undeniable. Influences raged from Delta blues to folk to pure hip-hop. He played a trademark Weissenborn, a hollow-neck lap slide guitar designed by Herman Weissenborn in the Twenties. And his lyrics pleaded for equality, fellowship and self-determination.

Harper was brought up in Southern California, where he was taught to sing and play at an early age.

"My family runs a museum of acoustic musical instruments from all over the world. My grandfather is a luthier specializing in repair and restoration," Harper explained. "There are plenty of people who are raised around little to no music at all who become some of the greatest musical minds of our time.

But I would never take for granted that blessing in my life. The next step was to commit my life to music, survive and live on it. I've had plenty of day gigs, from boxing groceries to busing tables. But all that was around the music."

Fight for Your Mind showed Harper expressing his convictions on the marijuana anthem "Burn One Down," the churning "Ground on Down" and the buoyant folk-soul of "Gold to Me." His telephonic vocal treatment of "Excuse Me Mr." revealed a penchant for musical experimentation. He described what he did as "rhythm of life" music, out of place in the music industry.

"Most important is to keep creative control. There are a lot of people who walk through the doors of record companies and say, 'Make me into whatever it will take to be marketed.' It's not all record company wickedness that churns out this product. It's also people ready to conform. In order to make music, you must take part in business, and I feel fortunate to have the opportunity. But we're going an extra step, saying we want to guide what we do, because this is roots music from the earth. It's like a seed in the ground—it'll grow eternal." ■

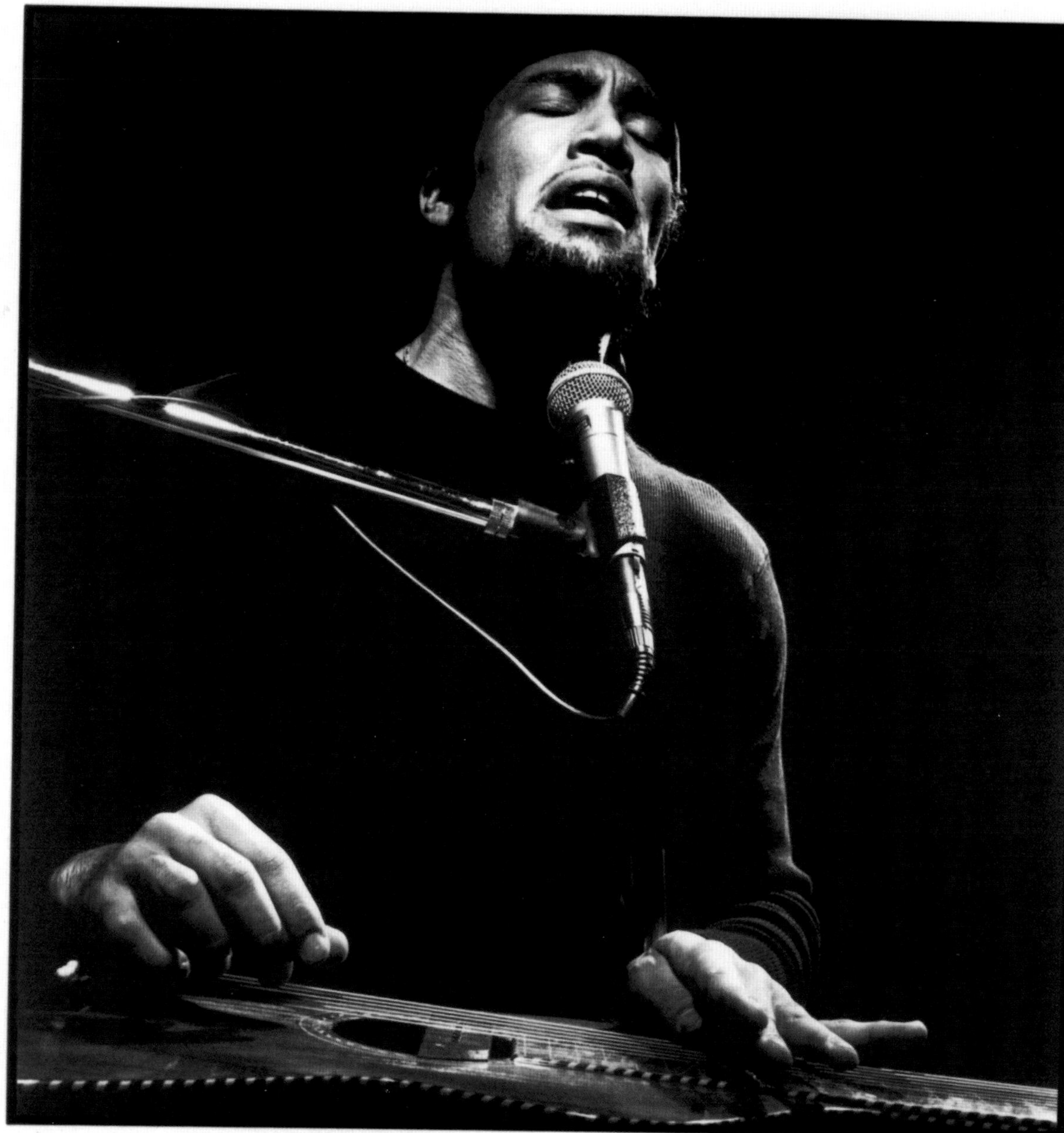

Photo Credit: William Howard 06/95

BEN HARPER

Virgin

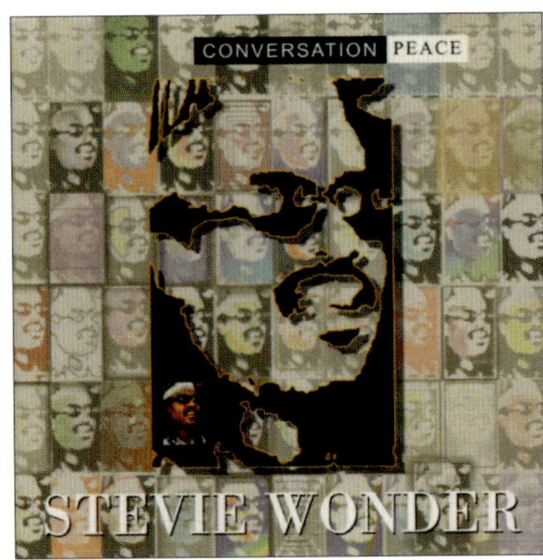

Billboard 200: *Conversation Peace* (#16)
Billboard Hot 100: "For Your Love" (#53)

***Conversation Peace* by the beloved Stevie Wonder was a sumptuously crafted record of mindful commentaries.**

APART FROM the 1991 soundtrack for Spike Lee's *Jungle Fever*, more than seven years had passed since the prodigiously creative Stevie Wonder's last album of new music. The drought ended with the release of *Conversation Peace*.

"You can't base your life on other people's expectations—fortunately, I'm still around, and I'm excited," Wonder said. "I'm very happy with my life. I'm always in love, that goes without saying. I look forward to getting married again. I'm very blessed with family—I'm the father of four. Yet I'm very similar to Duke Ellington—music has been my mistress for a long time. I thank God for the opportunity to love it and express my feelings through it."

Blind since birth (he was born Steveland Morris and raised in Detroit), Wonder was revered by his peers as much as by the public. When "Fingertips—Pt. 2" became a No. 1 hit in 1963, he was dubbed "the 12-year-old genius." And though Wonder grew to manhood, the term "genius" still applied. He didn't burn out, as sometimes occurs with highly gifted children. He continually improved his singing, writing, producing and performing skills.

His real impact on pop music dated to his mature work of the early Seventies. Making the synthesizer and studio his personal instruments, he created the tour de force albums *Music of My Mind*, *Talking Book*, *Innervisions*, *Fulfillingness' First Finale* and *Songs in the Key of Life*. During the Eighties, he hit the top of the charts twice with "I Just Called to Say I Love You" and "Part-Time Lover." The latter established him with the longest span of No. 1 hits (22 years and three months) in *Billboard* Hot 100 history. Some argued that Wonder could have added that record if he just wouldn't take so long to complete an album, but it had nothing to do with his ego.

"I don't get off on people waiting for my music," he said. "I'm a perfectionist, and my bottom line is good music. I have to feel that it's right. Your heart tells you when you're finished with a record. You put it out and whatever happens, happens, but obviously I want to be successful."

Wonder wrote a lot of the songs for *Conversation Peace* in Ghana. "I went there in the latter part of '93 and returned again in '94. I was able to have some time away from telephones and the things that distract me in New York and Los Angeles. I love the weather, and the people are very warm." Wonder was still a hitmaker—the single "For Your Love" was a vivid, carefully developed pop R&B song which won two Grammy Awards. He had plenty of plans for the coming years.

"There's a lot more to happen in my life, both good and unfortunate. People need to see that it's not as easy as turning on a television and watching a saga in a few hours. They need to see the reality—the perseverance, the hard work, the disappointment. We have to climb the ladder. That's what *Conversation Peace* is about, and it was a blessing to come up with those words. As Kahlil Gibran wrote, 'Children don't come from us but through us.' I'll take what I've learned and pass it on for as long as they're willing to reach out." ■

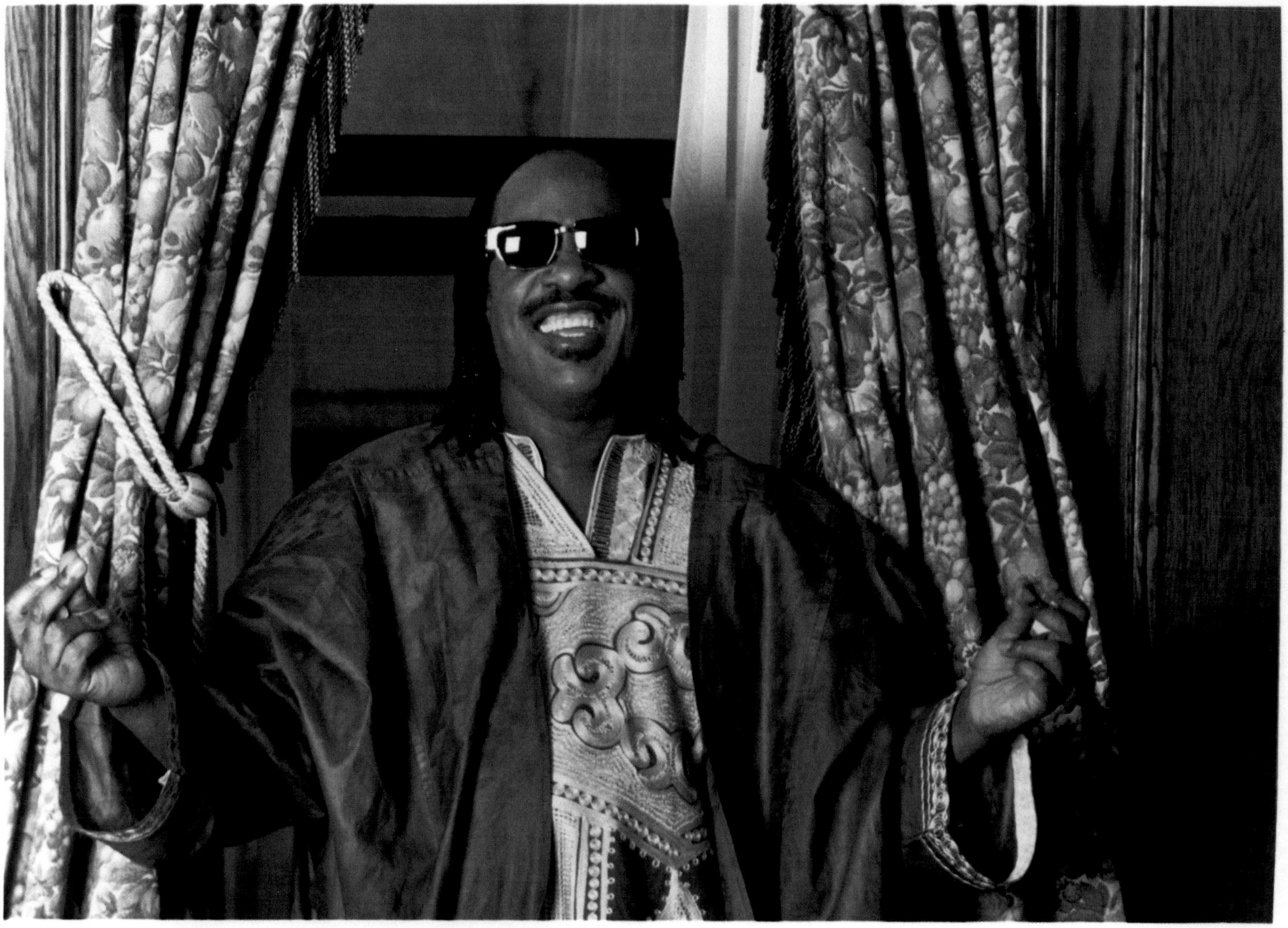

STEVIE WONDER

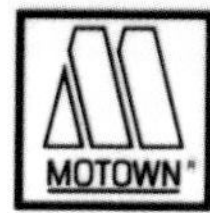

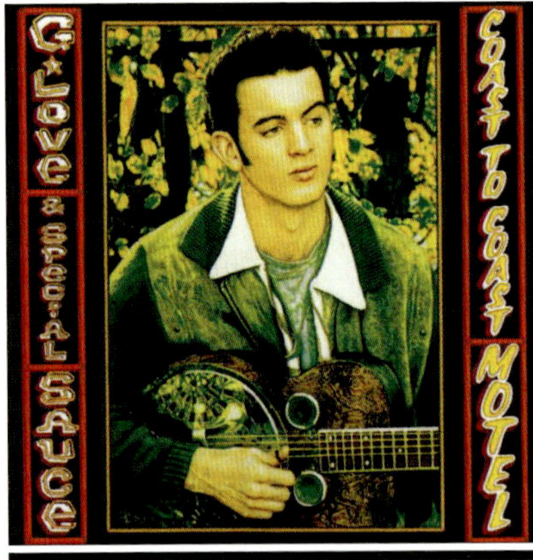

Billboard 200: *Coast to Coast Motel* (#122)

With *Coast to Coast Motel*, G. Love & Special Sauce found a receptive young audience for their groovy interplay.

HE WAS a lean 6-foot-3 with slicked back hair and long sideburns. He sported the finest thrift-store duds and spoke in an acquired Delta drawl. G. Love was "a white kid from Philly" who'd adopted the persona of an itinerant bluesman.

"I feel the accusations. People want to know what gives me the right to play that music," Love said. "But among musicians and music lovers, all those lines are crossed. The people who call our music blues probably never listened to Lightnin' Hopkins, y'know? We call our music 'ragmop.' I don't think it's blues in the traditional sense. It's our own form."

Love, whose real name was Garrett Dutton, couldn't remember a time when he didn't play guitar. "I've always played acoustic. When I was 17, I got my first John Hammond record, *Country Blues*, just him solo. I had never really listened to any blues, and the minute I put it on, it changed my life. I proceeded to learn every song off that record by Jimmy Reed and John Lee Hooker and Howlin' Wolf, all those cats."

He moved to Boston, and G. Love was born. "I was always trying to get a gig—I played Harvard Square, the subway," he explained. "I eventually got one playing in the balcony of this hard-rock dive. Everyone hung downstairs where they could hear the jukebox, so I'd be in the loft area some nights playing my heart out for nobody but me and a passed-out bum. The club booked me as 'Glove.'"

Love hooked up with drummer Jeffrey Clemens and bassist Jimmy Prescott, and they became a band. The sound of *G. Love & Special Sauce*, the first record, was tagged as "hip-hop porch music," a combination of the rhythm section's wide-open backbeat and Love's earthy playing on harmonica, guitar and dobro. Love muttered raps about such lowdown pleasures as shooting hoops, hanging out on the street and drinking a "Cold Beverage" (a song that got in rotation on MTV)—"That's reflective of my life, which is what the blues is supposed to be."

The album *Coast to Coast Motel* decreased the hip-hop element for a more standard blues delivery. On the classic New Orleans R&B groove of "Kiss and Tell," Memphis producer Jim Dickinson, who had a reputation for extracting peak performances out of eccentrics like Alex Chilton and Paul Westerberg, fleshed out the rustic sound.

"He's not a technical guy—he don't touch the buttons and mikes," Love said. "He's straight-up to you about your songs, but he don't get involved in the arrangements. He sets up an atmosphere—he tells stories about playing golf with Aretha Franklin."

Love talked, wrote and sang in a style appropriated from Black America's roots, but his intentions were sincere and he avoided sounding jive. "The bottom line is, when you pick up your guitar, everyone can tell who's feeling it and who's trying to be something else. We're playing the kind of music that we're passionate about—you can see it comes from a good place." ■

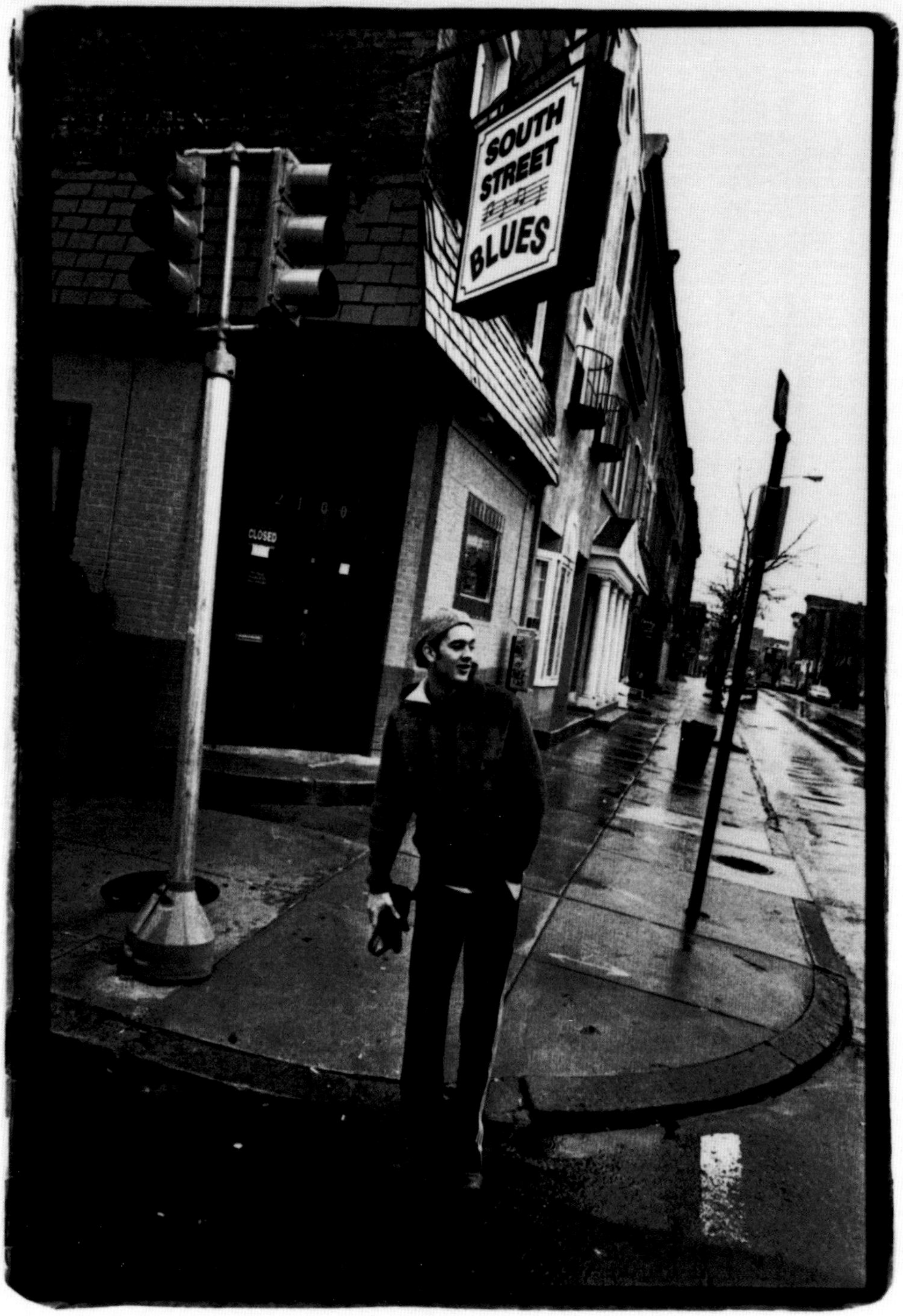

PHOTO CREDIT: DANNY CLINCH

OKeh

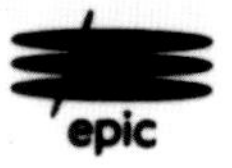

G. LOVE & SPECIAL SAUCE

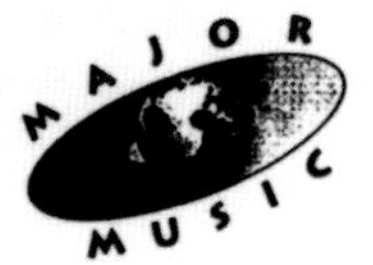

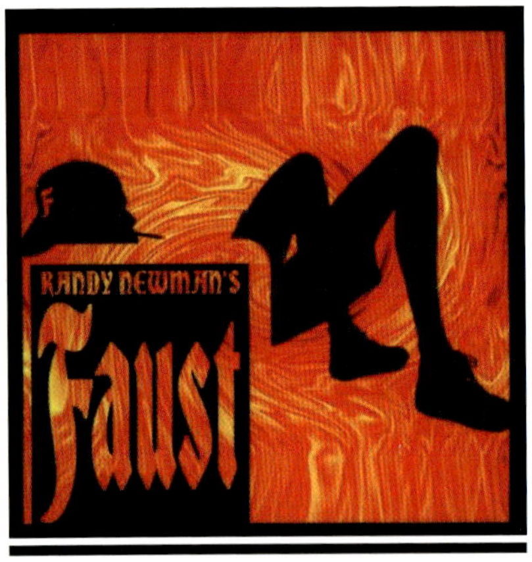

Rallying famous friends to sing parts, Randy Newman wrote a musical based on *Faust*, Goethe's morality play.

ONE OF the most acute and subtly outrageous singer-songwriters of the rock era, Randy Newman was simply in a class of his own. The 1972 album *Sail Away* included the wryly acerbic "Political Science" and the title track, a capsule study of racism that packed a bigger wallop than any protest song; in "God's Song (That's Why I Love Mankind)," God got a kick out of humanity's cluelessness in the face of disaster. A native Angeleno, Newman spent an important part of his childhood in the South, where his mother was born; it inspired the masterly *Good Old Boys*, from 1974, and he scandalized the masses with "Rednecks" ("We're rednecks, we're rednecks, we don't know our ass from a hole in the ground"). Newman made his name with his biggest (and ludicrously misunderstood) hits "Short People" and "I Love L.A.," but all his albums included masterpieces of startling ambiguities and compassion that were unequalled in pop.

Randy Newman's Faust, his ambitious modern opera version, had God and the Devil vying for the soul of a college student. The project had a limited run at La Jolla Playhouse in San Diego, which coincided with the release of a concept-album version. The latter's bombastic production featured Newman himself as the Devil (Mephistopheles in Goethe's version) and guest artists James Taylor (God), Don Henley (the student), Elton John, Linda Ronstadt and Bonnie Raitt (who sang the worldly wise "Feels Like Home" in her role).

"The musical starts with the Devil getting expelled from Heaven and he goes down to hell to reign, but he wants to go back to Heaven because it's comfortable there, with golf courses and rollercoasters and stately homes," Newman said. "And the Devil isn't allowed to have anything like that. The Devil's home is more sort of stucco and AstroTurf."

With 1981's *Ragtime* soundtrack, Newman had started making his bread and butter by writing songs and musical scores for a wide range of films. In a sense, he was joining the family business—his uncles Alfred and Lionel Newman were both respected motion picture composers. Over the years, Newman did the scores for *The Natural*, *Parenthood*, *Avalon* and *The Paper*. The Academy of Motion Picture Arts and Sciences recognized his talents with multiple Oscar nominations—without an actual win.

Another empty-handed evening came after his nomination for "You've Got a Friend in Me," one of his three original songs from Disney-Pixar's 1995 box-office smash *Toy Story*. "I never leave the (Oscars) disappointed—sometimes I'm disappointed because I had to sit there for five hours, but I'm always happy to be nominated," Newman said. "I've been nominated eight times, and always I lose out to a singing lobster or something. When I write my diseased love songs for my own albums, it's hard work. But when I get an assignment from Disney, it's easy—I'll sell out in a second. 'You've Got a Friend in Me'? You don't got a fucking friend in me." ■

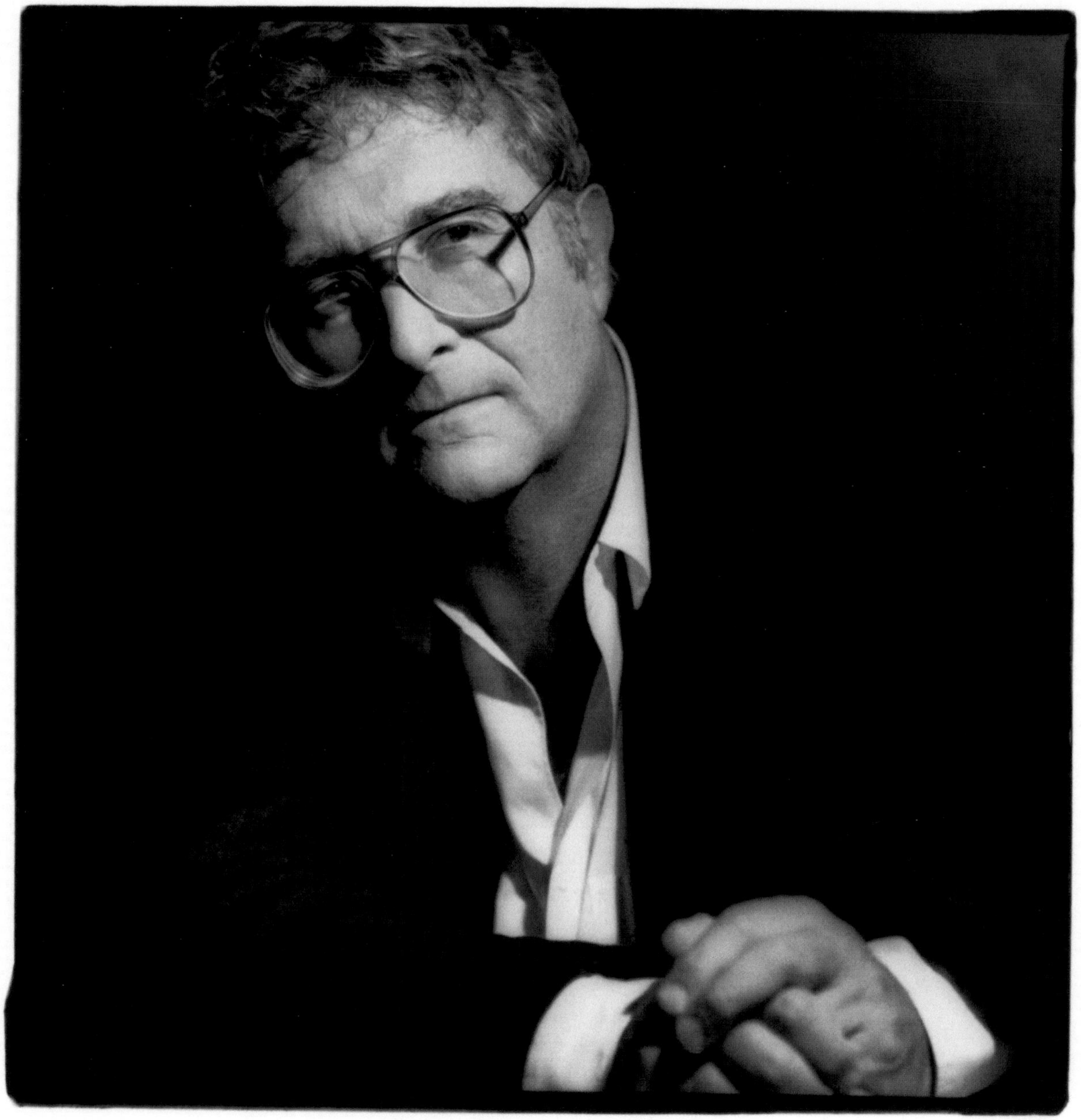

Photo Credit Pamela Springsteen

RANDY NEWMAN

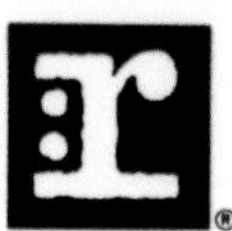

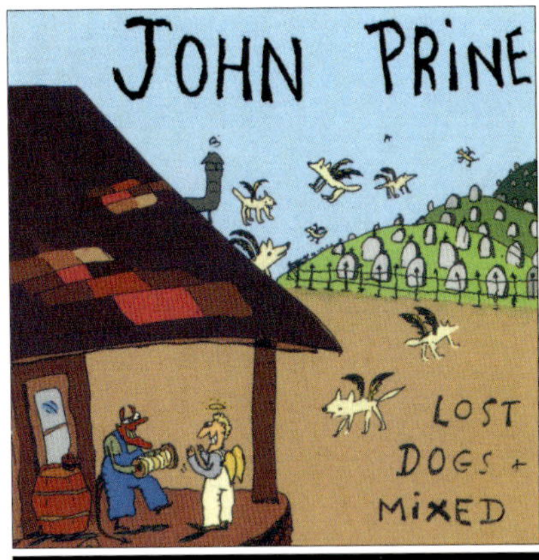

Billboard 200: *Lost Dogs and Mixed Blessings* (#159)

More than two decades into John Prine's career, the mainstream finally caught up with the Grammy-winning bard.

IN THE Seventies, John Prine's work won critical approval and great renown among his fellow performers, but the folk-based singer-songwriter never scored a hit of his own. In the Eighties, he called it quits with the big companies and formed his own Oh Boy Records, releasing several fine low-key, low-budget albums. After 1986's *German Afternoons*, he seemed on the verge of pulling a disappearing act. "I toyed with the idea of going back to school," Prine admitted.

But help arrived in the form of Howie Epstein, the bassist for Tom Petty & the Heartbreakers and a longtime fan. He and Prine drew on old friends for *The Missing Years* (Petty, Bonnie Raitt and Bruce Springsteen added background vocals), and the song "Big Old Goofy World" showed Prine's writing at its bittersweet best. *The Missing Years* won a Grammy award.

Prine had a featured role in *Falling from Grace*, a movie produced and directed by John Mellencamp. He played "the apologetic brother-in-law, the guy whose pants are a little too short and whose pockets are a little too tight." "I'd been asked back in the Seventies to be in movies, but they were ex-convict or biker movies, so I took a pass on them," Prine explained. "Now I'd like to do some Wallace Beery remakes."

Prine returned with the songs on *Lost Dogs and Mixed Blessings*, also produced by Epstein. "It was an exciting time, no rules to follow—just write the album and play it as we rolled along," Prine said. "The working title of the album was *As You Like It*, taken, of course, from Billy Shakespeare's play. I figured if the people out there liked *The Missing Years*, then we'd give 'em something they would really like. We were really cocky."

Prine adapted his hoarse vocals to "Lake Marie," and "Ain't Hurtin' Nobody" was chosen to be a music video.

"I had returned to L.A. from my first Australian tour," Prine said. "I had no new songs, just a bunch of ideas and the studio booked at two the next afternoon. I wrote 'Ain't Hurtin' Nobody,' a song about a fellow, Lucky LaRue, who was walking down the street thinking about his sweetheart. Not making the world a better place, but certainly not screwin' it up. I looked out my window at about 5:30 a.m. and figured about 6,700,033 lights were on. That's when I knew we were on our way to a new album."

Lost Dogs and Mixed Blessings earned Prine another Grammy nomination. ■

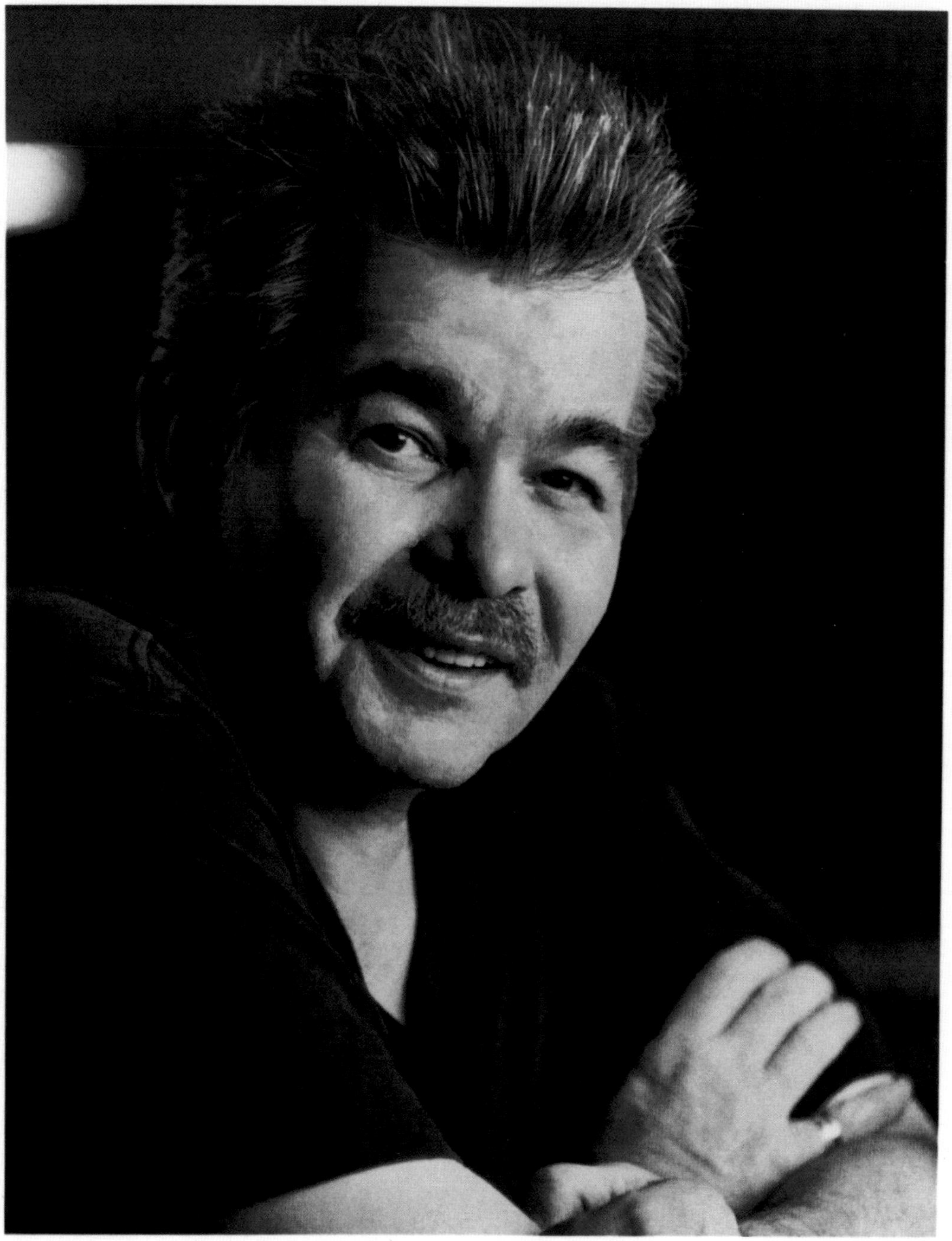

JOHN PRINE

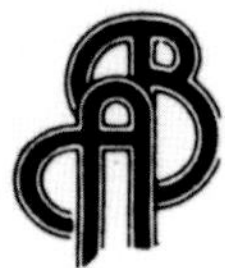

Al Bunetta Mgmt., Inc.
33 Music Square West, Suite 102A
Nashville, Tennessee 37203
(615)742-1250 ● Fax (615)742-1360

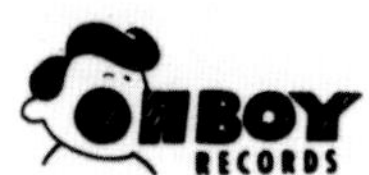

33 Music Square West
Suite 102A
Nashville, TN 37203
(615)742-1250

Monterey Artists, Inc.
901 18th Avenue South
Nashville, TN 37212
(615)321-4444

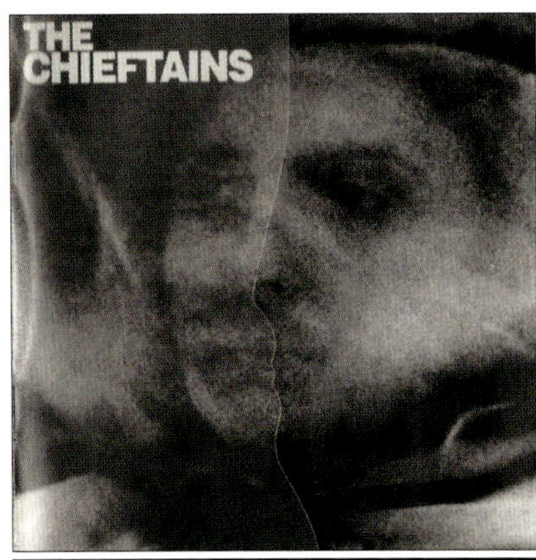

Billboard 200: *The Long Black Veil* (#22)

The Chieftains, one of Ireland's wonderful cultural exports, recorded *The Long Black Veil* with famed rock stars.

PADDY MOLONEY formed the Chieftains in 1962, and over the years the veteran Irish folk group had come to be regarded as the world's most popular exponents of traditional Irish music. The Chieftains had pulled off a long, interesting list of achievements, playing on authentic instruments at the Taj Mahal, on the Great Wall of China, for the Pope—you name it.

"I don't qualify as a brilliant classical master—I never did finish out my studies, I'm more or less self-taught," Moloney, the leprechaun-like founder and indefatigable guiding spirit, proudly proclaimed. "But I overcame it when I sat down and wrote for pipes and an orchestra way back in 1977. I love a challenge."

The Chieftains' popularity had reached a new peak. After decades of cult status in America, the group deftly blended the centuries-old range and variation of Irish fare with the world of rock music. *The Long Black Veil* was filled with friends—Sting, the Rolling Stones, Van Morrison, Mark Knopfler, Ry Cooder, Marianne Faithfull, Tom Jones and Sinead O'Connor—and became the Chieftains' first gold album, reaching countless people who had no idea that the instruments Moloney played were called uilleann pipes and tin whistles.

"There was no clash breaking down personality barriers—and once that disappears, it becomes an Irish party for me," Moloney explained. "I didn't stick a score in front of the guests—I don't think any of them read. It was a jam session, two or three times over, and then we had it. It was a great, happy feeling before we ever sat down to record."

It was apparent in the track done with the Stones—there was a bit of "Satisfaction" thrown into the middle of "The Rocky Road to Dublin." "Keith (Richards) was rather curious with me—'Whose idea was this?' He thought somebody put me up to it. I said, 'No, I thought it'd be nice.' He said, 'Great, let's do it,' and that was that."

Morrison accompanied the Chieftains on a version of his song "Have I Told You Lately That I Love You?" The recording won the Grammy Award for Best Pop Collaboration with Vocals.

"This is what people have been noticing and enjoying about Ireland and our music—for such a small country, the folk art is so strong," Moloney said. "It's so vast, a tremendous variety of rhythms and themes and songs. You can't go wrong." ■

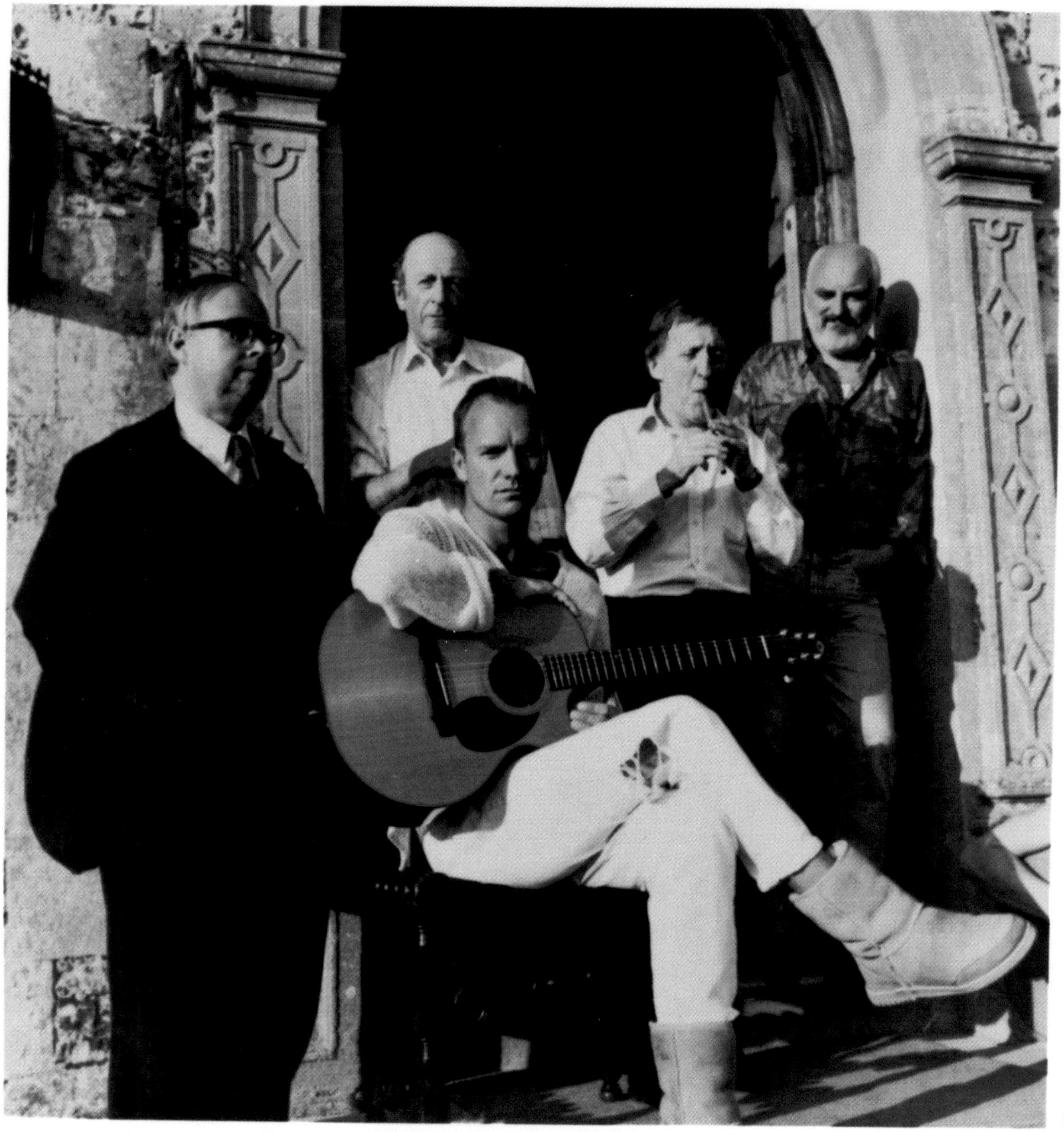

Photo: Claire Carnegie

Members of The Chieftains with Sting (seated)

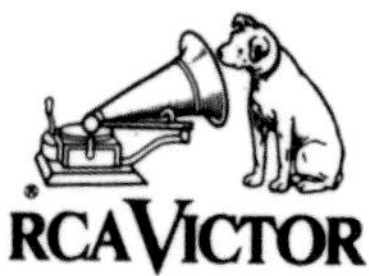

THE CHIEFTAINS
THE LONG BLACK VEIL

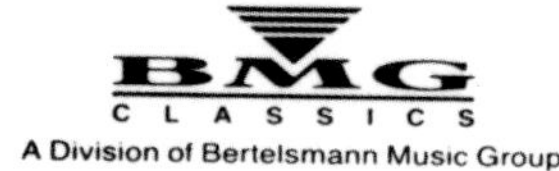

A Division of Bertelsmann Music Group

Taking rockabilly and surf guitar sounds, Los Straitjackets celebrated the glory days of instrumental rock 'n' roll.

WITH AN brash, willful take on twangy, reverbed guitar instrumentals, Los Straitjackets were making their mark on a younger generation.

"Instrumentals are my favorite kind of music, I have always enjoyed them, and they've been around a long time, back before rock 'n' roll," guitarist Danny Amis said. "They never really went away, and I don't understand why there haven't been more hit instrumentals in the last 20 years. But there is a resurgence in popularity. We just put together the type of band that we would like to go to see."

Amis had played in the Raybeats, an instrumental band from the new wave era. He wound up in Nashville circa 1988 and hooked up with guitarist Eddie Angel and drummer L.J. Lester. They began playing around town as Amis switched to guitar and brought in Scott Esbeck on bass. "And we decided to add a few extra things to present the band in a unique way," the soft-spoken Amis said.

The group called itself Los Straitjackets in honor of early Mexican rock 'n' roll heroes. "I've got a record collection that I built up on trips to Mexico—groups like Los Teentops and Los Rockin' Devils and Los Jokers," Amis said. "I always thought the English noun with the Spanish article in front of it was a real cool sound."

And to keep their identities a "secret," they wore gaudy Mexican *luchador* wrestling masks. "I'd gone to the Mexican wrestling matches down there and picked up some of the masks they wear. We found four that fit, and it seemed like a fun idea to wear them onstage. It's a very colorful style. The wrestlers are like superheroes to kids in Mexico. They're worshipped like Batman and Superman are here."

But there was no kidding around when it came to Los Straitjackets' sonic assault. After a few practices, the four guys spent a day and a half recording live in a Nashville studio. *The Utterly Fantastic and Totally Unbelievable Sound of Los Straitjackets* offered rowdy, razor-sharp ditties, from spy music ("G-Man") to surf ("Fury").

"There are a lot of instrumental acts that stick to the traditional 'surf sound' format. I love those bands, but we don't feel like we have to do that. I like to think of it as legitimate instrumental rock 'n' roll," Amis said.

The band's frenzied, goofy live shows rocked audiences of greasers, punks, cowboys and everyone else into a sweat. What made it work was the combination of Amis' deft touch and Angel's force.

"Eddie is a Link Wray-inspired guitar player, more rock 'n' roll than roots-based," Amis explained. "My style is more compositional—my favorite group would be the Shadows (from England). Together, it doesn't go so far in one direction that it gets to sounding stale. The recent converts have never been into instrumentals before, so it's a new type of music for them to listen to." ■

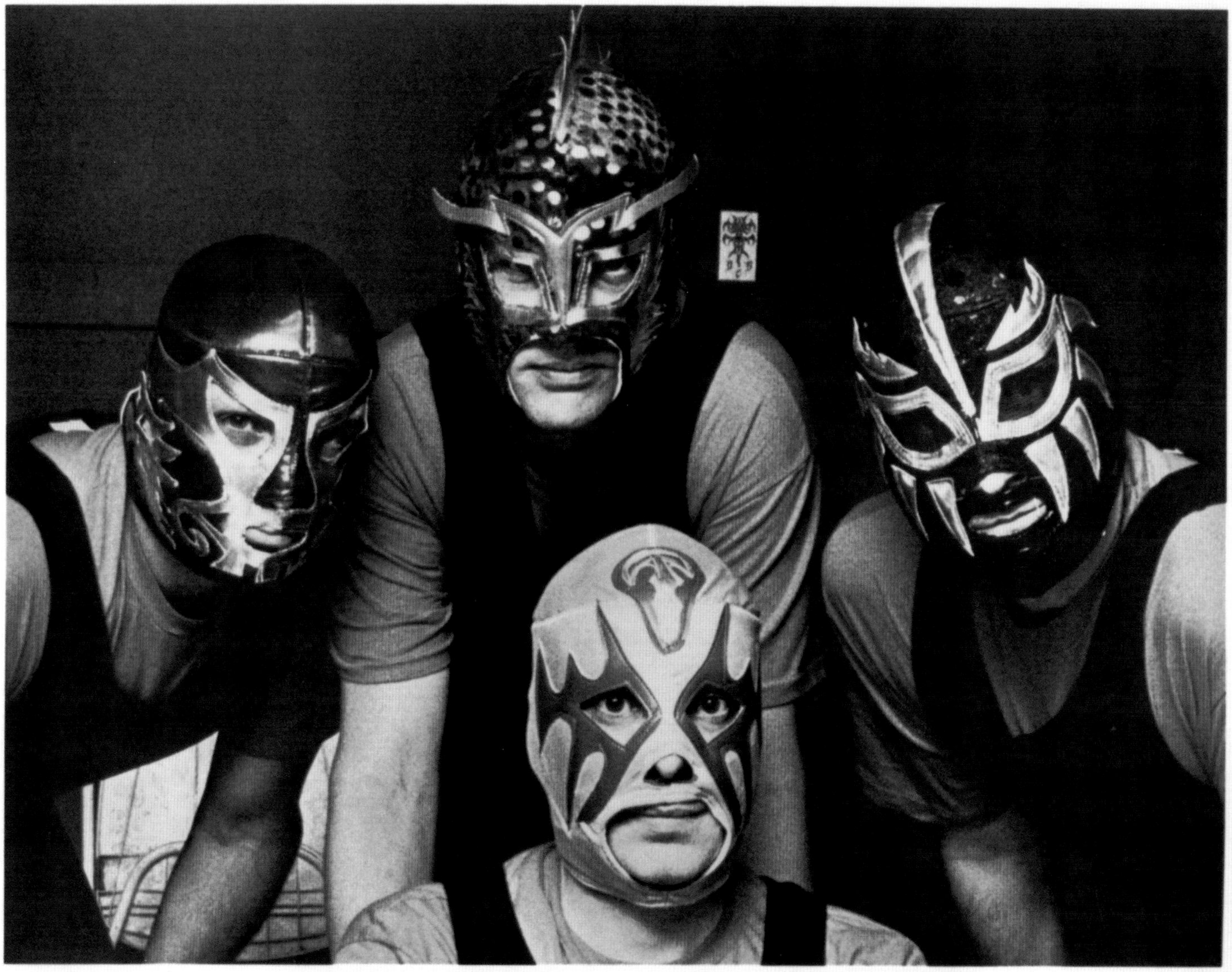

Photograph by Chris Peltier

Upstart Records

•

P. O. Box 44-1418
W. Somerville, Mass. USA 02144
617/354-0700 • Fax 617/491-1970

LOS STRAITJACKETS

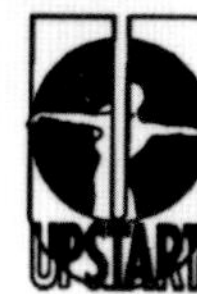

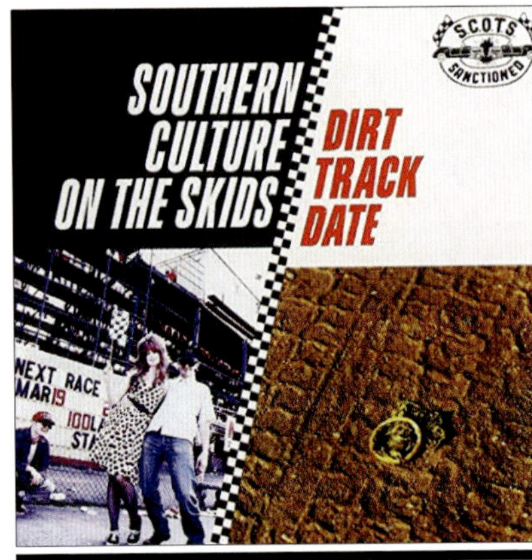

Southern Culture on the Skids got a taste of national attention with the backwoods brilliance of "Camel Walk."

IT WAS best to experience Southern Culture on the Skids at one of the band's frenetic live shows—like when frontman Rick Miller hurled buckets of fried chicken into the audience, invited fans onto the stage to dance with the pieces and wore the KFC box as a hat.

"I don't like the 'extra crispy,' only because when people throw it back at us, it hurts—it's like getting hit with a dirt clod. And I don't like 'rotisserie,' because it doesn't come in parts—it's harder to hold," Miller said. "So I like 'original recipe.' Just call me traditional."

Guitarist and vocalist Miller played up his band's goofy "white trash" image like they were the victims of too much inbreeding, but he was no fool. He started Southern Culture on the Skids in 1984 while bored at the University of North Carolina.

"We hated all the bands that were playing at the time—they were all R.E.M. clones. So we decided to take the rockabilly of the Cramps—we liked the simple, primitive approach—but with the roots music from the South. Our first gig was as a warmup to a porno movie, *Café Flesh*—my roommate worked at the theater. It started off on the right foot, something really different."

Bassist Mary Huff auditioned for SCOTS and recruited an old friend, drummer Dave Hartman. Over the course of three indie releases and numerous singles, the band had honed its "swamp rock" sound, running together punk, country, R&B, rockabilly, surf and lounge styles. *Dirt Track Date*, the band's major-label debut, featured the stomping "Camel Walk," with a playful lyric about a ludicrous snack-cracker fetish.

But it was the chicken-tossing performances that spread the party band's reputation. At times, the mysterious masked wrestler Santo appeared to guzzle Tabasco and keep things loose. The crowds worshipped at the Church of Pabst Blue Ribbon. Miller said he'd been burned playing with Southern stereotypes.

"We've never had a problem with fans. Once you've seen us, it puts everything in perspective—we're conscious of having fun. But when we were getting going, a lot of critics were negative. They wanted to overintellectualize it—they wanted it to be an art-rock thing, they didn't want the humor in it. But we have a different attitude than a lot of bands who consider themselves to be musicians above entertainers. The main thing is to have songs where people want to dance. For me to enjoy a show, I want a physical reaction to our music. That beat is what rock 'n' roll is all about." ■

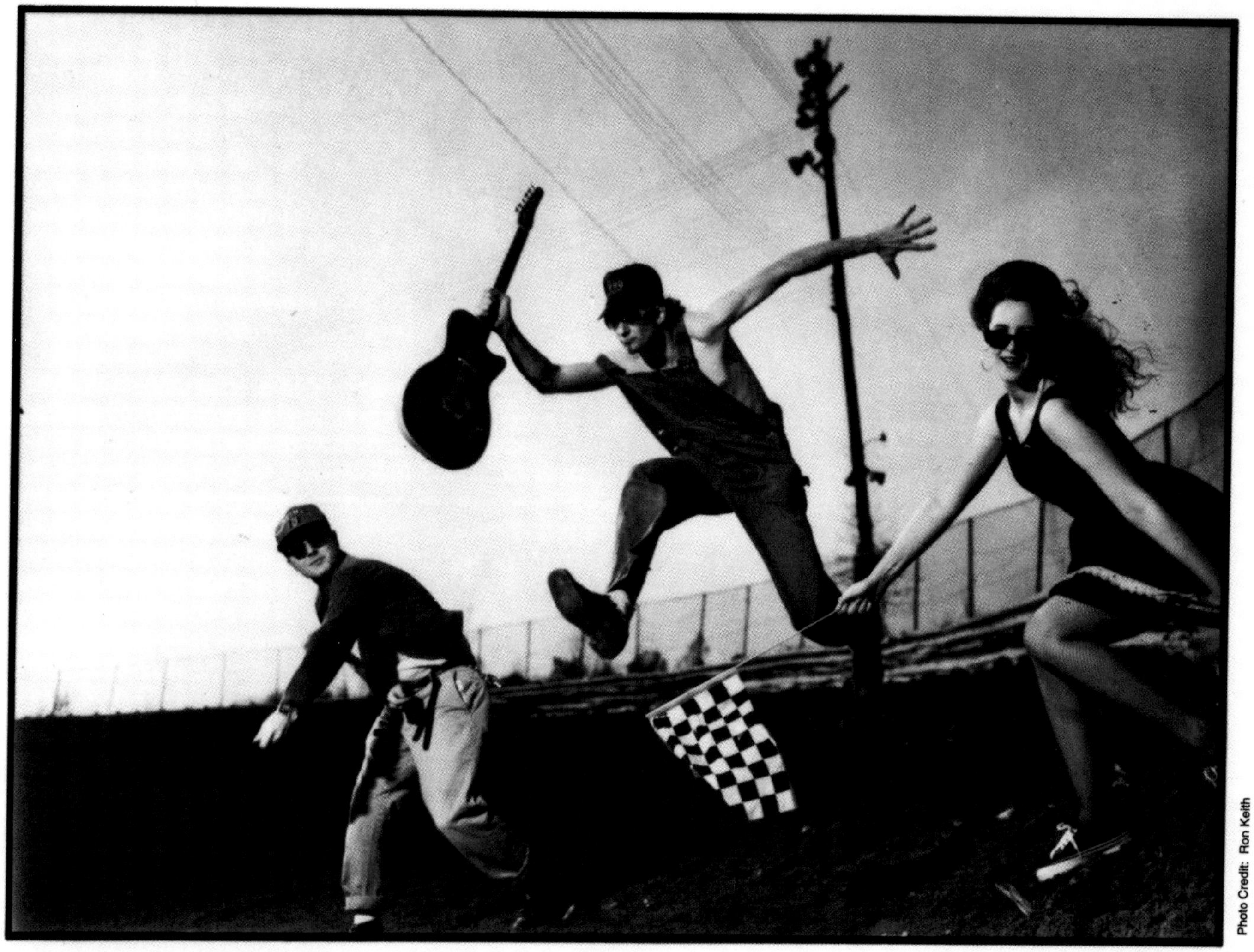

Photo Credit: Ron Keith

Dave Hartman   Rick Miller   Mary Huff

SOUTHERN
CULTURE ON THE SKIDS

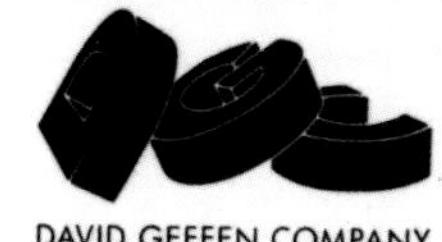

DAVID GEFFEN COMPANY

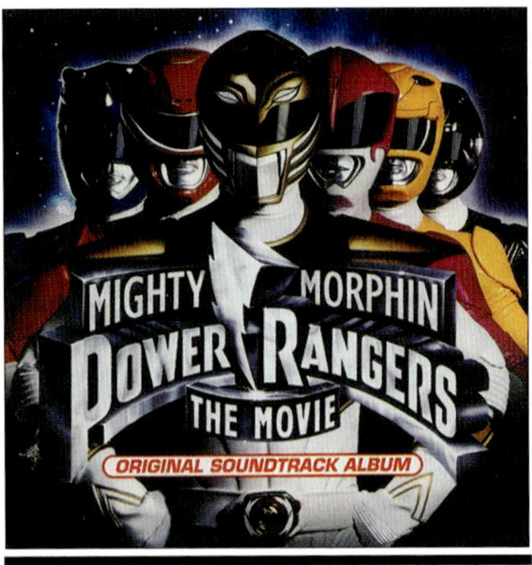

Moving more merchandise than music, Mighty Morphin Power Rangers unlocked their abilities in a theme song.

IN 1993, Egyptian-born entrepreneur Haim Saban introduced a group of multicultural teenage superheroes to America. His campy adaptation of stock footage from a low-budget Japanese serial, *Mighty Morphin Power Rangers*, had since dominated children's television ratings—and caused small riots in toy stores.

And the most recognizable theme song among kids of all ages was "Go Go Power Rangers." Like other rock songs from the TV series, it featured the performance of Aaron Waters - The Mighty RAW.

"RAW are my initials," producer, arranger and engineer Ron Aaron Wasserman explained. "I wanted a different identity as an artist, and I had fun tying into the Power Rangers concept with 'Aaron Waters - The Mighty RAW.'"

Saban's show was a No. 1 hit on the Fox Kids programming block, and the Power Rangers enjoyed remarkable media and merchandising success. Saban had started out in the late Seventies with his Paris-based record company. "He sold millions, primarily in the European kids market—not a single record in the US," Wasserman said.

Saban looked at music as commerce when the Power Rangers took off in America. Atlantic Records promoted a four-minute "Euro mix" of "Go Go Power Rangers" (the song with sound bites mixed in) at rock radio stations. Programmers said it came off sounding like early Kiss.

"Believe it or not, Haim Saban is a tremendously talented musician," Wasserman said. "He hummed that ditty to me, and we went in the studio. I took a production role—we were looking for something energetic, and it came together in a very short time. What you hear was actually a demo, all done on keyboard because I don't play guitar. The final mix is a rough mix, and the vocal is a guide vocal. I played it to Haim and said, 'I'm gonna do more to this and that.' And he said, 'Are you crazy? This is great!'"

In Britain, "Go Go Power Rangers" topped the charts. In the US, an original soundtrack album attached to *Mighty Morphin Power Rangers: The Movie* featured a newly arranged and re-recorded "Go Go Power Rangers" theme performed by the Power Rangers Orchestra, a collaboration featuring Guns N' Roses drummer Matt Sorum.

"It's all very confusing now," Wasserman said of his nom de guerre. "I wish I would have stuck with just my name." ■

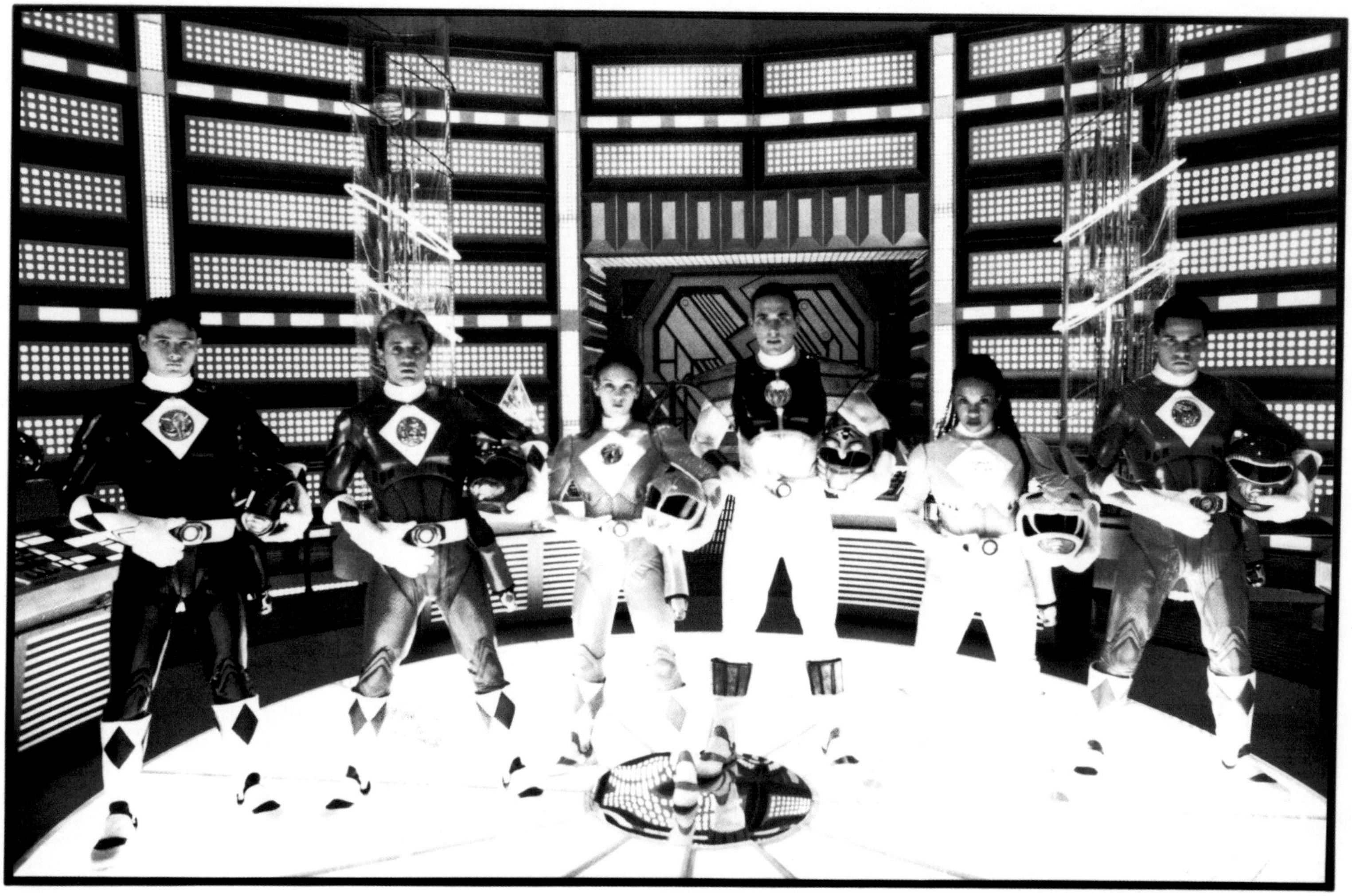

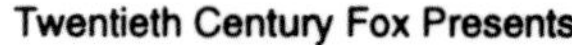

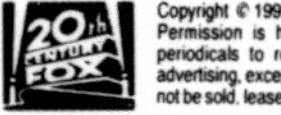

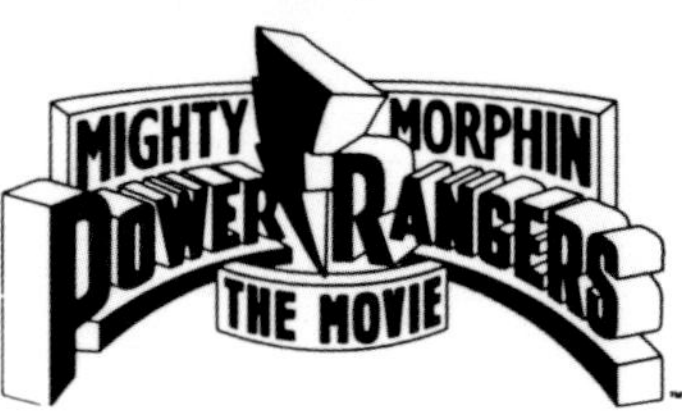

MMPR-1 (From left) **JOHNNY YONG BOSCH** is Adam, the Black Power Ranger; **DAVID YOST** is Billy, the Blue Power Ranger; **AMY JO JOHNSON** is Kimberly, The Pink Power Ranger; **JASON DAVID FRANK** is Tommy, the White Power Ranger; **KARAN ASHLEY** is Aisha, the Yellow Power Ranger, and **STEVE CARDENAS** is Rocky, the Red Power Ranger in **"MIGHTY MORPHIN POWER RANGERS™: THE MOVIE."**

Photo credit: Jim Townley

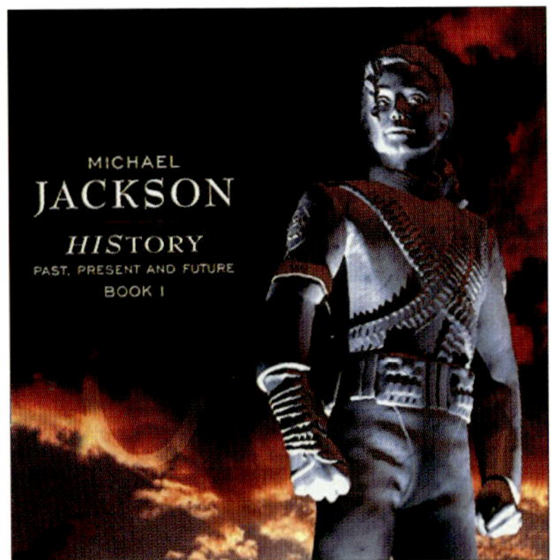

Debuting at No. 1, *HIStory: Past, Present and Future, Book I* by **Michael Jackson** eventually became the best-selling multiple-disc release of all-time.

Billboard 200: *HIStory: Past Present and Future, Book I* (No. 1)
Billboard Hot 100: "Scream" (#5); "You Are Not Alone" (No. 1); "They Don't Care About Us" (#30); "Stranger in Moscow" (#91)

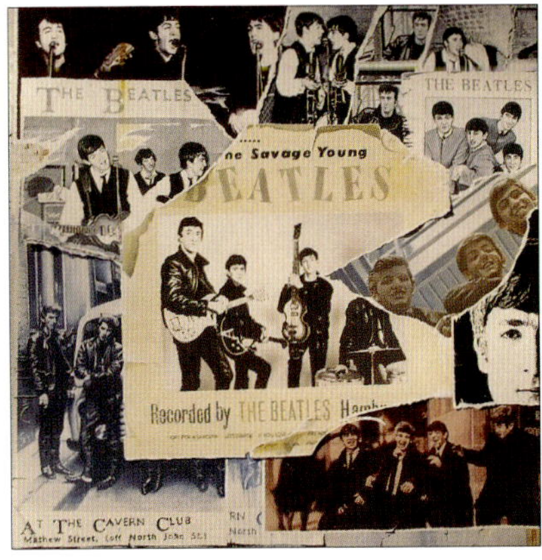

The Beatles' *Anthology 1* added "Free as a Bird," a John Lennon demo from 1977 gilded with overdubs, billed as the first new Beatles song in 25 years.

Billboard 200: *Anthology 1* (No. 1)
Billboard Hot 100: "Free as a Bird" (#6)

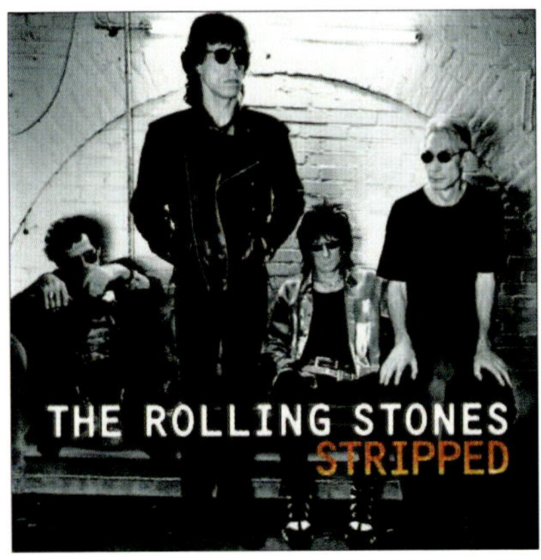

The Rolling Stones' *Stripped* emphasized an "unplugged" recording of Bob Dylan's "Like a Rolling Stone" and live tracks from the "Voodoo Lounge" tour.

Billboard 200: *Stripped* (#9)

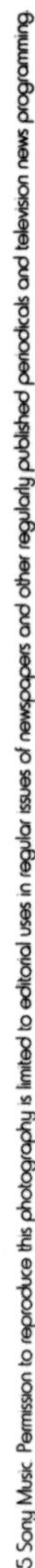

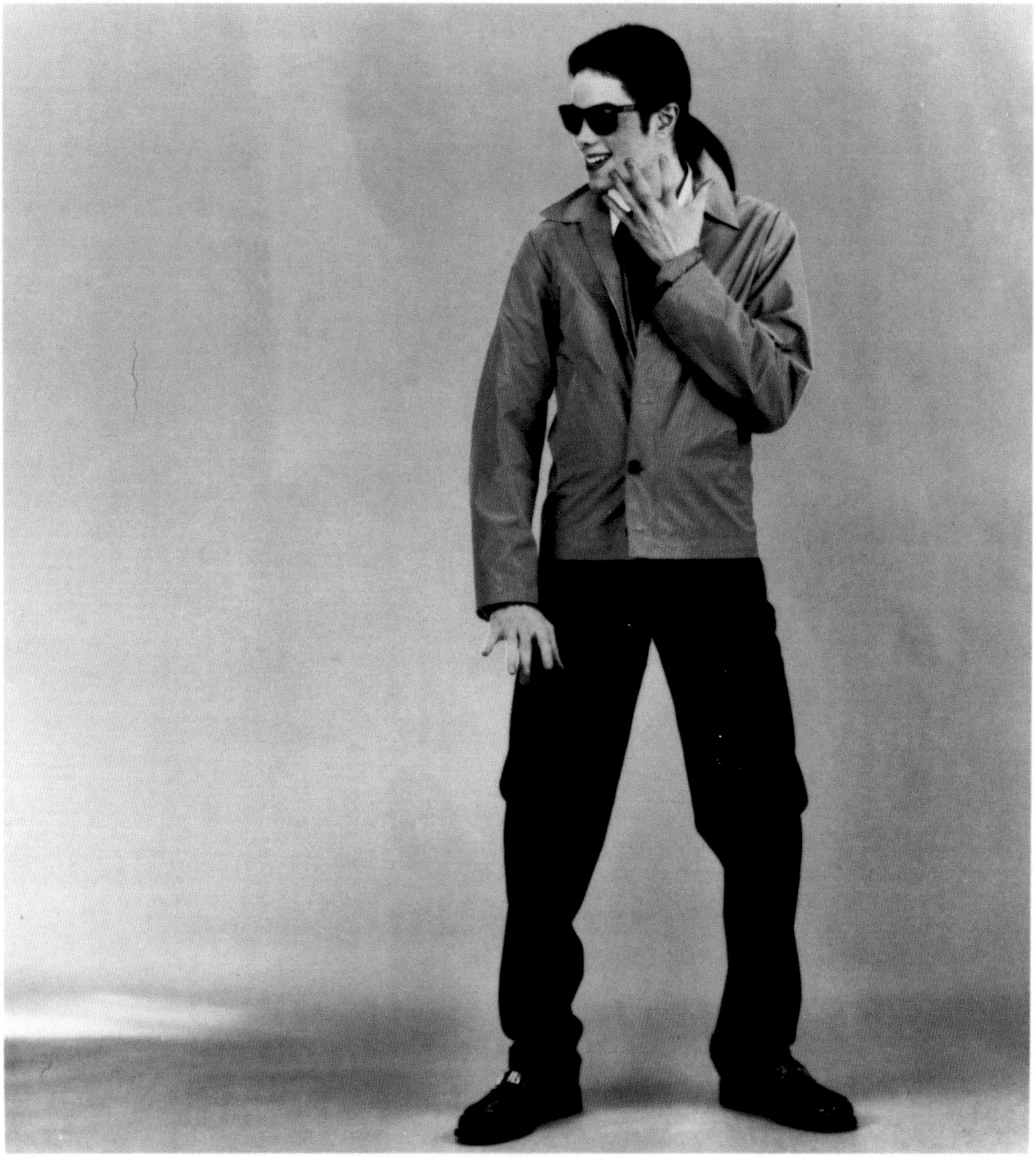

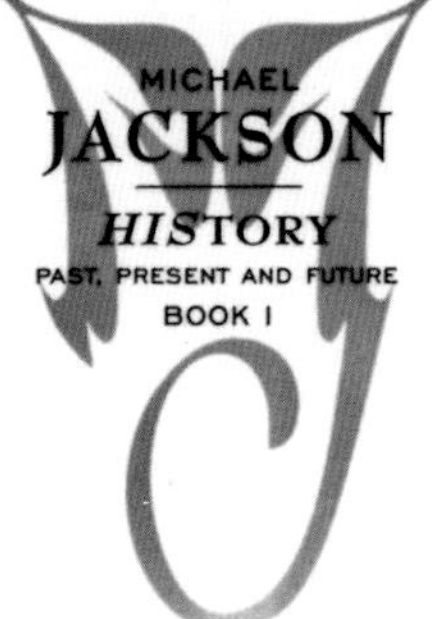
MICHAEL
JACKSON
HIStory
PAST, PRESENT AND FUTURE
BOOK I

epic
9506

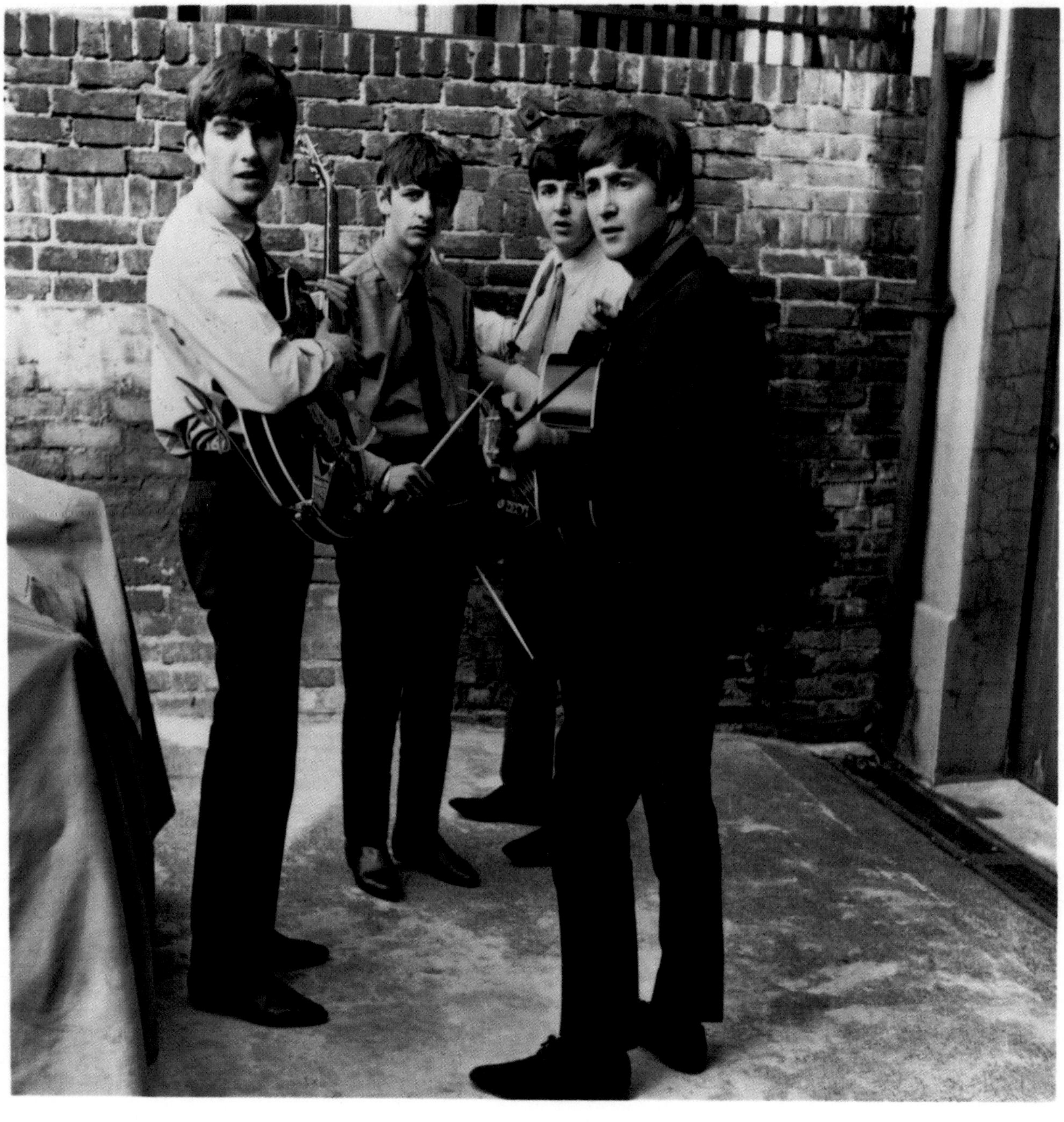

1995 / 36976

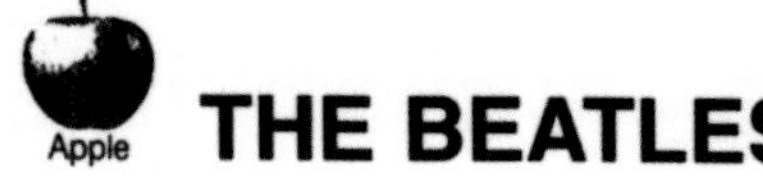

THE BEATLES IN THE ALLEYWAY NEXT TO EMI'S ABBEY ROAD STUDIOS, 1 JULY 1963, JUST BEFORE GOING INSIDE TO RECORD THEIR FOURTH SINGLE, AND THIRD NUMBER ONE, "SHE LOVES YOU"

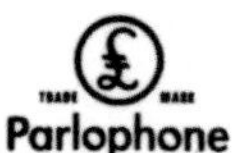

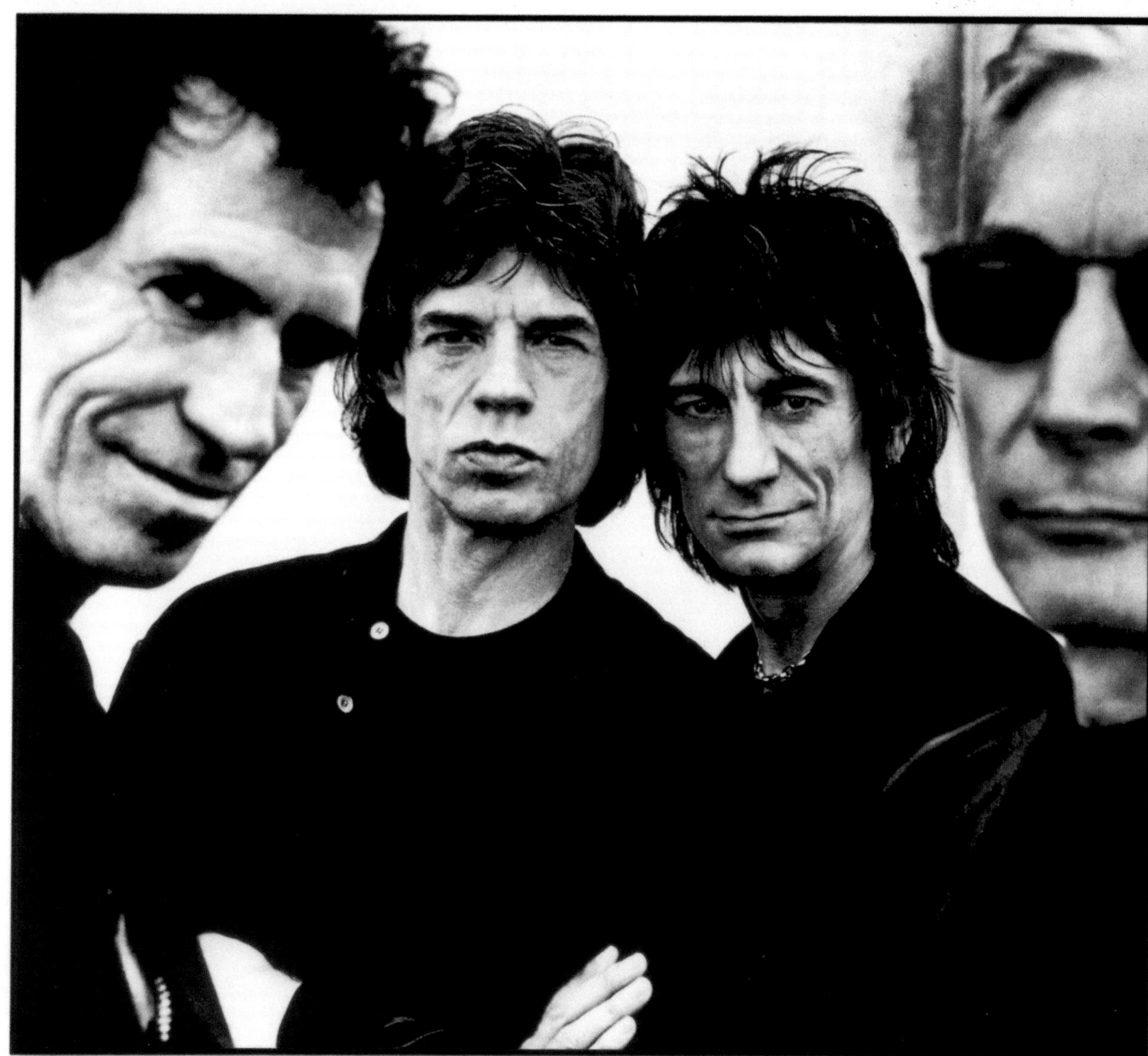

Photo Credit: Anton Corbijn 8/95

THE ROLLING STONES

Virgin

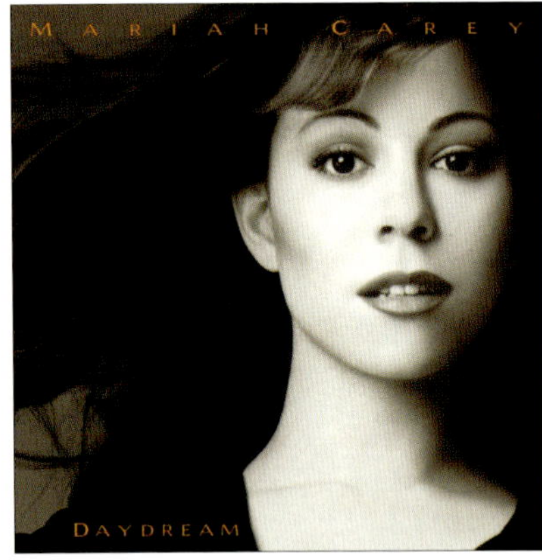

Mariah Carey's *Daydream* held the chart-toppers "Fantasy," "Always Be My Baby" and "One Sweet Day," which lodged at No. 1 for a record 16 weeks.

Billboard 200: *Daydream* (No. 1)
Billboard Hot 100: "Fantasy" (No. 1); "One Sweet Day" (No. 1); "Always Be My Baby" (No. 1)

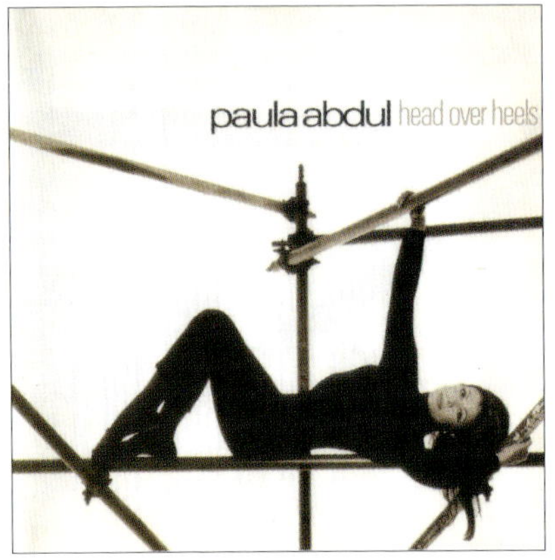

A blending of R&B elements with Middle Eastern instrumentation, **Paula Abdul**'s sensual "My Love Is for Real" topped the dance club songs chart.

Billboard 200: *Head over Heels* (#18)
Billboard Hot 100: "My Love Is for Real" (#28); "Crazy Cool" (#58)

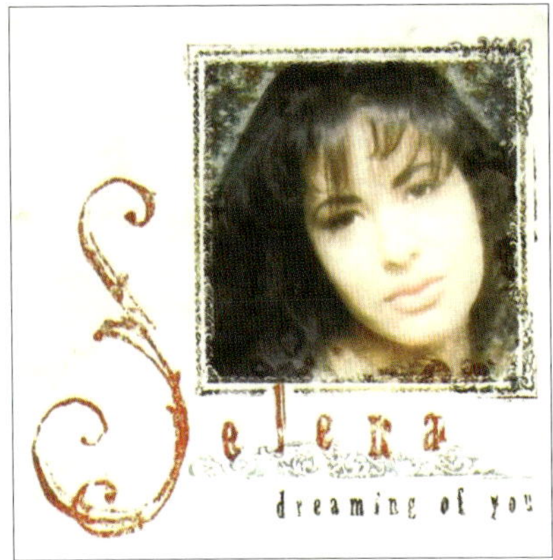

Issued posthumously, *Dreaming of You* debuted at No. 1 on the pop charts, making beloved Tejano singer **Selena** the first Latin artist to manage the feat.

Billboard 200: *Dreaming of You* (No. 1)
Billboard Hot 100: "Dreaming of You" (#22)

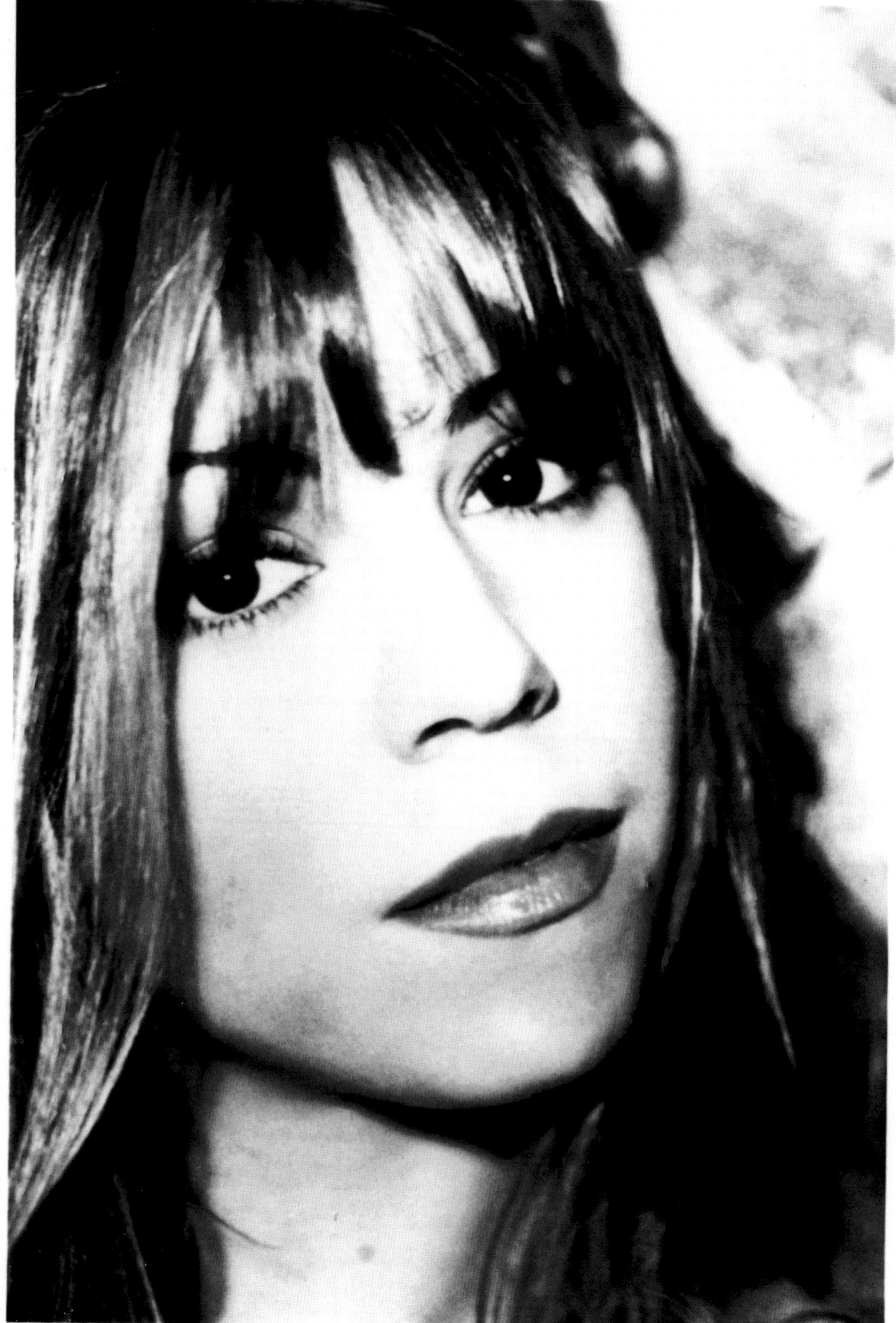

PHOTOGRAPH: DANIELA FEDERICI

HOFFMAN ENTERTAINMENT INC

MARIAH CAREY

COLUMBIA 9509

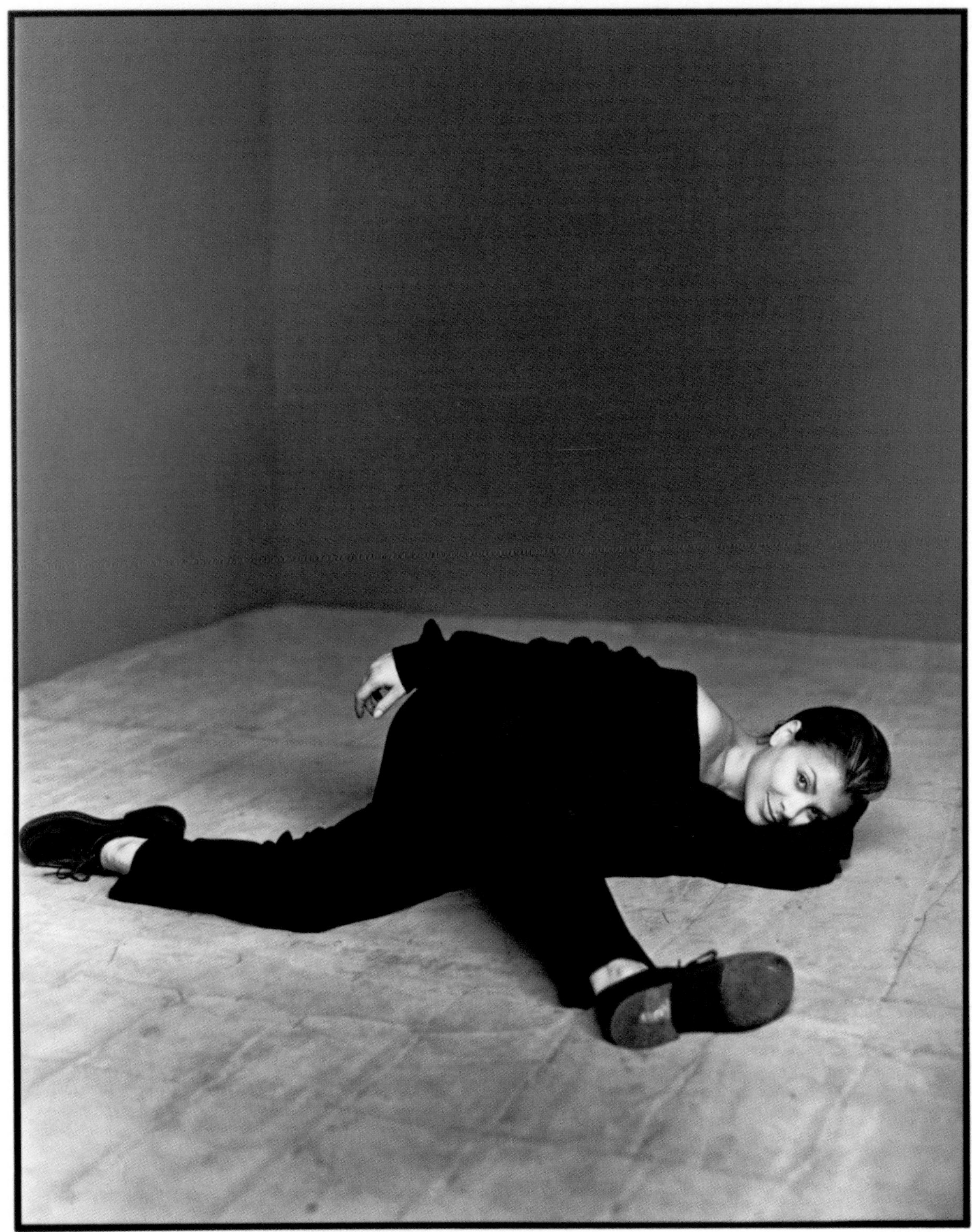

Photo Credit Walter Chin 4/95

PAULA ABDUL

Virgin

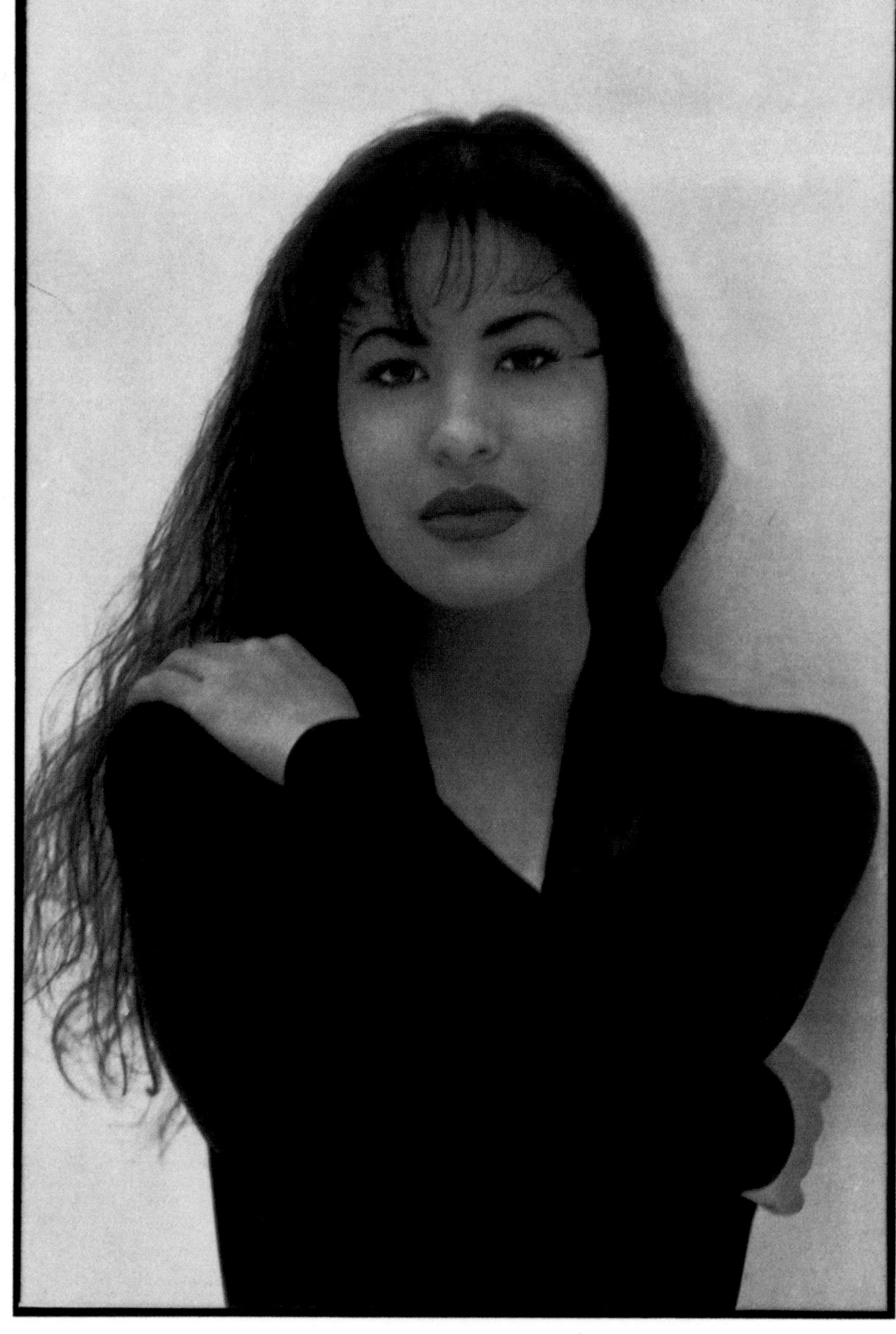

Photo credit: MAURICE RINALDI

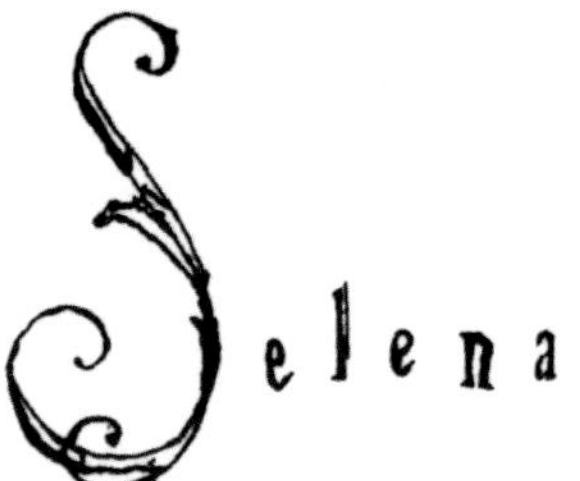

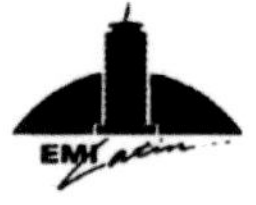

EMI Records

EMI

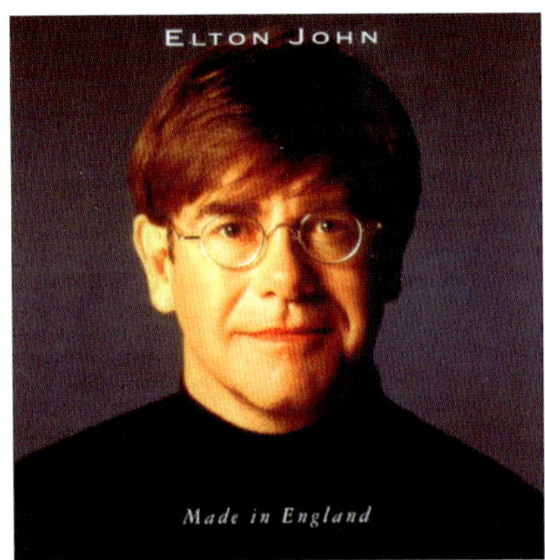

Yielding the charting hits "Believe," "Blessed" and the autobiographical title track, *Made in England* extended the comeback of rock survivor **Elton John**.

Billboard 200: *Made in England* (#13)
Billboard Hot 100: "Believe" (#13);
"Made in England" (#52); "Blessed" (#34)

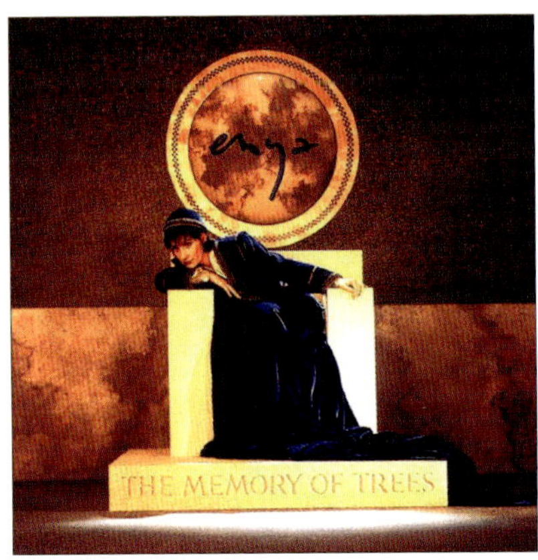

Irish singer-songwriter **Enya** spent nearly four years recording *The Memory of Trees*, her multimillion-selling fourth album and first Top 10 record in the US.

Billboard 200: *The Memory of Trees* (#9)

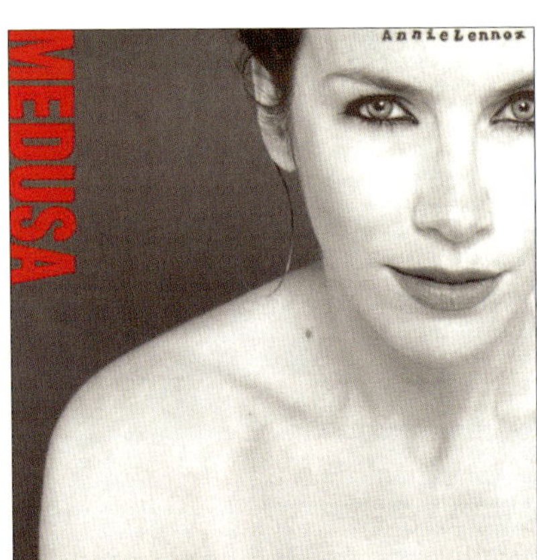

From *Medusa*, **Annie Lennox**'s all-covers set, the alluring "No More 'I Love You's" picked up the Grammy Award for Best Female Pop Vocal Performance.

Billboard 200: *Medusa* (#11)
Billboard Hot 100: "No More 'I Love You's" (#23)

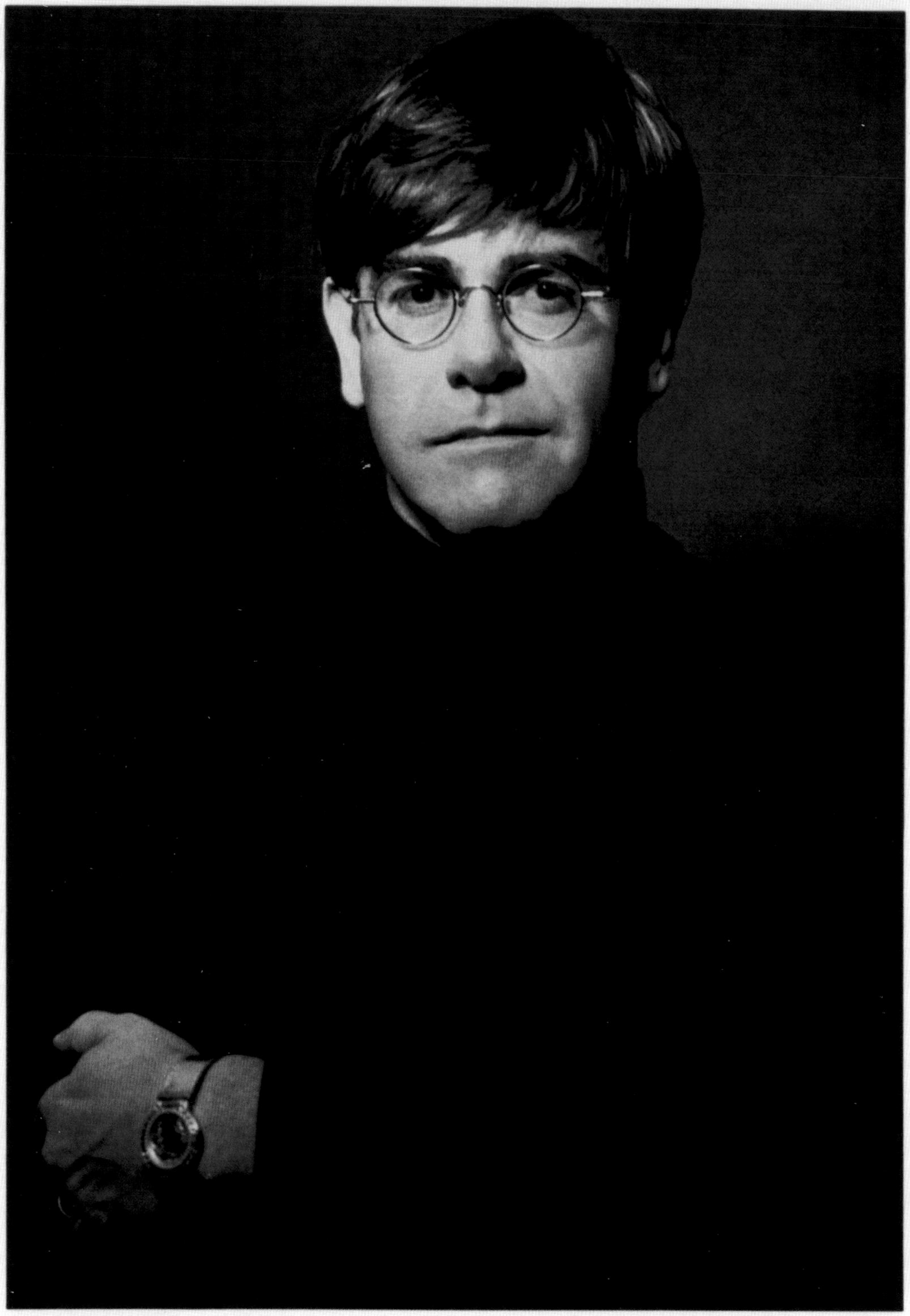

Photo Credit: Greg Gorman

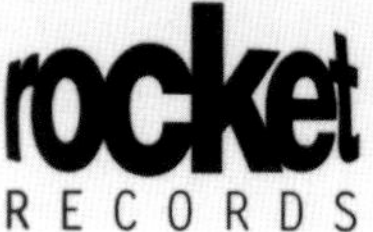

ELTON JOHN

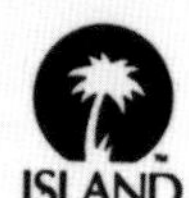

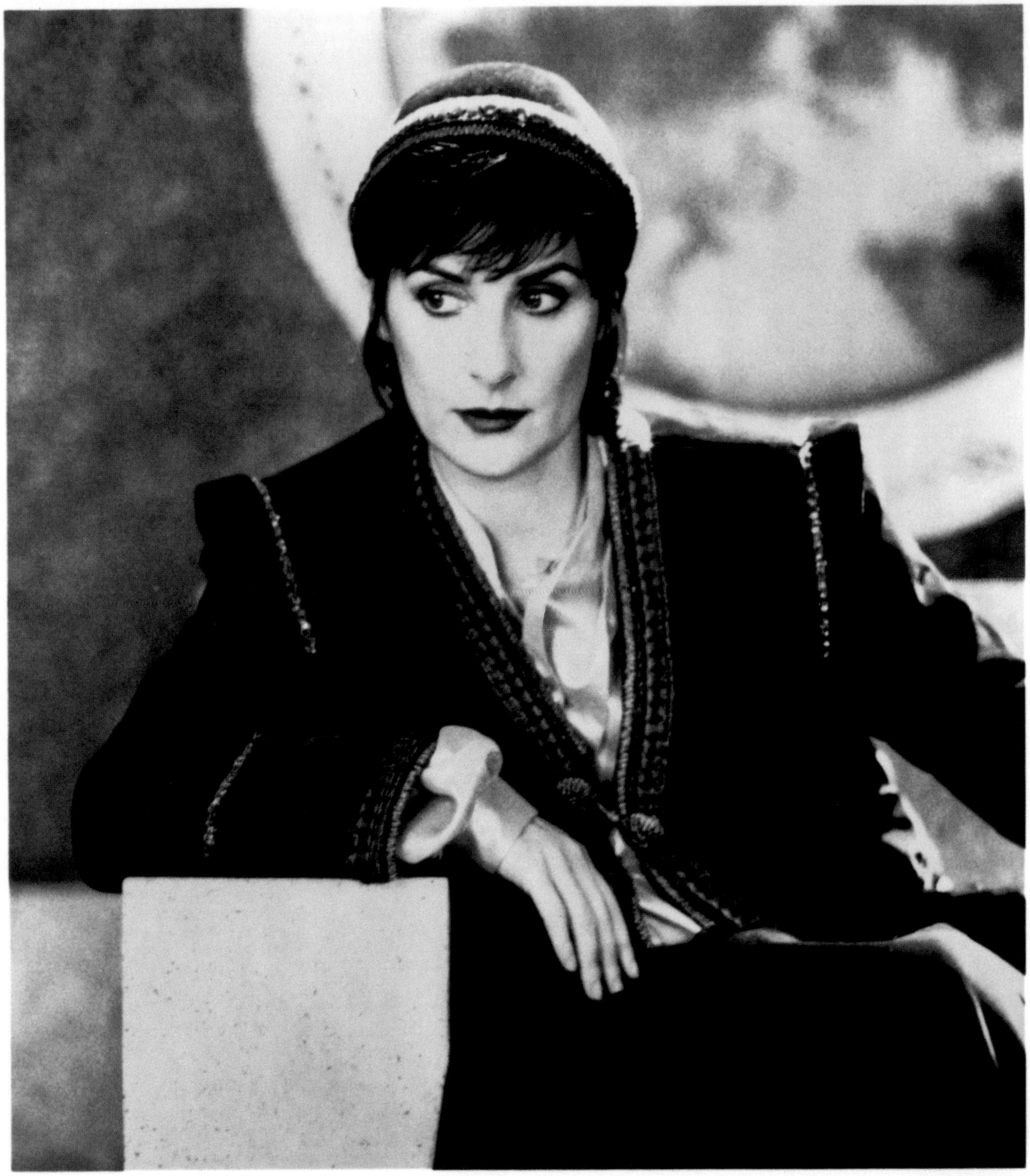

Photo Credit: David Scheinmann

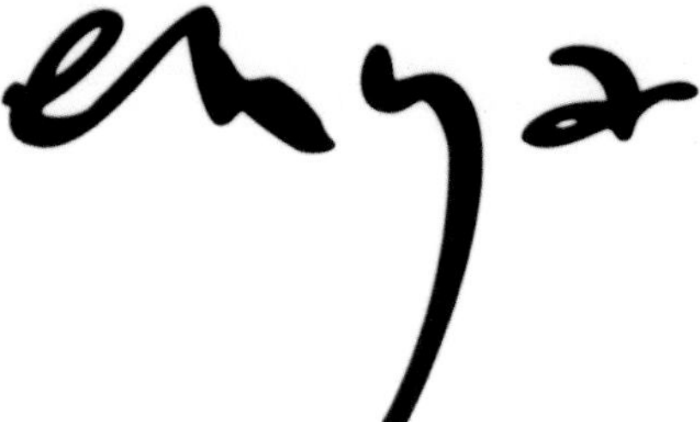

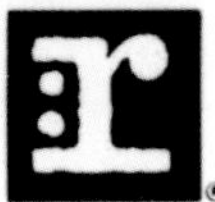

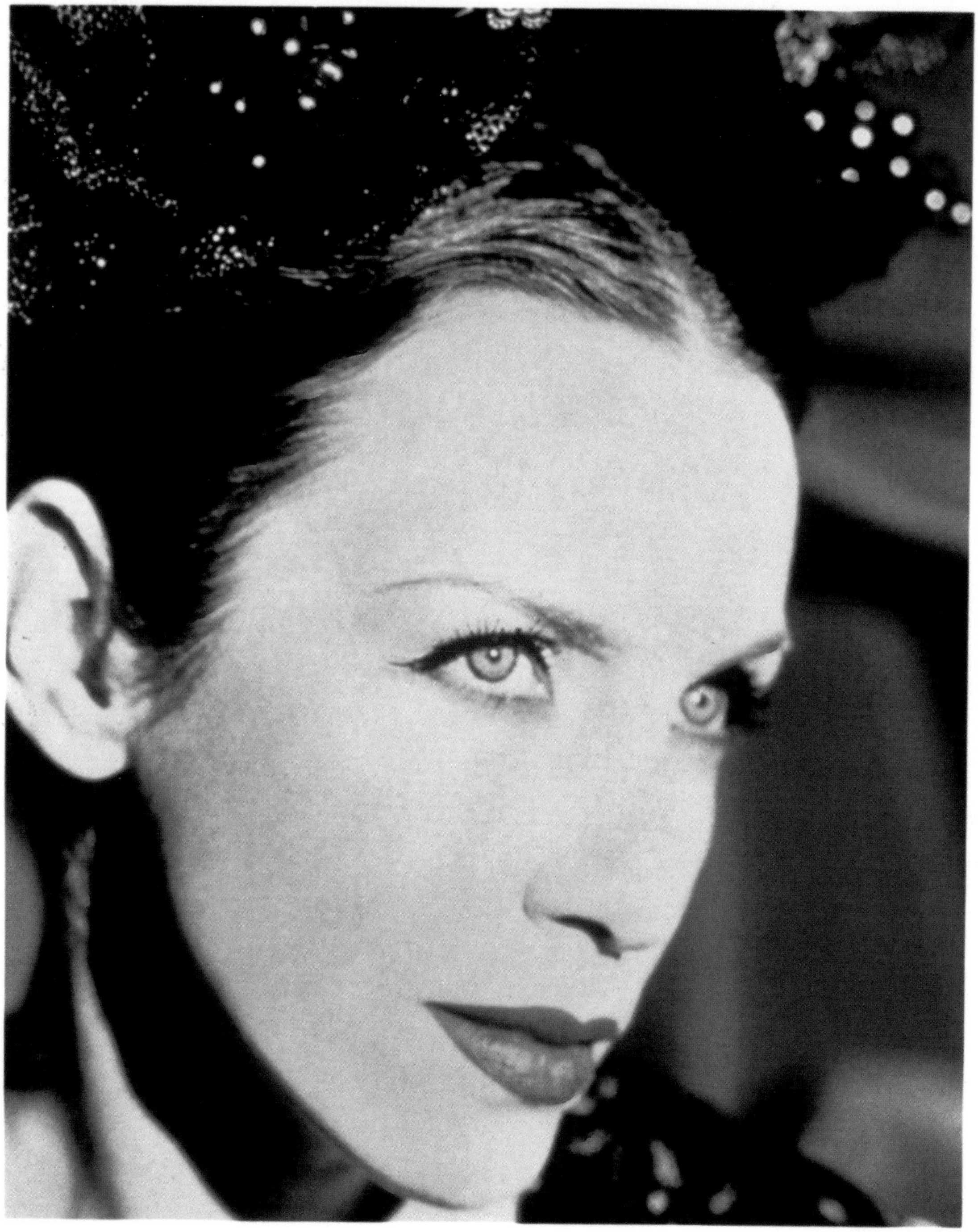

Photo: Pamela Hanson

A n n i e L e n n o x

Management:
Simon Fuller @ 19 Management Limited

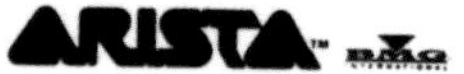

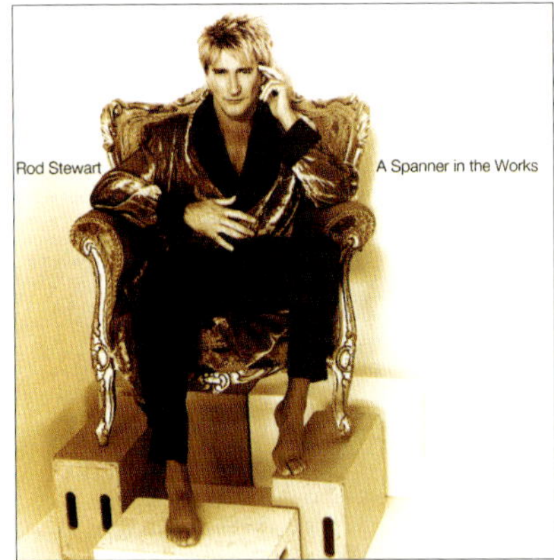

For *A Spanner in the Works*, **Rod Stewart** was convinced to record "Leave Virginia Alone," a Tom Petty song that emerged as an adult contemporary hit.

Billboard 200: *A Spanner in the Works* (#35)
Billboard Hot 100: "Leave Virginia Alone" (#52)

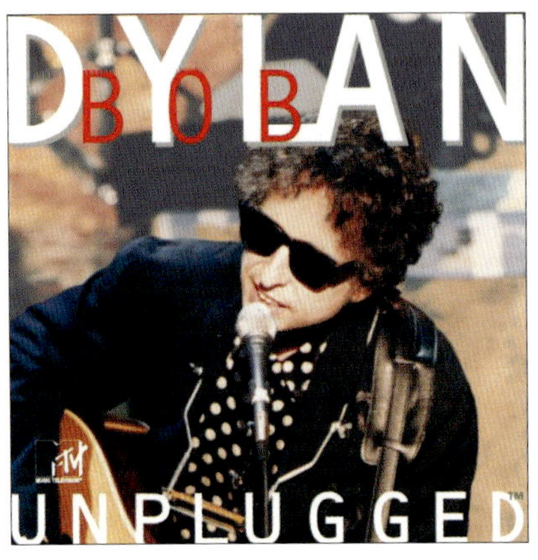

MTV Unplugged, a live record showcasing **Bob Dylan**'s appearance on the popular acoustic music series, generated his biggest sales of the decade.

Billboard 200: *MTV Unplugged* (#23)

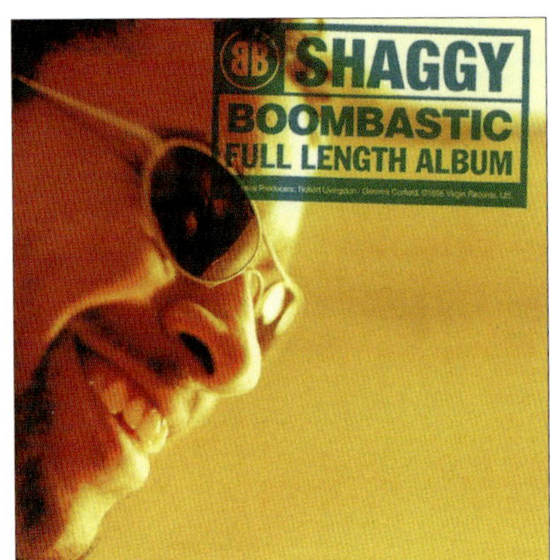

Reggae artist **Shaggy** scored an inescapable hit with "Boombastic," a song which gained renown after being featured in a TV commercial for Levi's.

Billboard 200: *Boombastic* (#34)
Billboard Hot 100: "Boombastic"/"In the Summertime" (#3)

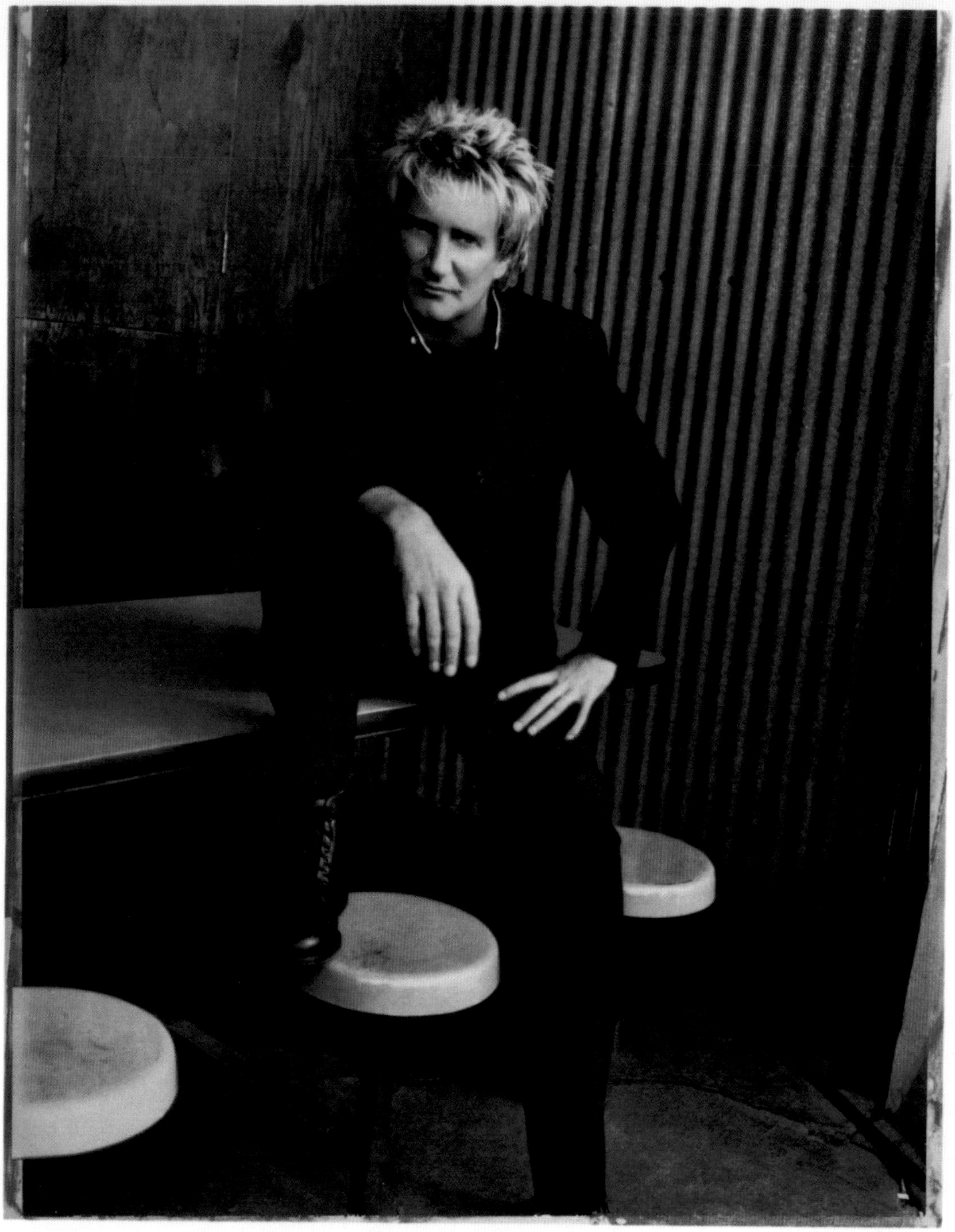

PHOTO CREDIT · Guzman

Rod Stewart

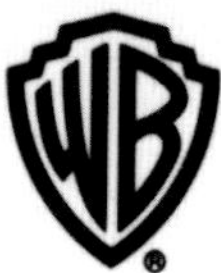

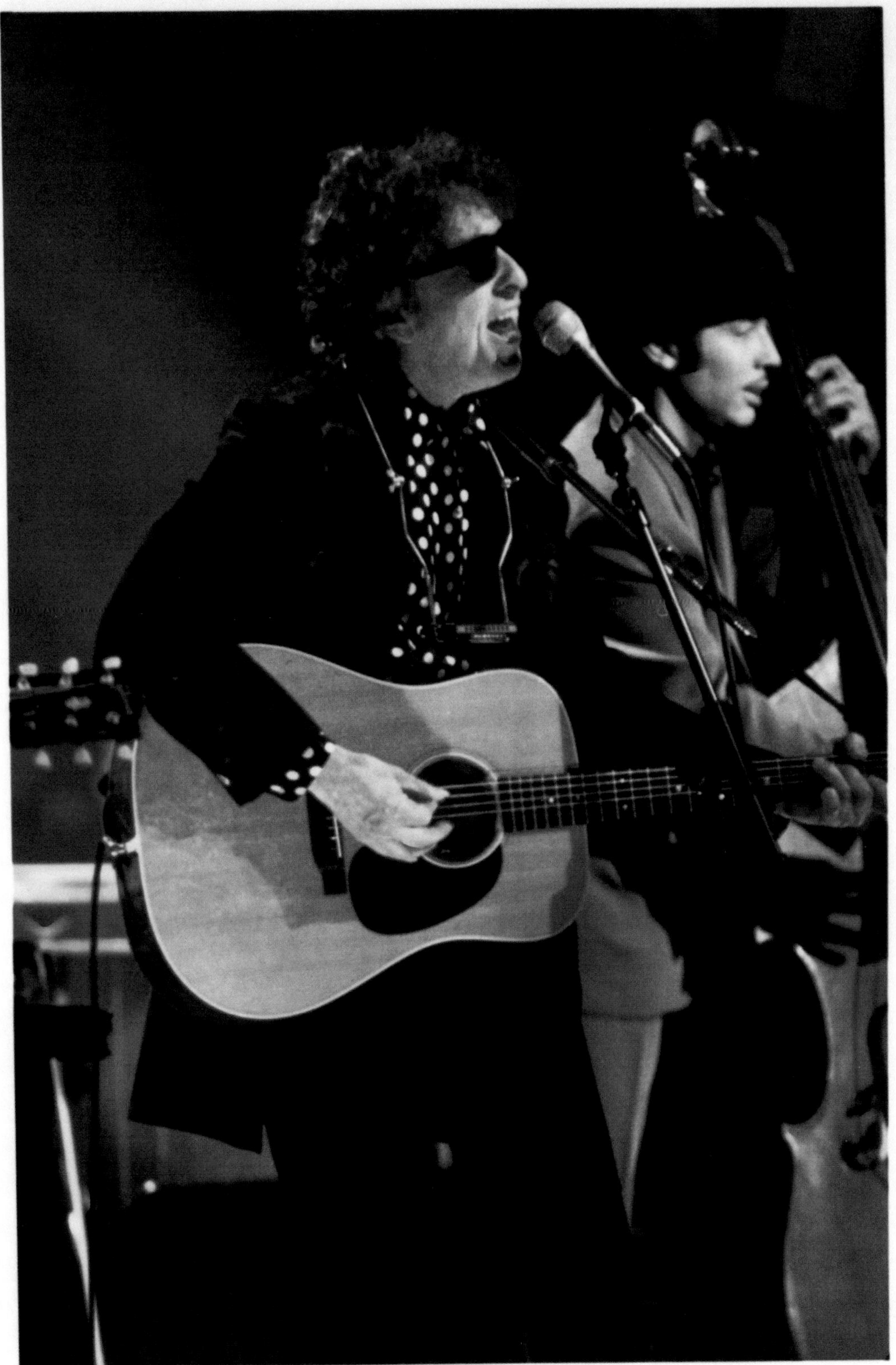

PHOTOGRAPH: FRANK MICELOTTA

BOB DYLAN

COLUMBIA
9411

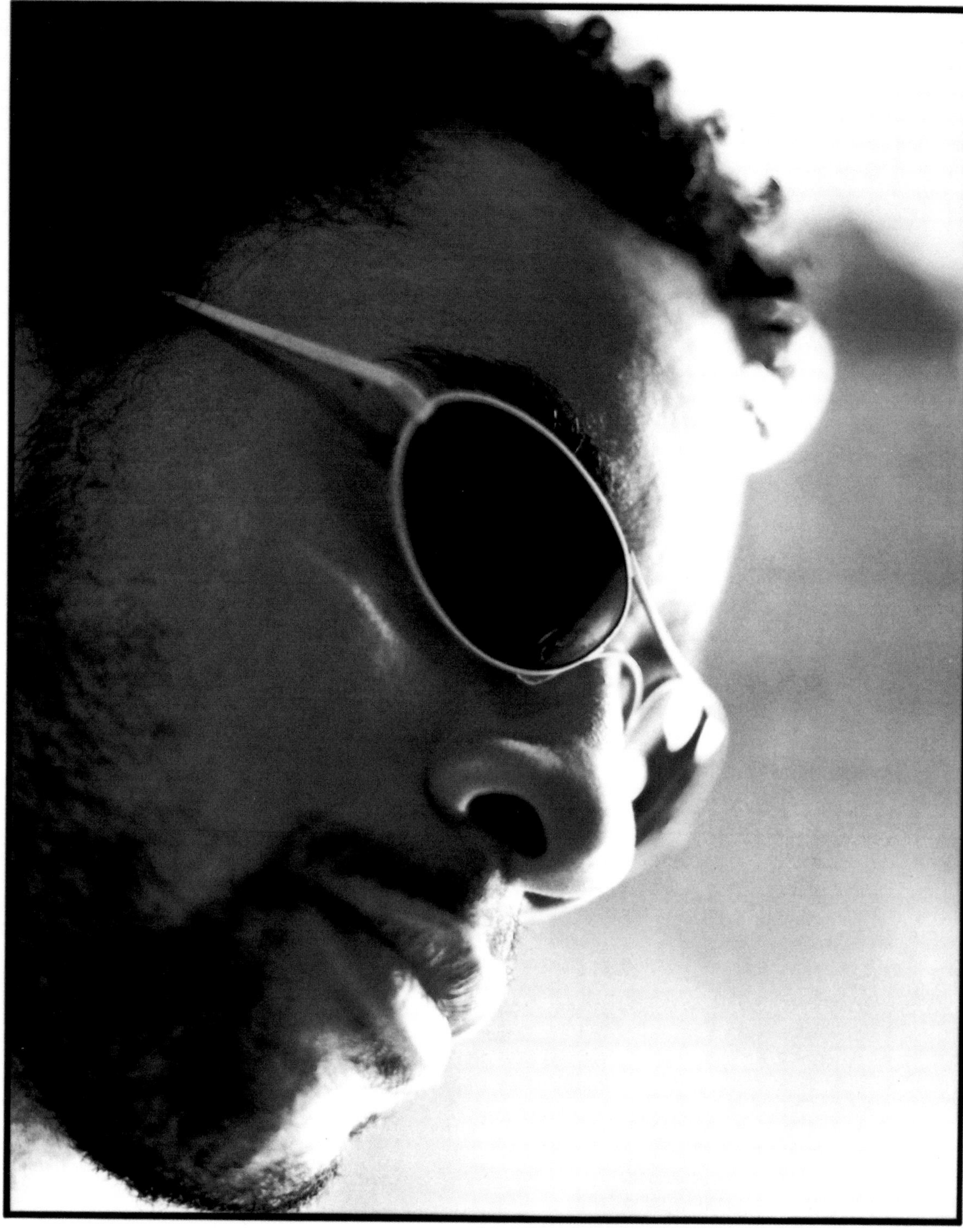

Photo Credit Jake Chessum 5/95

SHAGGY

Virgin

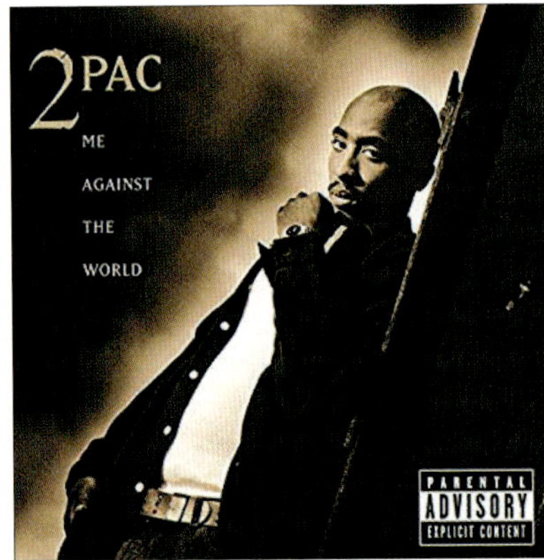

Gangsta rap icon **2Pac** proved he was suited for reflection on *Me Against the World*, led by the intimate, thoughtful "Dear Mama," a tribute to his mother.

Billboard 200: *Me Against the World* (No. 1)
Billboard Hot 100: "Dear Mama" (#9);
"So Many Tears" (#44); "Temptations" (#68)

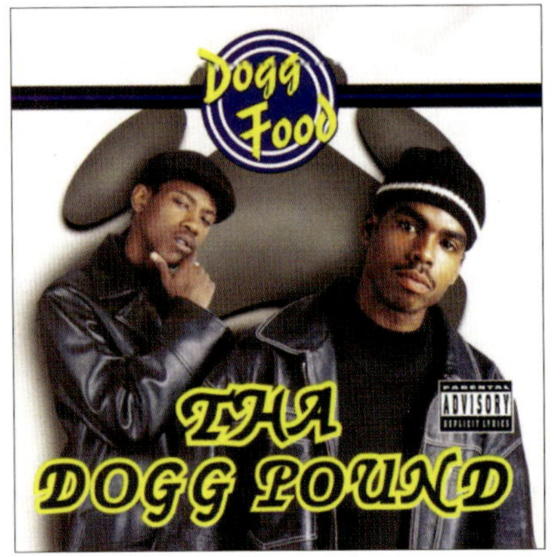

Pilloried by conservative groups prior to its release for vulgar and violent content, *Dogg Food* by hip-hop duo **Tha Dogg Pound** debuted atop the charts.

Billboard 200: *Dogg Food* (No. 1)
Billboard Hot 100: "Let's Play House" (#45)

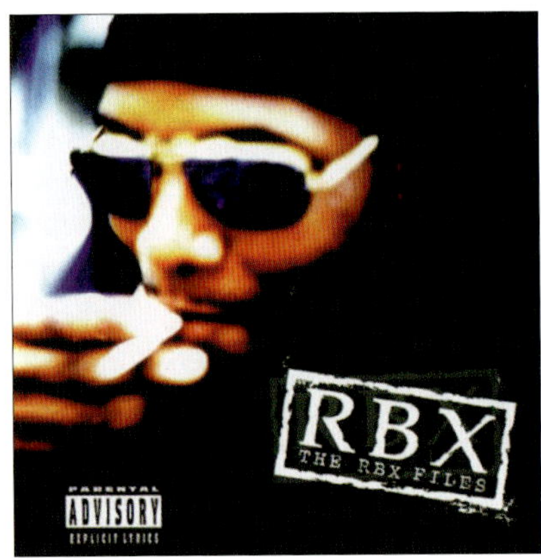

L.A. rapper **RBX** released "A.W.O.L.," a forcible attack on Death Row Records, as Dr. Dre's label had delayed the release of the album *The RBX Files*.

Billboard 200: *The RBX Files* (#62)

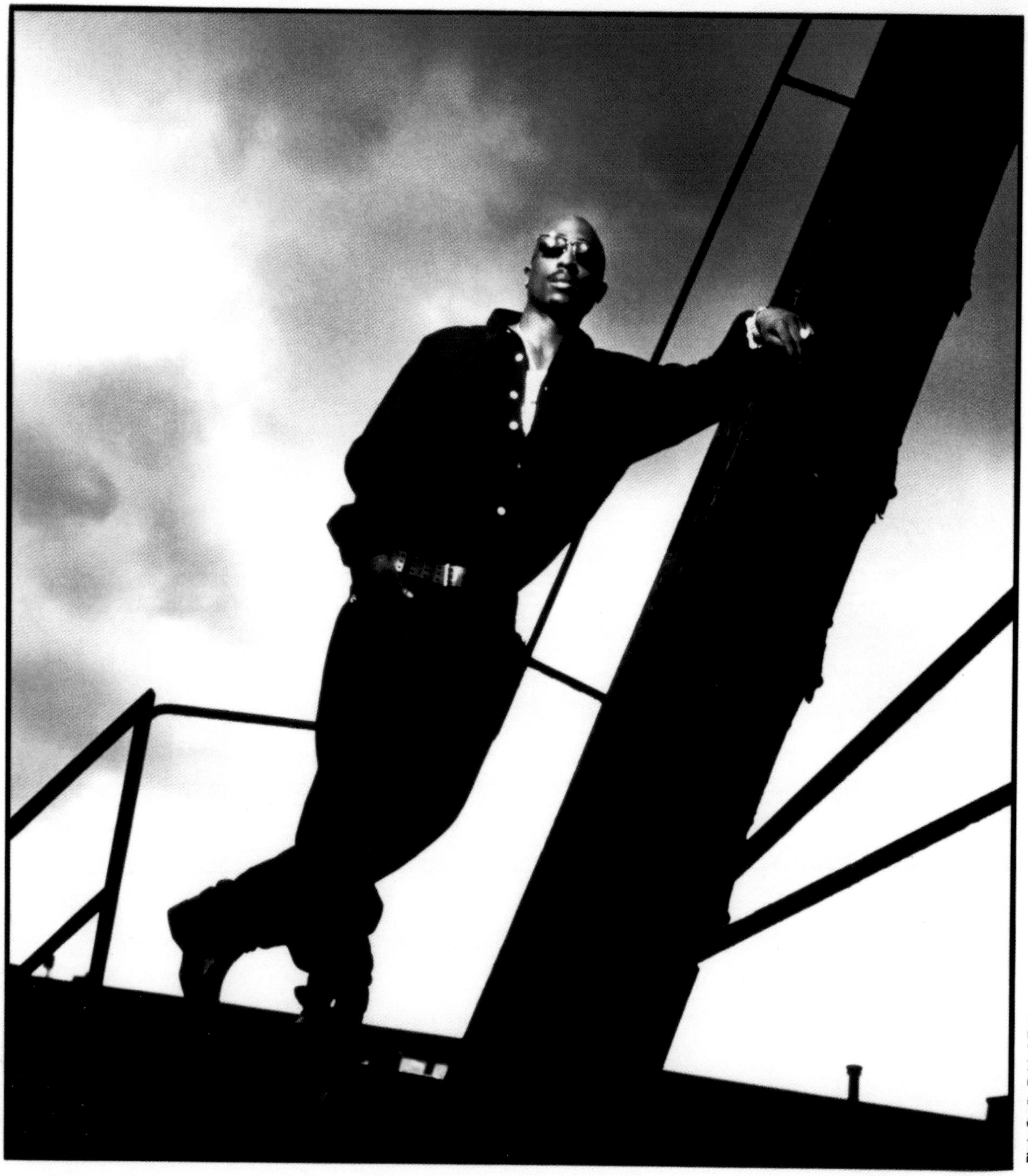

Photo Credit: Reisig & Taylor

2PAC

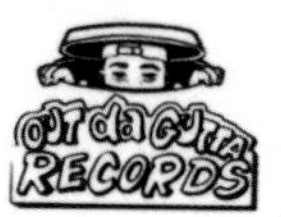

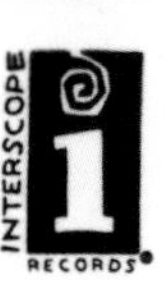

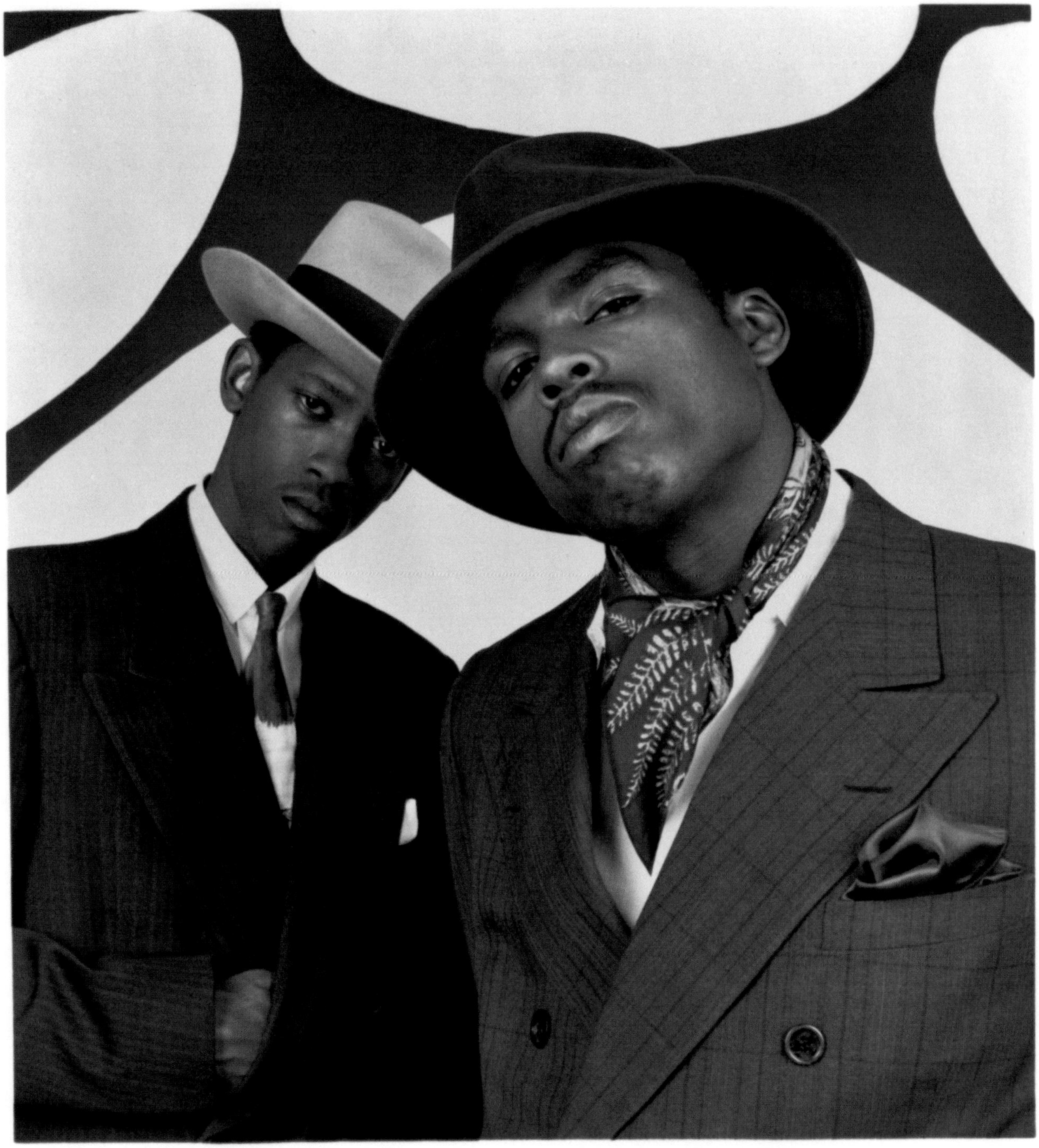

Kurupt

Daz

THA DOGG POUND

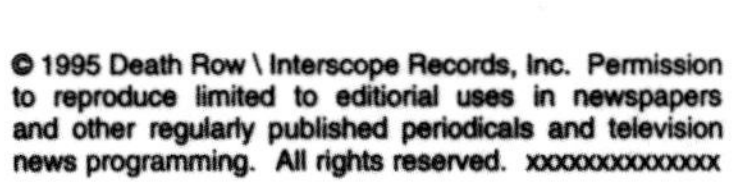

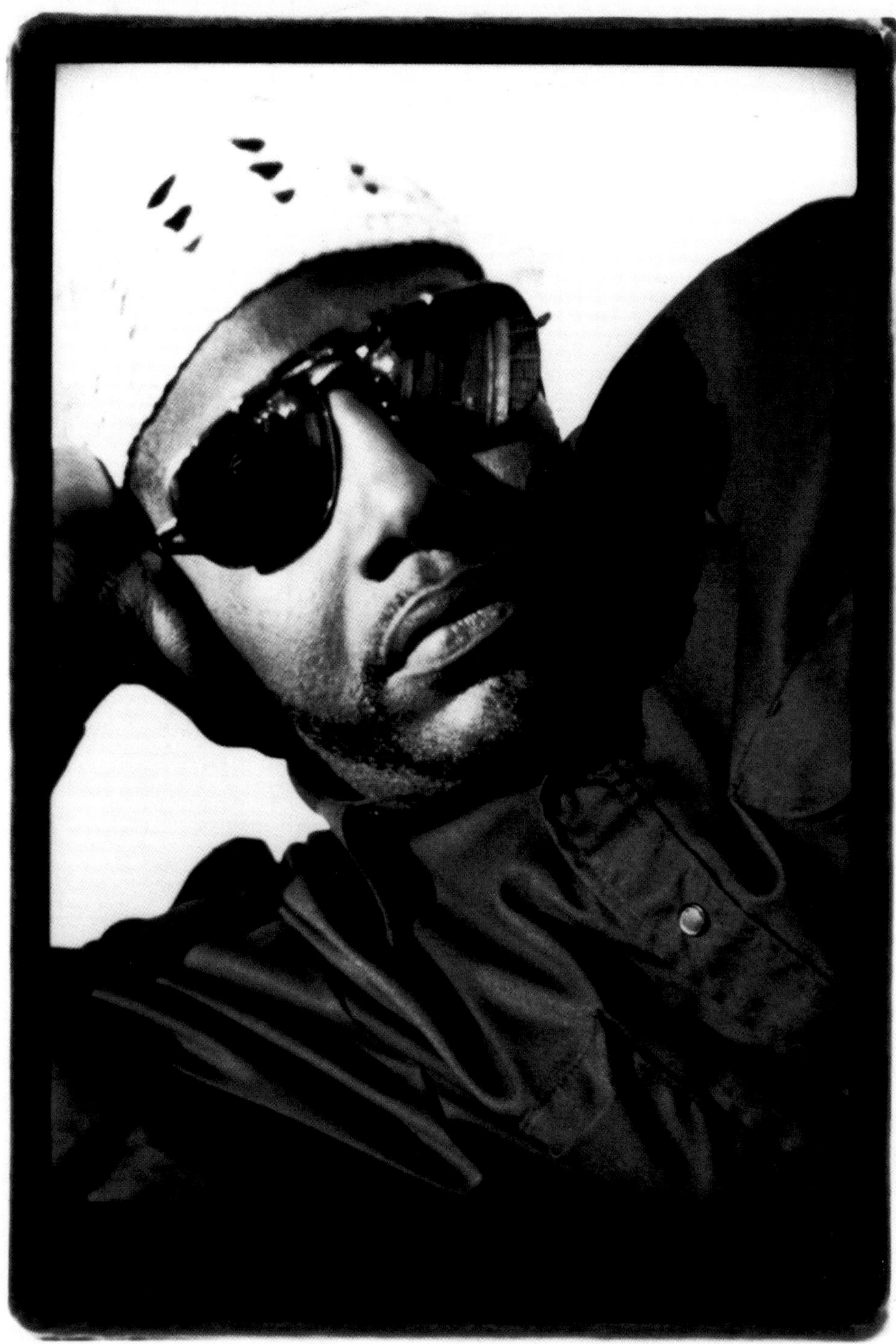

PHOTO CREDIT· Annalisa

RBX

PREMEDITATED

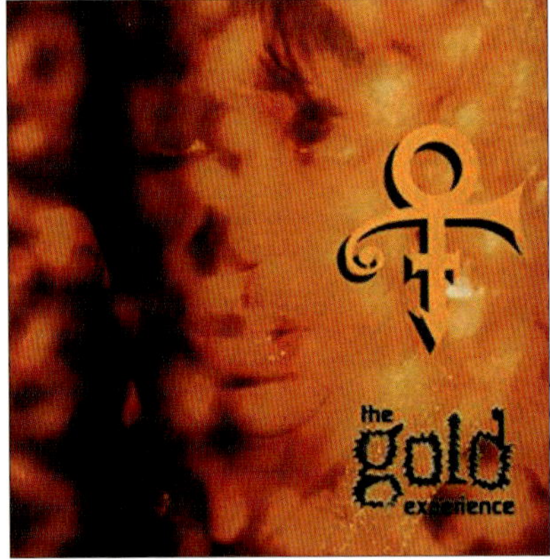

Under his new stage name, an unpronounceable symbol, **Prince** rode the momentum of "The Most Beautiful Girl in the World" on *The Gold Experience*.

Billboard 200: *The Gold Experience* (#6)
Billboard Hot 100: "The Most Beautiful Girl in the World" (#3), "I Hate U" (#12); "Gold" (#88)

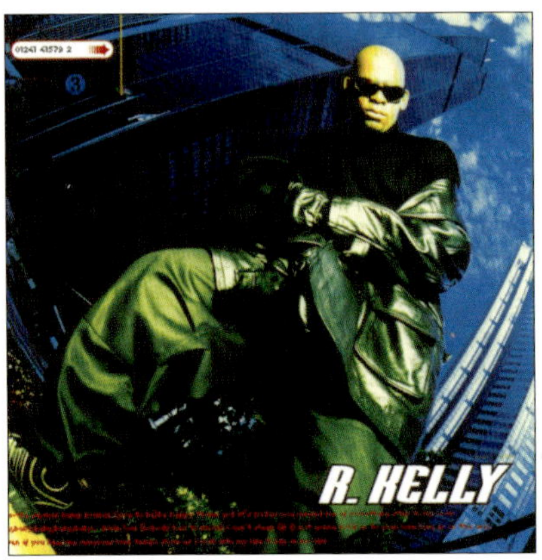

Lascivious soul man **R. Kelly**'s second album of bedroom funk and ballads reached No. 1 on the pop and R&B charts and sired three platinum singles.

Billboard 200: *R. Kelly* (No. 1)
Billboard Hot 100: "You Remind Me of Something" (#4); "Down Low (Nobody Has to Know)" (#4); "I Can't Sleep (Baby If I)" (#5)

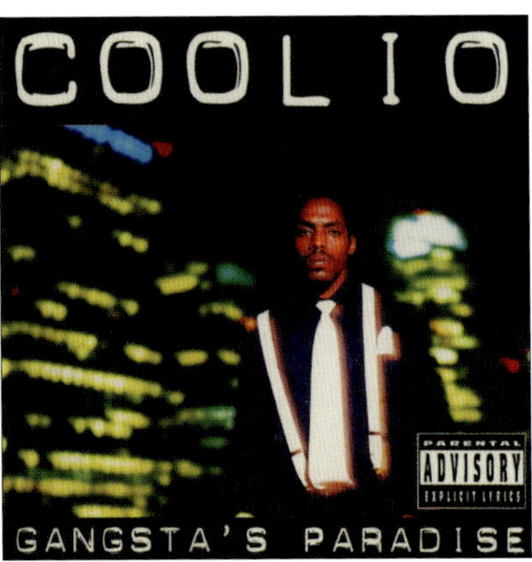

Made for the movie *Dangerous Minds*, "Gangsta's Paradise" catapulted **Coolio** to global stardom and won a Grammy for Best Rap Solo Performance.

Billboard 200: *Gangsta's* Paradise (#9)

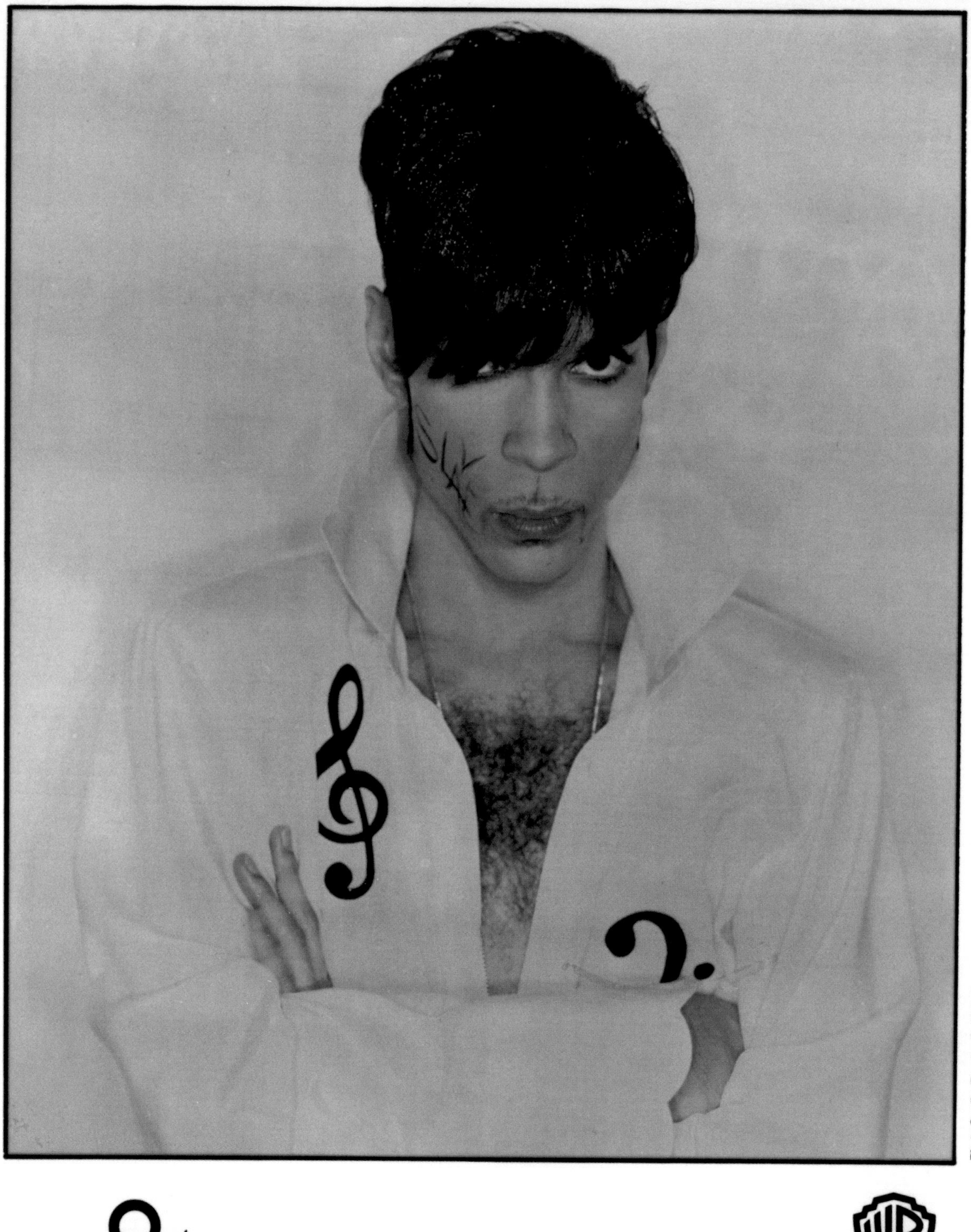

Photo Credit : Randee St. Nicholas

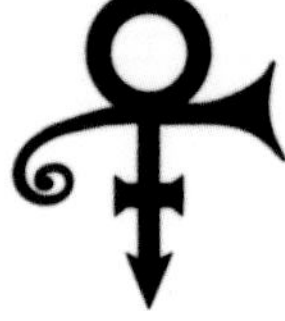

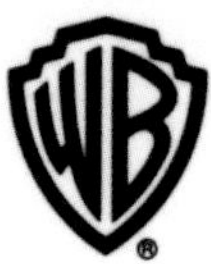

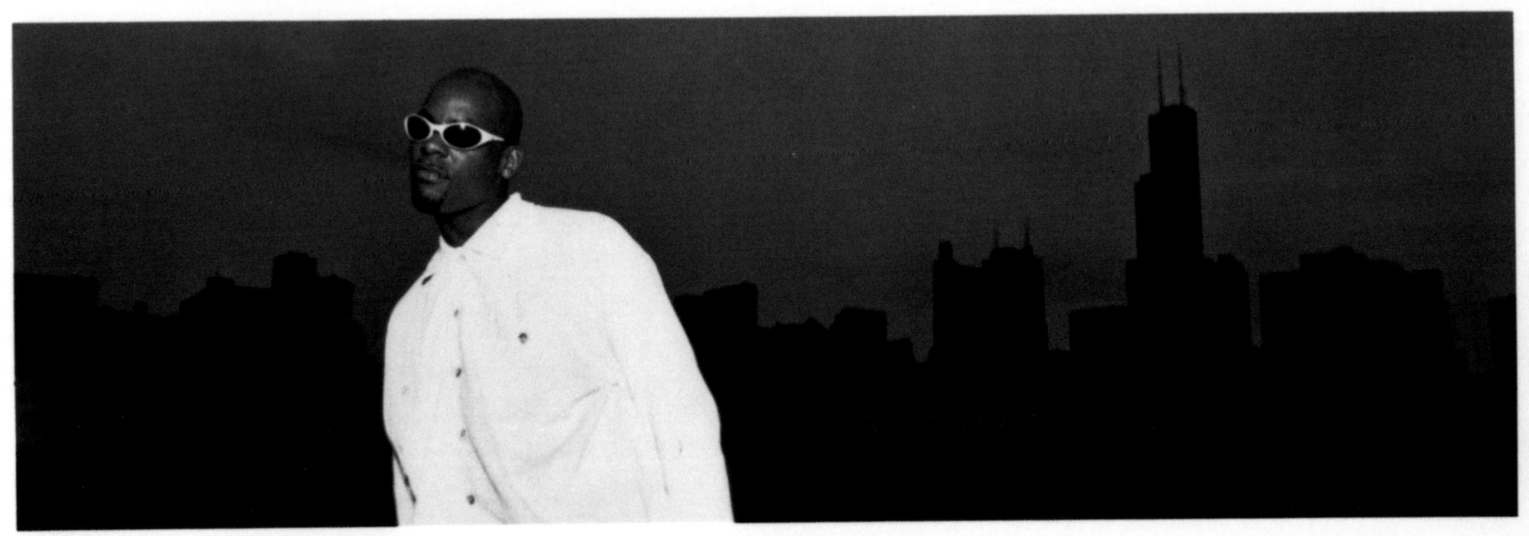

PHOTO CREDIT MICHAEL LAVINE

R. KELLY

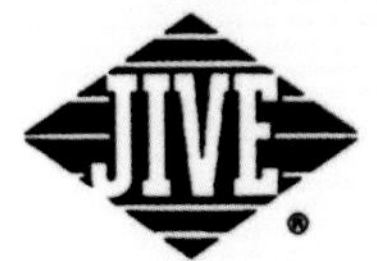

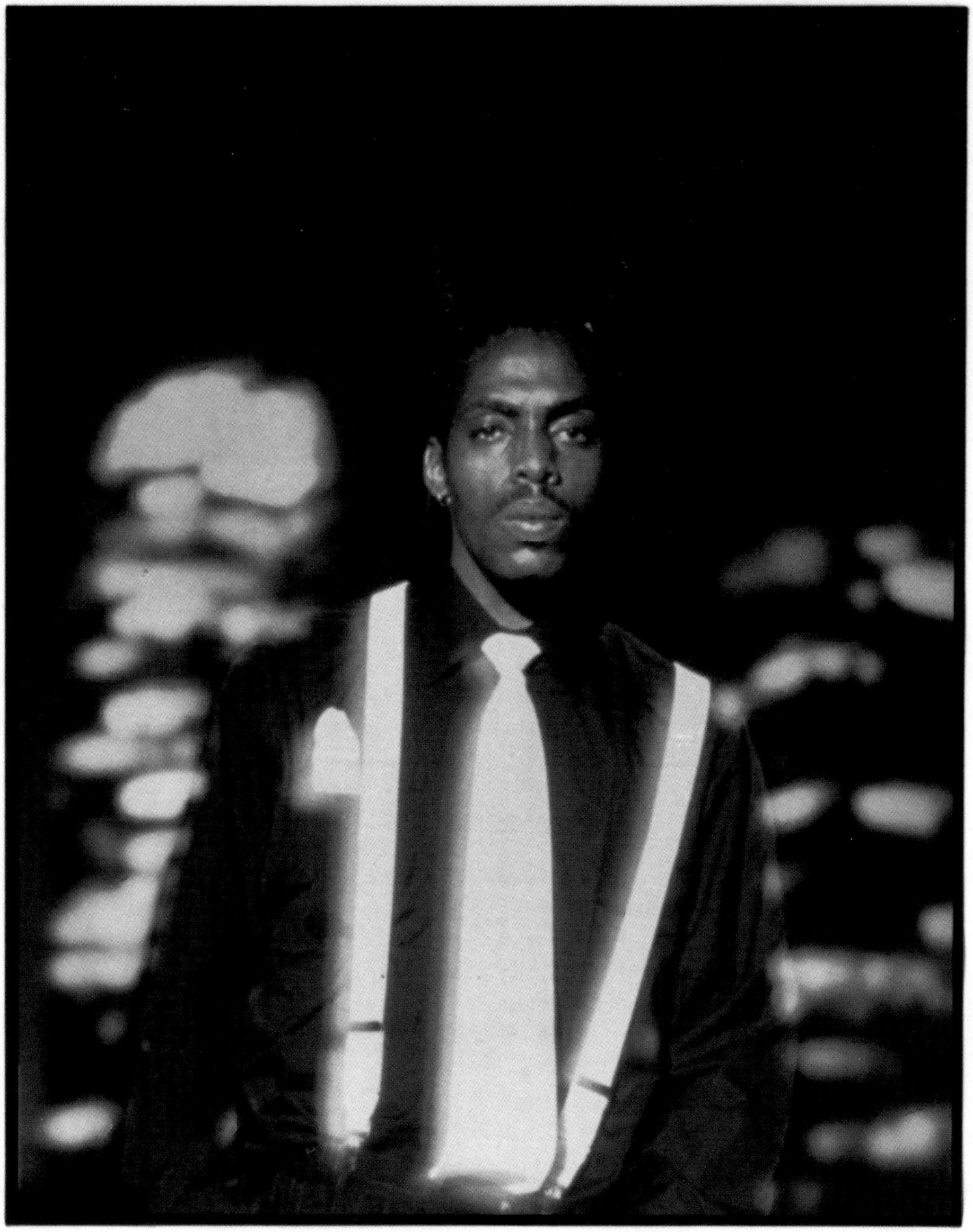

Photo: Michael Miller

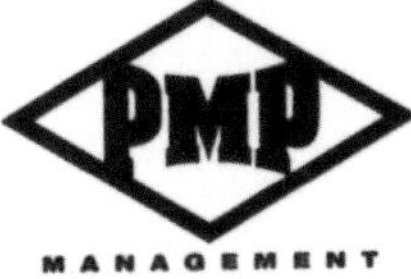

COOLIO

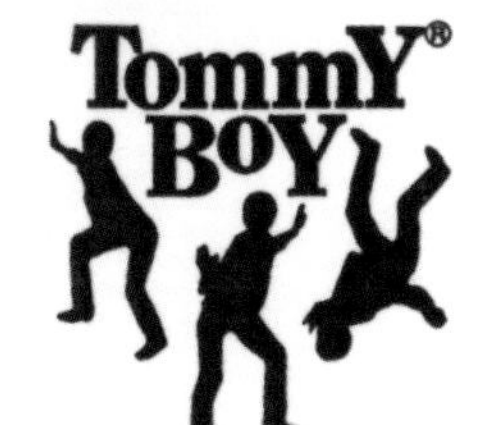

By dint of its allusions to the Mafia and organized crime, Wu-Tang Clan member **Raekwon** started a gangsta-rap subgenre on *Only Built 4 Cuban Linx...*

Billboard 200: *Only Built 4 Cuban Linx...* (#4)
Billboard Hot 100: "Glaciers of Ice"/"Criminology" (#43); "Incarcerated Scarfaces"/"Ice Cream" (#37)

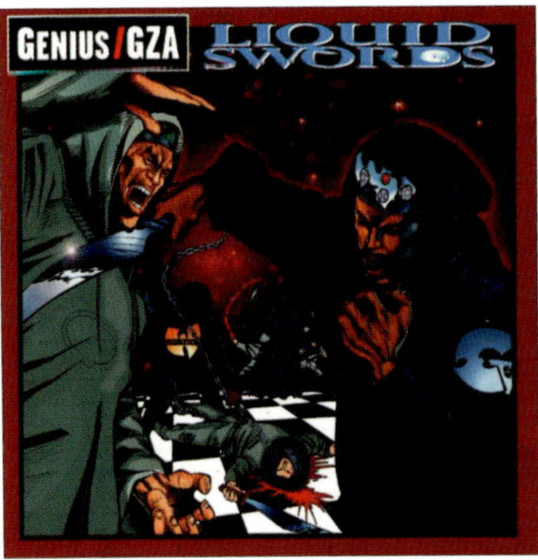

Known as a founder of Wu-Tang Clan, rapper **Genius/GZA** began a solo career with the somber, hard-hitting lyrical artistry of his *Liquid Swords* album.

Billboard 200: *Liquid Swords* (#9)
Billboard Hot 100: "Liquid Swords" (#48); "Cold World" (#97); "Shadowboxin'" (#67)

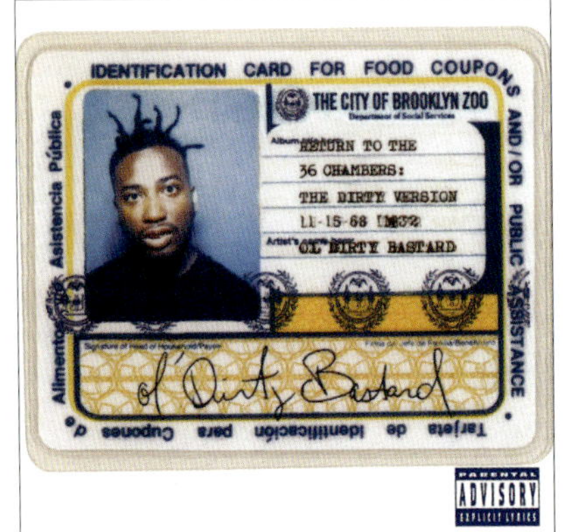

Ol' Dirty Bastard, an initial contributor to Wu-Tang Clan, went out on his own with the RZA-produced *Return to the 36 Chambers: The Dirty Version.*

Billboard 200: *Return to the 36 Chambers: The Dirty Version* (#7)
Billboard Hot 100: "Brooklyn Zoo" (#54); "Shimmy Shimmy Ya" (#62)

CHEF RAEKWON & GHOSTFACE KILLER

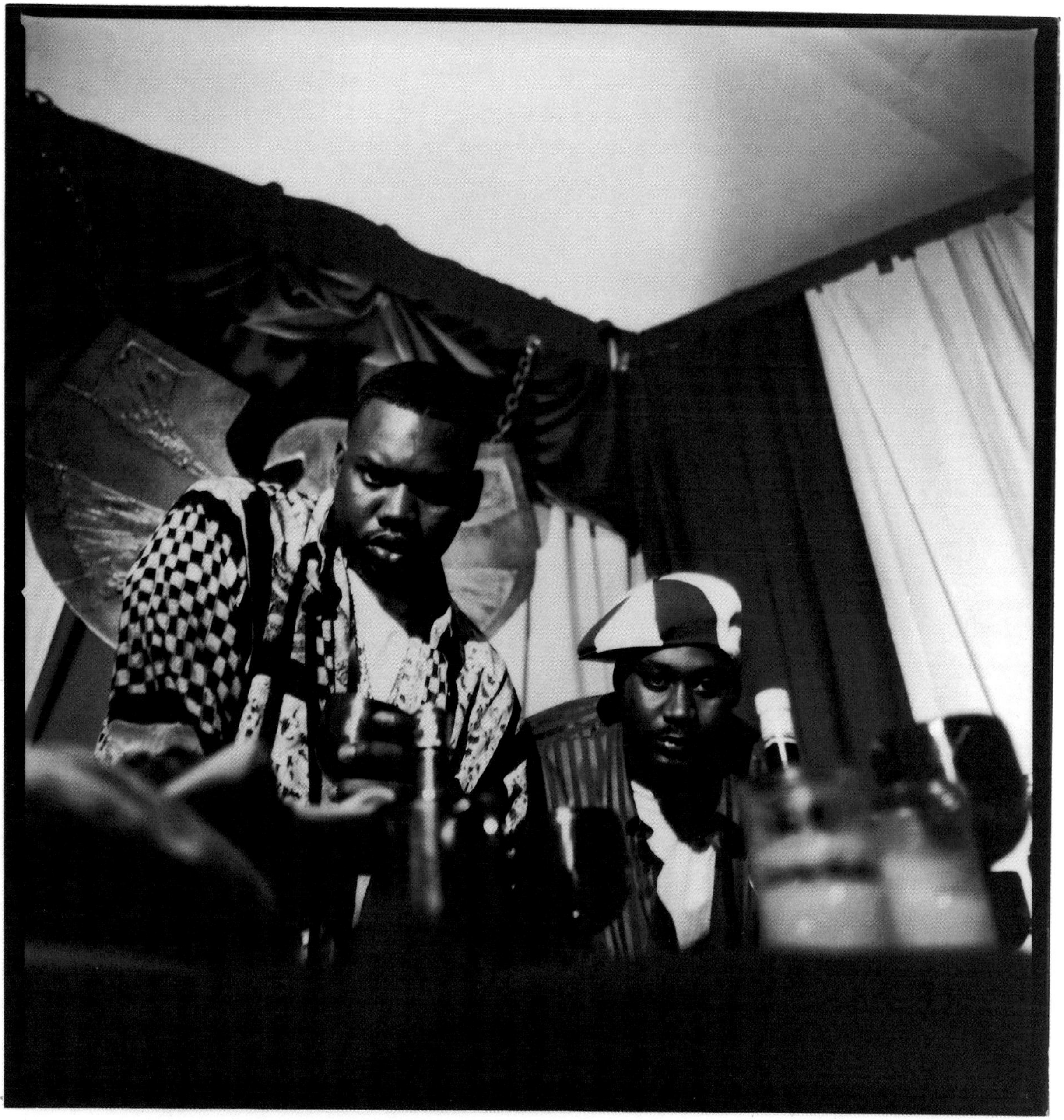

Wu-Tang Productions (718) 442-7757

Chef Raekwon
AKA Lou Diamonds

Ghostface Killer
AKA Tony Starks

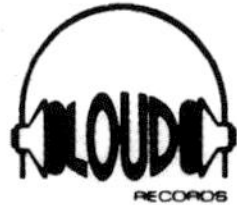

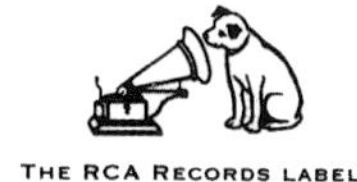

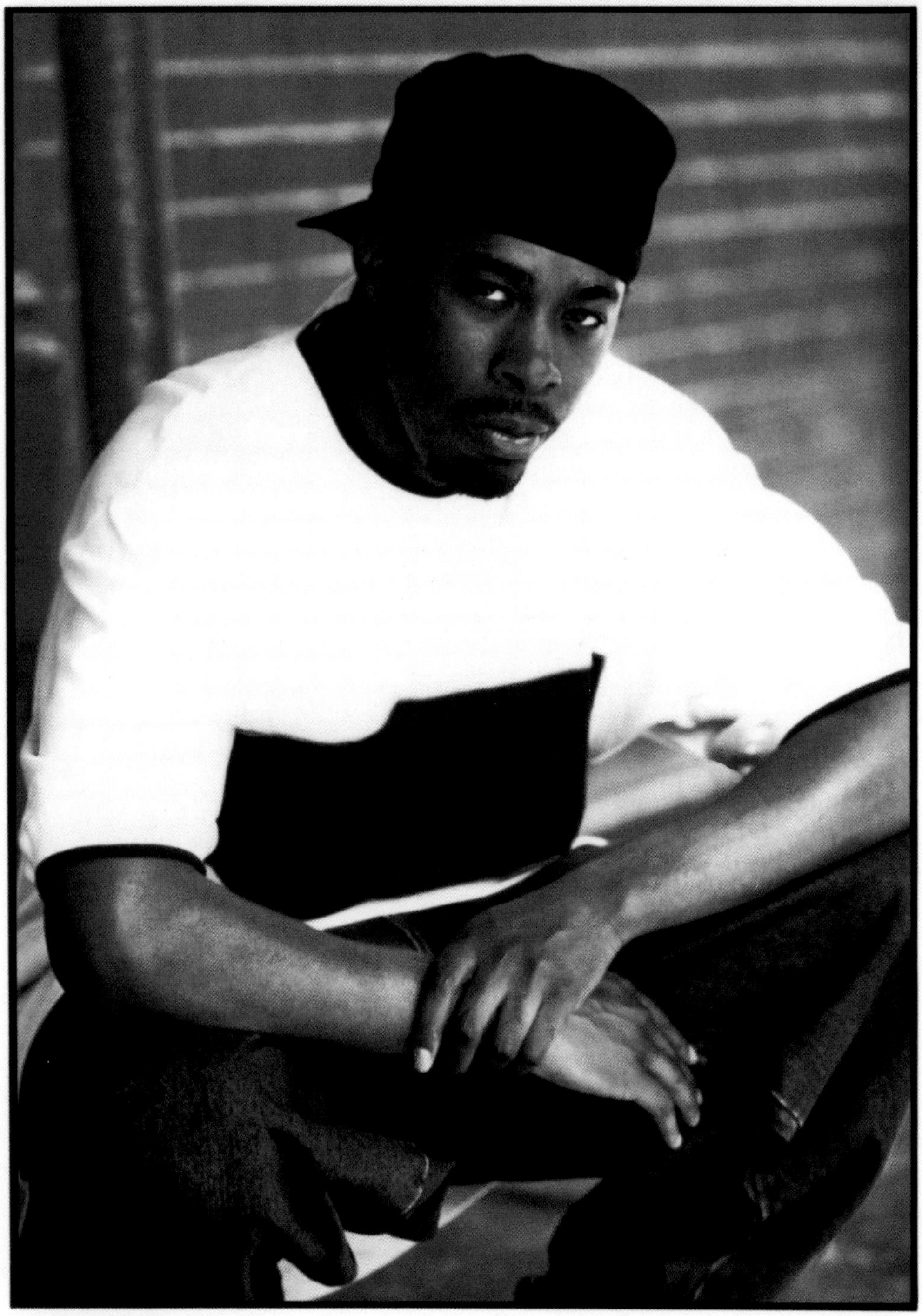

Photo Credit: Mark Humphries

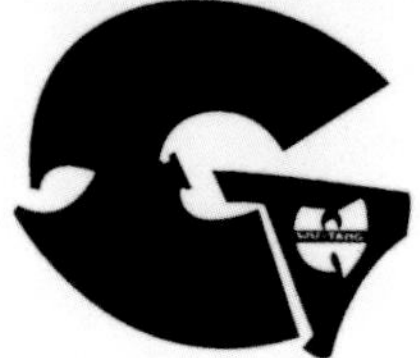

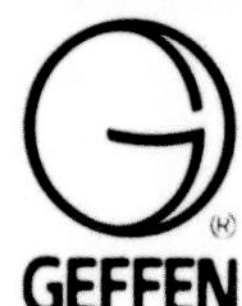

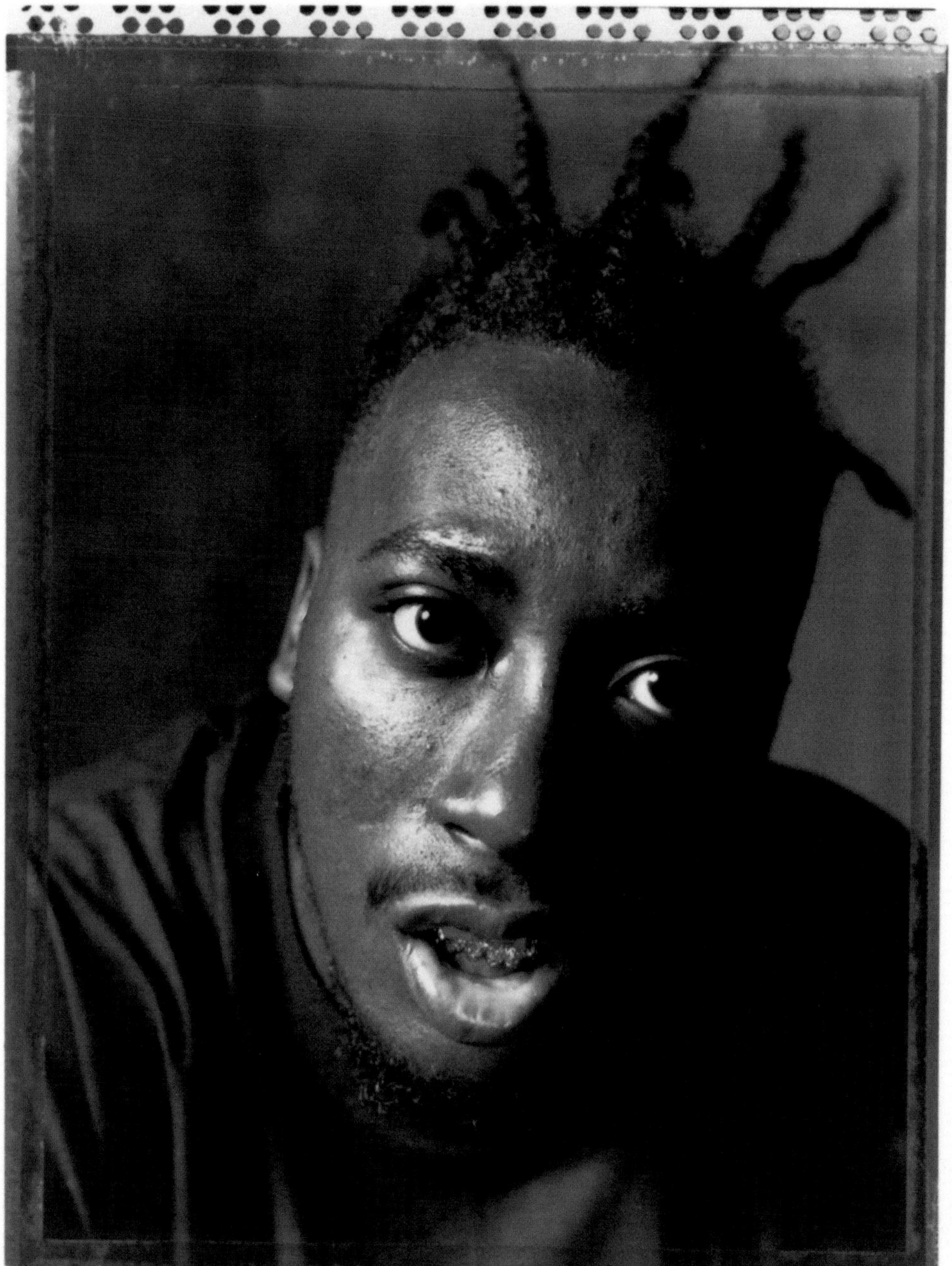

PHOTO CREDIT: DANNY CLINCH / 1995

OL' DIRTY BASTARD

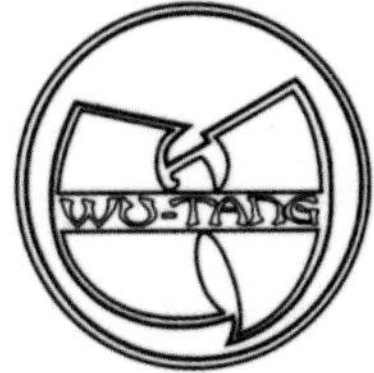

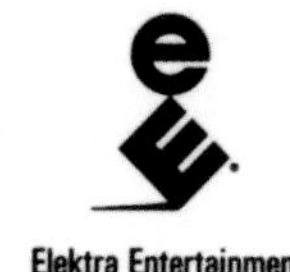

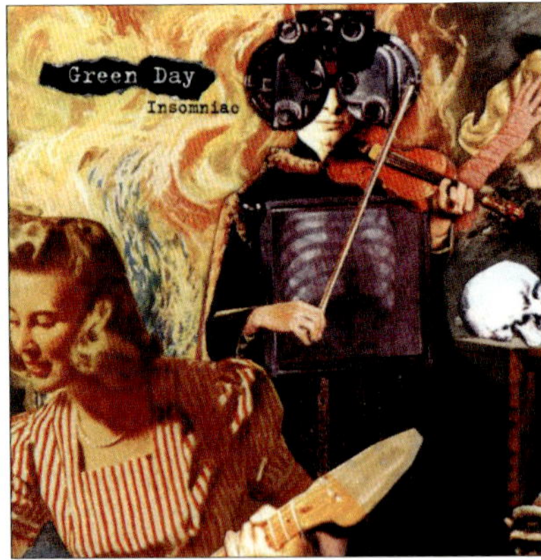

Insomniac, **Green Day**'s darker follow-up to the hit *Dookie*, saw "Geek Stink Breath" and "Brain Stew/Jaded" emerge as pop-punk favorites on rock radio.

Billboard 200: *Insomniac* (#2)

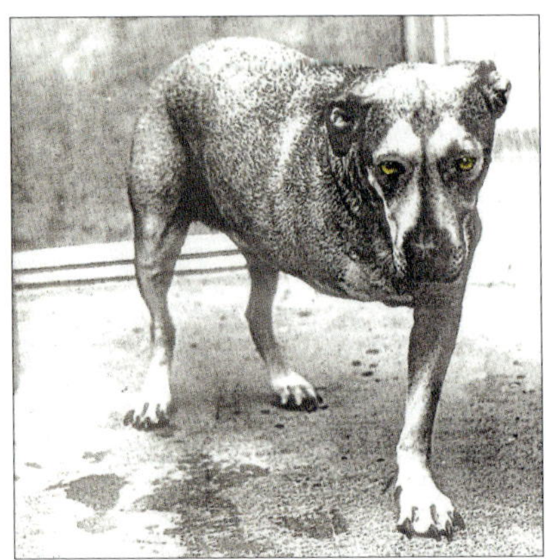

Alice in Chains' eponymous third album debuted at No. 1 on the charts, fortifed by the ominous "Grind" and "Again" and the ballad "Heaven Beside You."

Billboard 200: *Alice in Chains* (No. 1)

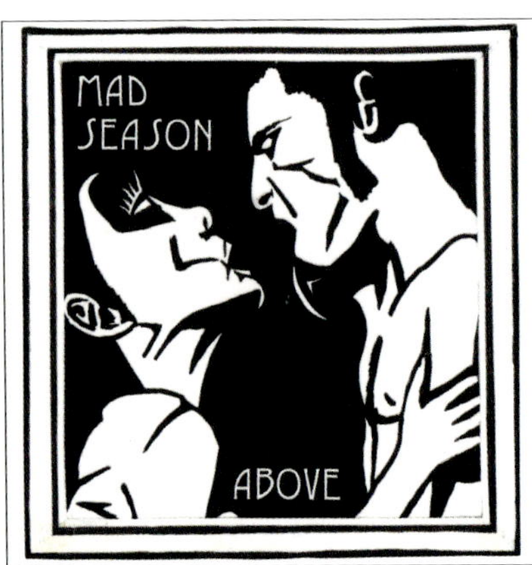

A Seattle grunge supergroup featuring members of Alice in Chains, Pearl Jam and Screaming Trees, **Mad Season** scored a radio hit, "River of Deceit."

Billboard 200: *Above* (#24)

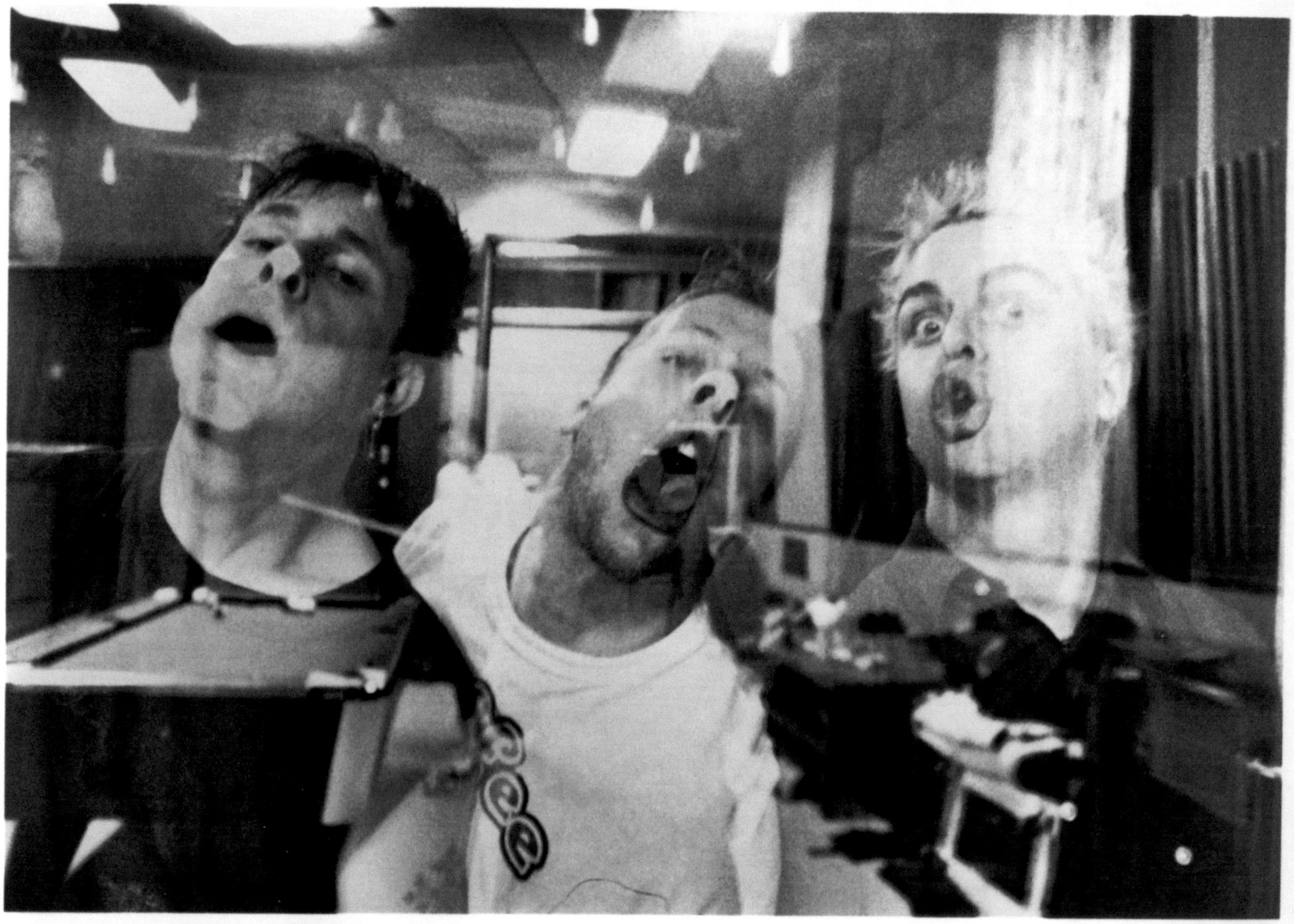

Photo Credit: Eva Janey

Green Day

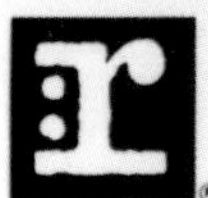

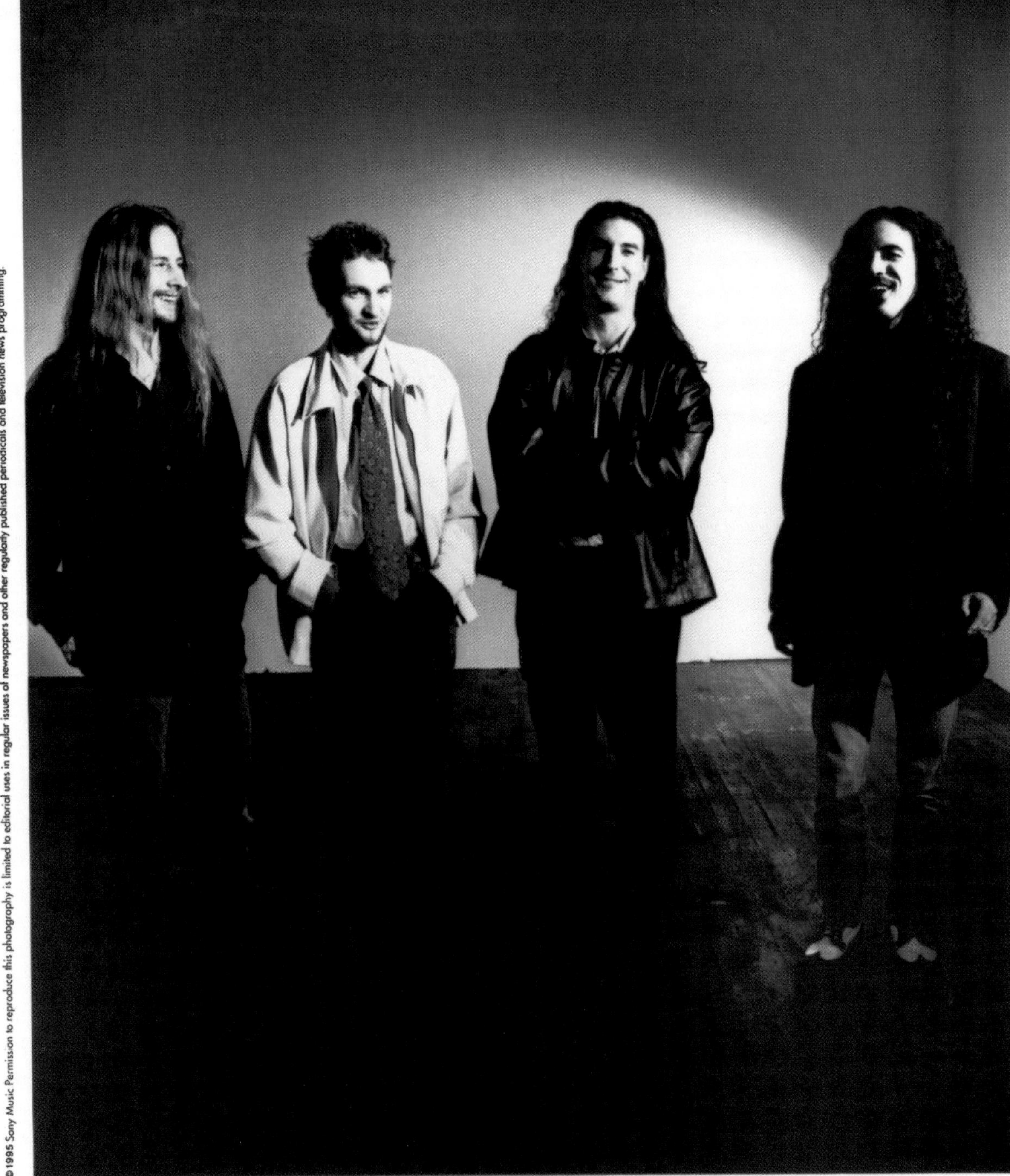

PHOTOGRAPH: ROCKY SCHENCK

Jerry Cantrell Layne Staley Sean Kinney Mike Inez

ALICE IN CHAINS

COLUMBIA
9511

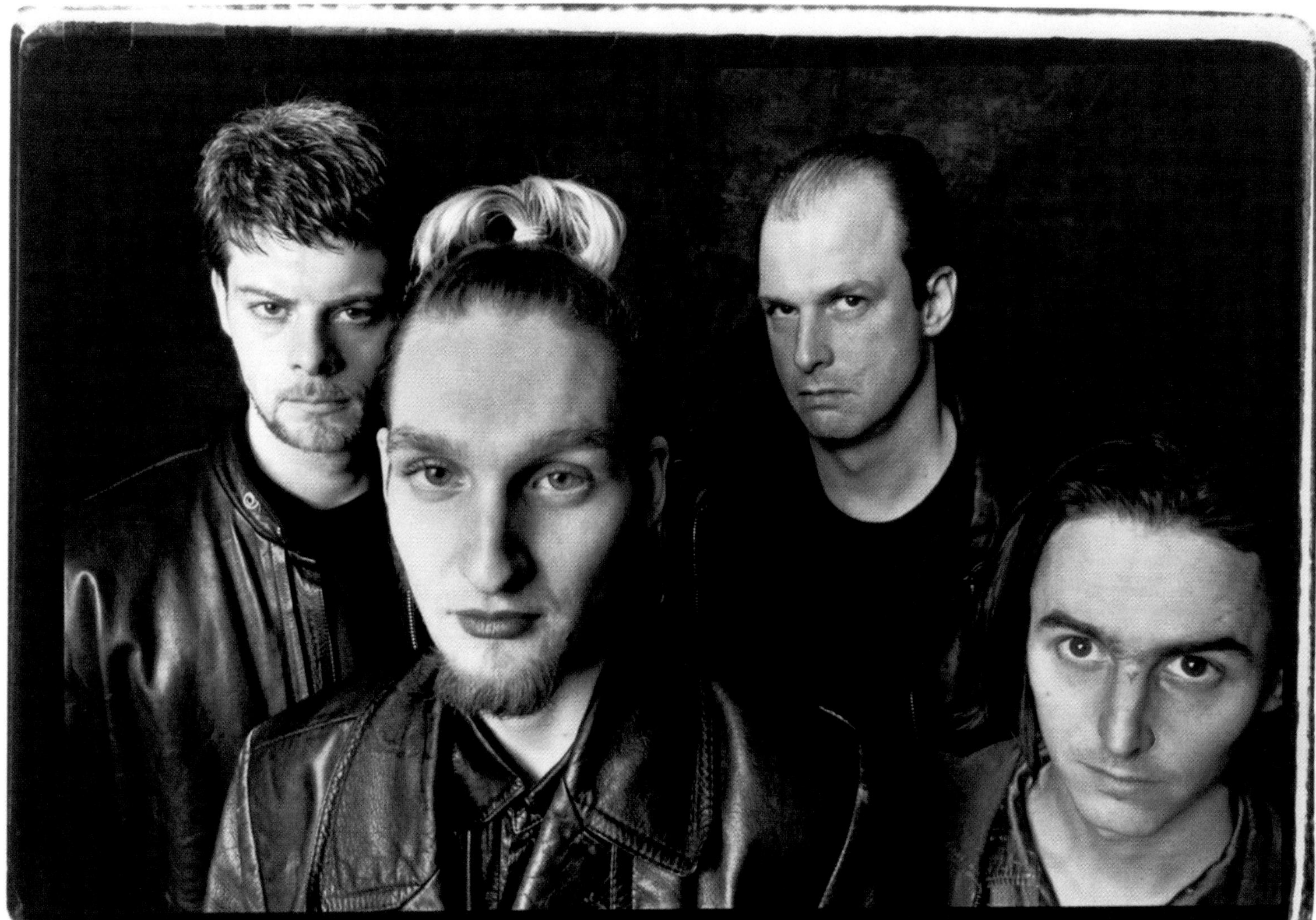

photo credit: Lance Mercer

BARRETT MARTIN **LAYNE STALEY** **BAKER** **MIKE McCREADY**

MAD SEASON

COLUMBIA

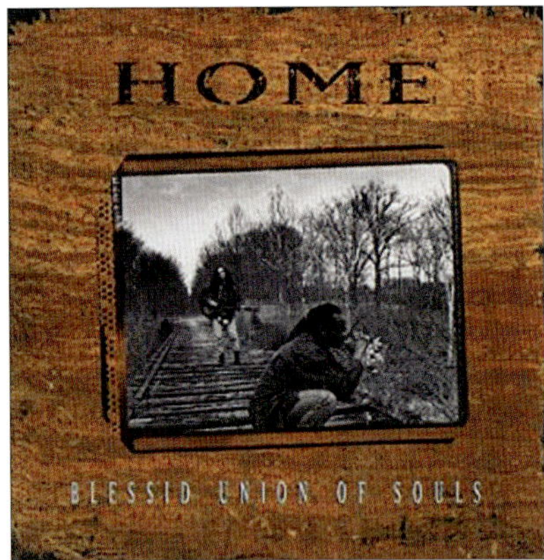

Benefiting from DJs who spread the word in the quartet's hometown of Cincinnati, the song "I Believe" put **Blessid Union of Souls** on the musical map.

Billboard 200: *Home* (#78)

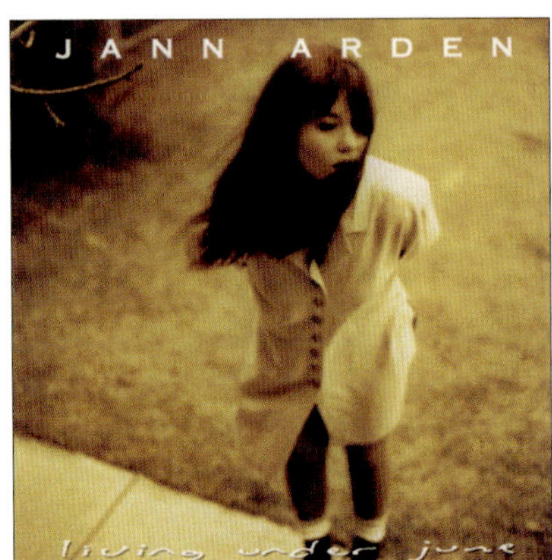

Living Under June by Canadian darling **Jann Arden** generated six Top 10 hits in her home country, with the ballad "Insensitive" her biggest hit worldwide.

Billboard 200: *Living Under June* (#76)
Billboard Hot 100: "Insensitive" (#12)

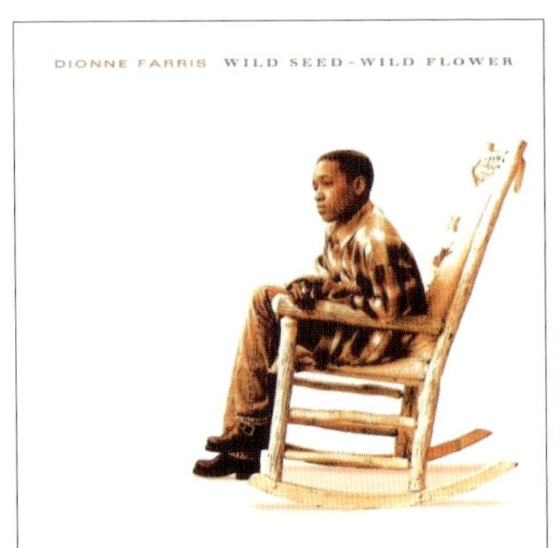

After a stint with the alternative hip-hop group Arrested Development, **Dionne Farris** delivered the striking hit single "I Know" and dominated the airwaves.

Billboard 200: *Wild Seed - Wild Flower* (#57)
Billboard Hot 100: "I Know" (#4)

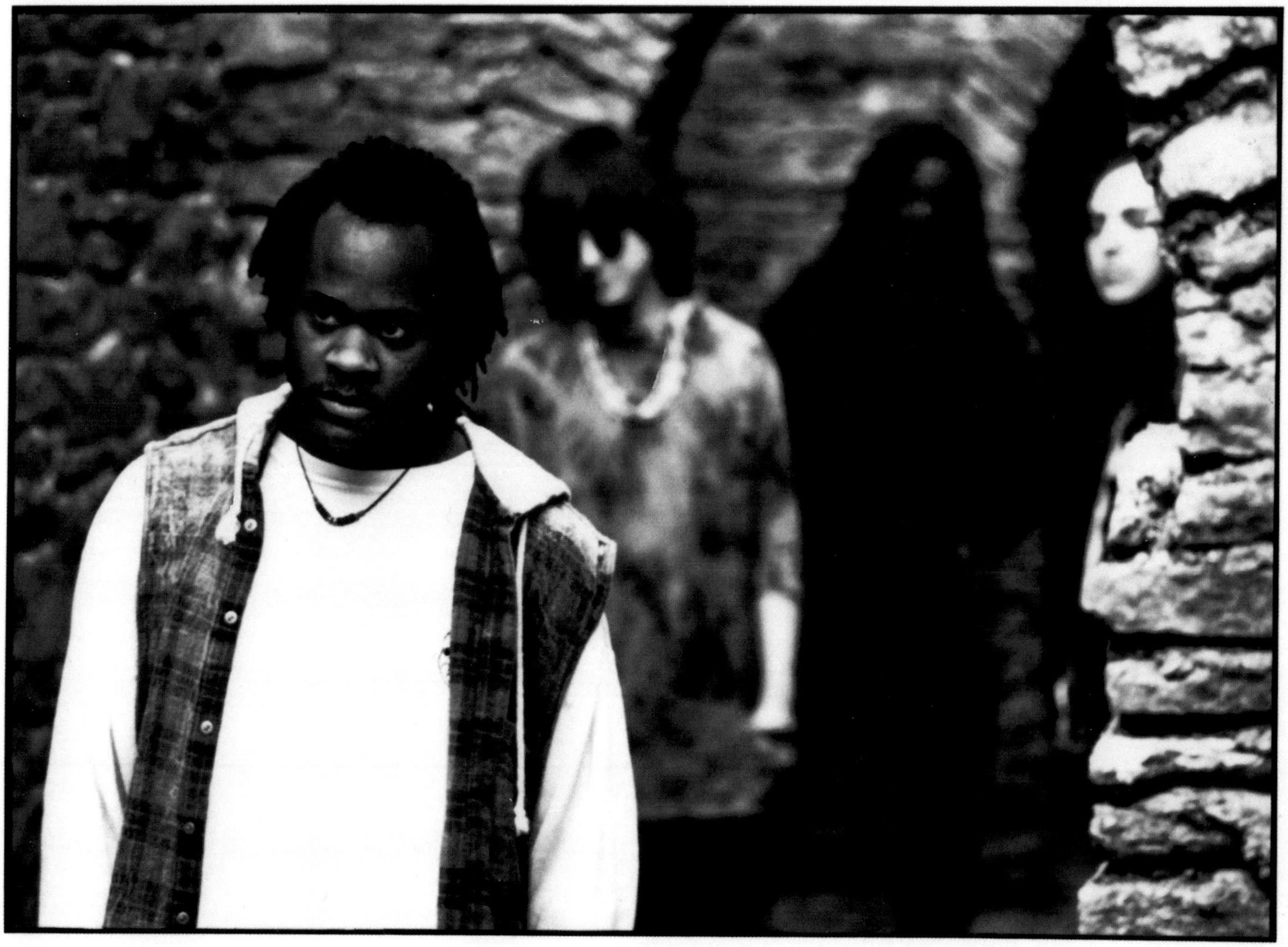

Photo credit: TODD SLATER

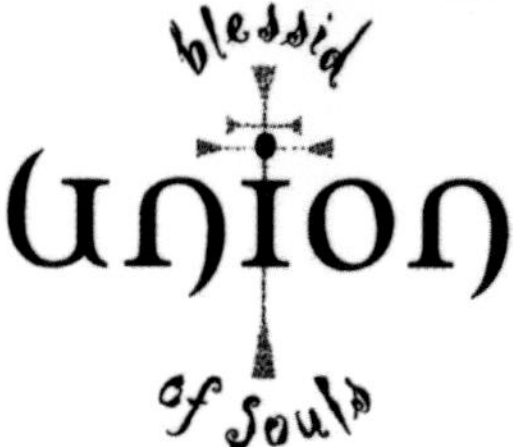

EMI Records

EMI

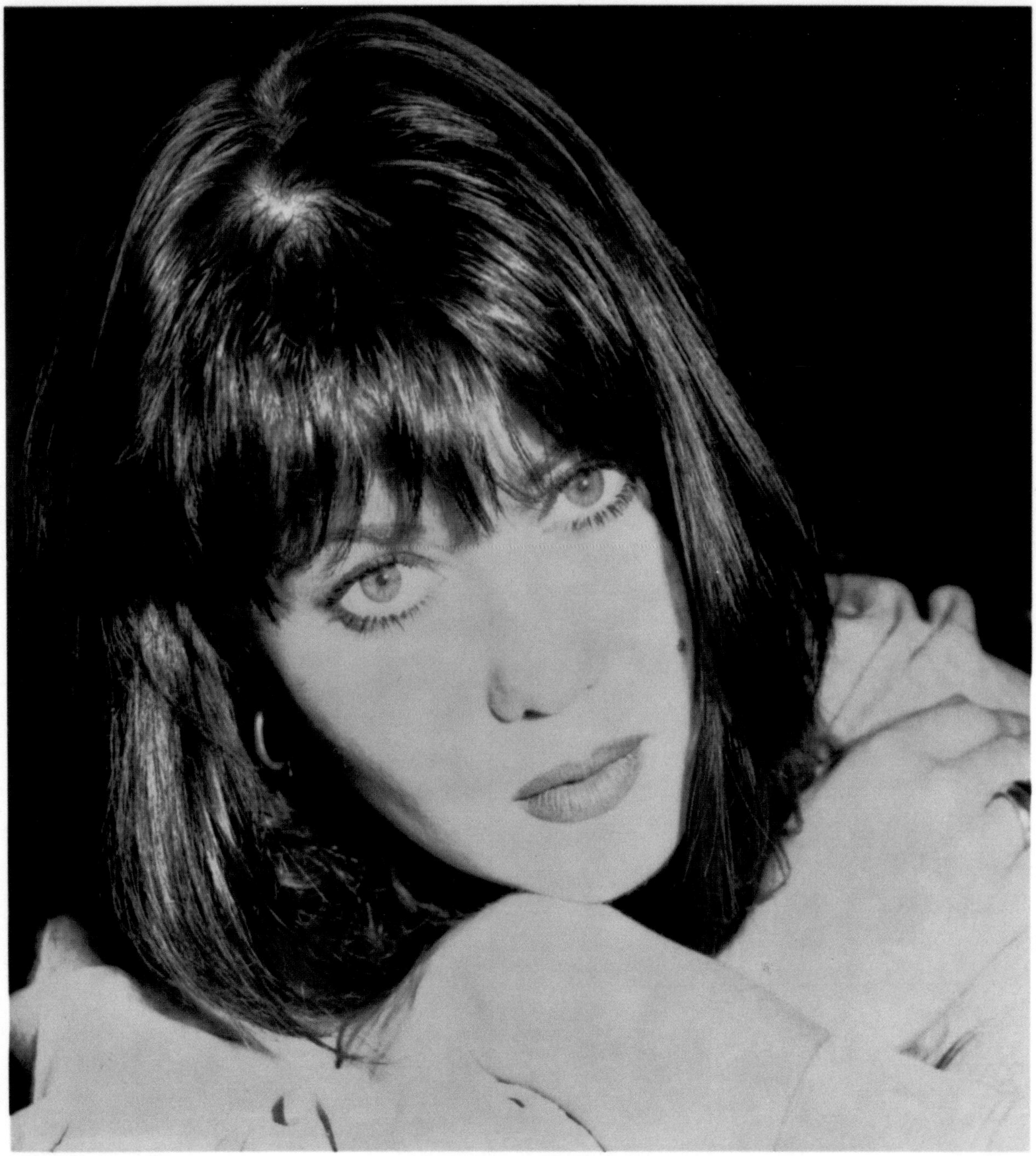

MUSICWORKS INC.
NEIL MacGONIGILL / RUDI LeVALLEY
#207 1501 17th AVE. S.W.
CALGARY, ALBERTA CANADA
PHONE - (403) 245-0425
FAX (403) 244-7129

JANN ARDEN

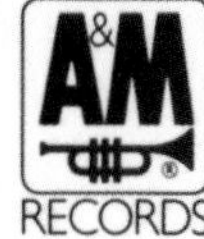

Photo: Andrew MacNaughton 3/95

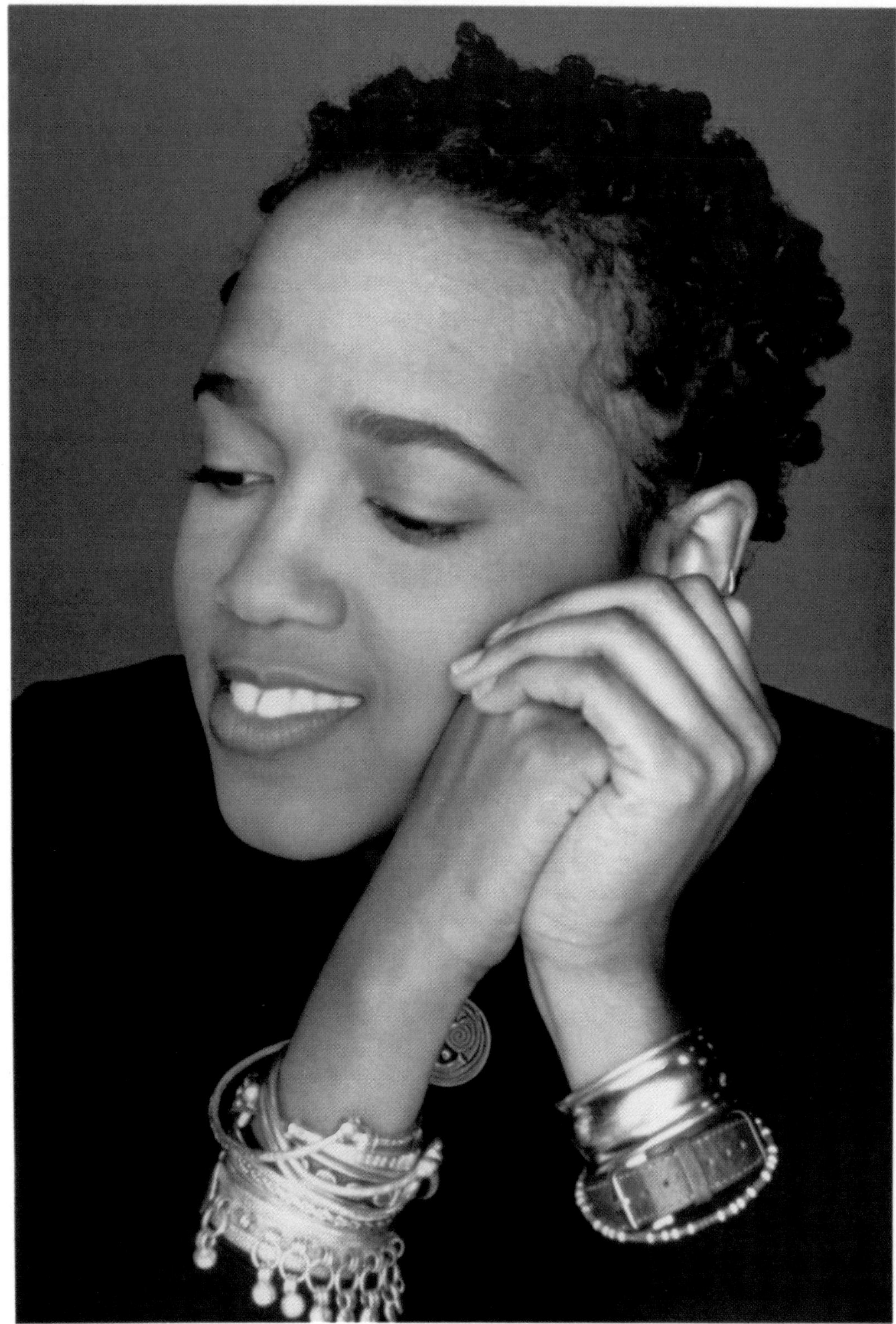

PHOTOGRAPH: EDIE BASKIN

DIONNE FARRIS

COLUMBIA
9506

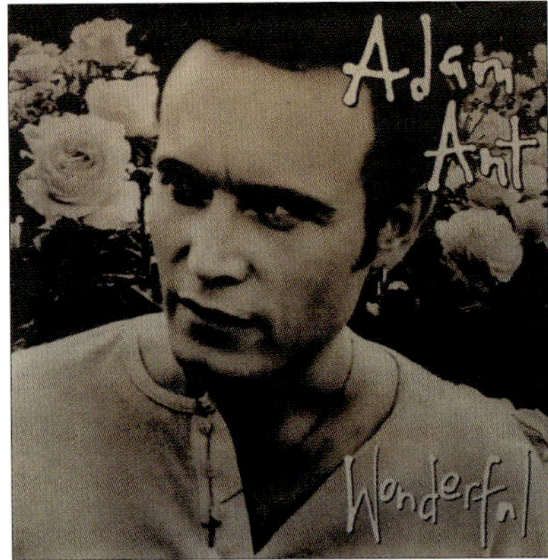

More than a dozen years after Adam & the Ants ruled British pop, **Adam Ant** made an abrupt comeback, emerging with *Wonderful* and the Top 40 title track.

Billboard 200: *Wonderful* (#143)
Billboard Hot 100: "Wonderful" (#39)

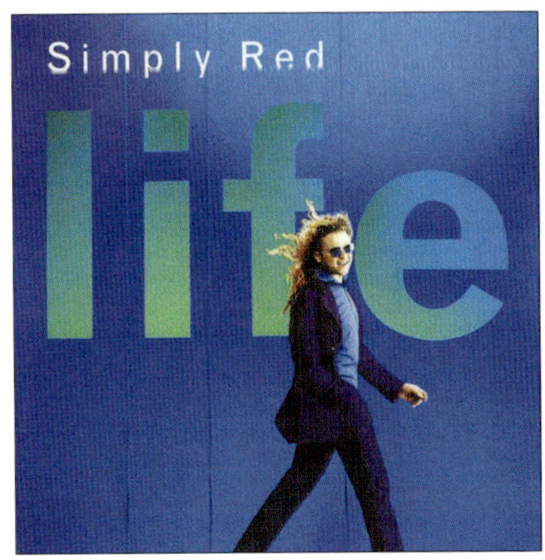

Led by Mick Hucknall, British blue-eyed soul act **Simply Red** reached No. 1 in the UK with "Fairground," and *Life* topped the album charts all over Europe.

Billboard 200: *Life* (#75)

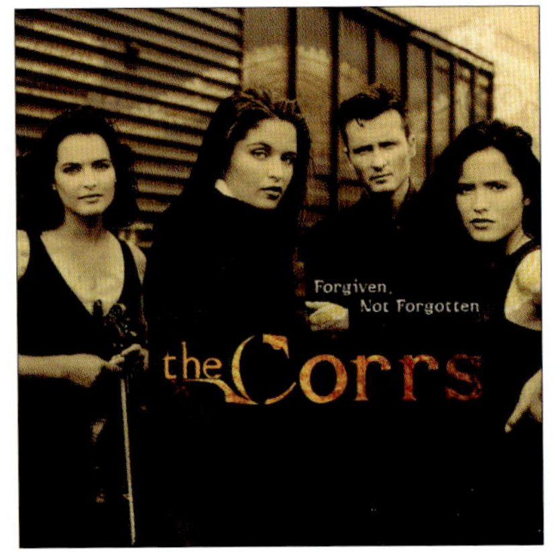

The Corrs, an Irish pop group consisting of photogenic siblings, recorded their debut, *Forgiven, Not Forgotten*, and "Runaway" was a modest hit in the US.

Billboard 200: *Forgiven, Not Forgotten* (#131)
Billboard Hot 100: "Runaway" (#68)

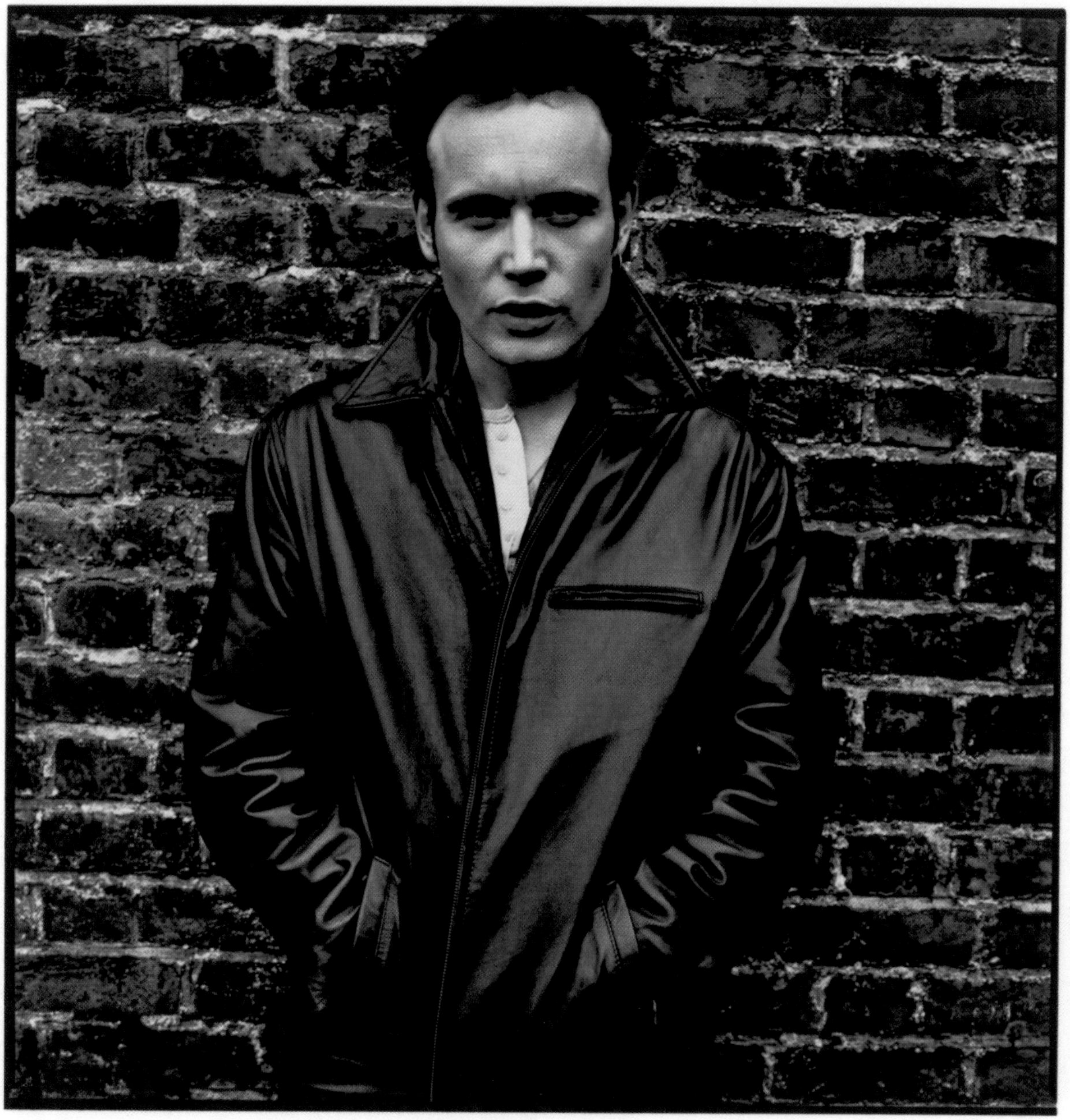

Photo credit: Anton Corbijn ©1994

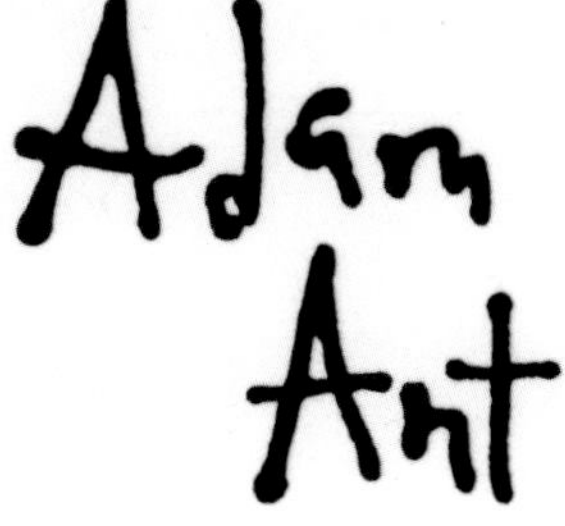

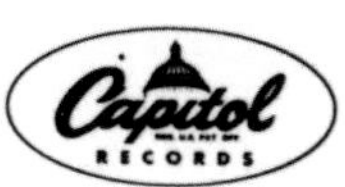

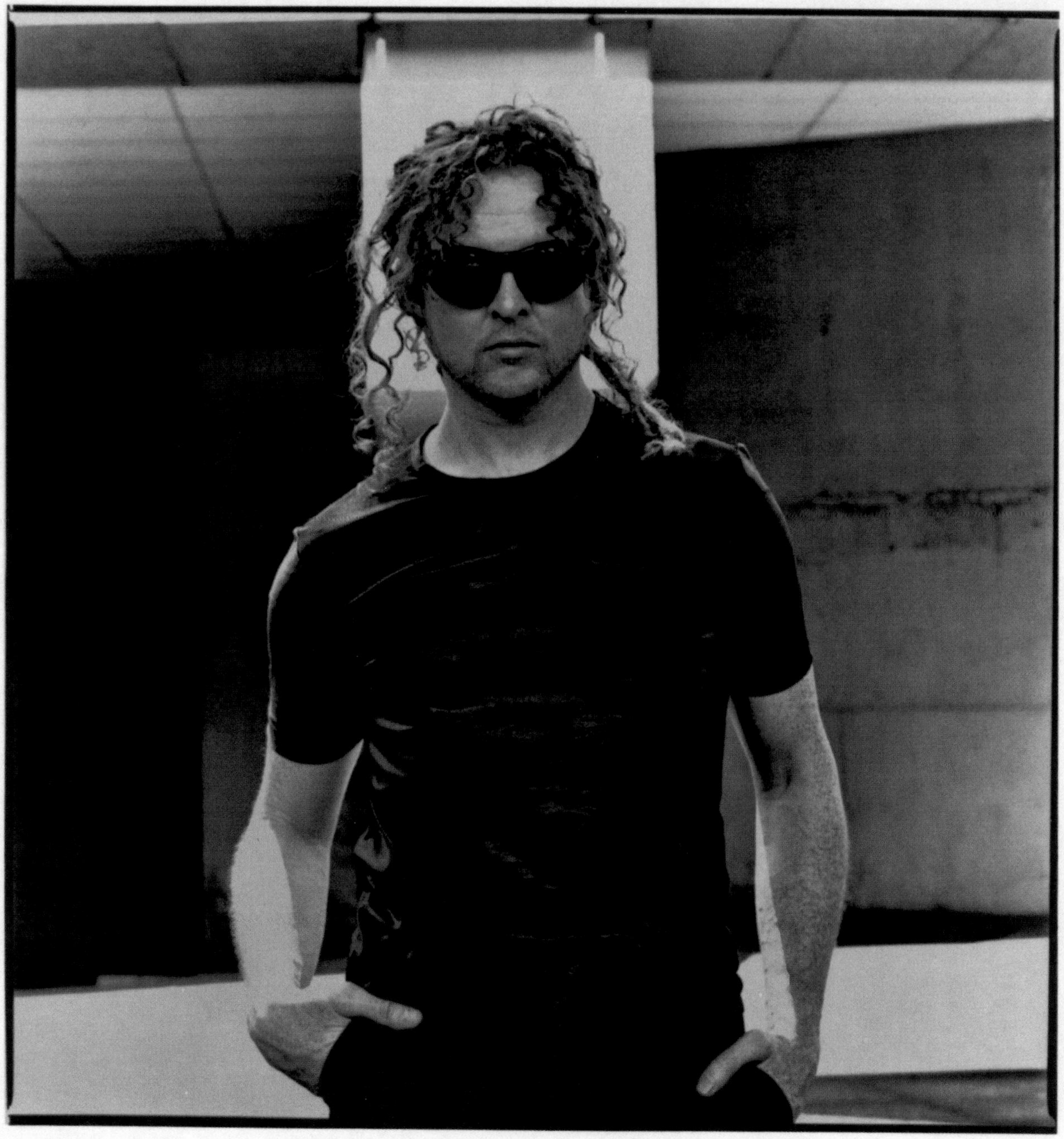

PHOTO CREDIT ANTON CORBIN 1995

SIMPLY RED

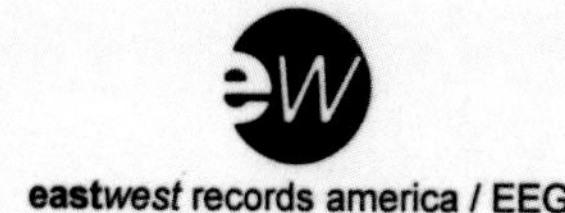

east*west* records america / EEG

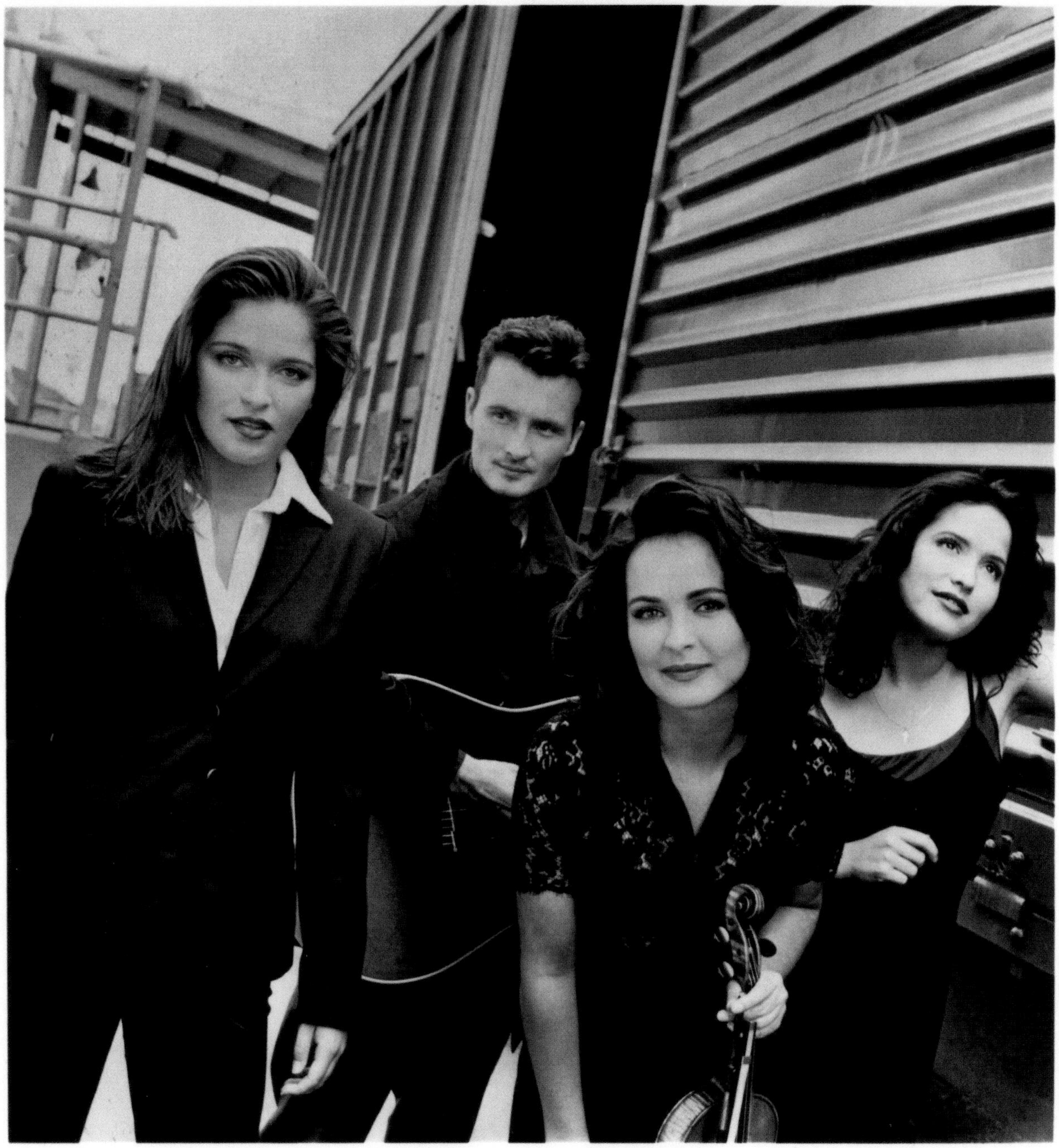

Photo Credit: Guzman

CAROLINE CORR **JIM CORR** **SHARON CORR** **ANDREA CORR**

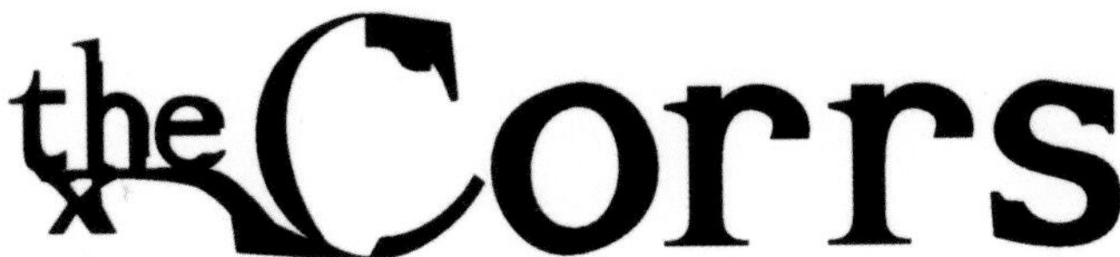

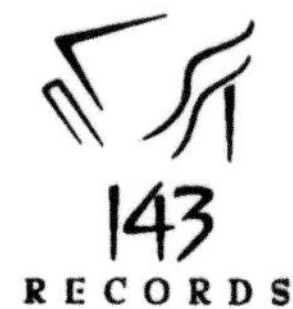

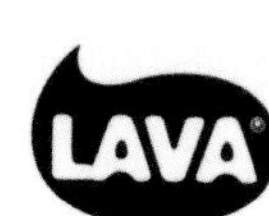

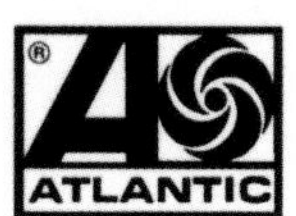

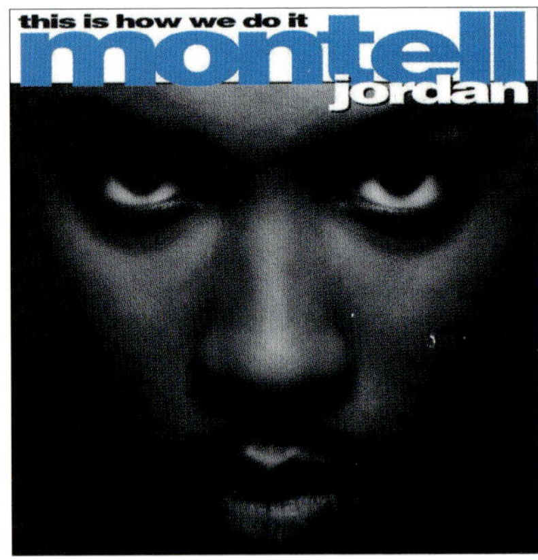

Montell Jordan's "This Is How We Do It," a party track from his album of the same name, remained at No. 1 on the pop and R&B charts for seven weeks.

Billboard 200: *This Is How We Do It* (#12)

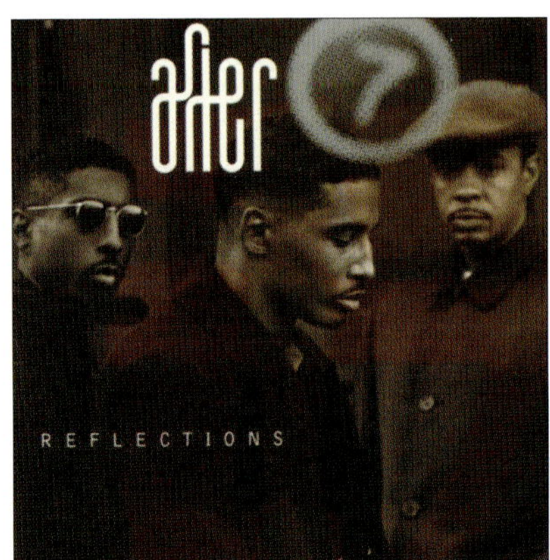

Reuniting After 7 with producer Babyface and his partner L.A. Reid, the gold-selling *Reflections* was the final album before the refined vocal group split.

Billboard 200: *Reflections* (#40)

Billboard Hot 100: "'Til You Do Me Right" (#31)

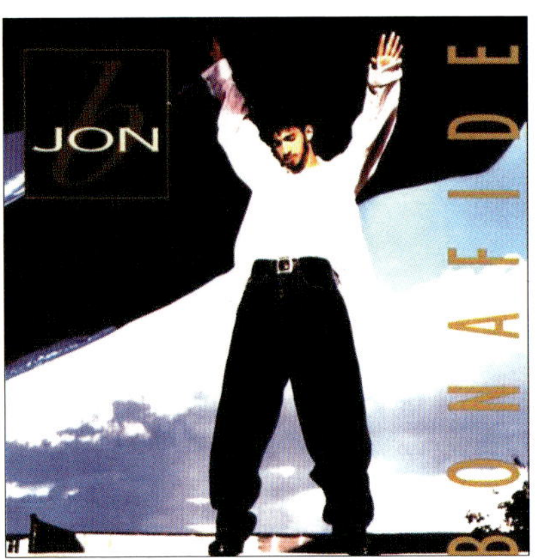

A songwriter for others before becoming known, Jon B. released his platinum debut, *Bonafide*, led by a duet with Babyface, the single "Someone to Love."

Billboard 200: *Bonafide* (#7)

Billboard Hot 100: "Someone to Love" (#10); "Pretty Girl" (#25)

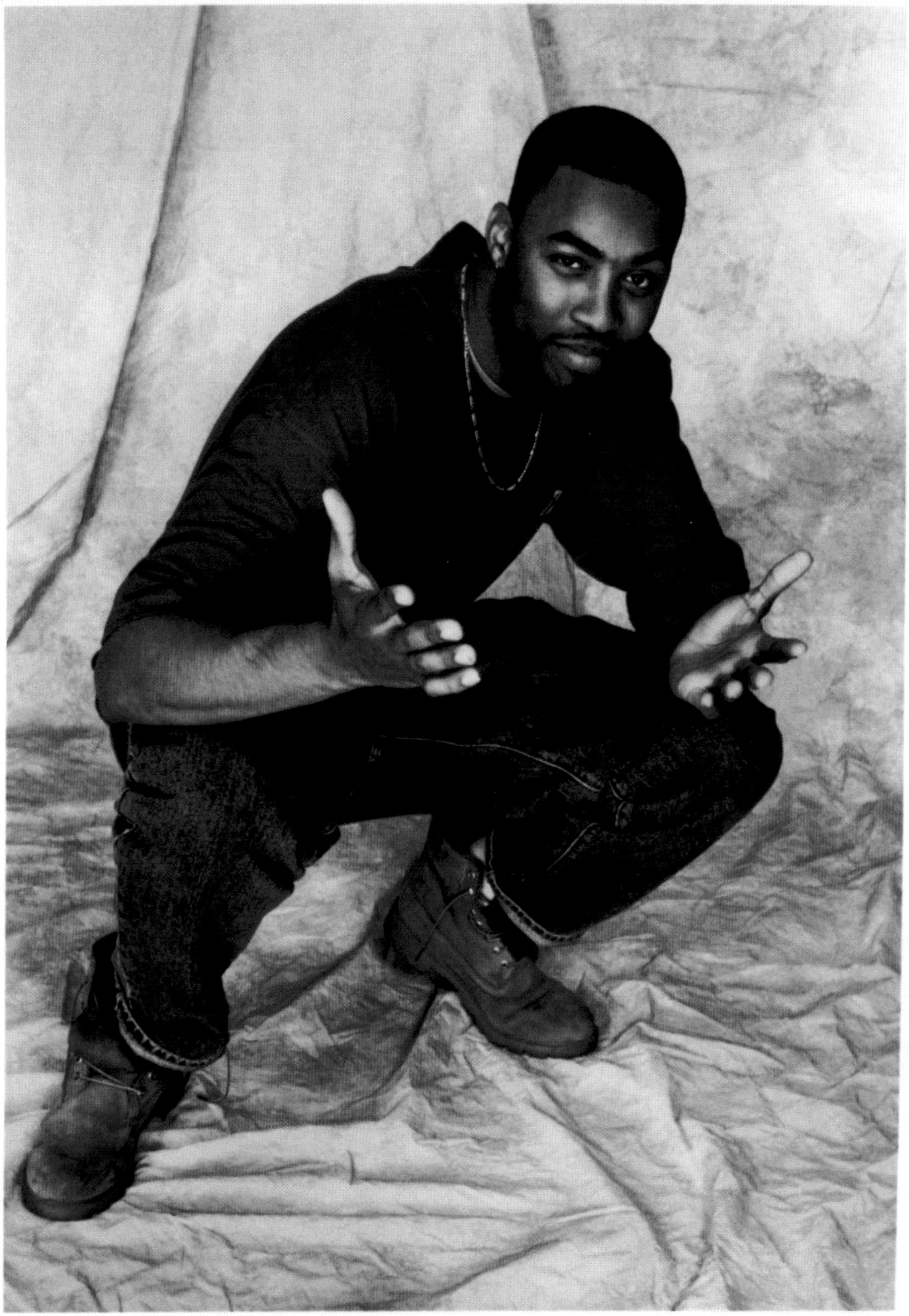

Photo Credit: TONY CUTAGAR

montell jordan

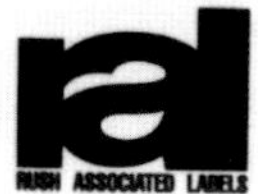

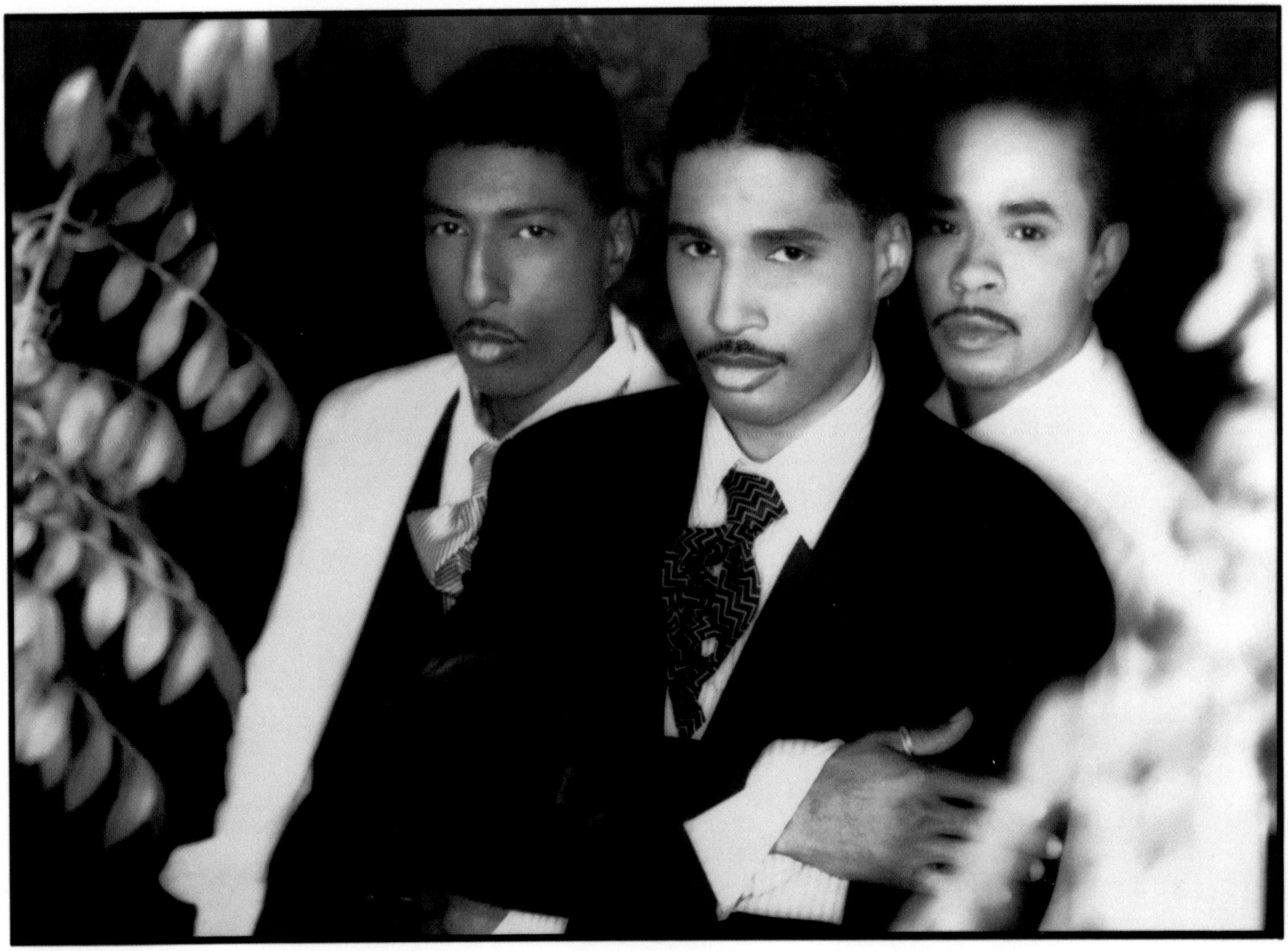

Melvin Edmonds Kevon Edmonds Keith Mitchell

Photo Credit Randee St. Nicholas 6/95

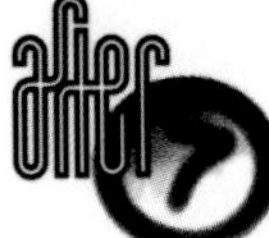

Virgin

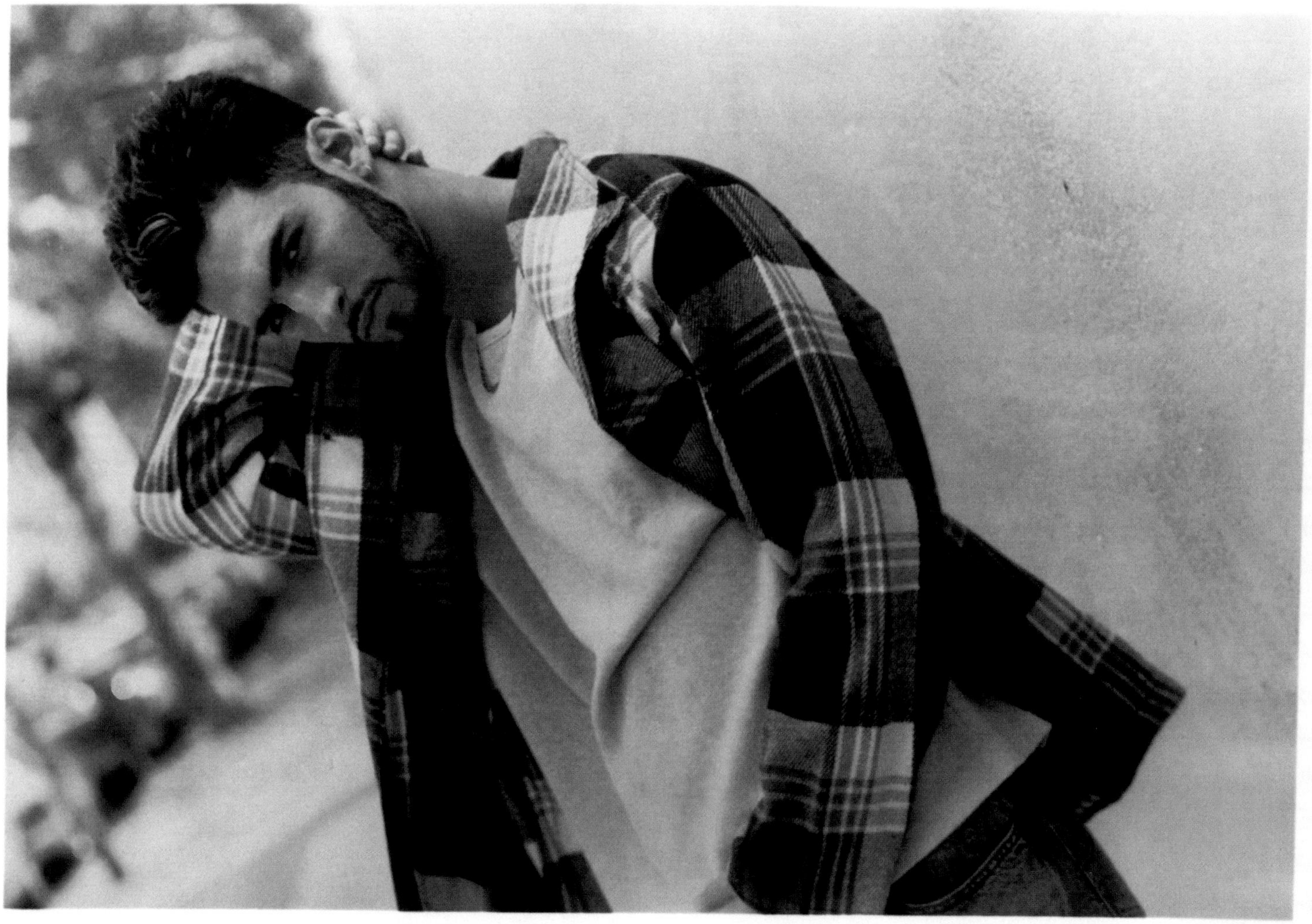

Photo Credit: HOSEA L. JOHNSON

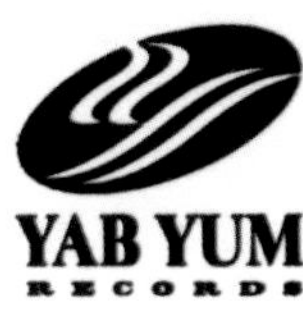

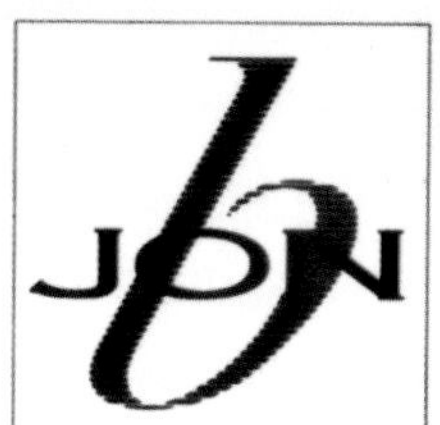

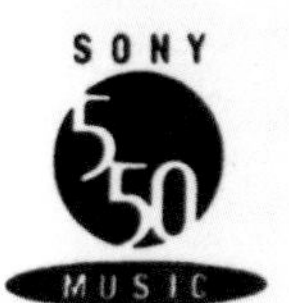

Soon after **Skee-Lo**'s "I Wish" became a hit on radio and MTV and was nominated for a Grammy, the rapper retired, claiming his label took the profits.

Billboard 200: *I Wish* (#53)
Billboard Hot 100: "I Wish" (#13)

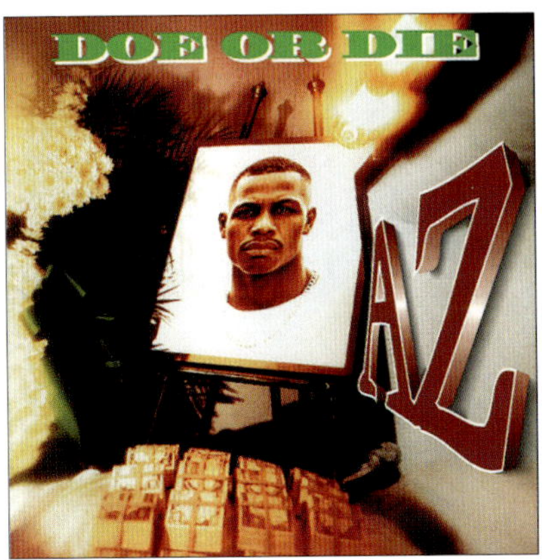

Featuring a guest appearance by his musical comrade Nas, **AZ** released *Doe or Die*, a debut album of mafioso rap containing a gold single, "Sugar Hill."

Billboard 200: *Doe or Die* (#15)
Billboard Hot 100: "Sugar Hill" (#25)

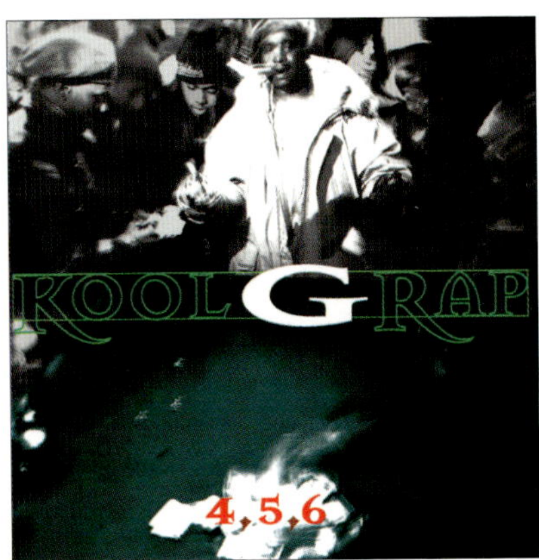

After a run with DJ Polo as part of the Juice Crew, Queens crime rapper **Kool G Rap** embarked on a solo career with a garrulous street odyssey, *4, 5, 6*.

Billboard 200: *4, 5, 6* (#24)
Billboard Hot 100: "Fast Life" (#74)

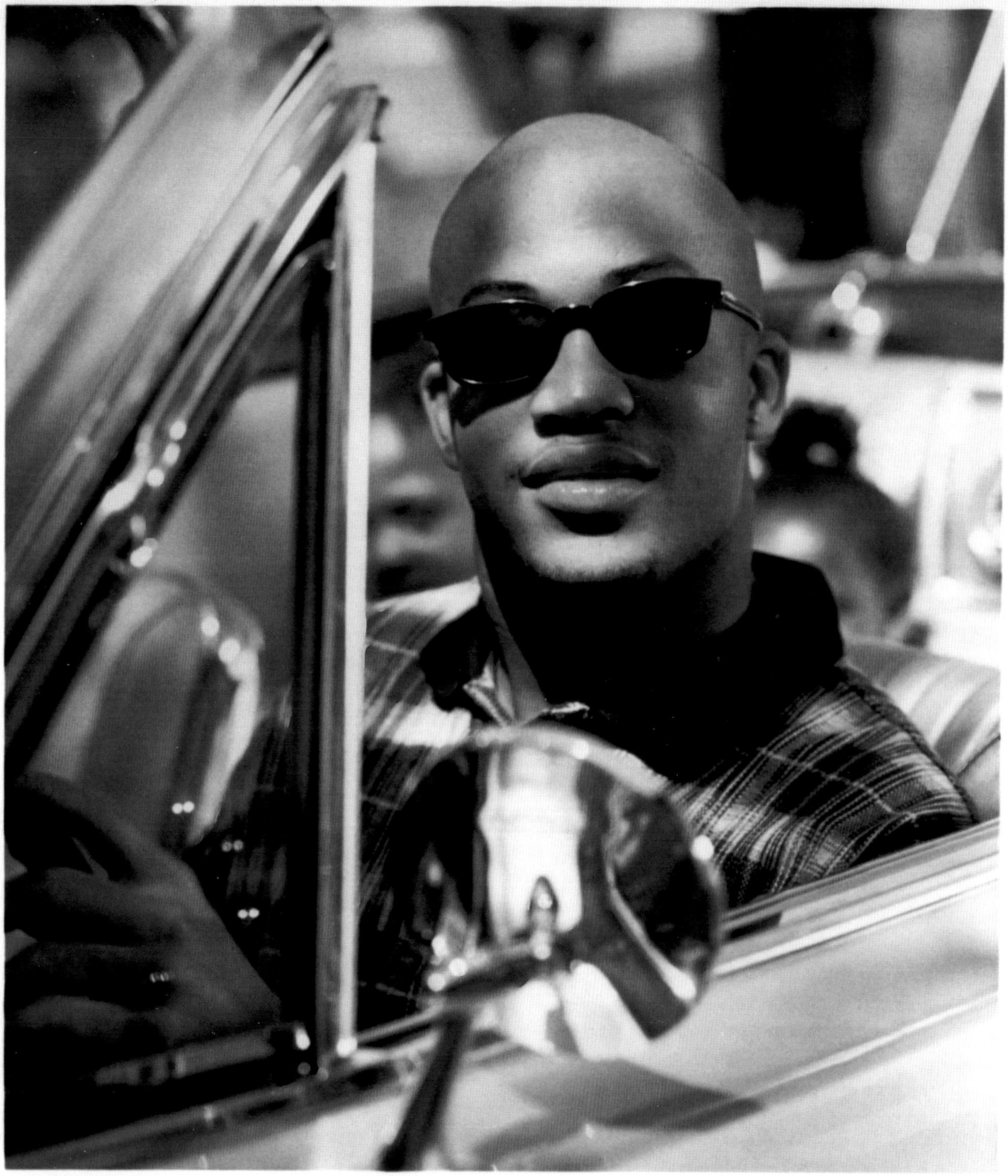

Photo Credit: Johnny Buzzerio

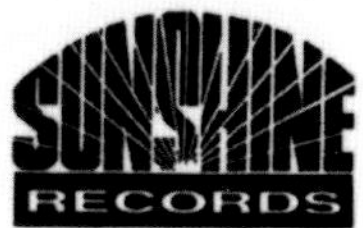

Skee-Lo

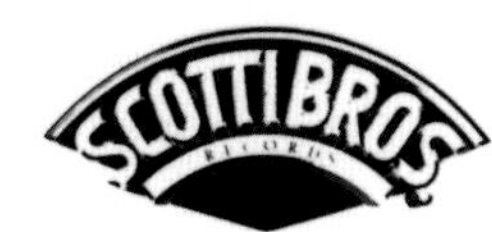

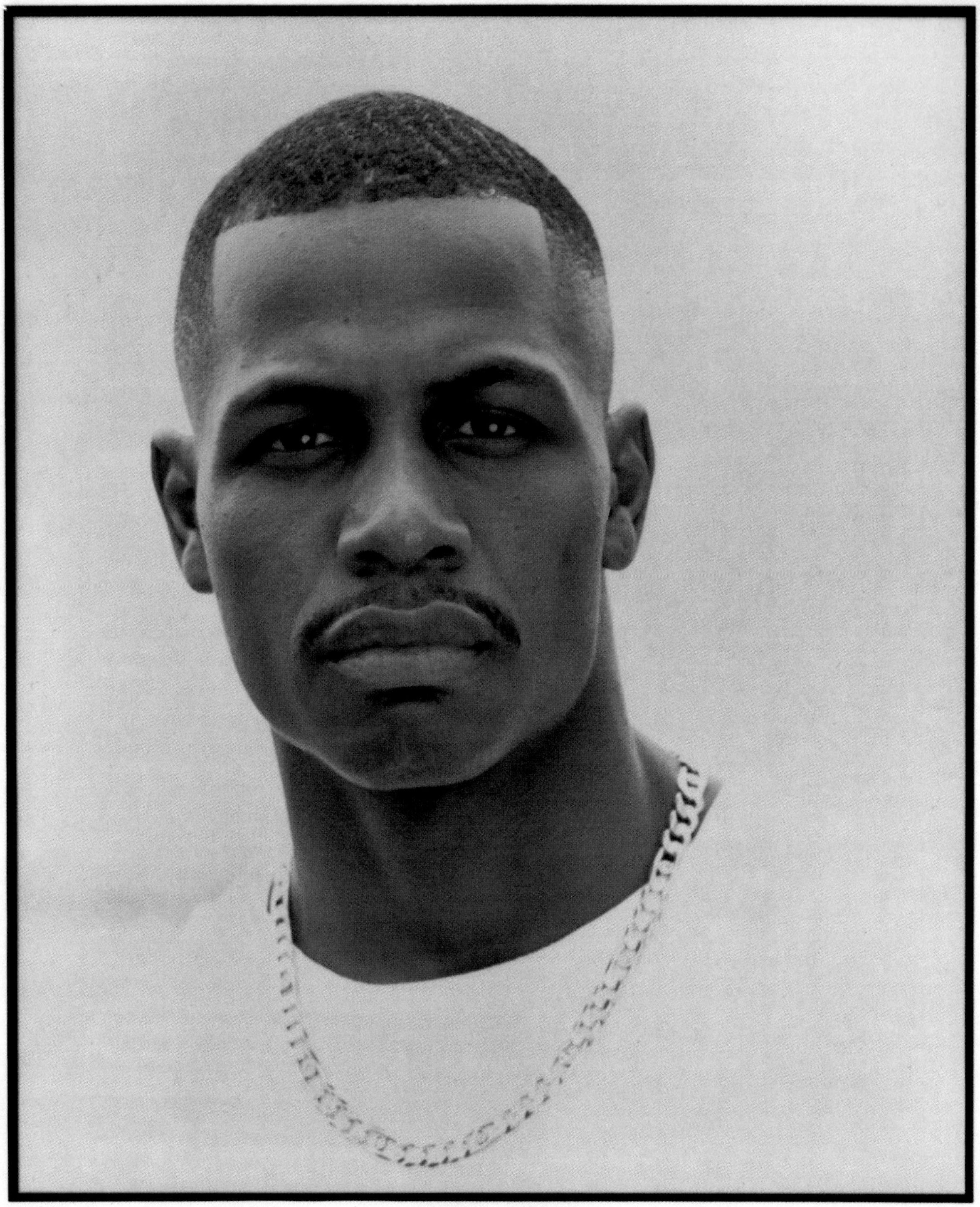

Photo credit: DANIEL HASTINGS

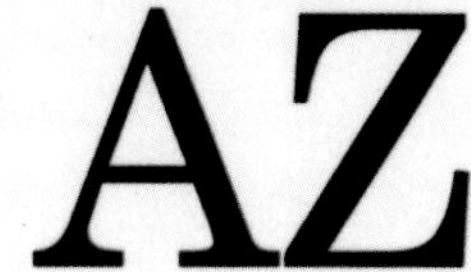

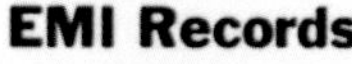

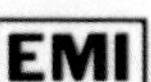

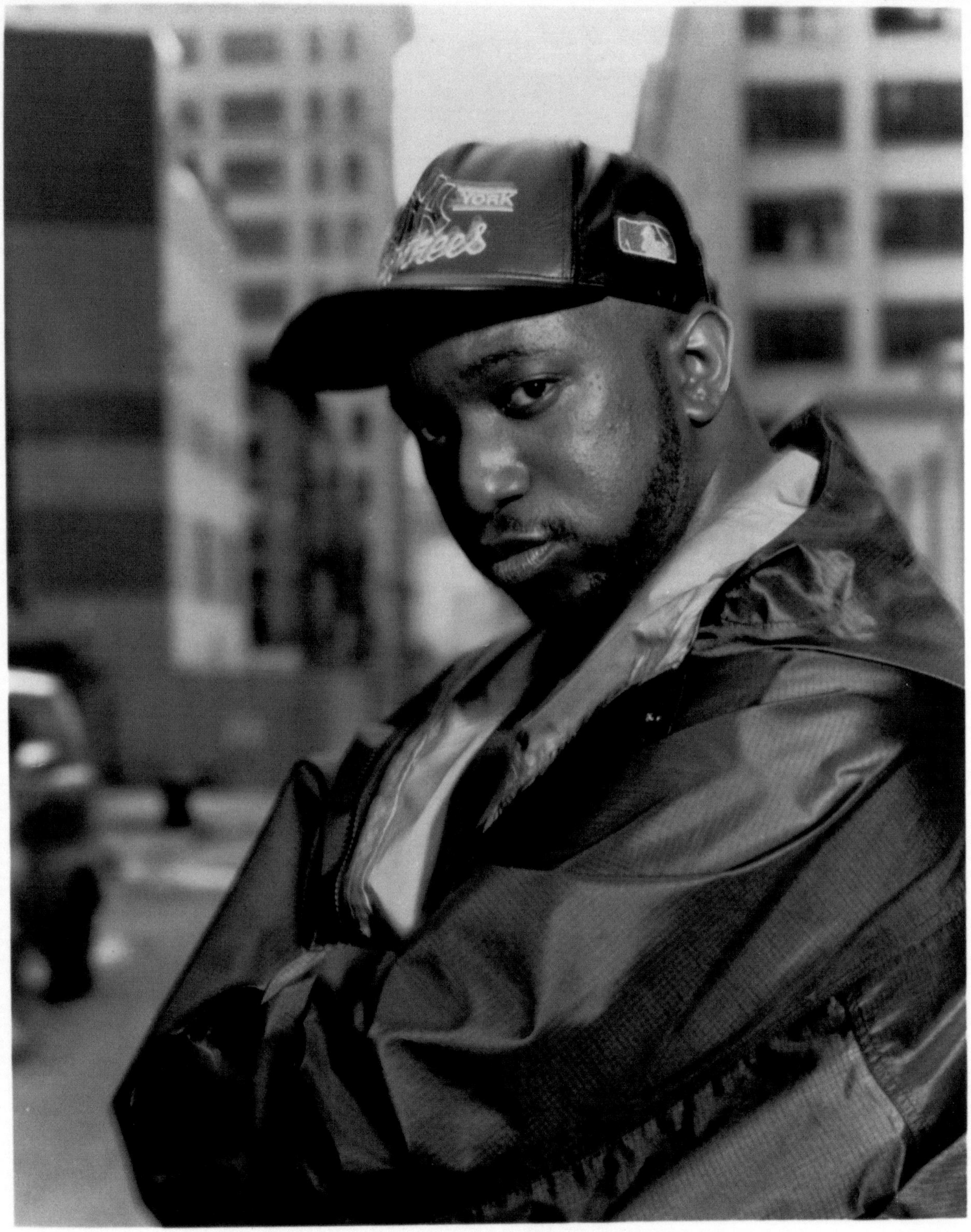

Photo Credit SUE KWON

Cold Chillin'

KOOL G RAP

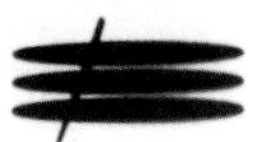

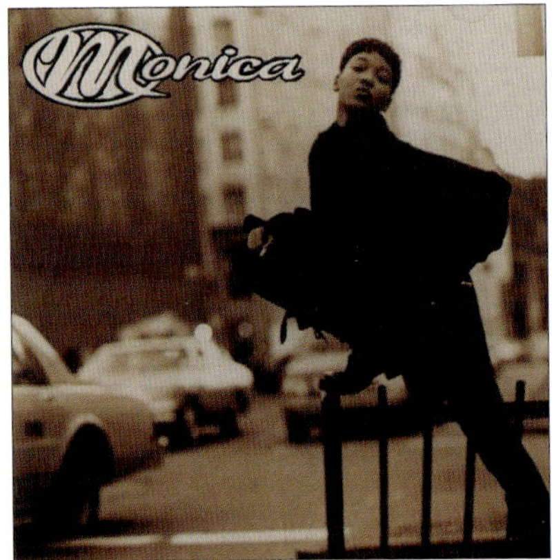

Two No. 1 R&B hits sprang from **Monica**'s *Miss Thang* album: "Don't Take It Personal (Just One of Dem Days)" along with "Before You Walk Out of My Life."

Billboard 200: *Miss Thang* (#36)
Billboard Hot 100: "Don't Take It Personal (Just One of Dem Days)" (#2); "Before You Walk Out of My Life"/"Like This and Like That" (#7); "Why I Love You So Much"/"Ain't Nobody" (#9)

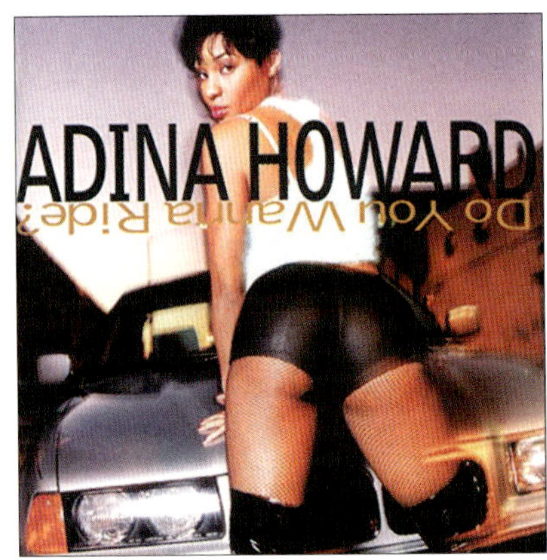

R&B singer **Adina Howard** made a name for herself via the funky bump-and-grind of "Freak Like Me," the Michigan native's platinum-selling debut single.

Billboard 200: *Do You Wanna Ride?* (#39)
Billboard Hot 100: "Freak Like Me" (#2); "My Up and Down" (#68)

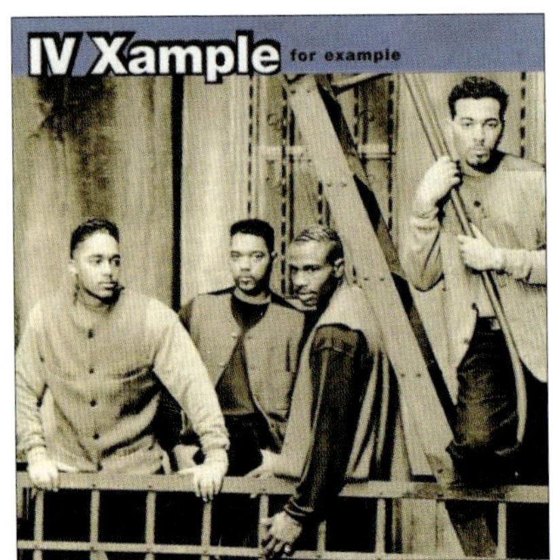

Los Angeles-based vocal quartet **IV Xample** recorded the album *For Example* and saw the single "I'd Rather Be Alone" make it to the pop and R&B charts.

Billboard Hot 100: "I'd Rather Be Alone" (#44)

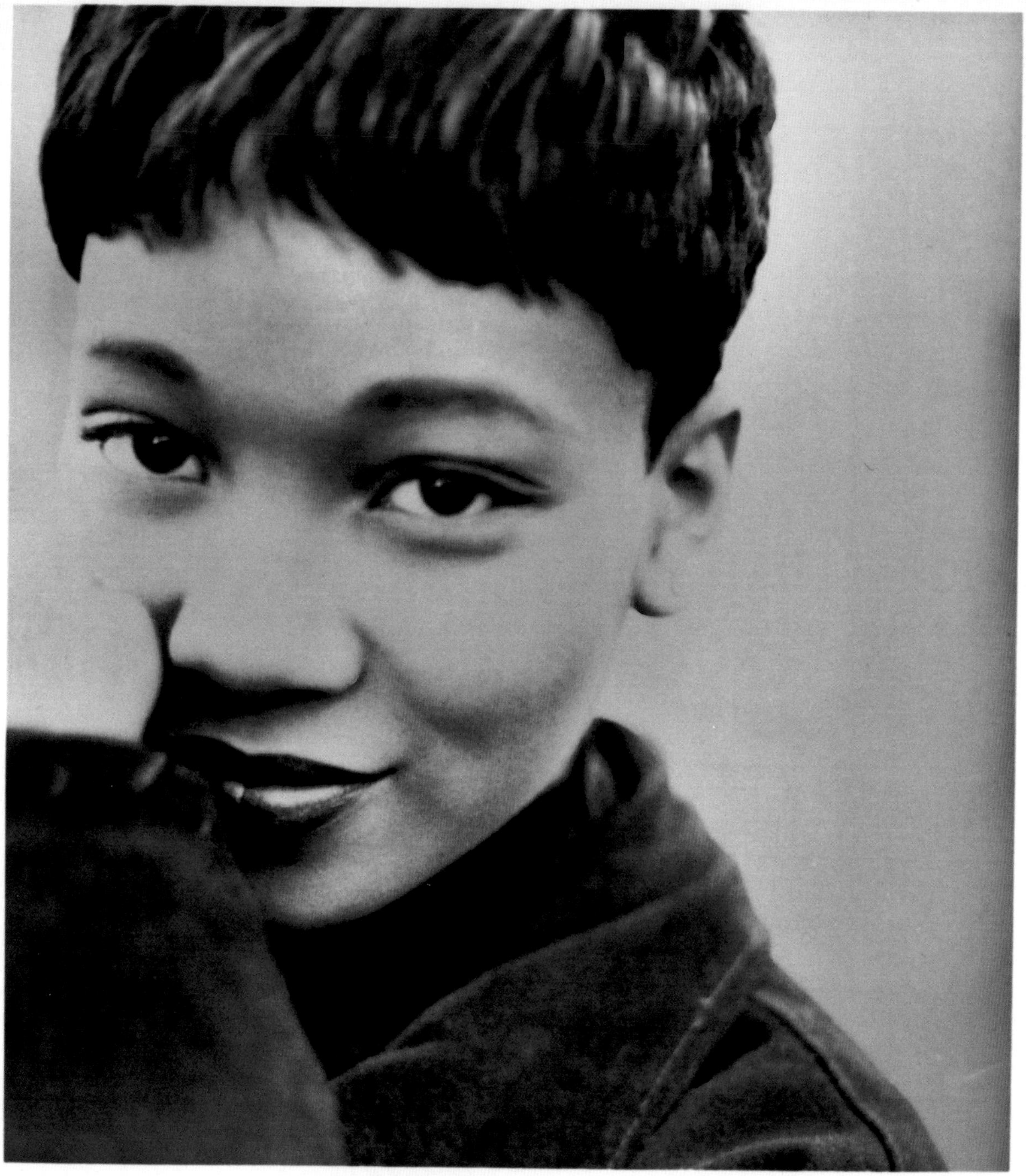

photo: Daniel Hastings

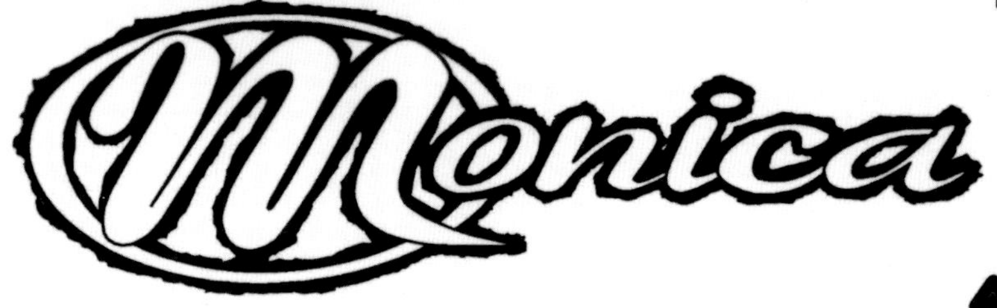

ROWDY.

ARISTA

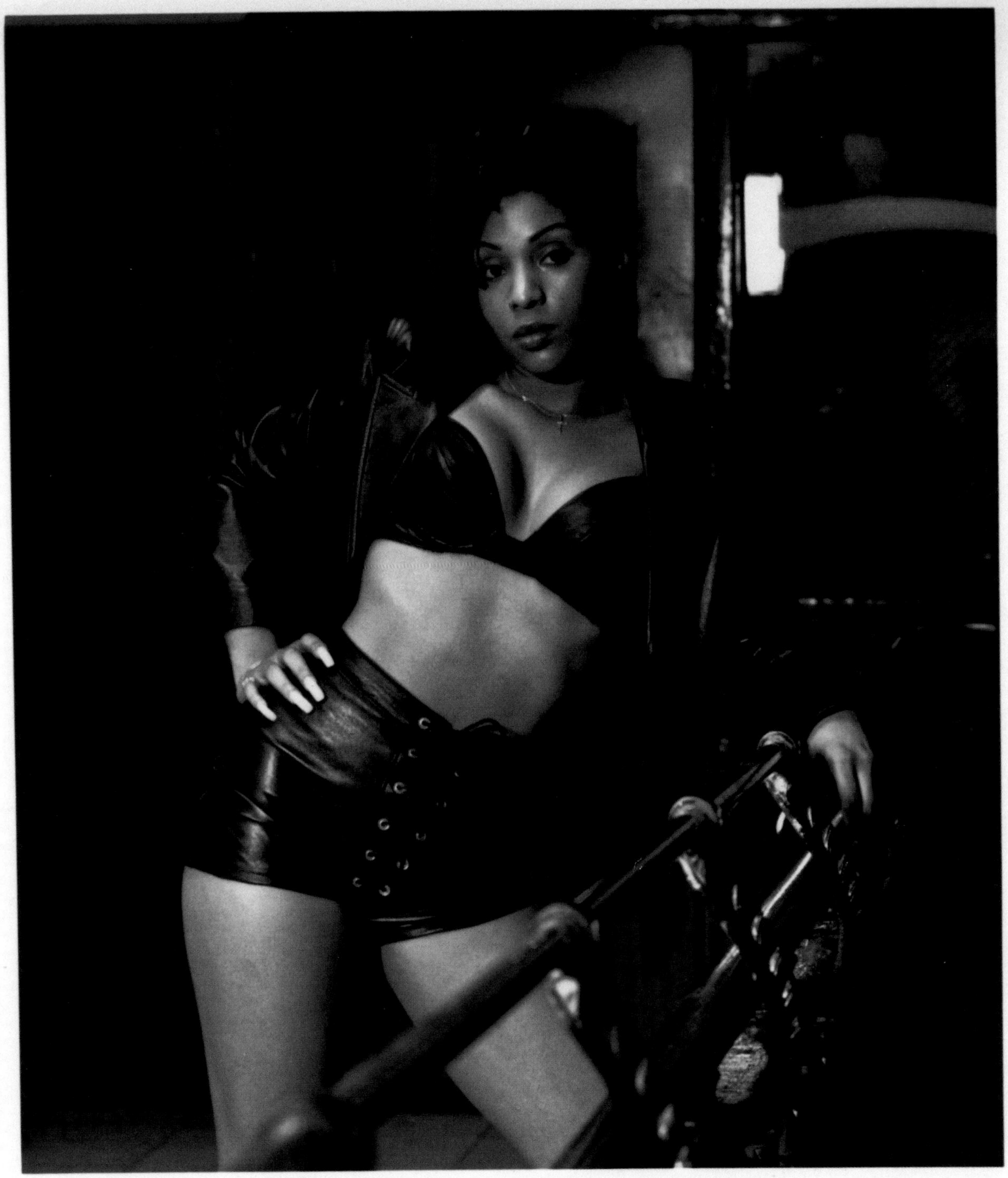

PHOTO CREDIT: KWAKU ALSTON

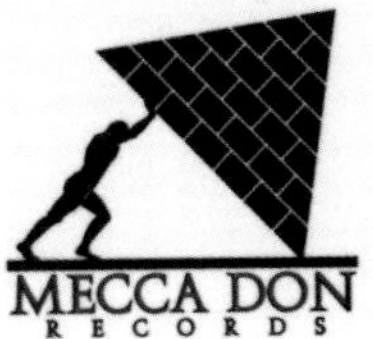

ADINA HOWARD

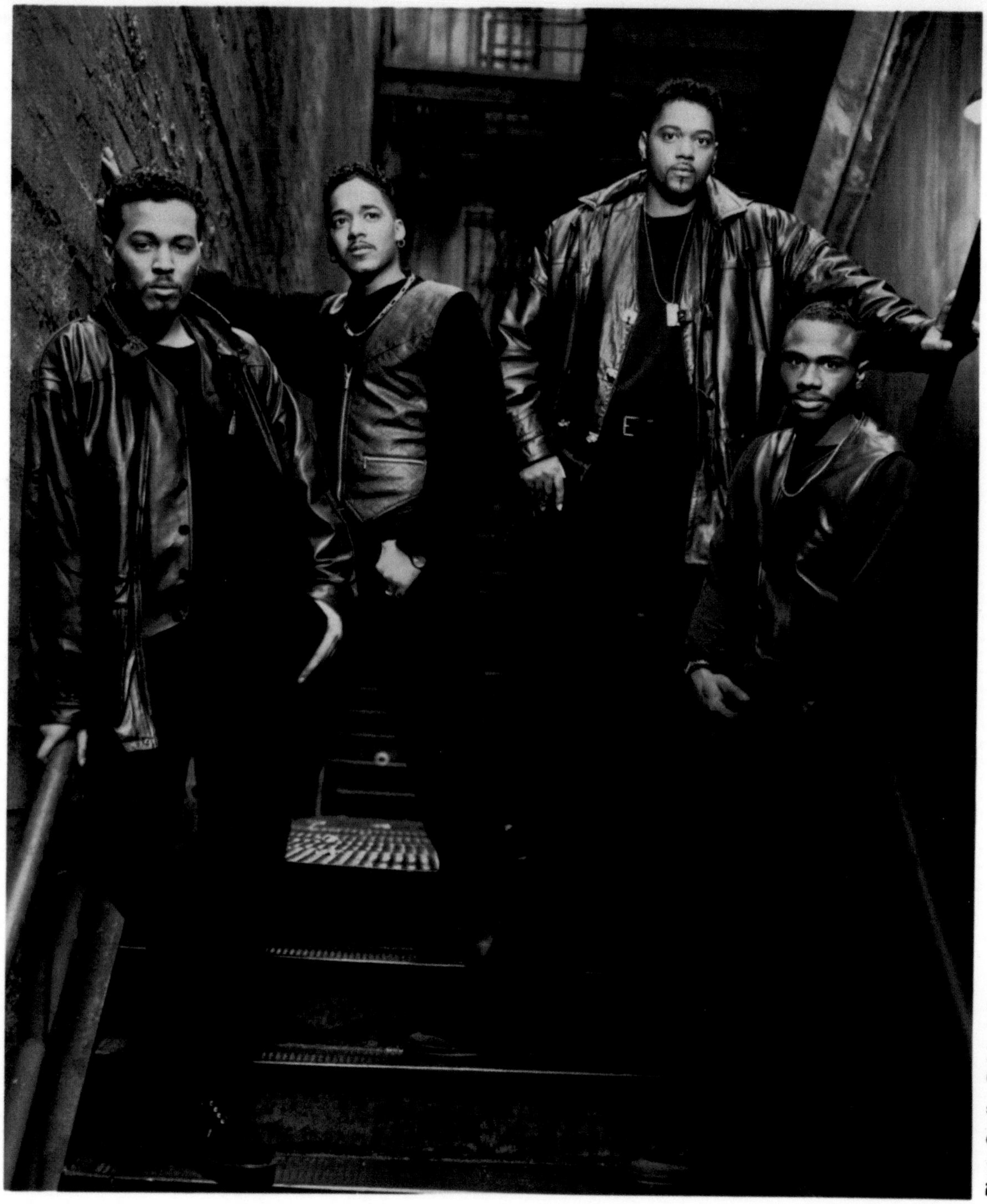

Photo Credit: Reisig & Taylor

ANDRE ALLEN	ATHEMUS CHEVIS "BC"	RAYMOND CHEVIS "RUNNI RAE"	LUCIUS

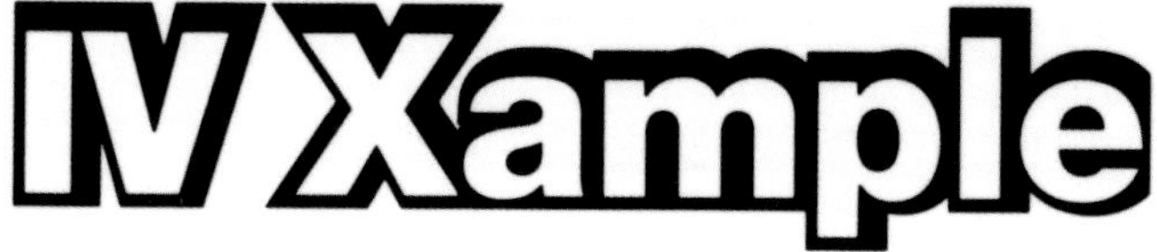

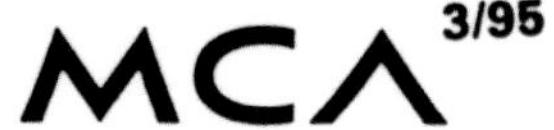

3/95

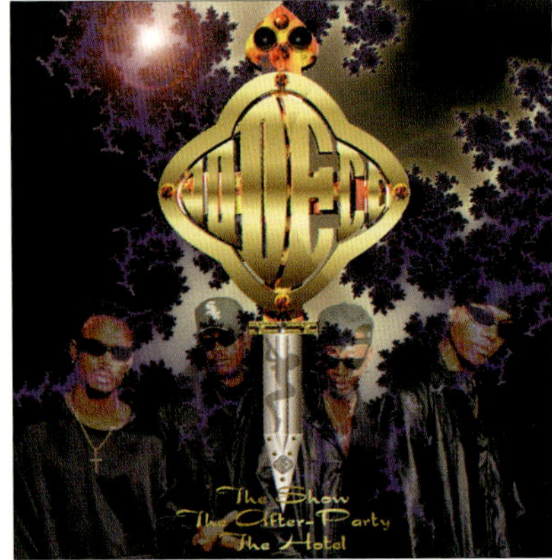

Jodeci's *The Show, the After Party, the Hotel,* a concept album spinning a tale of the new jack swing act's backstage naughtiness, topped the R&B charts.

Billboard 200: *The Show, the After Party, the Hotel* (#2)
Billboard Hot 100: "Freek'n You" (#14);
"Love U 4 Life" (#31); "Get on Up" (#22)

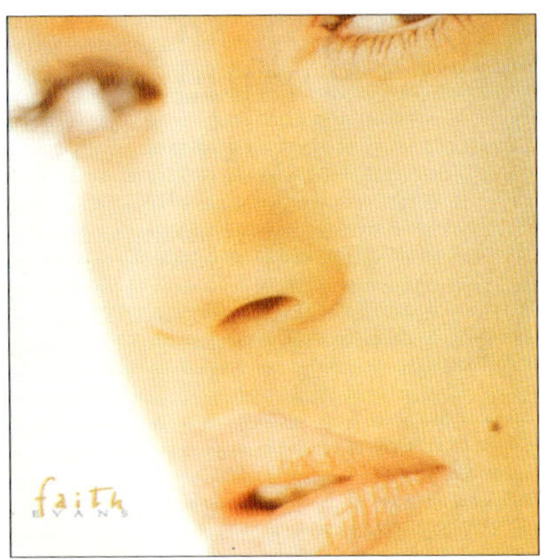

Leveraging the popularity of "You Used to Love Me" and "As Soon as I Get Home," R&B songstress Faith Evans' debut *Faith* attained platinum status.

Billboard 200: *Faith* (#22)
Billboard Hot 100: "You Used to Love Me" (#24);
"Soon as I Get home" (#21); "Ain't Nobody" (#67)

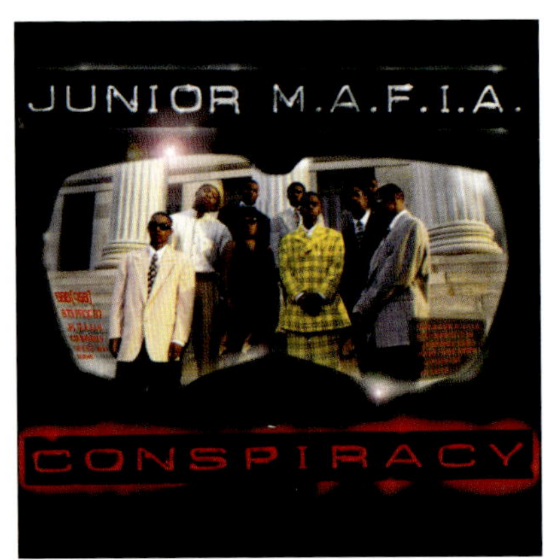

Guided by the Notorious B.I.G., a childhood ally, Junior M.A.F.I.A. snagged renown with the album *Conspiracy* and an emblematic hit, "Player's Anthem."

Billboard 200: *Conspiracy* (#8)
Billboard Hot 100: "Get Money" (#17); "Player's Anthem" (#13)

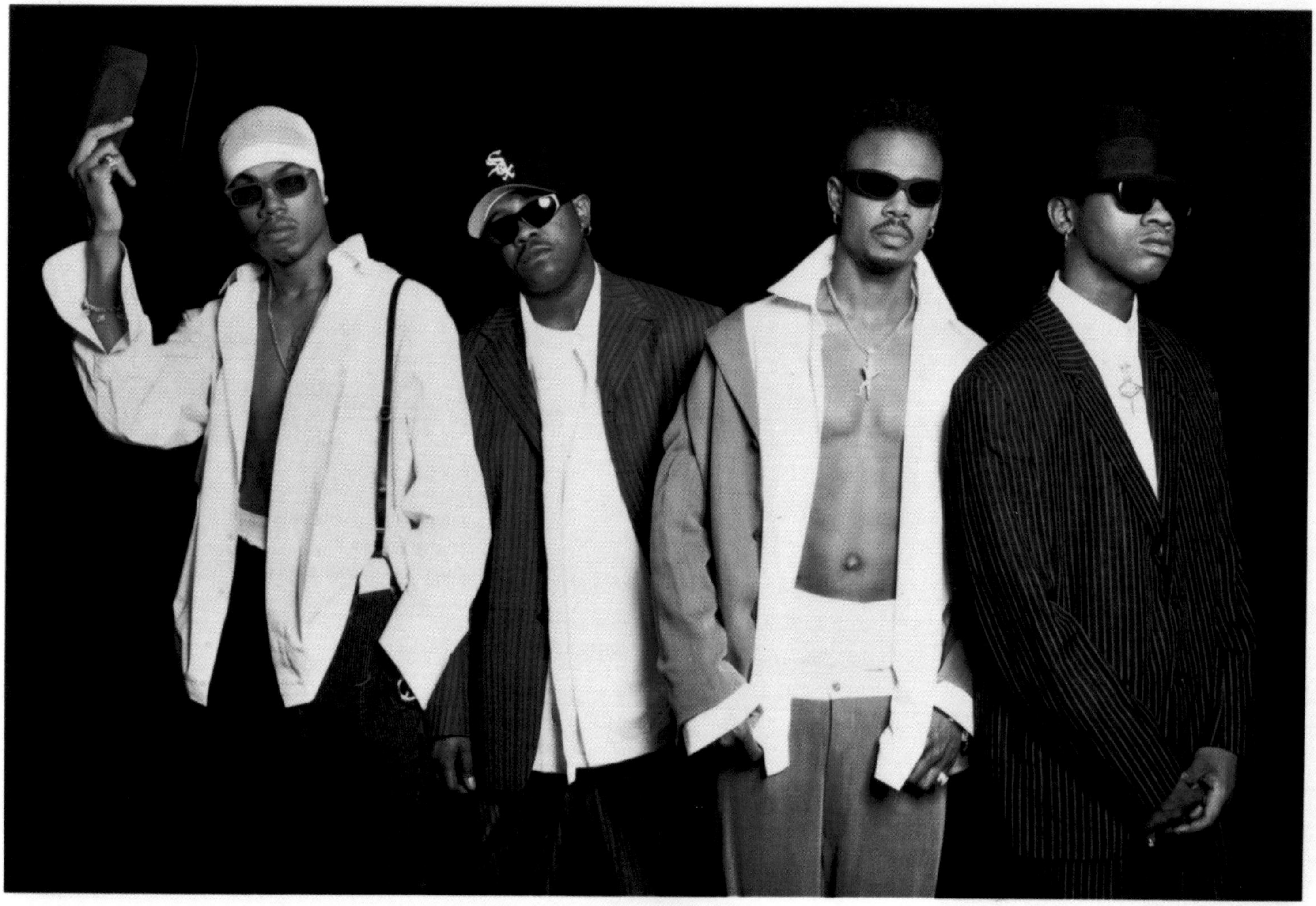

PHOTO: UPTOWN / MCA RECORDS

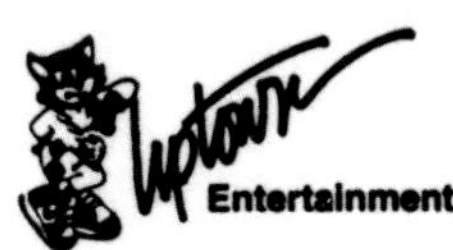

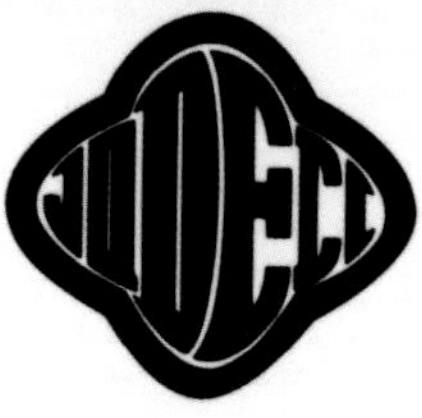

MCA

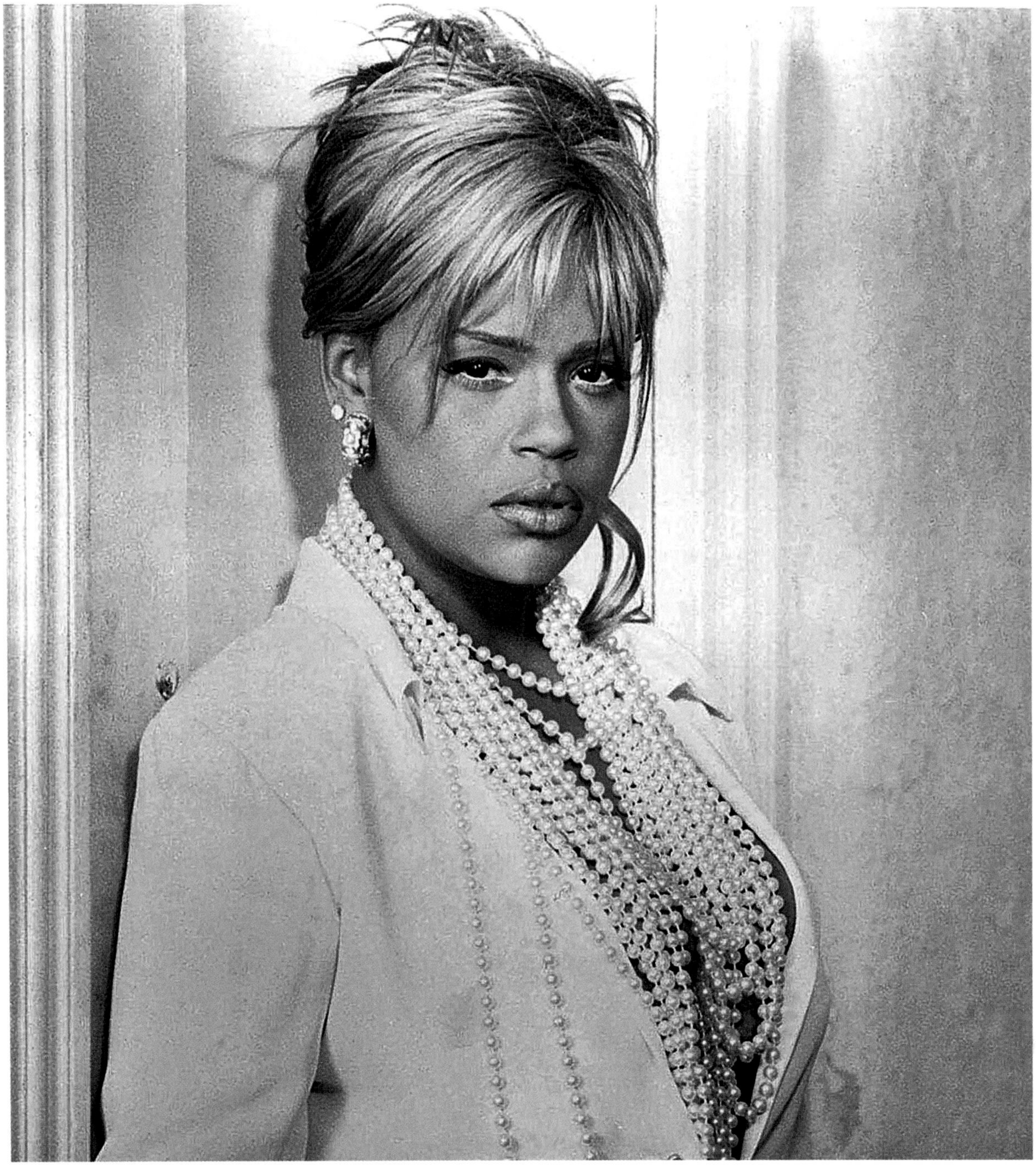

faith

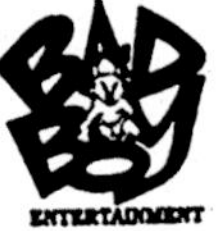

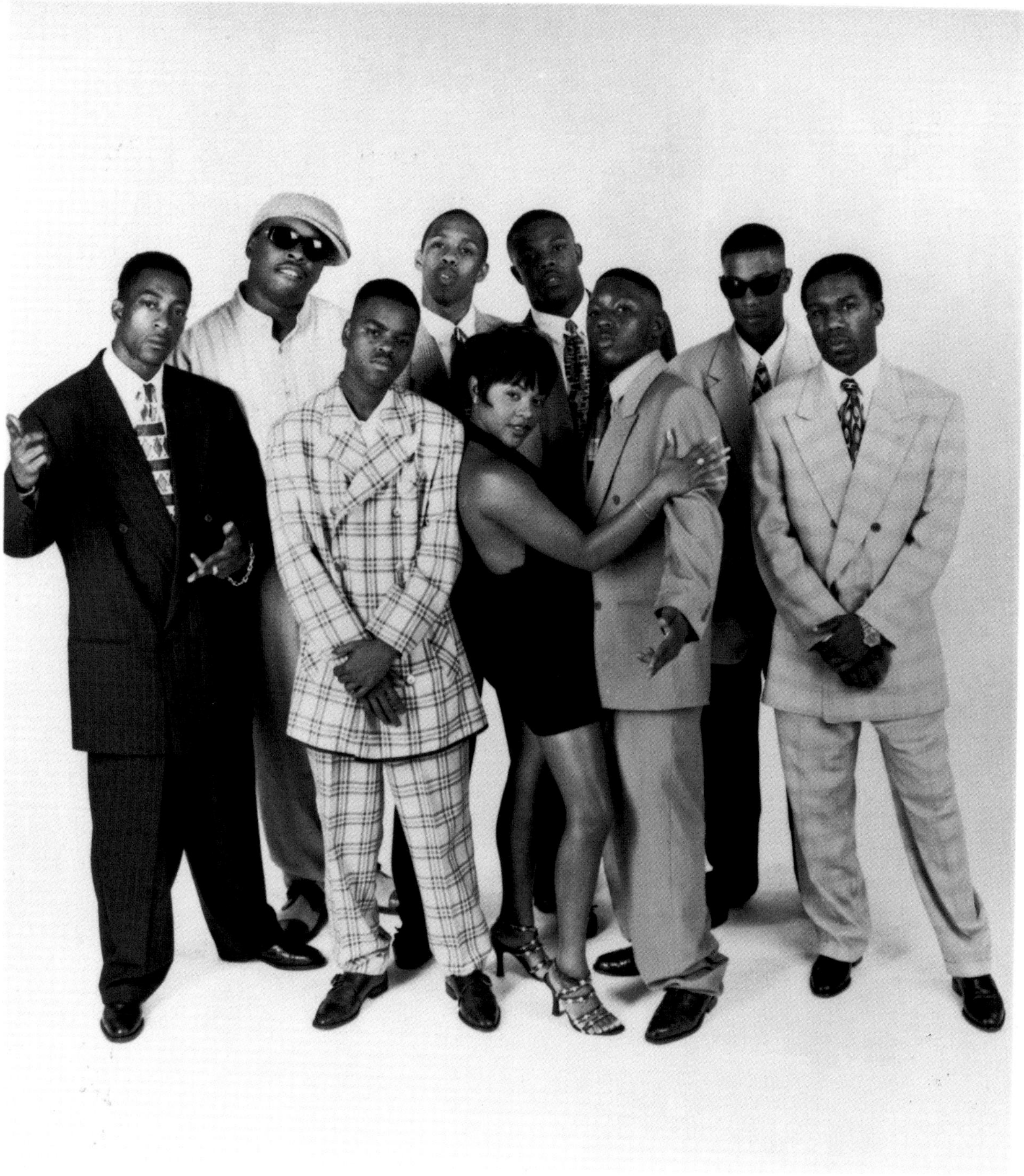

Photo Credit: Chi Modu

JUNIOR M.A.F.I.A.

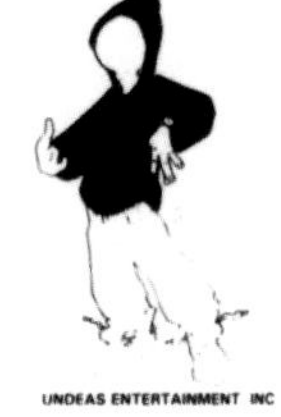

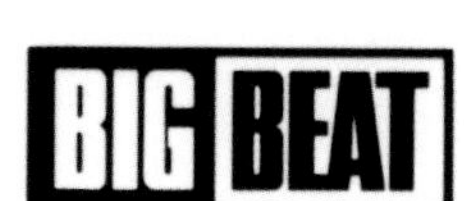

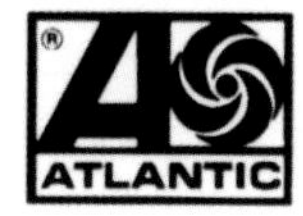

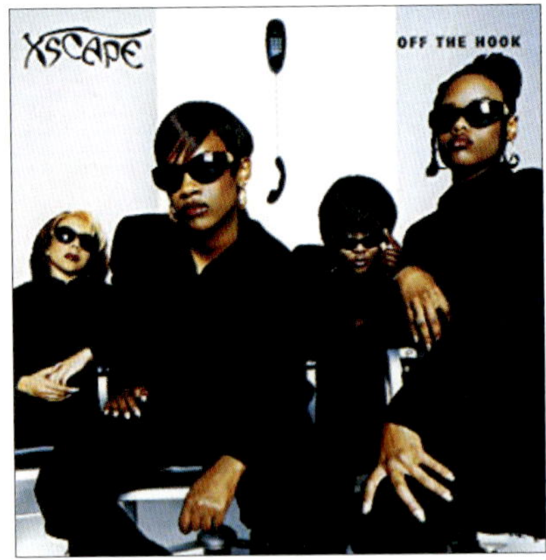

Supervised by Atlanta producer and songwriter Jermaine Dupri on various tracks, **Xscape** issued *Off the Hook*, the R&B quartet's second platinum effort.

Billboard 200: *Off the Hook* (#23)
Billboard Hot 100: "Feels So Good" (#31); "Who Can I Run To" (#8); "Do You Want To"/"Can't Hang" (#50)

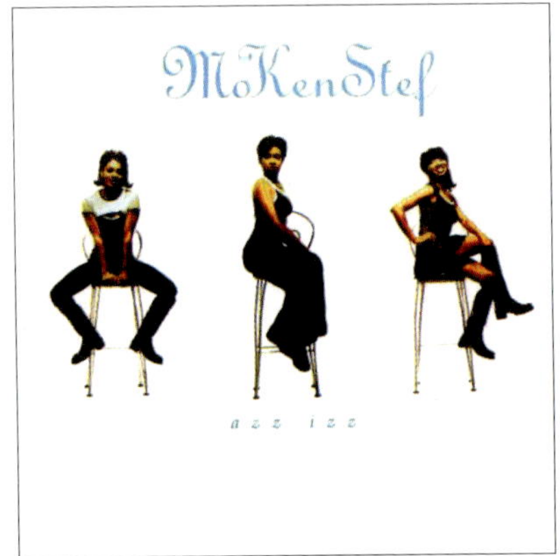

Los Angeles-based girl group **MoKenStef**—the first syllable of each member's name combined to form the moniker—debuted with a slow jam, "He's Mine."

Billboard 200: *Azz Izz* (#117)
Billboard Hot 100: "He's Mine" (#7)

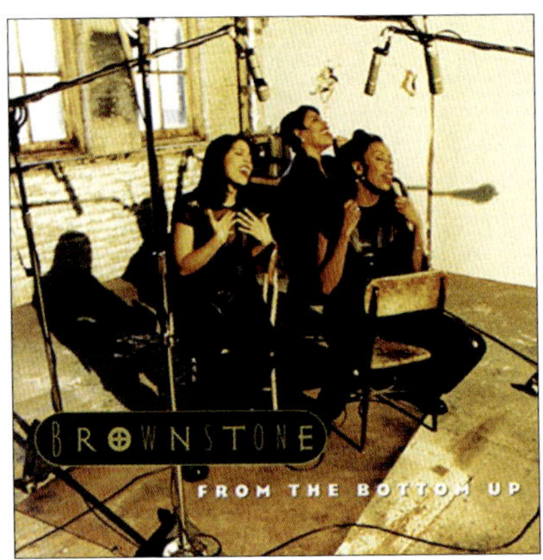

Brownstone's *From the Bottom Up* spawned "If You Love Me," a hit single earning the vocal trio a Grammy Award nomination for Best R&B Performance.

Billboard 200: *From the Bottom Up* (#29)
Billboard Hot 100: "If You Love Me" (#8); "Grapevyne" (#49); "I Can't Tell You Why" (#54)

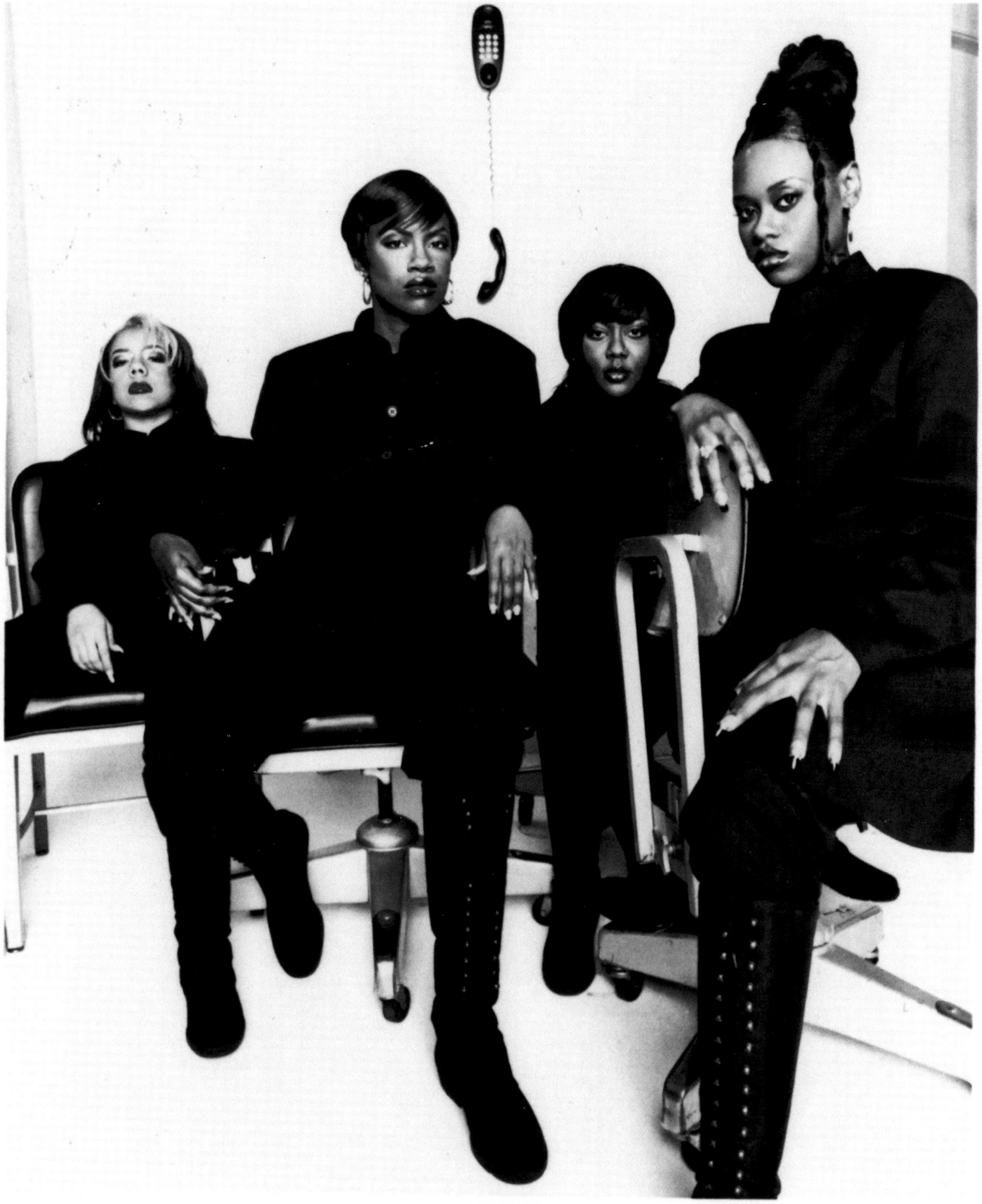

PHOTOGRAPH: DAH-LEN

Tiny Kandi Latocha Tamika

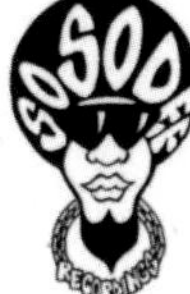

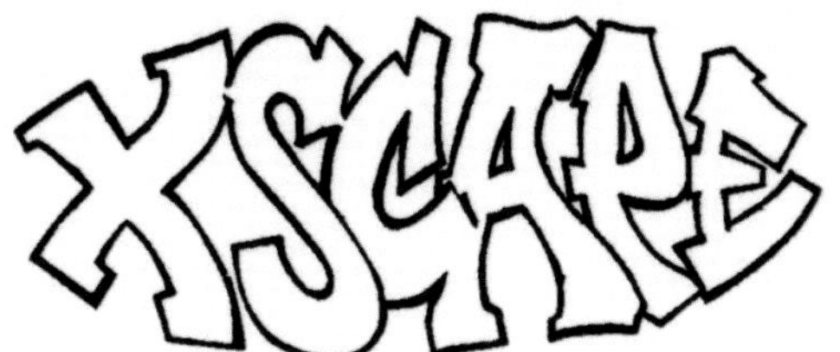

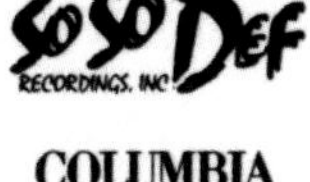

COLUMBIA
9506

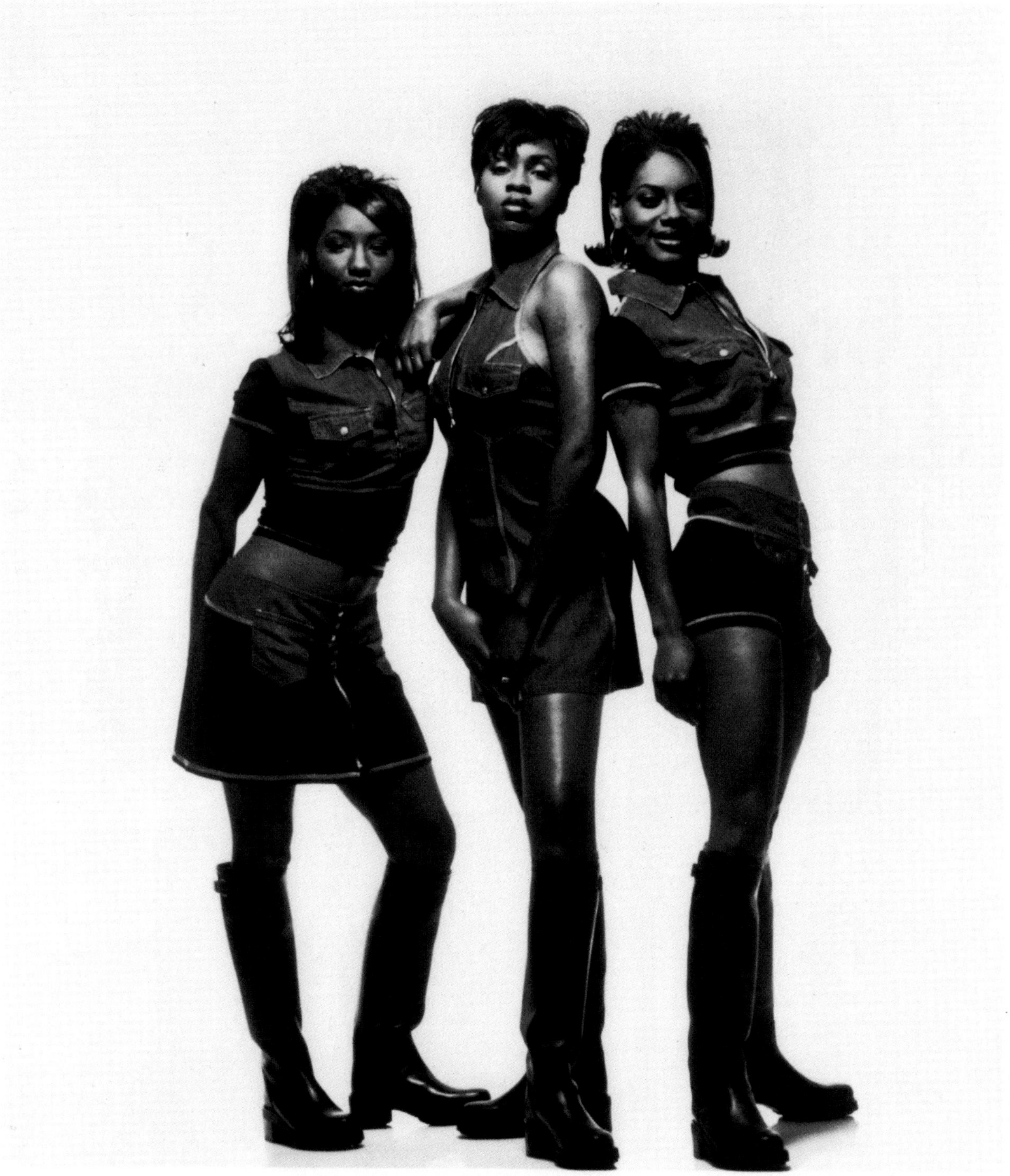

Photo Credit: ZHLEMA JACOME

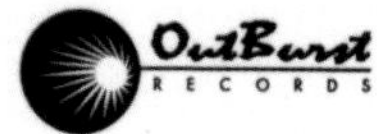

MoKenStef

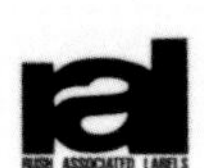

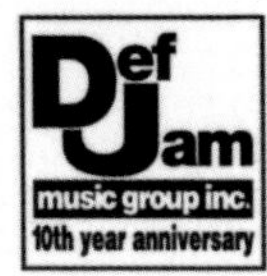

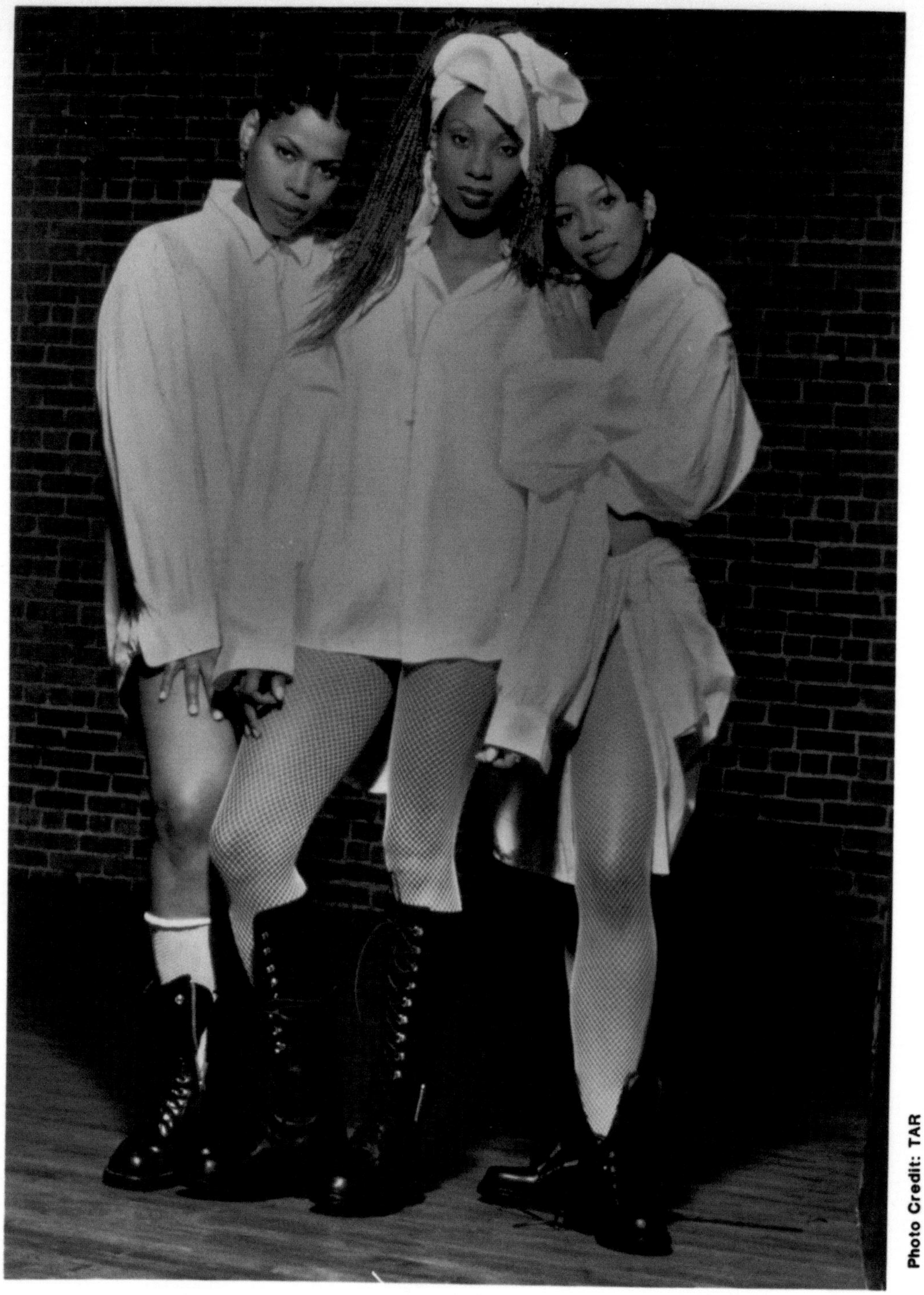

Photo Credit: TAR

NICCI MAXEE MIMI

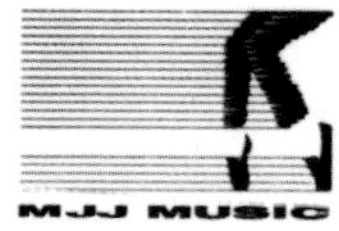

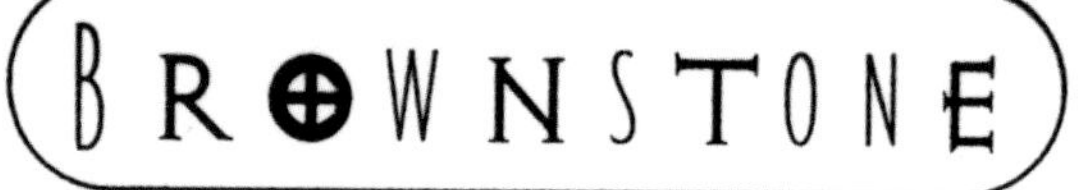

9408

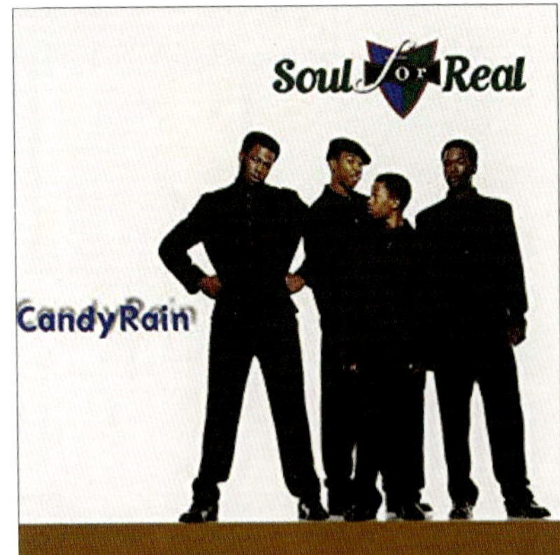

Consisting of four brothers, **Soul for Real** celebrated the marvelous "Candy Rain," a seductive offering from the group's platinum-selling debut album.

Billboard 200: *Candy Rain* (#23)
Billboard Hot 100: "Candy Rain" (#2); "Every Little Thing I Do" (#17)

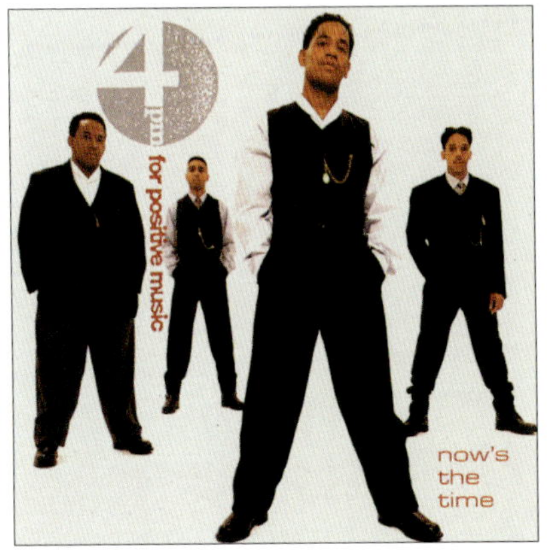

4 P.M.–an acronym meaning For Positive Music–remade Kyu Sakamoto's 1963 hit "Sukiyaki," and the soothing a cappella version reached the Top 10.

Billboard 200: *Now's the Time* (#126)
Billboard Hot 100: "Sukiyaki" (#8)

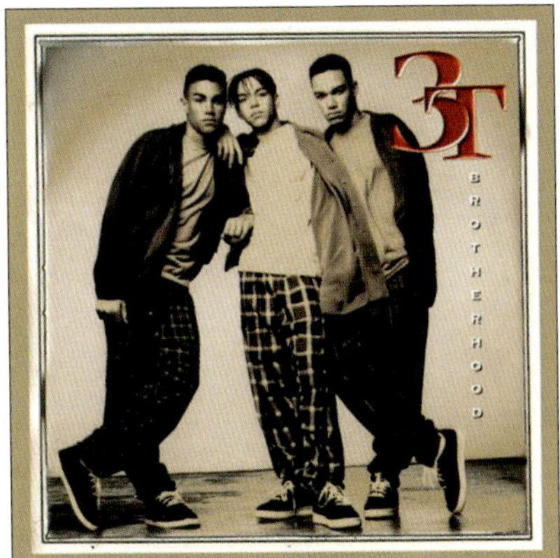

Featuring the sons of Tito Jackson, R&B trio **3T** released *Brotherhood* and attained a global smash with "Anything," produced by uncle Michael Jackson.

Billboard 200: *Brotherhood* (#127)
Billboard Hot 100: "Anything" (#15)

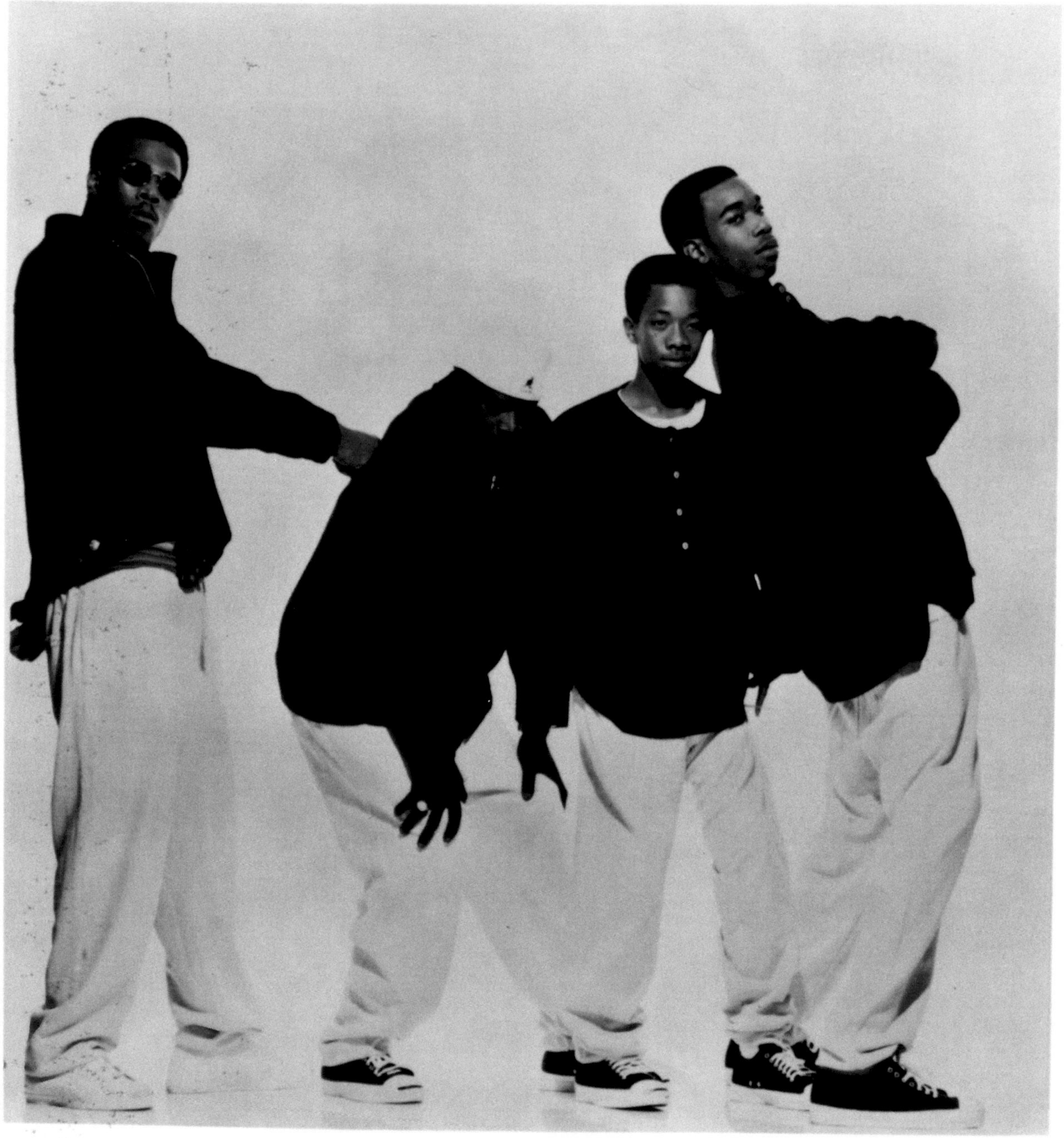

Photo Credit: Mark Contratto

MCA

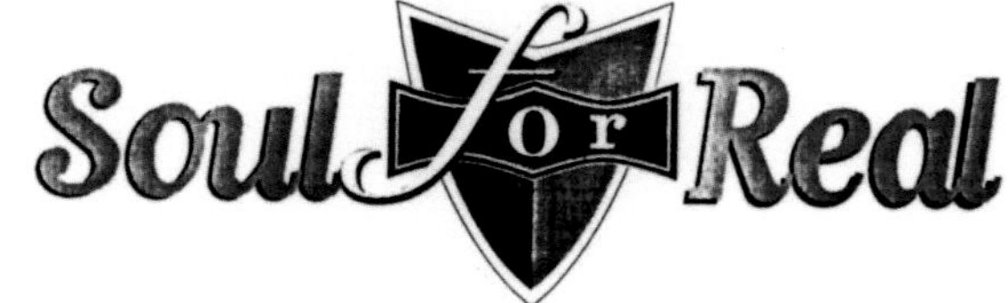

1/95

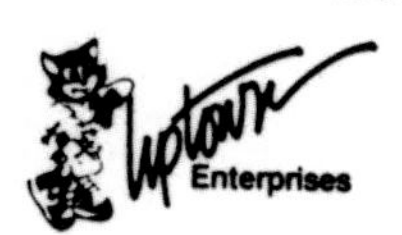

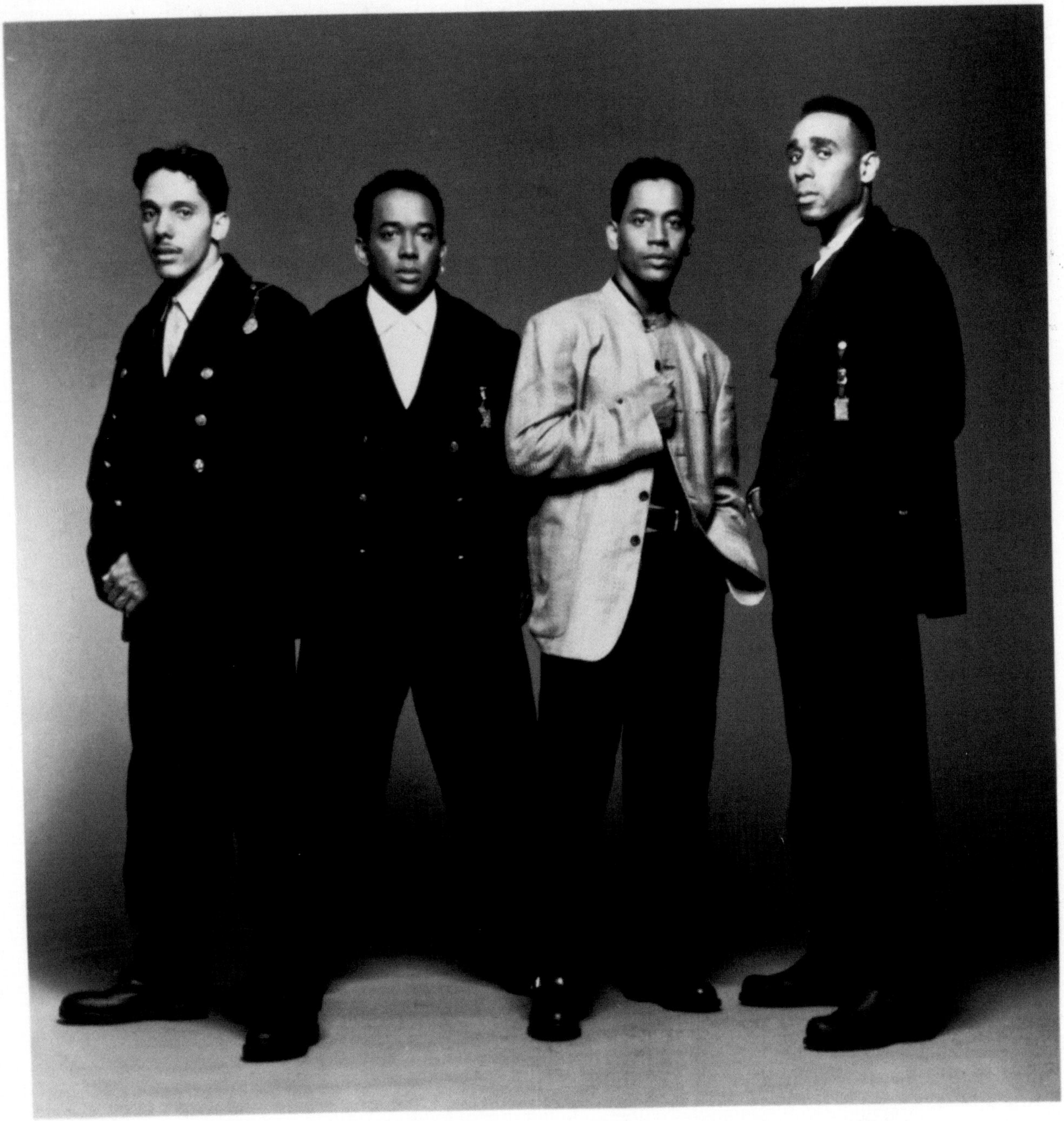

Larry Bobby Ray Marty

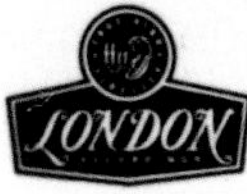

4 P.M.
(For Positive Music)

TRU-PLATINUM ENTERTAINMENT
395 SOUTH END AVENUE#20D NEW YORK, N.Y. 10280
TELEPHONE (212) 432-5866 FAX AND INFORMATION LINE (212) 432-7872

TAJ T.J. TARYLL

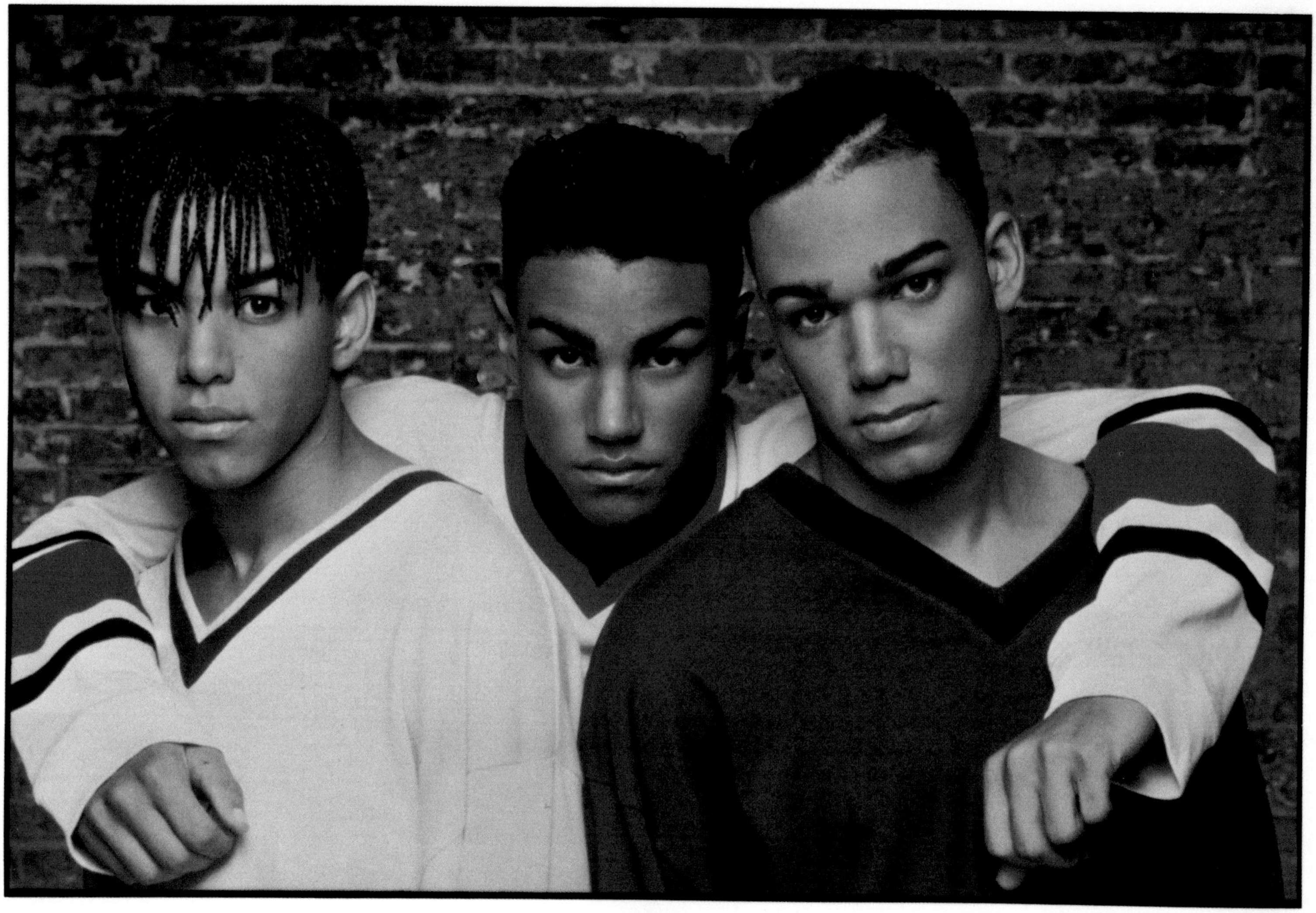

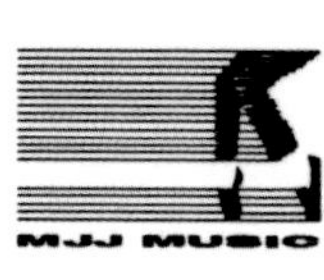

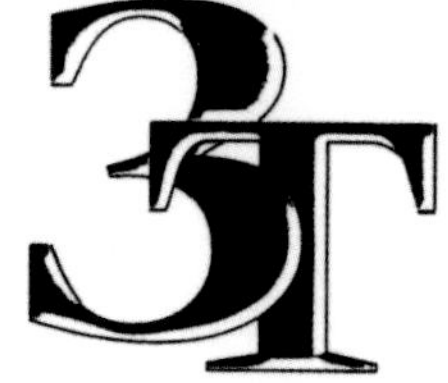

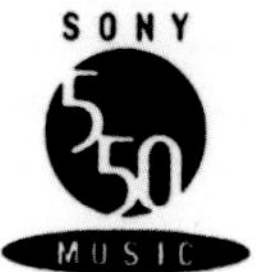

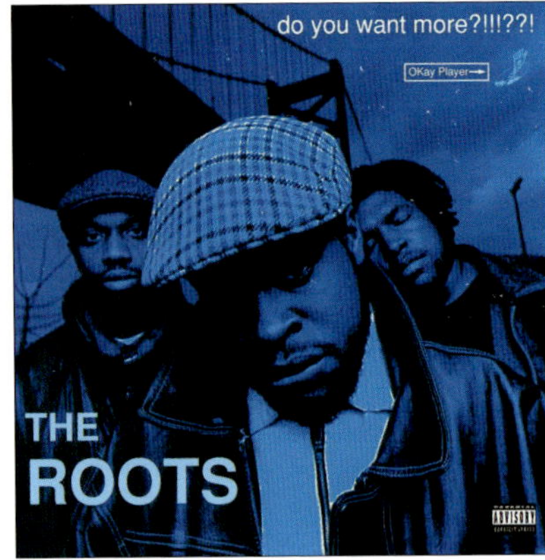

The Roots' *Do You Want More ?!!!??!* eschewed sampling for live instrumentation, unveiling the Philadelphia-based act's style of "organic hip-hop jazz."

Billboard 200: *Do You Want More?!!!??!* (#104)

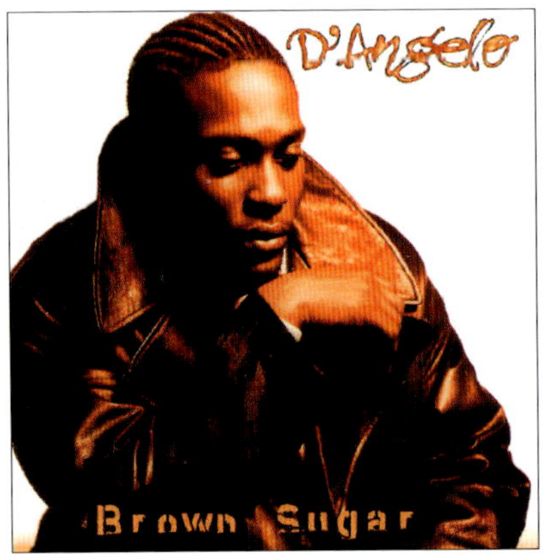

The "neo-soul" sound of *Brown Sugar*, D'Angelo's debut solo album, soon became popular by ratifying and facilitating classic R&B in the hip-hop age.

Billboard 200: *Brown Sugar* (#22)
Billboard Hot 100: "Brown Sugar" (#27); "Cruisin'" (#53); "Lady" (#10); "Me and Those Dreamin' Eyes of Mine" (#74)

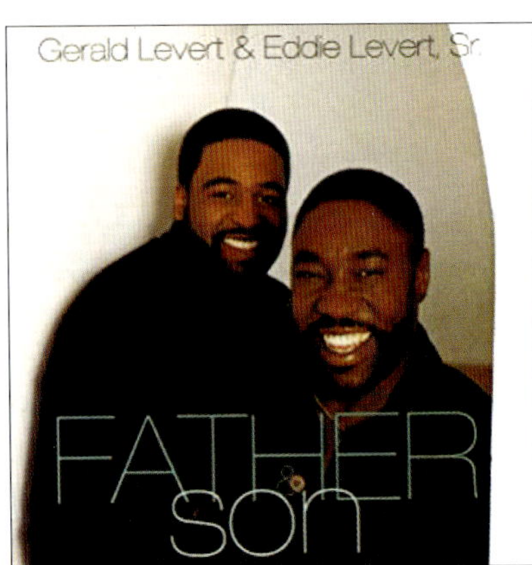

Sharing the recording studio, singers Gerald Levert & Eddie Levert, Sr. testified to their mutual devotion and deference on the soulful *Father and Son*.

Billboard 200: *Father and Son* (#20)
Billboard Hot 100: "Already Missing You" (#75)

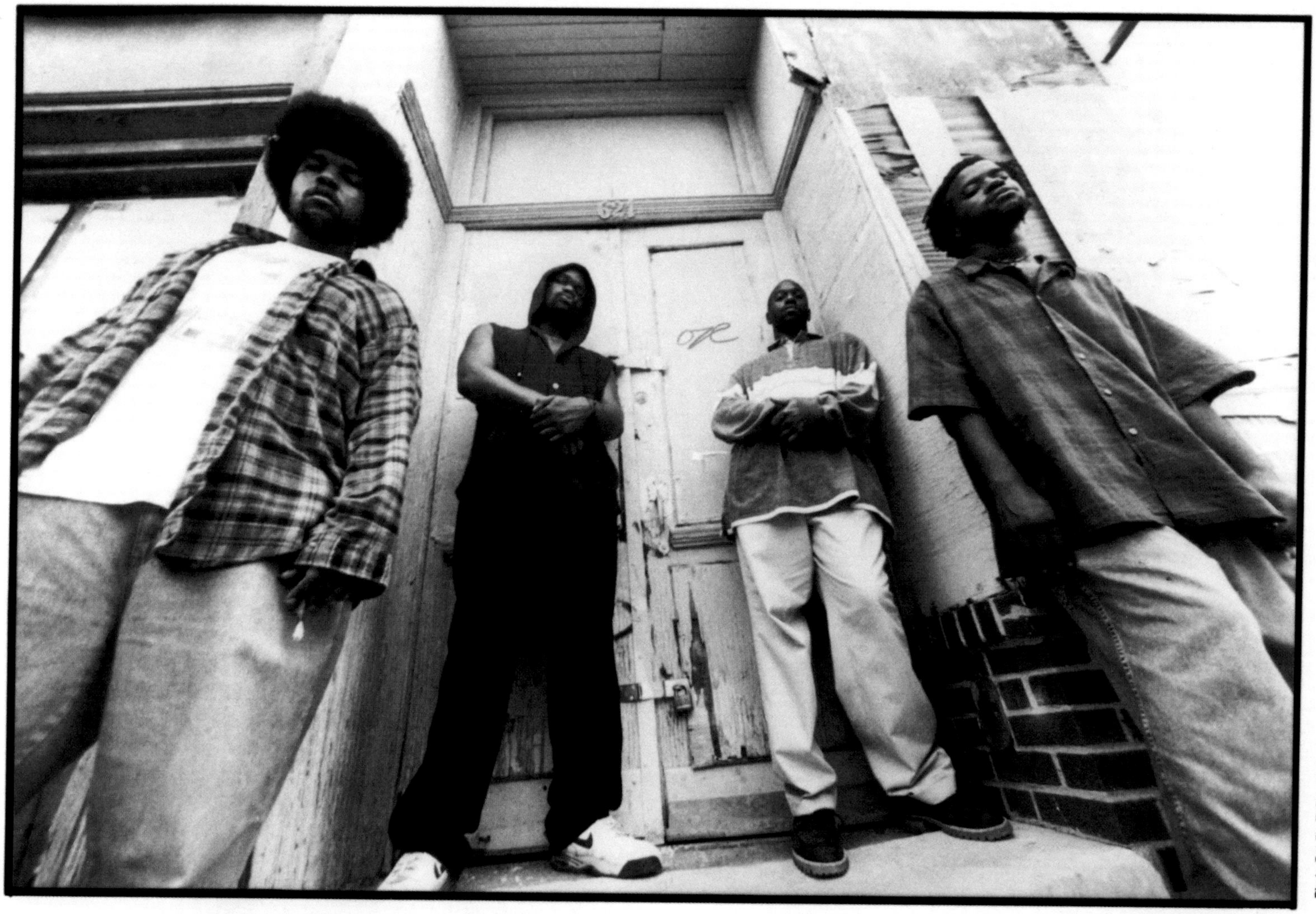

Photo Credit: T. Eric Munroe

B.R.O. the R.? Hub Malik B. Black Thought

THE ROOTS

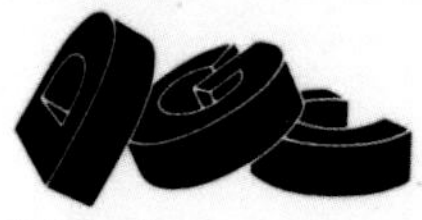

DAVID GEFFEN COMPANY

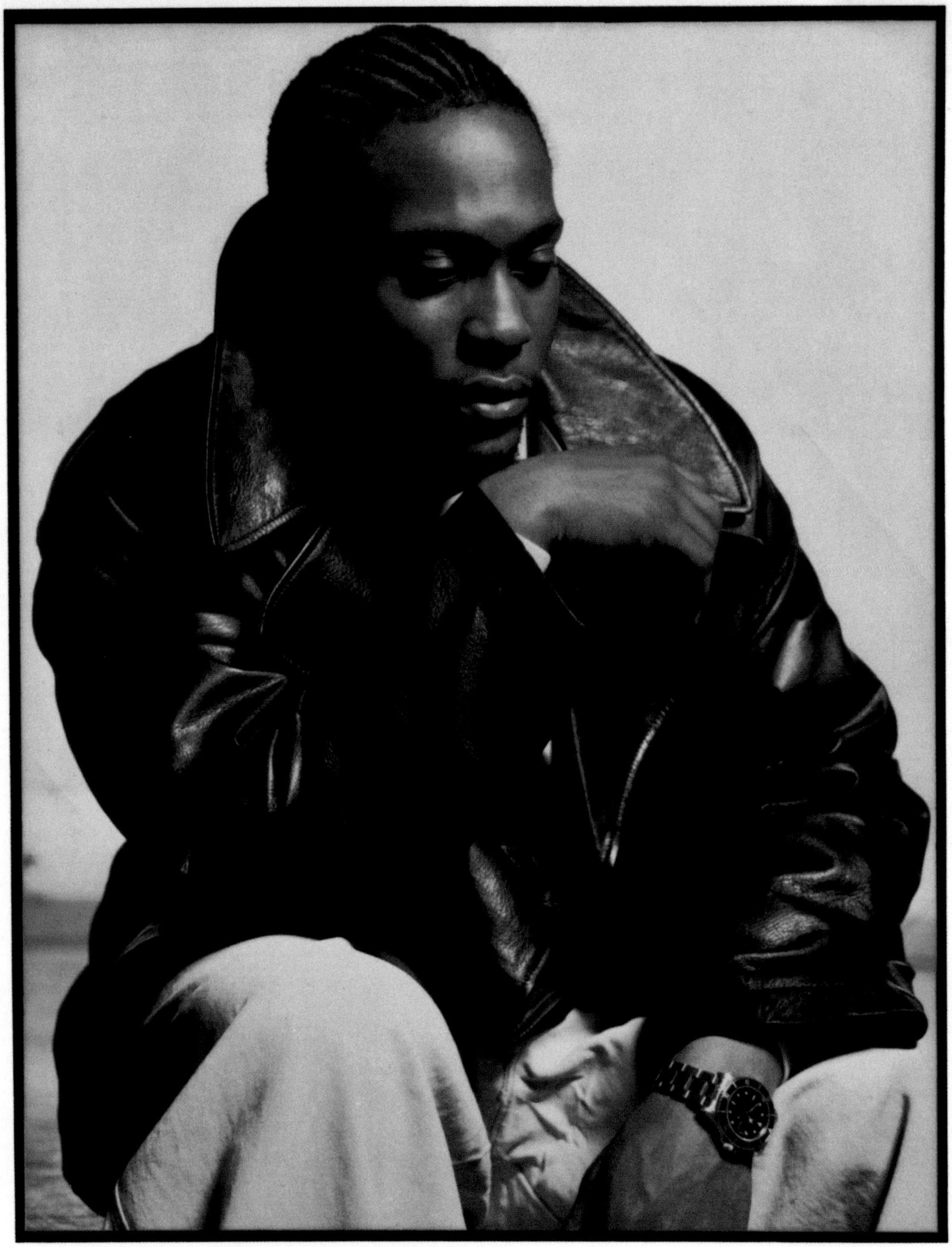

Photo credit: PER GUSTAFSSON

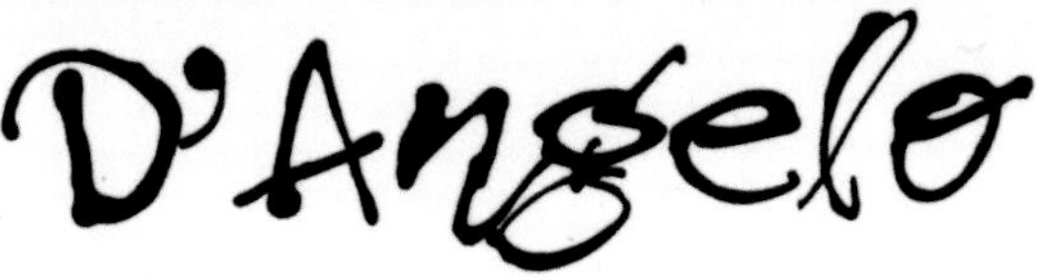

EMI Records

EMI

Management: Kedar Entertainment

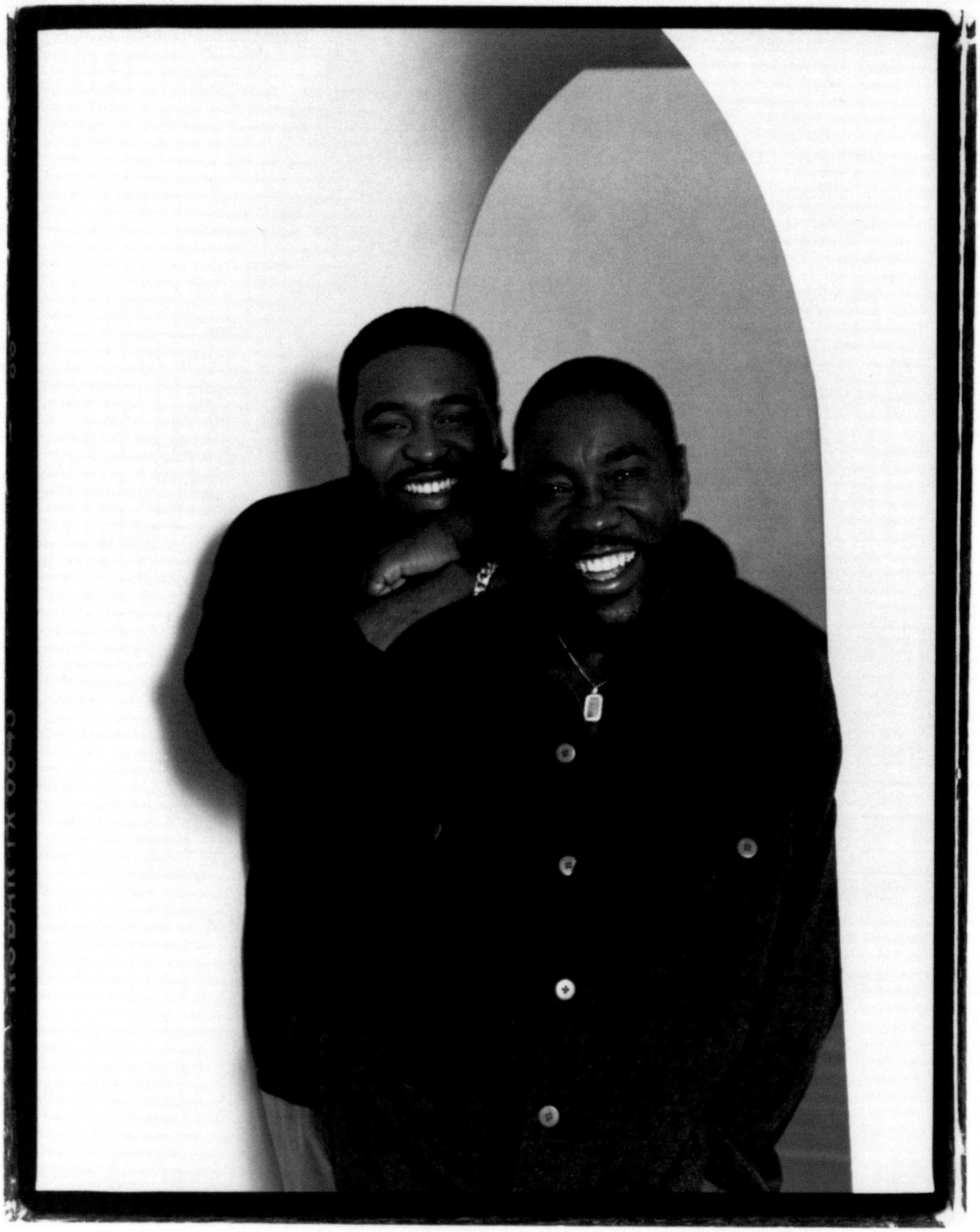

Eddie Levert, Sr. appears courtesy of EMI Records

PHOTO CREDIT DANIEL BORIS

Gerald Levert & Eddie Levert, Sr

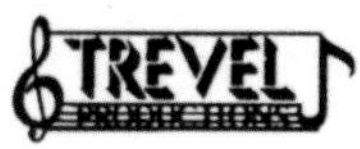

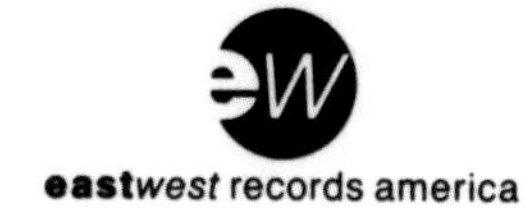

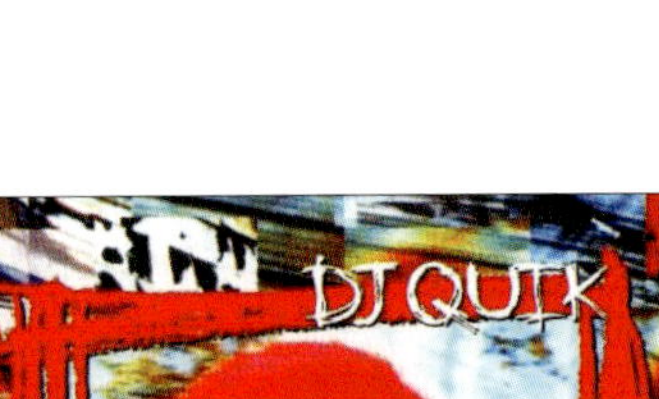

Operating under an arrangement with Suge Knight, rapper and producer **DJ Quik**'s *Safe + Sound* reached No. 1 on the R&B and hip-hop album charts.

Billboard 200: *Safe + Sound* (#14)
Billboard Hot 100: "Safe + Sound" (#81)

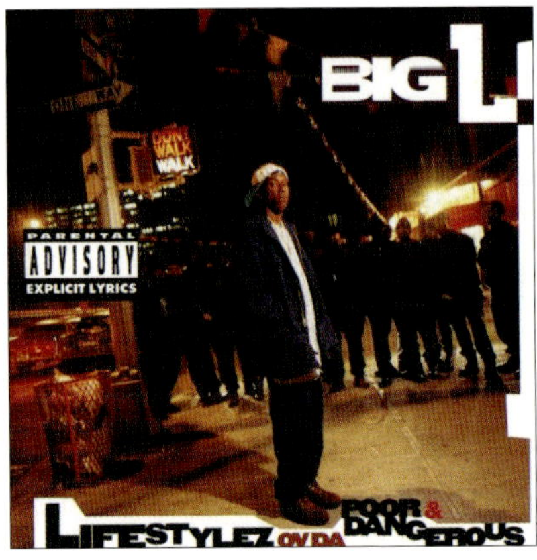

Earning praise for his aggressive, unapologetic lyricism and wordplay, Harlem MC **Big L** released his debut album, *Lifestylez ov da Poor & Dangerous*.

Billboard 200: *Lifestylez ov da Poor & Dangerous* (#149)

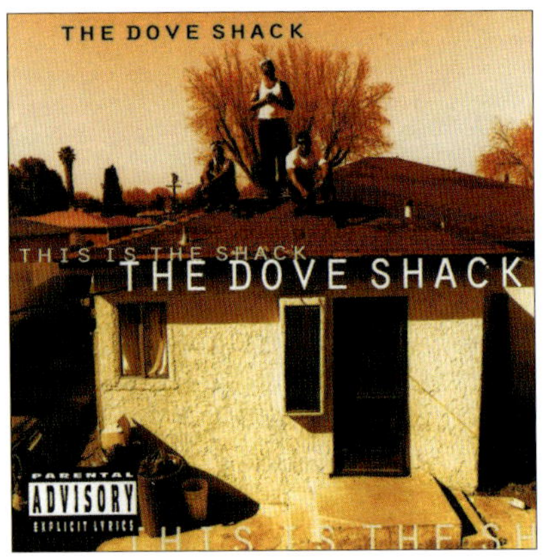

The Dove Shack, a G-funk group from Long Beach, California, peaked with its first release and "Summertime in the LBC," a song featuring Arnita Porter.

Billboard 200: *This Is the Shack* (#68)
Billboard Hot 100: "Summertime in the LBC" (#54)

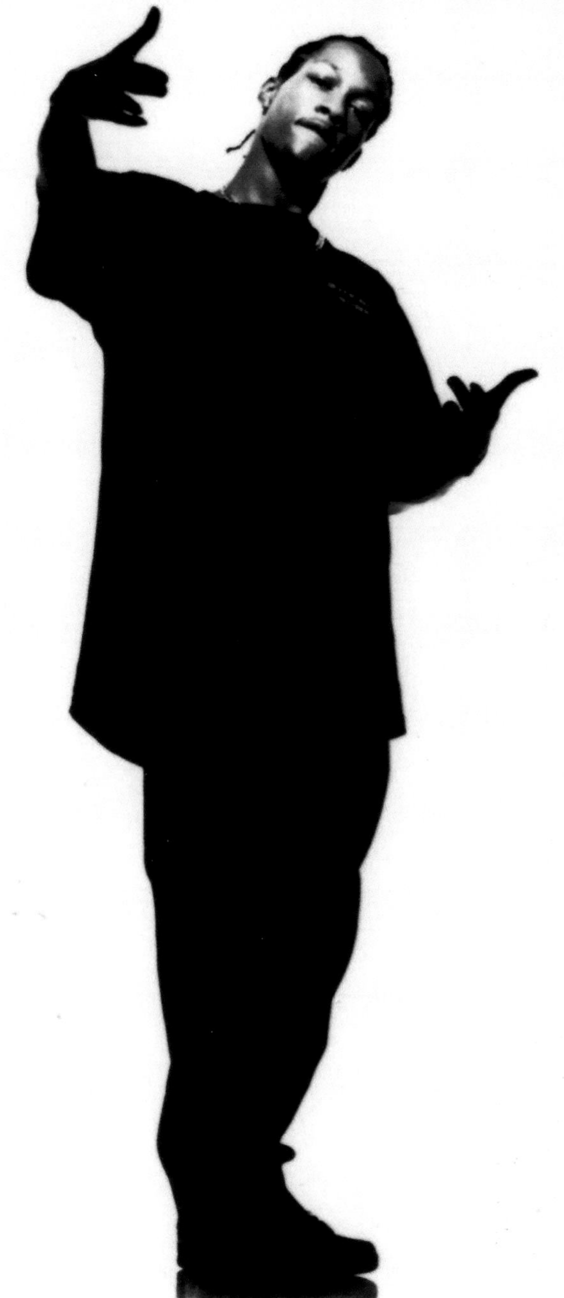

PHOTO: KLAUS SCHÖENWIESE

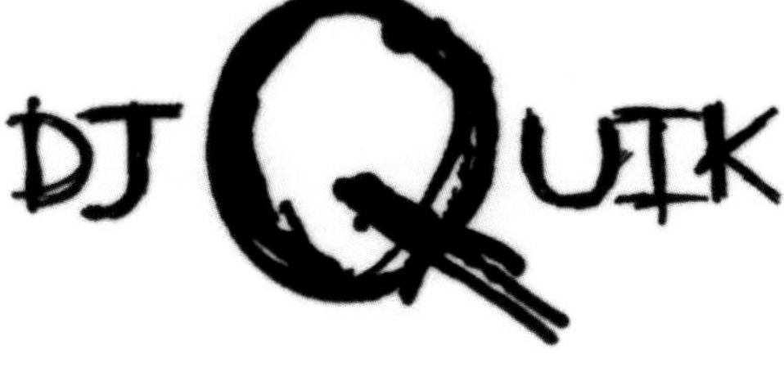

PROFILE

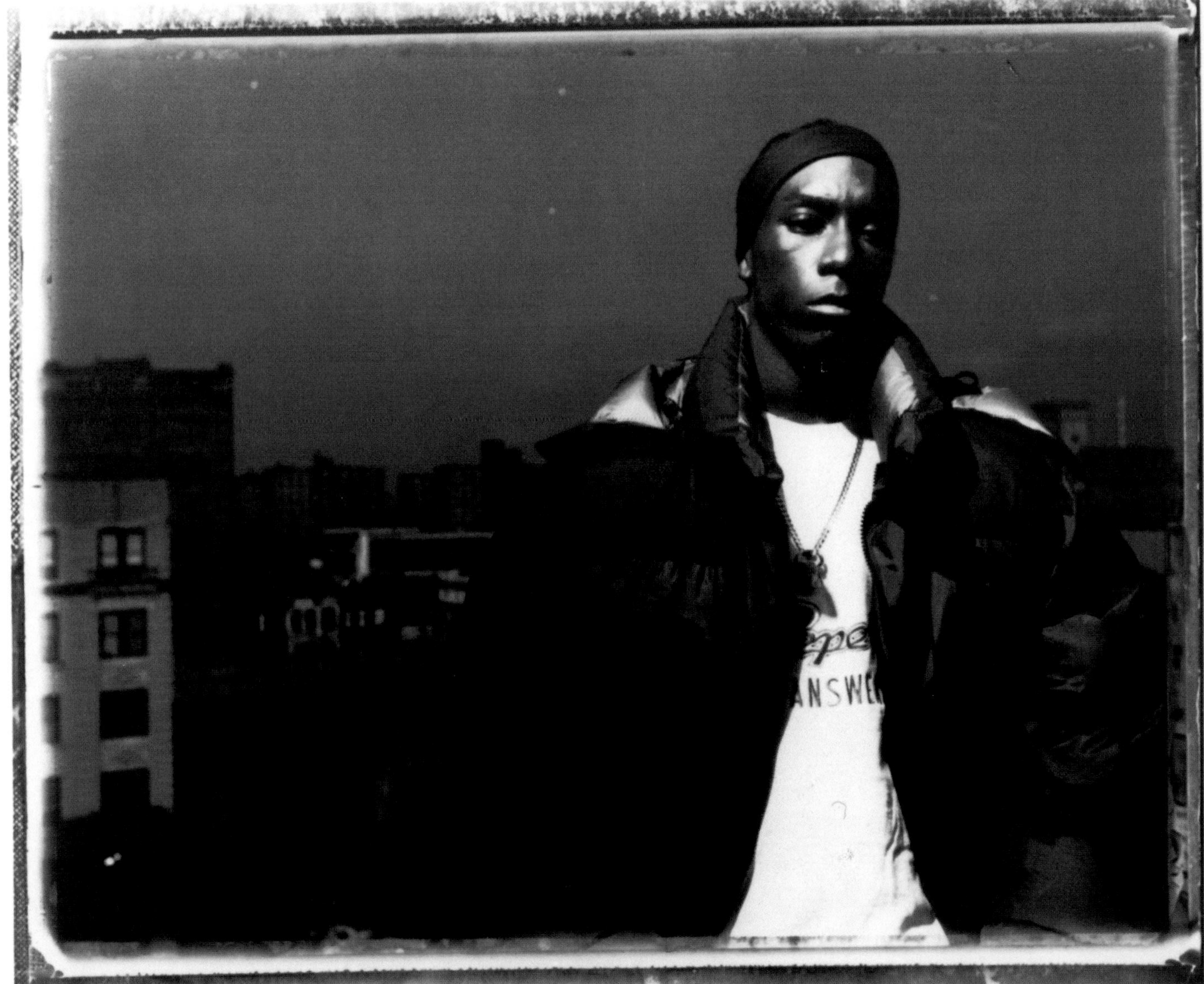

PHOTOGRAPH: DANNY CLINCH

BIG L

COLUMBIA
9501

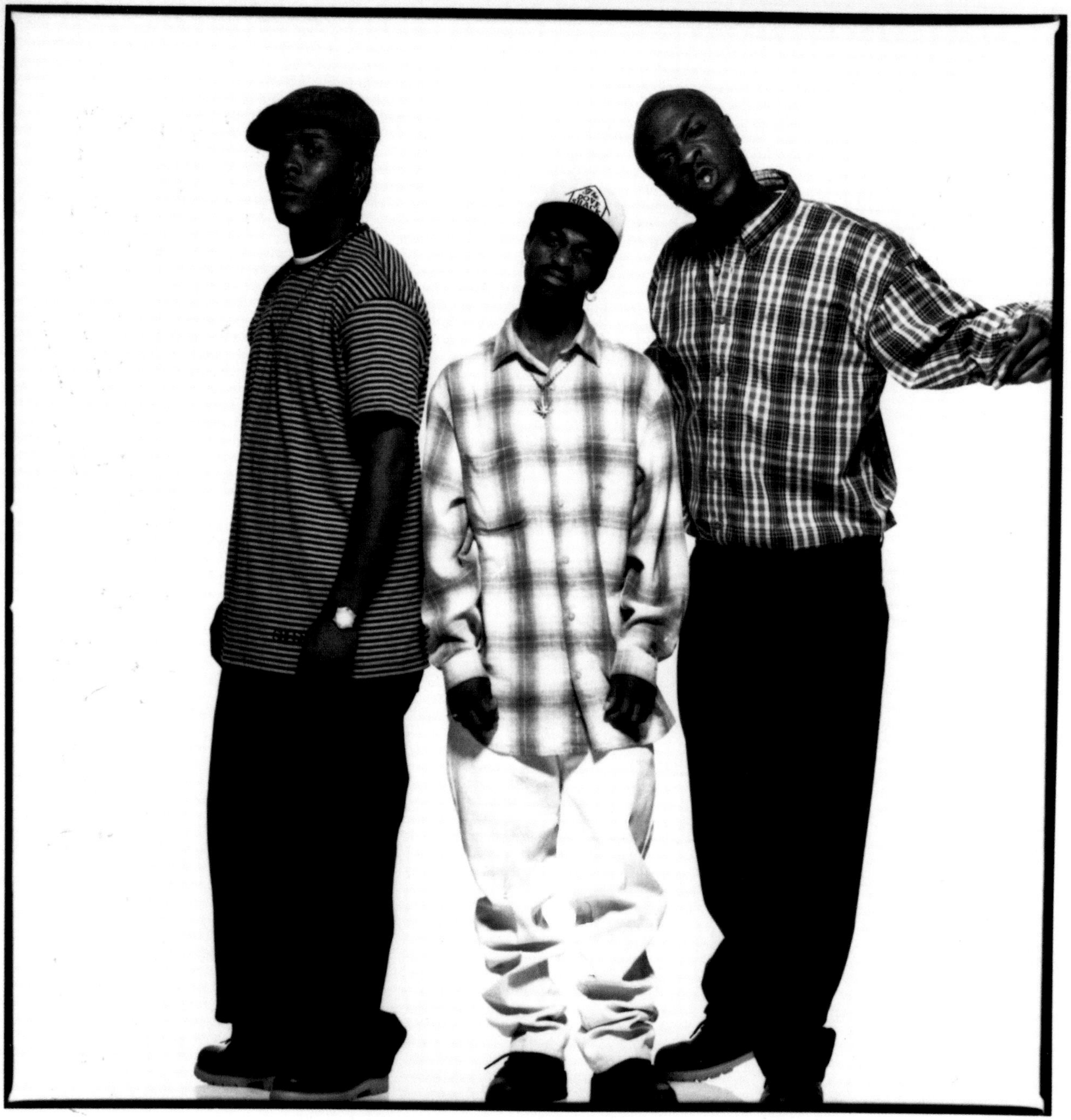

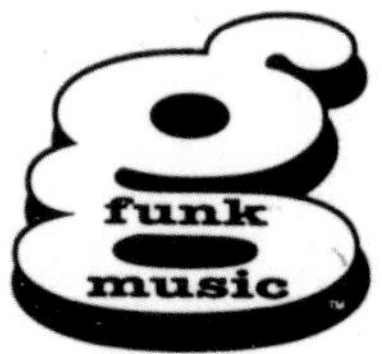
g
funk
music

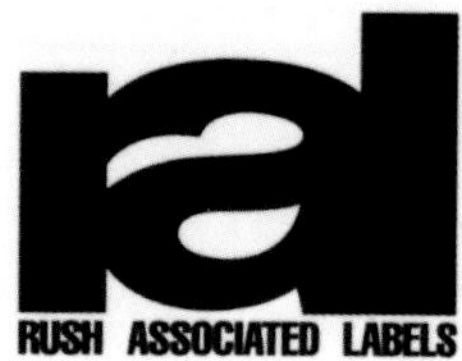
ral
RUSH ASSOCIATED LABELS

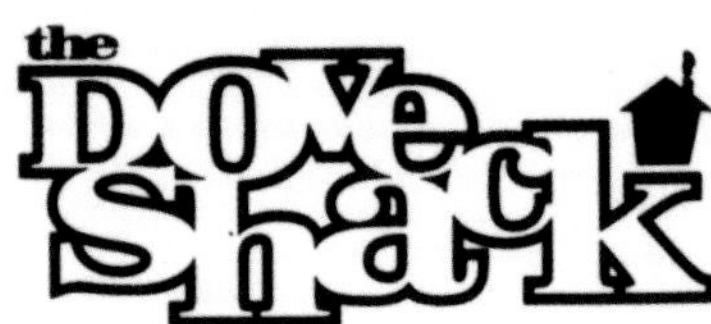
the
Dove
Shack

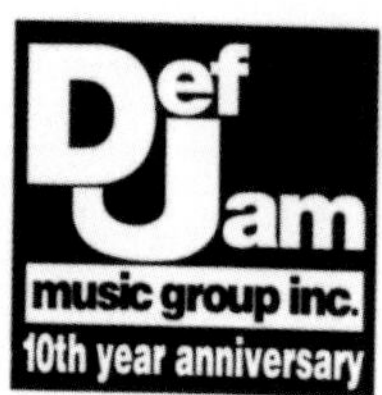
Def
Jam
music group inc.
10th year anniversary

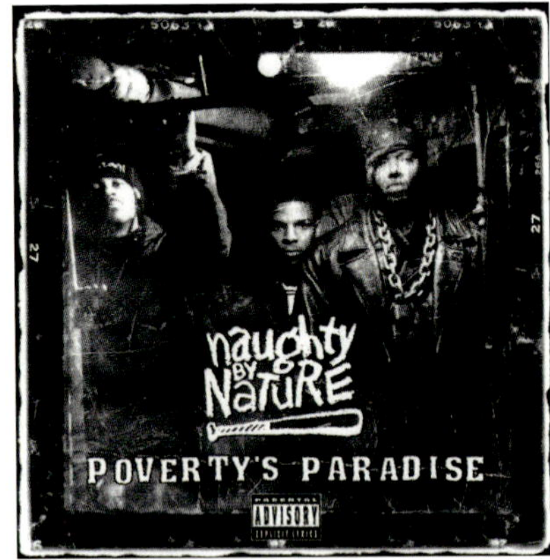

Naughty by Nature's *Poverty's Paradise* hit No. 1 on the hip-hop charts, spawned the hit "Feel Me Flow" and won a Grammy in the new rap category.

Billboard 200: *Poverty's Paradise* (#3)
Billboard Hot 100: "Feel Me Flow" (#17); "Craziest" (#51)

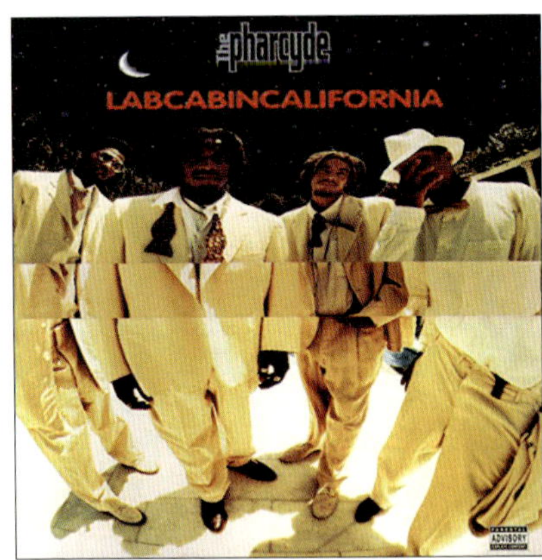

The Pharcyde released *Labcabincalifornia*, a contemplative, calmer follow-up to the eccentric good humor of the West Coast rap group's lauded debut.

Billboard 200: *Labcabincalifornia* (#37)
Billboard Hot 100: "Runnin'" (#55); "Drop" (#93)

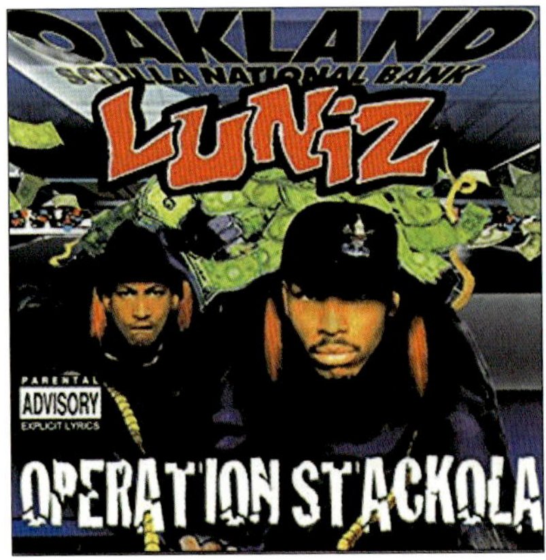

Yukmouth and Numskull of Luniz dropped the album *Operation Stackola*, and the duo from Oakland scored a booming worldwide hit, "I Got 5 on It."

Billboard 200: *Operation Stackola* (#20)
Billboard Hot 100: "I Got 5 on It" (#8)

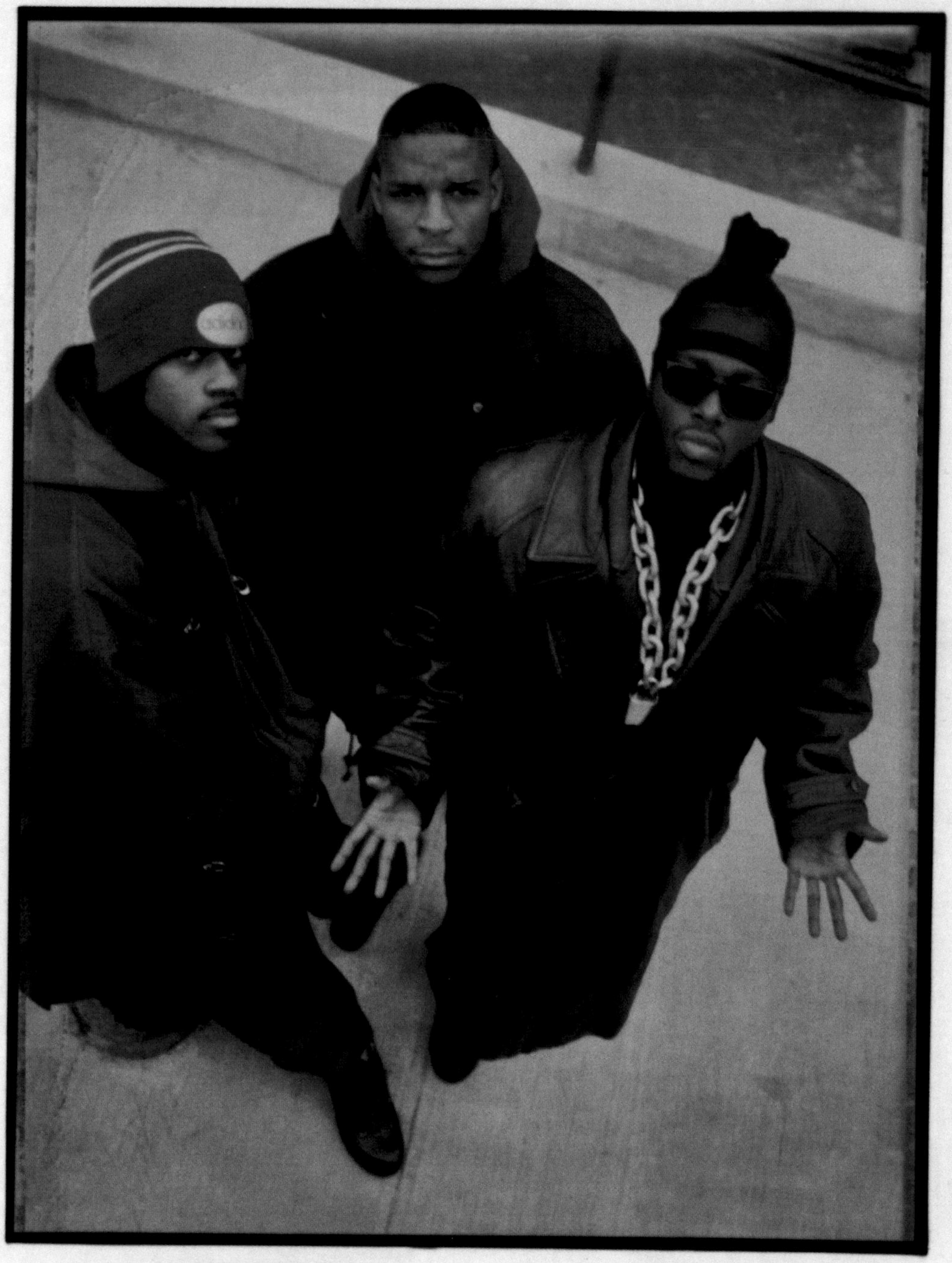

PHOTO BY: JAMES MINCHIN III

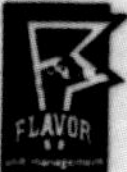

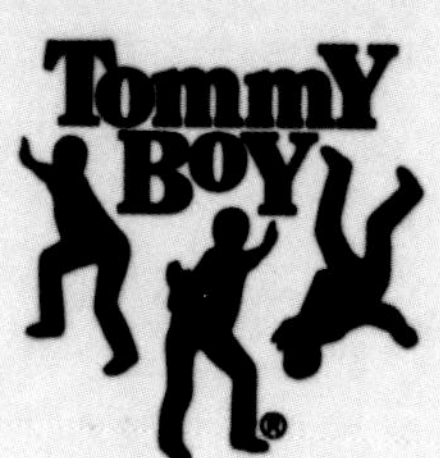

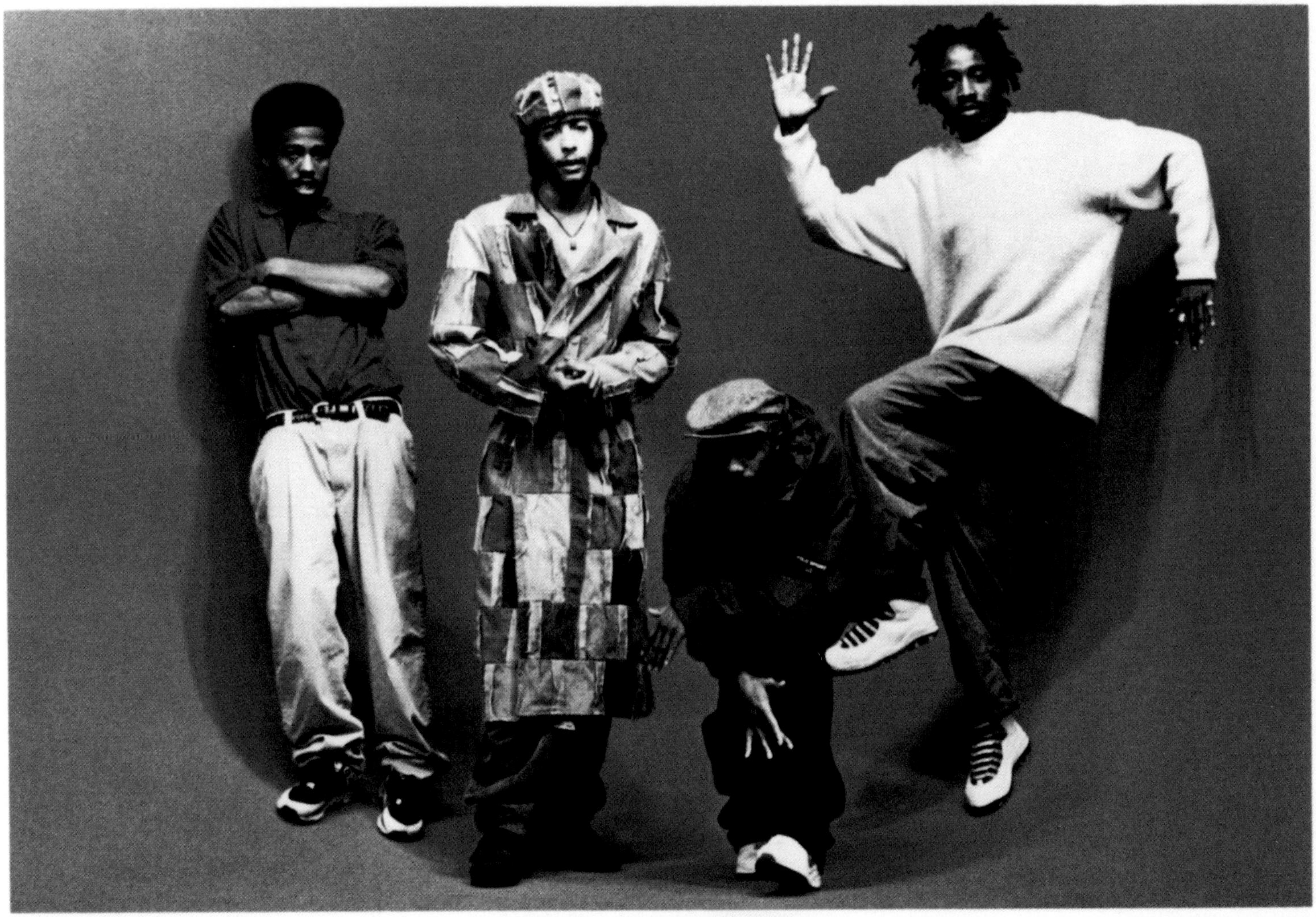

BOOTIE BROWN SLIMKID 3 FATLIP IMANI

PHOTO CREDIT: B+

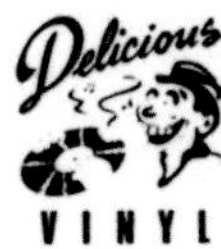

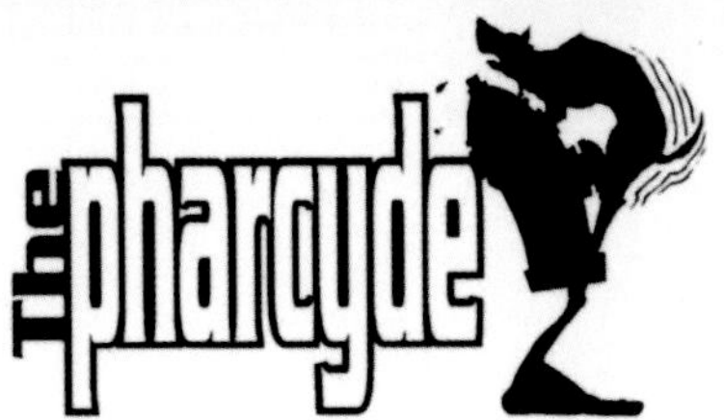

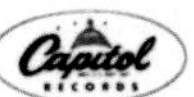

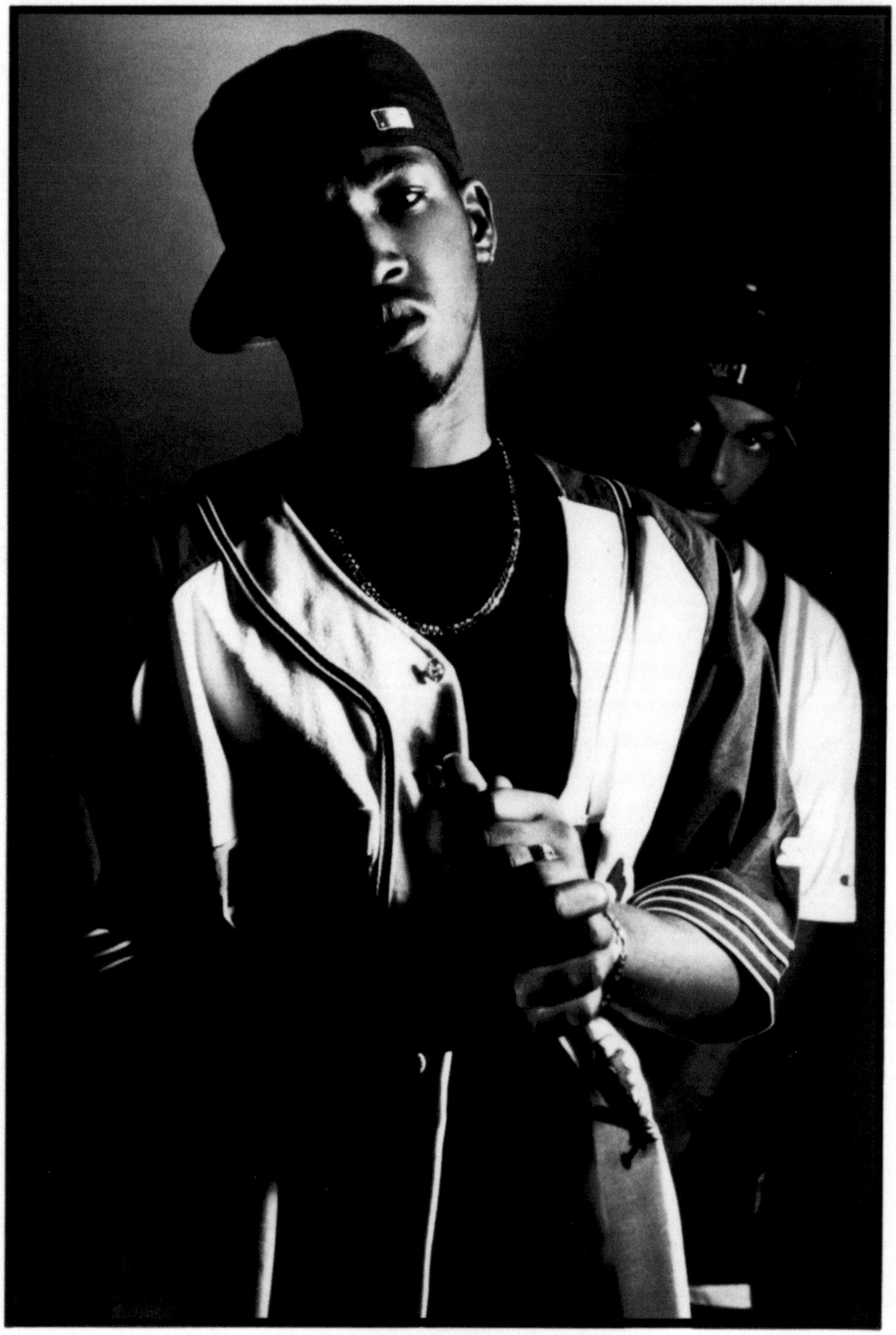

Photo Credit Victor Hall 3/95

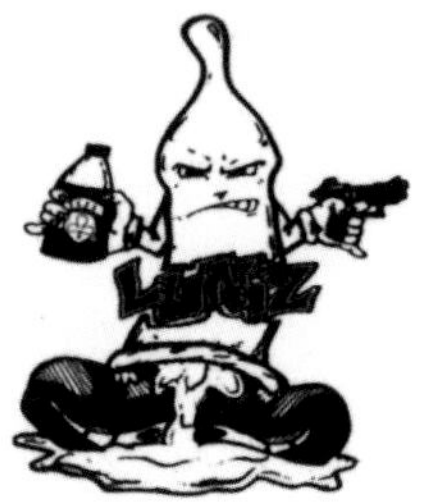

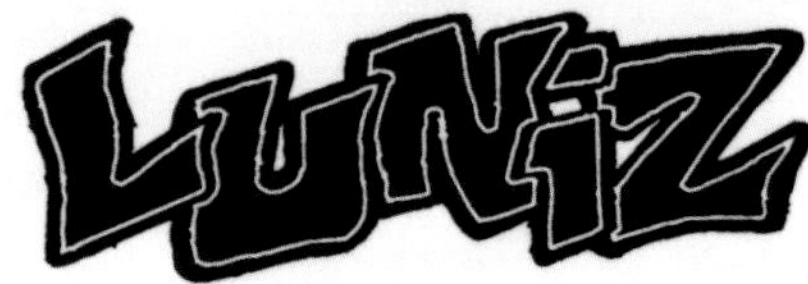

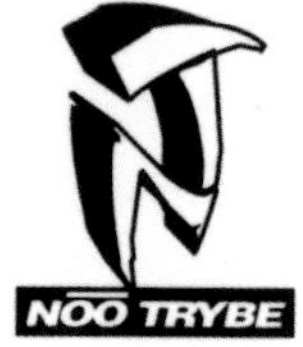

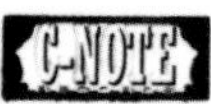

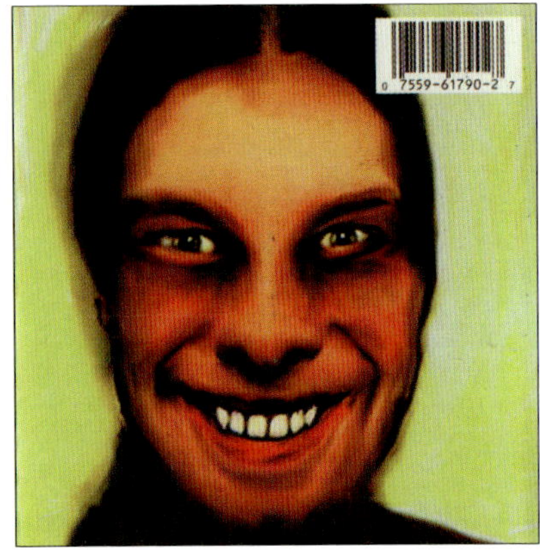

...I Care Because You Do by **Aphex Twin**, aka electronic musician Richard D. James, deftly mixed abrasive rhythms with symphonic and ambient elements.

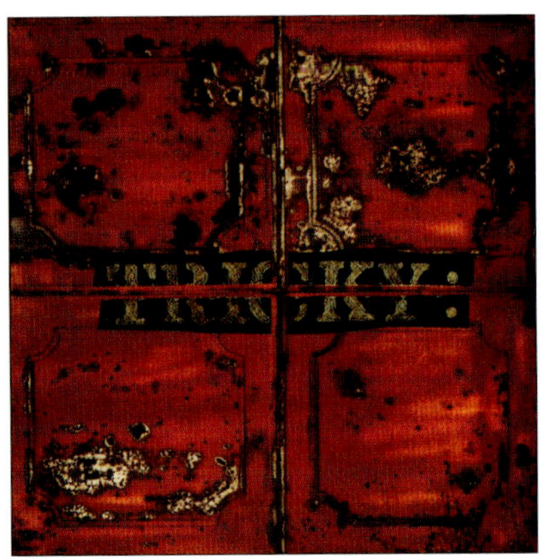

An original member of Massive Attack, English rapper and producer **Tricky** prospered with *Maxinquaye,* a vibrant release in the burgeoning trip-hop genre.

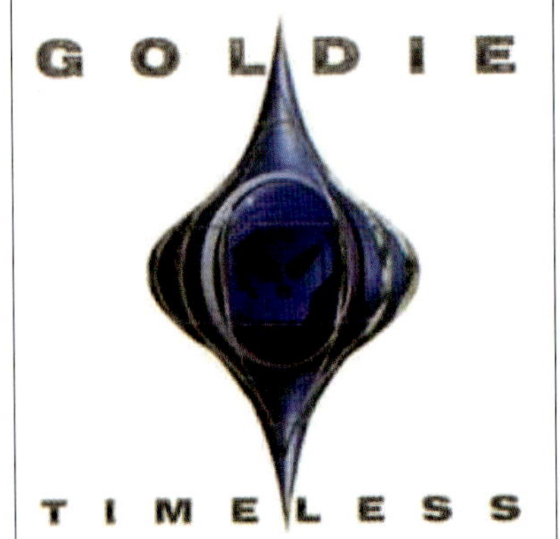

Timeless by British electronic musician **Goldie** popularized jungle, a fusion of bass lines and breakbeats with orchestral strings, airy textures and soulful vocals.

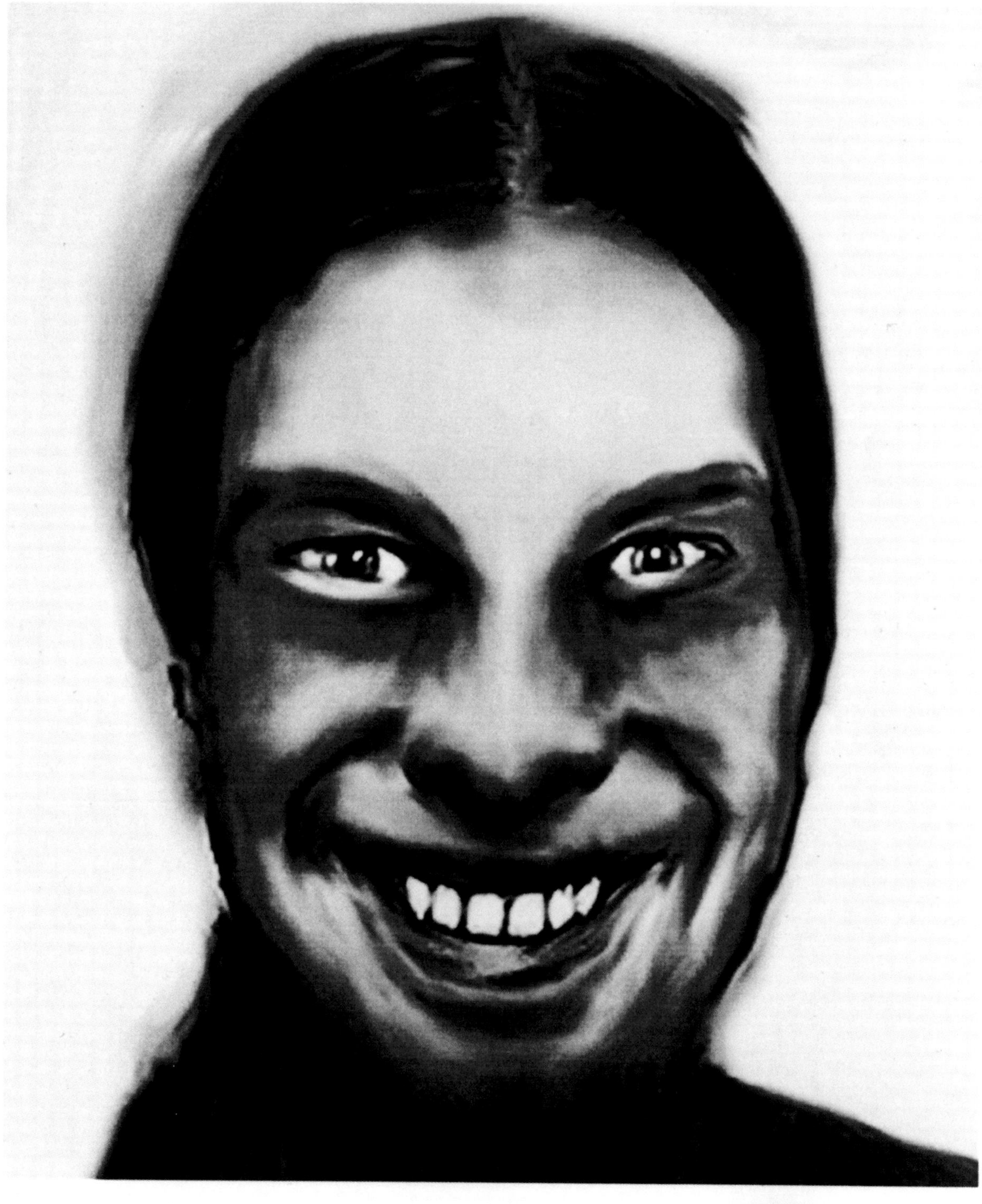

aphex twin

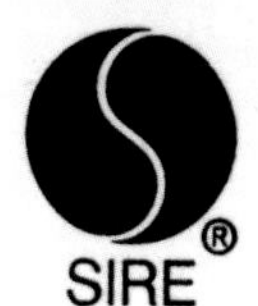

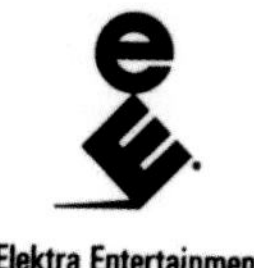

TRICKY

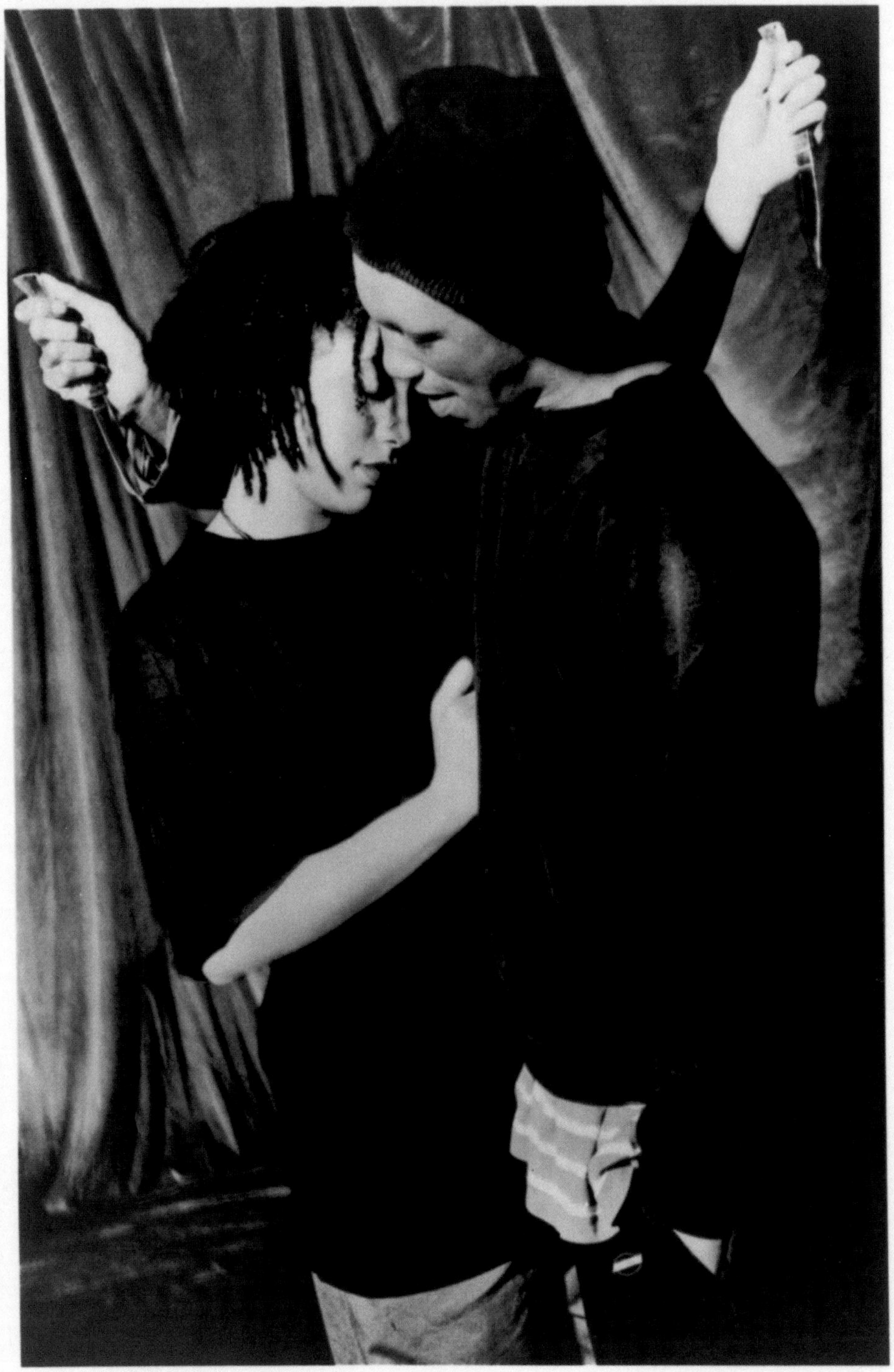

PHOTO CREDIT: PAUL RYDER

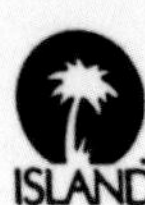

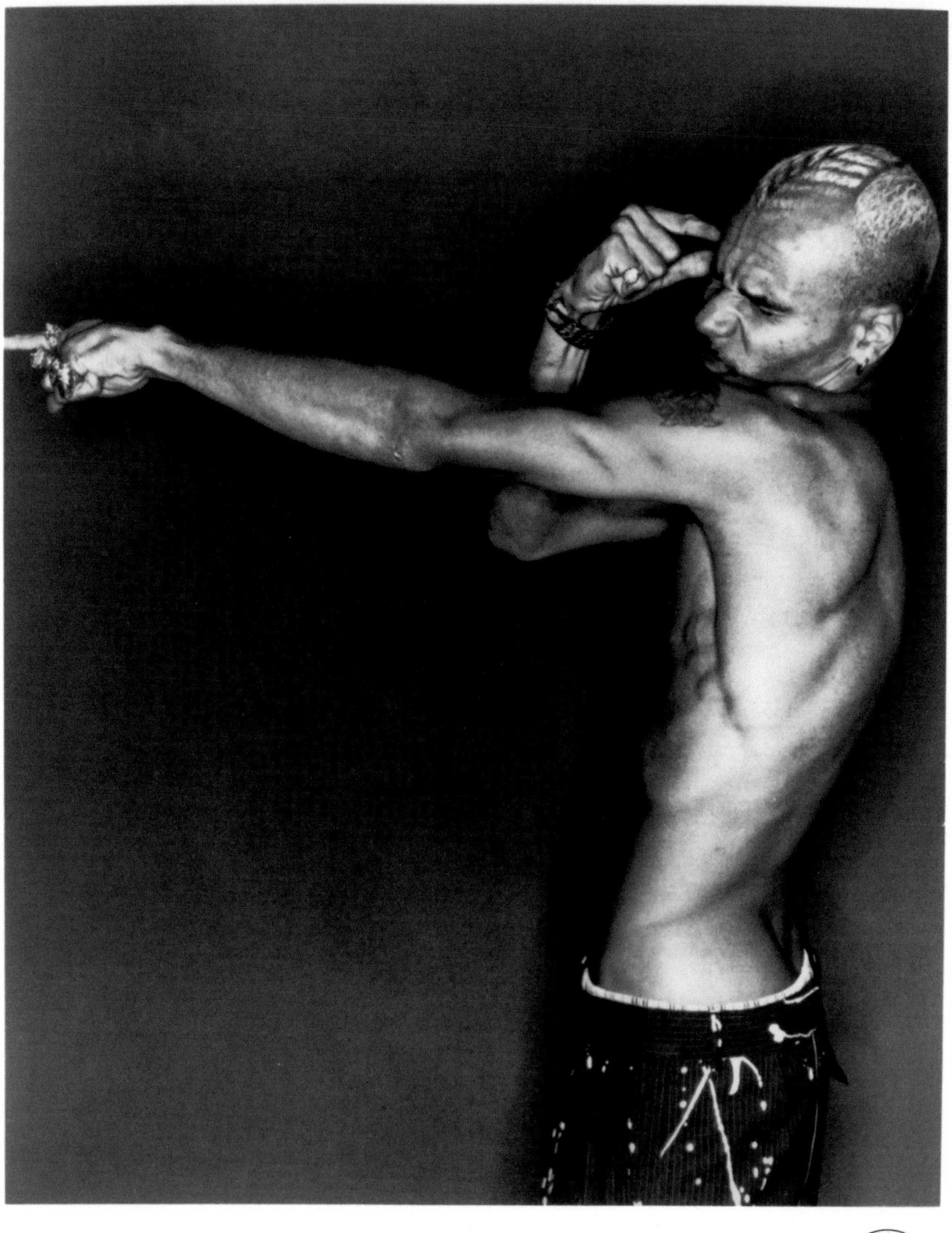

GOLDIE

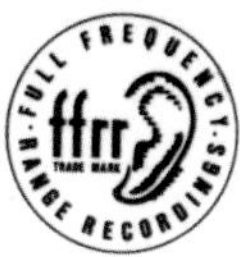

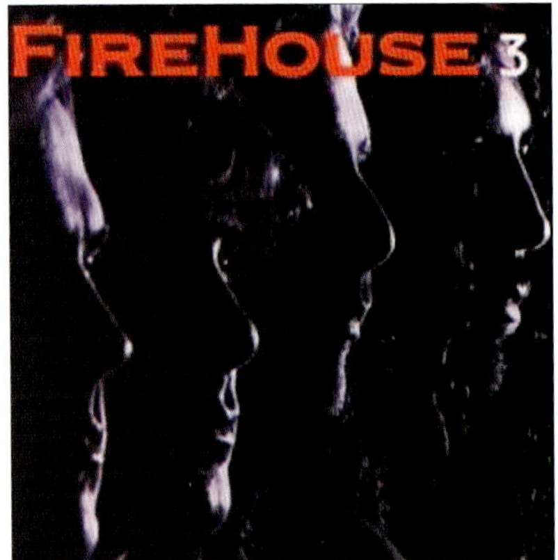

In the midst of post-grunge developments, pop-metal troupe **FireHouse** managed another power-ballad hit with the commercial "I Live My Life for You."

Billboard 200: *3* (#66)
Billboard Hot 100: "I Live My Life for You" (#26)

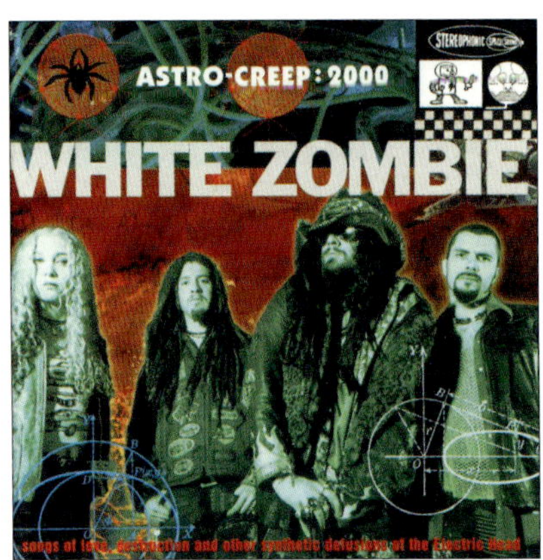

From *Astro Creep: 2000*, "More Human than Human" earned the horror-obsessed **White Zombie** another Grammy nomination for Best Metal Performance.

Billboard 200: *Astro Creep: 2000* (#6)
Billboard Hot 100: "More Human than Human" (#53)

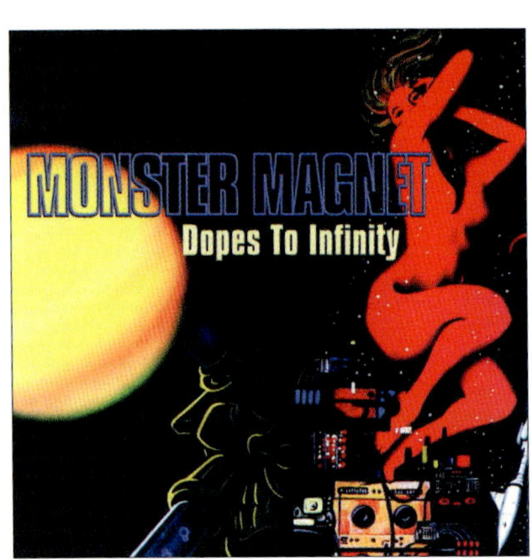

Monster Magnet's sludgy but sleek "Negasonic Teenage Warhead," the New Jersey retro rockers' first successful single, got play on rock radio and MTV.

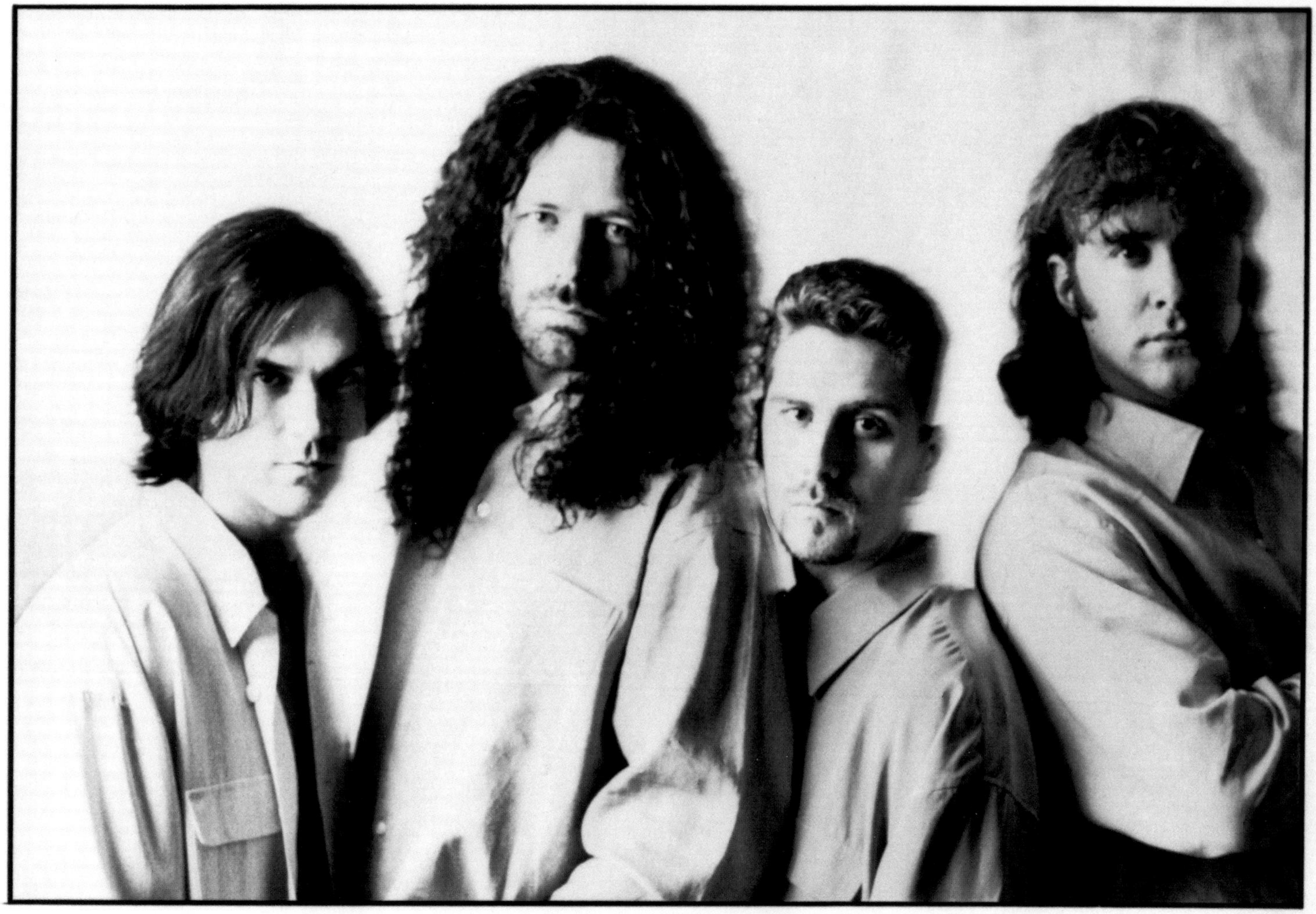

PHOTO CREDIT: PAUL ARESU

BILL LEVERTY PERRY RICHARDSON MICHAEL FOSTER C.J. SNARE

FIREHOUSE

MGMT:
HARD TO HANDLE MGMT
610-889-3166

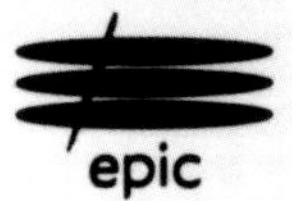

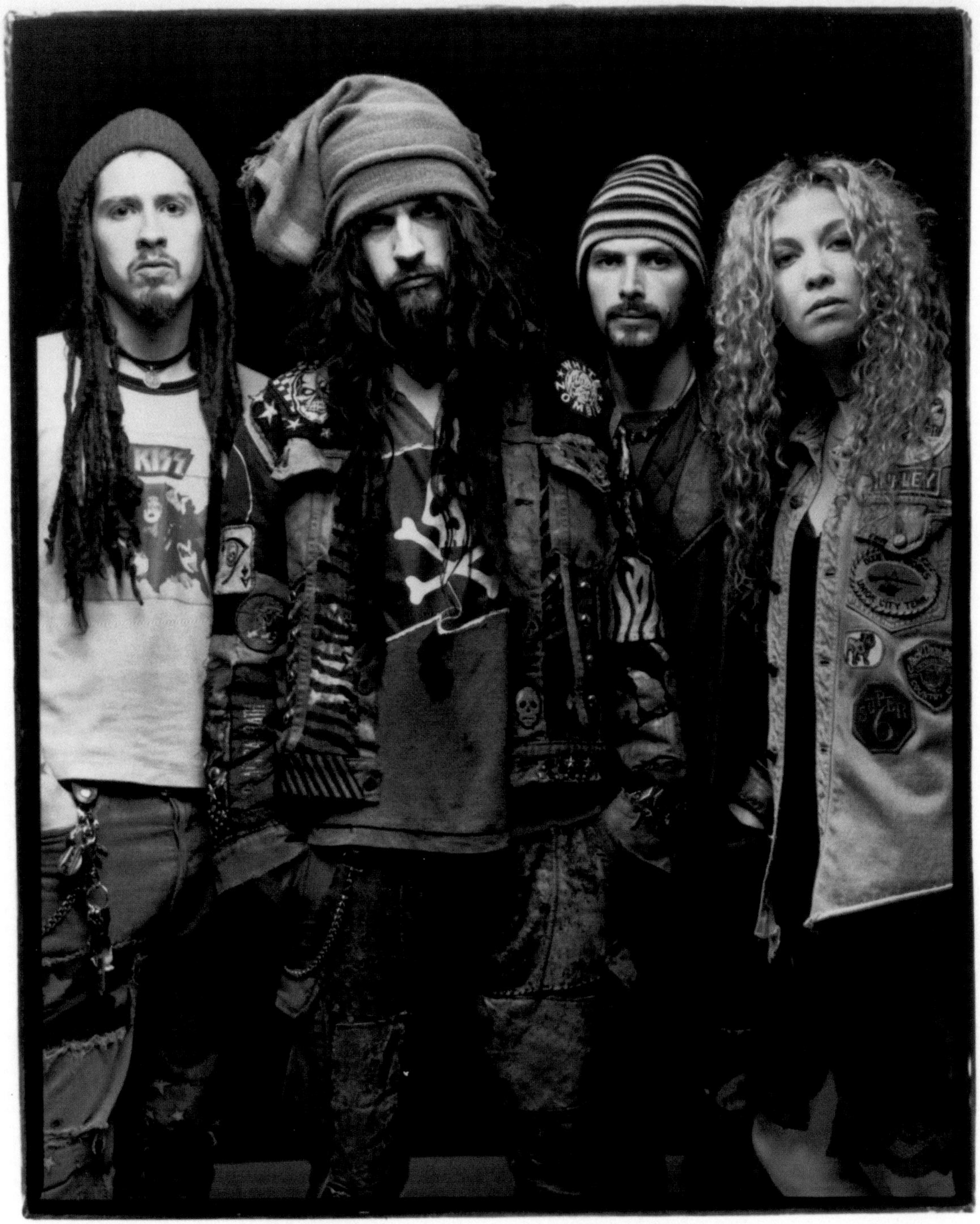

Photo Credit: Chris Cuffaro

J. Rob Zombie John Tempesta Sean Yseult

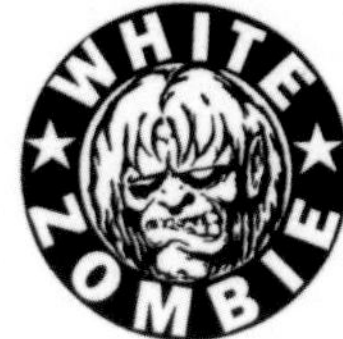

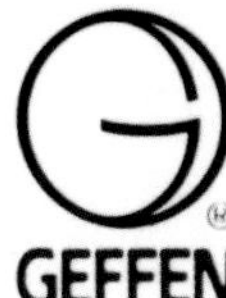

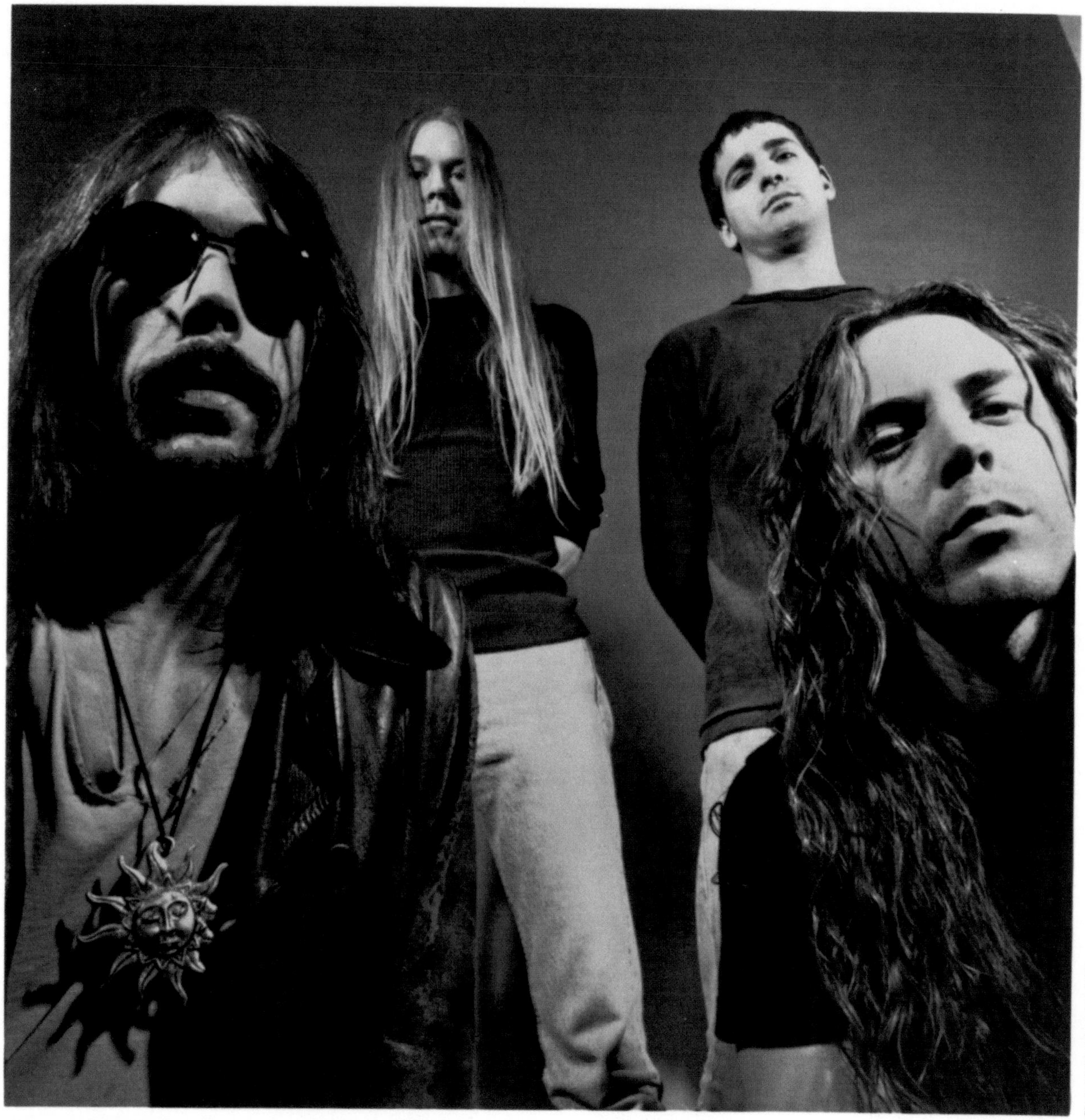

Photo: Michael Lavine 1/95

Dave Wyndorf Ed Mundell Jon Kleiman Joe Calandra

MONSTER MAGNET

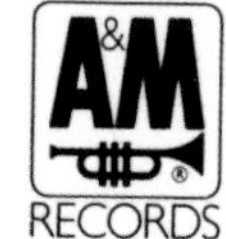

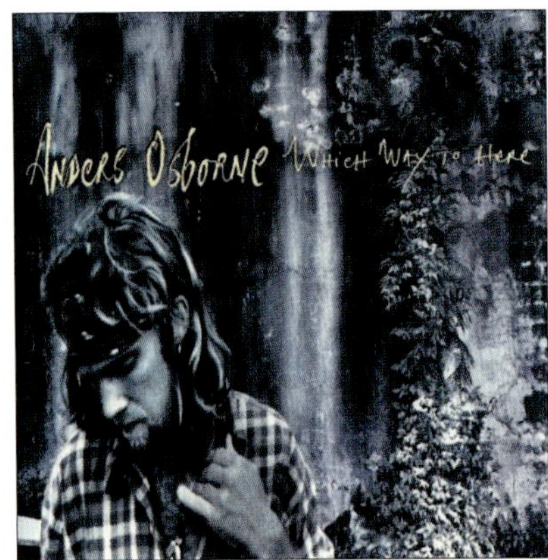

Anders Osborne's *Which Way to Here* earned the Swedish-born singer and guitarist notice with the roots-based tunes "Favorite Son" and "Pleasin' You."

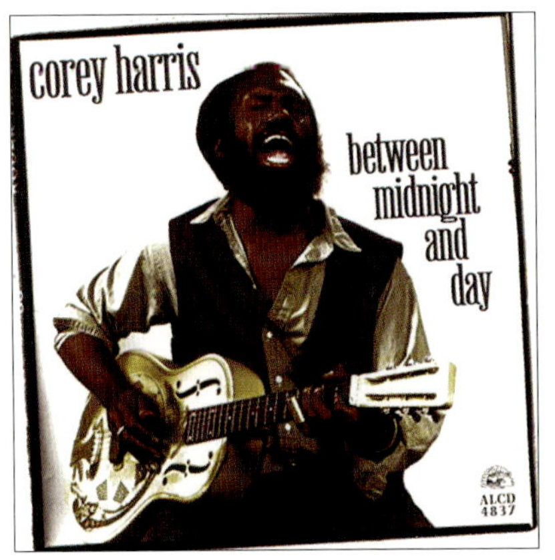

Between Night and Day by **Corey Harris** turned a spotlight on acoustic Delta blues guitar styles, covering songs from Muddy Waters to Charley Patton.

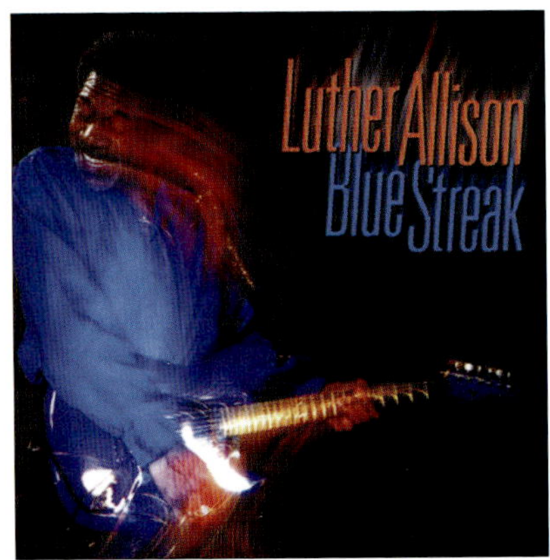

Featuring "Cherry Red Wine," the album *Blue Streak* earned guitarist **Luther Allison** five more W.C. Handy Awards, including Contemporary Blues Album.

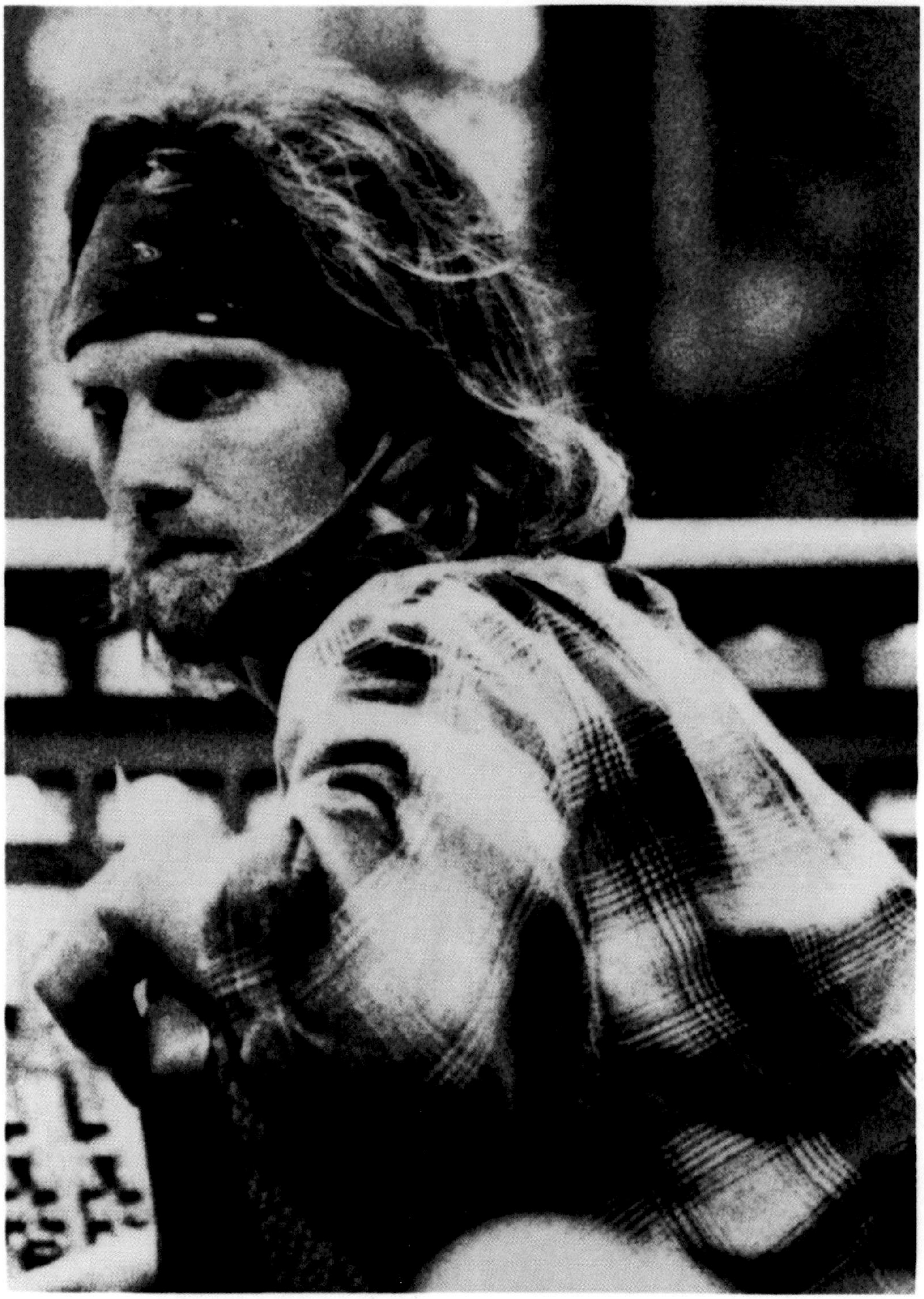

PHOTO CREDIT KENT G. HUTSLAR

OKeh

Anders Osborne

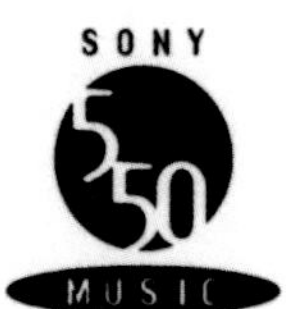

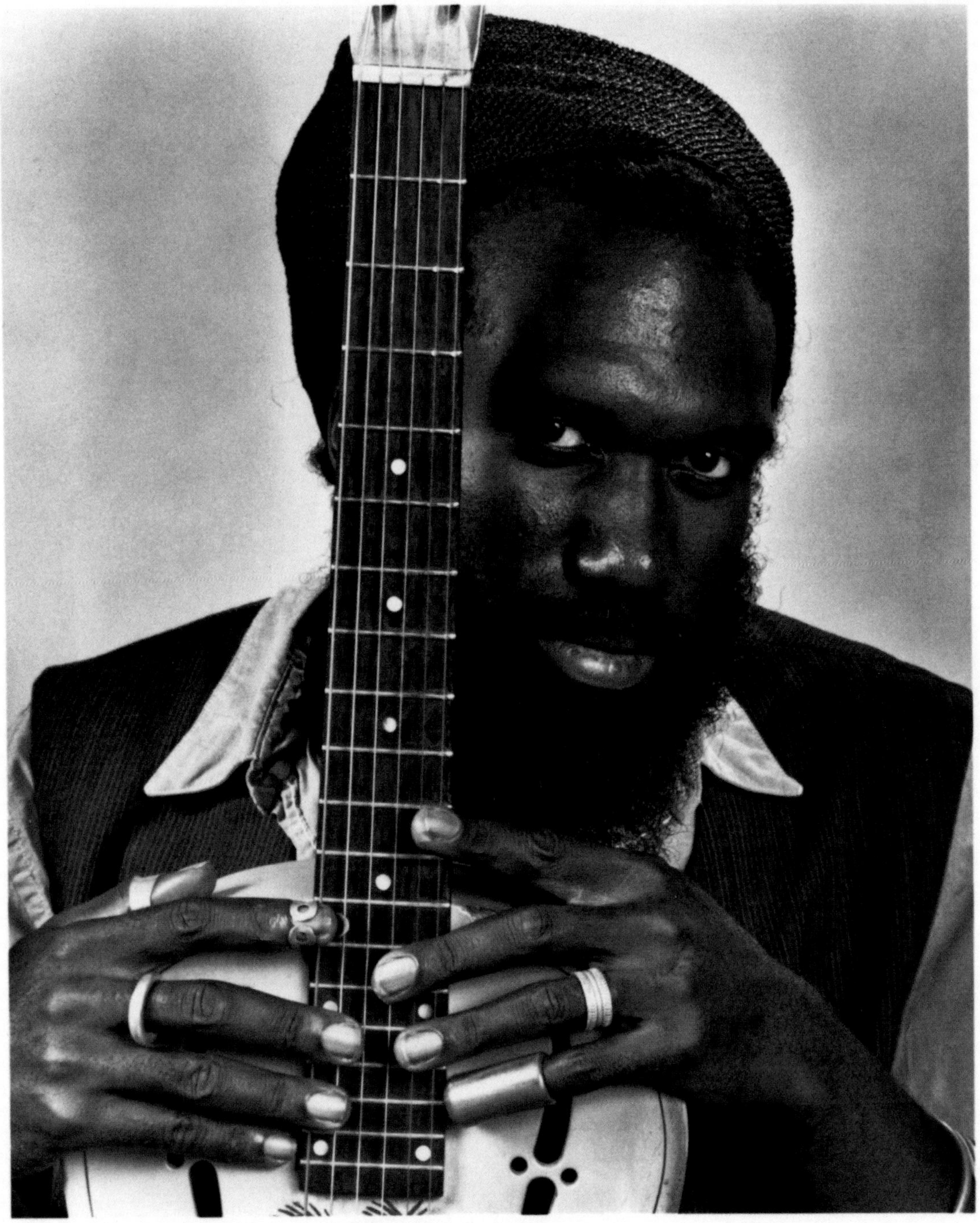

PHOTO: MICHAEL SMITH

ALLIGATOR RECORDS
P.O. BOX
60234
CHICAGO, IL 60660
(312) 973-7736

Corey Harris

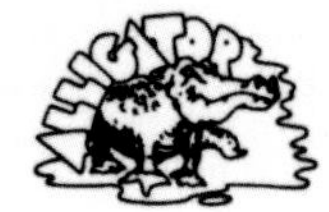

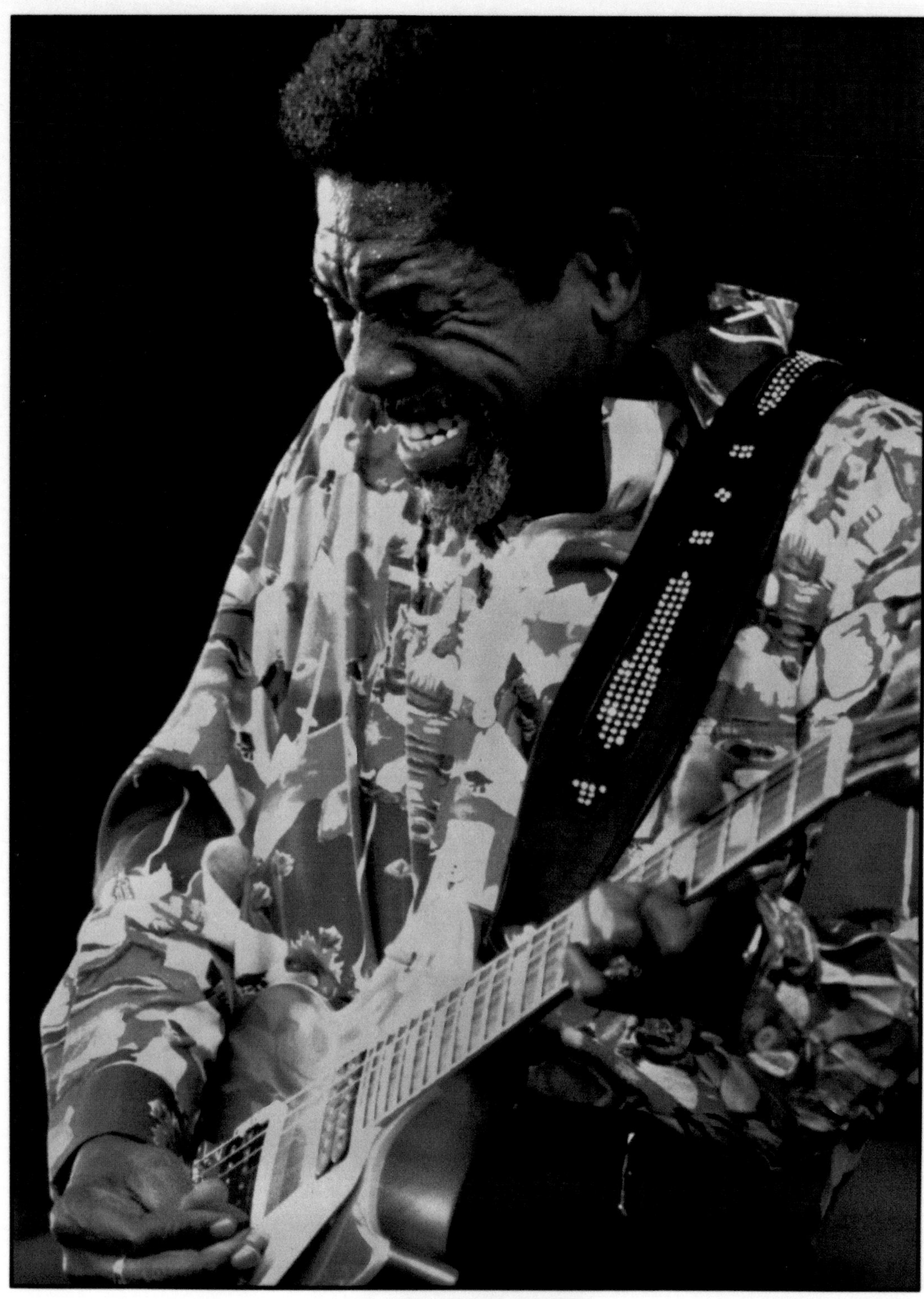

PHOTO: LES GRUSECK

BOOKING:
Rosebud Agency
(415)386-3456
Fax: (415)386-0599

LUTHER ALLISON

ALLIGATOR RECORDS
P.O. BOX
60234
CHICAGO, IL 60660
(312) 973-7736

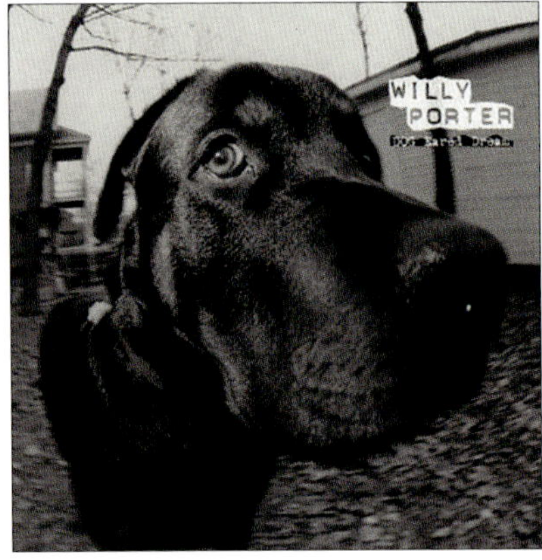

"Angry Words" appeared on **Willy Porter**'s *Dog-Eared Dream* album and established the Midwest artist's vivid acoustic guitar work and rich songwriting.

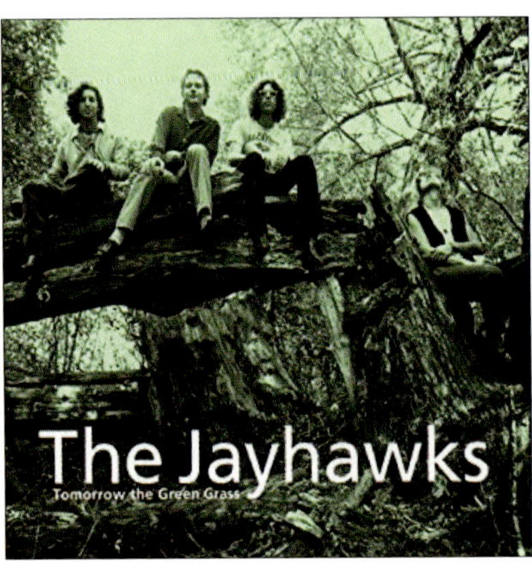

The Jayhawks' *Tomorrow the Green Grass*, the alt-country band's last release prior to co-founder Mark Olson quitting, was led by the melancholic "Blue."

Billboard 200: *Tomorrow the Green Grass* (#92)

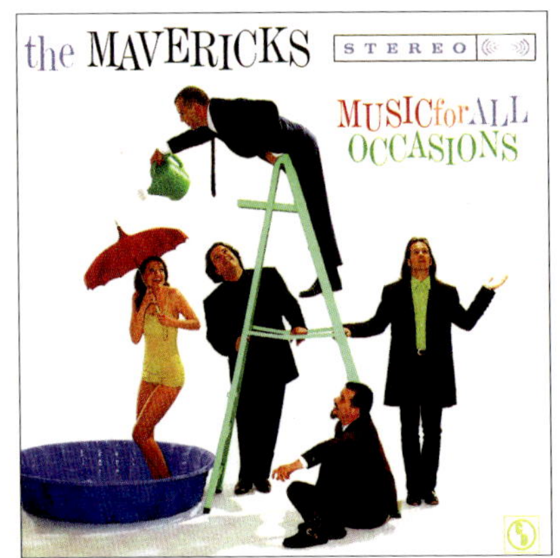

The Mavericks delivered the country hits "Here Comes the Rain," a Grammy winner, and "All You Ever Do Is Bring Me Down," featuring Flaco Jimenez.

Billboard 200: *Music for All Occasions* (#58)

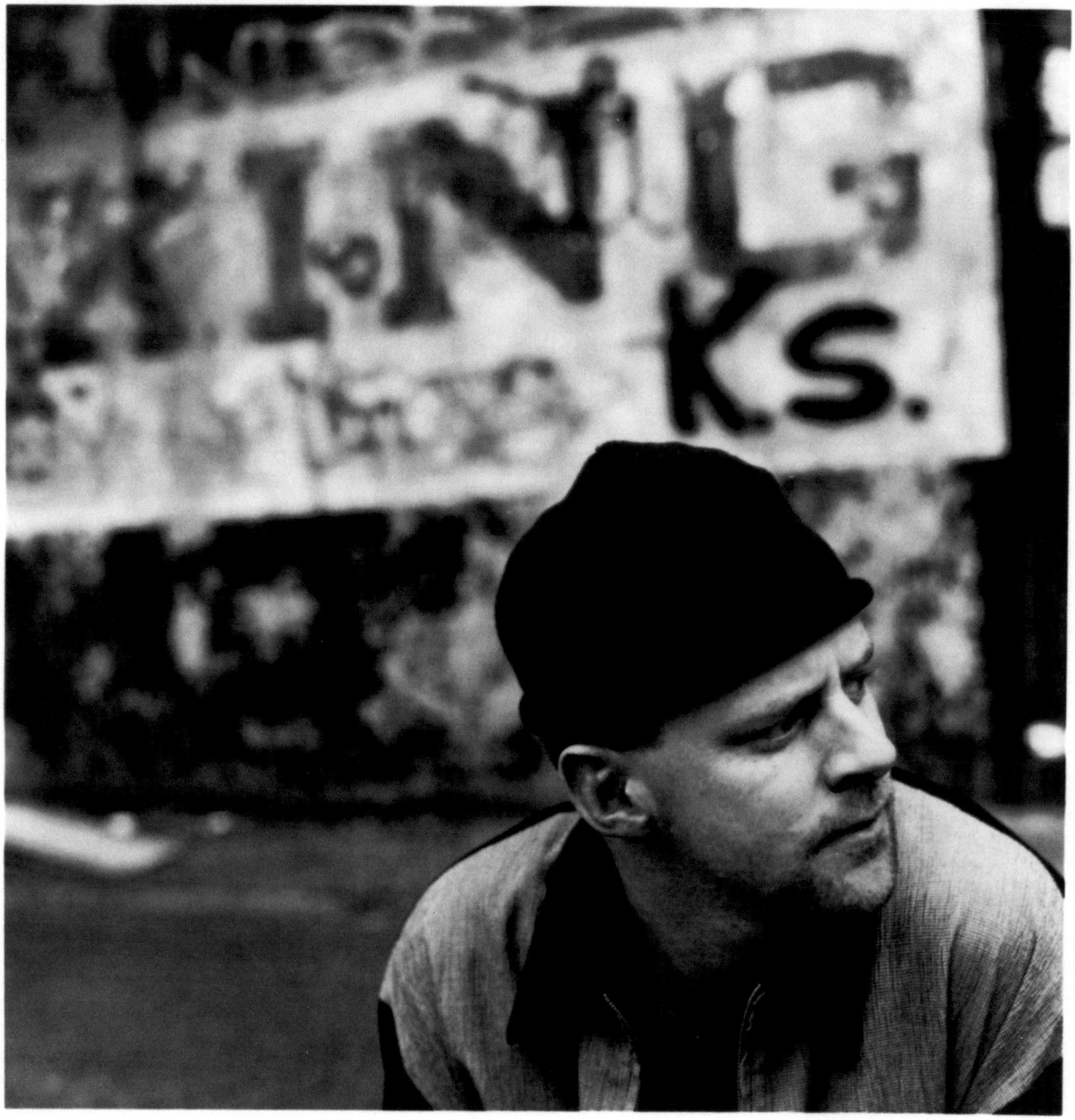

Photo Credit: Michael Wilson

WILLY PORTER

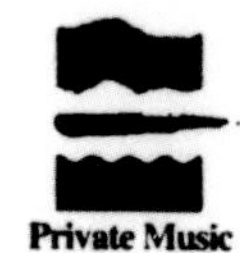

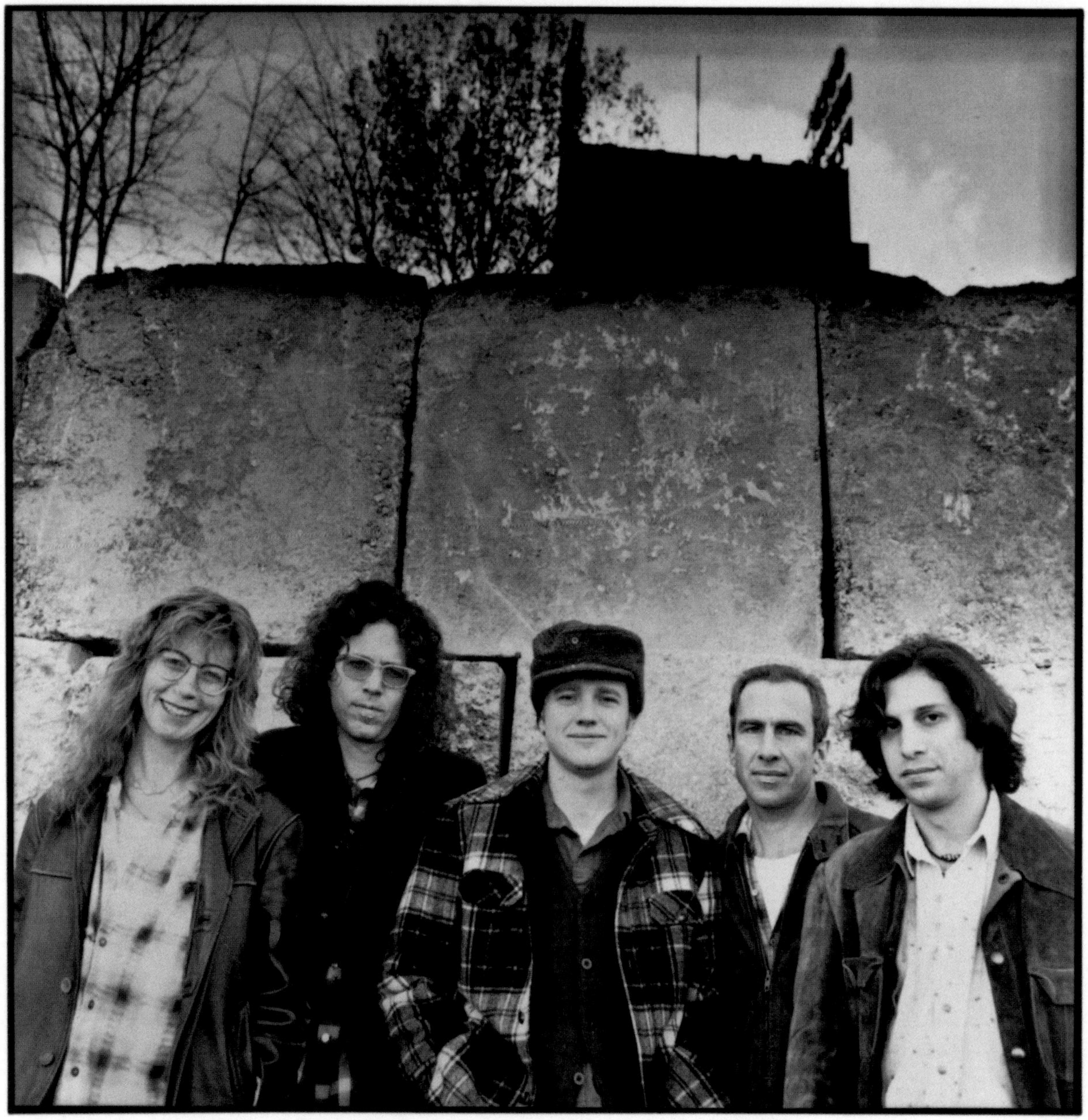

Karen Grotberg Gary Louris Mark Olson Tim O'Reagan Marc Perlman

The Jayhawks

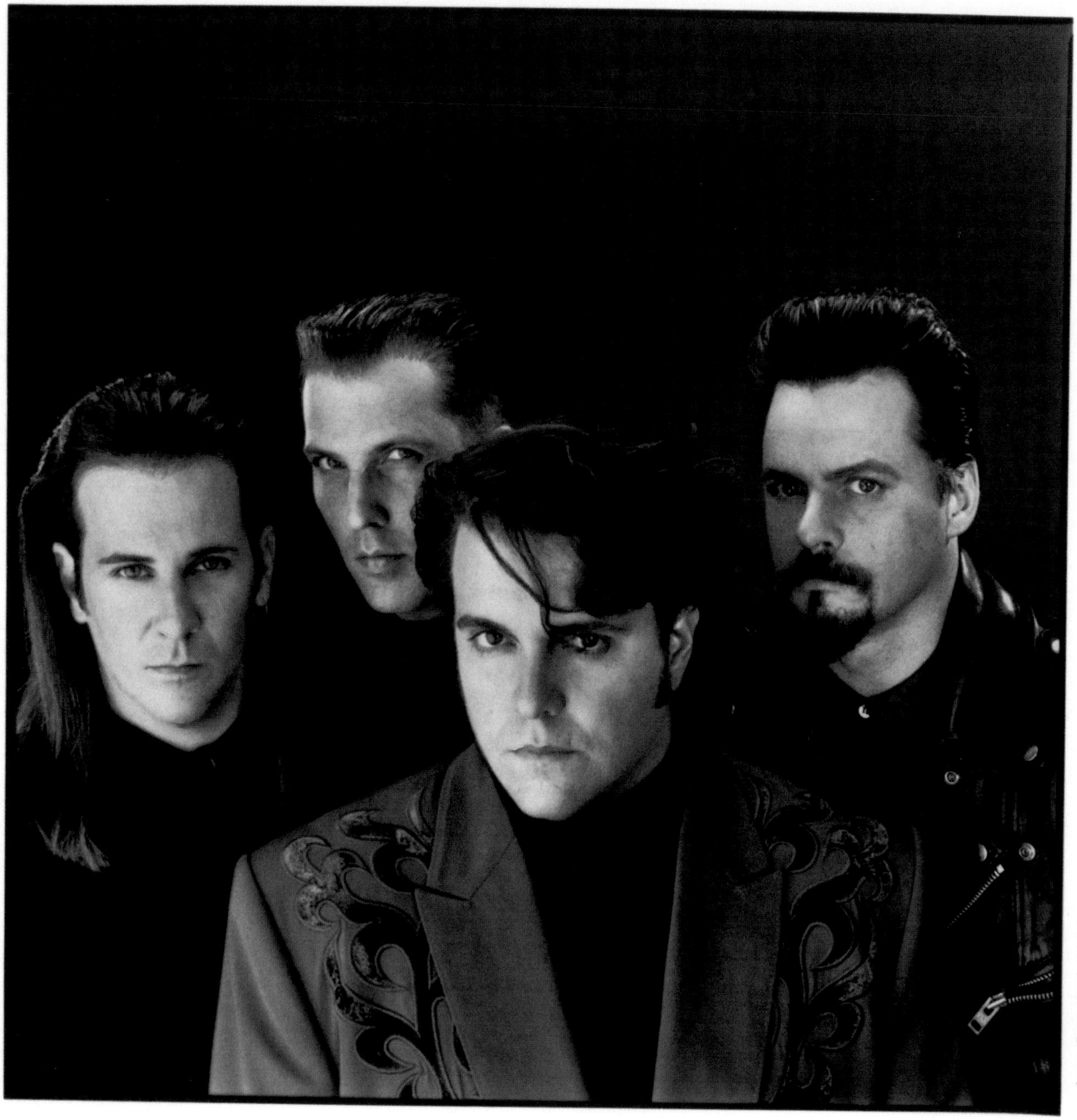

photo: Peter Nash 0195A

Robert Reynolds Paul Deakin Raul Malo Nick Kane

THE MAVERICKS

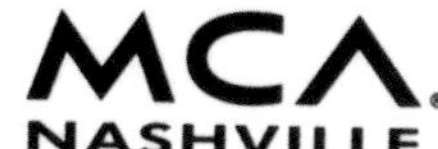

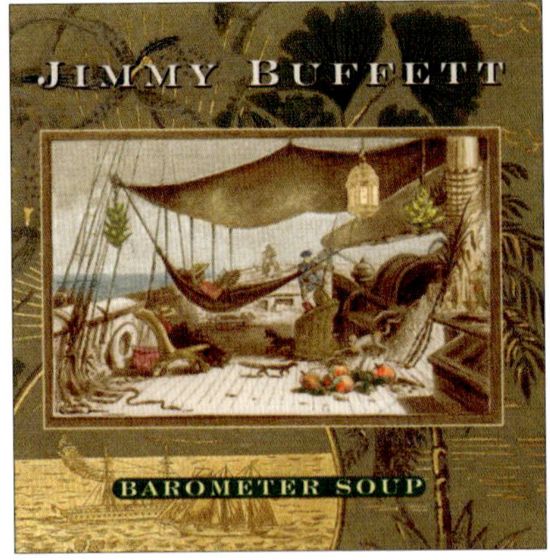

The last track on singer-songwriter **Jimmy Buffett**'s *Barometer Soup*, a cover version of James Taylor's "Mexico," kept in tune with his philosophy on life.

Billboard 200: *Barometer Soup* (#6)

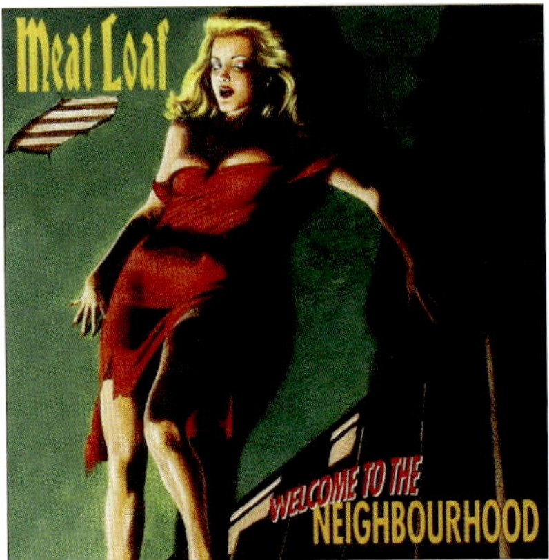

Meat Loaf retained his popularity with *Welcome to the Neighbourhood* and the hit "I'd Lie for You (And That's the Truth)," a stagy duet with Patti Russo.

Billboard 200: *Welcome to the Neighbourhood* (#17)
Billboard Hot 100: "I'd Lie for You (And That's the Truth)" (#13);
"Not a Dry Eye in the House" (#82)

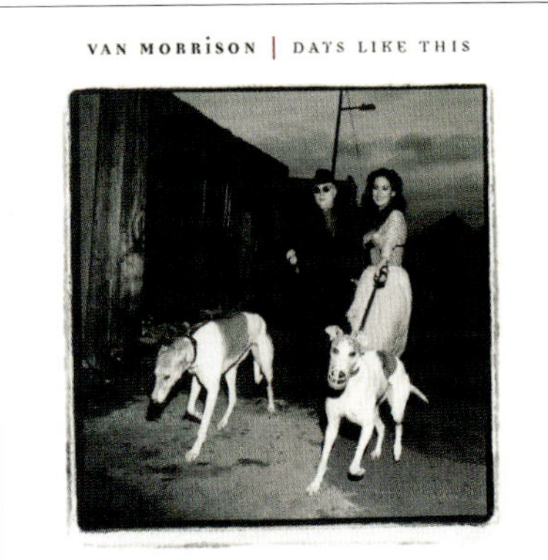

Van Morrison's daughter Shana sang on several tracks from *Days Like This*, and the title song became a concert favorite for the Irish singer-songwriter.

Billboard 200: *Days Like This* (#33)

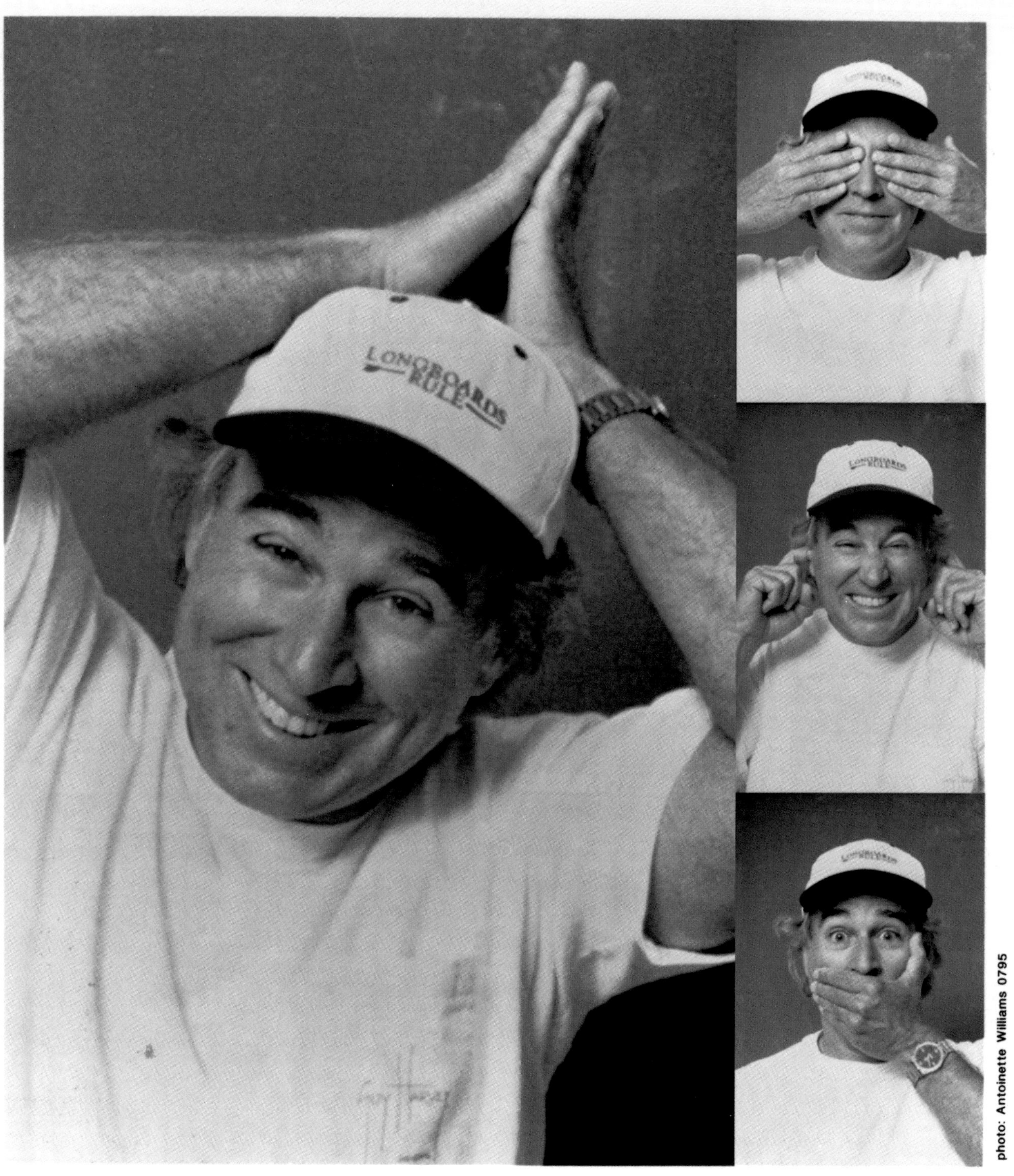

photo: Antoinette Williams 0795

JIMMY BUFFETT

Margaritaville RECORDS

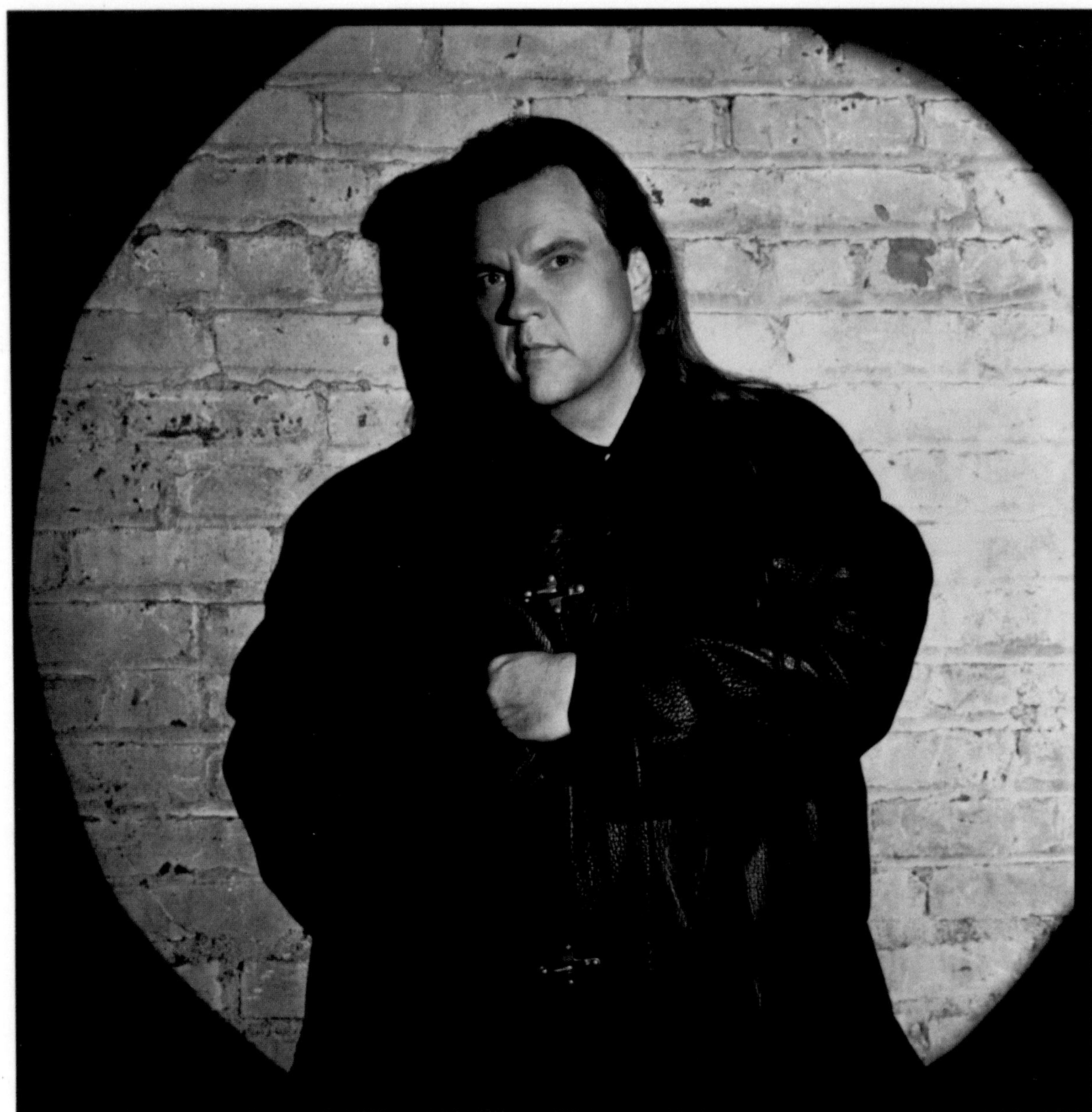

PHOTO CREDIT: NORMAN WATSON

Meat Loaf

MCA 10/95

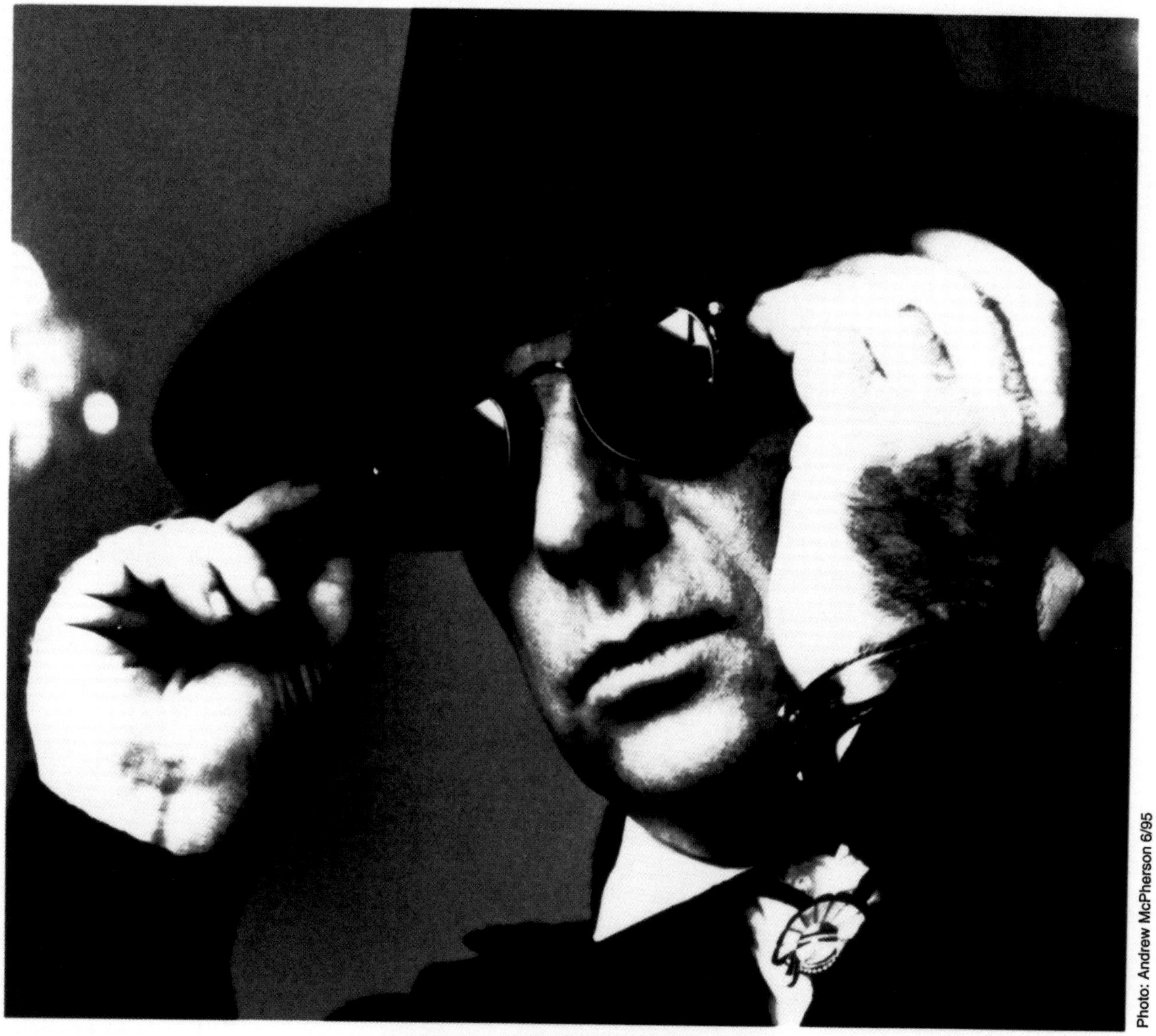

Photo: Andrew McPherson 6/95

VAN MORRISON

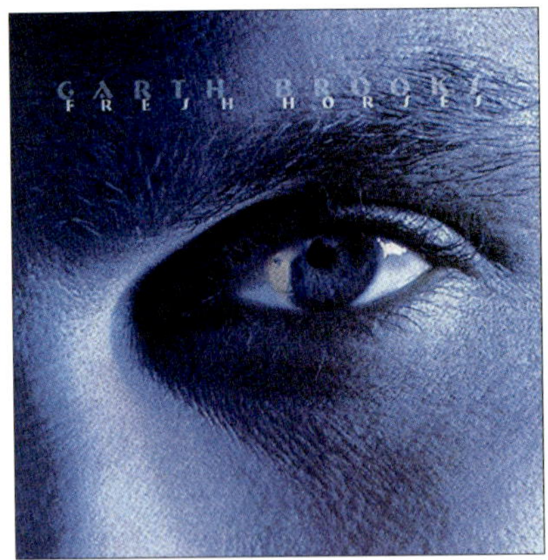

Garth Brooks' *Fresh Horses* contained two No. 1 country singles—"She's Every Woman" and "The Beaches of Cheyenne"—and an Aerosmith song, "The Fever."

Billboard 200: *Fresh Horses* (#2)

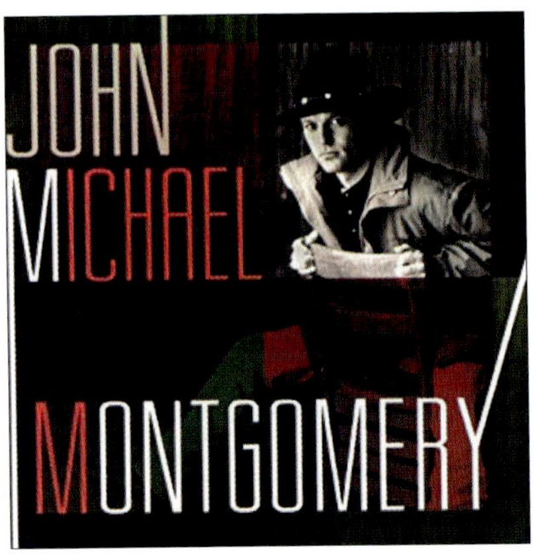

"I Can Love You Like That" and "Sold (The Grundy County Auction Incident)," both No. 1 country hits, rose from **John Michael Montgomery**'s third album.

Billboard 200: *John Michael Montgomery* (#5)

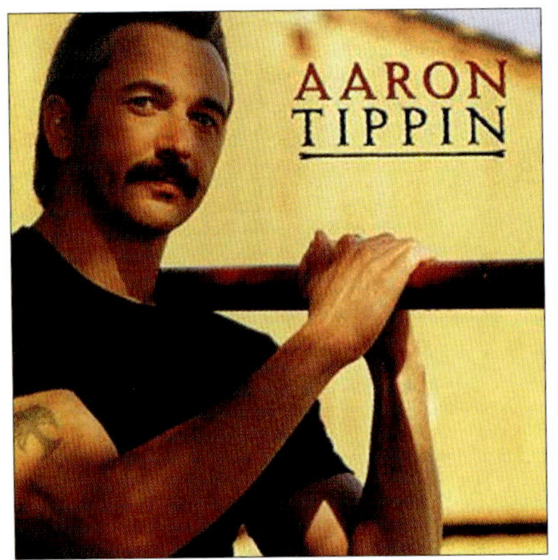

From *Tool Box*, singer **Aaron Tippin** supplied his second No. 1 on the country music charts, the soulful ballad "That's as Close as I'll Get to Loving You."

Billboard 200: *Tool Box* (#63)

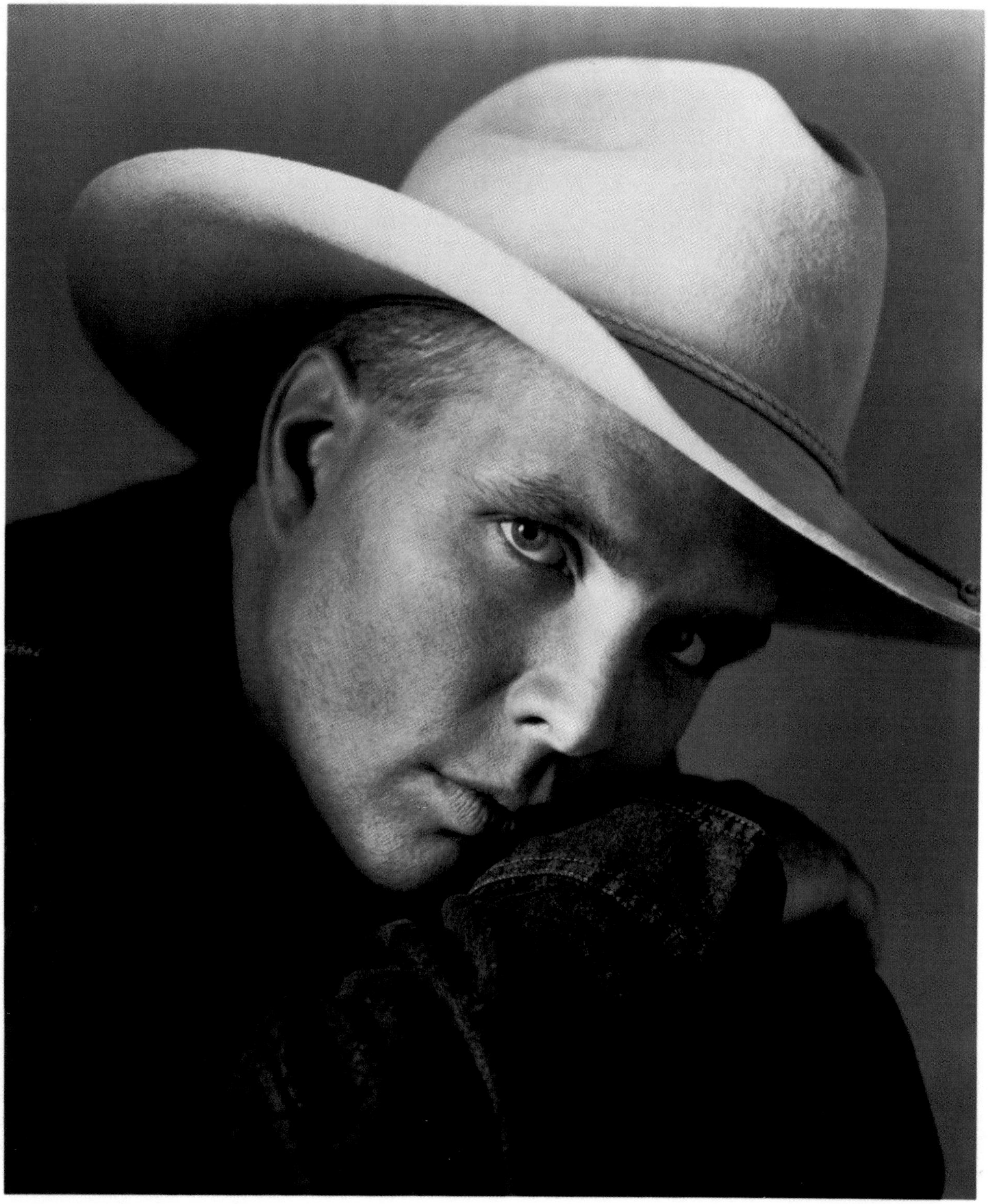

photo: Beverly Parker 10/95A

GARTH BROOKS

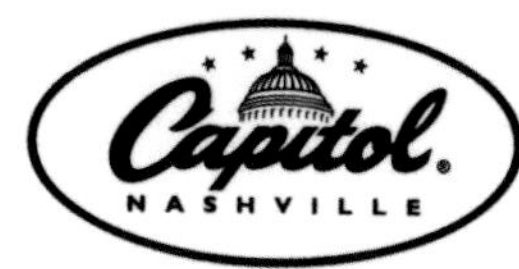

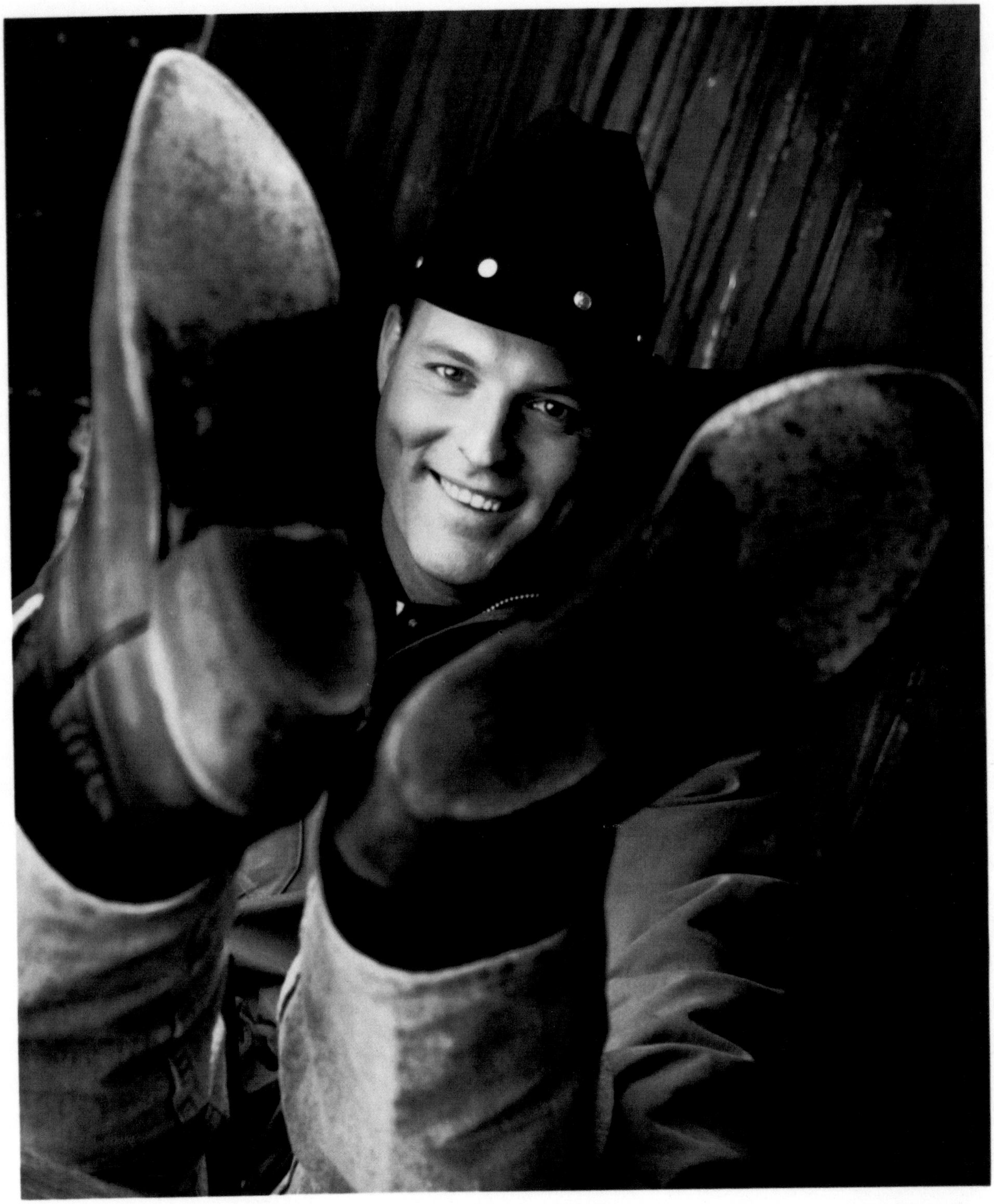

photo: Mark Tucker

JOHN MICHAEL MONTGOMERY

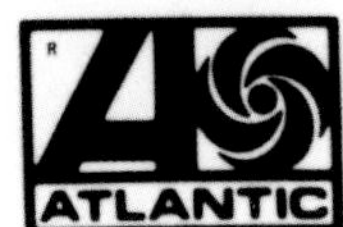

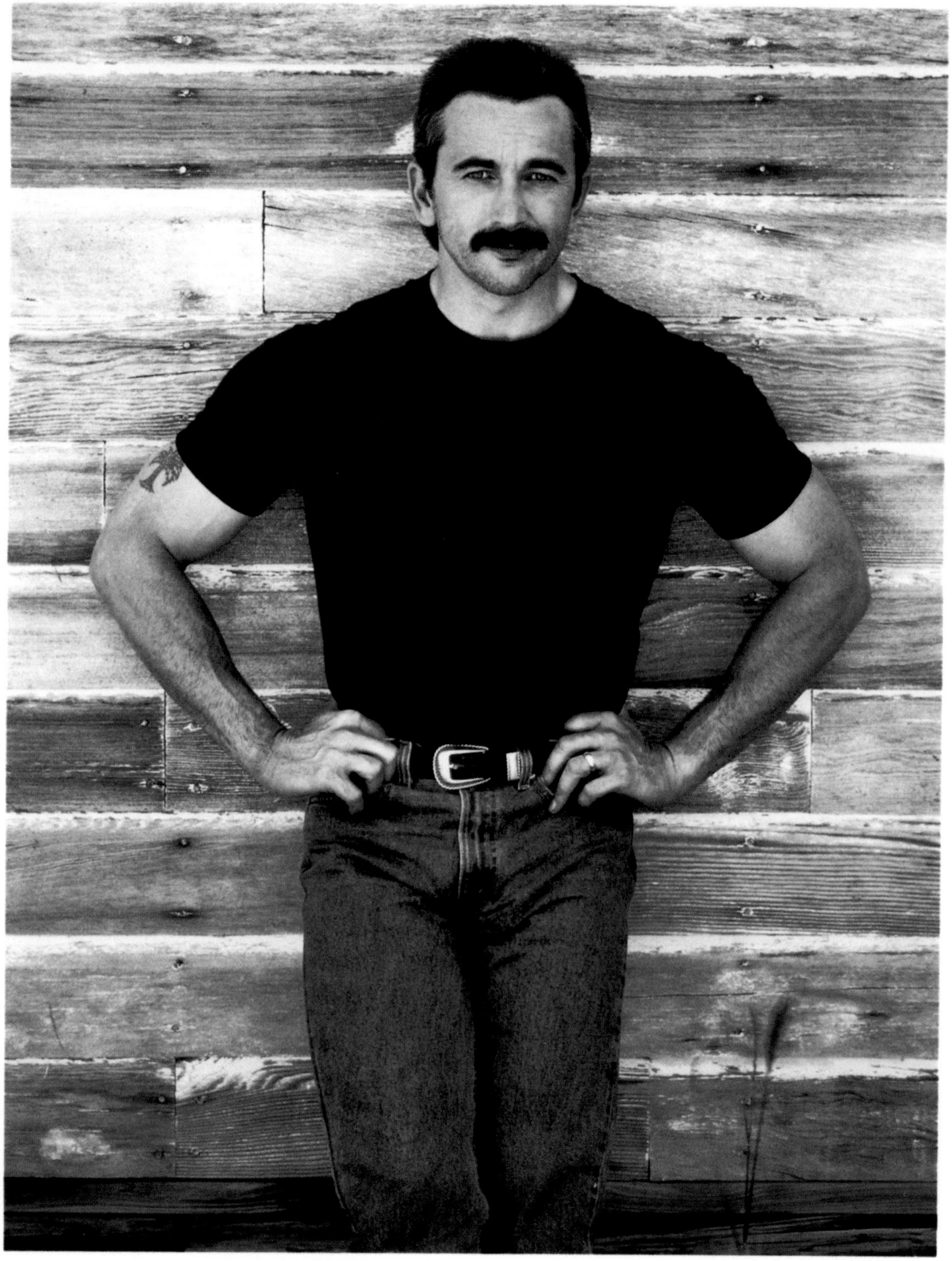

photo: Chuck Kuhn

AARON TIPPIN

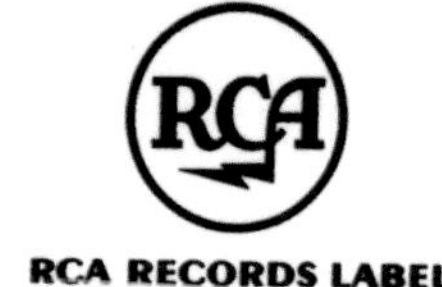

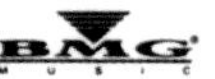

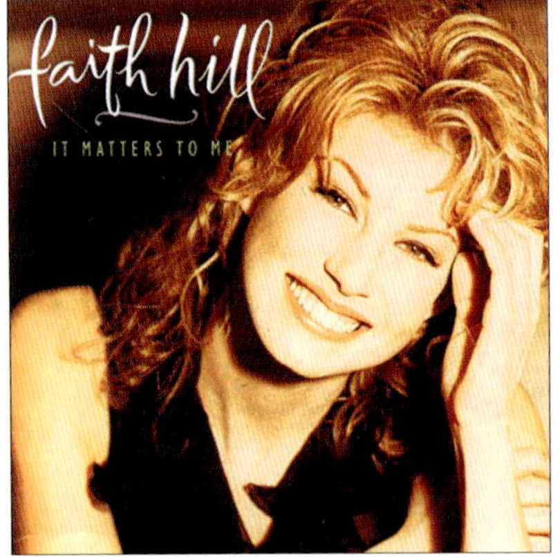

Singer **Faith Hill**'s second album, *It Matters to Me*, produced five Top 10 songs on the country charts, including the title track, her third No. 1 single.

Billboard 200: *It Matters to Me* (#29)
Billboard Hot 100: "It Matters to Me" (#74)

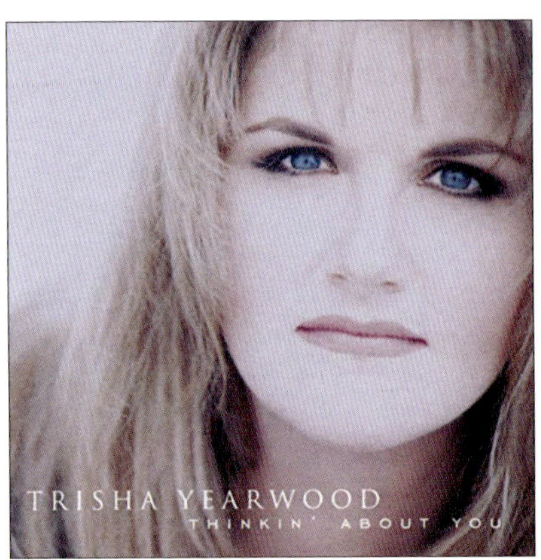

Trisha Yearwood delivered back-to-back No. 1 country hits: first, the lighthearted "XXX's and OOO's (An American Girl)," and then "Thinkin' About You."

Billboard 200: *Thinkin' About You* (#28)

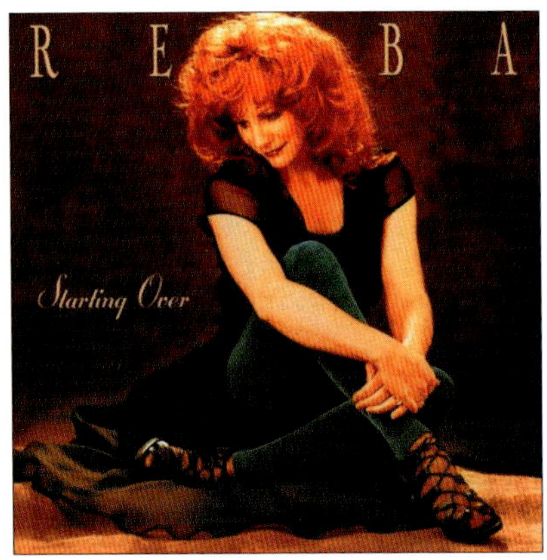

The charming *Starting Over* collected songs originally recorded by **Reba McEntire**'s favorite musical acts, a commemoration of her formative influences.

Billboard 200: *Starting Over* (#5)

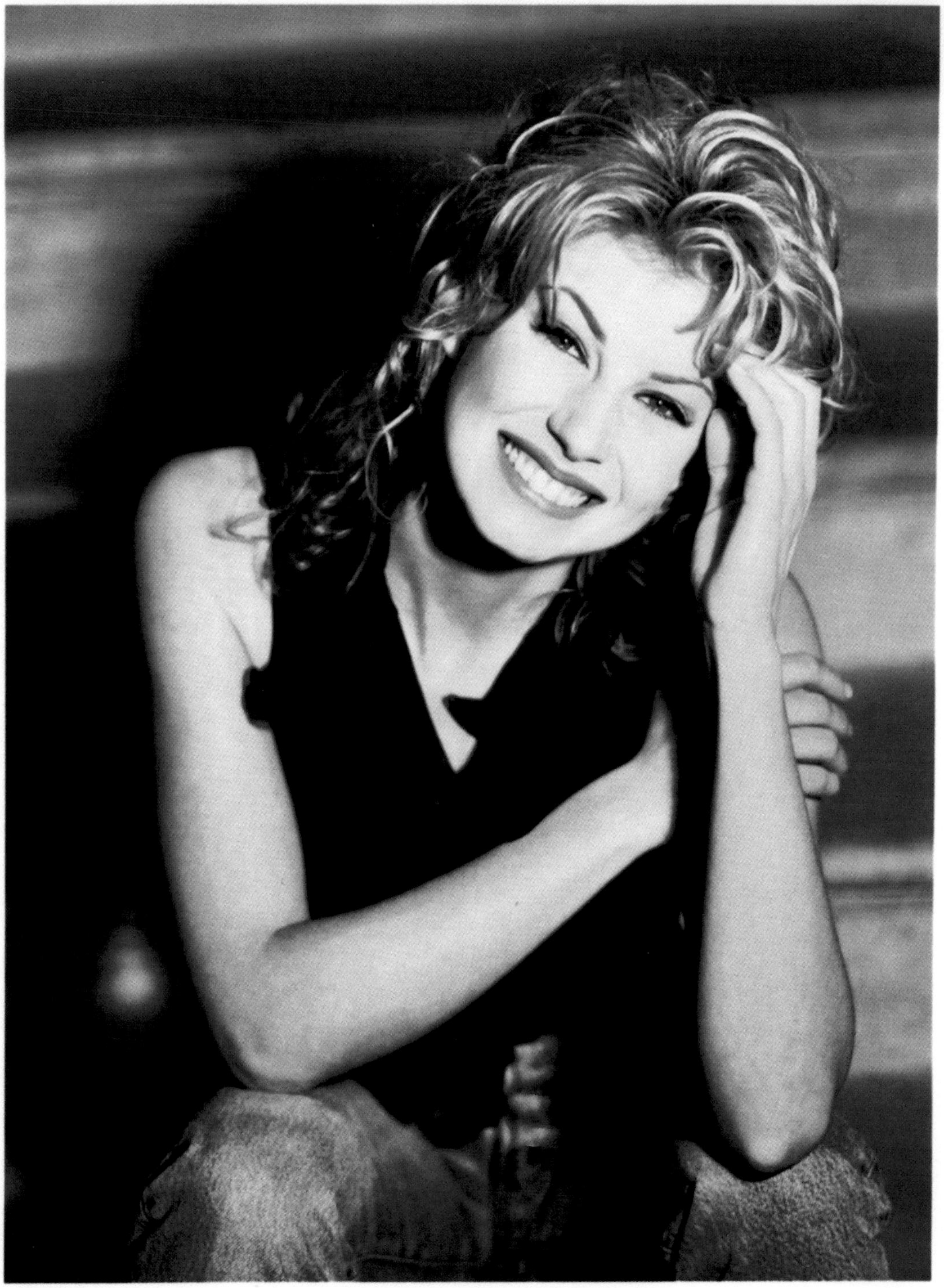

Photo Credit Randee St. Nicholas

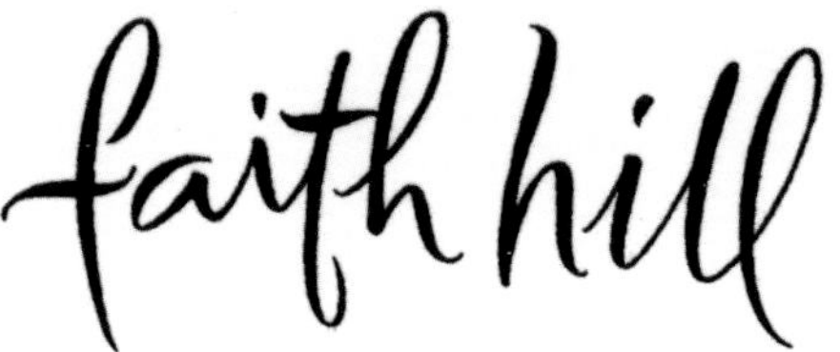

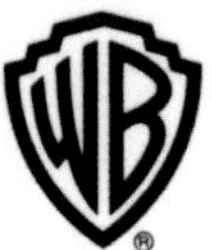

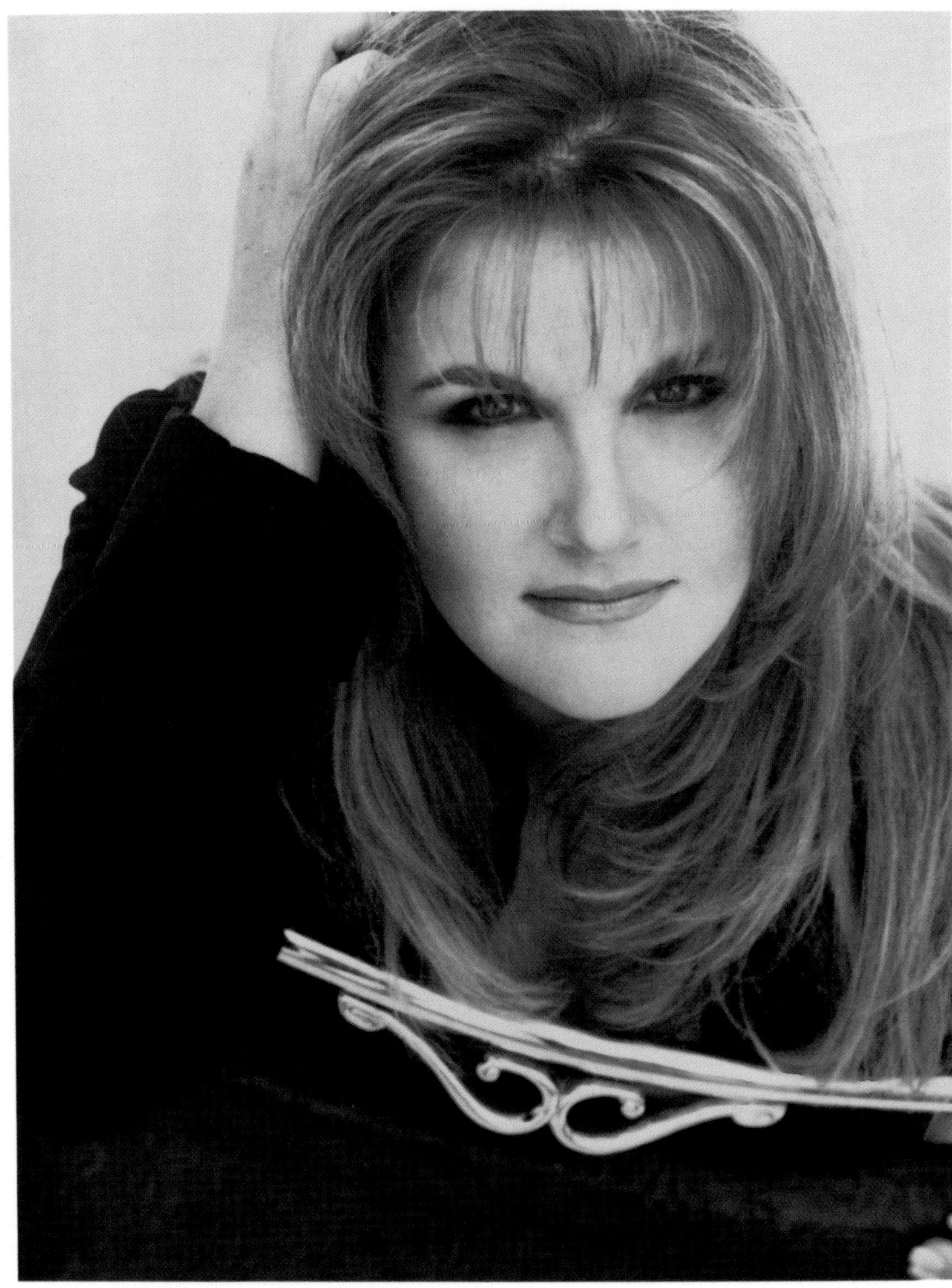

photo: Russ Harrington 0195A

TRISHA YEARWOOD

MCA NASHVILLE

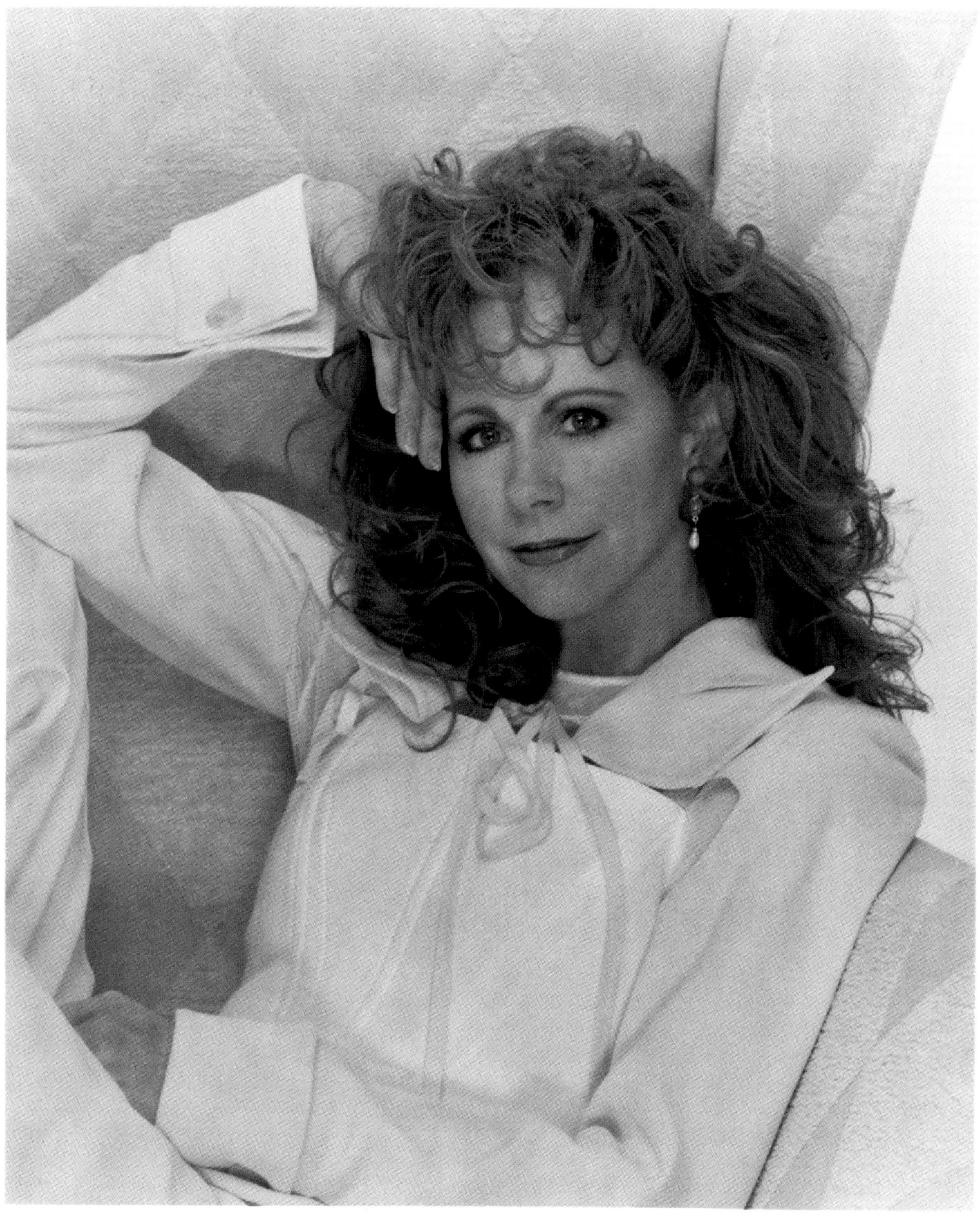

photo: Mark Tucker 0995A

REBA McENTIRE

MCA
NASHVILLE

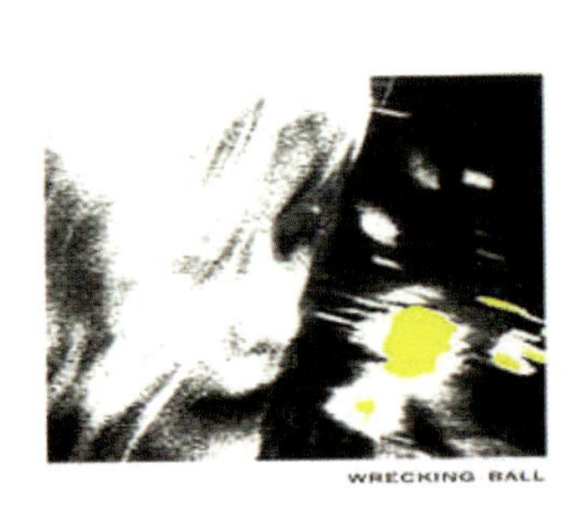

Produced by Daniel Lanois, the atmospheric *Wrecking Ball* reforged **Emmylou Harris**' artistry, bringing her to the attention of an alternative-rock following.

Billboard 200: *Wrecking Ball* (#94)

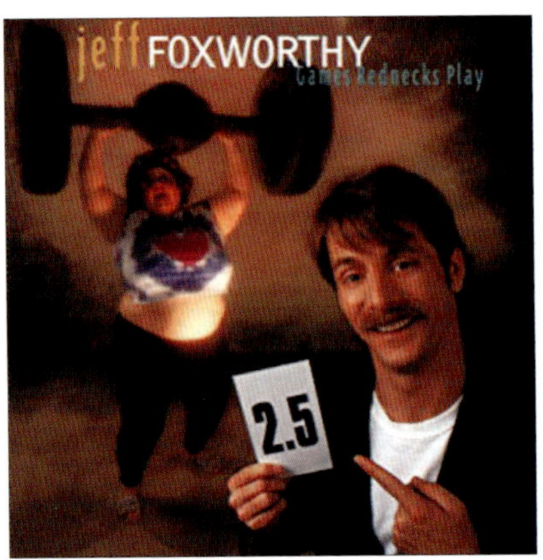

Comedian **Jeff Foxworthy**'s *Games Rednecks Play* added "Party All Night," a music track featuring Little Texas and Scott Rouse that made the country charts.

llboard 200: *Games Rednecks Play* (#8)

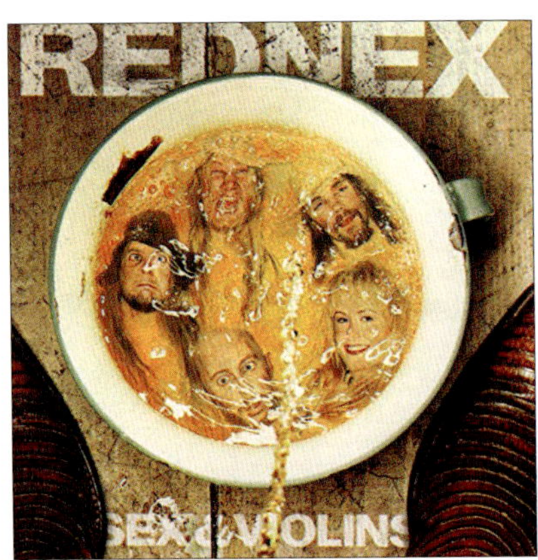

The Swedish dance act **Rednex** left the farm with the novelty hit "Cotton Eye Joe," a techno twist on the traditional American folk song "Cotton-Eyed Joe."

Billboard 200: *Sex & Violins* (#68)
Billboard Hot 100: "Cotton Eye Joe" (#25)

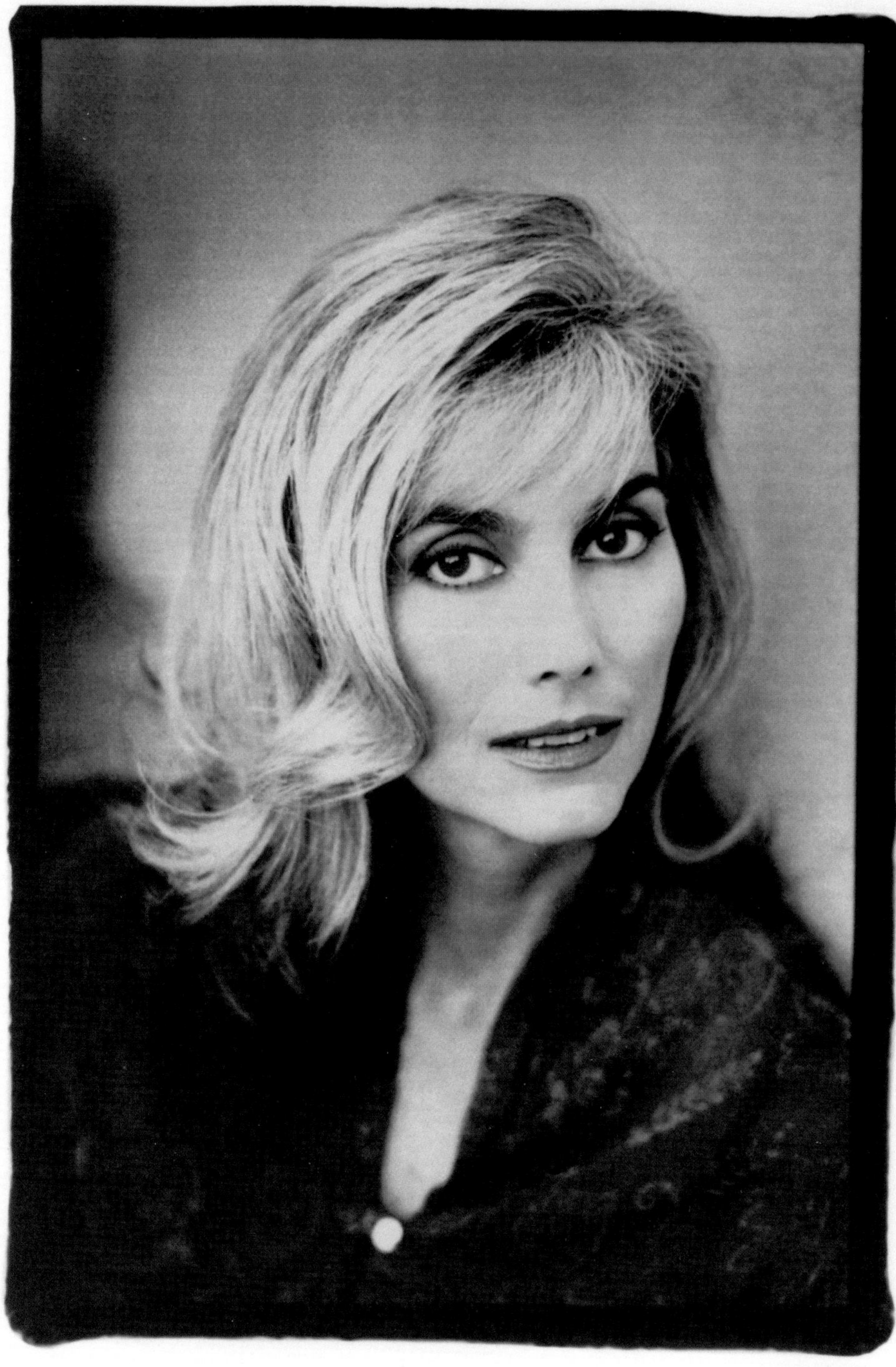

Photography by : Caroline Greyshock

EMMYLOU HARRIS

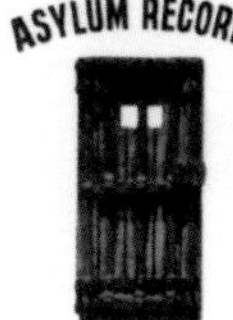

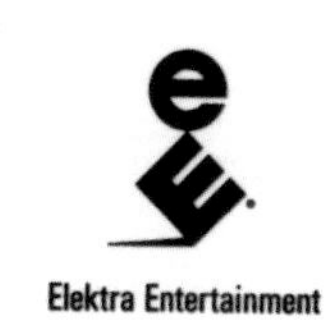

Elektra Entertainment

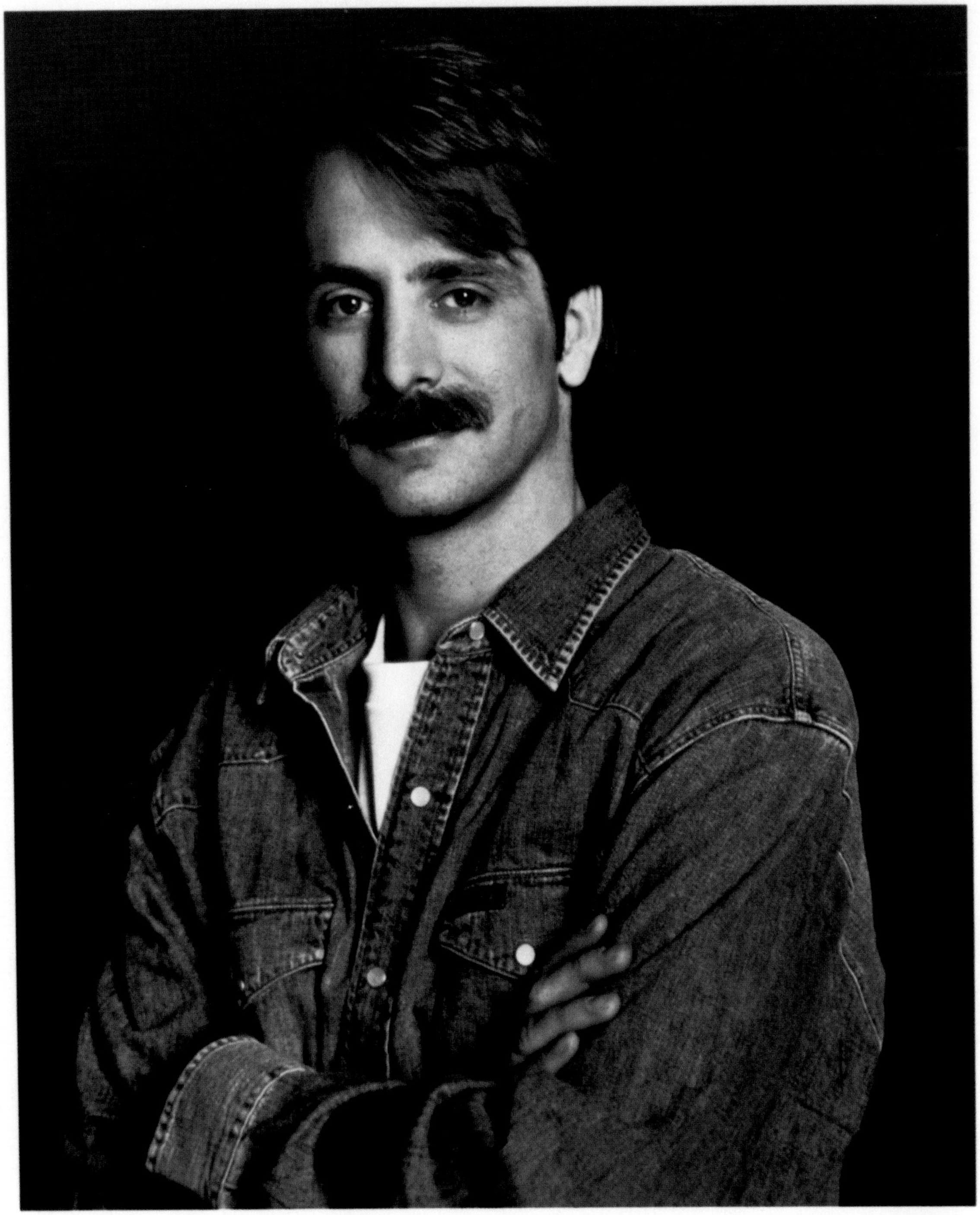

photo: Steve Sigoloff

JEFF FOXWORTHY

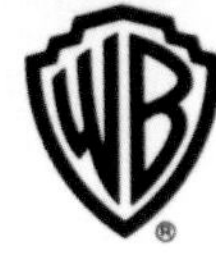

REDNEX

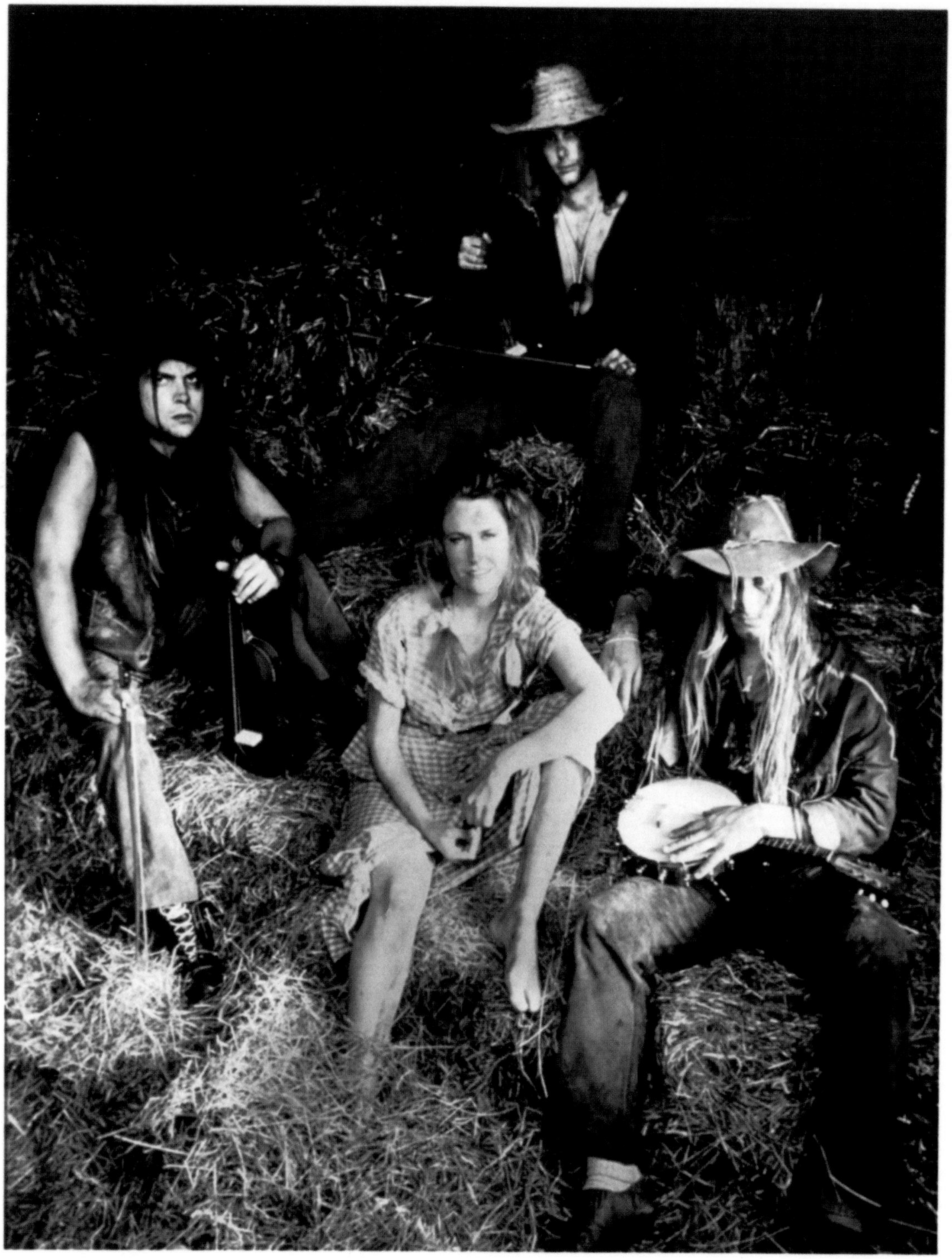

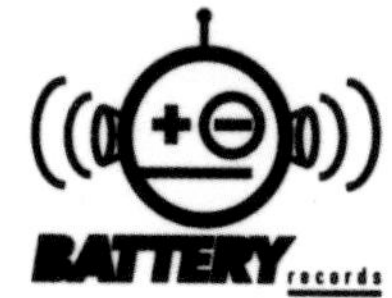

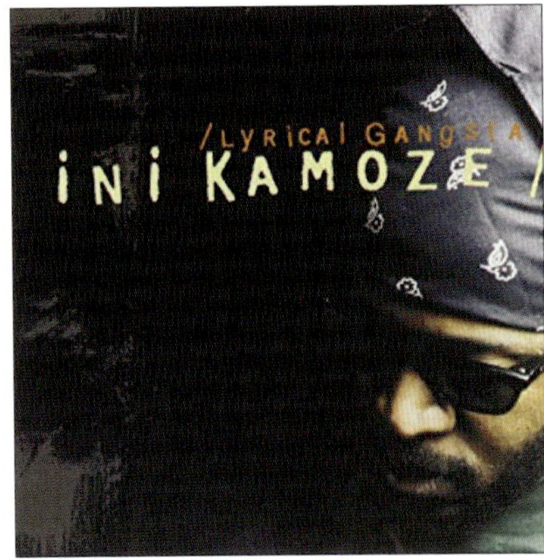

Ini Kamoze built on the success of his signature song "Here Comes the Hotstepper," further developing his mix of reggae and hip-hop on *Lyrical Gangsta*.

Billboard Hot 100: "Listen Me Tic (Woyoi)" (#88)

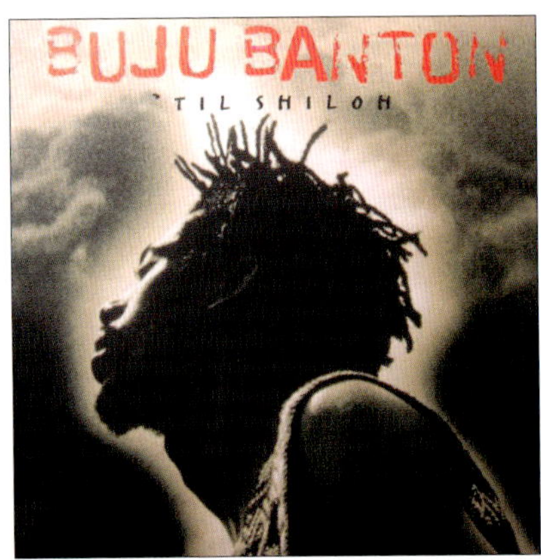

Embracing his Rastafari faith, Jamaican dancehall artist **Buju Banton** was moved to introspection on the album *'Til Shiloh* and the gentle "Untold Stories."

Billboard 200: *'Til Shiloh* (#148)

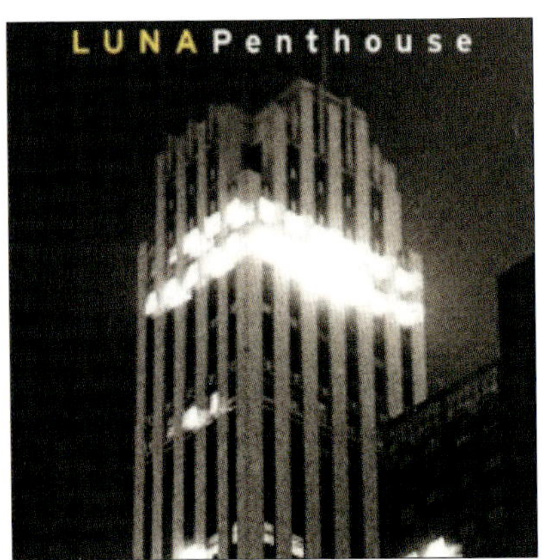

Dean Wareham, the former leader of Galaxie 500, formed a new alternative band, **Luna**, and put out the expressive, dreamy *Penthouse* to critical raves.

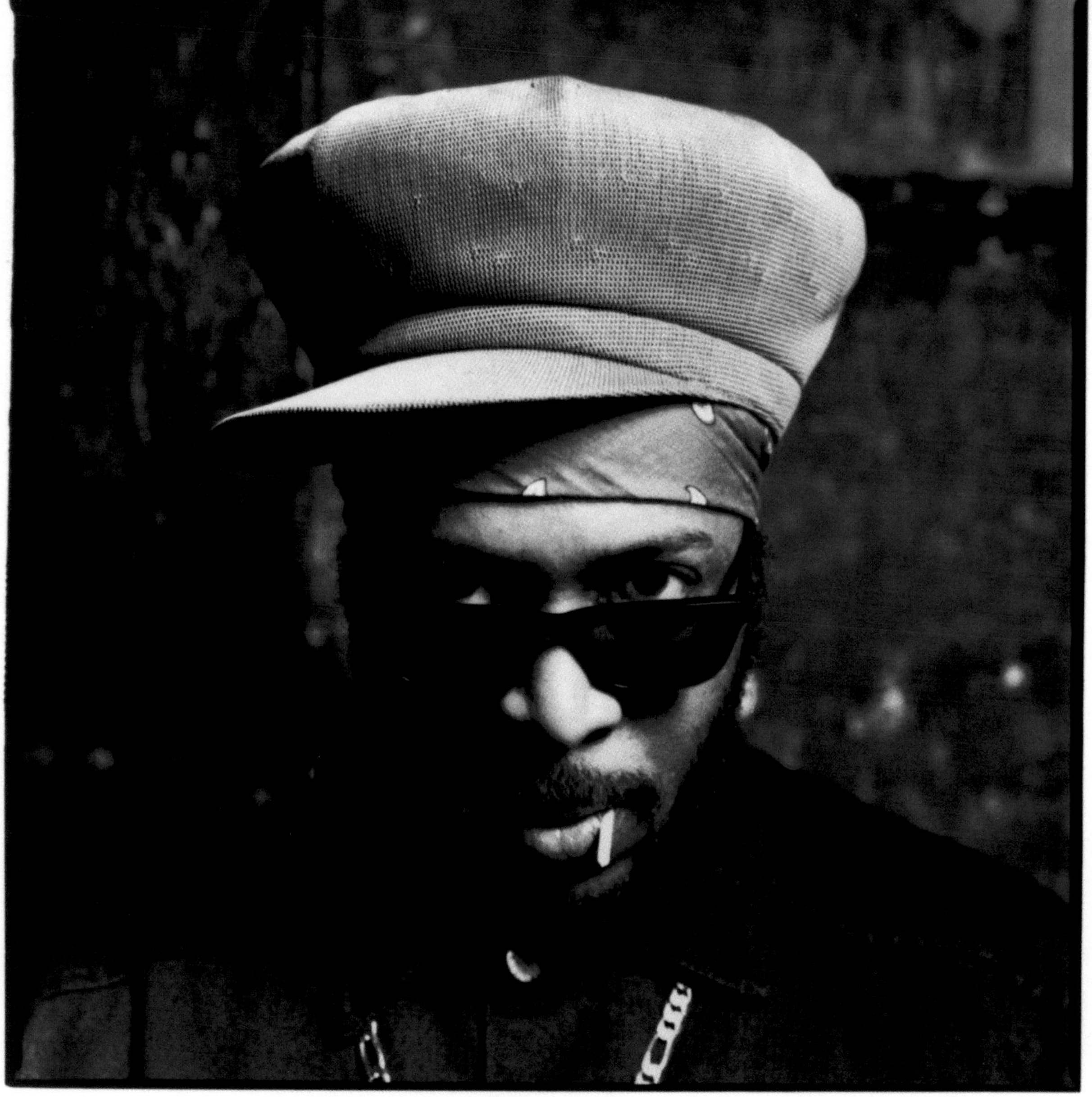

PHOTO CREDIT KWAKU ALSTON

INI KAMOZE

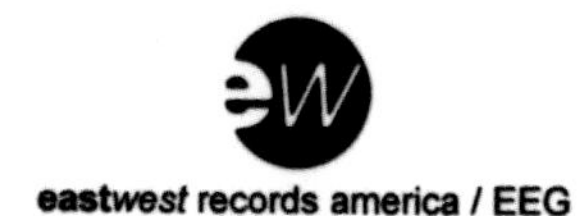

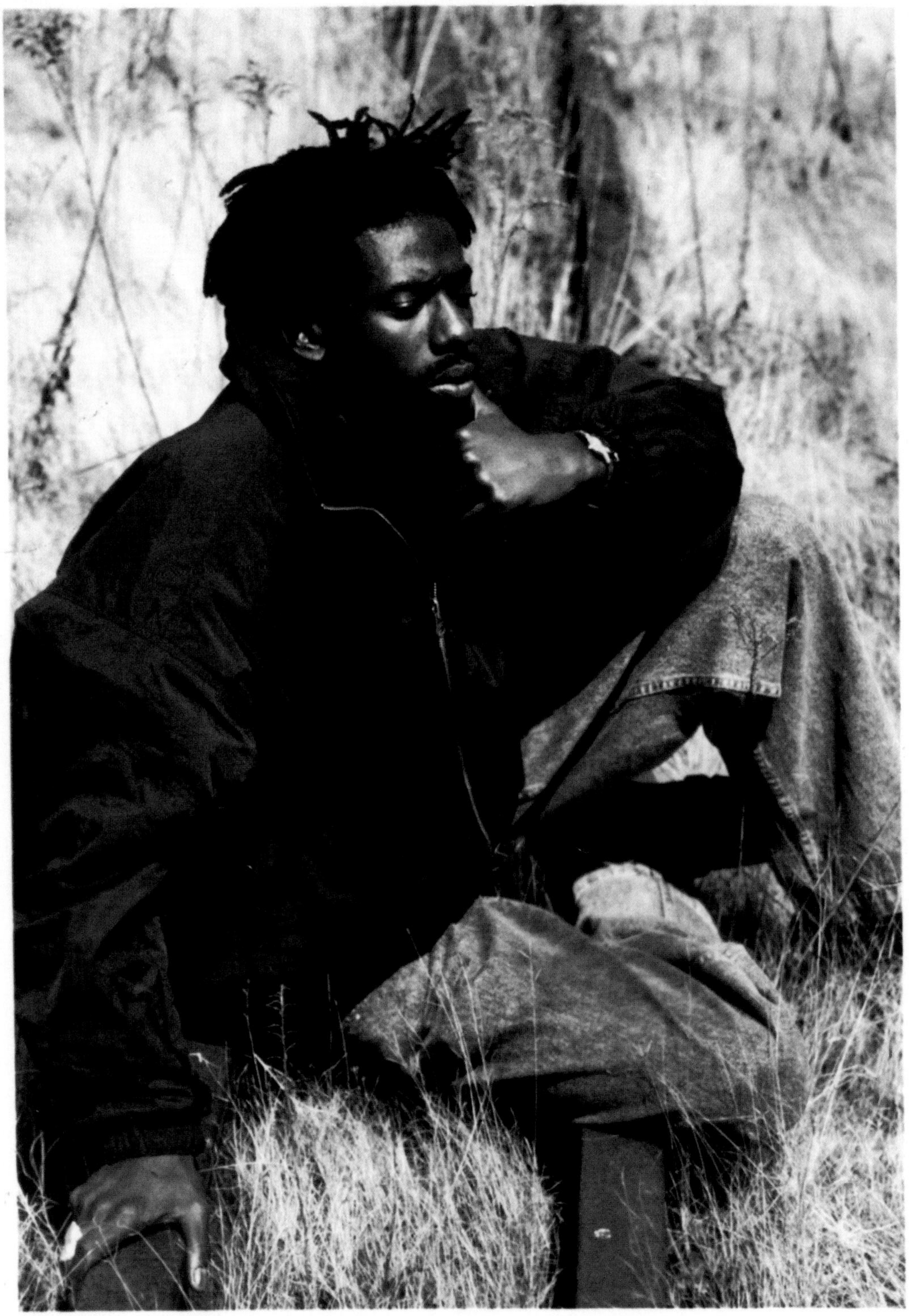

Photo Credit: Geoffroy DeBoisMenu

Penthouse Recording Co.
56 Slipe Road
Kingston 5 Jamaica
809-929-7446
809-968-2051 fax

BUJU BANTON

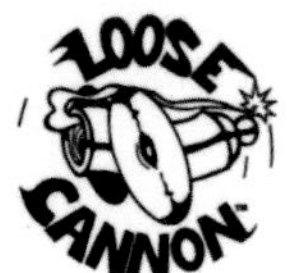

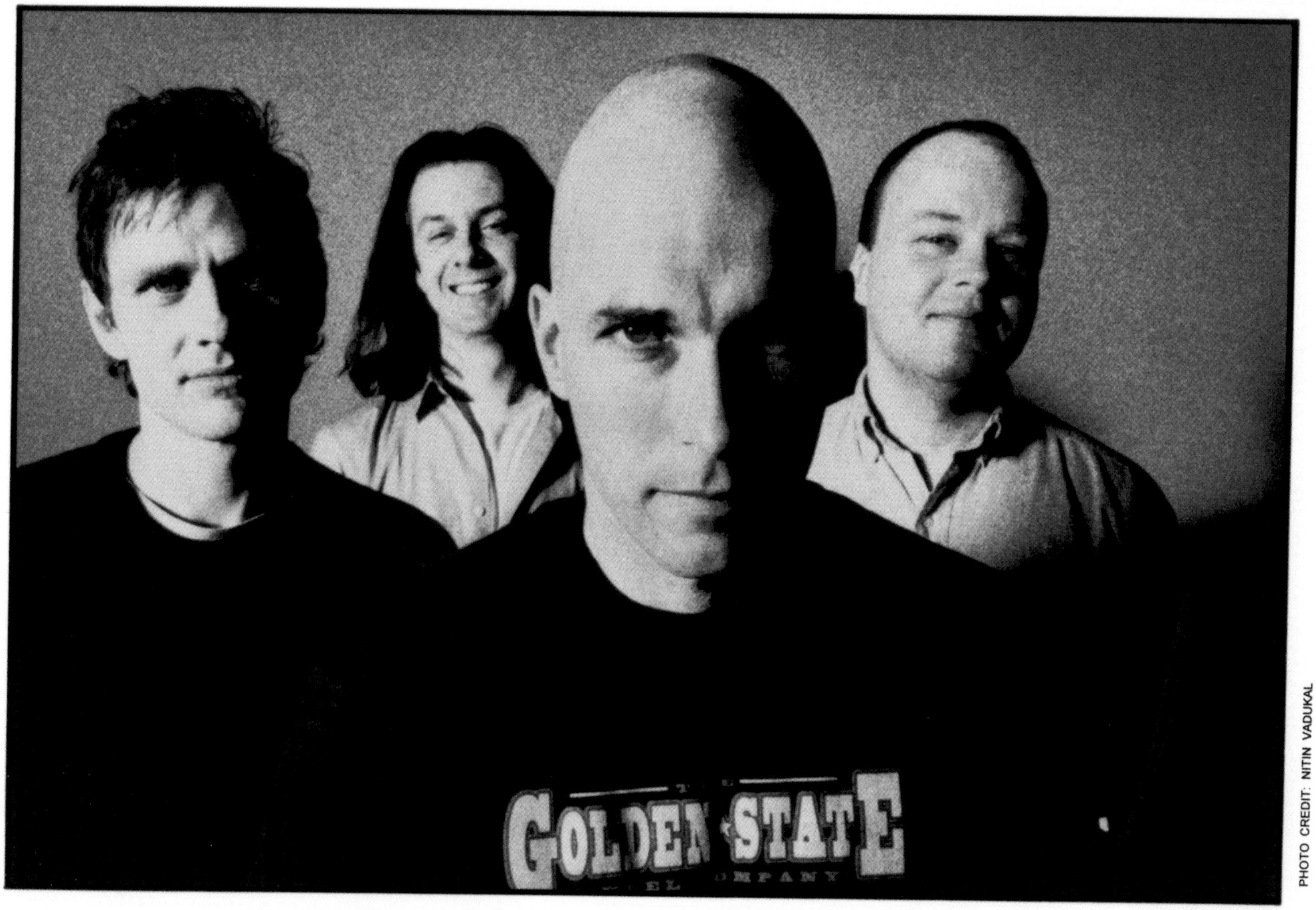

PHOTO CREDIT: NITIN VADUKAL

L R : DEAN WAREHAM, SEAN EDEN, JUSTIN HARWOOD, STANLEY DEMESKI

LUNA

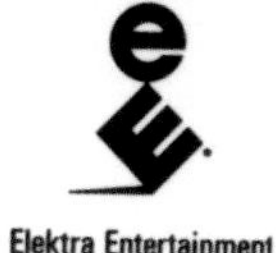

Elektra Entertainment

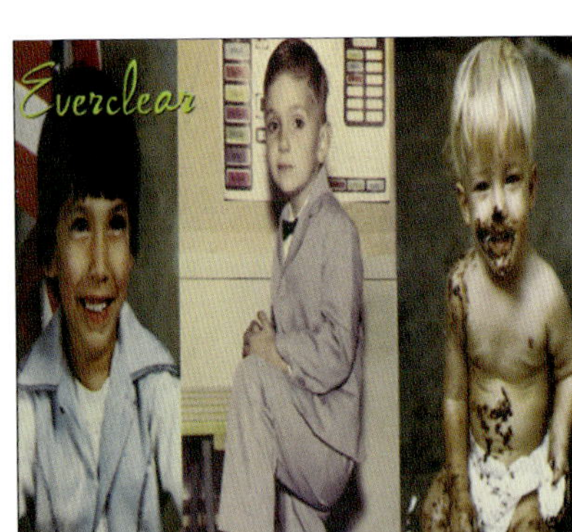

Guided by Art Alexakis, **Everclear** debuted on a major label with *Sparkle and Fade*, and "Santa Monica" reached a robust audience on alternative radio.

Billboard 200: *Sparkle and Fade* (#25)
Billboard Hot 100: "Santa Monica" (#29); "Heartspark Dollarsign" (#85)

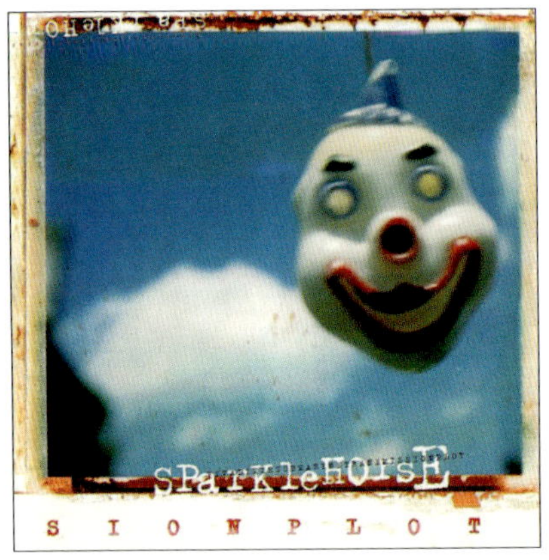

Indie rock outfit **Sparklehorse**, led by Mark Linkous, scored a college radio hit with "Someday I Will Treat You Good," crafted by Cracker's David Lowery.

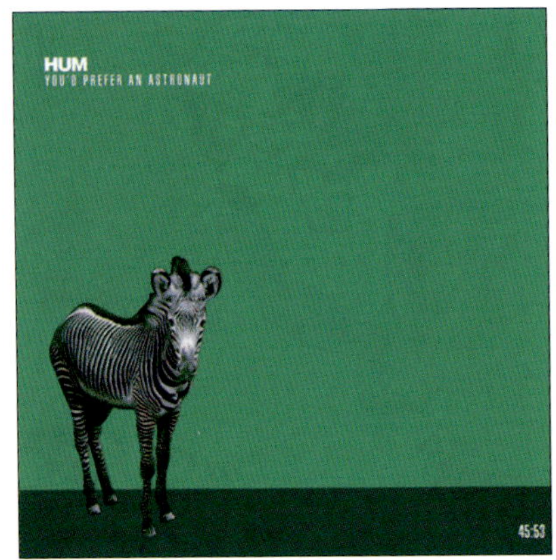

Coming out of Champaign, Illinois, alternative rockers **Hum** distributed the album *You'd Prefer an Astronaut* and secured a breakthrough song, "Stars."

Billboard 200: *You'd Prefer an Astronaut* (#105)

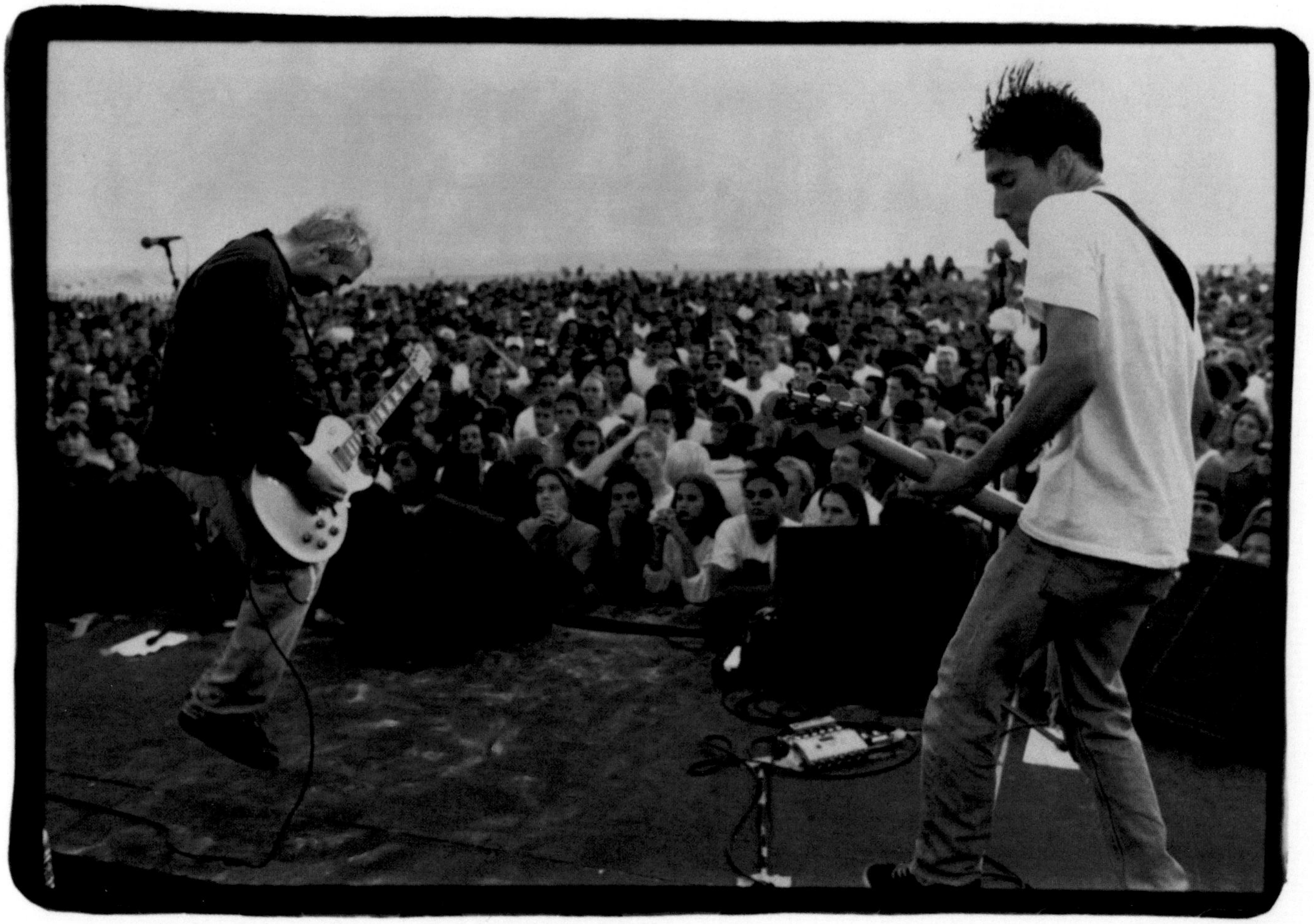

Photo Credit: Henry Diltz

Everclear

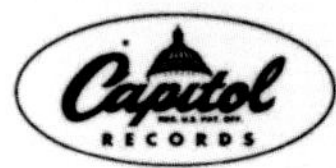

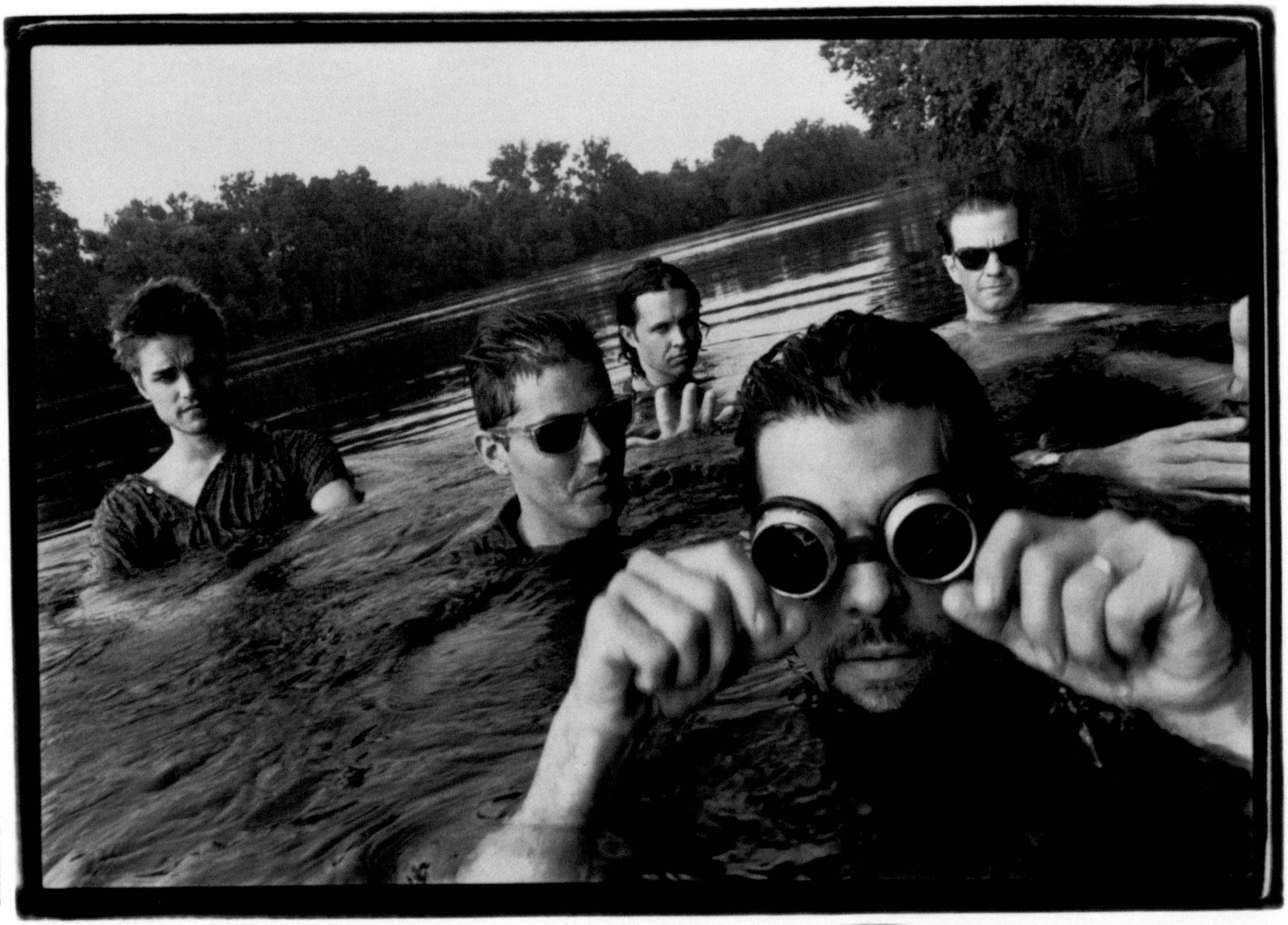

Location: Bremo Bluff, VA

Photo Credit: Danny Clinch/1995

Scott Fitzsimmons, Scott Minor, Johnny Hott, (front) Mark Linkous, Paul Watson

SPARKLEHORSE

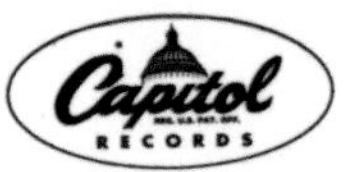

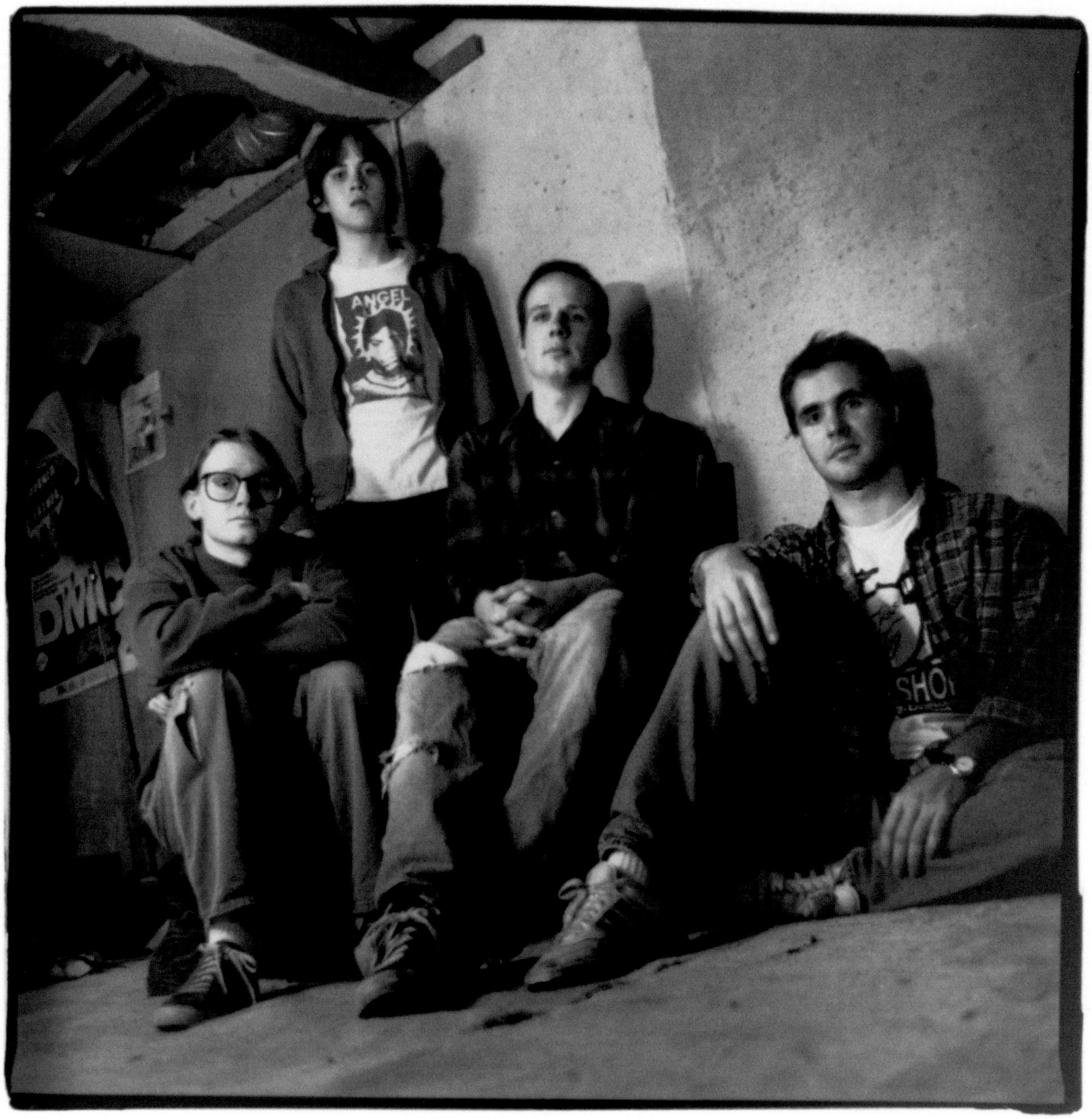

Matt Talbot Tim Lash Jeff Dimpsey Bryan St.Pere

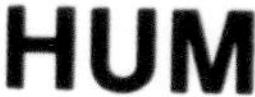

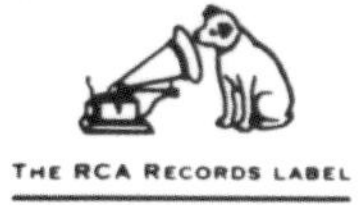

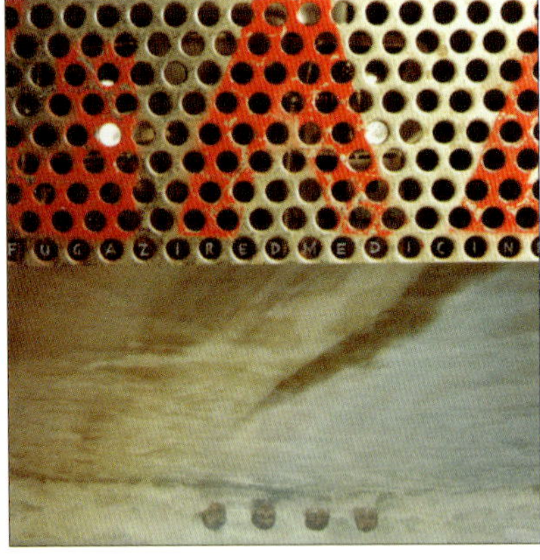

Having avoided all contact with the corporate music industry, the Washington, D.C. hardcore-punk act **Fugazi** hit on experimental rock with *Red Medicine*.

Billboard 200: *Red Medicine* (#126)

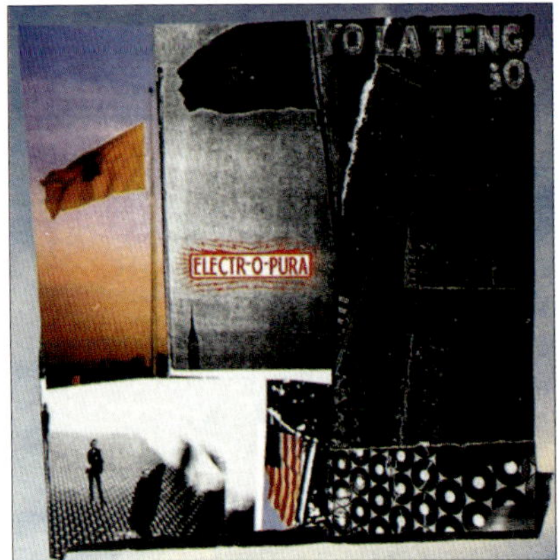

The Hoboken, New Jersey-based indie-rock band **Yo La Tengo** extended its range of sonic textures on *Electr-O-Pura* and the exuberant "Tom Courtenay."

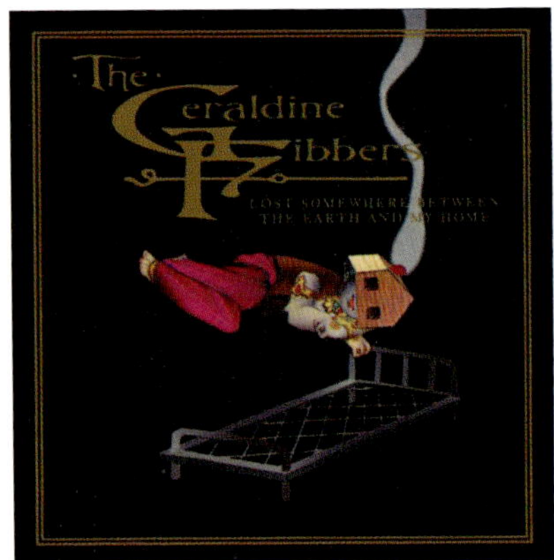

The Geraldine Fibbers, an alt-country band fronted by Carla Bozulich, debuted with the striking *Lost Somewhere Beneath the Earth and My Home* album.

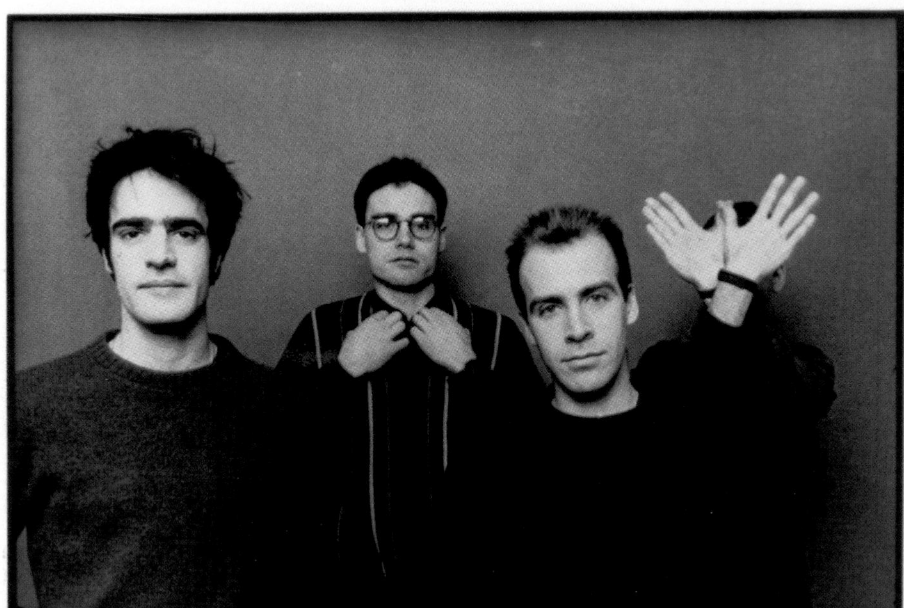

photo: John Falls

FUGAZI

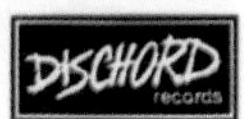

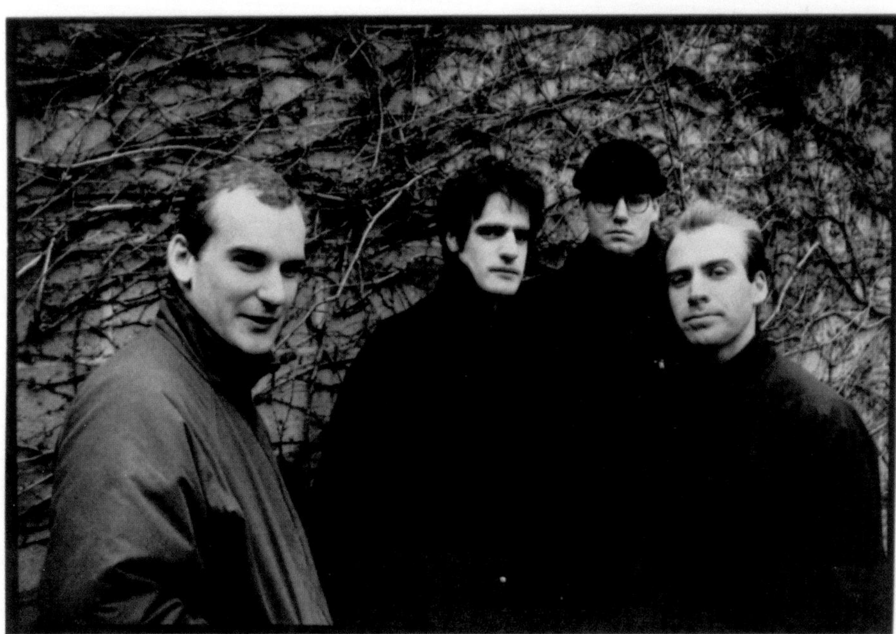

photo: John Falls

FUGAZI

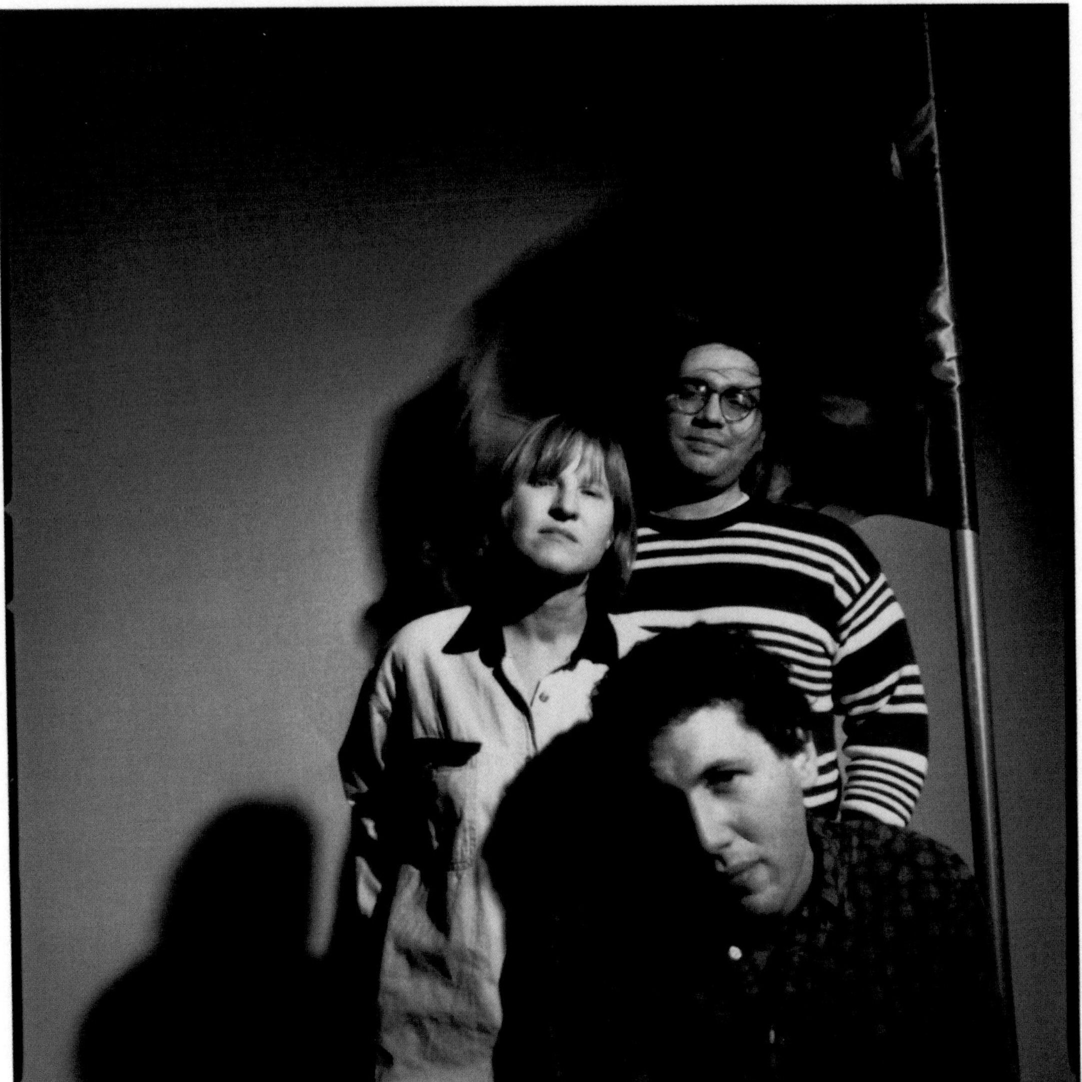

PHOTO: MICHAEL LAVINE

YO LA TENGO

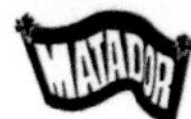

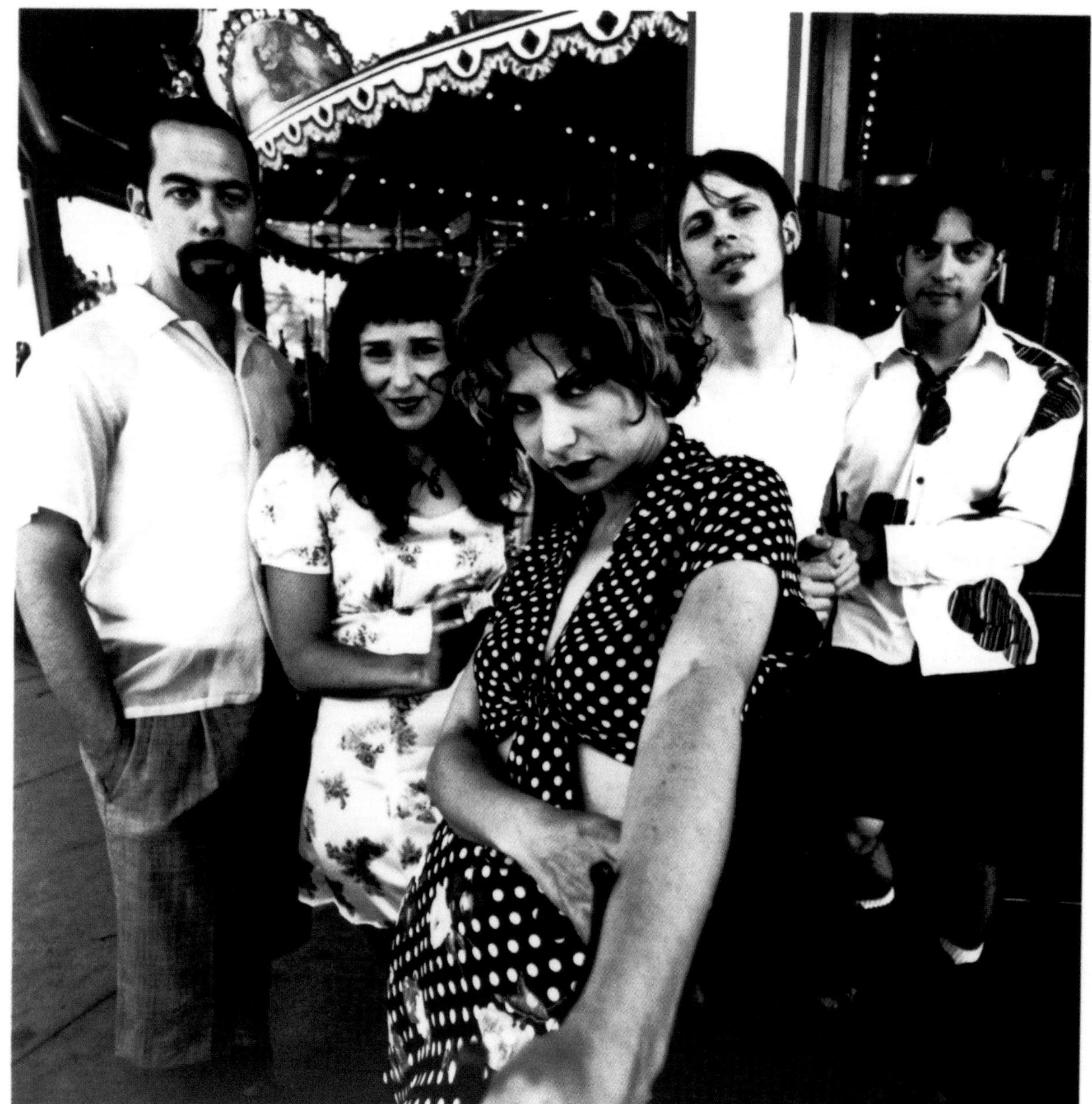

Photo Credit Melanie Nissan 7/95

THE GERALDINE FIBBERS

Virgin

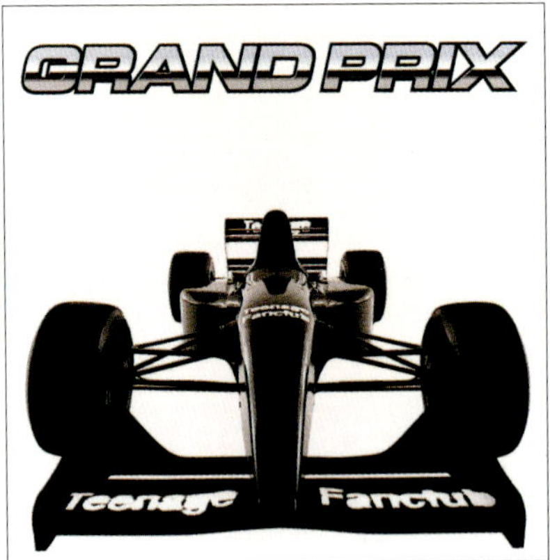

Teenage Fanclub's woefully undervalued *Grand Prix*, the Scottish band's fifth album of illustrious guitar-based popcraft, garnered solid critical approval.

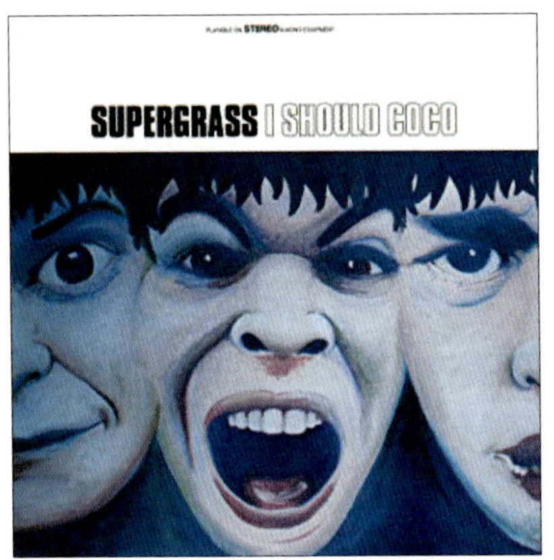

From the debut album *I Should Coco*, a No. 1 UK hit, the ebullient single "Alright" established a buzz around the youthful British rock band **Supergrass**.

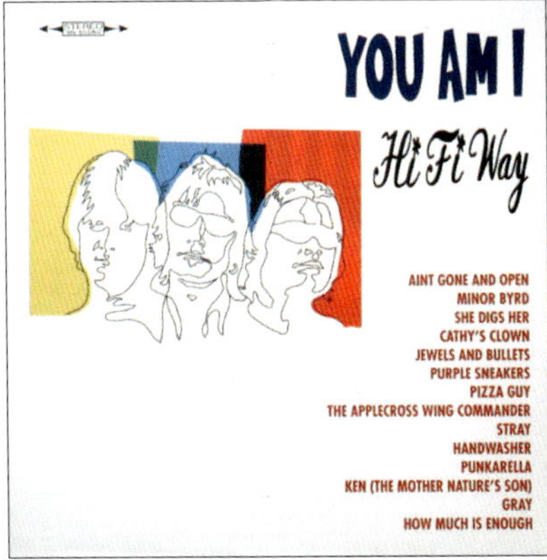

Working with Sonic Youth's Lee Renaldo as producer, Australian rockers **You Am I** recorded *Hi Fi Way* and debuted at No. 1 on the charts Down Under.

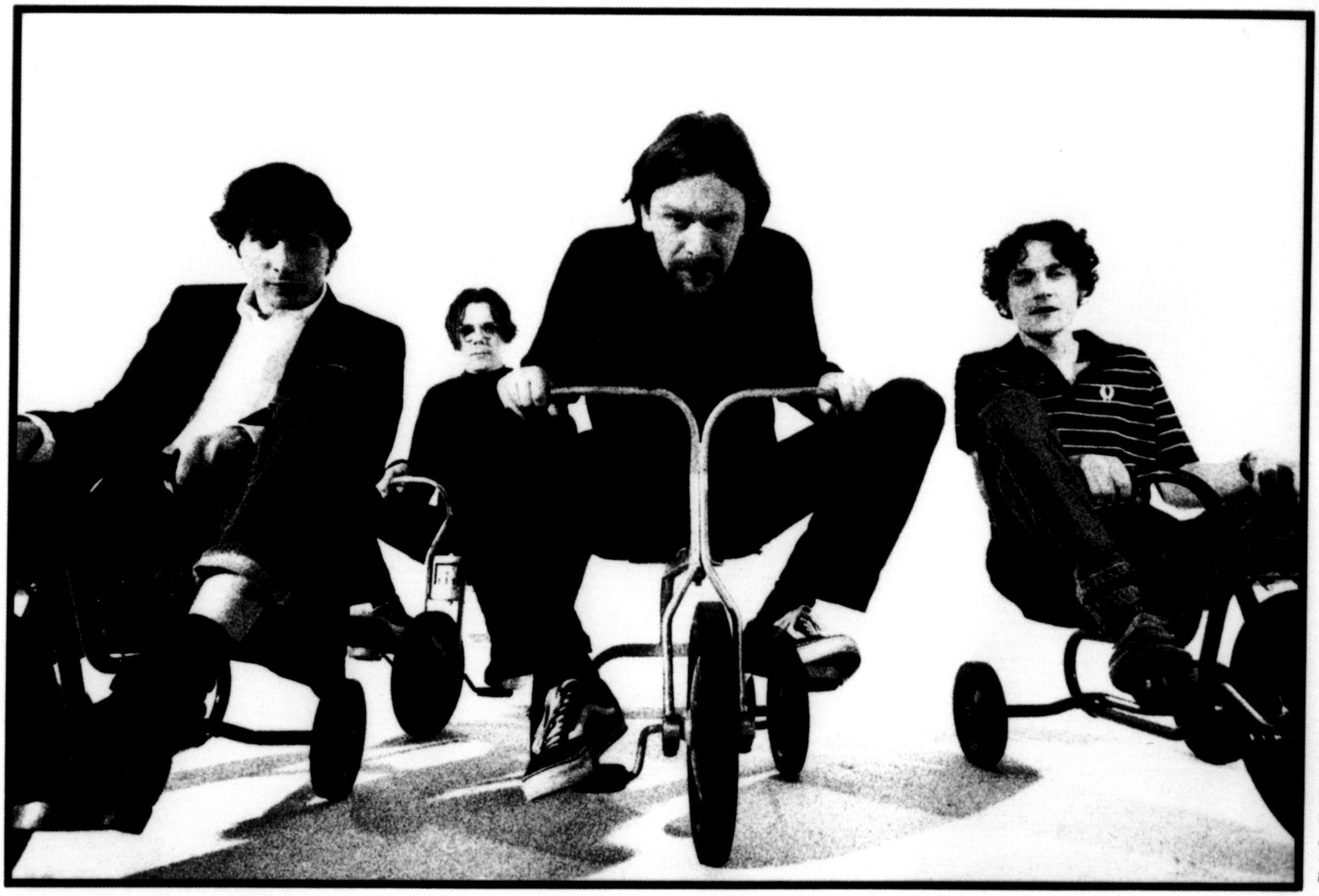

Photo Credit: Nitin Vadukul

Raymond McGinley Paul Quinn Gerry Love Norman Blake

Teenage Fanclub

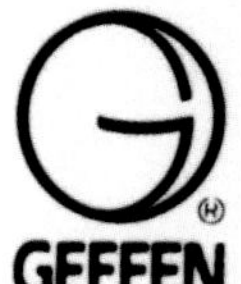

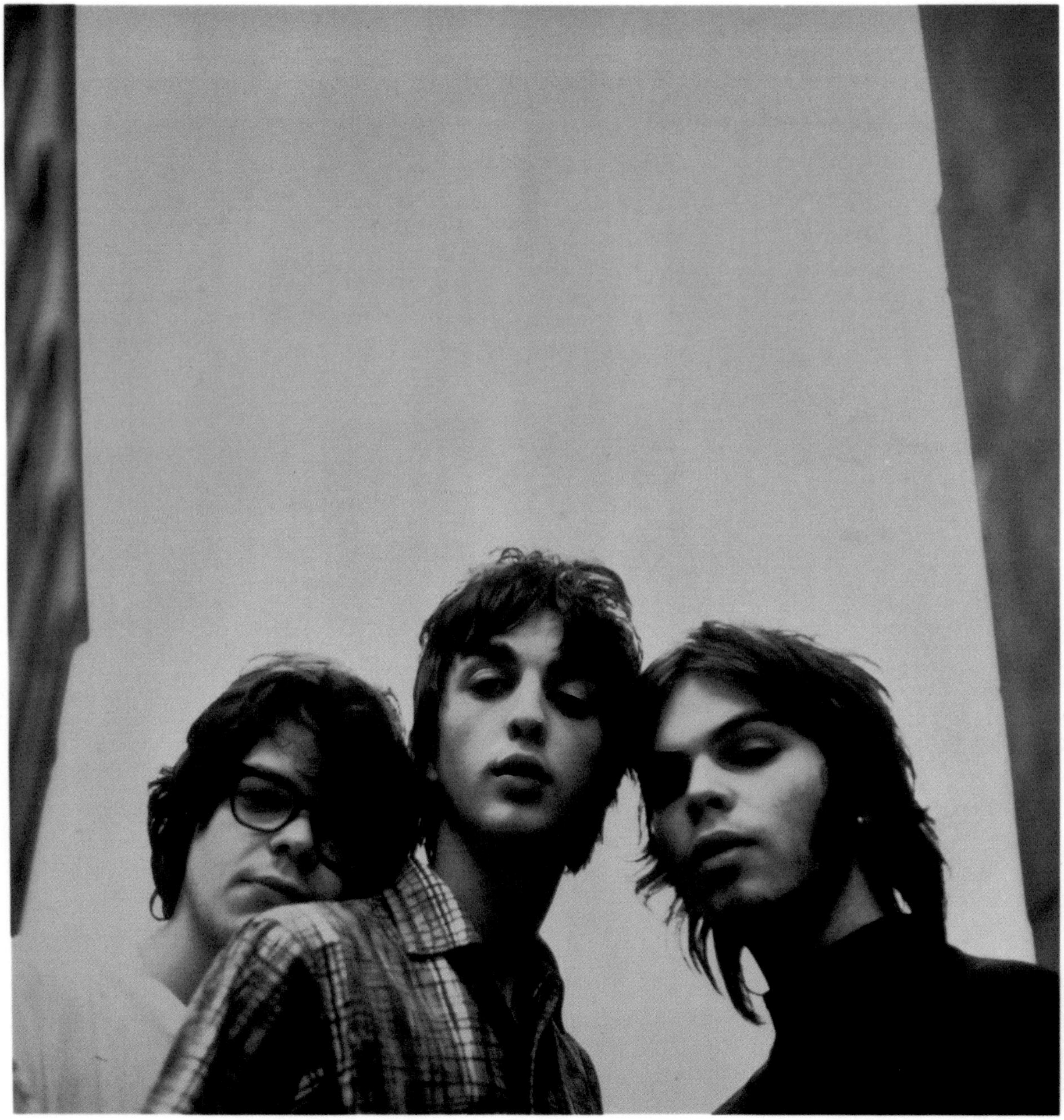

Photographer: Donald Milne/1995

Mickey Quinn **Danny Goffey** **Gaz Coombes**

SUPERGRASS

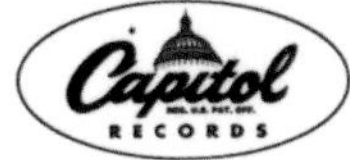

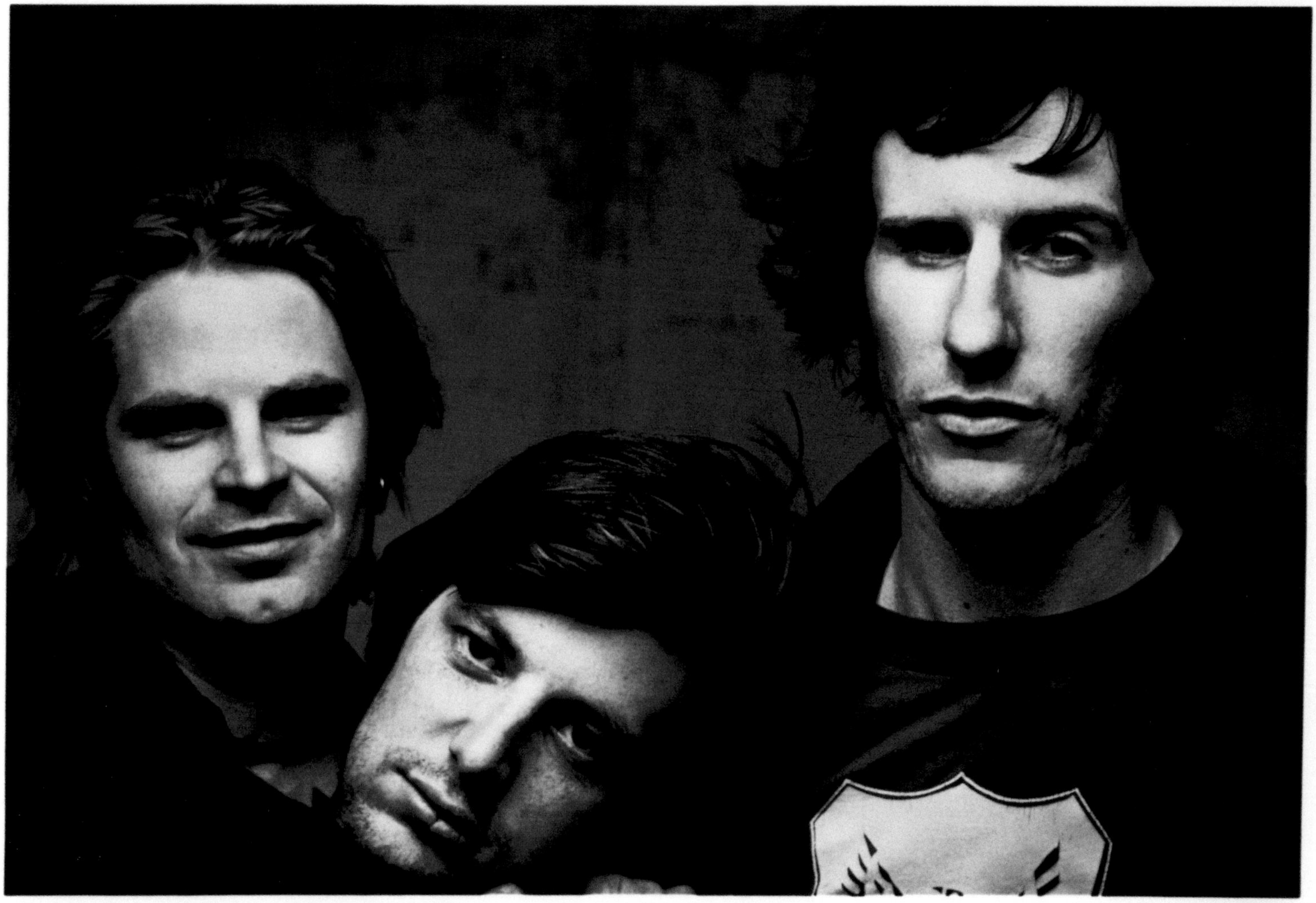

PHOTO CREDIT: Dennis Montalbetti

YOU AM I

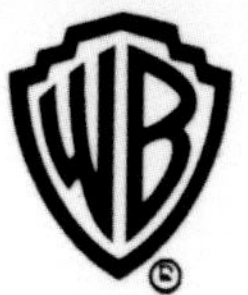

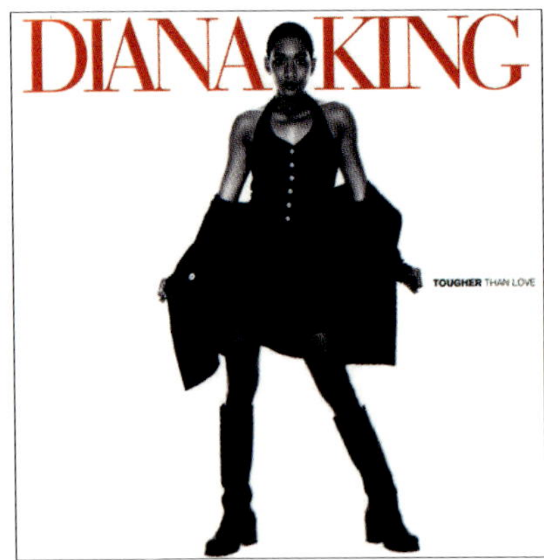

Jamaican vocalist **Diana King**'s "Shy Guy," a reggae fusion song, emerged on both her debut album *Tougher Than Love* and the soundtrack of *Bad Boys*.

Billboard 200: *Tougher Than Love* (#179)
Billboard Hot 100: "Shy Guy" (#13); "Ain't Nobody" (#94)

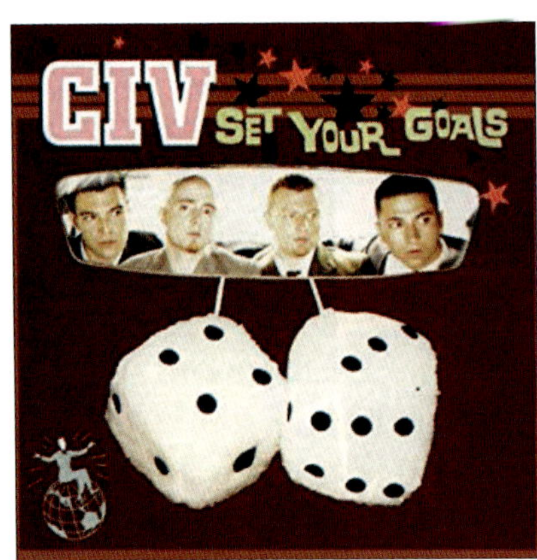

Named for lead singer Anthony "Civ" Civocelli, New York punk band **CIV** brought out *Set Your Goals* and a modern rock hit, "Can't Wait One Minute More."

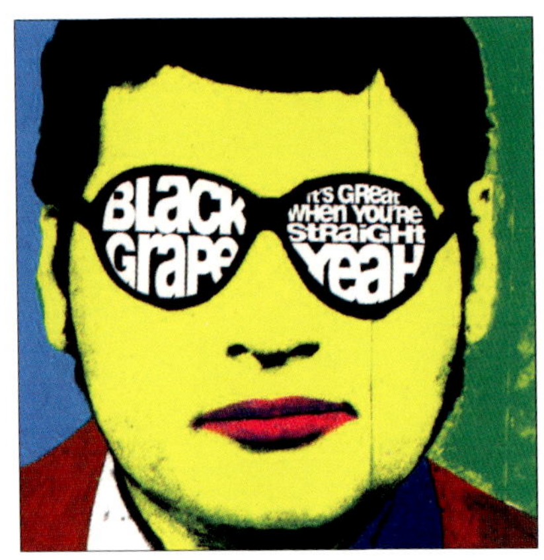

Run by Shaun Ryder, a former Happy Mondays member, **Black Grape**'s debut album *It's Great When You're Straight...Yeah* came in the UK charts at No. 1.

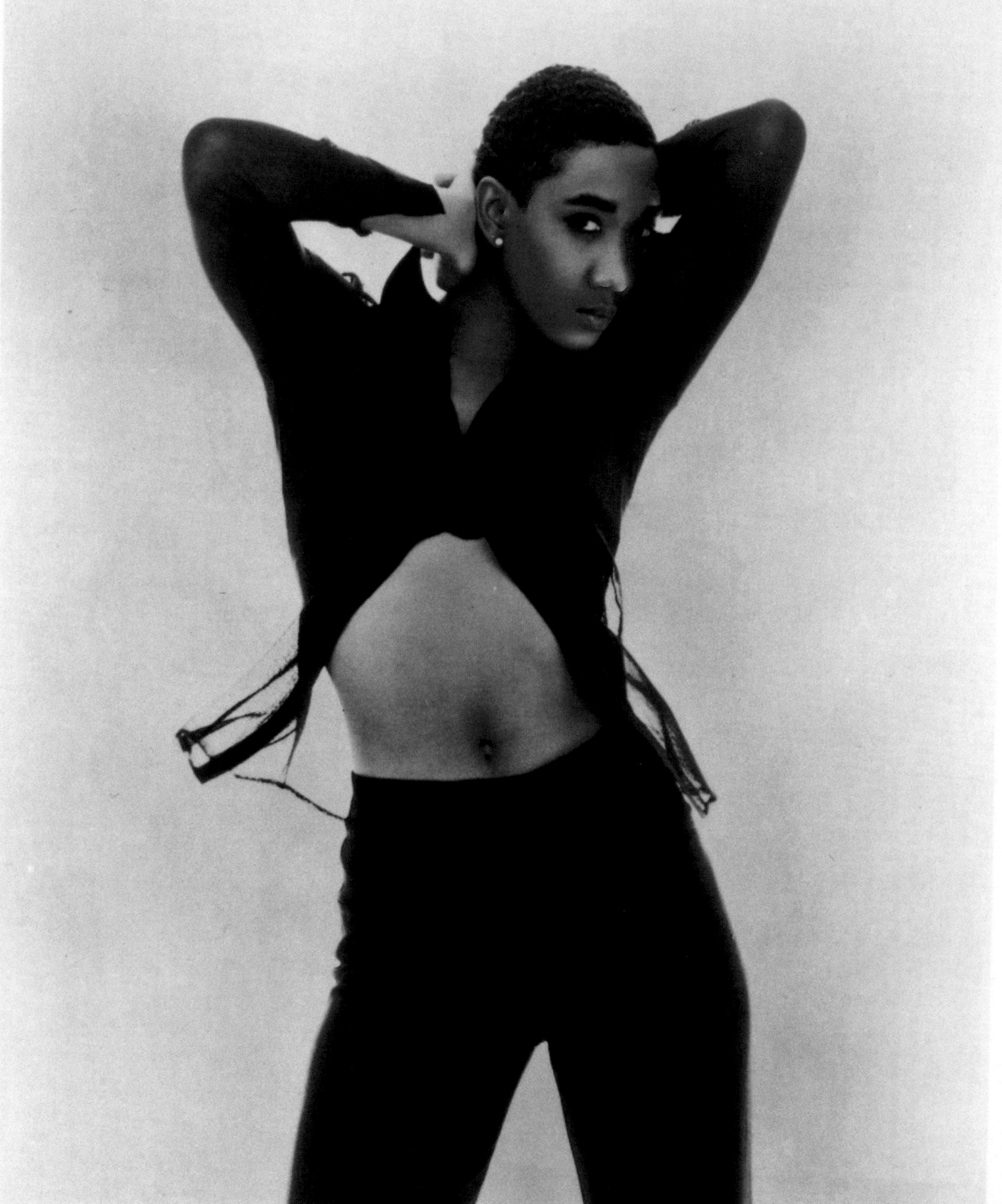

Photo Credit: David Factor

DIANA KING

WORK

9503

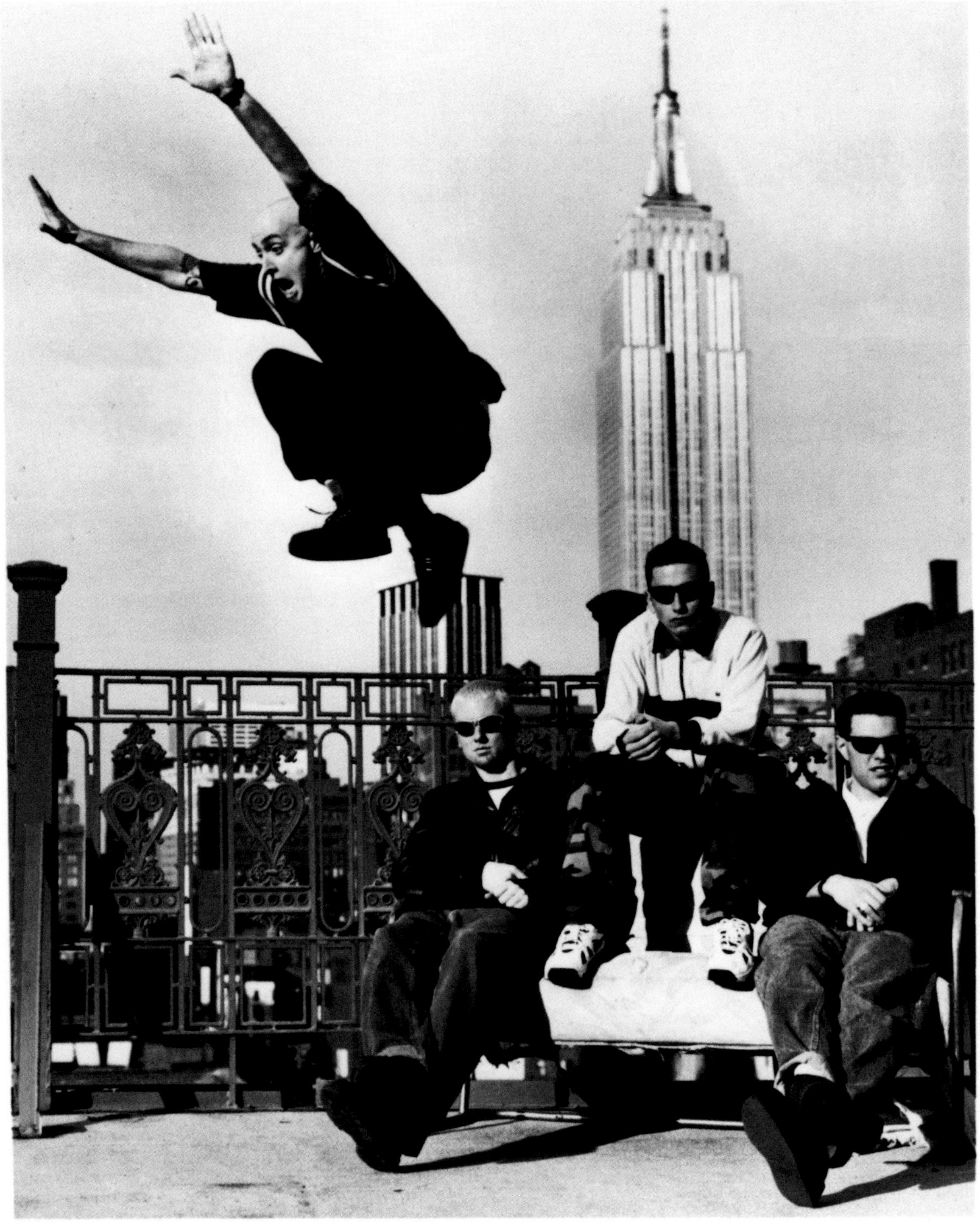

CIV CHARLIE SAMMY ARTHUR

Photo Credit: Patrick Mulligan

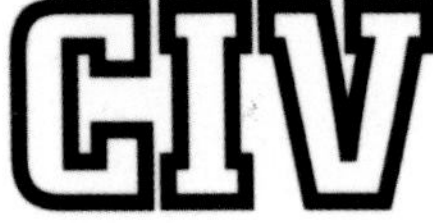

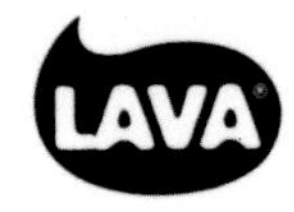

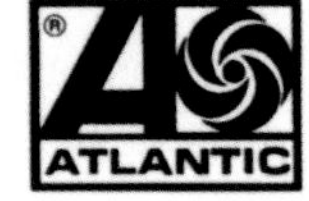

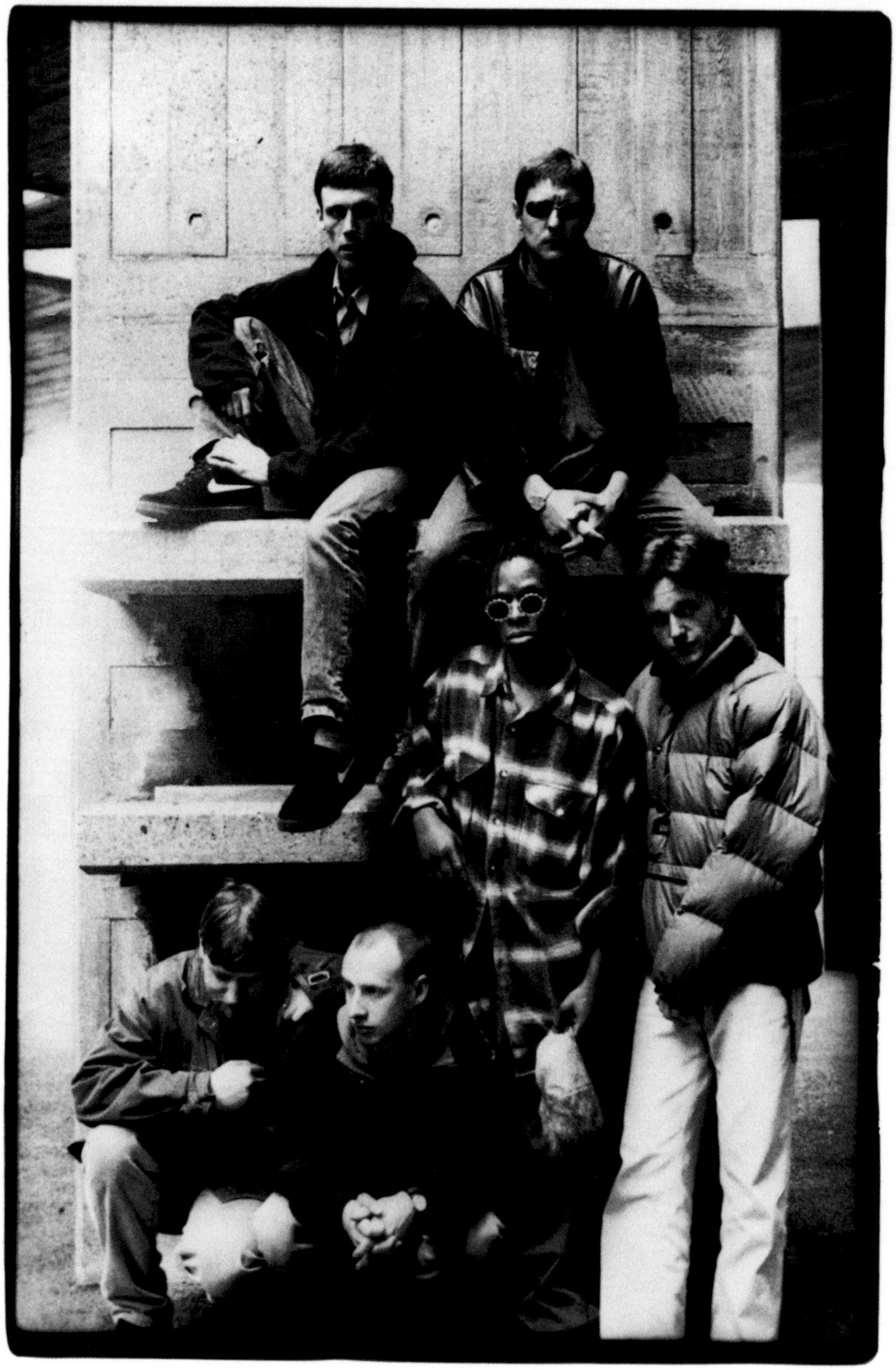

Photo Credit: Pennie Smith

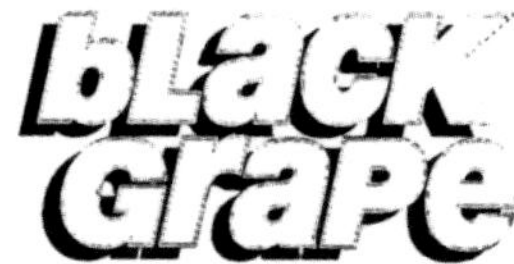

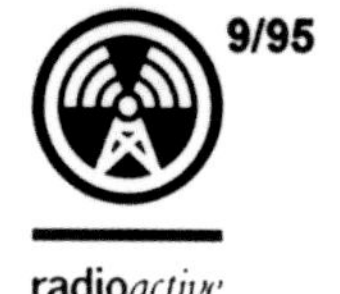

On *Boheme*, the French duo **Deep Forest** fused the melodies of Eastern Europe with electronic sounds and won the Grammy for Best World Music album.

Billboard 200: *Boheme* (#62)

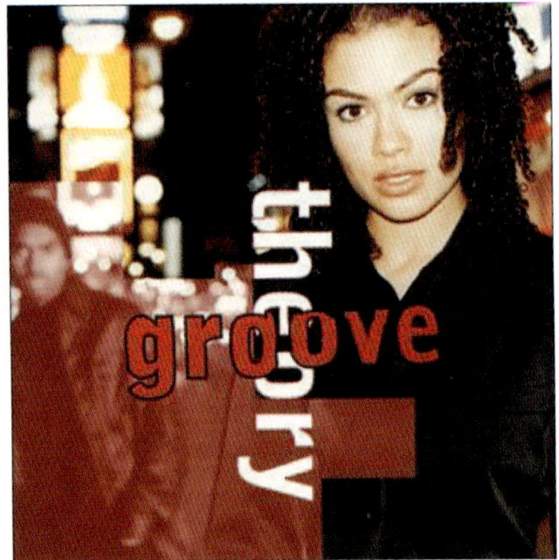

Groove Theory, a duo of vocalist Amel Larrieux and producer Bryce Wilson, reached the Top 5 of both the pop and R&B charts with the alluring "Tell Me."

Billboard 200: *Groove Theory* (#69)
Billboard Hot 100: "Tell Me" (#5); "Keep Tryin'" (#64); "Baby Luv" (#65)

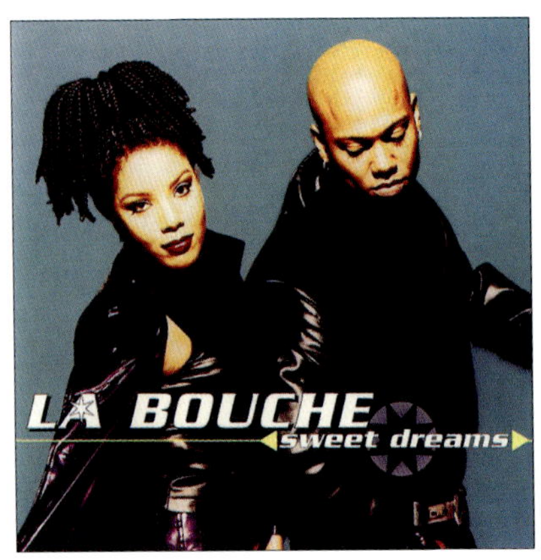

A twosome developed by Frank Farian, the German producer behind Milli Vanilli and Boney M, **La Bouche** hit No. 1 on US dance charts with "Be My Lover."

Billboard 200: *Sweet Dreams* (#28)
Billboard Hot 100: "Sweet Dreams" (#13); "Be My Lover" (#6)

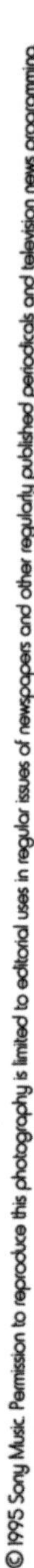

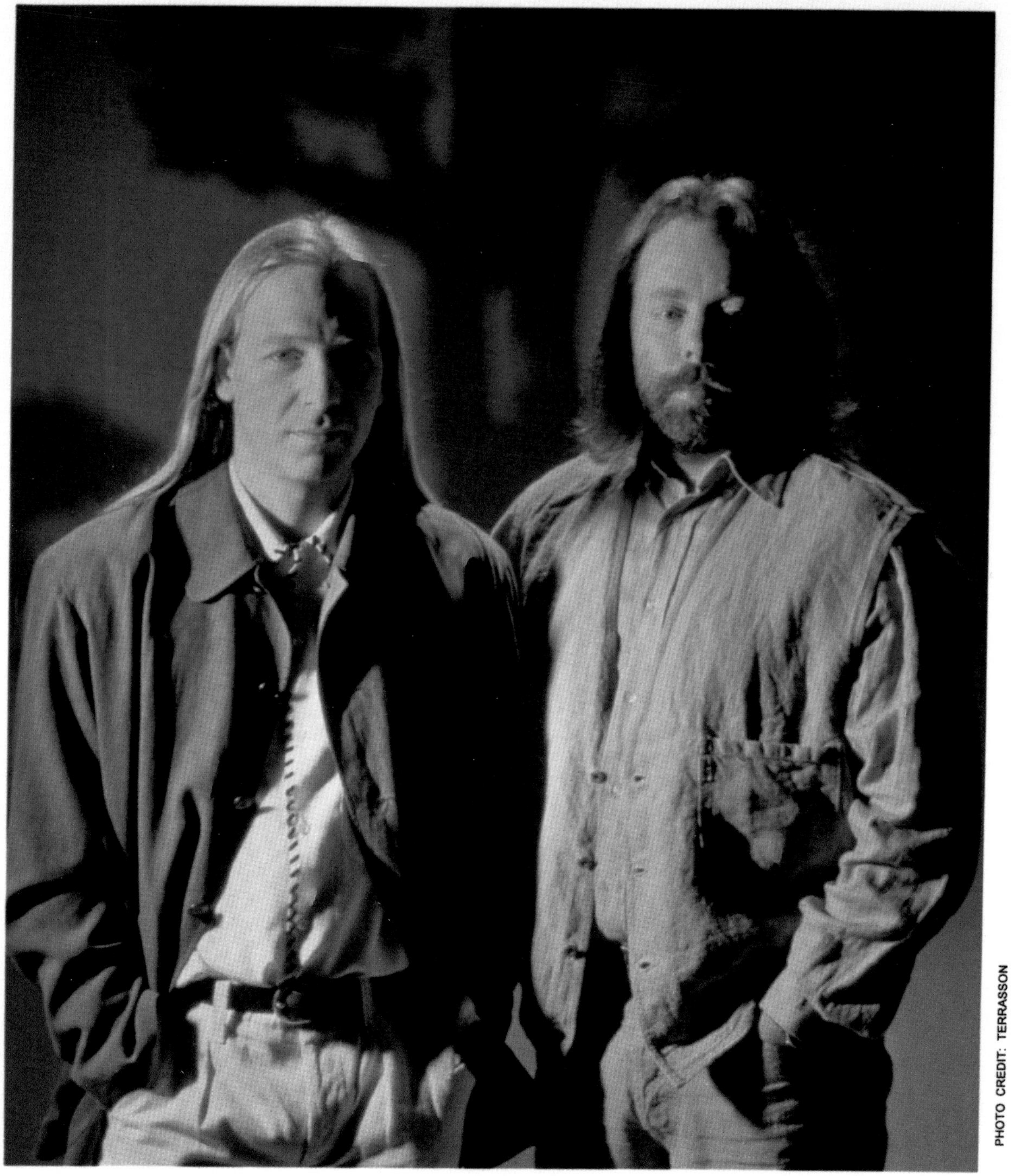

PHOTO CREDIT: TERRASSON

ERIC MOUQUET

MICHEL SANCHEZ

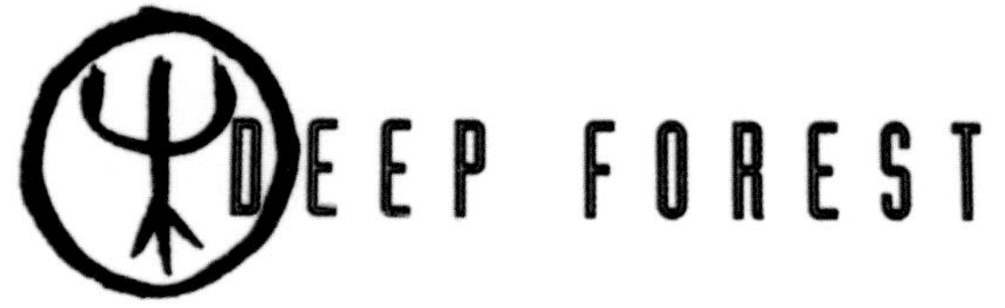

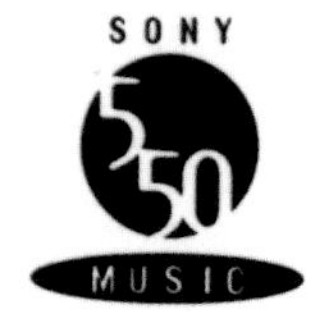

9506

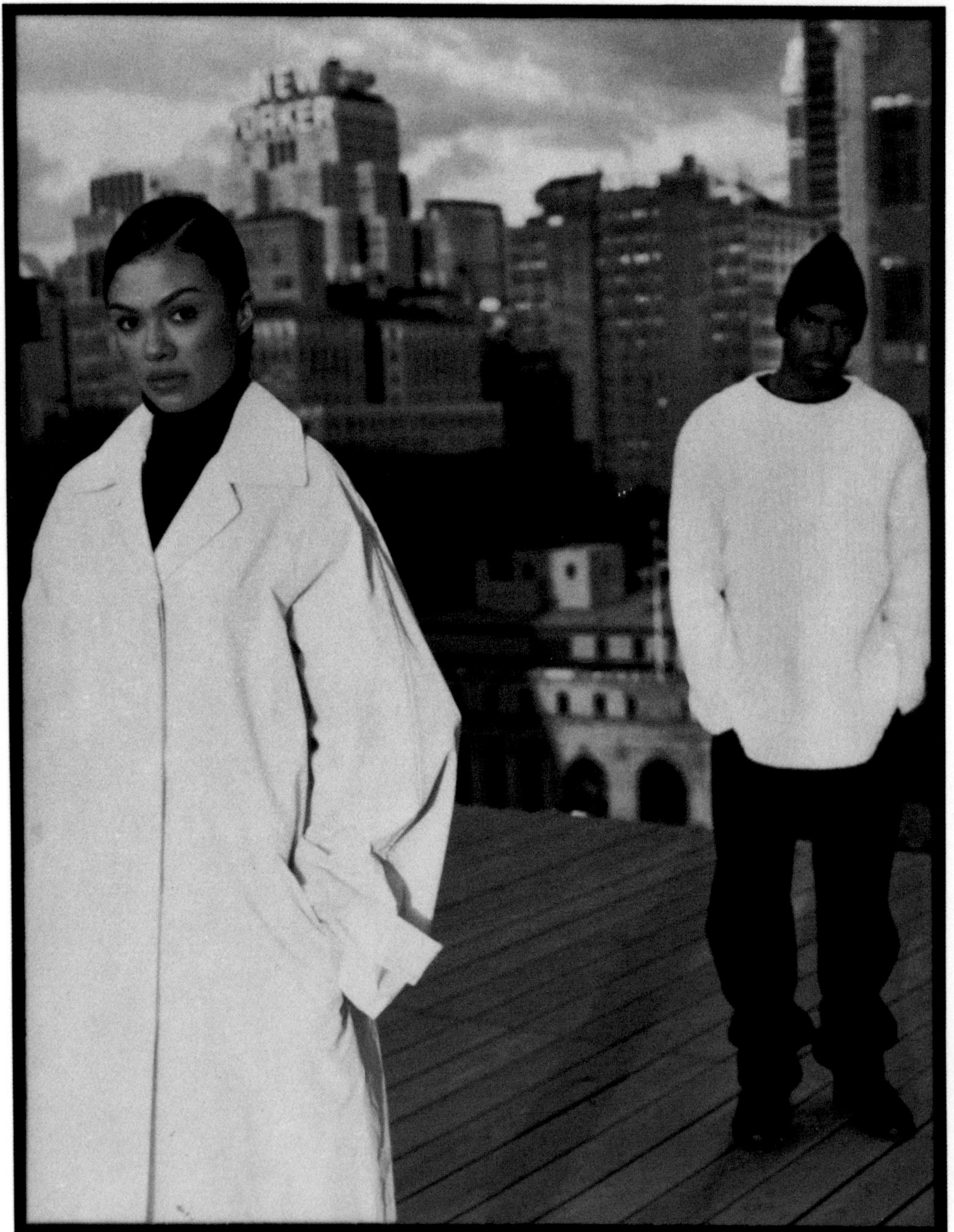

Photo Credit: TROY HOUSE

groove theory

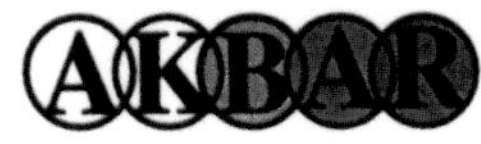

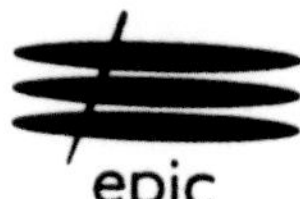

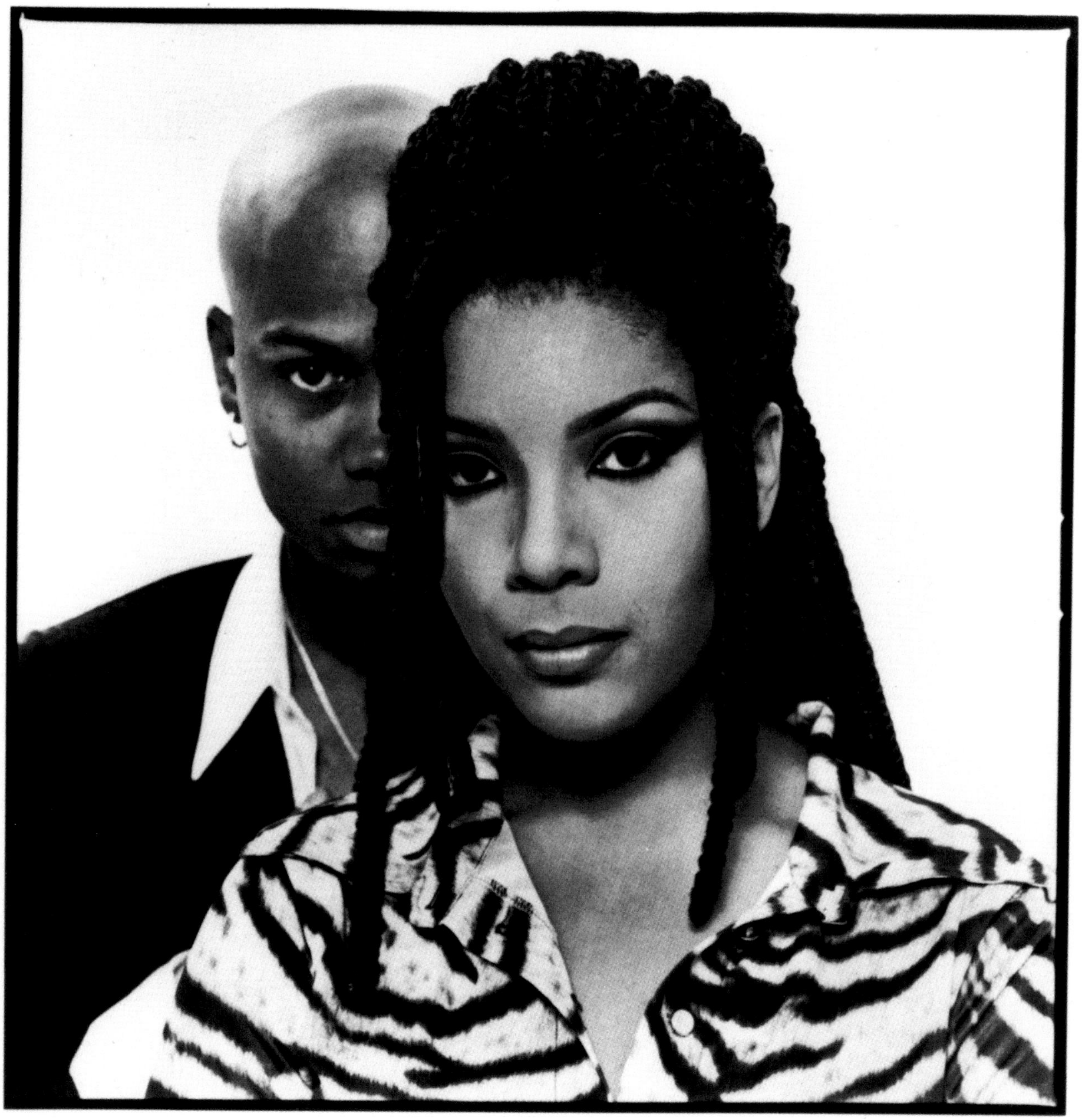

LA BOUCHE

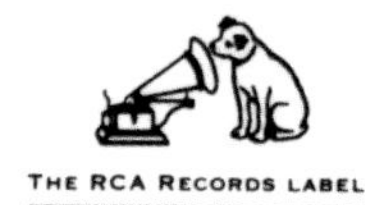

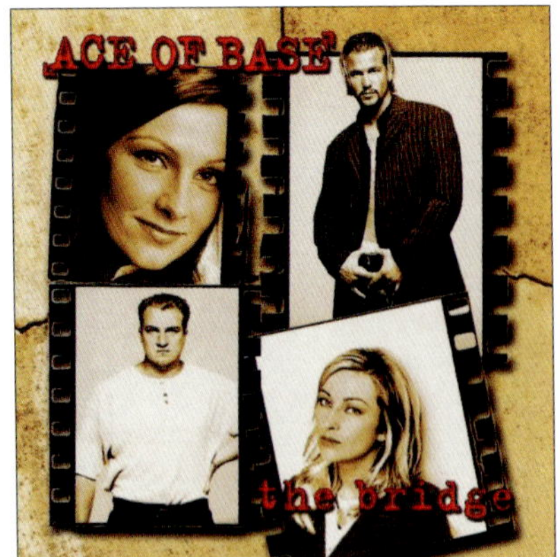

Swedish quartet **Ace of Base** continued to score American hit singles, as *The Bridge* yielded the club-savvy dance songs "Beautiful Life" and "Lucky Love."

Billboard Hot 100: "Beautiful Life" (#15); "Lucky Love" (#30)

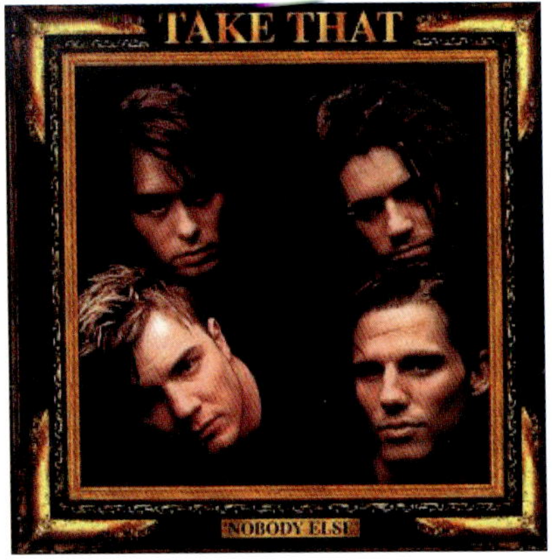

A teen-pop sensation in the UK, **Take That** arrived in the US with "Back for Good," a single which reached No. 1 in many other nations around the world.

Billboard 200: *Nobody Else* (#69)
Billboard Hot 100: "Back for Good" (#7)

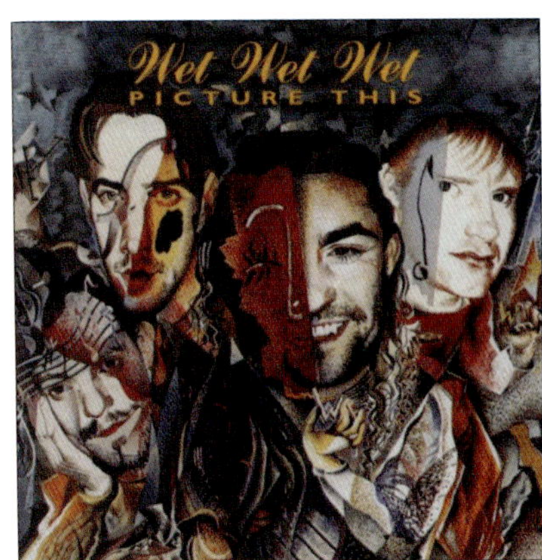

Wet Wet Wet achieved global fame when a cover of the Troggs' "Love Is All Around" was used in the soundtrack to the film *Four Weddings and a Funeral.*

Billboard Hot 100: "Love Is All Around" (#41)

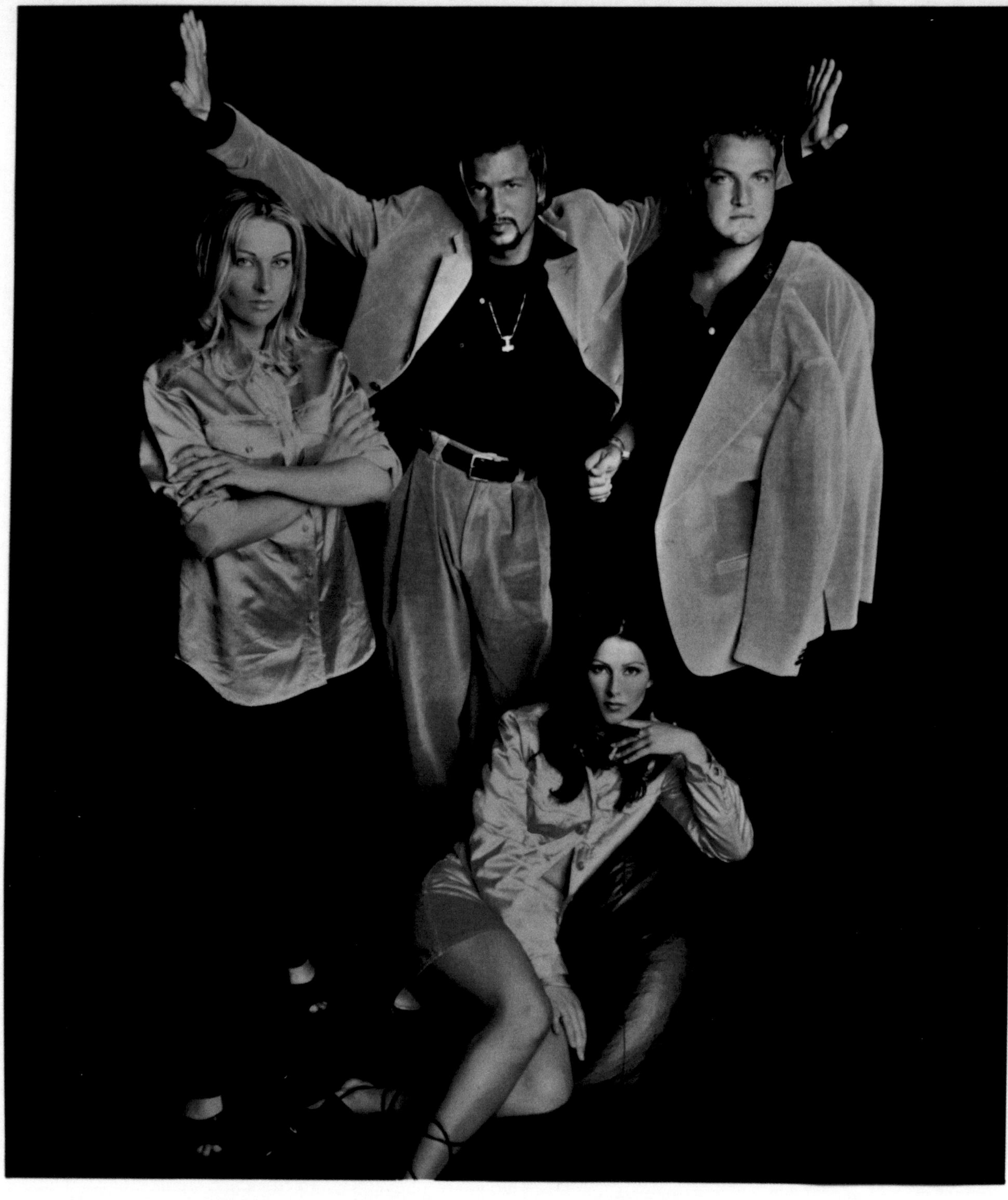

Left to Right: LINN BERGGREN, ULF EKBERG, JONAS BERGGREN, JENNY BERGGREN (in front)

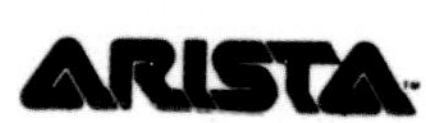

ACE OF BASE

Management:
Siljemark Productions
Gardslager 2 S-171 52
Solna Sweden

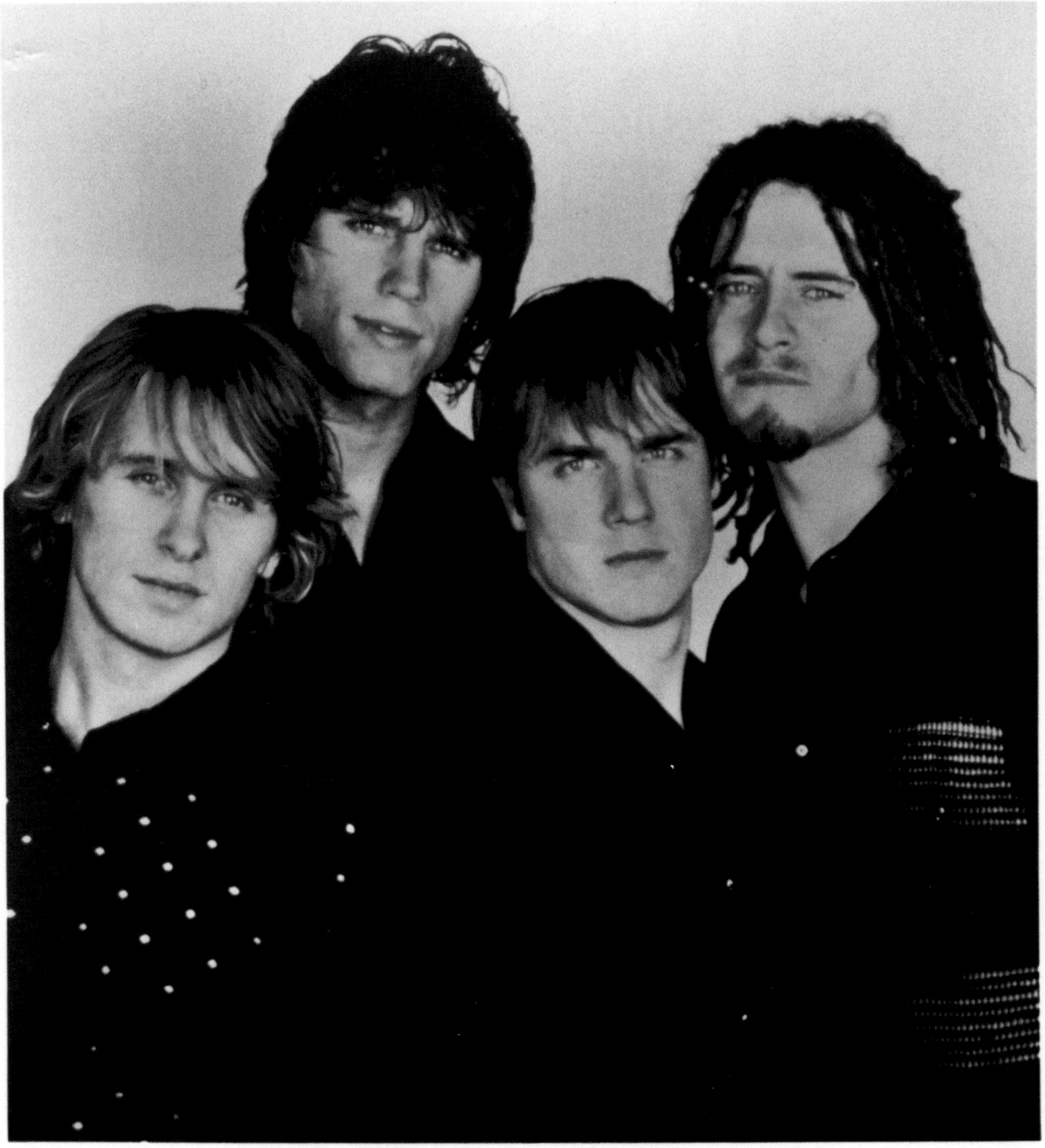

Photo:Robert Walker

TAKE THAT

Management:
Nigel Martin-Smith

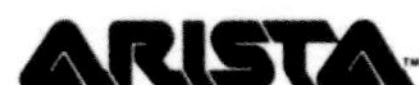

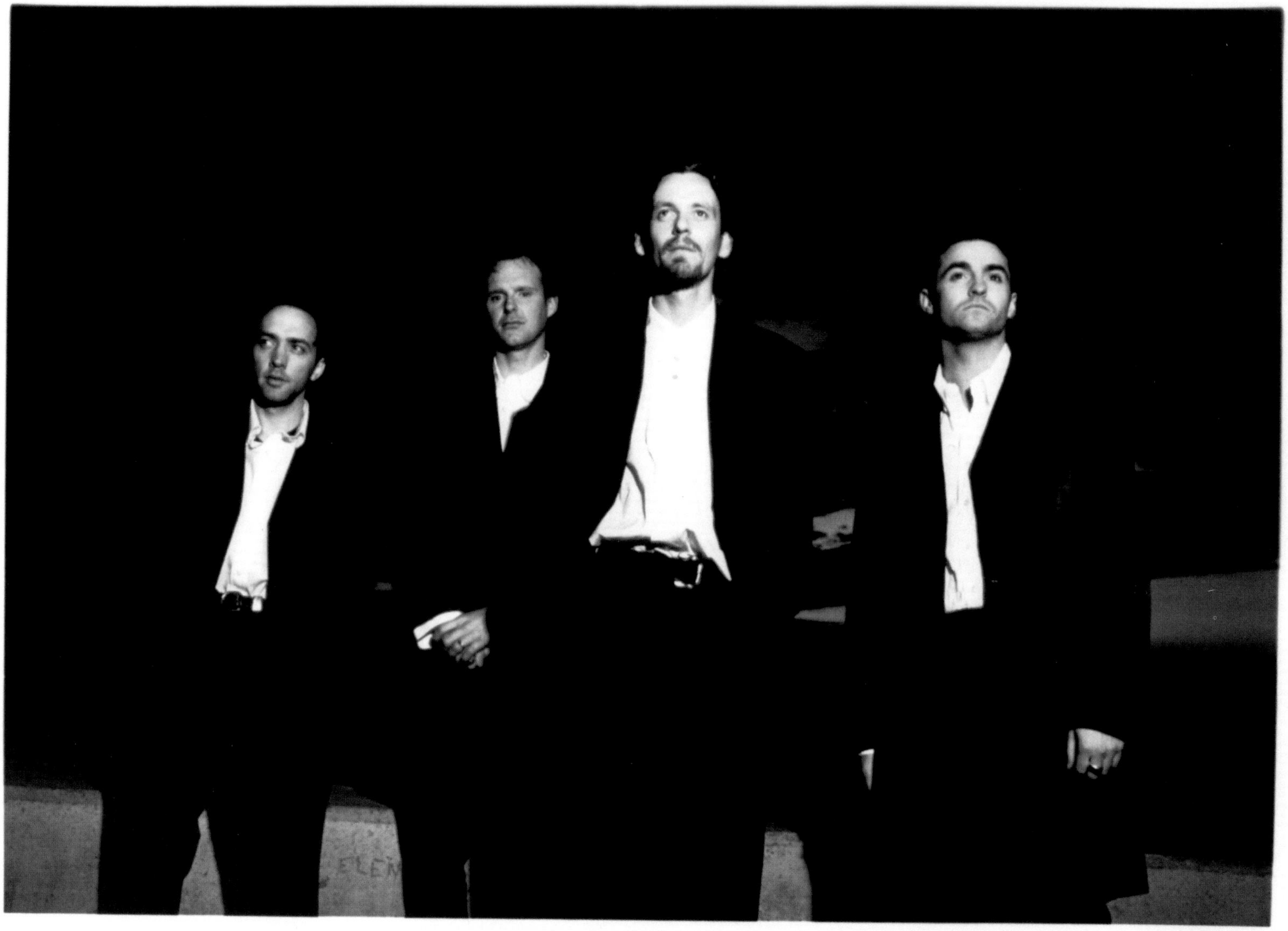

WET WET WET

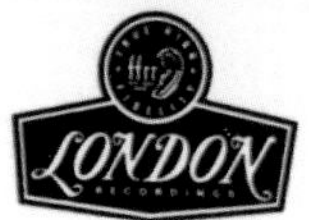

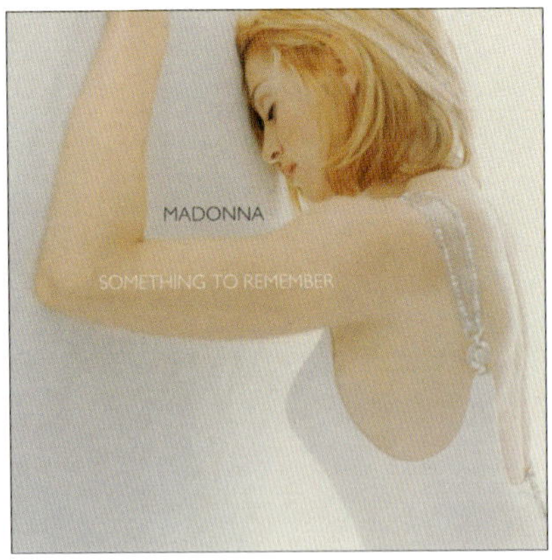

Something to Remember, a set of ballads spanning Madonna's career, emphasized a new acoustic song, "You'll See," to soften her provocative image.

Billboard 200: *Something to Remember* (#6)
Billboard Hot 100: "You'll See" (#6); "Love Don't Live Here Anymore" (#78)

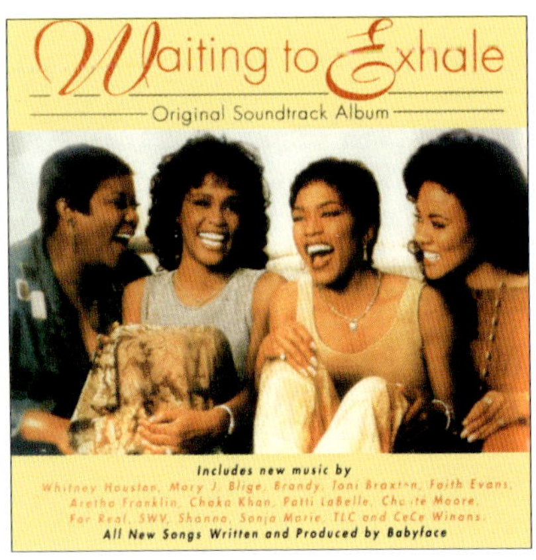

The *Waiting to Exhale* soundtrack offered two No. 1 hits, "Exhale (Shoop Shoop)" by the film's star, Whitney Houston, and Toni Braxton's "Let It Flow."

Billboard 200: *Waiting to Exhale: Original Soundtrack Album* (No. 1)
Billboard Hot 100: "Exhale (Shoop Shoop)" (No. 1);
"Sittin' Up in My Room" (#2); "Not Gon' Cry" (#2); "Count on Me" (#8);
"Let It Flow" (No. 1); "Why Does It Hurt So Bad" (#26)

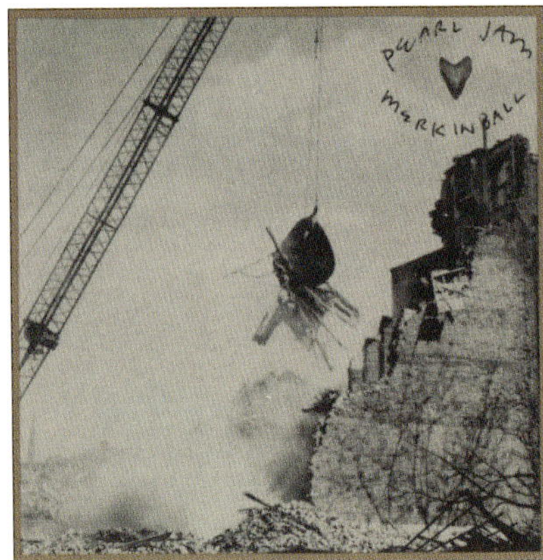

A companion to Neil Young's *Mirror Ball*, where members acted as his backing band, Pearl Jam issued *Merkin Ball*, featuring "I Got ID" and "Long Road."

Billboard Hot 100: *Merkin Ball* (#7)

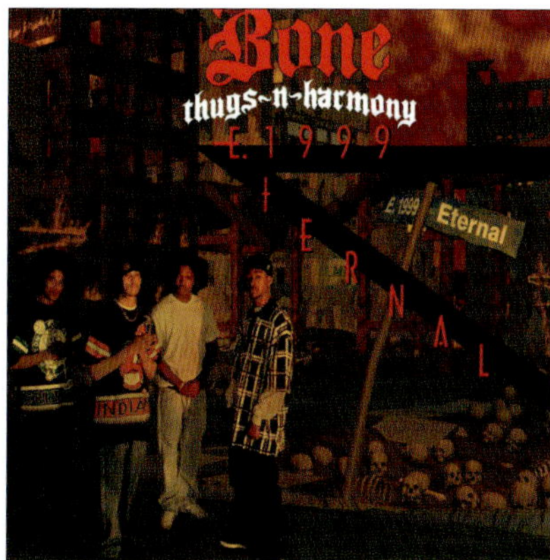

Bone Thugs-N-Harmony's *E. 1999 Eternal* included "Tha Crossroads," a tribute to mentor Easy-E, the recently deceased West Coast gangsta rapper.

Billboard 200: *E. 1999 Eternal* (No. 1)
Billboard Hot 100: "1st of tha Month" (#14); "East 1999" (#40), "Tha Crossroads" (No. 1)

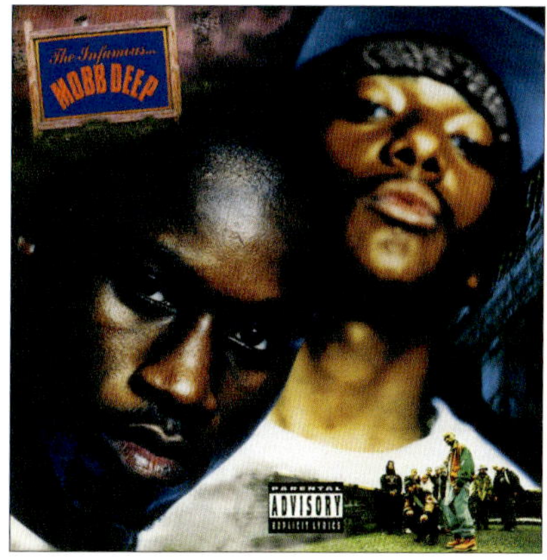

Mobb Deep, a hardcore hip-hop duo from Queens, saw success with *The Infamous*, an album evoking indelible, poetic narratives of street life's dark side.

Billboard 200: *The Infamous* (#18)
Billboard Hot 100: "Shook Ones (Part II)" (#59); "Survival of the Fittest" (#69)

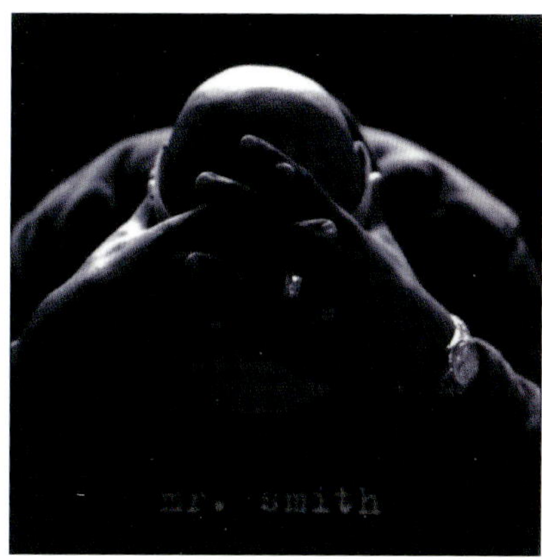

Mr. Smith introduced two of rapper **LL Cool J**'s biggest hits, the steamy "Doin' It" and the Grammy-winning "Hey Lover," a duet featuring Boyz II Men.

Billboard 200: *Mr. Smith* (#20)
Billboard Hot 100: "Hey Lover" (#3); "Doin' It" (#9); "Loungin'" (#3)

"Hold Me, Thrill Me, Kiss Me, Kill Me," performed by **U2** as the end credits rolled in *Batman Forever*, was put out as a single from the film's soundtrack.

Billboard 200: *Batman Forever: Music from the Motion Picture* (#5)
Billboard Hot 100: "Hold Me, Thrill Me, Kiss Me, Kill Me" (#16)

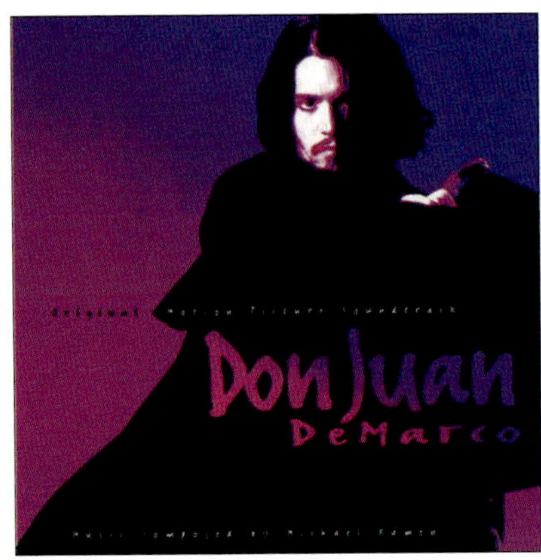

"Have You Ever Really Loved a Woman?," recorded by **Bryan Adams** for the movie *Don Juan DeMarco*, received an Oscar nomination for Best Original Song.

Billboard 200: *Don Juan DeMarco: Original Motion Picture Soundtrack* (#99)
Billboard Hot 100: "Have You Ever Really Loved a Woman?" (No. 1)

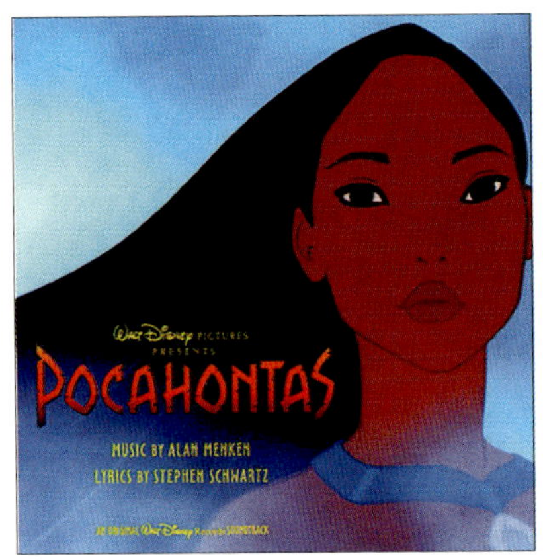

"Colors of the Wind" by **Vanessa Williams**, featured on the soundtrack to the Disney animated movie *Pocahontas*, won an Academy Award and a Grammy.

Billboard 200: *Pocahontas: An Original Walt Disney Records Soundtrack* (No. 1)
Billboard Hot 100: "Colors of the Wind" (#4)

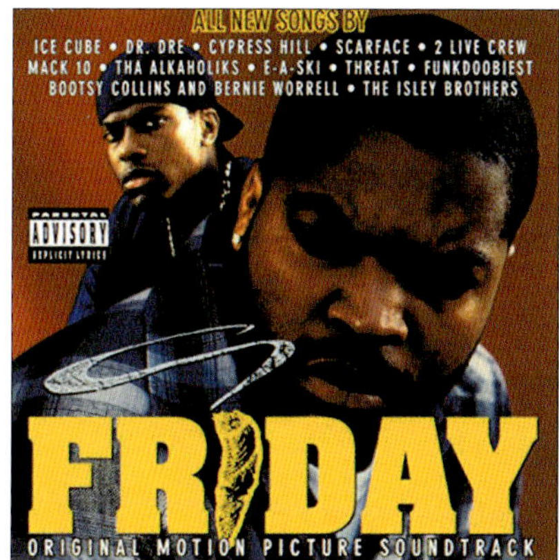

From the soundtrack album for the comedy film *Friday*, the **Dr. Dre**-provided track "Keep Their Heads Ringin'" peaked at No. 1 on the rap charts.

Billboard 200: *The Original Motion Picture Soundtrack Friday* (No. 1)
Billboard Hot 100: "Keep Their Heads Ringin'" (#10)

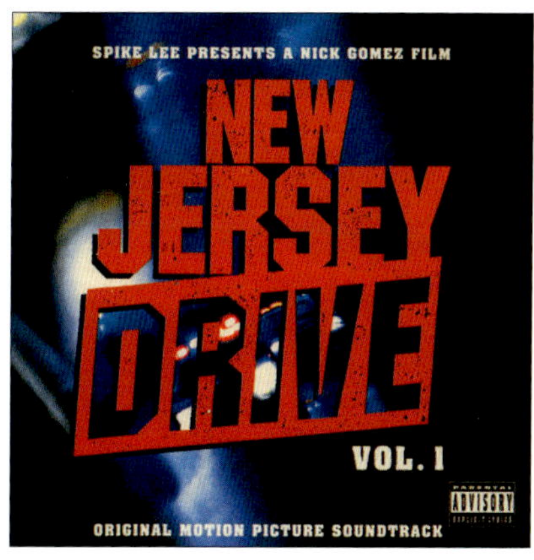

The first of two soundtracks to the film *New Jersey Drive* set forth a gold record, "Can't You See," a banger that launched the R&B girl group **Total**.

Billboard 200: *New Jersey Drive, Vol. 1* (#22)
Billboard Hot 100: "Can't You See" (#13)

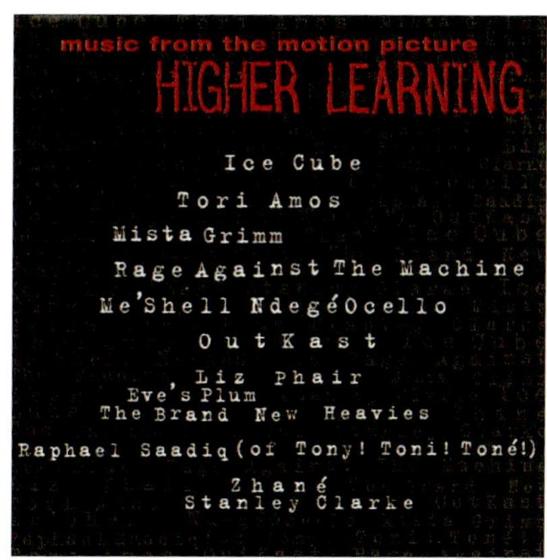

The single "Ask of You," from the soundtrack to *Higher Learning*, turned out to be **Raphael Saadiq**'s biggest hit, reaching #2 on the hip-hop charts.

Billboard 200: *Music from the Motion Picture Higher Learning* (#39)
Billboard Hot 100: "Ask of You" (#19)

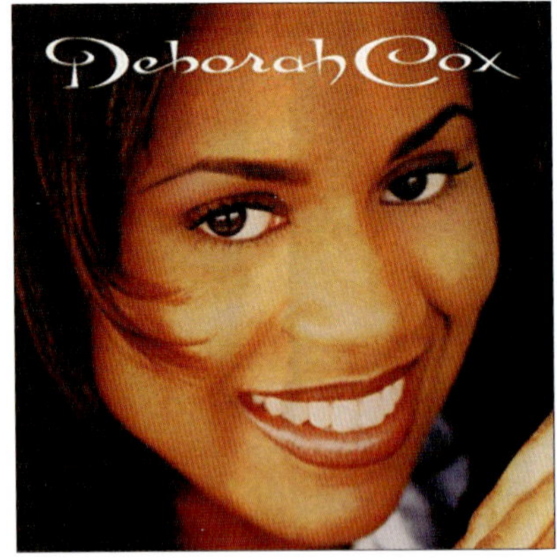

A protégé of music executive Clive Davis, who recruited some expert R&B producers, vocalist **Deborah Cox** made good with the dance hit "Who Do U Love."

Billboard 200: *Deborah Cox* (#102)
Billboard Hot 100: "Sentimental" (#27); "Who Do U Love" (#17); "Where Do We Go from Here" (#48); "The Sound of My Tears" (#97)

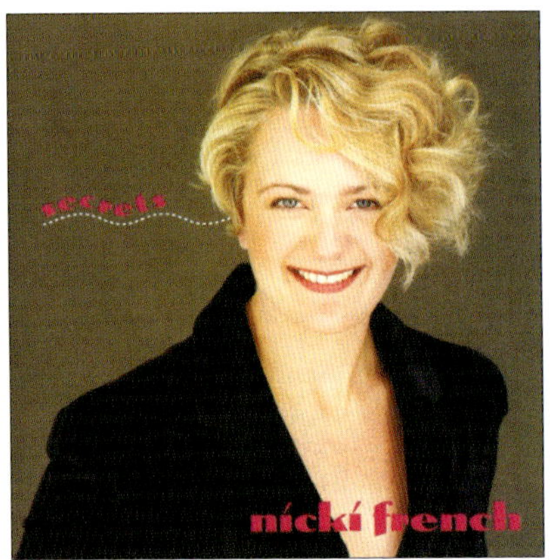

British singer **Nicki French**'s club-oriented cover of Bonnie Tyler's 1983 torch song "Total Eclipse of the Heart" occupied the pop charts for six months.

Billboard 200: *Secrets* (#151)
Billboard Hot 100: "Total Eclipse of the Heart" (#2)

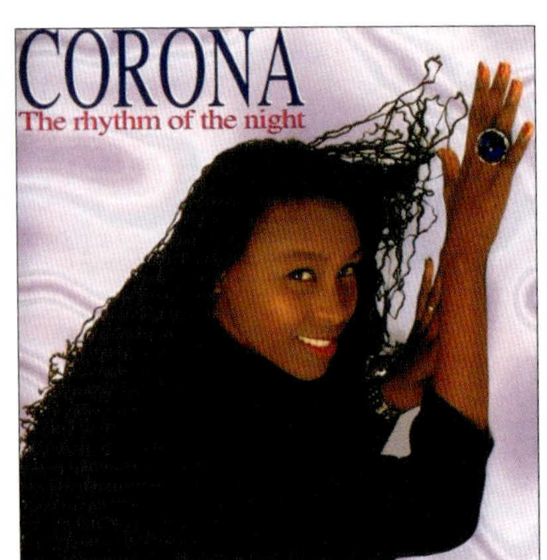

Well after scoring colossal success in Europe, the Italian dance band **Corona** saw "The Rhythm of the Night" gain US exposure on radio and in clubs.

Billboard 200: *The Rhythm of the Night* (#154)
Billboard Hot 100: "The Rhythm of the Night" (#11); "Baby Baby" (#57)

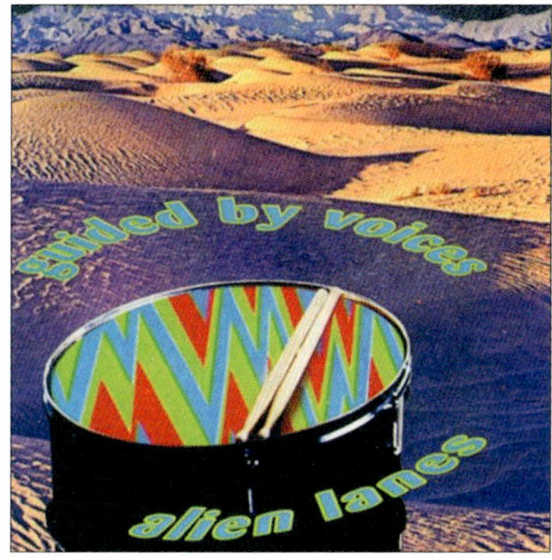

Led by Robert Pollard, **Guided by Voices** grew its cult audience with *Alien Lanes*, which the lo-fi band shaped out of cheap home-recorded fragments.

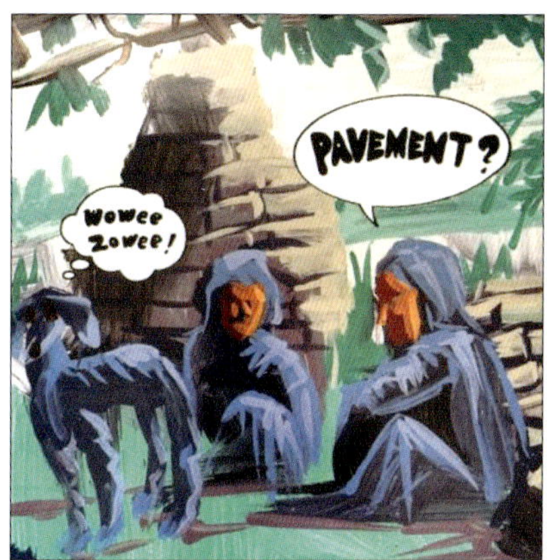

After nearly engineering its way into the mainstream with "Cut Your Hair" in 1994, indie rock band **Pavement** evinced an eclectic side on *Wowee Zowee*.

Billboard 200: *Wowee Zowee* (#117)

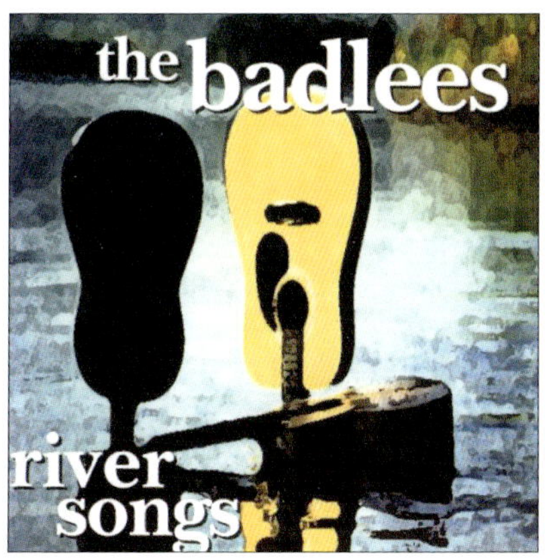

The Badlees, earnest roots rockers from the Pennsylvania music scene, were finally thrust into the spotlight with *River Songs*, their first national release.

Billboard Hot 100: "Angeline Is Coming Home" (#67)

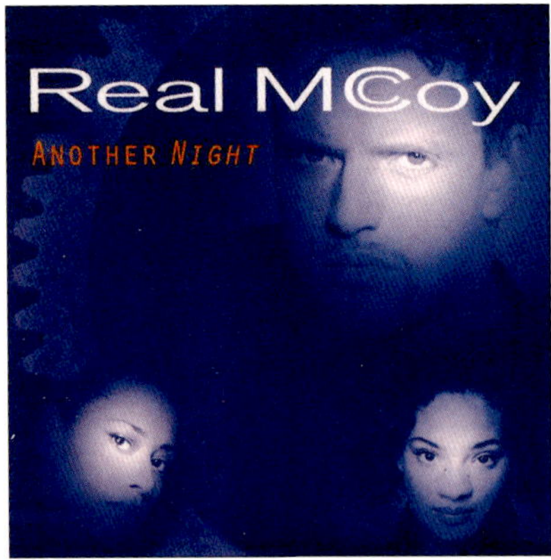

Real McCoy, a German Europop project, ruled the pop and dance charts, thanks to "Another Night," "Run Away" and a "Come and Get Your Love" redo.

Billboard 200: *Another Night* (#13)
Billboard Hot 100: "Another Night" (#3); "Run Away" (#3); "Come and Get Your Love" (#19); "Automatic Lover (Call for Love)" (#52)

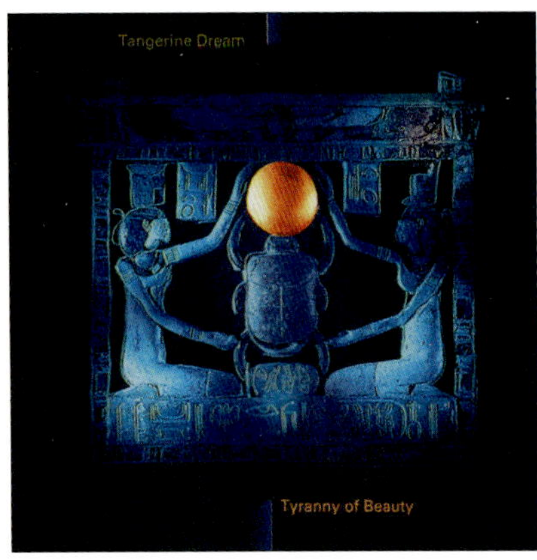

Electronic music pioneers who had recorded more than fifty albums, German band **Tangerine Dream** watched *Tyranny of Beauty* scale the new age charts.

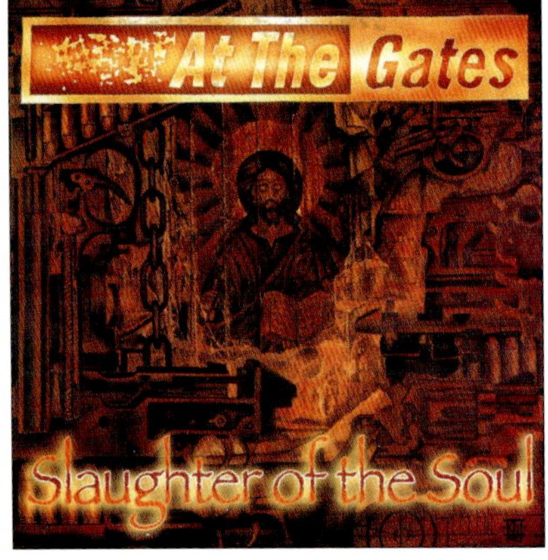

The Swedish band **At the Gates** circulated its furious sound around the world with the compelling *Slaughter of the Soul*, an album of melodic death metal.

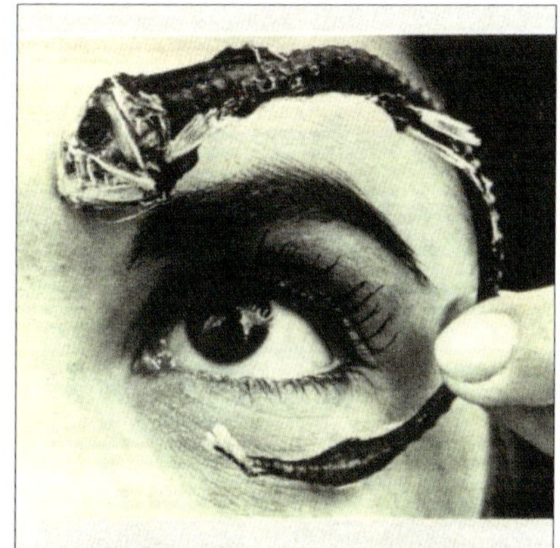

Mr. Bungle, a side project for Faith No More's Mike Patton, shifted to an abstruse and preposterous musical style on its second album, *Disco Volante.*

Billboard 200: *Disco Volante* (#113)

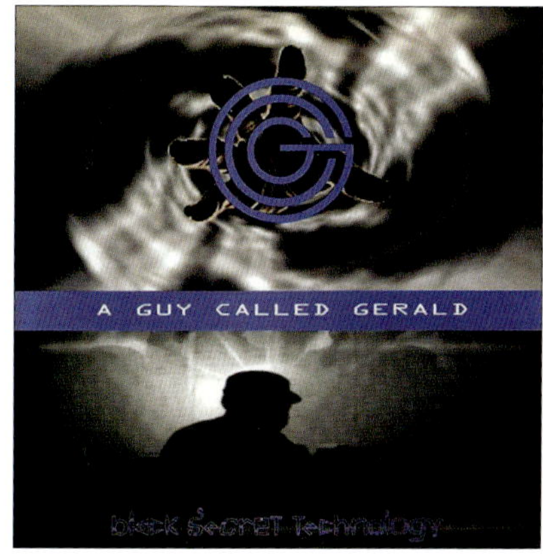

A Guy Named Gerald—electronic music producer Gerald Simpson, an early member of 808 State—was feted by jungle fans for *Black Secret Technology*.

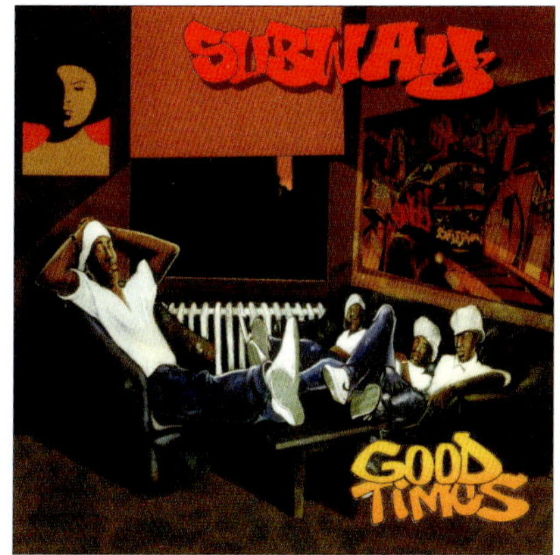

"This Lil' Game We Play," featuring vocals by labelmates 702, sold nearly a million copies for **Subway**, the highlight of the quartet's short-lived career.

Billboard 200: *Good Times* (#101)
Billboard Hot 100: "This Lil' Game We Play" (#15); "Fire" (#91)

{ IN MEMORY OF SUSAN JANE }

ACKNOWLEDGMENTS

Many people were essential to the creation of this book. My first thanks go to my amazing publishing team—Jon Rizzi for bringing his special brand of editorial wit and intelligence, and Kate Glassner Brainerd for her design artistry and unflagging pursuit of excellence. Special appreciation goes to Eric Pirritt's The Love We Bring Foundation and the Michael & Patricia Matthews Fund, whose facilitation was indispensable, as well as John Cerullo and Kevin Votel.

Mike Dickson, Chip Garofalo, Jennifer Soulé, Mark Zaremba, Peter Marcus, Matt Rue, Jay Elowsky, Dave Zobl and Mark Lewis contributed expertise and resources. I am especially indebted to my dear friend Michael Jensen, as well as Sue Satriano, Janice Azrak, Bryn Bridenthal, Byron Hontas, Kathy Acquaviva, Shelly Selover, Sue Sawyer, Glen Brunman, Rick Ambrose, Bob Merlis, Bill Bentley, Heidi Ellen Robinson, Les Schwartz, Rick Gershon, Jim Merlis, Judi Kerr and Susan Blond—all of whom supported my efforts.

I specifically treasure the beneficence of Dave Rothstein, Greg Phifer, John Tope, Kevin Knee, Dick Merkle, Jeff Cook, Michael Brannen, Zak Phillips, Rich Garcia, Jason Minkler, Burt Baumgartner, Mitch Kampf, Don Zucker, Carl Walters, Charlie Reardon, Robin Wren, Jimmy Smith, Sharona White, John Ryland, Geina Horton, Michael Linehan, Mike Prince and Jeffrey Naumann, who all graciously furnished information and assistance.

I gratefully acknowledge the editing and reviewing skills of Dick Kreck, Tom Walker, Diane Carman, Mike Rudeen, Ed Smith, Jay Whearley, Mark Sims, Jeff Bradley and Peggy McKay.

I also salute David Gans, Leland Rucker, Steve Knopper, David Menconi, Jon Iverson, Gil Asakawa, Mark Bliesener, Butch Hause, Ricardo Baca, John Moore, Justin Mitchell, Michael Mehle and Harvey Kubernik, whose writings formed a vital index for the music-obsessed.

Finally, I would like to acknowledge with gratitude my beloved wife, Bridget, for her constant devotion and kindness. I cherish her—the love of my life.

EDITOR | **JON RIZZI**
ART DIRECTOR | **KATE GLASSNER BRAINERD**

ISBN 978-0-9915668-9-1 PRINTED IN CHINA | Asia Pacific Offset

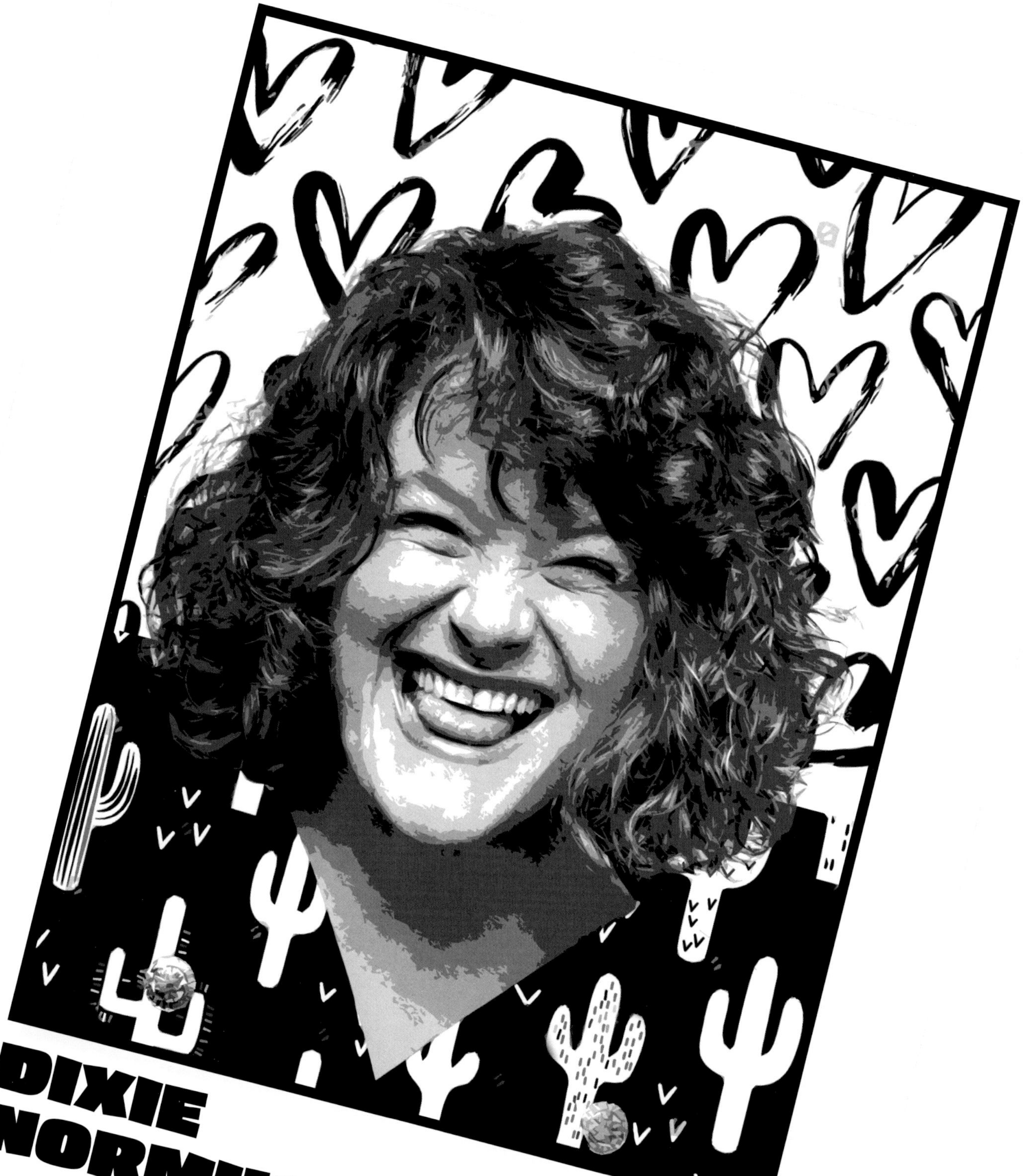

DIXIE NORMUSS

The hit album **Don't Fiddle with Love**
Featuring the single "Doll-Faced Hick"

MANAGEMENT
Sidney Q. Weldonburgerstein
P.O. Box 1932
Boulder, Colorado 80306

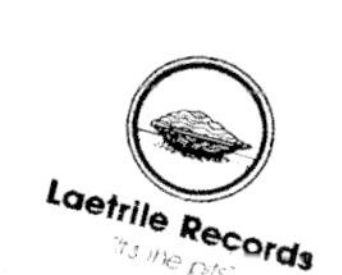

Next in the *ON RECORD* book series

Vol. 7 1979

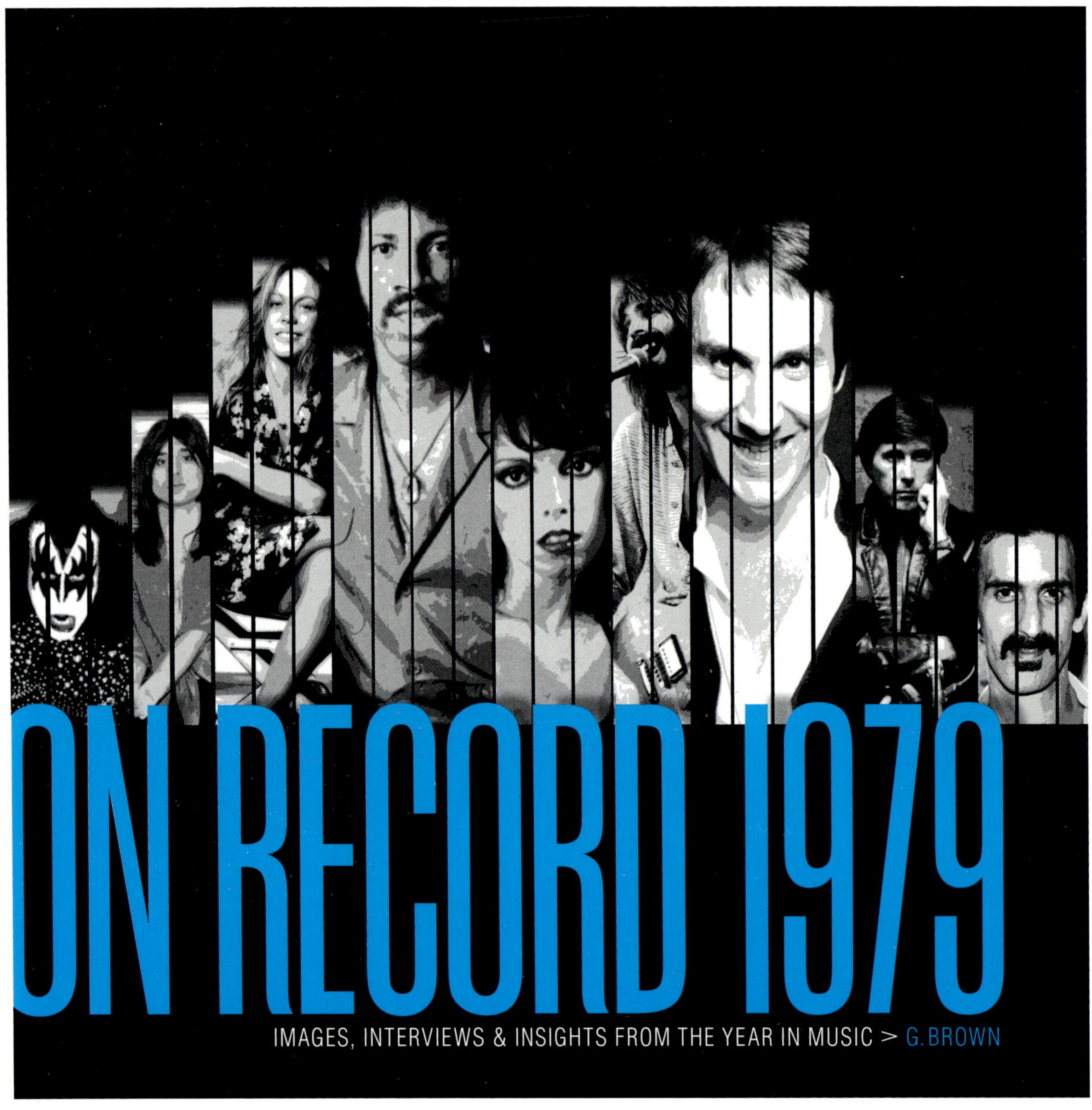